Past is Prologue

Past is Prologue

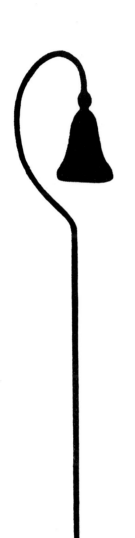

Some Historical Reflections
1961-1991

by

MSGR. FRANCIS J. WEBER

The Archival Center gratefully acknowledges the
dedicated interest of the Ernest and Helen Chagon
Foundation in the publication of this book.

Library of Congress Cataloging-in-Publication Data

Weber, Francis J.
  Past is prologue: some historical recollections, 1961-1991/by
Francis J. Weber.
  ISBN 0-87461-931-9
  1. Catholic Church--California--History. 2. Catholic Church-
-United States--History. 3. California--Church history. 4. United
States--Church history. I. Title.
BX1415.C2W418   1992
282'.73--dc20   92-13618
                                                    CIP

Preface

In 1987, shortly after the appearance of *Days of Change. Years of Challenge*, a collection of the homilies, addresses and talks compiled and edited for the late Timothy Cardinal Manning, an interesting proposal arrived by mail at the Archival Center in Mission Hills from a graduate student at UCLA: "Might I suggest that you consider preparing an anthology of the essays you have published over the past thirty years in various historical and literary journals?"

The correspondent pointed out that "many of those writings appeared in now-defunct publications which are often difficult to locate. Would it not make some sense to breath new life into those old wineskins?"

Over the next few months, I submitted the idea to ten of my closest friends and advisors, six of whom are themselves historians and/or churchmen. It was their positive response that motivated this book.

It took almost a year to "gather up the fragments" and arrange them into categories. It was decided that footnotes should remain in place, since they were valuable keys to further information.

In order to maintain the character and integrity of the original essays, it seemed best to leave them substantially unchanged. With very few exceptions then, the writings in this book remain in their original form, with all their blemishes and shortcomings.

It is important to note that this anthology is not complete. Excluded, for example, are any essays that appeared in "California's Catholic Heritage," a series that has appeared in *The Tidings* and other Catholic newspapers since 1962. Also omitted are any articles that later became chapters of books, monographs or miniature books. The collection was chiefly meant to feature materials not readily accessible to scholars and others.

There are those who feel that archivists should not be historians or *vice versa*. Personally, I feel that one discipline enhances the other. In my own case, the handiness of the materials at the Archival Center, Archdiocese of Los Angeles, has been both a blessing and a challenge.

My good friend, Dr. Doyce B. Nunis, Jr., agreed long ago to be my literary executor. The publication of this book should lessen the burden of that task when the Lord calls me to His great archives in the sky. It is a pleasure to thank Gladys Posakony once again for reading and correcting the galleys.

Msgr. Francis J. Weber

Table of Contents

1

This essay on "American Catholic Historical Societies" is taken from *Church History* XXXI (September, 1962), 350-356.

S oon after Pope Leo XIII's pastoral letter on historical studies, *Saepenumero considerantes*[1], was published on August 18th, 1883, a renewed interest in the field of Catholic historical research became apparent. Once again, great scholars came forward "to undertake the writing of history for the purpose of showing what is true and genuine" in the drama of international ecclesiastical development.

There were, of course, many aspects of this new historical enthusiasm but perhaps none was more important than the flood of Catholic historical societies that blossomed around the world "to act as clearing-houses for historical investigation and controversy."[2] On the continent such great reviews as *Revue Benedictine* (Maredsous, 1884), *Revue d'Histoire ecclesiastique* (Louvain, 1900), and *Revue Mabillon* (Paris, 1905) soon emerged as the truly remarkable journals in the field of ecclesiastical history.

Response to the papal call for a revival of historical activity was no less obvious in the United States. Of the several hundred historical societies functioning at the turn of the century, not a few of them were operating under Catholic auspices, endeavoring to put into effect the ideals of Leo XIII:

> To meagre narrations, let there be opposed a laborious and mature investigation; to rash assertions, a prudent judgement; to opinions lightly hazarded, a learned selection of facts. No effort should be spared to refute inventions and falsehoods; for writers should always bear in mind, that *the first law of history is not to utter falsehood; the second, not to fear to speak the truth.*[3]

The year 1844 witnessed the foundation of three Catholic historical societies, two of which subsequently developed into the leading societies in the country. On July 22nd,[4] a group of priests[5] and laymen founded the *American Catholic Historical Society of Philadelphia*.[6] The chief objects of the Society were "to aid Catholic writers and speakers, to make the truth known and to found a library and a cabinet." Also included among the aims of the Society was the collection, preservation and publication of documentary material pertinent to the history of the Catholic Church in America. After 1895 the Society used the Nicholas Biddle mansion at 715 Spruce Street in Philadelphia as its headquarters. In the early 1940s part of the collection was moved to Saint Charles Seminary, Overbrook. Two years after its foundation, in November of 1886, the Society began publication of a quarterly known as the *Records of the American Catholic Historical Society* which is now in its seventy-second volume. An *Index* of the first thirty-one volumes (1886-1920) was published with almost one hundred thousand references to various pertinent Catholic historical developments. A second *Index*, released in 1956, covers the period between 1921 and 1930. In 1912 the *American Catholic Historical Researches*, established by Martin I. J. Griffin in 1884, was incorporated with the *Records*.[7]

On a Tuesday in December of 1884, John Gilmary Shea and Richard H. Clarke founded the *United States Catholic Historical Society* of New York City, the objects of which were "to gather and preserve all these rapidly disappearing evidences of what God has wrought by our ancestors..."[8] Unfortunately in its early years, the Society was not active even after an unsuccessful attempt was made to merge it with the *American Catholic Historical Society of Philadelphia*. Three volumes of annual *Proceedings* were published in 1885 and 1886.

On January 1st, 1887, Shea breathed new life into the organization with the publication of the *United States Catholic Historical Magazine*, the official journal of the Society which continued to be issued until Shea's death in 1892. In 1899 the Society began publishing its *Historical Records and Studies*[9] which subsequently ran over thirty volumes. Since 1902, the Society has put out various monographs, many of which are highly significant contributions to Catholic American historiography.

As far back as 1879, Andrew Arnold Lambing tried to inaugurate a Catholic historical society in Pittsburgh to collect data on the Church in that area, but his plans never materialized. In February of 1884, Monsignor Lambing formed the *Ohio Valley Catholic Historical Society*[10] with objects more-or-less similar to those adopted some months later by the *American Catholic Historical Society of Philadelphia*. At that time, he began the publication of a small quarterly magazine entitled *Historical Researches in Western Pennsylvania Principally Catholic*, which he changed in July of 1885 to the simpler title *Catholic Historical Researches*. The quarterly was taken over by Martin I. J. Griffin in 1886 and published as the *American Catholic Historical Researches* until its demise in 1912. Subsequent activities along these veins were attempted by the *Catholic Historical Society of Western Pennsylvania*.

Another foundation of short duration was organized on February 22, 1892, by Marc F. Vallette and George E. O'Hara. Known originally as the *Long Island Catholic Historical Society*, its name was changed in 1894 to the *Brooklyn Catholic Historical Society*. Purpose of the Society was to collect "all matters of an historical nature relating to the Catholic Church, especially in Long Island." In the brief span of its existence, the organization made several notable contributions to American Church historiography and was responsible for Brooklyn's Peter Turner Memorial as well as the movement leading to the foundation of the Mitchell Memorial Scholarship at The Catholic University of America. A small publication entitled *Records* was issued in April of 1901.

The *New England Catholic Historical Society* was founded on June 13th, 1900, by Reverend William Byrne with headquarters at Boston. It was envisioned "to promote Catholic historical research and a wider knowledge of the origins of the Catholic Church in New England..."[11] In the years from 1901 through 1904 the Society issued five publications. Founders of the group were intent "that an effort should be made to have an historical record of every parish in New England secured and gathered together as a part of the preparation for a suitable celebration of the centenary of the Archdiocese of Boston in 1908."[12] Unhappily, the Society ceased to meet after 1904.

On April 25th, 1905, the *Saint Paul Catholic Historical Society*[13] was founded under the auspices of Archbishop John Ireland and the suffragan bishops of the province of Saint Paul. Its purpose was to study the Catholic history of the old northwest. The Society published five volumes between 1907 and 1918 under the title *Acta et Dicta* outlining the origin and growth of the Church in that area. Its avowed purpose was "to gather and place before its readers all available information in regard to the establishment and progress of the Church in the northwest..." Between 1918 and 1933 there was no activity but in that latter year the Society sent a questionnaire to the pastors of the archdiocese requesting information on parochial histories. *Acta et Dicta*[14] was reactivated in October of 1933 and published four additional volumes. Since October, 1936, however, there has been no further progress. In 1955 a *General Index* for the seven volumes of *Acta et Dicta* was issued under the editorship of Rev. Patrick Ahern at Saint Paul's Seminary.

On July 16th, 1908,[15] the *Maine Catholic Historical Society* was launched and perdured for about four or five years. The motivating cause behind its beginning was "the research and publication of what-ever is important in person, fact or document regarding the origin and growth of the Catholic Church in the present State of Maine."[16] The publication of the *Maine Catholic Historical Magazine* was begun in July of 1913 and appeared on a monthly basis until 1920, when it became a quarterly. It evolved into an official bulletin for the diocese of Portland and took on the added task of publishing "all important unpublished historical documents on the past and present conditions of the Catholic Church in Maine." In 1916 the officers of the Society announced that "the threads of the Catholic history of Maine from 1604 have been gathered up and the chief historic events have been carefully recorded, while the chronology of the present and all important Church events have been printed..."[17] Eight volumes appeared between 1913 and 1919 containing among other things a critical study of Catholic progress in Maine but the *Magazine* was discontinued in the early 1930s.

The organization of the *Catholic Historical Society of Saint Louis*, on February 7, 1917, is best described as "the result of a century's endeavor."[18] An earlier attempt had been made to set up a society in 1878 when the *Ecclesiastico-Historical Society* was established by certain clergymen of the Saint Louis diocese, who were "impressed by the fact that every age is the maker of its own history, that none can be more truthful witnesses to the events transpiring than the actors in its ever changing scenes."[19] After a few meetings, however, the original enthusiasm waned. Shortly thereafter, the *Catholic Union of Missouri* took over the task of gathering and preserving historical materials relating to the German Catholics in Missouri. Many valuable historical essays on the subject were published in the *Central Blatt and Social Justice*. Archbishop Glennon suggested the formation of the *Catholic Historical Society of Saint Louis* in 1917, it being the centennial of the Church in Saint Louis. The first number of the *Saint Louis Catholic Historical Review* appeared in October of 1918. Quarterly issues followed until October, 1923, when the *Review* ceased publication. It was a fine journal, steeped in scholarly and historical value. The documents and catalogues of manuscripts and sources were exceptionally well received and it has been said that nothing comparable to the *Review*[20] had previously appeared in Catholic American literature.

The Illinois Catholic Historical Society was established early in 1918 in anticipation of the centenary of Illinois' entry into the Union. Under the editorship of Rev. Frederick Siedenburg, and with the approval of the bishops of the Metropolitan Province, the *Illinois Catholic Historical Review* was inaugurated and ran through eleven volumes, issued on a quarterly basis. In July of 1928, its name was changed to *Mid-America* and a broader policy and wider scope enhanced even further the attractive *Review*. For the past three decades *Mid-America* has dealt primarily with Catholic life and history in the Mississippi Valley area and has now reached its forty-fourth volume.

Father Peter Guilday established the *American Catholic Historical Society* at Cleveland on December 30th, 1919, with the goal of widening the field of church history to a national level. The central offices of the Society were located at The Catholic University of America and since 1919 annual meetings have been held throughout the country. In 1922 the *Catholic Historical Review*, founded seven years earlier by Bishop Thomas Shahan and Father Guilday, became the official organ of the Society.

A unique organization was founded on May 15th, 1923, during the twentieth annual convention of the Texas State Council of the Knights of Columbus at Austin, Texas. Its formal name is the Texas Knights of Columbus Commission. In cooperation with the University of Texas and the State Historical Association, the Commission spent the early years of its existence collecting all types of information on early Catholic life in Texas. The purpose of the *Commission* was the preparation of a centennial history ending in 1936. The *Texas Catholic Historical Society* was launched in 1926 with headquarters at Saint Edward's University in Austin. It was incorporated in 1936. Publication of *Preliminary Studies of the Texas Catholic Historical Society* was an extremely valuable organ for Carlos E. Castaneda's subsequent *Our Catholic Heritage in Texas*.

The *Catholic Historical Society of Indiana* was started on the 27th of October in 1926, in the capital city. Its object was to prepare for the centennial of the Diocese of Vincennes-Indianapolis scheduled for 1934. The Society has published only one small volume entitled *Bulletin*.

The *Iowa Catholic Historical Society* was formed at Dubuque in March of 1928 with Archbishop James Keane as President, assisted by the faculty members of Columbia College.[21] Among its aims was the assembling of all materials relevant to the Catholic history of the old northwest. A publication appeared briefly under the name of *Collections* and in January of 1930, the first number of the *Iowa Catholic Historical Review* was issued as the official organ of the Society. This Review continued publication for nine volumes but has been on the inactive list since February of 1936.

In the midwest, the *Kansas Catholic Historical Society* was founded in 1930 at Saint Benedict's College, Atchison, Kansas. At one time, it had a fine collection of books and pamphlets and other materials pertaining to the state's Catholic background. For a number of years it remained inactive but was revived briefly in 1939 although no publications have appeared under its label.

April of 1944 witnessed the beginnings of the *Academy of American Franciscan History* at Washington, D.C. "It understands its scope as a review of inter-American cultural history... to include history, economics, sociology, ethnology, literature and folklore."[22] Official organ of the Academy is *The Americas* which first appeared in July of 1944 and is now in its eighteenth volume. Strictly speaking, the *Academy* is not an historical society although many of its functions are analogous.

The *Academy of California Church History* was organized in the late 1940s by Rt. Rev. James Culleton. Although technically not an historical review, its aims were similar, v.g. to publish short articles on important events in California Catholic history. *Academy Scrapbook* appeared in July, 1950, and continued through five volumes, the last being issued in 1959. "The subjects herein discussed are of varying types and must be blended together under their proper headings."[23] The *Scrapbook* was discontinued with the publication of its fifth volume although future works, entitled *California Yesterdays*, are promised by the Academy Guild Press of Fresno.

Last among the Catholic historical societies founded in the United States is the *Catholic Historical Society of Wisconsin*, organized at Ashland, in April of 1959.

Successes and failures have been recorded in the endeavor to form local historical societies, with perhaps the emphasis on the latter. Nevertheless, their value, even though short-termed, is incomparable for they have provided innumerable essays of great merit on matters of historic interest to students of American Catholic Church history which might never have come to light. And those diligent historians who worked so hard to put into effect the directives of Leo XIII can rest confident that they fulfilled his primary wishes...

> We bid all those of good will to join in this work and to count on Our special affection.... For the opinions of men cannot but yield to solid arguments; and truth herself will vanquish the attacks on truth that have been made so persistently.[24]

Notes to the Text

1. Issued at the Vatican, August 8, 1883. The letter is translated in the London *Tablet*, LXII, 321-323.
2. Rev. John P. Cadden, *The Historiography of the American Catholic Church*, (Washington, 1944) p.35.
3. Leo XIII, *Saepenumero Considerantes.*
4. *Records of the American Catholic Historical Society*, I, 16.
5. Rev. Thomas C. Middleton was chosen president.
6. The Society was founded after the closing of the Third Plenary Council of Baltimore and was greatly encouraged by Cardinal McCloskey and Archbishop Corrigan.
7. *Records of the American Catholic Historical Society*, XXIV, 65.
8. *United States Catholic Historical Magazine*, I, 1.
9. Charles G. Herbermann, "The United States Catholic Historical Society," *Catholic Historical Review*, II, 302-306.
10. "The Story of a Failure," *Catholic Historical Review*, I, 435-438.
11. Rev. Peter Guilday, "Catholic Historical Societies," *Official Catholic Yearbook, 1928.*
12. *Ibid.,*
13. The Society was reorganized in late 1912 and, on March 22nd, 1913, voted to change its name to the *Catholic Historical Society of Saint Paul.*
14. July 1907-July 1910; July 1914-July 1918; October 1933-October 1935.
15. Actually, the Society was only tentatively launched by Bishop Walsh in 1908 and did not take its permanent form until April of 1911.
16. Bishop Louis Walsh, "The Preface," *Maine Catholic Historical Magazine*, I, 1, p.5.
17. Guilday, *op. cit.*, p. 643.
18. Rev. John Rothensteiner, "The Catholic Historical Society of Saint Louis, the Result of a Century's Endeavor," *Saint Louis Catholic Historical Review*, I, 11.
19. *Item supra*, p. 12.
20. Cf. Waldo G. Leland, "Concerning Catholic Historical Societies," *Catholic Historical Review*, II, 389ff.
21. Now Loras College.
22. *The Americas*, I, 111.
23. Rt. Rev. James Culleton, "Background and Future Plans," *Academy Scrapbook*, V, ii
24. Leo XIII, *op. cit.*

2

Several hundred of the nation's parish stories have been written along the lines suggested in "A Note on Parochial Histories" which initially appeared in the *American Ecclesiastical Review* CL (February, 1964), 118-120. It was reprinted numerous times in the United States and Australia.

From a geographical point of view, the parish is the smallest juridic unit in Church administration. Nonetheless, in the words of the late Peter K. Guilday, "it is precisely in proportion to the accuracy and completeness of the printed history of the parish that the diocesan historian will be enabled to present us with a general picture of Catholic life and action, so desirable and indeed peremptory."[1]

With few exceptions, parish histories produced up to this time have been works of slight scientific value and even though these little volumes now constitute a fair sized library,[2] they are the despair of those interested in the future of American Catholic historiography. While it is true that not all parishes need to have their histories written, all parochial centers should prepare for the day when such an activity will be necessary by carefully preserving all the source materials revealing local spiritual and temporal growth.

No set of general rules for parish histories can be given which are applicable to the entire nation. But an author can be advised not to launch into the writing phase until he is at least armed with answers to the following questions:[3]

1. What is the official name of the parish and was it ever known by any other title ?
2. What city is the parish in and was that city ever known by another name?

8

3. From what earlier parish(es) was the jurisdiction originally formed and what were its original boundaries?

4. Have there been any additions or subtractions to the original boundaries?

5. Where was Mass first celebrated in the area? (approximate location or address)

6. What was the location of the property, date of construction, names of architects and contractors, size, type of material used (frame building, stucco exterior, stone reinforced, concrete and steel, brick facing on steel frame) and any other useful data of the permanent buildings in the parish plant?

7. What later additions were made, for what reason and by whom?

8. What were the dedication dates associated with the parish and the prelate who presided at the event?

9. What religious community staffed the parochial school and was there ever any change of communities? Dates of arrival?

10. Were there any outstanding lay pioneers associated with the early days of the parish? If so, give details.

11. Enumerate (with dates) the pastors and administrators of the parish. If there was a transfer to or from secular administration, give the date of this event.

12. List any extra parochial academies, convents, schools or charitable institutions within the parish boundaries.

"It is a rare parish which has all the requisite information ready at hand for the amateur historian to transform into some kind of interesting and connective narrative,"[4] hence research will consume much time and will extend to parochial registers, announcement books, diocesan newspapers, parish bulletins, aged parishioners, old maps, etc. Local historical societies will sketch the ethnic, political, social and industrial background of the area. If the parish is old enough, it might be useful to consult early national journals such as the *Records of the American Catholic Historical Society*, the *Catholic Historical Review* and others. When the research is completed, then the author must judiciously select those facts which are found useful, and couch them in discrete language that is at once true and attractive to prospective readers.

The historian must keep in mind that "he is more than a recorder; he is an interpreter of trends and movements and motives, if he is to make his narrative reasonably intelligible and interesting."[5]

When the major events bearing on the growth of the parish as a distinct institutional unit have been amassed, the final stages of work are finished and all that remains is the composition. It often happens that as many as ten or twelve drafts are made before the final version falls into place and most authors would do well to seek the judgment and advice of others before sending off the finished product for the *imprimatur.*

While it is generally recommended that the historical aspect of the text be entrusted to a priest, there is every reason to encourage participation by skilled parishioners in the work, especially in the layout and photographic formats of the monograph. Great care must be used in selecting a printer and it is always suggested that a minimum of three bids be handed in on a competitive basis. As in other matters, quality is expensive and there are no short cuts in the printing business. Cost is usually proportionate to the amount of type needed, quantity of cuts, and types of binding. Most parochial histories now being issued are profit-making ventures. By selling advertising the production costs can normally be met and the book sold at a modest price. If advertising is used, it is preferable to group the advertisements in one section of the monograph rather than scattering them throughout the narrative.

When the completed booklet is ready, copies should be sent to the local chancery archives, city newspapers, state and local libraries, Library of Congress, The Catholic University of America and all national Catholic historical societies.

Some years ago, an eminent authority noted that

> The parochial historian is the hewer of wood and the drawer of water for the diocesan and national Church historian. His duty it is to assemble and make accessible the materials for the story of the Church within his limited chosen area. The value of his parochial history depends upon the use which the specialist makes of original records; and its ultimate lasting qualities depend upon the amount of unpublished material which be brings to light in his researches. This note should be struck at the outset, because false quantities have crept into much of what has been written in the parochial historical field.[6]

Notes to the Text

1. The Writing of Parish Histories," *American Ecclesiastical Review* XCIII (September, 1935), 246-247.
2. The library at the Catholic University of America has set aside a special section for parochial histories and now numbers almost a thousand entries.
3. Based on a questionnaire sent out to the clergy of the Archdiocese of Los Angeles.
4. George Zimpfer, "The Parish Historian," *Homiletic and Pastoral Review* XXXVII (May, 1937), 826
5. *Ibid.*, p. 828.
6. Peter K. Guilday, *op. cit.*, 247.

3

"John Carroll and a Vernacular Liturgy" is the topic of this essay reproduced from *The Furrow*, XV (April, 1964) 228-230.

K nown as the "charioteer whom God has set over the American Church", John Carroll remains today an unequalled champion of progressive thought and nowhere is that more clearly exemplified than in his observations on the use of English in the liturgy. As early as 1787 Father Carroll made a strong plea for the vernacular, stating his opinion that the continued use of Latin was a major obstacle to a proper understanding of the Church by Protestants. In a letter to Father Joseph Berington,[1] Carroll remarked that:

> I cannot help thinking that the alteration of the Church discipline ought not only to be solicited, but insisted upon as an essential to the service of God and benefit of mankind.[2]

Carroll goes on to admit that:

> It may not have been prudent, for ought I know, to impose a compliance in this matter with the insulting and reproachful demands of the first reformers; but to continue the practice of the Latin liturgy in the present state of things must be owing either to chimerical fears of innovation or to indolence and inattention in the first pastors of the national Churches in not joining to solicit or indeed ordain this necessary alteration.[3]

Carroll's views were publicized in the British Isles where they elicited a sharp rebuke from the Archbishop of Dublin, John Thomas Troy. The Dominican prelate wrote to Carroll that the vernacular question was so controverted in Ireland that he had recently written a sixty-page pastoral objecting to its introduction. That Dublin's archbishop was anxious to silence the young American priest was obvious enough although his effect was negligible.

Troy's appeal notwithstanding, Carroll stated shortly thereafter:

> Before I had thought of ever being in my present station I expressed a wish that the pastors of the Church would see cause to grant to this extensive continent jointly with England and Ireland, etc., the same privileges as are enjoyed by many Churches of infinitely less extent; that of having their liturgy in their own language; for I do indeed conceive that one of the most popular prejudices against us is that our public prayers are unintelligible to our hearers. Many of the poor people, and the negroes generally, not being able to read, have no technical help to confine their attention.[4]

Nonetheless, always a minute observer of Church discipline, Carroll pointed out that Berington's interpretation of his attitudes on the vernacular

> ...attributes to me projects which far exceed my powers, and in which I should find no cooperation from my clerical brethren in America, were I rash enough to attempt their introduction upon my own authority.[5]

There is no question that Carroll's position as Superior of the Missions of the United States gave added prominence to his views. In one of his letters to Carroll, Berington appeared quite eager to see a mitre placed on the head of one "with your liberality of mind".[6] Berington's remarks had a prophetic sound for on 6 November 1789 a mitre was placed on Carroll's head when he became the first bishop in United States Catholic history.

If the holy oils tempered Bishop Carroll's views on the liturgy, there is no evidence to sustain it for in the First Synod of 1791 the priests were instructed to read the Sunday Gospel in the vernacular and especially at Vespers "it would be desirable for certain hymns and prayers to be sung in the vernacular tongue"[7] It was further recommended that the Our Father, Hail Mary, Apostles' Creed and Acts of Faith, Hope and Charity be said in the mother language.

There is no explicit testimony to indicate that English was ever used in the Mass or other liturgical functions prior to 1810 although the regulations adopted on 19 November of that year indicate some lack of conformity to the traditional practices. Among their observations the nation's five prelates noted that:

It is being made known to the archbishops and bishops that there exists a difference of opinion and practice among some of the clergy of the United States concerning the use of the vernacular language in any part of the public service, and in the administration of the sacraments, and it is hereby enjoined on all priests not only to celebrate the whole Mass in the Latin language, but likewise when they administer Baptism…[8]

Although Carroll's views on the delicate subject of a vernacular liturgy were somewhat modified between 1787 and 1810, there remains no doubt that the first member of the American hierarchy anticipated by 177 years that legislation promulgated on 16 February 1964 by the presently reigning pontiff, Paul VI.

Notes to the Text

1. Berington was the well-known author of *State and Behavior of English Catholics from the Reformation to the Year* 1780 (London, 1780).
2. Quoted in Peter K. Guilday, *The Life and Times of John Carroll* (New York, 1922), p. 130.
3. *Ibid.*
4. Quoted in John Gilmary Shea, *History of the Catholic Church in the United States*, 1763-1815 (New York, 1888), II, 234-5.
5. Peter K. Guilday. *op. cit*, p. 131.
6. *Ibid.*, p. 132.
7. *Concilia Provincialia Baltimori habita ab anno 1829 usque ad annum* 1849 (Baltimore, 1850), p. 20.
8. For the full text, cf. Martin I. J. Griffin, *History of Rt. Rev. Michael Egan, First Bishop of Philadelphia* (Philadelphia, 1893), Pp. 44 thru 48.

4

This talk was first delivered to the Newman Club of Los Angeles at the Statler Hilton Hotel on November 21, 1963. It later appeared as "Shadows over American Catholicism" in *Front Line* III (Summer, 1964), 23-28.

Some years ago Fr. Thomas A. Judge made the following observation about Catholics in America:

> We have in the United States at present scarcely touched the good-willed effort of our Catholic people. How to provoke it into action, lead it and conserve it, should be the constant thought of priests in their meditations. It is like the scattered waters of the meadow — a vast, idle flood. These waters, gathered into a conduit and given flow, make a vast power for good. Think what might be done with the waste products of leisure moments in the lives of our people. There are great impulses for good in the hearts of our men and women and the pity of it is that these receive so little expression. They must be led and their good impulses must be fostered and encouraged in action. The hope of our generation lies with the faithful.[1]

The indisputable fact that the Church in the United States is growing has as its corollary that all is not as it could be, that there are weaknesses. Yet like the hopeful man, it is the hopeful society that can look calmly and constructively at its failings. Indeed an analysis of its weaknesses will reveal those areas where the future growth of the Church is to take place. For the vitality of the Church will stem from her grappling with the problems now besetting her. And if challenge is a condition for her growth; then complacency is a sign of her decline.

Recently a leading churchman said in an address to the graduates of The Catholic University of America, "you are taking degrees at a time when Roman Catholicism is losing ground in the United States in spite of increased prosperity and prestige." He went on to point out that materially the Church is richer here than in any other country of the world, a fact which is witnessed to by 561 seminaries, 282 colleges and universities, more than 14,000 elementary and secondary schools and over 1,000 hospitals. The election of a Catholic president, the world-wide popularity Pope John XXIII enjoyed, the sympathetic coverage by the mass media of the Second Vatican Council all would seem to indicate the high level of prestige the Church in this land now enjoys. But with all this, we continue to lose ground.

> Here are a few cold figures that point to disaster unless the present trend is reversed. The number of converts is decreasing by 3,700 a year while the population continues to explode. In 1955, there were 151,000, in 1958 146,000, in 1961 128,000 and in 1962 125,000. Last year it took 340 Catholics 365 days to make one American like their Church well enough to join it. In the same length of time thirteen enthusiastic Mormons and nine Jehovahs Witnesses achieved a corresponding success. We can admit that it is easier to become a Jehovahs Witness than it is to become a Catholic-but is it thirty-three times easier? Meanwhile the number of living adults that vanishes each year from the Catholic Directory almost equals the number of converts. Last year, 125,000 came in and 118,000 left us. The main reasons seem to be bad marriages and birth control, the paganism of American higher education and the general deterioration of American morals. [2]

This breakdown could well come as a shock to complacent Catholics who read that there are in the United States today some 43,000,000 members of the Mystical Body. It is all too true that "Catholics count much more on births than on conversions. It is easier to produce a child than to convert a nation."[3]

In the United States today there are 65,000,000 people professing no religion at all. Many indifferentists have left the religion of their childhood; many others have never received any religious training. J. K. Kirwin feels this is because "our approach has been determinedly negative."[4] In many cases Catholics have closed in on themselves rather than going forth as Christ commanded. Soldiers raising walls for defense never conquer new lands. And this defensive attitude, seen in the phrase "keeping the faith" is self-destroying since the Catholic Faith can only be kept by giving it away. Cardinal Suenens says that the true answer to the catechism question is "God made us to know Him and to make Him known, and to love Him and make Him loved, to serve Him and make Him served."

We would suggest that the scarcity of converts is due to a lack of apostolic spirit, especially among the laity. It is true enough that converts are instructed by the clergy but they are attracted to the Church by the people they meet in everyday life. The expression "I didn't know you were a Catholic" is an all too frequent indictment. One hears of converts wondering why Catholic friends they had known for years never approached them about religion. Why do Catholics lack this spirit? Is it because only 50% of our students are attending Catholic schools? Maybe so, but even those who do seem to lack the missionary spirit. Since this spirit requires a living faith, perhaps the paucity of converts can be traced to inadequate religious education. The missionary implications of baptism and the apostolic commitment of confirmation have not been made real enough to certain Catholics. In a recent editorial, Fr. John Sheerin pinpoints this inadequacy as it applies to the Negro problem: "The Catholic proves to be as anti-Negro as the agnostic next door who never goes to Church.... I feel that the root problem... is education that does not touch the conscience. The Catholic child must learn more than the definition of love. He must learn to live it."[5] Our religious education is not real then if it is not regarded as a way of living Christ's life and helping Him to redeem the world.

As the zeal of Christians increases so will the number of converts. Lenin once said he could conquer the whole world if he had six men like Francis of Assisi. Mediocre Catholics are characterized by a sort of departmentalized attitude to their religion and often "Sunday Catholics" are indistinguishable from others in their weekday activities. One authority mentions that Catholics' adaptation to American society where external manifestations of religious belief are not permitted is "perhaps too successful" and he goes on to say that American Catholics are "weak in initiative" and leave "the inauguration of projects and their direction largely... to the clergy."[6]

Another grave cause for concern to the Church in America is related to the challenge of the apostolate. There is the oft-repeated charge that Catholics form a "ghetto," a group cut off from the mainstream of American life. It has been convincingly argued that among the reasons why Catholicism does not appeal to American non-Catholics is the view that the Church does not meet modern problems and needs. Others say she holds outdated ideas, is against progress or wholly disinterested in ameliorating life in this world. This attitude was pointed out by Bishop John Wright: "American Catholics are said, on the one hand, to be virtually indistinguishable in their behavior from non-Catholic Americans.

17

And on the other hand, American Catholics are also said to be rather separatist...non-involved with much of the ongoing work of our society, whether it be in the social, political, or cultural order."[7] The fact that nineteenth-century Catholicism in America was largely immigrant resulted in a membership composed of the lower socioeconomic class. But this does not excuse the present "ghetto" situation.

Does the Church in the United States, in her members, really address herself to the reconstruction of the social order? What about concerted Catholic effort to alleviate the material poverty of many Americans. Can we say that there is social justice in a nation where the top one-fifth of the population obtains more of the national income than the bottom three-fifths?

The apostolate requires an active concern for the welfare of people and this must be emphasized because too many Catholics feel that their religion is a private matter only.

Among the primary causes of adults leaving the Church, according to Gannon, are bad marriages, birth control, and the general deterioration of American morals. Time and again it is noted that morals of Catholics are no better than those of others. "The State Supreme Court of California last year threw out as unconstitutional certain local ordinances and laws governing narcotics, traffic, pornography, prostitution and the like."[8] Is this not an indication that the moral climate of our nation is rapidly going downhill while the courts seemingly hasten the process along by accommodating the law to what they think is the majority viewpoint of morals? This moral crisis involves all the commandments of God. Divorce, economic dishonesty, and social injustice are but a few of the more frequent violations.

American bishops in their 1948 Pastoral point to the cause of this moral decline: "The greatest moral catastrophe of our age is the growing number of Christians who lack a sense of sin because personal responsibility to God is not a moving force in their lives."[9]

Another partial index of the vitality of the Church and the morality of its members is the level of Mass attendance. According to the conclusion of such reliable pollsters as Gallup and the University of Michigan Research Center, "Some 70% of American Catholics attend Church regularly and the attendance increases as social and economic status improves. The skeptics argue that such survey material depends on the respondents telling the truth and that Catholics are obviously lying about their church-going habits."[10] Attendance, they find, is worst in the far West. Since attendance at Mass is required under pain of mortal sin, one wonders about the religious attitude of the one-third who violate this law of their Church.

What is the cause of this lack of religious fervor and conviction, this loss of the sense of sin? Again, the American hierarchy point out secularism as the main cause of modern ills and they define it as "the practical exclusion of God from thinking and living."

Closely linked to this are materialism and hedonism, so prominent in American society. Unhappily many Catholics practically agree in "identifying our national greatness with our material luxury."[11] Lack of the poverty of spirit, especially in clergy and religious is often criticized and too often Catholics seeking wealth and pleasure appear to be submerged in strictly material values. One writer analyzes the weaknesses of the Catholic Church as a whole: Hollywood's hedonism, the breakdown of family life, divorce, birth control... alcoholism."[12]

What has the Church done in the south? How many of our people there are openly prejudiced? Sociological studies reveal alarming figures: The most notable and continuing example of opposition to a progressive hierarchy occurs in Louisiana where a minority of the laity are in open and expressed defiance of the program for Catholic school desegregation. These people seem to refuse to recognize the race problem as a moral and theological issue and one needs only recall the reaction to Archbishop Joseph F. Rummell's decision to verify this assertion.

It would seem also that obligations of charity are overlooked. Rare indeed are the white homes which allow a Negro to enter by the front door and rarer still the family tables at which a Negro may break bread with white friends. Great scandal has been caused by separate Catholic churches and schools for colored people and certainly we cannot deny that this failure on our part must account for the scarcity of Negro Catholics. Of the 18,000,000 Negroes in the United States, only 664,000 are Catholic.

Indeed the Church seems to be at its weakest in the south. In the ten states from the Mississippi to the Atlantic less than 5% of the population is Catholic, over one-half of these living in one part of Louisiana. Many of the 607 counties in the United States with no priests are in this area. It is not unheard of that one priest has for a parish an area larger than the whole of Belgium and the Netherlands combined.

Our late Holy Father, John XXIII, in his last encyclical, might have been thinking of the United States when he noted that, "Our era is penetrated and shot through by radical errors, it is torn and upset by deep disorders. Nevertheless, it is also an era in which immense possibilities for good are opened to the Church."

Notes to the Text

1. In Lawrence Brediger, *Sparks of Faith* (Westminster, 1961), p. 56.
2. Robert I. Gannon, "Commencement Address Given at The Catholic University of America," manuscript courtesy of the author. Address dated June 9, 1963.
3. R. L. Bruckberger, *Roman Catholicism and the American Way of Life* (Notre Dame, 1960), p. 40.
4. *Politics...Government...Catholics* (New York, 1961), p. 104.
5. *Catholic World*, 196 (1963), 333.
6. Gustave Weigel, "An Introduction to American Catholicism," in *The Catholic Church, U.S.A.* (Chicago, 1956), p. 17.
7. In Donald McDonald, Religion, *Series of Interviews on the American Character* (Santa Barbara, 1962), p. 34.
8. *Ibid.*, p. 58.
9. In Theodore Roemer, *The Catholic Church in the United States* (St. Louis, 1950), p. 388.
10. Andrew M. Greeley, "Catholicism Among College Graduates," *Catholic World*, 197 (1963), 96.
11. John Ryan, "Are We Education Conscious," *Catholic World*, 186 (1962), 21.
12. Joseph B. Gramillion, "The Catholic Church in Louisiana," in *The Catholic Church, U.S.A.*, *op. cit.*, p. 219.

5

This essay on "American Church-State Relations: A Catholic View" appeared in *A Journal of Church and State* VII (Winter, 1965), 30-34.

It might be well to preface these remarks by observing that the delicate subject of church-state relations is not a religious question, but rather one of civil liberties and constitutional law. The First Amendment has nothing whatever to do with the truth or falsity of any or all religious beliefs nor with the validity of any mode of worship. Rather, it deals primarily with the delegation of powers from the states to the national government guaranteeing every citizen the right to worship God in a manner consistent with his conscience and devoid of all outside influence.

The eminent F. Ernest Johnson of Columbia University has remarked that ignoring "the distinction between church and state would be disastrous both to religious and political freedom. But to make the doctrine a rule of thumb to be invoked against every measure that brings church and state into some cooperative relationship is to travesty important principle and thus to make it more obscure."[1]

The point of conflict, if indeed there really be one, centers around the precise manner in which church and state should cooperate or, more basically, whether such cooperation is even tolerable. Jefferson's "wall of separation"[2] has grown to ironcurtain proportions and seeks to block any official contact between these two basic units of society despite the fact that the so-called "separation of church and state" doctrine is not in the First Amendment itself, but is exhumed from subsequent writings of Jefferson and Madison, as if these observations actually formed part of our constitutional provisions. This strange approach to the problem was commented on by the Appellee's brief in the *McCullom* case.

Are we now, 160 years after the Amendment was explained by
Madison, to examine his writings and speeches outside of the legislative chamber, and from them to seek to determine what was
his own personal political philosophy as to the relationship of
Church and State, and then, disregarding his words at the time of
the framing of the Amendment, ascribe to the Amendment the
meaning thus gleaned?[3]

The wording of the First Amendment is quite plain: "Congress shall
make no law respecting an establishment of religion, or prohibiting the
free exercise thereof..." The only other mention made of religion in the
Constitution is that in Article VI, section 3: "No religious test shall ever
be required as a qualification to any office or public trust under the
United States." This crystal-clear terminology has been examined in
relation both to the *times* in which it was written and to the *men* instrumental in its formation and adoption. A study of this type shows that
much of the present-day interpretation has strayed considerably from the
original intention of the framers.

The name of God is nowhere to be found in the Constitution. Joseph
Story and Charles Warren agree on the basic reasons for this a-religious tone
of the Constitution, contending that 'the framers wished to restrict the federal government from exercising *any* control over any religion. In addition,
these eminent constitutional lawyers feel that the religious beliefs of the people were so diverse that the federal government would have found it wholly
impractical to attempt any kind of uniformity in matters religious.

An "establishment of religion," as understood in the eighteenth century,
was a common feature in the colonies for there were nine such established
churches in the thirteen colonies at the outbreak of the Revolution, [4]
although their number was reduced to five by the time the First
Amendment was drafted.[5] Variations in the different colonies obviously
existed but it was not uncustomary for inhabitants in "established states" to
tithe and attend religious services even under penalty. Frequently the right
to vote or hold public office depended on submission to a religious test.[6]
judging from all available evidence, this arrangement was precisely what our
early statesmen hoped to prevent on a national scale by enactment of the
First Amendment. It hardly was envisioned that this Amendment would
prohibit the federal government from recognizing religion in *general* for by
its very definition "...establishment of religion is meant the setting up or
recognition of a state church, or at least the conferring upon one church of
special favors and advantages which are denied to others."[7]

During the debates prior to the adoption of the First Amendment, six different proposals were considered. Five of these six incorporated the term "establishment of religion." The third suggested that "Congress shall make no laws touching religion or infringing the rights of conscience." This version, rejected by Congress, embodies the principle prevalent in certain *dicta* of the Supreme Court through the years. Nonetheless, the final draft was accepted with its ban on "an establishment of religion" and it is around *that wording* that all discussion must center. Obviously, the 1789 framers were chiefly concerned lest the setting up of an "exclusive" religion in America would bring discrimination to all others.[8] This interpretation is sustained by an examination of the individual states ratifying the Constitution, some even with the express *proviso* that a Bill of Rights be adopted embodying this sentiment. In fact, insistence on a ban forbidding the federal government to have a national church formed part of several of the state ratifying conventions. Virginia's action is of particular significance for her framers observed

> that religion or the duty which we owe to our Creator, and the manner of discharging it can be directed only by reason and conviction, not by force or violence, and therefore all men have an equal, natural and inalienable right to the free exercise of religion according to the dictates of conscience, … no particular religious sect or society ought to be favored or established in preference to others.[9]

Here the distinction between "religious freedom" and an "established religion" is logically spelled out. In none of the conventions was there any reference to aid to or cooperation with religion *in general*. The resultant amendment itself contained no ban on equal attitudes to all religions, nor did it mention schools or education, even though they be parochial. The federal government concerned itself therefore, not with separation, but with *equality*. Joseph Story says that "the real object of the Amendment was to exclude all rivalry among Christian sects, and to prevent any national ecclesiastical establishments which should give to a hierarchy the exclusive patronage of the national government."[10]

A proper understanding of the historical development of this matter demands some reflection on the philosophy of James Madison who drew up the Amendment in its final form. He was an ardent student of John Locke's theory of religion as an inward conviction; Locke viewed a man's faith as inviolable and demanded its protection at all costs, provided only that there be no threat to the commonweal. Another influencing factor in Madison's life was his early association with John Witherspoon, a strong advocate of toleration in ecclesiastical matters.[11] The future president was gradually led to the personal conviction that a successful republic must emphasize preservation of freedom under the law even to the exclusion of equality. "The right of every man is to liberty, not to toleration."

In addition to Madison's thoughts as embodied in the First Amendment, other recorded observations of this respected statesman can be found in the *Annals of Congress*. For instance, he believed that Congress should not establish or enforce the legal observance of religion by law, nor compel men to worship God in any manner contrary to their conscience. Even had Madison foreseen the confusion existing in our own day, he could hardly have used clearer terms than these. References to his *Remonstrances*, cited by proponents of the "wall of separation," are surely not applicable to this discussion, written as they were four years earlier and concerned with a completely different aspect of this delicate question.

An investigation of Madison's actions as congressman are additional clues to his private interpretation of the First Amendment. He served on a joint committee which arranged for the chaplain system, financed by public funds, for use in both houses of Congress. And even in later years when he questioned the constitutionality of this action, he was concerned not with the use of public funds to support the project but about the "principle of a national establishment" which excluded Roman Catholics and Quakers who, by virtue of their personal convictions, could not participate actively in this program. Here again Madison focused attention on this traditionally strict determination of avoiding an "establishment of religion" which might undermine the rights of certain minorities.

Obviously then, Madison's interpretation of the First Amendment simply involved a denial to the federal government of the power to confer on any particular religious organization an official or privileged position, injurious to all others. Any other conclusion could hardly be supported by the historical facts and would lead us to conclude with James Milton O'Neill, in his commentary on the *Everson Case*, that "Justice Rutledge gave us Eckenrode's *interpretation* of what Madison wrote about *something else* from which he deduces what Madison meant by the First Amendment but he omits to tell us what Madison said he meant in plain English."[12]

There remains little historical doubt that the First Amendment was anything more than a legislative act forbidding a monopoly of state favors to one particular religion. It is unsound, therefore, to read into the First Amendment a prohibition against the government either dealing with religion as such or assisting all religions equally.

Notes to the Text

1. F. Ernest Johnson, "Religion and Public Education," *Proceedings of the Thirty-First Annual Convention, Secondary School Principals* (1947), p.96.
2. Thomas Jefferson seems to be the first to use the term "wall of separation." See *Writings of Thomas Jefferson* (20 vols.; Washington, D.C.: Thomas Jefferson Memorial Association of the United States, 1905), XVI, 282.
3. McCullom vs. Board of Education, *Appellee's Brief*, p. 43.
4. The Congregational Church was established in Massachusetts, Connecticut and New Hampshire; the Anglican Church in New York, Virginia, Maryland, North and South Carolina and Georgia. Rhode Island, Delaware, New Jersey and Pennsylvania had no form of establishment.
5. Only Massachusetts, Connecticut, Maryland, New Hampshire and South Carolina retained established churches at this time.
6. Marcus W. Jernegan, *The American Colonies* (New York, Longmans, Green & Co., 1929), p. 350.
7. Thomas M. Cooley, *The General Principles of Constitutional Law in the United States* (Boston: Little, Brown and Co., 1891), p. 213.
8. Not so in England
9. Charles C. Tansill, *Documents Illustrative of Formation of the Union of the American States* (Washington: Government Printing Office, 1927) p.1030.
10. Joseph Story, *Commentaries on the Constitution*; (2 vols.; Boston: Little, Brown and Co., 1891), II, 1874 and 1877.
11. Anson Phelps Stokes, *Church and State in the United States* (3 vols.; New York: Harper and Brothers, 1950), 1, 339.
12. James Milton O'Neill, "Church and State in the United States," *Historical Records and Studies* XXXVII (New York, 1948), 36.

6

"Thomas Conaty Confronts Problems of His Day" is taken from the *American Benedictine Review*, XVI (December, 1965) 557-564.

In his younger days, Thomas Conaty, second Rector of The Catholic University of America, was described in terms as realistic as they were poetic:

> We can easily imagine him a Peter waking up Europe to the crusades, but would find it hard to see in him the same Peter in a hermit's cell...God made him an active man, and in every agitation for the people's health he is the angel who, stronger than the rest, can best stir the waters.[1]

Thomas James Conaty was born in Kilnaleck, County Cavan, Ireland, on August 1, 1847,[2] the son of Patrick and Alice Lynch Conaty. Two years later the infant was brought to the United States by his parents who settled in Taunton, Massachusetts.[3] The boy grew up in the Old Colony State and after attending the local public schools, he entered Montreal College on December 30, 1863, transferring four years later to Holy Cross in Worcester. Under the patronage of a cousin, Conaty returned to Montreal in 1869 and enrolled at the Grand Séminaire. He was ordained for the Diocese of Springfield in the chapel of the Grand Séminaire on December 21, 1872, by the Most Reverend Ignatius Bourget.[4]

The following spring Father Conaty was named curate at Saint John's Church in Worcester and in 1880, when the parochial boundaries were adjusted, Conaty was given charge of the newly erected parish of the Sacred Heart.

That the years of his pastorate were filled with activities is understandable in view of his reputation as an "agitator who loves the work of the multitude."[5] A school, rectory, convent, gymnasium and finally a church were built and within a few years the parish had no less than sixteen societies to coordinate its many-phased apostolate.

Early in life, Conaty interested himself in the temperance movement. He was a strong proponent of Henry Edward Cardinal Manning and Monsignor James Nugent who introduced the League of the Cross in England as a legion of total abstinence. The Worcester pastor was even more sympathetic to the program brought to the United States from Ireland by the Reverend Theobold Mathew in 1849. An outgrowth of the Father Mathew movement was the establishment, on February 22, 1872, of the Catholic Total Abstinence Union of America, set up at Baltimore by representatives of various local units throughout the nation. Its avowed purpose was "the moral elevation of others and the salvation of souls, by aiding in suppressing the evils of intemperance."[6] Indeed, the C.T.A.U. was "different from any other Catholic society in United States history" and to a certain extent "it was the incarnation of Archbishop Ireland's ideal of a prosperous, civic minded, Americanized Catholicism." [7]

It was an attempt to revitalize and strengthen this work that motivated Father Thomas J. Conaty to organize the Springfield Diocesan Temperance Union at Fall River on May 30, 1877[8]. The obstacles were many in the early years and it was January of 1885 before Conaty could establish, in his own parish, the Catholic Young Men's Lyceum "for the advancement of temperance, and for the moral, mental, and physical improvement of its members."[9] Once organized, progress was rapid and within a decade the Lyceum had "achieved a reputation coextensive with the confines of the state."[10] To its members, the entire movement was "an apostolate by which to reach to the source of private and public life, to preach self-denial and sacrifice for the sake of humanity, to redeem humanity from the ills which intemperance brings."[11]

The pastor of Sacred Heart parish first attracted national attention in 1885 when he was elected vice president of the C.T.A.U. Two years later he became president of the society and during his term he crisscrossed the nation telling audiences, in the words of Manning:

> Temperance is good; total abstinence is better. We are pledged to temperance by the words of our baptism. No one is bound to total abstinence. It is the free choice of those who aspire to live by the council of a higher life. Happy are those who have taken the pledge not for any need of their own, but to save others by word and example from spiritual death.[12]

Wherever he spoke, Conaty emphasized that the 60,000 members of the C.T.A.U. in every state of the union find their "ethics in the plain teaching of Christian virtues" by promoting the "great end of the spiritual welfare of man."[13]

Conaty was able, during his tenure as president, to return to the land of his birth and while there he told almost incredulous multitudes that at least 70 per cent of the C.T.A.U. membership had never tasted liquor, underscoring his belief that the alcoholic "is the smallest, and probably the least important part of the total abstinence work, for I am one who has so far lost faith in human nature, that I think the prospect of the permanent reformation of the confirmed drunkard is slight indeed."[14]

In contrast to his mentor, Father Theobold Mathew, Conaty's views on total abstinence made him no friend of the prohibitionists for he was quick to point out that "men sometimes forget that Catholic total abstinence and party prohibition are totally different. The former hates drunkeness, the latter hates drink." He never hesitated to say that "Catholic total abstinence may accept prohibition in certain cases as a method of curtailing a traffic grown into monstrous proportions," but he viewed such actions "an extreme remedy, a sort of war measure."[15]

The Worcester pastor, adroitly avoided creating a paper dragon of his campaign and constantly reiterated that "total abstinence is not a substitute for religion, but a real help to religious life, making the practice of religion easier and more effectual."[16]

There was opposition to Father Conaty's work among many conservative church leaders who expressed uneasiness at the C.T.A.U.'s willingness to cooperate with Protestants. John Lancaster Spalding, the Bishop of Peoria, once worried aloud that "these people, if they had the power, would make us a sect of Methodists."[17] Nonetheless, although unable to guide the anti-liquor forces toward the goals won in 1919, the C.T.A.U. people can be credited with trying to increase happiness without abandoning the traditional American concept of personal liberty.

To the charge that his movement was "political," Conaty replied that "the Catholic Church leaves its members free to act as their consciences may direct and to vote as their best interests may demand, urging solely that the common welfare be the guide of action."[18] In a similar vein, at a rally of the Springfield C.T.A.U., Conaty said that "no matter what our creed, or nationality, or politics, we are all one in belief that intemperance is a great evil, and we are one in honoring the temperance that ennobles our mankind, enriches our labor and strengthens our state."[19]

Esteem for Father Theobold Mathew was widespread in the East and when Conaty spoke at Salem in 1887 for the dedication of a statue of the

Irish Capuchin, all the city's liquor stores closed for the event[20]" During his address on that occasion, Conaty pointed out that "Father Mathew never advocated that total abstinence is all the religion a man needs or that the pledge is a charm guaranteeing against all temptation,"[21] and he brought out how the entire program was merely a "means" to higher perfection.

The New York *Freeman's Journal* relates[22] how Father Conaty spearheaded attempts to establish at The Catholic University of America a Chair dedicated to the memory of Father Theobold Mathew during his presidency of the C.T.A.U. to "thus fittingly celebrate the centenary of our apostle, and to erect to his memory a monument, more enduring than block of stone or figure of bronze and stamp his movement with the high and noble characteristic of education."[23] It was as a former president of the Union and one of its strongest advocates that Conaty gave the first "Father Mathew Lecture" at The Catholic University of America in 1895. Therein he expressed his belief that "Father Mathew's principles have accomplished an amount of good in our country we can never adequately acknowledge. Whatever of success we Irish have been able to secure in the United States has been in great measure owing to our adoption of his principles."[24]

Conaty's prominence on the national scene was considerably enhanced by his presidency of The Catholic Summer School of America from 1892 onwards. And although he possessed no formally earned degrees, the Irish-born priest's activities as a temperance worker and educator were said "to embrace every chapter of his life, for even as an unknown priest his thoughts were always bent toward the educating and humanizing of his fellows."[25] It came then as no surprise when Pope Leo XIII selected Conaty's name from the terna submitted in 1896 for the rectorship of The Catholic University of America. Soon after the formal bulls were released on November 22, the press hailed the appointee "as an ardent advocate of the cause of temperance, which he has nourished, fostered, and developed in this country."[26]

In speaking of the departure of Father Conaty from Worcester, a city "representative of all the ancient narrowness as well as all the potential greatness of New England character," one journal "doubted whether a higher tribute of praise has ever been tendered to any man." "It is well to remember," noted the *Catholic World*, "that this ovation was the spontaneous expression of New England devotion to a Catholic priest, and that this Catholic priest won his way to the New England heart because he entered the arena of public life and took a bold stand for Temperance and good citizenship."[27]

Although the multitudinous activities of running a large, problem-ridden university left little time for temperance work, Conaty's interest in the movement never abated and commenting on the twenty-fifth annual convention of the Springfield Union in 1901, Monsignor Conaty noted:

> The recollections of the past twenty-five years of temperance work in our Union are most pleasing. I recall the difficulties of the early years and their subsequent successes. From the beginning, there were devoted men in the temperance work, anxious only for the welfare of the people and the glory of the Church.... My wish at its Twenty-Fifth Anniversary is that the spirit which created it and which permitted it great successes may lead it to greater energy in the cause which lies so near to the spiritual and temporal interests of the people.... We need it to safeguard the individual life, to protect the home, to give value to labor and honor and glory to God.... The badge of the Union as the pledge of Total Abstinence is always to me a source of greatest pride, consolation, and encouragement.[28]

Despite a personal vow to abstain from alcohol, Conaty never objected to those who used such beverages moderately and remarked on several occasions that "you will always find the Catholic Church opposed to the theory of any man or set of men which asserts that drink is in itself evil, and an evil to be absolutely and universally condemned."[29] That Conaty himself was no prude is obvious from a letter he wrote acknowledging a gift of wine on the occasion of his consecration to the Titular See of Samos on November 24, 1901:

> I am deeply grateful to you for...the bottles of Samos wine which you were so thoughtful to send me. I was very proud to have been able to use the wine at the banquet in Baltimore, and thus give my friends, especially those around the Cardinal, a taste of my diocesan production.[30]

With completion of Conaty's term at Washington, the Archbishop of San Francisco, Patrick W. Riordan, asked that the second Rector of The Catholic University of America be named Bishop of Monterey-Los Angeles in far-away California. The Holy See acquiesced and papal bulls to that effect were dispatched from the Vatican on March 27, 1903. Soon after hearing of the appointment, the Los Angeles newspapers reprinted a farewell speech of Senator George F. Haar in which the nationally known legislator saluted Conaty as a man who had stood for temperance, for sobriety, for honest living, for courtesy, for charity, for piety."[31]

The magnetic personality and restless zeal of the Irish-born prelate soon won over his California flock. One Angelino spoke of the Bishop to the President of the United States in these words:

He does not hesitate to express himself freely upon a point and will surely do a very great amount of good in this state. He is respected and beloved by all our citizens, without regard to their religious affiliations, and he is certainly a power in this part of the country.[32]

Any thought that the new Bishop of Monterey-Los Angeles might bring the temperance movement to the west coast were soon dispelled though, for Conaty felt that the C.T.A.U. was needed mostly "in the great industrial centers of the East" where "the pastor of souls cannot fail to recognize the dangers of intemperance."[33] The bishop preferred to carry on such work in California's southland within the framework of existing organizations and, in this regard, endorsed the work of the Federation of Catholic Societies.

Though he felt that Los Angeles was not the place for a formal unit of the C.T.A.U., Conaty retained his affection and appreciation for the movement and in a speech to the Ancient Order of Hibernians he said:

Long ago I resolved what I could do to crush down the terrible blight of intemperance that lies in wait, ready to crush them to the earth. I vowed myself a pledge of total abstinence that I might say, "Follow me!" This is the kind of prohibition I believe in.[34]

Notes to the Text

1. John J. McCoy, *History of the Catholic Church in the Diocese of Springfield* (Boston, 1900), p. 273
2. There is only secondary evidence to substantiate this statement. In 1962 the author visited the Very Reverend Patrick Gaffney, pastor of Crosserlough in the Diocese of Kilmore only to find that the original Saint Mary's Church and its records had been destroyed by fire about 1884.
3. Charles Nutt, *History of Worcester and Its People* (New York, 1919), II, p. 871.
4. *"Actes des Ordinations et autres,* 1857-1932."
5. John J. McCoy, *op. cit.,* p.273.
6. Morgan M. Sheedy, "The Catholic Total Abstinence Union," *American Ecclesiastical Review* XII (March, 1895), 188.
7. Sister Joan Bland, *Hibernian Crusade* (Washington, 1951), p. 267
8. *Catholic Messenger,* July 4, 1908.
9. *The Gleaner,* October 3, 1894. The Catholic Young Women's Lyceum was established in the parish on March 25, 1888.
10. Philip J. Tighe, *Souvenir of the United Catholic Total Abstinence Societies of Worcester* (Worcester, 1896), n.p.
11. "Ethics of Catholic Total Abstinence," *Temperance Truth* III (December, 1894), 12.
12. A quotation from an address of *Cardinal Manning to the Thurles Convention of the League of the Cross,* July 23, 1899.
13. "Ethics of Catholic Total Abstinence,"*op. cit.,* p. 3.

14. An Address to the Father Mathew, O.S.F.C. *Total Abstinence League of the Sacred Thirst* (Liverpool, 1889), p. 3.
15. "Catholic Total Abstinence," *Catholic World* XLV (August, 1887), 685.
16. Annual Address of Rev. Thomas J. Conaty, D.D., President of the *Catholic Total Abstinence Union of America* (Cleveland, 1889), p. 3.
17. Archives of the University of Notre Dame, John Lancaster Spalding to Daniel Hudson, Peoria, August 13, 1894.
18. *The Catholic Church and Total Abstinence* (Saratoga, 1894), p. 8. *Worcester Telegram*, September 7, 1896.
20. Maurice Dinneen, *The Catholic Temperance Movement in the Archdiocese of Boston* (Boston, 1908), p.200.
21. Archives of the Archdiocese of Los Angeles, "Address in Salem," October 10, 1887.
22. November 3, 1888.
23. *Annual Address... op. cit.*, p.6.
24. *An Address...*, *op. cit.*, p. 13.
25. The *Catholic School and Home Magazine* V (January, 1897), 225.
26. *Saint Louis Church Progress*, December 5, 1896.
27. "Editorial Notes," *LXIV* (February, 1897), 707.
28. Archives of The Catholic University of America, Thomas J. Conaty to John J. O'Malley, Washington, October 5, 1901. Quoted in Peter E. Hogan, *The Catholic University of America, 1896-1903: The Rectorship of Thomas J. Conaty* (Washington, 1949), p. 16.
29. *The Catholic Church and Total Abstinence*, *op. cit*, p. 3.
30. Archives of the Catholic University of America, Thomas J. Conaty to John Furey, Washington, December 18, 1901. Quoted in Peter E. Hogan, *op. cit.*, p. 1 5.
31. Los Angeles *Times*, April 19, 1903.
32. Library of Congress, Ms. in Taft Papers, 194, John J. Davis to William Howard Taft, Los Angeles, September 22, 1908.
33. Archives of the Archdiocese of Los Angeles, *An Address*, n.d. *(circa 1913)*
34. *The Tidings*, July 4, 1903.

7

This treatise on "Episcopal Appointments in the U.S.A." appeared in the *American Ecclesiastical Review* CLV (September, 1966), 178-191.

Vatican II's *Decree Concerning the Pastoral Office of Bishops in the Church* re-affirms that "bishops (are) chosen from various parts of the world in ways and manners established or to be established by the Roman Pontiff...."[1] The electoral procedure has been variously modified in the course of history; yet certain essentials have never been sacrificed, though in the constitution of her chief agents "the Church has always sought to take cognizance of the social and political conditions of the world in which they were to exercise their influence."[2]

In the United States, as elsewhere, "ecclesiastical discipline on the selection of candidates for the Episcopacy has changed with the growth of the Church."[3] On March 12, 1788, the priests working along the Atlantic seaboard addressed a request to Pope Pius VI asking for creation of an episcopal seat in the infant nation. As a special concession, the petitioners asked "that the election[4] of the bishop, at least for the first time, be permitted to the priests, who now duly exercise the religious ministry here and have the care of souls."[5] The Holy Father acquiesced and permission was given "for this time only, to name the candidate for presentation."[6] Of the twenty-six ballots subsequently cast, all but two favored Father John Carroll, superior of the American Missions. The action of the clergy was ratified by the Sacred Congregation of Propaganda Fide on September 14, 1789, and on November 6th the Holy Father made the formal appointment.

During the First National Synod, held on November 7, 1791, "the question of the appointment of a Bishop as suffragan of Baltimore, or Coadjutor, was discussed."[7] Bishop Carroll subsequently wrote to Rome proposing that "the ten oldest clergymen here, and five others to be nominated by myself, be the electors of the new bishop."[8] Leonardo Cardinal Antonelli, the Prefect of Propaganda, responded affirmatively on September 28, 1792, enjoining the Bishop of Baltimore to propose, "with the advice of his older priests,"[9] a qualified cleric of the American Mission for the Coadjutorship.

When the episcopal candidate, Dominic Lawrence Graessl, died, the same procedure was used by Carroll in submitting the name of Father Leonard Neale, the first man consecrated within the borders of the United States.

When the vast Baltimore jurisdiction was divided into a metropolitan province with an archdiocese and four suffragan sees, on April 8, 1808, the Holy See accepted Carroll's recommendation of candidates for Boston (John Cheverus), Philadelphia (Michael Egan) and Bardstown (Benedict Flaget). Pope Pius VII was careful to note, however, that in the future, "whenever a vacancy occurs in any of the said Sees,"[10] the presentation of *episcopabiles* would be reserved.

Two years later, in November of 1810, at the first meeting of the American hierarchy, the bishops "humbly and respectfully suggested to the Supreme Pastor of the Church to allow the nomination for the vacant Diocese to proceed solely from the Archbishop and Bishops of this ecclesiastical province."[11] This request Rome apparently chose to ignore.

Though he bad been "rather contemptuously informed that neither the Archbishop of Baltimore nor his suffragans had the right to nominate the vacant sees," Archbishop Ambrose Marechal suggested to Propaganda Fide that " for the welfare of religion" the congregation should "write us and hear our reasons before proceeding to the nomination of subjects recommended only by intriguing monks at Rome or by outside Bishops who have not the least knowledge of Church affairs."[12] That Marechal's annoyance was well taken is obvious for on June 3, 1822, the American bishops were given the limited right to "recommend" candidates for vacancies.

Prior to 1833, there was no definite procedure outlined for presenting episcopal candidates, however, and several distinct methods were employed. From time to time Rome directly appointed bishops for New York (Richard Concanen and John Connolly), Charleston (John England) and Richmond (Patrick Kelly); Archbishop Marechal of Baltimore nominated a coadjutor for Bardstown (John David) while the Bishops of Cincinnati (Edward Fenwick and John Purcell) and Boston (Benedict Fenwick) were nominated by the suffragans without recourse to the metropolitan.

At the Second Provincial Council, assembled at Baltimore during October of 1833, the prelates drafted a wholly new method for selecting bishops, which, with a few alterations, was approved by the Sacred Congregation of Propaganda Fide. The decree on the "Mode of Filling Vacant Sees," issued on June 14, 1834, specified that:

> When a see becomes vacant all the bishops of the province vote upon those candidates they deem worthy of being appointed to the vacancy. Since this voting can be done more accurately and easily at a Provincial Council, if a council is to be held within three months of the death of the bishop, the bishops of the province should not vote upon the names of the candidates, but should wait till they meet in council before sending the names to the Sacred Congregation. Assembled in such a case, after a discussion, they shall determine what priests merit appointment to the vacant see or to a coadjutorship according as the case may be.

> However, when the see becomes vacant at a time when no Provincial Council is to be held, another plan should be followed. In order that a see might not be too long without an incumbent, it is necessary and fitting that each bishop keep sealed and directed to his vicar general, to be opened at his death, a duplicate list of the three priests whom he deems best fitted to succeed him. The vicar general should take care to send one of these lists to the archbishop and the other to the neighboring bishop or to the senior of the neighboring bishops. On reception of the list the neighboring bishop will write to the archbishop enclosing his opinion regarding the candidates. When this has been done or within a reasonable period if the neighboring bishop does not write, the archbishop will communicate to all the bishops of the province, the neighboring bishop included, the names of the proposed candidates together with his personal opinion in the matter. He may add other names to the list proposed by the deceased bishop if the candidates do not seem to him to be the best selection. After receiving the letter of the archbishop, each suffragan will write directly to Propaganda expressing his choice and giving his opinion concerning the three or six candidates.

> In the case of the vacancy of the metropolitan see, the letter of the deceased archbishop designating the names of the three priests should be sent by the vicar general to both the neighboring and the senior suffragan bishop. Then the senior suffragan will do all those things which are determined in the case of a suffragan's election to be performed by the archbishop.

If among the letters of the deceased prelate there is not found one designating three names to succeed him, the vicar general must immediately inform the neighboring bishop or the senior of two neighboring bishops, so that the names of three priests chosen by the neighboring bishop may be sent by letter to the archbishop. The archbishop having received the letters will write to all the bishops following out the prescriptions already indicated when the letters of the deceased bishop or metropolitan are found. If the neighboring bishop should neglect entirely to write to the archbishop, the latter will send three names to all his suffragans, the neighboring bishop included.

If it is a question of the election of an archbishop, the senior suffragan will do all those things to be done by the archbishop in the election of a candidate to a suffragan see. When it is a question of the election of a coadjutor, except where the Holy See might determine a different method of action, the bishop who desires the coadjutor will send a list of three names to the archbishop and suffragan bishops along with a petition requisitioning the coadjutor to the Sacred Congregation. The archbishop and the suffragan bishops will communicate to the Congregation their views on the matter.

The Congregation insists that all these prescriptions are to be followed carefully and wishes to emphasize that the names thus sent are not really nominations, elections or requests, but properly and solely recommendations, imposing no obligation on the Congregation to select any of the candidates mentioned.[13]

The 1834 legislation remained in force and was generally observed until the Seventh Provincial Council when the bishops felt that certain alterations were needed because of an increase in the number of ecclesiastical jurisdictions. Acting on the American hierarchy's recommendations, the Sacred Congregation, on August 10, 1850, directed "that for the future, over and above previous prescriptions, the archbishop in whose province the vacancy occurs, will transmit the names proposed to the other archbishops of the nation. Each archbishop then will send his observations on the priests recommended to the Holy See."[14]

Eight years later, at the First Plenary Council of Baltimore, the assembled prelates suggested that the clergy be given some voice in the episcopal selection since "for the bishops to have consultors was always in accord with the general practice of the Church."[15] The directive did not have the force of law but its framers "considered it opportune to exhort the bishops whenever possible, to select some mature priests with out-standing ability in their diocese,"[16] to act in that capacity.

In August of 1856, Propaganda dispensed the Provinces of Baltimore, Saint Louis, New Orleans, and Cincinnati from sending proposed candidates to other metropolitans, unless they were externs, in which case, both the metropolitan and proper ordinary should be informed. As a corollary, Rome directed, on August 7, 1859, that "all the archbishops were to be afforded a deliberative vote in the selection of an ordinary for any metropolitan see."[17]

In May of 1859, Rome asked the American hierarchy to re-examine the whole process of selecting bishops in order to insure that future prelates would be "learned, prudent, experienced, pious, and suitable to bear the episcopal office worthily."[18] After receiving suggestions from a number of bishops, the Sacred Congregation of Propaganda Fide augmented the decrees of June 14, 1834, and August 10, 1850, by a papal encyclical, dated January 21, 1861, obliging each residential ordinary to send triennially to Rome and to the metropolitans, names of eligible candidates.

Five years later, in October of 1861, the nation's seven archbishops, thirty-seven bishops, two procurators and two abbots, directed further that:

> Whenever a See, metropolitan or suffragan, falls vacant, all the prelates qualified to make recommendations for the vacancy, should meet in a special synod, there to discuss the characters and the abilities of the proposed candidates.

> Prior to this meeting, however, each bishop should send the metropolitan or senior suffragan of his province, a list of candidates he considers eligible for nomination.

> The qualities of those chosen should be discussed publicly in a meeting at which the archbishop or senior suffragan presides. The vote is then taken secretly by means of balloting.

> Minutes of the meeting are to be sent to the Sacred Congregation of Propaganda Fide by the presiding officer.[19]

A *scrutinium* of fourteen points accompanied the conciliar decrees concerning the character of the candidates. The consultees were directed to:

1. Give the candidate's full name, age and place of birth;
2. Name the diocese and ecclesiastical province to which the candidate belongs;
3. Ascertain with what success the candidate made his theological studies;
4. Enumerate the candidate's academic degrees;

5. Inquire if the candidate was ever a professor and in which branches he excelled;
6. Describe the candidate's activities in the sacred ministry;
7. List the languages spoken and/or understood by the candidate;
8. Outline what offices the candidate has discharged and his success therein;
9. Give a judgment as to whether the candidate displays prudence in his deliberations and actions;
10. Note whether the candidate is sound in body, discreet, patient and versed in the administration of temporal affairs;
11. State the candidate's tenacity of purpose;
12. Investigate the candidate's good name and whether he has ever been wayward or forgetful of his state;
13. Discover if the candidate is attentive and solicitous in the exercise of his priestly office, if he conducts himself edifyingly and if he is strict in his observance of the rubrics;
14. Finally, make a prudent appraisal as to whether the candidate bears himself with gravity and priestly decorum in habit, in gait, in word.[20]

It was known that Archbishop Martin J. Spalding of Baltimore favored allowing the priests a share in the election "so as, in some way, to give the second order of the clergy a voice in the presentation of candidates for episcopal office. He would have given the diocesan councillors the right to present a list of names to be sent to Rome with that of the bishops." The prelate felt that such legislation "would bring us nearer the general discipline of the Church."[21] In any event, no action along these lines was taken at that time.

However, the Spalding proposals were to be brought up again at the Third Plenary Council, held in the premier see during November and December of 1884. Just a year earlier, Father Patrick Corrigan, Pastor of Our Lady of Grace Parish in Hoboken, had written a small monograph on *Episcopal Nominations: Do the Interests of the Church in the United States Require that the Priests Should have the Power of Nominating Bishops?*

Though suppressed by Bishop Winand Wigger of Newark, the publication apparently succeeded in convincing the nation's prelates of the merits attached to a more representative form of ecclesiastical government in the United States. The final form of the council's decrees submitted and approved by Rome considerably broadened the overall procedure.

I. When a diocese falls vacant, whether by the death, resignation, transfer, or removal of the bishop, and when, in consequence, three candidates are to be chosen whose names shall be proposed or recommended to the Holy See for the vacant bishopric, the consultors and the irremovable rectors of the vacant diocese shall be called together, v.g. thirty days after the vacancy occurs. It will be the right and the duty of these consultors and rectors, thus properly assembled, to select three candidates for the vacant see. The candidates thus chosen shall be submitted to the bishops of the province, whose right it will be to approve or disapprove of them.

II. The meeting of the consultors and irremovable rectors is called and presided over by the metropolitan of the province to which the vacant diocese belongs; or, if the metropolitan is lawfully hindered, by one of the suffragan bishops of the same province, to be deputed for this purpose by the metropolitan. Where there is a question of choosing three candidates for a metropolitan see which is vacant, the meeting of the consultors and irremovable rectors of the vacant metropolitan see is called and presided over by the senior suffragan bishop, or, if he is hindered, by another bishop to be deputed by him.

III. Before they cast their votes, the aforesaid consultors and rectors shall swear that they are not induced to cast their votes for a candidate because of unworthy motives, such as that of expecting favors or rewards. They shall vote by *secret ballot*. This vote is merely consultive, *i.e.*, it is simply equivalent to a recommendation that one of the candidates be appointed to the vacant see.

IV. The president of the meeting shall cause two authentic copies of the minutes of the meeting containing an accurate list of the candidates chosen, to be drawn up and signed by the secretary. He shall forward one copy directly to the S. C. de Prop. Fide; the second to the other bishops of the province. A third copy may also be drawn up and placed in the diocesan archives.

V. Thereupon, on a day fixed beforehand, *v.g.* ten days after the above meeting of consultors and rectors, the bishops of the province shall meet and openly discuss among themselves the merits of the candidates selected by the consultors and rectors or of others to be selected by themselves. Then they vote by secret ballot, and make up a list to be sent to Rome. From this it will be seen that the Bishops have a right to approve or disapprove of the candidates chosen by the clergy. But if they disapprove of them, they are bound to give the reasons upon which they base their disapproval to the S. C. de P. F.

VI. In everything else the bishops shall observe the instruction of the S. C de P. F. dated Jan. 21, 1861, and given in the Second Plenary Council of Baltimore, n. 106, 107. In other words, the bishop shall state in writing the qualifications and merits of the various candidates, according to the questions given in the Second Plenary Council of Baltimore, n. 107. The minutes of the meeting of the bishops shall then be sent to the S. C. de P. F. by the archbishop, or the senior bishop of the province.

VII. When there is question of appointing a *coadjutor-bishop* (with the right of succession), the rules laid down above under Nos. I, III, IV, V, and VI, shall be strictly adhered to. Rule II, will, however, be changed thus: The meeting of the consultors and irremovable rectors will be presided over, not by the archbishop of the province, or his deputy, but by the archbishop or bishop *for whom the coadjutor is to be chosen*, or where he is hindered, by the vicar-general, or other priests, deputed by him. Moreover, in this case, the bishop for whom the coadjutor is to be named can, if he desires, suggest or point out the names of the candidates who would be most acceptable to him for the coadjutorship.

VIII. When there is question of electing a bishop for a diocese *newly erected*, the rules given above under Nos. II, III, IV, V, and VI, shall be observed. However, Rule I shall be changed thus: When there is question of proposing to the Holy See the names of candidates for the new diocese, *the consultors of the diocese, or dioceses, from which the new see has been formed*, and the irremovable rectors of the newly-erected diocese, shall be called together, and it will be their right and duty to select three candidates for the new bishopric. This rule is based on the fact that a newly-erected see will, of course, have no consultors until after the first bishop, having been confirmed, appoints them. Hence the consultors of the old diocese or dioceses properly take the place of the future consultors of the new diocese, for the purpose of naming the first bishop.[22]

The so-called *terna* method remained in force for the next three decades until July 25, 1916, when the Consistorial Congregation issued the format currently in effect. The preamble refers to the manner in which names were formerly proposed to the Holy See and observes that the procedure is no longer workable chiefly because of the long delay it involves.

1. At the beginning of Lent, 1917, and thereafter every two years at the same season, all Bishops shall indicate to their

Metropolitan the names of one or two priests who they judge fit for the office of Bishop. The candidate may be from outside the diocese or province; but it is required *sub gravi* that he be personally known through long acquaintance to the proponent. The age, origin, and location of the candidate, and the principal office he now holds, should also be stated.

2. Before deciding upon the names to be sent in, the Bishops and the Archbishop shall ask the diocesan consultors and the irremovable pastors, in the manner hereinafter to be defined, to name some priest whom they regard, in the sight of God, as especially worthy to receive the charge of a flock in some diocese.

a) This inquiry is to be made of the consultors and pastors, not in a body, but singly, imposing upon each of them *sub gravi* the obligation of secrecy, and the injunction to destroy any correspondence that may take place in regard to the matter.

b) The Bishops shall not disclose to any one the advice they have received, except at the meeting of Bishops, as hereinafter provided.

3. The Bishops may also ask other prudent men, even of the regular clergy, both for candidates to be proposed, and to obtain information regarding the qualifications of any one; but on condition that the rules laid down in paragraphs (a) and (b) of Article 2, above, be exactly observed.

4. The Bishops may, but are not bound to follow the advice they shall have received under Articles 2 and 3, being responsible in this matter, to God alone. But they are to disclose to no one except the Archbishop, the names of the one or two priests whom they shall propose in accordance with Article I.

5. After receiving from his suffragans the names of candidates, the Archbishop shall add his own candidates to the list, draw up the list alphabetically, without the names of the sponsors, and send it to each of the suffragans, so that they may make suitable investigations regarding the qualifications of such of the candidates as are not personally and certainly known to them.

6. These investigations are to be conducted with even greater caution, as regards secrecy, than is provided for in Article 3, above. The Bishops may withhold, and with prudent caution conceal, the reason for the investigation. If they fear disclosures, they should abstain from further inquiry.

7. After Easter, at a time and place to be fixed by the Archbishop, all the Bishops of the province shall meet with their Metropolitan to select the names of those who are to be proposed to the Holy See for the episcopal office. The meeting shall be without solemnity, as for a friendly reunion so as to attract no attention, least of all on the part of newspapers, and to give no encouragement to idle curiosity.

8. At the meeting, after invoking the divine assistance, all, including the Archbishop, shall take an oath on the Sacred Gospels to keep secrecy, so that the bond binding all shall be even more sacred. Then the rules governing the election shall be read.

9. One of the Bishops present shall be chosen as secretary.

10. Then follows the discussion in a moderate tone, as a means to the selection of the best candidates from among so many. The very importance of the matter absolutely requires that the discussion and all else be conducted as if under the eye of Christ Himself present, every merely human consideration being put aside, yet with discretion and charity, and having in view only the supreme welfare of the Church, the glory of God, and the salvation of souls. The religious fidelity and reverence of all the Bishops demand this.

11. The candidates should be mature, but not too old; of good judgment, tried in actual service; of learning, sound and above the ordinary; devoted to the Holy See; especially noted for rectitude and piety. Besides, attention should be paid to the candidate's executive ability, financial condition, character, and state of health. In a word, the question is whether be has all the qualities which are required in an excellent pastor, so that he may rule the people of God with success and edification.

12. When the Archbishop shall have closed the discussion, the vote shall proceed in the following order:

a) Those whom it shall have been decided by unanimous consent in the discussion, to expunge from the list of candidates, for any reason, shall not be voted on. All others, even the most highly thought of, shall be voted on.

b) A vote shall be taken upon each one by secret ballot, beginning with the first of the candidates in alphabetical order.

c) Each of the Bishops, including the Metropolitan, shall have for each candidate, three tokens, one white, for approval, another black, for rejection, and a third of some other color to indicate abstention from voting, for any reason.

d) Each of the prelates, beginning with the Archbishop, shall then deposit in an urn prepared for the purpose, the token which expresses his vote on the candidates in question, regarding it as a grave obligation before God to vote according to conscience; the two unused tokens shall be deposited in another urn. Likewise secretly.

e) After all have voted, the Archbishop, assisted by the secretary, shall, in the presence of all, count the tokens of each kind, and record the result in writing.

13. When all have been voted on, the Bishops may if they choose, or if anyone asks it, decide by a new ballot which one is to be preferred among candidates who have received all, or an equal number of favorable votes. For this purpose each voter writes the name of the candidate to be preferred on a slip of paper, and deposits it in the urn. The votes are then examined as provided above in n. 12, (e).

14. Although the Holy Father reserves to himself the right, in case of the vacancy of any diocese or archdiocese, to obtain timely counsel from the Bishops and Archbishops, either through the Most Reverend Apostolic Delegate or in some other way, so as to appoint to the vacant diocese the person who, among all those who are approved, seems the most worthy;[23] yet it is permissible, and even advisable, that the Bishops at this very meeting give some general indications as to the diocese for which they regard the various candidates as best fitted; for example, whether for a small, well-ordered, and peaceful diocese, or also for a more important one, or one in which there is considerable organizing to be done; for one of mild climate and even territory, or of another sort, etc.

15. The Bishop acting as secretary shall during the discussion carefully note what is said about each candidate by each of the prelates; the conclusion reached upon each one; the result of the first vote, and of the second if there was one; and the special remarks referred to under n. 14.

16. Before the Bishops leave, they shall have read to them for their approval, the report of the secretary regarding the names proposed, the qualities of the candidates and the votes they received.

17. A copy of the proceedings, signed by the Archbishop, the secretary, and the other Bishops present, shall be sent most securely to this Sacred Congregation, through the Apostolic Delegate. The original record shall be kept by the Archbishop in the most secret archives, but shall be destroyed after one year, or if imminent danger of violation of secrecy arises, even earlier.

18. The Bishops are always free, on the occasion of the proposing of a candidate or the vacancy of any see, particularly an important one, to write to this Sacred Congregation or to the Holy Father himself, to express their mind about the qualifications of persons, either absolutely or with regard to the particular diocese in question.[24]

On March 28, 1927, the Sacred Consistorial Congregation issued a Commentary on the above legislation noting that faithful adherence to the 1916 decree had wrought great benefits to the Church in the United States. The congregation reminded the American hierarchy of the need to interpret most strictly both the letter and the spirit of the directive and, in this regard, singled out four points for special mention:

1. It is necessary that the Most Reverend Archbishops and Bishops, when in virtue of article 7 of the Decree, they assemble, shall have acquired, previously and separately a sufficient and, as far as possible a full knowledge of every candidate proposed; so that the discussion to be held and the decisions to be taken in respect to the candidates shall not be left to the proposing bishop alone but rather be the business and the acts of all the bishops. To this end, before the meeting, the regulations laid down in articles 1 to 6 must be accurately observed; that is to say, the Consultors and the Irremovable Pastors must be interrogated with the necessary precautions; the names selected must be sent in good time to the Archbishop so that he may have time to send them to the other Suffragans; and each Suffragan must make inquiry into the fitness of the candidates thus signified to him.

2. The number of candidates proposed should, naturally, be limited, considering the purpose of the meeing, which is to find *"pauci sed electi."*

3. The Most Reverend Archbishops and Bishops should bear in mind that it is the resolute will of the Holy See that they should enjoy the fullest liberty in the matter of proposing candidates. There is, therefore, no reason why any Bishop should fear to expose the

merits of any candidate he may have to the discussion of the assembled Bishops; and much less should any Bishop hesitate to propose a candidate because of an eventual probability of a contrary vote. The rules governing this matter are laid down in articles 10 and 11.

If a Bishop believes that a candidate proposed by him is the object of disfavor because of a motive extraneous to the candidate's merits, or because of the candidate's nationality, or because of the candidate's relation to some person or to some religious body, or for any other unjust reason, the Bishop not only is free but even is exhorted to expose the fact to the Holy See, which will not fail to make prudent investigations and ascertain all necessary information.

4. While all this concerns, as it were, the immediate preparation of the future bishops, let the Most Reverend Ordinaries give themselves also, and as far as they are able, to the remote preparation of such subjects. This is to be done by cultivating in many, especially in those endowed with exceptional qualities of mind and heart, all that goes particularly to enhance the government of a diocese, as e.g., a complete course in Canon Law and the study of those languages which, according to the respective localities, are useful and necessary in the episcopal office.

Throughout all of ecclesiastical history, selection of worthy bishops has been of paramount importance to the Holy See. The high standard of the almost 1000 Americans raised to the episcopate since 1789 is the measure of success for that extensive canonical legislation which, at one time or another, has governed this vital function for the Catholic Church in the United States.

Notes to the Text

1. *Decretum de pastorali episcoporum munere in Ecclesia* (Rome, 1965), p. 9.
2. Maurice F. Hassett, "Primitive Episcopal Elections," *Catholic University Bulletin*, III (October, 1897), 404.
3. John Daniel Barrett, S.S., *A Comparative Study of the Councils of Baltimore* (Washington, 1922), p. 56.
4. The term "election" is here taken to mean the act of legitimately designating or calling a candidate to a vacant ecclesiastical jurisdiction. Since "election" confers nothing more than a *jus ad rem*, the Roman Pontiff, and he alone, is *per se* exclusively the competent authority to confirm those duly "elected" by local procedures.
5. Quoted in Peter K. Guilday, *The Life and Times of John Carroll* (New York, 1922), p. 348.
6. Patrick William Browne (trans.), *Etat de l'Eglise Catholique ou Diocése des Etats-Unis de l'Amérique Septentrionale par Jean Dilhet* (Washington, 1922), p. 168.
7. John Gilmary Shea, *History of the Catholic Church in the United States* (New York, 1888), II, 397.
8. John Carroll to Charles Plowden, Baltimore. Quoted in John Carroll Brent, *Biographical Sketch of the Most Rev. J. Carroll, First Archbishop of Baltimore* (Baltimore, 1843), pp.154-155.
9. Thomas O'Gorman, *A History of the Roman Catholic Church in the United States* (New York, 1895), p. 278.
10. For the entire decree, see Donald C. Shearer, O.F.M., Cap., *Pontificia Americana* (Washington, 1933), pp.98-100.
11. Quoted in Peter K. Guilday, *A History of the Councils of Baltimore* (New York, 1932), p. 75.
12. Frederick James Zwierlein, *Les premiéres nominations épiscopales aux Etats-Unis* (Louvain, 1914), II, 553.
13. *Collectanea S. Congregationis de Propaganda Fide* (Rome, 1893), p. 23.
14. *Acta et Dicta Concilii Plenarii Baltimorensis* II (Baltimore, 1868), p. 72.
15. Charles Florence McCarthy, "The Historical Development of Episcopal Nominations in the Catholic Church of the United States," *Records of the American Catholic Historical Society*, XXXVIII (December, 1927), 341.
16. *Concilium plenarium totius Americas Septentrionalis Foederatae Baltimori habitum, anno 1852* (Baltimore, 1853), p. 45.
17. Vincent A. Tatarczuk, "Past and Present Practice in the Selection of Candidates for Bishoprics in the United States," *The Jurist*, XVI (July, 1956), 314.
18. Quoted in Charles Florence McCarthy, *op. cit.*, 343.
19. *Acta et Dicta, op. cit.*, pp. 73-74.
20. *Ibid.*, pp. 74-75.
21. John Lancaster Spalding, *The Life of the Most Reverend M. J. Spalding* (New York, 1873), pp. 311-312.
22. *Acta et dicta concilii plenarii Baltimorensis tertii* (Baltimore, 1886), pp. 12-14. Translation used is that of Sebastian Bach Smith, *Elements of Ecclesiastical Law* (New York, 1887), I, 152-154.
23. Upon receiving the recommendations, the Apostolic Delegate conducts a thorough investigation of the proposed candidates. A *scrutinium* or questionnaire is sent to selected individuals asking for their conscientious opinions of the candidates and their fitness for the bishopric. Those interrogated are bound by the strictest secrecy concerning their involvement in the process.
24. T. Lincoln Bouscaren, S.J., *The Canon Law Digest* (Milwaukee, 1934), I, 195-199.

8

"A Missionary's Plea for Governmental Assistance" is the title of this essay about Father Eugene Casmir Chirouse which appeared in the *Records of the American Catholic Historical* Society LXXVII (December, 1966), 242-249.

EUGENE CASMIR CHIROUSE, O.M.I. (1821-1892) spent half of his forty-four missionary years working among the Indians of Puget Sound. The French-born cleric, a member of the Oblates of Mary Immaculate, was a man of surprising ingenuity and uncommon industry. He established the Church of Saint Francis Savier des Snohomish on September 14, 1858, at Priests' Point and in the eight years after 1861 managed to support a school for his people with the meagre sums gathered from concerts played in the lumber camps and frontier settlements of the area. The determined efforts of Father Chirouse on behalf of the Indians were rewarded, however, when the first United States Government contract-school under religious auspices was opened on September 12, 1869.

The following letter, reproduced with the permission of James Francis Cardinal McIntyre from the Chancery Archives of the Archdiocese of Los Angeles, was written by Chirouse on August 28, 1865, to James Willis Nesmith (1820-1885), Democratic Senator from Oregon between 1861 and 1867. In order to insure accuracy, the fifteen page document is presented here with no alteration in style, punctuation or capitalization, except that indicated with brackets [ ].

With a view to further the spiritual and temporal welfare of the Indians, and the benefit of our Govemment, I am happy to comply with your request in submitting to you, the following statements.

In the year 1847, I left my native country and came to this Territory as a Missionary Priest among the natives, since that time I have been engaged in the instruction of these poor children of nature. Eighteen years of experience has made me thoroughly acquainted with their character, and the manner in which they should be treated, in order to forward the designs of the Government. I have not the slightest doubt, that the intention of the Government is most correct; I am aware that large sums of money have been appropriated, and all the means furnished to fulfil [sic] the Treaty [of Point Elliott], but, I regret to say, without the beneficial results that might naturally be expected.

Therefore I take the liberty of representing to you the actual wants of our pupils, and to submit to your consideration, the best system in my mind to be adopted for the education of all the Indians of the [Puget] sound; so as to save the Government as much expense as possible, and enable the Department to succeed in collecting together all the able children of each and every tribe, and from among these, establish a school, on a sound and solid basis, with respect to the immediate wants of our school, they are particularized in my annual reports herewith enclosed. I will add but a few additional remarks.

The school is now in working order, so far as our limited means will allow, and certainly not without much fatigue and incessant application have we so far succeeded as every one in the country are [sic] well aware, the number of our pupils being always on the increase, obliges us to be more pressing for government aid, without which it will be utterly impossible for us to make any satisfactory progress.

If the Government does not make some new appropriations, the money already set apart, is by no means sufficient to supply the necessary requirements, there being only $3,000, while the Tulalip establishment, being the central agricultural and industrial school for all the Indians of Puget Sound, and in fact the only one actually existing; it would require according to the following testimony of the agent of the place,

48

1st Principal Teacher salary per annum		$1,000
2nd Asst. Teachers.	do	800
3rd 2 Sisters of Charity	do	1,200
4th I Laborerdo	do	800
5th For maintenance of school supplying the necessary provisions(that cannot yet be raised on Reservation) furnishing clothing tools plow and working cattle.		2,000
6th A carpenter for two years		1,200
TOTAL		$7,000

In my capacity of Missionary, I visit annually all the Indians of the Sound, and I am thoroughly acquainted with their disposition and feelings and I have every reason to fear that the bad Indians (so long as they remain so) can never be induced to send their children to school, in fact all schools opened up to this time for their children on the local reservations, have been complete failures. I know by experience, that the children of the good Christians only can be induced to remain at school; hence by conviction, that if the seven thousand dollars ($7,000) spent annually for nominal or useless schools, were applied by the Government for the support of *one central and general school* on the main reservation; in the first place, a better education could be given to all the Indians and halfbreed children of the Sound; and secondly there would be an actual saving of Three Thousand Dollars *per annum* to the Government. The youths selected from each tribe, would thus enjoy the benefit of an education in proportion to their capacity, and their stay at Tulalip would prepare them for the future meeting of all the Indians of the Sound, on the main Reservation, in conformity with the intentions expressed by Gov't in the Treaty of Point Elliott.

I must add, that, the farther away the children are from their parents, the better for themselves; as I know by experience that the Indian Children living in close proximity with their parents and friends, cannot be got to attend school regularly. With regard to the means of rendering an agricultural and industrial school successful, I would suggest the following brief remarks.

The pupils must find in their teacher, a true and fond father, entirely devoted to their present and future welfare. Of this they must have no doubt, and as they have been nurtured in bad and wicked habits, too much attention cannot be bestowed in order to eradicate them. Not only frequent, strong, and plain explanations of the will and judgement of God, must be given them, but sound and practical example alone shall convince them. As they shall have to work, in order to obtain an honest livelihood, and as labor is assuredly the antidote against all vice, they must learn to work and acquire a love of it, which is at the present stage of their reformation extremely repulsive to their natural inclinations. Therefore in order to encourage them and give them good example it is expedient that the teacher work with them with attention and pleasure. A laborer should be appointed to help them in their various employments, and in order to fulfil [sic] the design proposed, implements of husbandry, such as are specified in another part of this communication should be furnished immediately. Working cattle, milch [sic] cows, swine, and poultry could tend very much to assist them and increase their stock of provisions as they cannot at present raise enough for their maintenance.

The Pupils have to spend a great portion of their time every year in fishing and are thus obliged to lose a considerable portion of their time that should otherwise be devoted to study. On these occasions I am obliged to furnish their own fishing tackle and hooks, for which reason, I would request that they be furnished with a Seine as indispensable to the advancement of the school. The pupils must be by all means encouraged and that monotonous life they lead, rendered more various, by the introduction of some inanely and amusing employments suitable to their age and acquirements, therefore a Gymnasium with some musical instruments should be furnished which would enable me to organize a band and thus tend to promote their further advancement in civilization.

I also require for them a larger quantity of clothing than that at present furnished by the Department, which is far insufficient for their wants; under which circumstances, I must earnestly request some addition be made to the usual supply.

It is also necessary that a sufficient stock of provisions be on hand in order to promote and preserve health amongst the pupils, such as flour and molasses, *etc*, as at present we are unable to raise any corn on the reservation.

Barns, stables and sheds are very much needed and should be erected as soon as possible.

Many of the pupils are entirely without school requisites, such as books, and slates; and others who are fit for writing are deprived of the opportunity, for want of writing materials; a stock of copy books, pens, slates and pencils, are indispensable to the proper management of the school, and it is expedient, that the books furnished should accord with their religious principles.

The domestic department is very much in want of many necessaries, as dishes, brooms, lampoil, soap, combs, and thread, which things are indispensable so long as the boys are required to keep themselves clean, and do their own washing.

At the distributions of annuities, some special favor should be made to the parents who urge their children to study and industry, and who are thus deprived of their services when they are in need of them. The pupils who have distinguished themselves for conduct should be also specially rewarded, as it would tend to promote a desire to excel in order to obtain the reward, or merit; it would have also the effect of increasing the number of the pupils and incite them to more energy and perseverance for both parents and children would see that they derive some benefit by their application and attention to the instructions that are given them. I will add here a few general remarks.

Many persons are very much mistaken in their idea that religion has no influence in the reformation of the Indians. My experience has, however, convinced me to the contrary. I firmly believe it to be a most potent auxiliary and am of [the] opinion that if the Indians are not taught by word and example to fear God, they certainly never can be induced to fear man, and consequently they will despise the commands of the Agent as they [do] the commands and laws of God. I am satisfied there is no permanent civilization for the Indians, if a religious education is wanting and all they can gather from their communication with the bad whites will, I am sure, tend more to their destruction and ruin, than to their amelioration.

The immediate erection of a church, the laying out of ground for a cemetery, I consider to be of paramount importance, and should be put in hands for execution as soon as possible, and the

Missionaries instead of being restrained in their efforts to promote civilization among the Indians, should be aided and encouraged in their arduous and difficult undertaking. Drunkenness, gambling, public and tumultious [sic] performances, superstitions, and that most degrading vice, adultary [sic], and all others which cause troubles and contentions, and which deter the Indians from becoming civilized should never be tolerated on the Reservation, but should be put a stop to, and punished by the agent without regard or distinction of persons.

Good and practical example being a more powerful incentive to reformation than any other teaching, it is expedient that the employees should be men of sound moral character, just and patient, and for such reason I would suggest that married men get the preference; this I am sure would tend very much to the annihilation of that besetting vice of concubinage so reninous [sic] to morality, and which should never be allowed to take root on the reservation.

The good, honest, trustworthy Christians amongst the Indians deserve to be encouraged, rather than despised; they should at least have that credit awarded them that their exemplary conduct so justly merits, and should be by all means preferred to those Indians of bad repute, who (it is strange to say) very often get the preference among the whites. As up to this period, no other principles but those taught by the Catholic Church, have been diffused amongst all the tribes of the sound, and as many of the Indians have been received members of that Church, it is to be desired that the Chief employees on the Reservation should be of the same denomination, or at least, persons of liberal opinions, and divested of that party feeling which is so prejudicial to the unity of views that should exist among us.

Prostitution should be necessarily abolished, and labour and other honest means of obtaining a living, substituted, and the Indians, expecially the female portion, protected at all times, against the furious and brutal passions of some of the poor demoralized whites. The Indians being like other children susceptible to good or bad example, good advice should be by all means given them respecting their duties to God and man, and by doing so, the employes on the Reservation, would gain more esteem, respect and confidence.

Let the Indians be once convinced that the officers of the Government are their real protectors and guardians and they, on their part, will carry out their orders and commands with cheerfulness and willingness.

The present system adopted in the payment of annuities, I am of opinion tends to their degradation, than otherwise. The drunkards, theives [sic] etc, receiving (and that against the spirit of the Treaty) as much as the good and honest Indians, giving to the former additional means of going on in their debauchery, and the latter just complaints in making them believe that the Government is not just in its administration.

Besides this, a large reunion of Indians of opposite opinions and of different feelings towards each other, is I fear the cause of great disturbance and always brings ill consequences in its train. It is therefore to be desired that such distributions should be made on each local reservation, as it would be the means of giving satisfaction to many peaceable Indians, who refuse very often to come to Tulalip in order to avoid the bad company and worse crimes that are there to be met with.

Let the chief employes explain to the Indians the true meaning of the Treaty, and let it be fulfilled on both sides and then justice will be done. A worthy sub-agent should be selected for each local reservation where the Indians make some effort to improve themselves, and let them not be alone without protection or redress, when molested by their wild and stupid neighbors.

According to the terms of the Treaty, a carpenter, a blacksmith, and a farmer should be appointed without delay, who should not only reside on the Central Reservation, but also help and instruct the Indians efficiently in their various occupations. The buildings erected by the Indians alone, are quite inefficient and cannot last but a very short time. Consequently a great quantity of lumber, nails, and tools, are uselessly wasted and otherwise destroyed, thus incurring great expense to the Government, without any beneficial results.

Implements of husbandry should be furnished only to those, who are capable and willing to make good use of them, and not to those idle, Indians who, very often dispose of them, in order to obtain the means of drinking and gambling. An exact account of the tools should be kept, and every Indian on the Reservation should be required to show to the agent at determined times, the tools given him so that the agent may have the opportunity of giving credit to those who are deserving, and punish those who spoil or wilfully [sic] damage the tools entrusted to them without doing any work. As to what concerns the farming of the Indians besides, the individual fields are invariably neglected, and producing little or no support to the owner, a large and commonfarm called the "Reservation farm," should be established by the agent, and attended to by the farmer. In order to supply the wants of the Indians, who should work on this farm, and be kept on the Reservation. The agent should hire as many Indians as would be necessary, and pay them as good, if not better wages than they could get from any other source, and this out of their annuities; and when the over-plus of the annuities are being divided, let it be distributed among the industrious and faithful followers of the Department regulations; and among the old and infirm and let the drunkards, gamblers, thieves and idlers, get nothing but what they justly merit, viz; sharp repramands [sic] and punishment, which they will undergo by obliging them to show a certain amount of work, done by them, on the reservation farm.

The common farm should be furnished with various domestic animals guch as cows, oxen, swine and poultry, etc. and an equitable distribution of all the produce should be made to benefit the sturdy Indian settlers, and show that they are better off than their indolent and drunken neighbors. A store should not be allowed on the Reservation, except for the benefit of the Indian settlers only, and such store should not be kept, or attended to, by any of the farmer[s], or any other employee whatsoever, are store keepers for his or their benefit, the duty for which he or they have been specially appointed is sure, to be more or less neglected, and if the Indians are obliged to pay exorbitant prices as is generally the case, they shall have just cause of complaint, and will eventually leave the reservation.

No whites should be allowed to erect houses on the Reservation or reside thereon, as the Indians are quite opposed to it, and it would always tend to cause troubles and contentions.

A seine should be furnished exclusively for the Indian settlers on the Reservations so that they could salt and dry enough of fish for their own use and for sale.

Let there be a good sawyer employed to run the mill and teach some Indians in order that they may understand how to perform the work themselves.

Let the Agent hire the Indians to cut and carry them to the mill, and pay them with goods taken out of the annuities.

If any timber should be sold on the reservation let the Indians be made aware, that it is set apart for their benefit an[d] never let a logging camp be fixed too near the Indian settlement. It sometimes occurs that the Indians require money, and they always say they have too [sic] leave their homes to work for the whites in order to procure it; as they say they can never get as much as one single cent on the reservation. It would be therefore advisable that they should be paid occasionally in money at the same rate generally fixed among the whites, so that they may have no excuse for being a long time away from home.

It is extremely difficult and almost impossible to have all the Indians settled at one place; they being so numerous, diseases and contentions would very often spring up among them, which might be the occasion of serious troubles and inconveniences.

It is therefore expedient that those who prefer the town should live together near the agency and if there be any good land at an other place on the reservation, let those who are satisfied to remain in the country fix their homes there, at such convenient distance however, that they can be visited when deemed necessary. A large piece of land should be cleared for the purpose of raising grass, so as to enable the Indians to raise and feed stock.

I consider the erection of a jail to be a matter of great importance, as I am satisfied it would tend to the decrease of abuse, and to a certain extent, promote honesty, industry, and sobriety among the Indians.

The appointment of a Doctor would be a great boon, or, at least, some of the employees who may understand the use of medicine, should be furnished with a medicine chest, containing such simple remedies as may meet the wants of the sick and thus contribute the "Indian Doctors" and scorcerers [sic], who do all in their power, to deter the Indians from becoming civilized and who diffuse amongst them, darkness and most extravagant superstitions. It is an astonishing fact that the Indians are dying off in great numbers since the whites came amongst them, and if not speedily reformed from their brutal habits, if prostitution and drunkness be not immediately abolished, the consequences shall be ruinous to the Indian race. It is a matter of very great difficulty in fact almost impossible to civilize the old Indians of the Sound, although with patience and perseverance there might be some hopes yet entertained of their amelioration, if conducted with judgement and discretion and I fear not to assert that our Indian youths even the off-spring of the most stupid and dull parents, and far inferior to many other Indians, are nevertheless endowed with sufficient faculties, if properly developed, to become honest farmers enjoying the benefit of an ordinary civilization and in time become useful members to the whites. Religious, Industrial and Agricultural instruction, I am of opinion are the only means that can be resorted to in order to make of them a new generation; to restore health, increase their numbers, make them happy and save them from utter ruin, being as they are by nature condemned to be an inferior and sequestered race, and very few amongst them capable of great attainments, or ever reaching high offices, an ordinary knowledge of reading, writing and arithmetic will be quite sufficient for their use. I believe the education of the flatheads to be the most difficult task undertaken, nevertheless with patience, perseverence, and a sufficient support from Government and with proper use of means thus supplied, the difficulty may in course of time be surmounted.

9

The following historical survey on "Monsignorial Appointments in the U.S.A." is taken from the *American Ecclesiastical Review* CLVII (August, 1967),113-120.

Though the Second Vatican Council discussed in considerable detail the "variety of ministries" instituted for the nurturing and growth of the People of God, its decree on the hierarchial structure of the Church conspicuously omitted any reference to that 3.2% of the world's Catholic clergymen who fall into one or the other of the monsignorial categories. The title itself is given to prelates as a mark distinguishing them from all other clerics or *signori*. As it developed in the United States, the term is reserved for those *prelaturae gratiae* or honorary prelacies conferred on certain individuals without any notion of corresponding ecclesiastical jurisdiction.

Generally speaking, the office is derived from one of the sixteen categories[1] of personal or domestic service rendered to the Holy Father by those attached to the papal household. In those areas where the honor is bestowed on non-resident Romans, the position is completely supernumerary, though certain rights and privileges are conceded to the recipient, such as distinctive style and color of choir dress[2] and limited liturgical privileges. Ordination is not a *sine qua non* requirement. In 1897, for example, Raphael Merry del Val, then only a theological student, was named a private chamberlain and sent with the papal delegation to England for Queen Victoria's golden jubilee celebrations.[3] Normally, appointment to prelatial rank is made by a rescript from the Vatican Secretariate of State, the validity of which does not depend on the designee's willingness to accept. In view of current canonical legislation, it would seem that the appointment cannot be renounced since it is not purely a personal favor.[4]

With few exceptions, clerics in United States Catholic annals have been named to only three of the many categories of honorary papal service.[5] The most advanced of these is the Protonotary Apostolic *(Proto-Notarius Apostolicus ad instar participantium)*.[6] Next is the Domestic Prelacy *(Antistes Urbanus)*. Last group is that of Private or Papal Chamberlain *(Cubicularius Intimus adlectus supra numerum)*.[7] In this final enumeration, the appointees are regarded as the pope's personal officers and, as such, must be confirmed by each succeeding pontiff.[8]

It has been an almost inviolable practice that no appointments to honorary papal titles are conferred without the recommendation, or at least the endorsement, of the recipient's ordinary and/or the ordinary of the place. Presently, the Holy See advises that clerics ordained less than seven years not be nominated. The various privileges, rules, and traditions governing honorary prelacies were codified by Pope Pius X in the papal document *Inter Multiplices* of February 21, 1905,[9] and revised by Pius XI in his *Ad Incrementum* of August 15, 1934.[10]

From the sparse evidence available it would seem that prior to 1775 no honorary prelatial titles were bestowed on priests living outside the confines of Rome itself. Pope Pius VI, apparently the first pontiff to allow externs to hold non-residential status in the papal family, is on record as nominating three clerics to the monsignorate. His successor, Pius VII, was responsible for another fourteen such distinctions. The practice was suspended during the pontificates of Leo XII and Pius VIII but revived shortly after the accession of Bartolomeo Cappellari as Gregory XVI in 1831.[11]

Conferral of honorary prelatial dignities received its greatest impetus during the thirty-two year reign of Pius IX. As that genial Pope gathered the powers of the papacy more firmly into his bands, the Ultramontane emphasis on the *Privilegium Petri* gained ascendancy and brought about a period of centralization in ecclesiastical machinery. One undeniably effective method of counteracting the strong nationalistic tendencies prevalent in certain areas was the distribution of "Roman titles—and particularly that of monsignor—more widely" on priests living outside the Eternal City.[12] Thus it came about that Pius IX "made more foreign monsignors than his predecessors for two centuries."[13] The actual number of such appointees, however, remained relatively small and as late as 1866 the title of monsignor, not common even in Italy, was conferred rarely on non Europeans and then only "in consideration of learning, birth or some adventitious quality."[14]

The following two decades saw the trend reversed. By 1884 the Sacred Consistorial Congregation sent out letters on behalf of Leo XIII to all the bishops requesting them to seek honorific distinctions for their clergy more rarely and cautiously.[15]

Honorary papal titles were undoubtedly conferred in the New World as far back as the pontificate of Gregory XVI (1841-1846). There is a letter on file in the Archives of the Sacred Congregation of Propaganda Fide, written on July 17, 1838, wherein a certain Father J. F. Rost asked the Pope to bestow on him the domestic prelacy.[16] There is no record as to whether the Mexican cleric succeeded in convincing Roman officials about the expediency of such an appointment, but there is evidence that he enlisted several members of the curia to plead his cause.

The first recorded bestowal of an honorary papal title on a citizen of the United States occurred in 1866 when the newly ordained Father Robert Seton[17] was named a Private Chamberlain at the papal court of Pius IX. As the first American monsignor, Seton assisted "at the Pope's Easter Pontificals and later at the laying of the cornerstone of the church of the English College."

Seton further recorded in his memoirs that he did weekly service at the Vatican while continuing his graduate studies. One of his highly-placed friends would send the red and gilded papal coach, drawn by longtailed horses, to bring him to the pontiff's residence as often as he "cared to perform Chamberlain service." Monsignor Seton related, with apparent satisfaction, how his position made it possible for him to carry "the peacock feathers at Pontifical Mass or in the procession of *Corpus Christi* around the colonnade of Saint Peter's."[18] On August 17, 1867, shortly before leaving the Eternal City for Newark, Monsignor Seton was made a Protonotary[19] Apostolic, again the first in the nation raised to that dignity.

It was a dozen years before the next American priest, Father Patrick F. Allen of New Orleans, was designated a Domestic Prelate. The exclusive character of the distinction was retained in the years immediately following, at least as far as the United States was concerned.[20]

When preparations were being made for the convocation of the Third Plenary Council of Balitmore in 1884, the Coadjutor Archbishop of New York, Michael A. Corrigan, suggested that the nation's monsignors be formally invited to the episcopal conclave. Corrigan sent a letter to Archbishop James Gibbons enumerating the names of those monsignors he then knew to be living in the United States. The Empire State's coadjutor was especially anxious that Monsignor George H. Doane of Newark be invited, since he was not likely to be asked by his own bishop, "who knew not Joseph."[21]

The Archbishop of Baltimore designated Monsignor Seton to act as chief notary of the council, observing in his invitation that "your exact knowledge, and zeal in what you undertake, as well as the title with which the H. See has honored you, eminently fit you, in my judgment, for the office."[22] Indeed, the appointment was historically significant for it has been the duty of protonotaries since the fourth century "to record carefully all the decrees and enactments concerning the faith and discipline of the Church."[23]

According to the journal of the council, ten of the nation's sixteen monsignors actually attended the third and last plenary assemblage.[24] As far as the record is concerned, the council marked the final time that any official recognition was accorded to the country's *prelaturae gratiae.*

By 1897, three decades after the initial appointment had been made, the number of those raised to papal honors in the United States had not reached fifty.[25] Gradually, however, in ensuing decades, the earlier reluctance of Rome toward granting such distinctions to American clerics was abrogated and each successive year since the turn of the century has seen the number multiplied. A half century after his own appointment, the nation's first such appointee observed that "the Monsignorship has become ridiculously common in the United States, and is too often considered only a consolation prize for missing the Mitre."[26]

The actual number of monsignors currently represents a small percentage of all ordained clerics. According to statistics released in 1965, there are 346,998 priests in the world. Of that total number, 3.2% fall into the overall category of *prelaturae gratiae.* Restricting the enumeration to the 233,556 secular or diocesan priests, the percentage rises to 4.7% (0.4% Protonotaries Apostolic, 3.0% Domestic Prelates and 1.3% Private Chamberlains). In round numbers, about 11,000 priests have been honored with papal titles of various kinds.

This proliferation, small though it is in relative figures, has prompted criticism in certain quarters. One well-known authority recently suggested that "it would hardly harm the Church if the gaudy garb and pompous titles of Monsignors were to disappear."[27] Another writer wondered if "the custom of setting certain priests apart from the rest, giving them a fancy title, and vesting them in robes reminiscent of ancient nobility" might not be a meaningless type of clerical segregation.[28] An outstanding historian, himself a domestic prelate, wrote that "the whole matter of the monsignori has gotten sufficiently out of hand in some dioceses as to threaten disedification, if not scandal, were it for nothing else than the amount of money that is expended by the clergy for the ecclesiastical raiment involved."[29]

A recent national survey among diocesan priests conducted by Father Joseph Fichter of the Cambridge Center for Social Studies indicated that 73% of the American clergy favored dropping the title of monsignor."[30] What favorable attitude remains for *prelaturae gratiae* is further discounted by another writer who feels that "in a changing Church, the minor features of the past soothe the sense of insecurity" in those finding difficulty adjusting to ecclesiastical updating.[31]

Perhaps a middle course between retention and abolition might be a system whereby honorary papal titles or their equivalents would be attached always and only to specified positions,[32] such distinctions to perdure as long as the appointee fills the designated office. Under this plan, the vicar general, chancellor, and vicar for religious, *etc.*, would automatically attain one or the other categories of the monsignorate by virtue of appointment. The distinctive garb for each of these positions could be restricted to a color variation of the traditional sash worn with the black cassock.

While the relevancy of papal honors may be open to discussion in a period of decentralization, this writer bows out of the controversial aspects of the question by calling attention to the sentiments penned by Robert Bellarmine at the time of his appointment to the College of Cardinals. The Archbishop of Capua told a priest friend that purely honorary distinctions, even in ecclesiastical circles, "are wonderful and great, if we cleave to earth and forget our true country. But if we judge aright, like good scholars of the school of Christ, if we have studied with attention the Gospels and Saint Paul, if we seriously consider ourselves strangers and pilgrims on earth, what are all these things but a cloud that appears for a little time, and what is our life but grass, and what is its glory but a flower of the field." As for those actively seeking such distinctions, the eminent churchman said that he marvelled at them. "I pity them too, for they seem not to care for the glory of the Eternal King if only they may gain some fleeting, counterfeit honors and the shadow of renown."[33]

Notes to the Text

1. John F. Sullivan, *The Visible Church* (New York, 1921), p. 17.
2. See John Abel Nainfa, *Costume of Prelates of the Catholic Church* (Baltimore, 1926). The Sacred Congregation of Ceremonies issued a pamphlet describing the exact color for various prelatial robes on June 24, 1933.
3. It should be noted that the distinction granted to Raphael Merry del Val was different from that usually conferred on laymen. An interesting insight into the latter classification can be seen in *Francis Augustus MacNutt, A Papal Chamberlain* (London, 1936).
4. See Aidan M. Carr, O.F.M. Conv., "But I don't want to be a Monsignor," *Homiletic and Pastoral Review*, LXIV (October, 1963), 82-84.
5. See Paul R. E. Francis, "Monsignor," *The Catholic Digest*, XXVII (June, 1963), 5-10. For an official description of these various offices, *cf.* the current issue of the *Annuario Pontificio* under the appropriate headings.
6. See "Protonotaries Apostolic," *American Ecclesiastical Review*, XXXI (Novernber, 1904), 445–454.
7. See Joacbim Nabuco, *Jus Pontificalium* (Paris, 1956), pp. 32-37. It is still the basic law of the Church that any benefice, including a parish, held by a domestic prelate or papal chamberlain is reserved to the Holy See upon the death, promotion, resignation, or transfer of the holder. See "Papal Reservation of Appointment to Parishes," *American Ecclesiastical Review*, LXXXIX (October, 1933), 432-434. A list of those countries currently obliged by this legislation is in *L'Attivitá della Santa Sede* (Rome, 1965), p. 740.
8. The first monsignorial appointment not renewed for the United States was that of the Very Reverend John Henry Clüever of Albany whose prelatial status was allowed to lapse with the death of Pope Leo XIII.
9. This decree is reproduced in the appendix of Nicholas Hilling, *Procedure at the Roman Curia* (New York, 1907), pp. 249-276.
10. *Acta Apostolicae Sedis*, XXVI (September, 1934), 497-521. For a detailed elaboration of the various internal organization of the papal household, see Paul F. Schreiber, *Canonical Precedence* (Washington, 1961).
11. T. Ortolan, "Cour Romaine," *Dictionnaire de théologie catholique* (Paris, 1938), III, 1975.
12. E. E. Y. Hales, *Pio Nono* (Garden City, 1954), p. 293.
13. See Roger Aubert, *Le Pontificat de Pie IX* (Paris, 1952), pp. 287-289.
14. Robert Seton, *Memories of Many Years* (1839-1922) (New York, 1923), p. 188.
15. *Collectanea Sanctae Congregationis de Propaganda Fide* (Rome, 1893), 114. The decree was dated September 16, 1884.
16. See Finbar Kenneally, O.F.M., *United States Documents in the Propaganda Fide Archives* (Washington, 1966), p. 280.
17. Father Seton was a grandson of Blessed Mother Elizabeth Seton.
18. *Op. cit.*, p. 185.
19. There seems little justification for spelling this word "prothonotary" though it appears as such in many sources. The Latin, Italian, French, and Spanish retain the term "proto" but writers in English seem to vacillate. See P. A. Baart, *The Roman Court* (Cincinnati, 1895), Preface.
20. There are several examples in United States Catholic annals of papal bestowal of non-prelatial titles on clerics. In May of 1887, for example, Father Patrick J. Toner (1833-1897) was appointed "Missionary Apostolic" by Pius IX, apparently at the behest of the Archbisbop of Naples. Several other priests were subsequently given similar distinctions, though the title is apparently no longer granted in the New World. See Francis X. Reuss, "Catholic Chronicles of Lancaster, Pa.," *Records of the American Catholic Historical Society*, IX (June, 1898), 216.
21. Archives of the Archdiocese of Baltimore, Michael A. Corrigan to James Gibbons, New York, April 28, 1884.
22. Quoted in John Tracy Ellis, *James Cardinal Gibbons, Archbishop of Baltimore* (Milwaukee, 1952), I, 228.

23. Henry J. McCloud, *Clerical Dress and Insignia of the Roman Catholic Church* (Milwaukee, 1948), p. 33. Supernumerary Protonotary Apostolics date from the 16th century.

24. *Acta et decreta concili Plenarii Baltimorensis term* (Baltimore, 1886), pp. xlvi-xlix

25. Francis X. Reuss, *Biographical Cyclopaedia of the Catholic Hierarchy* (Milwaukee, 1898), pp. 128-129.

26. Robert Seton, *op. cit.*, p. 188.

27. J. D. Conway, "On Revising Canon Law," *Commonweal*, LXXX (April 24, 1964), 144.

28. Joseph P. Kiefer, Steubenville *Register*, July 29, 1965.

29. John Tracy Ellis, "Revising Canon Law," *Commonweal*, LXXX (May 29, 1964), 301. Economy-minded priests can take heart that one nationally known clerical tailor offers monsignors a cassock complete with red buttons, buttonholes, duster, cuff-cord, collar-lining, and seam-to-seam piping for only $9.50 more than the traditional black cassock!

30. A synopsis of the survey appears in the *National Catholic Reporter*, December 14, 1966. Obviously, the poll excluded monsignors themselves as well as pastors.

31. Quoted in Richard M. McKeon, S.J., "The Church and Nobility," *Homiletic and Pastoral Review*, LXV (February, 1965), 398.

32. This practice already exists canonically for vicars general, who are equated with protonotaries apostolic for the duration of their tenure. See Stanislaus Woywod, O.F.M. "The Second Book of the New Code of Canon Law," *American Ecclesiastical Review*, LVIII (January, 1918), 42.

33. James Broderick, S.J., *The Life and Work of Blessed Robert Francis Cardinal Bellarmine, S.J., 1542-1621* (London, 1928), I, 406.

10

The following essay about "America's First Vernacular Missal" is here reproduced from the *American Ecclesiastical Review* CLXI (July, 1969), 33-39.

Though bibliophiles have long regarded John England's publication of *The Roman Missal* a treasured collector's item, scholars have yet to accord that proto-American rendition the place it so richly deserves in the nation's liturgical annals. Such an oversight can probably be attributed to the volume's rarity. Indeed, the 1822 edition had become so scarce by the 1920's, that Peter Guilday, the widely recognized historian of American Catholicism, was unable to locate a copy for consultation while preparing his monumental two-volume biography on the Bishop of Charleston.

It was in order "to instruct the members of the Roman Catholic Church on the nature of the most solemn act of their religion," that John England began work on the first American vernacular edition of the *Missale Romanum* shortly after his installation at Charleston, on December 30, 1820. Despite the many other demands on his time, the bishop had finished the compilation, along with an exhaustive ninety-eight page "Explanation of the Mass" by mid-1821.[1] On September 13, he secured a copyright for *The Roman Missal Translated Into the English Language For Use Of the Laity.* The book was set in type at the New York press of B. Bolmore and published in the summer of 1822, by William H. Creagh.[2]

In his edition of the missal, which England prepared under the most unfavorable circumstances,[3] the prelate relied on Richard Challoner's translation for the scripture readings. The prayers, prefaces, sequences and other passages were mostly adaptations of texts then being used in England and Ireland. Generally speaking, "the arrangement of the Missal is good, the rubrics are clear, and the whole work serves its purpose of enabling the reader to assist at Mass with understanding and devotion."[4] A comparison of England's rendition of the Roman Canon, now Eucharistic Prayer I, with the revised version of the International Committee on English in the Liturgy,[5] clearly demonstrates the effect that 146 years can have on the pliability of a language.

The 1882 Edition

We therefore, humbly pray and beseech thee, most merciful Father, thro' Jesus Christ thy Son, our Lord, that thou wouldst vouchsafe to accept and bless these gifts, these presents, these holy unspotted sacrifices, which in the first place we offer thee for thy holy Catholic Church, to which vouchsafe to grant peace; as also to preserve, unite, and govern it throughout the world: together with thy servant N. our Pope and N. our Bishop, as also all orthodox believers and professors of the catholic and apostolic Faith.

Be mindful, O Lord, of thy servants, men and women, N. and N., and of all here present, whose Faith and Devotion is known unto thee, for whom we offer; or who offer up to thee this sacrifice of praise for themselves, their families, and friends; for the redemption of their souls, for the health and salvation they hope for, and for which they now pay their vows to thee, the eternal, living and true God.

Communicating, and honouring in the first place, the memory of the ever glorious Virgin Mary, mother of our Lord and God Jesus Christ; as also of the blessed Apostles and Martyrs, Peter and Paul, Andrew, James, John, Thomas, James, Philip, Bartholomew, Matthew, Simon and Thaddeus, Linus, Cletus, Clement, Xystus, Cornelius, Cyprian, Lawrence, Chrysogonus, John and Paul, Cosmas and Damian, and all of thy saints; by whose merits and prayers grant that we may be always defended by the help of thy protection through the same Christ our Lord. Amen.

We therefore beseech thee, O Lord, graciously to accept this oblation of our servitude, as also of thy whole family; dispose our days in peace, preserve us from eternal damnation, and rank us in the number of thine elect. Thro' Christ our Lord. Amen.

Which oblation do thou, O God, vouchsafe in all respects, to bless, approve, ratify, make reasonable, and accept; that it may be made for us the body and blood of thy most beloved Son Jesus Christ our Lord.

Who on the day before he suffered, took bread into his holy and venerable hands, and with his eyes lifted up towards heaven, giving thanks to thee, God his Father Almighty; he blessed, brake and gave to his disciples, saying: Take and eat ye all of this, FOR THIS IS MY BODY.

In like manner, after he had supped, taking also this excellent chalice into his holy and venerable hands, also giving thee thanks, he blessed, and gave to his disciples, saying: TAKE AND DRINK YE ALL OF THIS, FOR THIS IS THE CHALICE OF MY BLOOD OF THE NEW AND ETERNAL TESTAMENT: THE MYSTERY OF FAITH: WHICH SHALL BE SHED FOR YOU, AND FOR MANY, TO THE REMISSION OF SINS. As often as you do these things, ye shall do them in remembrance of me.

Wherefore, O Lord, we thy servants, as also thy holy people, calling to mind the blessed passion of the same Christ thy Son our Lord, his resurrection from the dead, and admirable ascension into heaven, offer unto thy most excellent Majesty of thy presents and gifts bestowed upon us, a pure Host, a holy Host, an unspotted Host, the holy bread of eternal life, and chalice of everlasting salvation.

Upon which vouchsafe to look, with a propitious and serene countenance, and to accept them, as thou wert graciously pleased to accept the presents of thy just servant Abel, and the sacrifice of our Patriarch Abraham, and that which thy High Priest Melchisedech offered to thee, a holy sacrifice and unspotted victim.

We most humbly beseech thee, Almighty God, command these to be carried by the hands of thy holy angel to thy altar on high, in sight of thy divine Majesty, that as many as shall partake of the most sacred body and blood of thy Son from this altar, may be filled with every heavenly grace and blessing. Thro' the same Christ our Lord. Amen.

Be mindful, O Lord, of thy servants N. and N. who are gone before us with the sign of Faith, and rest in the sleep of peace. To these, O Lord, and to all that sleep in Christ grant, we beseech thee, a place of refreshment, light and peace: thro' the same Christ our Lord. Amen.

Also to us sinners, thy servants, confiding in the multitude of thy mercies, vouchsafe to grant some part and fellowship with thy holy apostles and martyrs: with John, Stephen, Matthias, Barnabas, Ignatius, Alexander, Marcelline, Peter, Felicitas, Perpetua, Agatha, Lucy, Agnes, Cecily, Anastasia, and with all thy saints: into whose company we beseech thee to admit us, not in consideration of our merit, but of thy own gratuitous pardon. Thro' Christ our Lord.

By whom, O Lord, thou dost always create, sanctify, quicken, bless, and give us all these good things. By him and with him, and in him, is to thee, God the Father Almighty, in the unity of the Holy Ghost all honour and glory. For ever and ever. Amen.

The 1968 edition

We come to you, Father, with praise and thanksgiving, through Jesus Christ your Son. Through him we ask you to accept and bless these gifts we offer you in sacrifice. We offer them for your holy catholic Church, watch over it, Lord, and guide it; grant it peace and unity throughout the world. We offer them for N. our Pope, for N. our Bishop and for all who hold and teach the catholic faith that comes to us from the apostles.

Remember, Lord, your people, especially those for whom we now pray, N. and N. Remember all of us gathered here before you. You know how firmly we believe in you and dedicate ourselves to you. We offer you this sacrifice of praise for ourselves and those who are dear to us. We pray to you, our living and true God, for our well-being and redemption.

In union with the whole Church, we honor Mary, the ever-virgin mother of Jesus Christ our Lord and God. We honor Joseph, her husband, the apostles and martyrs Peter and Paul, Andrew, James, John, Thomas, James, Philip, Bartholomew, Matthew, Simon and Jude; we honor Linus, Cletus, Clement, Sixtus, Cornelius, Cyprian, Lawrence, Chrysogonus, John and Paul, Cosmas and Damian, and all the saints. May their merits and prayers gain us your constant help and protection. Through Christ our Lord. Amen.

Father, accept this offering from your whole family. Grant us your peace in this life, save us from final damnation, and count us among those you have chosen. Through Christ our Lord. Amen.

Bless and approve our offering; make it acceptable to you, an offering in spirit and in truth. Let it become for us the body and blood of Jesus Christ, your only Son, our Lord.

The day before he suffered he took break in his sacred hands and looking up to heaven, to you, his almighty Father, he gave you thanks and praise. He broke the bread, gave it to his disciples, and said: Take this, all of you, and eat it: this is my body.

When supper was ended, he took the cup. Again he gave you thanks and praise, gave the cup to his disciples, and said: Take this, all of you, and drink from it: this is the cup of my blood, the blood of the new and everlasting covenant — the mystery of faith. It will be shed for you and for all men so that sins may be forgiven. Whenever you do this, you will do it in memory of me.

Father, we celebrate the memory of Christ, your son. We, your people and your ministers, recall his passion, his resurrection from the dead, and his ascension into glory; and from the many gifts you have given us we offer to you, God of glory and majesty, this holy and perfect sacrifice: the bread of life and the cup of eternal salvation.

Look with favor on these offerings and accept them as once you acccepted the gifts of your servant Abel, the sacrifice of Abraham, our father in faith, and the bread and wine offered by your priest Melchisedech.

Almighty God, we pray that your angel may take this sacrifice to your altar in heaven. Then, as we receive from this altar the sacred body and blood of your Son, let us be filled with every grace and blessing. Through Christ our Lord. Amen.

Remember, Lord, those who have died and have gone before us marked with the sign of faith, especially those for whom we now pray, N. and N. May these and all who sleep in Christ, find in your presence light, happiness and peace. Through Christ our Lord. Amen.

For ourselves, too, we ask some share in the fellowship of your apostles and martyrs, with John the Baptist, Stephen, Matthias, Barnabas, Ignatius, Alexander, Marcellin, Peter, Felicity, Perpetua, Agatha, Lucy, Agnes, Cecilia, Anastasia, and all the saints. Though we are sinners, we trust in your mercy and love. Do not consider what we truly deserve, but grant us your forgiveness, through Christ our Lord.

Through him you give us all these gifts. You fill them with life and goodness, you bless them and make them holy. Through him, with him, in him, in the unity of the Holy Spirit, all glory and honor is yours, almighty Father, for ever and ever. Amen.

Beyond the terminological similarity of the translations, there is also an historical parallel in the stormy reception accorded the two editions. Indeed, the widespread criticism that greeted the rendition of the English canon in 1965, was hardly less vehement than the flurry caused in Rome's curial circles by its 1822 prototype.[6]

That historians generally regard John England as "the foremost ecclesiastic in the Catholic Church of the United States during the years he presided over the Diocese of Charleston"[7] does not blind them to the obvious fact that few of England's activities found favor with such contemporaries as Archbishop Ambrose Marechal. Ostensibly, the metropolitan based his original refusal to authorize publication of the missal on the grounds that such approbation could be granted only by the Holy See. Privately, however, the archbishop expressed doubts to Rome about his suffragan's "theological and biblical knowledge" to undertake a task of that magnitude![8]

Marechal apparently labored under the mistaken assumption that England was preparing a wholly new translation, rather than a compilation of already approved renditions. In any event, when word of Rome's discomfort reached Bishop England, be wrote several explanatory notes to the Sacred Congregation of Propaganda Fide offering a polite but firm *"apologia"* for his work. The fact that none of his letters on the subject was answered, as he later complained,[9] was undoubtedly due to the frantic barrage of correspondence Roman officials were busily raining on the British Isles in an attempt to ascertain whether the "typical" missal used there had the proper ecclesiastical approbation. In a move of almost utter desperation, the impatient Bishop of Charleston informed Francisco Cardinal Fontana that he was ready to put aside his mitre any time the Prefect of Propaganda might find such a move expedient.

Meanwhile, a copy of the newly published missal caught up with Archbishop Marechal who was absent in Europe on business. After personally examining the book and communicating with Bishop William Poynter, the Vicar Apostolic of the London District, Marechal withdrew his earlier reservations and advised Rome against any attempts to suppress the volume.[10] The machinery at Propaganda was not so quickly reversed, however, and as late as mid-1823, the congregation was advised to inform Bishop England that, for the present, *"non gradisce simili versioni, benche le tolleri."*[11]

It was too late, by the time the missal was fully exonerated, to effectively offset the negative image implanted in the public mind by Roman officials and certain of Bishop England's less talented, but more influential episcopal confreres. Though the 1822 *Roman Missal* represented a giant forward step in the nation's liturgical life, the circumstances of its birth militated against the book's wide circulation,[12] at least in the initial edition. That such a volume ever took form is another reason for regarding the Bishop of Charleston as a "prelate who accomplished more good with less means and in the face of greater difficulties" than any other ecclesiastic of his generation.[13]

Notes to the Text

1. A second edition was released in 1843 by Eugene Cummiskey of Philadelphia. In 1861, Cummiskey issued a "first revised edition" of the work.
2. Another version, differing "somewhat in a portion of its contents" from that used in the missal appears as "Explanation of a Church, the Vestments of the Clergy, and the Nature and Ceremonies of the Mass" in Ignatius Aloysius Reynolds' edition of *The Works of the Right Rev. John England* (Baltimore, 1849), III, 305-349.
3. See "Letters from Right Reverend John England, D.D., to the Honorable William Gaston, LL.D.," *Records of the American Catholic Historical Society* XVIII (December, 1907), 378.
4. John K. Ryan, "Bishop England and the Missal in English," *American Ecclesiastical Review* XCV (July, 1936), 33.
5. Released in 1968 by the National Conference of Catholic Bishops in the United States.
6. Peter K. Guilday, *The Life and Times of John England* (New York, 1927), I, 330.
7. Ella M. E. Flick, "John England," *Records of the American Catholic Historical Society* XXXVIIII (December, 1927), 375.
8. Archives of the sacred Congregation of Propaganda Fide (hereafter referred to as ASPF), *Ambrose Marechal to Propaganda Fide, Paris,* September 7, 1822.
9. ASPF, John England to Propaganda Fide, Charleston, May 2, 1822.
10. ASPF, Ambrose Marechal to Robert Gradwell, Rome, October 1, 1822.
11. ASPF, Unsigned Memorandum, c. May, 1823.
12. In addition to the copy in the Archives of the Archdiocese of Los Angeles, there are five known editions of the 1822 missal in the United States, at Georgetown University, the Peabody Institute, Saint Louis University, the University of South Carolina and the Public Library of Philadelphia.
13. Jeremiah J. O'Connell, O.S.B., *Catholicity in the Carolines and Georgia* (Westminster, 1964), p. 49.

11

This essay about "Francisco Garcia Diego and Santa Barbara Mission" was the subject of an address delivered at the Old Mission on March 8, 1987. It appeared in *Noticias* XXXIII (Winter, 1987), 76-85.

S anta Barbara Mission can rightly be called the "Cradle of Catholicity" for Western Americana, not alone because it was and is the Queen of the Missions, or because it is the architectural gem of *El Camino Real* or even because it has been in continual operation since its establishment in 1786.

Rather, Santa Barbara Mission qualifies for that unique title because the first bishop of California lived there during his brief tenure, because its church was his pro-cathedral and because he is buried in its sanctuary.

Over the years, Santa Barbara Mission has become known throughout the world for its admittedly pivotal role during the provincial era. I would like to reflect on another, possibly even more important aspect of its service, one related to its being the seat of episcopal government in California during the crucial and formative years, 1842-1846. It's really a sad story, for the time in question was one of sowing, not reaping. What occurred then stands out mostly because it involved the agonizing ordeal of birth pains. Only now, in the late 1980's, can the interested bystander begin to appreciate what transpired in the mid 1840's.

Initially, Francisco Garcia Diego expected to live and die at San Diego, the geographical center of his vast jurisdiction. Indeed, the bulls appointing him *Obispo de Ambas Californias* specified that his see city would be San Diego. However, it didn't take the friar-bishop long to become disenchanted with the area, its 150 inhabitants and the bleak prospects for development.

When a wealthy merchant offered free transportation to Santa Barbara, the bishop readily acquiesced. His arrival there, in January of 1842, was enthusiastically announced by exploding skyrockets and pealing Mission bells. The surviving Indians, many of whom remembered Francisco Garcia Diego from an earlier era, were pleased at the prospect of having a bishop in their midst.

Alfred Robinson happened to be on hand for that happy occasion and he described the scene this way:

> All was bustle; men, women and children hastening to the beach, banners flying, drums beating, and soldiers marching. The whole population of the place turned out to pay homage to the first Bishop of California. At eleven o'clock the vessel anchored. He came on shore, and was welcomed by the kneeling multitude. All received his benediction—all kissed the pontifical ring. The troops, the civic authorities, then escorted him to the house of Don Jose Antonio, where he dined. A carriage had been prepared for His Excellency, which was accompanied by several others, occupied by the President and his friends. The females formed, with ornamental canes, beautiful arches, through which the procession passed; and as it marched along, the heavy artillery of the Presidio continued to thunder forth its noisy welcome. At the time he had left the barque she was enveloped in smoke, and the distant report of her guns was heard echoing among the hills in our rear.
>
> At four o'clock the bishop was escorted to the Mission, and when a short distance from the town, the enthusiastic inhabitants took the horses from the carriage, and dragged it themselves. Halting at a small bower on the road, he alighted, went into it, and put on his pontifical robes; then resuming his place in the carriage, he continued on, amidst the sound of music and the firing of guns, till he arrived at the church, where he addressed the multitude that followed him.

After receiving several petitions and numerous personal appeals, Bishop Garcia Diego decided to make Santa Barbara his permanent home, much to the apparent satisfaction of both the natives and the *gente de razón*. He wrote Pope Gregory XVI, telling how the "most cordial hospitality as well as demonstrations of affection, respect and loyalty" had convinced him of the feasibility of relocating in a place where "security, population and commerce affords easy communication from one extremity" of his jurisdiction to the other. Citing the favorable disposition of the city's inhabitants, the bishop presumed that the Holy Father would endorse his decision.

After several weeks enjoying the hospitality of local families, the bishop took up residence at the Old Mission, occupying the first two rooms along the front corridor closest to the church. One account described the building of those days as being,

> very large and having many rooms. The bishop was placed in a small room which was partitioned so that he could have a bedroom and an office; both were so small that in the office only a table, a portable altar which at times was used to say Mass, a small bookstand and some chairs, and in the bedroom only a bed, trunk and a chair could be placed. I heard the bishop say after living there for some time: "Ah, my son, I cannot breathe in this cage; it appears they have selected for me the worst rooms."

Another glimpse into the prelate's living arrangements can be gleaned from the memoirs of Captain George Simpson, a representative with the Hudson Bay Company, who visited Santa Barbara Mission shortly after the bishop's arrival there.

> From the gate where we were received by the bishop, we were conducted into an apartment of ordinary size, lighted by a small grated window. This room and its contents presented a contrast which besides being agreeable in itself, was interesting as an evidence at once of the simplicity of the old fathers, and of the ostentation of their episcopal successor. The walls were whitewashed, and the ceiling consisted of rafters while articles of furniture that would not have disgraced a nobleman's mansion occupied the floor. The carpet was the work of the Indians of Mexico; the table was covered with crimson velvet, on which lay a pillow of the same material, adorned with gold; and the sofa and chairs had seats of the same costly and showy description. But the gem of the whole was a throne, with three steps in front of it. It was hung with crimson velvet, which was profusely trimmed with tissue of gold; and its back displayed an expensively framed miniature of the reigning pope painted by a princess, and sent by Gregory to the bishop, along with his diamond ring as a gift. In this his own chair of state, the good prelate insisted on placing me, though I am afraid that, in this planting a heretic before his most highly valued memorial of His Holiness, he must have sacrificed in some degree his orthodoxy to his politeness.

What the well intentioned Garcia Diego probably intended as a formal reception was obviously misinterpreted by Simpson who felt that the prelate was "overloaded with finery." Their conversation, however, went well enough and was described by the visitor as both "agreeable and amusing."

Accommodations were also made in another area of the Old Mission for the handful of seminarians who accompanied the bishop to California. Classes were held there until more permanent quarters could be provided at Santa Inés. For the first time in California history, Bishop Garcia Diego conferred the major orders on three seminarians at Santa Barbara Mission in June of 1842. Miguel Gomez became the proto priest ordained in the Golden State.

Meanwhile, in the flush of his earliest weeks in Santa Barbara, Bishop Garcia Diego drafted and completed his second pastoral letter. After formally outlining the litany of projects envisioned for the diocese the friar,-bishop acknowledged that "these great and beneficent projects cannot be affected unless the faithful are willing to cooperate with us in a very substantial way."

By "substantial" the prelate had in mind tithing, an ancient practice whose history he carefully explained. He pointed out that he had been forced to commence his episcopal apostolate in the Californias "without a single penny." Though much had been promised by the government, little had ever materialized. It was indeed a moving appeal and one which should have elicited a reasonably generous response. The letter, written in the episcopal chambers at the Old Mission, was then sent out to be read at all of the Masses in the diocese. Unhappily, practical though it may have been, the appeal struck an unresponsive cord and there is no indication that the Catholics of the area took the bishop's words seriously.

As is abundantly clear from even a cursory reading of a "Sermon for Independence," which Garcia Diego had delivered at Zacatecas on November 11, 1821, the bishop was a committed nationalist, outspoken against the "great evils in America during the years of its [Mexico's] subjection to Spain." Though one suspects that events occurring during the ensuing years did much to mollify the prelate's enthusiasm for the independence movement, he did voluntarily and perhaps even joyfully take the required Oath of Allegiance to the Mexican government's new constitution at the Old Mission on October 15, 1843.

One of the areas that caused the bishop considerable concern at Santa Barbara was that pertaining to marriages. Though the Law of the Indies had recognized ecclesial competency in such matters, the new regime early on claimed an equal if not paramount right to decide on any issue brought before it, irrespective of traditional canonical procedures.

A celebrated case in point involved Santa Barbara residents Casilda

Sepúlveda and Teodoro Trujillo. Casilda claimed that her marriage to Teodoro was null. *Fray* Tomas Estenaga had advised Casilda to bring the matter before a secular judge, probably because of the annexed property claims over which the judge would also exercise jurisdiction. On May 3, 1842, Bishop Garcia Diego wrote to Santiago Argüello, complaining that the judge had exceeded his authority by issuing a decree of marital nullity. He pointed out that "Your Excellency will readily ascertain my displeasure at seeing ecclesiastical authority encroached upon by the civil tribunal."

In asserting what he referred to as "the Church's undeniable rights," the bishop didn't want Arguello to think he was "looking down on civil officials," but he felt obligated to point out that the case in question was "absolutely reserved" to the Church's domain. The bishop concluded by invalidating the earlier decision, directing Casilda to re-institute her case in canonical court. In retrospect, it would appear that both the governor and the bishop had an obsolete understanding of the legal and canonical complexities resulting from the Mexican independence movement. It was fortunate for Garcia Diego that he was spared a prophetic glance into the following century!

The myriad of challenges that faced the Franciscan prelate in Santa Barbara are mirrored in the 197 letters, documents and related materials still extant in archival repositories. The passage of time did nothing to alleviate the bishop's problems. On October 27, 1843, he wrote to the Minister of Justice about the "very drastic straits" in which he found himself. Houses-of-worship had been closed for lack of priests and services throughout the diocese had been sharply curtailed. There were only twenty priests in the entire jurisdiction, most of them aged and infirm. Garcia Diego felt that the return of the administration of the Pious Fund to the diocese would help to "restore the nation's honor."

He warned that in the event of his death, Rome likely would not "name a successor...and even should someone be nominated, who would want to govern a diocese so completely lacking the most basic items and one without any type of subsistance?" Garcia Diego pleaded with the Minister to "make these facts known to the President, whose generous nature will certainly incline him to look compassionately on this fair territory, where religion languishes and its ministers are severely hampered."

On August 8, 1845, in a letter to Jose Maria Hijar, the prelate said that "we are being threatened by the greatest possibility of the Church's total ruination." The lack of ministers had, in the bishop's view, "brought about the abandonment of some *pueblos*." Lacking all resources, almost devoid of clergy, hope and protection, "the Church can only foresee its complete destruction." He saw, as the only reasonable solution for the many problems, that "the government support the Church, by setting up a relevant, energetic and just system, in tune with local circumstances to reverse the factors bent on its destruction." He saw such action as the only alternative to the ruination that would surely ensue. Garcia Diego said "that any other solution would destroy my patience, already wasted by five years of labors, embarrassments and privations." He threatened "to resign the bishopric" and give the Apostolic See an itemized account of the burdensome situation and the deplorable state to which he had been reduced.

One of the last of the prelate's letters, written to the President of the Republic, noted sadly that "the clergy in this diocese today consists of a few disconsolate friars anxious to retire, others too old or feeble to work and a few others who, despite their efforts, cannot possibly care for this vast territory in the proper manner."

From the first moment of his arrival in Santa Barbara, the bishop had grandiose plans for the Channel City. He envisioned a church, a seminary, school, episcopal residence and several charitable institutions. Unhappily, the ambitious plans were aborted for lack of support and/or interest on behalf of the populace. We are told that "large piles of stones were heaped up in several places for laying foundations of the above-mentioned edifices. The stones will undoubtedly remain for some years as monuments of the frailty of human speculation."

Hard pressed as he was for revenues, the bishop adamantly refused to implement the suggestion, even when offered by the governor, that he inaugurate stole fees. He pointed out that in former times services had been provided free for the people. This, he said, gained the good will of the faithful, sheltered churchmen from the cavils of the impious and the ill will of those with earthly interests. He firmly believed that even if the system were adopted, it would not support the church.

It will not furnish relief, and of this I am certain...Santa Barbara which is one of the most populous towns (not counting the Indians) has had in the past year fifty-five baptisms, four marriages, and twenty-six burials. The tariff of the Diocese of Guadalajara, which is the lowest, prescribed for each baptism (not including desired pomp) eighteen *reales*; for an ordinary marriage, seven *pesos*, besides the gift for the candles, the attendants, and for the use of the rings and token to the bride. In addition, for each announcement four *reales* are offered, so that the ordinary marriage costs eight and a half *reales*. For an ordinary burial the tariff prescribes six and a half *pesos*.

According to this, supposing all had paid the fees, what would be the result? The population of Santa Barbara in the preceding years would have produced an income of only 326.75 *pesos*! Can a parish priest maintain himself and the divine services at his church with such a paltry amount? If then, Santa Barbara under the fee system cannot support a pastor, what about the smaller places? Could they support him? Evidently not.

Though he spent the major part of his episcopate in Santa Barbara, there is surprisingly little evidence about his personal contact with the local inhabitants. Simpson remarked that "all but the better classes were unfriendly to the bishop."

The provincial authorities regarded him with an eye of jealousy as a creature and partisan of the central government; and the mass of the people dreaded any symptom of the revival of a system which had, in their opinion, sacrificed the temporal interests of the colonists to the spiritual welfare of the aborigines.

Father Doroteo Ambris, who came to Santa Barbara with Garcia Diego as a student, later recalled an unfortunate incident of which he was an eyewitness:

> In the same town [Santa Barbara] His lordship, the bishop, was taking a ride in his carriage along the outskirts, accompanied by this writer. A bull enraged by a crowd of people on foot and on horseback, appeared coming toward the carriage. The crowd continued exciting the bull until it came close to the carriage. Then they gave up their pursuit and celebrated with a loud noise the ferocity with which the bull struck the carriage killing the mule that was pulling it. On this occasion I saw the bishop shed abundant tears.

Another account of the episode stated that "no one knows whether the bull was chased outside [the plaza] intentionally or came out accidentally."

Some years later, Bishop Thaddeus Amat told Pope Pius IX about the incident and added that Garcia Diego was "hurt somewhat," in the crash and that he had "to return to the mission on foot while the men who saw what happened remained behind."

Though he was the most distinguished person ever to live at Santa Barbara Mission, Bishop Garcia Diego's love and concern for the people attached to the Old Mission was apparently never again reciprocated after the initial outburst of enthusiasm. Nor were the local residents responsive to the prelate financially. So poor was he that he had to borrow money to furnish his own quarters. Leandro Martinez felt that the people of Santa Barbara gave their bishop "an apparent show of respect" only.

One reason for the bishop's lack of popularity in Santa Barbara may have been his Mexican origins and education. The older Spanish families resented their New World counterparts and frowned upon the quality of their schooling. Actually, in Garcia Diego's case, that rationale was especially ludicrous because the bishop was born into a socially prominent family whose members had long been represented in the medical, legal, political and ecclesial sphere. Garcia Diego had been a schoolmate of Anastasio Bustamante, who became President of the Republic. Undoubtedly such factors as these were unknown to the people at the time and likely the bishop never realized their importance to his work. And the bishop's education towered above that of most Santa Barbarans of the time. His earlier published *Metodo de Misionar*, for example, gives ample evidence of his extensive philosophical and theological training.

But there were other factors too. Some of his contemporaries doubted the area needed a bishop. The biographer of Angustias de la Guerra Ord felt that Garcia Diego "was unfitted to overcome the difficulties he faced without priests or money," in as much as his only base of popular support was Santa Barbara and "rarely did the discouraged man leave his home." Eugéne Duflot de Mofras shared that opinion and predicted in 1841 that "the influence of the bishop...will not be widespread; his advanced age and his Mexican education will not permit him to take part in any spiritual conquests, nor augment the imposing foundations that are the glory of the Spanish Fathers."

A commentator on Santa Barbara's early history says that the city's *paisanos* resented the bishop's sermons, "which branded them as slothful while the leading Spanish families, the *gente de razón*, were embittered because Garcia Diego accused them of fornication and other immoralities." The same writer contended that "to show their contempt, whenever Bishop Garcia Diego was in the pulpit, the Barbaranos not only refused to attend Mass, but staged horse races, bear-and-bull fights, and other noisy sports within earshot of the Mission."

Apparently the prelate did not enhance his position with the stubbornness of his personality. Edward Fischer reported hearing repeatedly about what he called the hypocritical character of the bishop, noting that "his conduct appeared to confirm that description." An equally unimpressed, but openly antagonistic Guadalupe Vallejo classified Garcia Diego among those "prelates who suffered from an excess of silly pride." Another (even more prejudiced) observer recalled that "the bishop rules triumphant, and the wretched priest-ridden dupes would lick the very dirt from off his shoes were he but to will it." Obviously the ill feelings harbored by the *paisanos* or Californians for Mexican immigrants explains much of the personal antipathy for Francisco Garcia Diego. The bishop would doubtless have fared better if his cradle had stood in Spain rather than in Mexico.

Francisco Garcia Diego y Moreno gives every indication of having been unworldly, unselfish and well versed in the ecclesiastical disciplines. While he may not have been the strong character the stormy era desperately called for, "it is doubtful if any man could have been a great leader in the troublous times of Bishop [Garcia] Diego's episcopancy." Although chronologically the first Bishop for California, it remained the challenge of his successors to set the scene for a new culture. For his part, the bishop was destined to taste the stigma of the anticlericalism that pervaded the turbulent revolutionary Mexico. His natural death was hastened by the unfulfilled promises and the greedy chicanery of the men who governed California in the name of God and Liberty.

When the bishop died, on April 30, 1846, the entire population of Santa Barbara was invited to his funeral. That his services, even though conducted on Sunday, were not well attended, says a lot about his popularity and effectiveness.

In any event, what was denied Francisco Garcia Diego y Moreno by Santa Barbarans during his lifetime was lavished upon his remains in death. Shortly after his entombment in a vault of the sanctuary in his pro-cathedral, an artist was employed to design an elaborate monument for the bishop. It is the most elegant of any used for the state's subsequent prelates. The paradox is that Francisco Garcia Diego y Moreno was the poorest of them all.

The bishop's death brought down the curtain not only on his personal life but on the Hispanic era of Santa Barbara's history. A bare month after his funeral, Commodore Robert F. Stockton arrived to claim the Old Mission and its city for the United States. A century later, in an attempt to publicly atone for its earlier behavior, the people of Santa Barbara eagerly endorsed a suggestion by the Archbishop of Los Angeles that their newest Catholic institution be known as Bishop Garcia Diego High School.

So far, the school has experienced considerably more success than the friar-bishop whose name it bears.

12

This essay, entitled "Alemany Returns to San Francisco" is here taken from *California History* LXVII (December, 1988).

The centennial of Archbishop Joseph Sadoc Alemany's death was observed liturgically at Saint Mary's Cathedral in April 1988. Homilist for the memorial honoring San Francisco's proto-archbishop was Msgr. James Gaffey of Santa Rosa.

Over two decades ago, I was asked to serve as official agent for the Archdiocese of San Francisco in the complicated proceedings involved in returning Alemany's remains to California, a project that occupied a goodly portion of my time between November 1962 and February 1965.

The detailed log of correspondence kept during that time, together with records of earlier attempts to bring back the archbishop's restos, was placed on deposit at the Chancery Archives for the Archdiocese of San Francisco, Colma. What follows is an overview of those long, interesting but often frustrating negotiations.

With the acceptance of his resignation by Pope Leo XIII on March 27, 1884, Joseph Sadoc Alemany, the first Archbishop of San Francisco, brought to an end one of the great epochs in California's ecclesial heritage. His thirty-four-year episcopate behind him, the Titular Archbishop of Pelusium set out for his native Spain to spend his final years as a humble religious in the Order of Preachers.[1]

Death came to the Dominican archbishop on April 14, 1888 in the city of Valencia, where he had gone to help re-organize his order's ancient Province of Aragon. Although there is no evidence to determine his own wishes in the matter, Alemany's family asked that he be interred at Vich, his birthplace, in the *Iglesia de Santo Domingo*, the convent where he had begun his novitiate sixty years before.

A local newspaper account noted that the archbishop's remains were sent by rail and arrived at Vich on April 18th where a mourning city waited in respectful silence. Met there by members of the family, ecclesiastical dignitaries and civil officials, the body was taken to the Cathedral where it lay in state the rest of the day. At precisely ten o'clock the next morning, a Pontifical Mass was celebrated by the Bishop of Vich in the presence of most of the city's clergy. A spirited sermon, preached by Canon Narciso Villarasa, reviewed the notable accomplishments of the "Apostle of California."

With the completion of the ceremonies, the remains of the archbishop were borne in procession some few blocks to the Iglesia de Santo Domingo where they were buried in a chapel to the epistle side of the church. When the vault of his tomb was closed on April 19, 1888, hardly any more attention was paid to the noble California pioneer for the next thirty-three years.

The first concerted attempt to move Alemany's remains back to San Francisco seems to have taken place in the spring of 1921 when a formal petition was submitted to the Cathedral Chapter of Vich by Archbishop Edward J. Hanna. Apparently the proposal of Alemany's successor was received with some attention but the response was not favorable as is obvious from an examination of the response from the Bishop of Vich:

> We feel that it will be impossible at this time to accede to the wishes of Your Excellency which have been brought to our attention. After consulting with our chapter, the Alamany family[2] and others, we find ourselves unanimously opposed to transfering the archbishop from the humble city where he is interred.[3]

Thirteen years later another attempt was initiated by the Very Reverend James B. Connally, Dominican Provincial of Holy Name Province. The idea was to have Alemany "reinterred beneath the Chapel of the new College of Saint Albert the Great at the Dominican House of Studies" in Oakland.[4] With the enthusiastic support of Archbishop Hanna, two priests journeyed to Rome for consultation with the Dominican Master General, Very Reverend Martin Stanislaus Gillet. This second set of negotiations was considerably more productive, but was thwarted by the advent of Spain's Civil War. By the time the hostilities were over, there was such confusion about the actual site of the tomb that the matter was indefinitely postponed.

With the subsequent location of the grave, whose marker had been removed by the family to prevent its desecration, sentiments were again aroused to return the archbishop to California. It was at this juncture that the Alamany family filed a legal claim to the remains based on their contention that since they had paid the expenses of having the archbishop moved from Valencia to Vich after his death, they had a valid voice in determining whether the removal could take place, a claim that was judged valid by civil authorities. Antonio Alamany, the grand nephew of the archbishop, then disclosed his family's sentiments by stating that their consent would be given only "on the grounds that the process of beatification be taken up."[5]

A third overture was made by a certain Jaime Ensenat who was anxious that an exposition be staged in San Francisco of "the many and varied souvenirs and personal objects of the archbishop."[6] It was also proposed that Alemany's grand niece should come to the Bay City to supervise the exposition. The date of the event would coincide with San Francisco's centenary as an archdiocese.

About a year later, the matter came before Archbishop John J. Mitty of San Francisco; he showed no less enthusiasm about returning his illustrious predecessor than had Archbishop Hanna. It was pointed out that up until this time "the great obstacle to overcome in order to return the body of Archbishop Alemany to San Francisco was his family..." Apparently Mitty was not advised at this time about the previous condition regarding the beatification.[7]

Archbishop Mitty was confident that the transfer would then proceed along normal channels and expressed his delight with the arrangements: "I am very happy to learn that there will be no difficulty with the Dominicans, with the relatives or with the local Bishop." However, it was about that time that the family reminded Mitty about their reservations. It was their intention that the archdiocese would finance the cause. Apparently, to quote the rector of Rome's Angelicum College,

> The motive for consenting to the removal of the body together
> with the offer for the exposition of all the personal effects of the
> archbishop seem to indicate that there is a desire to stir up interest
> in the archbishop's cause.[8]

With the disclosure of the family's conditions, Archbishop Mitty cancelled further negotiations stating that such an undertaking "would have to be financed" by an archdiocese already confronted with a dire "shortage of priests." With this, Mitty concluded that "it looks as if I shall have to give up any hope of having the body of Archbishop Alemany here."[9]

There the matter rested for another decade until the summer of 1962, when I visited Barcelona seeking information on the history of Southern California. At that time I was the guest of the Alamany family for some weeks and discussed at length the possibility of reopening the whole question of moving the archbishop's remains. Antonio Alamany, grand nephew of the archbishop, still remembering quite vividly the details of his uncle's funeral in 1888, was extremely cordial as was his son José Alamany y Torner. Both of these gentlemen attended the Mass I celebrated at Sarría when Bishop Francisco Mora y Borrell was disinterred and both were eventually brought around to the logic of bringing the archbishop back to his California jurisdiction.[10] At long last, it seemed as if the state's first metropolitan would return.

It had been my personal desire that Alemany be interred in Los Angeles since that city lies within the territorial boundaries of Alemany's earlier jurisdiction of Monterey.[11] This matter had previously been discussed with the family but, as stated by José Alamany, "I can tell you that from my part I have no preference at all," although he did think "San Francisco has a right too."[12] I approached then Bishop Timothy Manning of Los Angeles and was advised to consult with Archbishop Joseph T. McGucken before making any definitive plans about the final disposition.

Within a week after approaching Archbishop McGucken the matter was brought before the Consultors of the Archdiocese of San Francisco and "they were all in favor of taking the steps to bring back to San Francisco the body of Archbishop Alemany."[13] McGucken authorized me to proceed as his agent in the removal process. That the decision to select San Francisco for the interment was well received by the family is obvious from a subsequent letter which stated that they were "very glad you have arrived at a final decision."[14]

Señor Ernesto Tell, a prominent Barcelona lawyer, was engaged to arrange the legal technicalities. An earlier communication from him indicated "there would be no difficulties in transferring the remains to California."[15]

A formal petition was drawn up and sent to San Francisco where it was translated into Spanish. Addressed to the Most Reverend Ramón Masnou Boixeda, Bishop of Vich, the petition expressed the wishes of San Francisco's Catholics to see the first archbishop interred in California.

> The undersigned, acting with the approval of his Archdiocesan Consulters, humbly petitions the Metropolitan Chapter of the Diocese of Vich for permission to move the remains of His

Excellency, the Most Reverend Joseph Sadoc Alemany to San Francisco, California, United States of America.

Assurance is hereby given that the remains of the archbishop will be interred with those of his illustrious successors with all respect and honor due the memory of California's first Archbishop. Señor Ernesto Tell (our legal counsel) has been commissioned by the undersigned as the official representative of the Archbishop of San Francisco in the removal process and is empowered to act in my name in all matters pertaining to the transfer of the archbishop.[16]

The petition was forwarded to Señor Tell on January 25, 1963 and was presented on February 2. It was at this juncture that complications again beset the process for, as the lawyer noted, "In the case of Archbishop Alemany, we will find complications from the fact that his remains...are publicly exposed in a church for many years."[17]

It had been suggested to Archbishop McGucken that the possibility of a refusal from either ecclesiastical or civil authorities would make it advisable "not to make any public announcement about this project until all the arrangements have been made."[18] This advice was given to Tell who had thought earlier that a public campaign in the Vich press would help the cause. However, news of the negotiations leaked out and Archbishop McGucken was forced to make a public announcement to the San Francisco papers on January 28, 1963.

The Archdiocese is planning to exhume the body of the first Archbishop of San Francisco—Friar Joseph Sadoc Alemany—from his family burial vault in Spain and fly it here...Archbishop Alemany will then be buried again in a special chapel of the Holy Cross Cemetery Mausoleum next to the bodies of Archbishops Riordan, Hanna and Mitty...The Archbishop said the Los Angeles historian, Friar [sic] Francis Weber returned from Spain recently and informed him that Archbishop Alemany's family was agreeable to bringing his remains to the United States.[19]

News of the press announcement was sent at once to Señor Tell who was advised, in view of the San Francisco release, "to remove the secrecy bond that was earlier imposed if you think it will work to the interest of everyone concerned.[20]

However, it would seem that the newspaper publicity was poorly received in Spain. Difficulties began multiplying and when Señor Tell was received by the Vicar General of the Diocese of Vich, he was told that the petition for removal would be refused on the "precedent" of the earlier denials. In response, it was pointed out that the 1921 decision was based on the "unanimous refusal" of both the chapter and the family. The basis for that earlier decision had been altered for the family "has not only given their permission but are now eagerly in favor of the move."[21] This response elicited no reaction from the Vich chancery.

Appealing to a higher ecclesiastical authority was ruled out by Archbishop McGucken who prudently pointed out that, "knowing the Spanish character, I do not think they will be much inclined to move on the basis of any challenge to jurisdiction. They are better than we are in arguing that field."[22]

It was then suggested that the Bishop of Vich might "care to come to San Francisco with the remains and to participate in the solemn ceremonies of his interment." McGucken also suggested that "it might be a good idea to stress the Spanish contribution to the christianization and the civilization of California, and the need of keeping alive here the memory of the valiant Spanish missionaries and Archbishops" by securing a letter from the local Spanish embassy.

His Excellency, Señor Mariano Sanz-Briz, Consul General of Spain in San Francisco, graciously acceded to this request and sent a cable directly to Doctor Don Ramón Masnou Boixeda, the Bishop of Vich, noting that if permission were eventually obtained, "it will be an honor for me to participate and represent Spain in the sacred acts that will be celebrated to commemorate [sic] this event."[23]

Early in May, Señor Tell informed me that negotiations in Vich had progressed about as far as he could carry them and advised that a personal representative be sent from San Francisco with authority to confer with Bishop Boixeda. It was hoped that California Archbishop McGucken might stop there on his way to Mallorca for the 250th anniversary of Junípero Serra's birth. The archbishop's facility with Spanish and his winning personality would have been forceful qualities in any private discussions with the local Spanish hierarchy. However, when the archbishop was forced to cancel his trip for reasons of health, the whole question of the removal was temporarily suspended.

Ernesto Tell and Antonio Alamany were received by the Bishop of Vich on August 26, 1963. On that occasion the prelate agreed to submit the matter of removing the archbishop's remains to his consultors and to abide by their advice in the matter. Bishop Masnou was aware from the beginning that Vich is a "very traditional and conventional town with great esteem for its illustrious pioneers."[24] A petition signed by seven members of the Alamany family was presented to the chapter in late

September and was passed favorably a few weeks later. Tell suggested the advisability of the Archbishop of San Francisco personally contacting Bishop Ramon Masnou Boixeda at the second session of Vatican Council II in Rome. Such a meeting did take place and the Catalan prelate assured Archbishop McGucken that personally "he had no objections" to the removal and would cooperate in every way possible.[25]

There were additional problems, however. Tell was informed that "the Parish of Santo Domingo, where the tomb is erected, and the civil people, are against the project."[26] Though he subsequently discovered very little real opposition to the removal, the matter encountered additional delays.

Tell suggested the need for further intervention by the Spanish Consul in San Francisco. Señor Mariano Sanz-Briz graciously complied. In a long communication to the *Presidente del Ayuntamiento de Vich*, Señor Antonio Bach Roura, he assured the *alcalde* and his council that California was, indeed, the most fitting and appropriate resting place for Archbishop Alemany.[27] The secretary of the *Ayuntamiento*, Señor Juan Duran Noguer, favored the removal and the Rector of Santo Domingo finally acquiesced provided the necessary expenses of the project would be assumed by the Archdiocese of San Francisco. Early in September, Duran reported that the town council was ready to issue its official *nil obstat*. The actual approval came on October 9th.[28]

Coincidentally, during that October, Señor Manuel Fraga Iribarne, the Spanish Minister of *Información y Turismo*, was in California on official government business. On meeting Fraga in Los Angeles, it was pointed out to him that his influence could do much to expedite the case.[29] The Spanish cabinet member received the request favorably and later, from his office in Madrid, he wrote that he would take all necessary measures to speed along affairs at Vich.[30]

Tell reported on November 4 that *the Ayuntamiento de Vich*, by initiative of its *alcalde*, reaffirmed its earlier action and granted unconditional approbation to the matter.[31] This was verified on November 9 by the Consul General of Spain in San Francisco; he wrote that "the Secretary of the *Ayuntamiento de Vich* and its Assembly has authorized the removal of the remains of Bishop Alemany."[32] Ecclesiastical approval, following closely on the decision of the *Corporación Municipal*, was formally granted on December 1.[33] Tell informed me that the chancery officials wished to make the transfer on Thursday, January 21.[34] The Archbishop of San Francisco was informed of the latest developments by Señor Mariano Sanz-Briz.[35]

With the approval in hand, I visited Archbishop McGucken on December 21 in order to make final arrangements for the actual transfer. The appropriateness of holding the ceremonies at old Saint Mary's, the cathedral Alemany built in 1854, was mentioned along with a proposed outline of procedural matters. Several alternate dates for the actual ceremony in San Francisco were discussed, though the archbishop noted that he would be out of town during the last days of January. In order to solemnize the events, and to leave a cushion time-period for unforeseen delays, it was decided to leave a reasonably safe lapse of time between the planned arrival of the remains in California and the official functions commemorating the event.[36] The same plan was utilized which I, aided by Señor Tell, had used in 1962 to bring back to Los Angeles the remains of Bishop Francis Mora from Barcelona.[37] Alemany's body would be received quietly in Los Angeles, re-casketed if necessary, and then placed in a receiving vault until the day of the ceremonies in San Francisco. The possibility of a Mass at Monterey in San Carlos Presidio Church, Alemany's first episcopal seat, was mentioned but later ruled out by McGucken as *de trop*.[38]

A subsequent visit to the Spanish Consul General in San Francisco brought up the possibility of having the Spanish ambassador in Washington, D.C., personally represent his government at the ceremonies in the Bay City. An invitation to that effect was issued and the Marqués Merry Del Val notified us that "you may be certain that I am looking forward with the greatest anticipation to this event in which the Catholics of San Francisco will honor the memory of my compatriot who was the founder of your great Diocese."[39]

Early in January, Archbishop McGucken wrote me that he had "talked with His Eminence, Cardinal McIntyre and Bishop Manning relative to the removal of the remains of Archbishop Alemany...and they have told me that it is perfectly agreeable to them for you to go to Spain to be present as official witness for the Archbishop of San Francisco on that occasion."[40]

Plans were immediately made to leave Los Angeles on January 17; arriving in Barcelona two days later. The archdiocese's lawyer was alerted to have all the necessary documentation readied by that time. On the appointed day I boarded an Italian plane for the journey to the "Queen of the Mediterranean."

Shortly after my arrival in Barcelona, the Ministry of Justice at Madrid announced that its Under Secretary, Carlos Oreja Elosequi, would personally come to Vich to represent the Caudillo of Spain, Generalisimo Francisco Franco. A request was also made to postpone the ceremonial observance until January 23 in order to allow the government time for more elaborate preparations.

The work of opening the tomb began at 3 o'clock in the afternoon on January 20 in the presence of the Most Reverend Ramón Masnou Boixeda, Bishop of Vich, and other civic and ecclesiastical officials. There was an obvious note of anxiety about this aspect of the work since the communists had defiled the grave during their occupation of Vich in the Civil War. A rather substantial tradition maintained, however, that they never actually found the remains and contented themselves with defacing the marble plaque attached to the adjoining wall.

At a level of approximately thirty centimeters, the workers unearthed the vaulted ceiling of a tomb. Further digging confirmed that the previously unopened subterranean enclosure did, in fact, house the metallic casket bearing the remains of Joseph Sadoc Alemany. When the tomb had been fully cleared, it was obvious that it had escaped despoliation, retaining intact the unbroken seals placed there in 1888.

After the recitation of appropriate prayers, the casket was removed and placed upon a catafalque directly in front of the altar in the little chapel where it laid in state until Saturday's ceremonies.

Early on the morning of January 23, the remarkably well-preserved remains of the first Archbishop of San Francisco were removed from their original container and placed in an African mahogany casket. The transfer was officially witnessed by the diocesan vicar general and chapter notary.

About 11 o'clock the visiting dignitaries were officially welcomed in the Chambers of the Vich *Ayuntamiento*. Among those attending the ceremonies were Under Secretary of Justice, Carlos Oreja Elosequi; the Governor of Barcelona, Antonio Ibañez Fraire; the Provincial Delegate of the Ministry of *Información*, Manuel Camacho; Court of Appeals Justice, the Marques de Castellflorite; the President of the Catalan *Audientia*, Elipidio Luzano Esolina; the Consul General of the United States in Barcelona, John W. Ford; the Director of the Institute of North American Studies, William Flauenselder; the *Alcalde* of Vich, Antonio Bach Roura and others.

When everyone had been assembled, a procession to the church started, winding its way through the streets, draped with American, Spanish and Papal flags. The Bishop of Vich greeted the assemblage at the entrance of Santo Domingo and led the officials to their places surrounding the elevated dais on which the archbishop's remains had been placed.

A beautifully executed tapestry bearing the coat-of-arms of the Archdiocese of San Francisco was hoisted at the entrance to the sanctuary during the *coram pontifice* Mass which I had the honor to celebrate as the representative of the San Francisco jurisdiction. Four deacons, vested in snow-white albs, served the Mass. The epistle and gospel were read in Catalan, Spanish and English and immediately after the Mass, Bishop Masnou imparted the final absolutions. The event was well chronicled and television coverage was extensive. Agents of the press took great care to have the sacred ceremonies well described and illustrated in the nation's newspapers.

Civic observances began about 2 p.m. in the *Casa Consistorialis*. Formal addresses were given by the Under Secretary of Justice and the *Alcalde* of Vich. A panegyric was delivered by Father Luis Cura Pellicer, who spoke for the bishop. John W. Ford, the United States Consul General at Barcelona, gave a brief address and was followed by myself who thanked the people of Vich in the name of the Catholics of California. Following this observance, the officials of Vich's *Ayuntamiento* gave a banquet for twenty-four of the attending officials in an old palace adjoining the *Museo de Jaime Balmes*.

The remains of Archbishop Joseph Sadoc Alemany reposed in the Blessed Sacrament Chapel of Santo Domingo until early Monday morning when they were taken by hearse to Barcelona, there to be loaded on a Lufthansa plane for California. The plane bearing the archbishop's remains arrived in Los Angeles early on the morning of January 27 and the remains were immediately taken to a mortuary in Hollywood where certain modifications were made on the casket.

Originally, it had been envisioned that a time-cushion of eight or nine days between the scheduled arrival date in California and the formal reception in San Francisco would ensure against any unforeseen delays in removing the remains from Vich. It was also planned, from the very outset, that the archbishop's body would be brought first to Los Angeles and then taken overland to Monterey for services in Alemany's first Cathedral of San Carlos. When the proposed ceremonies there were cancelled by Archbishop McGucken in mid-January, it was too late to alter the earlier plans. The presence of the archbishop's remains in California's southland was a source of some anxiety to at least one newsman who reported that, upon his arrival in the Golden State, the archbishop was taken, "of all places, to Los Angeles!"[41]

Meanwhile, final plans were being made for the San Francisco ceremonies by the Very Reverend Chester Thompson, vice chancellor for the archdiocese. On February 5, I accompanied the remains by air to the Bay City where delegations from the Spanish Embassy and the San Francisco

Chancery met the plane. An escorted procession sped the hearse and limousines to old Saint Mary's Church where Archbishop Joseph T. McGucken liturgically received his predecessor in the very church Alemany had built in 1853-1854. At the conclusion of the services, the body officially lay in state, guarded by alternating teams from the San Francisco Police Department. Placed atop the casket during the twenty-four-hour vigil was the mitre used at Alemany's consecration in Rome on June 30, 1850.

The formal ceremonies began on Saturday, February 6, at 12:10 p.m. In attendance were the Spanish Ambassador to the United States, Marques Merry del Val, the Mayor of San Francisco, John F. Shelley, six bishops and a church filled with eminent civic and ecclesiastical dignitaries. Father John B. McGloin of the University of San Francisco delivered the sermon. Dominican, Franciscan and Jesuit provincials assisted at the ceremonies as did representatives from all California's religious orders and communities. Archdiocesan seminarians provided the musical accompaniment and served the Pontifical Mass celebrated by San Francisco's archbishop.

At the end of the absolutions, the coffin was transported in a long funeral cortege, by way of Alemany Boulevard, to Holy Cross Mausoleum. There Marques Merry del Val spoke eloquently on the early life of Joseph Sadoc Alemany. The ceremony was appropriately concluded with the remarks of Archbishop McGucken who noted that "All that is good and noble in California's Catholic heritage derives from Spain and its generous priests and laity who have made this Golden State a jewel in the Crown of Mother Church. We rejoice today in the return of our first archbishop for his holy life epitomized the spirit of Christ which the Spanish realm left for our inheritance."[42]

With the entombment of Joseph Sadoc Alemany alongside his three successors, "the heart and affection" that California's first archbishop left in San Francisco were once again united to his earthly remains.[43] The gentle Dominican friar had returned to his people eight long decades after a tearful departure in 1885.

Notes to the Text

1. Alemany was Bishop of Monterey from 1850 to 1853 and Archbishop of San Francisco from 1853 to 1884.
2. While the archbishop preferred and generally used the Anglo spelling of his family name, most of the others then and now utilize the "a" rather than the "e." Both forms are considered correct.
3. Francis, Bishop of Vich to Edward Hanna, Vich, June 2, 1921.
4. Los Angeles *Tidings*, February 23, 1934.
5. Antonio Alamany to Manuel Montoto, O.P., Barcelona, December 7, 1952, Archives of the Archdiocese of San Francisco (AASF).
6. Jaime Ensenat to Manual Montoto, O.P., Barcelona, December 10, 1952, AASF.
7. Benedict Blank, O.P., to John Mitty, Rome, March 8, 1953, AASF.
8. Benedict Blank, O.P., to John Mitty, Rome, April 16, 1953, AASF.
9. John Mitty to Benedict Blank, O.P., San Francisco, April 21, 1953, AASF.
10. Francis J. Weber, "In Search of a Bishop," *Southern California Quarterly*, XLV (September 1963): 235-243.
11. Five of the prelates who governed the southern jurisdiction are buried within the Archdiocese of Los Angeles.
12. Jose Alamany to writer, Barcelona, December 5, 1962.
13. Joseph T. McGucken to writer, San Francisco, January 11, 1963.
14. Jose Alamany to writer, Barcelona, February 1, 1963.
15. Ernesto Tell to writer, Barcelona, December 22, 1962.
16. Joseph T. McGucken to Ramón Masnou Boixeda, San Francisco, January 24, 1963, AASF.
17. Ernesto Tell to writer, Barcelona, February 4, 1963.
18. Writer to Joseph T. McGucken, Los Angeles, December 28, 1962.
19. San Francisco *Examiner*, Janaury 28, 1963.
20. Writer to Ernesto Tell, Los Angeles, February 11, 1963.
21. Writer to Ernesto Tell, Los Angeles, February 18, 1963.
22. Joseph T. McGucken to writer, San Francisco, February 20, 1963.
23. Mariano Sanz-Briz to writer, San Francisco, March 5, 1963.
24. Ernesto Tell to writer, Barcelona, August 26, 1963.
25. Joseph T. McGucken to writer, Rome, November 25, 1963.
26. Ernesto Tell to writer, Barcelona, December 17, 1963.
27. Mariano Sanz-Briz to Antonio Bach Roura, San Francisco, January 23, 1964.
28. Ernesto Tell to writer, Barcelona, October 9, 1964.
29. Writer to Manuel Fraga Iribarne, Los Angeles, October 19, 1964.
30. Manuel Fraga Iribarne to writer, Madrid, October 28, 1964.
31. Don Juan Duran Noguer Statement, Vich, October 31, 1964.
32. Mariano Sanz-Briz to writer, San Francisco, November 9, 1964.
33. Decree of Vicar General, Diocese of Vich, December 1, 1964.
34. Ernesto Tell to writer, Barcelona, December 1, 1964. An alternate date of January 28th was suggested but not recommended.
35. Mariano Sanz-Briz to writer, San Francisco, December 10, 1964.
36. The date of February 5th-6th was ultimately decided upon.
37. See Weber, "In Search of a Bishop," pp. 235-243.
38. Joseph T. McGucken to writer, San Francisco, January 6, 1965.
39. Merry del Val to writer, Washington, January 11, 1965.
40. Joseph T. McGucken to writer, San Francisco, January 4, 1965.
41. San Francisco *Chronicle*, January 29, 1965.
42. *La Vanguardia*, February 8, 1965.
43. The *Monitor*, February 18, 1965.

13

"Thaddeus Amat—Fact versus Fiction" is the title of this essay which appeared in the *Records of the American Catholic Historical Society* LXXIV (September, 1963), 152-158.

Known as the "shrewdest man at the Vatican Council,"[1] Thaddeus Amat could be expected to provide his biographer with many challenges and this he has done with remarkable consistency. The documentation on the following pages indicates how the few meagre accounts of his life contradicted one another, to such an extent that we were eventually forced to disregard altogether secondary sources and center our attention on what original information could be discovered. It was decided almost immediately after our work began that nothing less than a personal visit to the areas of Amat's activities could unravel the puzzles caused by earlier chroniclers who seem, in many cases, to have invented facts where none existed and to have altered them where they did.

Realizing the importance of this preliminary research for an eventual biography of Amat, our program was endorsed by His Eminence, James Francis Cardinal McIntyre, and made possible by his generous patronage. Mindful of failures in the past and skepticism in the present, we launched forth using as our guide the sage advice of Newman that "nothing would be done at all if a man waited till he could do it so well that no one could find fault with it."[2]

Amat's Date of Birth

Thaddeus Amat's birthdate has been in question since 1898 when Francis X. Reuss published his *Biographical Cyclopedia of the Catholic*

Hierarchy of the United States.[3] Therein he stated that the future Bishop of Monterey-Los Angeles was born on December 31, 1810, giving as the source of his information Bishop Francis Mora, Amat's successor at Los Angeles. 1810 was also the date used by Thomas F. Meehan in his article for the Catholic Encyclopedia in 1907.[4] But by the time Joseph B. Code's *Dictionary of the American Hierarchy*[5] was published in 1940, it had been observed that the inscription on Amat's tomb[6] gave 1811 as the date of his birth. The earlier date seemed preferable[7] since Mora obviously supplied his data to Reuss some years after the tombstone had been erected and would have had no reason for changing it had not later evidence been discovered.

Records at Maison-Mere in Paris favor 1811 as we found after a personal investigation there in 1962.[8] In Barcelona, where Amat was known to have been born, the author spent several fruitless days in the Archivo Diocesano looking through baptismal registers of various city parishes including Santa Eulalia Cathedral. Up to this time we were unaware of a small volume of *Notas Biograficas de los que han pertenecido a la Congregacion de la Mision en Espana* by Benito Paradela, C.M.[9] Stumbling across this useful book in the archives of the Iglesia de San Vicente de Paul in Palma (Mallorca), it was noted that the entry for Amat carried this interesting item:

En la partida de Bautismo que en 1924 vimos en la parroquia del Pino, de Barcelona, consta fue bautizado alli en 31 de diciembre de 1811...[10]

Returning to Barcelona, a search was made through the parochial books of the Basilica de Nuestra Señora del Pino and the entry for Amat was quickly turned up. Written in Catalan it bore the date *"treinta y un de Desembre de mil vint cents y once"* (1811). It was further noted that the name "Tadeo" was conferred on the youngster in honor of that great apostle who is highly venerated in the basilica.

Only one chronicler[11] had given the names of Amat's parents and his information came from Paris. Known only as Pedro and Maria (Brusi), the Baptismal Register brought to light the additional information that Tadeo's father was a professional "arms-maker"[12] and a native of Barcelona. Maria Brusi, on the other hand, was born at Naples and hence not a member, as was thought, of the prominent Catalan Brusis who inaugurated the *Diario de Barcelona*.

Official documents at the Vincentian Motherhouse indicated that Thaddeus Amat was received into the Congregation of the Mission on January 4, 1832 at Barcelona. This data harmonized with the *"Catalogus*

Sacerdotum et Clericorum Congregationis Missionis Americanae Provinciae, 1816—"[13] which noted that he completed his minor seminary training in late December 1831. However, a discrepancy soon became obvious about the date of Amat's final vows. The *"Catalogus"* listed January 16, 1834, the date given in subsequent sketches. Nonetheless, the Paris *"Dictionnaire Du Personnel"* gave January 6th. No date at all is recorded by Jose Herrera in his *Historia de la Congregacion de la Mision*[14] although the chapel where the event took place is identified as Barcelona's *Iglesia de Nuestra Señora de la Merced*. In the absence of any further data, January 16th would seem a preferable date since it was also used by Paradela[15] who compiled his statistics from original documentation in Madrid.

The greatest puzzle of them all was the date and place of Amat's ordination to the priesthood. Usually these events took place either in the Chapel of Maison-Mere or at nearby Notre Dame Cathedral, depending on the wishes of the Vincentian Superior General. Reuss mentions only that he received holy orders at "Trinity Ordinations, 1838 at the House of the C.M., Paris France."[16] Code dropped the place of ordination and added the date, "June 9, 1838"[17] while the official historiographer of the Archdiocese of Los Angeles, Charles C. Conroy, listed "August 9, 1838."[18] Herrera did not venture an opinion on either the date or the place and both John Gilmary Shea[19] and Paradela noted only "1838."[20]

Much to our consternation, we discovered in Paris that there were no ordinations on either June 9 or August 9, 1838. A search of Notre Dame's registers also proved futile. More by accident than design, we noticed a marginal entry for December 23, 1837 stating that on that date the chapel at Rue de Sevres was being painted and renovated. Seeing no logical reason for such a comment in the *"Liber Ordinationum"* unless it was inserted for explanatory reasons, we judged that ordinations may have been scheduled for that day and transferred to another church[21] when the chapel became unavailable. A survey was then made of the immediate neighborhood and in the third church visited, now the Chapel of Paris' Catholic University,[22] we ran across the entry for Amat's ordination, dated December 23, 1837 and signed by Hyacinthe Louis de Quelen, the Archbishop of Paris.

Father Amat's early years as a missionary in the United States have also been the cause of confusion among chroniclers. He is known to have sailed from Liverpool in the summer of 1838 some weeks after receiving his appointment to the new American Province of the Congregation of the Mission.[23]

Soon after arriving at New Orleans on October 9th,[24] Amat was assigned to the faculty of Assumption Seminary[25] located a few miles down Bajou Lafourche. The young priest's presence there is attested to by a letter he sent to the Superior General on January 15, 1839[26] in which he describes some of the activities of parish life in Donaldsonville. One historian also notes that Amat was busily involved in missionary work and dedicated a Church to Saint Vincent Ferrer in that year.[27]

On March 5, 1841 Father Amat was sent to Saint Mary of the Barrens at Perryville, Missouri, to perfect his mastery of English. The following month he went to Cape Girardeau as Director of Novices.[28] A notation in the minute-book of the Vincention Superior General[29] states that on November 4, 1841 Amat was designated rector of Saint Mary's Seminary at the suggestion of the Very Reverend John Timon, C.M.

When the diocesan seminary was moved to Saint Louis in October of 1842, Timon informed the General that he wanted Amat made superior at Saint Louis.[30] The *Catholic Almanac* for 1843 mentions that he was also pastor of the newly created Parish of the Holy Trinity[31] and chaplain of Sacred Heart Convent. Except for a brief span as pastor at Donaldsonville, Amat administered both the seminary and parish at Saint Louis until July 8, 1844[32] when, acting again on the advice of Timon, Amat was named superior at Cape Girardeau. "Father Amat filled the office of President for a year or more when he was transferred to the Barrens and made superior of that Institution."[33] A check made of the entries in the parochial registers at Perryville reveal his name after this date and confirm his presence there.

There was some possibility in 1844 that Amat would be among those chosen to join the newly created Vincentian Province in Mexico. However, when asked about the availability of Amat, Bishop John Odin of Galveston answered that "though Mr. Amat was a very useful and well deserving member of the Congregation," his talents were sorely needed in the United States where he had become "one of the most valued priests...lured to America."[34]

The superiorship of the new Saint Charles Seminary in Philadelphia was entrusted to Amat on October 4, 1847 although he apparently did not arrive at his assignment until the beginning of the following year. He held that position until 1852.[35] His name was considered for the post of provincial in April of 1846[36] when it was learned that the Holy See was about to erect a diocese at Buffalo and name John Timon its first bishop. No definitive action was taken at the time and the appointment eventually went to the Reverend Mariano Maller, C.M.

Further examination of the Paris files revealed that the General Council named Amat Provincial and Director of the Daughters of

Charity in the Madrid Province in 1848 to succeed Buenaventura Codina who had been named Bishop of the Canaries.[37] But again there is no evidence that Amat ever received this news.

Acting on the recommendation of the First Plenary Council of Baltimore which had convened in May of 1852, Pope Pius IX created a metropolitan jurisdiction in California and promoted the Bishop of Monterey, Joseph Sadoc Alemany, O.P., to the new Archdiocese of San Francisco. Thaddeus Amat attended the council as theologian to Blessed John Neumann, the Bishop of Philadelphia.[38] That he became aware of his nomination to the vacant See of Monterey is now certain and explains his hasty retreat to Europe soon thereafter. It has been part of the record for many years that Amat accepted the mitre only after "vain appeals."[39] One Vicentian historian notes that "Amat came to Spain in the autumn of 1852 in order to escape being made Bishop of Monterey, California."[40]

The files at Paris showed that Amat had written to the General as early as May 20, 1852 asking him to suppress the nomination.[41] There is no indication, however, that the General took any action along those lines although he did approve Amat's transfer to Madrid as Rector of the Vincentian Novitiate.[42] This is also confirmed in a letter of the Reverend Jose Escarra written from Madrid on September 6, 1852 announcing the installation of the Congregation of the Mission in the new house ceded to them by the Government.[43] By October 9th, Amat had arrived in Madrid and was deeply immersed in the routines of his new appointment.[44]

The Holy See was persistent, however, and sought out Amat in Spain. The reluctant candidate again appealed to the General and this time the matter was discussed in the council meeting for May 30, 1853. It was proposed that Amat be named superior and director of the Daughters of Charity in Chile[45] although from the entries it is not clear whether the appointment was ever formally issued. We are led to believe he did receive the directive for one reliable source notes that on October 22, 1853 "*sale de Madrid el Sr. Amat para Chile.*"[46] This harmonizes with an earlier note from Archbishop Alemany which had mentioned that "as soon as he heard of his appointment, he withdrew from Philadelphia to Spain and thereafter passed on to France for the purpose of taking passage to Chile and so to hide himself."[47]

But by this time the bulls of his episcopal appointment had already been issued.[48] When this news reached him, Amat wrote directly to the Prefect of the Sacred Congregation of Propaganda Fide:

> I am greatly distressed because of my lack of knowledge, holiness and prudence and for these reasons I left Philadelphia last year.

Knowing full well my lack of qualifications I think God in His
infinite mercy has called me to the Congregation of the Mission
that I might lead a religious life and lacking the helps of this life I
fear I might lose my soul. Therefore, I pray you to allow me to
remain in my obscure place in the community...[49]

One final communication to Cardinal Fransoni was sent early the next
month after having received the bulls:

The letters ordering my submission to the burden of the episcopate have been received by our Father General who has left the
ultimate choice to me in this matter. I still think I should decline
because it is a threat to my salvation. But fearing that the judgment may be an effect of my weakness and fearing lest I resist the
will of God...I sought advice from my spiritual director and had
many Masses offered to find out God's Will. All these have convinced me that I should not accept this burden. Therefore, I plead
with you to tell His Holiness to relieve me of this burden.[50]

News of Amat's reluctance even found its way to California. The
Archbishop of San Francisco penned an interesting note to his vicar in
the southern jurisdiction:

The new Bishop of Monterey is the Rt. Rev. Thaddeus Amat of
Barcelona, a Father of the Congregation of Saint Vincent de Paul,
a man, I am assured, very distinguished for his humility and learning...The Propaganda is trying to forward the Bulls to him. It is
to be feared that he will decline and thus there will be another
delay of some additional months.[51]

But, in spite of all his pleas, Amat was finally obliged to acquiesce to
what he termed the "relentless insistence" of the Holy Father.

With Amat's consecration as Bishop of Monterey[52] on March 12, 1854
in the small chapel of Propaganda Fide in Rome, the first phase of this
remarkable man's life comes to a close. All the pieces of the interesting
but confusing puzzle now fit snugly into place and while our subsequent
research provided its challenges too, we look back on this preliminary
work and are tempted to agree with Newman's dictum that "The pleasure of a search, like that of a hunt, lies in the searching, and ends at the
point at which the pleasure of certitude begins."[53]

Notes to the Text

1. Quoted in Francis J. Weber, "Bishop Amat at the Vatican Council," *Educatio Christiana* (New York, 1962), VII, 19.
2. *The Knockberg Centenary Book* (Carlow, 1948), dedication page.
3. (Milwaukee, 1898).
4. I, 380-381.
5. (New York).
6. Thaddeus Amat was interred beneath the main altar of Saint Vibiana's Cathedral in 1878. In November, 1962, his remains were transferred to the Bishop's vault at Calvary Mausoleum.
7. 1810 was the date given as late as 1940 by Charles C. Conroy in *The Centennial* (Los Angeles, 1940), p. 22.
8. *"Dictionnaire Du Personnel Congregation de la Mission,"* Deuxieme Series, 1801-1900 (A-B), Book 446.
9. (Madrid, 1935).
10. *Ibid*, p. 157.
11. Code, *op. cit.*, p. 6.
12. *"armero"* is the term used.
13. Entry No. 51.
14. (Madrid, 1949).
15. p. 158.
16. p. 16.
17. p. 7.
18. p. 22.
19. *History of the Catholic Church in the United States* (New York, 1892) IV, 709.
20. p. 158.
21. This procedure would have presented no difficulties canonically, since the Vincentian Superior General is automatically Vicar General of Paris.
22. I.e., Eglise Saint-Joseph des Carmes.
23. The American Province had been founded on September 2, 1835.
24. Conroy, *op. cit.*, p. 22.
25. Placed under the patronage of Saint Vincent de Paul, the original institution burned and was later rebuilt in New Orleans.
26. *Annals de la Congregation de la Mission* (Paris, 1839), V, 83-87.
27. Roger Baudier, *The Catholic Church in Louisiana* (New Orleans, 1939), p. 383.
28. Archives of *Juventudes de la Medalla Milagrosa*, Anonymous manuscript. Dated "Philadelphia, 1903."
29. *"Registre Des Conseils,"* I, 137.
30. *Ibid.*, I, 232.
31. Presently this is Saint Vincent's Church in Saint Louis.
32. *"Registre,"* I, 324.
33. John Rothensteiner, *History of the Archdiocese of Saint Louis* (Saint Louis, 1928), II, 85. Amat's actual appointment was dated July 14, 1845. Cf. *"Registre,"* I, 368.
34. Ralph Bayard, C.M., *Lone Star Vanguard* (Saint Louis, 1945), p. 351.
35. And not until 1857 as stated by Shea.
36. *"Registre,"* I, 395.
37. *Ibid.*, I, 434.
38. Not as theologian to Alemany as stated by Conroy.
39. Shea, *op. cit.*, IV, 709.
40. Paradela, *op. cit.*, p. 158.
41. Archives of Saint Mary's Seminary (Perryville,Missouri), Amat to Superior General, Philadelphia, May 20, 1852.
42. In less than thirty years, the Vincentians gave five of their priests to the episcopacy. Pius IX was once heard to remark to the Superior General, "It is for you to plant the garden, for me to pluck the flowers."

43. *"Registre,"* II, 67.
44. *Archives of Juventudes de la Medalla Milagrosa.* A note reads, *"1852 9 Octubre llega a Madrid el Sr. Amat."* Cf. also "Registre," II, 81 (December 27, 1852).
45. *"Registre,"* II, 93.
46. *Annales Espana* (Madrid, 1854), sig. 52.
47. Archives of Santa Barbara Mission, III, 19. Bulls were dated July 29, 1853 and not July 28th as stated by Reuss.
48. *Ibid.,* III, 26. Alemany to Rubio, San Francisco, November 29, 1853.
49. Archives of the Sacred Congregation of Propaganda Fide, Amat to Fransoni, Paris, September 6, 1853.
50. *Ibid.,* Amat to Fransoni, Paris, October 3, 1853.
51. Archives of Santa Barbara Mission, III, 26, Alemany to Rubio, San Francisco, November 29, 1853.
52. Not Bishop of Monterey as reported by Paradela. The latter diocese is in Mexico.
53. *Grammar of Accent.*

14

This essay, "Candidate of Last Resort," appeared in the American *Benedictine Review* XIX (June, 1968), 193-202.

Isolated from its proper historical sequence, the two-year vacancy preceding John J. Cantwell's appointment to the Diocese of Monterey-Los Angeles could be erroneously interpreted as indicating that the Irishborn prelate was something of a desperation candidate. A careful investigation of the record reveals just the opposite; that his name was among the first considered when the incumbent of the Southern California jurisdiction died on September 18, 1915. To evaluate properly the events leading up to Cantwell's selection, it is necessary to sketch the overall perspective of the Province of San Francisco along with certain of the problems facing the ecclesiastical units then composing that metropolitan district.

The faltering health of Bishop Laurence Scanlan of Salt Lake had long been a matter of considerable anxiety and it was only the consistent prodding of San Francisco's Archbishop Patrick W. Riordan that finally resulted in the suffragan's agreeing to ask Rome for assistance in shouldering the burdens of the Utah Bishopric. It was a Phyrric victory for Riordan, however, inasmuch as none of those enumerated on Scanlan's preposterous *terna* were seriously "worthy of consideration."[1] Nonetheless, the Bay City prelate made a careful examination of each nominee before disgustingly confiding to the Apostolic Delegate, Archbishop John Bonzano, that Scanlan's respect for the Holy See should have prevented him from proposing such candidates.[2] Riordan advised the delegate to disregard the entire list in favor of appointing a coadjutor, a process which would place the burden of submitting a wholly new terna on the conference of provincial bishops.[3] Even with this precaution, Riordan thought that it would be difficult to find anyone willing to work alongside the ailing Bishop of Salt Lake. For his part, Scanlan persisted in demanding an auxiliary rather than a coadjutor, with the result that several outstanding clerics, among them the Vicar General of San Francisco, the Very Reverend John J. Cantwell, declined flatly to have his name even considered for the post.[4]

Salt Lake was not Riordan's only concern;[5] he was also worried about the health of his suffragan, Bishop Thomas J. Conaty of Monterey-Los Angeles. Though still able to look after the needs of his vast diocese, the former Rector of The Catholic University of America had asked advice about proposing the name of his Vicar General, the Right Reverend Patrick Harnett, as a candidate for the coadjutorship of the southland. To this suggestion, the archbishop replied: "I am convinced that an Auxiliary would be the best thing to have, but you want a young man. There is no use in taking one who is as old as yourself, and who would not be able to stand the strain of journeying...While no doubt Msgr. Harnett will be pleasing to you, and be a respectable man, yet he is too old to give you much assistance."[6] There matters stood when the hand of death swept away both Riordan and Conaty, the one on December 27, 1914, the other on September 18, 1915.

Five days after Archbishop Riordan's demise, the remaining ordinaries of the province met in the Bay City to draft a formal *terna* of candidates for the Archdiocese of San Francisco to submit, through the apostolic delegate, to the Holy See. The consultors and irremovable pastors had already agreed to present as candidates, the Right Reverend Edward J. Hanna, Auxiliary Bishop of San Francisco, the Very Reverend John J. Cantwell, Vicar General and the Reverend Peter C. Yorke, Pastor of Saint Peter's Church. As Hanna had been Archbishop Riordan's first choice,[7] the prelates decided to place his name as the *dignissimus* of their nominees.[8] The *terna* was then dispatched to the apostolic delegation in Washington and, on June 1, 1915, it was announced that the Holy Father had selected the first of the proposed candidates, Bishop Edward J. Hanna, to be the new Metropolitan of San Francisco.

The Diocese of Monterey-Los Angeles, which fell vacant three months later, was not so easily filled. Normally, the Holy See would have attached considerable importance to the recommendation of the provincial archbishop.[9] In this case, however, the impact of the metropolitan's suggestions were diminished by virtue of his own recent appointment. For what it was worth, Hanna championed the candidacy of Cantwell, and even the delegate himself mentioned later that from the beginning of the vacancy at Los Angeles, he had been "very favorable" to the nomination of San Francisco's Vicar General. However, Archbishop Bonzano could not "overlook the fact that Father Cantwell is Irish as are many of the priests of that diocese whose many abuses will need to be corrected.[10] The delegate felt that a complete outsider would be in a better position to handle the problems facing the "backward" Southern California jurisdiction. This, coupled with Cantwell's earlier refusal of the mitre at Salt Lake, explains the initial lack of enthusiasm on the part of Rome's Consistorial Congregation for the expressed candidate of the Archbishop of San Francisco.

Early in the summer of 1916, word leaked out that the Right Reverend John J. McCort, Auxiliary Bishop of Philadelphia, had been asked to accept the vacant see. On June 27, 1916, a Southland newspaper reported the actual appointment "according to press dispatches from Rome." The account further stated that,

Bishop McCort is not widely known in Los Angeles, although his reputation as a scholar and a churchman is widespread. The new bishop will succeed the late Bishop Conaty, who died last year. It has been believed by many that the diocese of Monterey-Los Angeles would be divided, but no intimation of this was contained in the cablegram. Bishop McCort is known as an excellent administrator."[11]

No official statement was ever released by the Chancery at Los Angeles but the diocesan newspaper reported that rumors about "the appointment of Bishop McCort to the See of Monterey-Los Angeles have not, thus far, been confirmed."[12] Speculation continued well into the winter months before a terse announcement was released to the press by Archbishop Edmond F. Prendergast's office in Philadelphia:

On Thursday, June 22, Bishop McCort was informed that the Holy Father had selected him to be Bishop of the Diocese of Monterey-Los Angeles. His Grace, the Most Reverend Archbishop, with the consent of the Right Reverend Bishop, immediately petitioned the Holy See, for grave and urgent reasons, which were subsequently submitted to the Holy Father, not to transfer Bishop McCort from Philadelphia. His Grace is pleased to announce that the Holy Father has graciously granted the request and that Bishop McCort will remain in Philadelphia.[13]

A further allusion to the incident was a 1916 Christmas message McCort sent to Archbishop Edward J. Hanna in which the Philadelphia auxiliary said he hoped the New Year "will soon bring such a suffragan as you need and desire for a certain diocese. You will not regret that I am still with the dear archbishop who needs me more than ever..."[14]

In a letter written to Bishop John J. Cantwell some years later, McCort rejoiced "that my successor is such a worthy one" and then went on to note his gratitude "to the Lord that the late Archbishop Prendergast fought so hard to keep me in the East, even though the price of it was beyond computation."[15] In his response, Cantwell chided McCort, by then the Bishop of Altoona, for his reluctance to move west and advised him to "come out some day and see Hollywood while you are still young, so that you may learn what you missed when you preferred Altoona to the City of the Angels. The very name should have inspired you to noble thoughts."[16]

To this gentle rebuke, Bishop McCort remarked that "The day before Archbishop Prendergast died—he said to me 'I presume that you will succeed me,' and I answered—'No, Your Grace, I will not succeed you.' 'Why not,' he asked and I replied, 'Los Angeles will come up again—and His Grace asked, 'What did you have to do with Los Angeles?' meaning of course that the action was entirely his own. I insert this so that Your Excellency may know that I never declined. It was an awful experience but the good God permitted it."[17]

It is only a half-century later that the actual story can be told in its totality but it does confirm one newspaper's observation that McCort's "great assistance to the elderly and infirm Archbishop Prendergast" induced the Ordinary of Philadelphia to cable "Rome a plea that the appointment of his assistant be rescinded."[18]

On February 10, 1917, another report from the East stated that Father William J. Kerby, Professor of Sociology in The Catholic University of America, had been asked to accept the Southern California mitre. Other prominent churchmen rumored as approached about the vacancy included the Reverends Charles A. Ramm, Chancellor of the Archdiocese of San Francisco, Edward A. Pace, Dean of the School of Philosophy at The Catholic University of America, Andrew Meehan, Professor of Canon Law at Rochester's Saint Bernard Seminary and the Very Reverend Patrick J. Fisher, Pastor of Holy Cross Church at Santa Cruz. The name of Bishop Joseph S. Glass, C.M., of Salt Lake was mentioned occasionally inasmuch as it was commonly known that the Vincentian prelate was amenable to the appointment and had, on one occasion, approached an influential layman to plead his cause.

On March 22, 1917, Los Angeles newspapers announced that Pope Benedict XV had named Peter J. Muldoon,[19] Bishop of Rockford, to the shepherdless Diocese of Monterey-Los Angeles. The news accounts reported that

> Bishop Peter J. Muldoon of Rockford, Ill., former auxiliary bishop of Chicago and one of the best known Roman Catholic dignitaries of the United States, today was named bishop of the diocese of Monterey-Los Angeles.
>
> According to Catholic laymen in Los Angeles, it was evident that the Pope in making the appointment disregarded some nominations which were submitted…This conclusion was based on the fact that the Pope first appointed the auxiliary bishop of Philadelphia, for the bishopric, and that the appointment was later withdrawn at the request of the bishop of Philadelphia. It has been understood that Bishop Muldoon has long desired to come to Los Angeles, but that he put aside that desire to remain near his mother who died recently.[20]

Monsignor Patrick Harnett, Administrator of the Diocese, added the weight of his office to the report by stating that "I have no official information on the subject, but I am convinced the report of the appointment is true."[21]

Muldoon's name was familiar to many Californians. A native of the Golden State, he had been discussed earlier as a possible successor to San Francisco's Archbishop Patrick J. Riordan. His visit to the Panama Pacific Exposition, in 1914, enhanced speculation about his eventual return to the west coast. Just a year later, Muldoon had been James Cardinal Gibbons' candidate to succeed James E. Quigley at Chicago because he was "well acquainted with its diocesan needs." Baltimore's metropolitan also suggested that Muldoon's "appointment would be a vindication for the unjust persecution he suffered there while he was auxiliary bishop."[22] However, that proved to be one of the rare times when Gibbons was over-ruled[23] and the appointment went instead to the Auxiliary of Brooklyn, George W. Mundelein.[24] Even though Muldoon was bypassed for Chicago, the Holy See remained aware of his organizational abilities and, in mid-December of 1916, Archbishop Mundelein approached Muldoon on the latter's availability for the Diocese of Monterey-Los Angeles. Contrary to press reports, the Bishop of Rockford clearly was not anxious to return to California and agreed to do so only if Rome insisted.[25]

Apparently, the Apostolic Delegate interpreted the "polite refusal...as a modest acceptance"[26] for wheels began turning and on March 22, 1917, the wire services reported that the Rockford *Morning Star*, quoting a Roman official, had announced that "Bishop Muldoon of Rockford, Ill., has been named Bishop of Los Angeles."[27] The bulls of appointment were dispatched in routine fashion. Msgr. Charles A. O'Hern of the North American College called at the Vatican secretariate for them and a newly-ordained priest for the Diocese of Monterey-Los Angeles, Father Henry G. Gross, was deputized as a courier and charged with bringing them to the appointee. When, from New York, Gross informed Muldoon of his mission the distressed bishop noted pessimistically in his diary, that "it does look like I go to Los Angeles."[28] When the young cleric arrived at the prelate's residence on June 7, he was requested to place the three tubular parcels on the mantlepiece, thereby avoiding any semblance that Muldoon, by accepting the bulls personally, had signified formal acceptance.[29]

In the meantime, the consultors and clergy of the Diocese of Rockford had petitioned Pope Benedict XV[30] to withdraw Muldoon's nomination, only to receive for their trouble a "sharp letter" from Archbishop John Bonzano, the Apostolic Delegate. Muldoon himself had written to Cajetan Cardinal De Lai, Secretary of the Sacred Consistorial Congregation, asking to be relieved of the appointment if such could be done without embarrassing the Pope. The complicated chain of events was finally concluded when Muldoon was notified by the delegate that "the Holy Father has deigned to accept your resignation as Bishop of the Diocese of Monterey-Los Angeles to which you were recently appointed."[31] In an obviously joyful strain, the Bishop of Rockford jotted in his diary that the affair had finally been settled in a satisfactory manner.[32]

The choice of Muldoon was a strange one if, as Archbishop Bonzano maintained, the Holy See was really concerned about the "Irish question" in Los Angeles. As far back as 1901, the then Chancellor of the Archdiocese of Chicago had so "aroused the bitter opposition of a score of Irish-born priests" in Chicago that a delegation journeyed to Washington with a formal protest "against Muldoon's elevation to the episcopacy."[33] Moreover, in the later years of Feehan's archiepiscopate, Muldoon had been the focal point of certain supposedly questionable activities in Chicago which one prelate characterized as "a stench in the nostrils of the better class of people and clergy."[34]

Public announcement of Muldoon's determination to remain in Illinois, released from the Apostolic Delegation in Washington, heartened the people of Rockford as much as it saddened those of Monterey-Los Angeles. Undoubtedly Muldoon's acceptance would have enhanced the fortunes of the Church in Southern California for "Los Angeles needed a public man and an administrator and a man of Bishop Muldoon's ability to head this vast expanding territory. Bishop Muldoon would have been that kind of man."[35]

As it became increasingly evident that few clerics were interested in the orphaned Monterey-Los Angeles jurisdiction, the candidacy of John J. Cantwell took on added dimensions. While acknowledging the difficulties that an Irish-born bishop would face in California's southland, Archbishop Bonzano admitted, perhaps reluctantly, that "these problems are not insurmountable, especially if Father Cantwell can rise above his personal and national sympathies."[36] The Archbishop of San Francisco assured the delegate that his confidence in Cantwell was well founded and went on to say, "...I feel, personally, any honor which comes to him. He has been to me a loyal and devoted friend."[37] Confirmation of his episcopal appointment came to Father Cantwell in a letter expressing Bonzano's personal pleasure "that the Holy Father has deigned to appoint you to the vacant Bishopric of Monterey-Los Angeles."[38]

It was a considerable challenge that faced the bishop-elect. His diocese extended from the Mexican boundary north to those portions of Santa Cruz, Santa Clara, and Merced counties lying south of the latitude of 37°, a territory embracing 80,000 square miles. Whatever may have been Cantwell's reaction about so formidable a charge is not evident, for in his first message to the southland, he rejoiced at the thought of going to a place so historic in its religious traditions.[39]

Cantwell's qualifications were widely heralded. One newspaper account portrayed the bishop-elect as "liberal in his views, possessed of the tenderest human sympathies, a jovial, handsome six-footer in the prime of life, extremely modest in discussing himself..."[40] The appointment was no less enthusiastically received in the south where the Administrator of the Diocese of Monterey-Los Angeles, Monsignor Patrick Harnett, stated that "Father Cantwell fills out in a very remarkable degree the measure of the bishop which this diocese demands."[41] The Vincentian Bishop of Salt Lake, a long-time Los Angeles resident, described the new appointee as one "trained at the side of Archbishop Riordan and Archbishop Hanna," a man who "has learned well the work of Episcopal administration, and has become thoroughly imbued with the fine qualities of the former and the charming spirit of the latter."[42]

The heretofore untold story behind John J. Cantwell's appointment to the Diocese of Monterey-Los Angeles can fittingly be concluded with the prelate's consecration on December 5, 1917, in Saint Mary's Cathedral. There Father William O'Ryan, Pastor of Saint Leo's Church in Denver, glanced ahead to Cantwell's three decades as ordinary with a remarkable accuracy;

You, dear Bishop Cantwell, will be a good bishop; I, a prophet of this hour, see you a great and wise and patriotic American bishop. I hear your life cry out: "They are Americans, so am I; they are the seed of free men, so am I; they are the ministers of the Gospel of Human Liberty; I am more; in many more watchings and labors that the light may burn not dim and murky from human exhalations but clear and bright, because nourished by the pure air that breathes from the mountains of God.[43]

Notes to the Text

1. Archives of the Archdiocese of Los Angeles (hereafter referred to as AALA), Thomas J. Grace to Thomas J. Conaty, Sacramento, May 17, 1915.
2. Archives of the Archdiocese of San Francisco (hereafter referred to as AASF), Patrick W. Riordan to John Bonzano, San Francisco, July 27, 1914.
3. For the historical and canonical background of the process used in selecting bishops in this country, see Francis J. Weber, "Episcopal Appointments in the U.S.A.," *American Ecclesiastical Review* CLV (Sept,, 1966), 178-191.
4. Although there is no available evidence supporting Cantwell's candidacy for Salt Lake, the bishop did make it known to several of his friends in later years, among them the present Bishop of Dallas-Fort Worth, Thomas K. Gorman.
5. The problem at Salt Lake solved itself on May 10, 1915, with Scanlan's death. Within ten days after the bishop's funeral, the vacancy had been filled, an indication that Rome had decided to take action even before the ailing prelate's death.
6. AASF, Patrick W. Riordan to Thomas J. Conaty, San Francisco, June 8, 1914. Whether Conaty was acting on his own behalf or solely for his consultors is not known for it is recorded that on April 14, 1915, the diocesan advisors "moved and seconded and unanimously carried the suggestion regarding the appointment of an auxiliary in the person of the Rt. Rev. Mons. Harnett, V.G., be approved." See *Acts of Council, 1893-1918*, p. 80, in AALA.
7. It is known that John J. Cantwell's name was on an earlier *terna* submitted by Riordan prior to Hanna's selection. See AALA, John Bonzano to Edward J. Hanna, Washington, D.C., Sept. 3, 1917.
8. AALA, Minutes of the Meeting of the Bishops of the Province of San Francisco, San Francisco, Jan. 1, 1915.
9. It had been the practice since the Third Plenary Council of Baltimore for the diocesan consultors and irremovable pastors of a vacant jurisdiction to present a terna of worthy episcopal candidates to the metropolitan. A subsequent meeting of the bishops in a province would then discuss the names, take a vote, and forward them to the Holy See through the Apostolic Delegate. However, there is no evidence that this procedure was followed after Conaty's death-perhaps because of an injudicious violation of secrecy in the meeting of December 12, 1902, which resulted in public disclosure of a candidate not acceptable to the Holy See. *(The Tidings,* for Jan. 31, 1903, reported to its readers that the diocesan consultors had expressed their "conscientious belief in his [Right Reverend Patrick Harnett's] eminent fitness for the position of Bishop of this diocese.")

10. AALA, John Bonzano to Edward J. Hanna, Washington, D.C., Sept. 3, 1917.
11. Los Angeles Evening *Herald*.
12. *The Tidings*, June 30, 1916.
13. Los Angeles Evening *Herald*, Nov. 10, 1916.
14. AALA, John J. McCort to Edward J. Hanna, Philadelphia, Dec. 22, 1916.
15. AALA, John J. McCort to John J. Cantwell, Altoona, Sept. 16, 1932.
16. AALA, John J. Cantwell to John J. McCort, Los Angeles, Sept. 21, 1932.
17. AALA, John J. McCort to John J. Cantwell, Altoona, Sept. 30, 1932.
18. Archives of The Catholic University of America (hereafter referred to as ACUA), "Diary of the Right Reverend Peter J. Muldoon," unidentified newspaper clipping.
19. For a sketch of the prelate, see Charles A. McMahon, "Right Reverend Peter James Muldoon, D.D., First Bishop of Rockford, 1863-1927," *Illinois Catholic Historical Review* X (April, 1928), 291-300.
20. Los Angeles Evening *Herald*, March 22, 1917.
21. *Ibid.*
22. Francis G. McManamin, "Peter J. Muldoon, First Bishop of Rockford, 1862-1927," *Catholic Historical Review XLVIII* (Oct., 1962), 372.
23. The Archbishop of Baltimore thus reversed a stand he had taken in 1902 when he vetoed the proposal that Muldoon succeed Archbishop Feehan in Chicago. Gibbons believed that the auxiliary "was incapable at the moment of restoring peace in the archdiocese." See David Francis Sweeney, O.F.M., *The Life of John Lancaster Spalding* (New York, 1965), p. 305n.
24. Cardinal Gibbons apparently had no hand in Muldoon's subsequent nomination to Monterey-Los Angeles for he later remarked to the Bishop of Rockford that "there never was any reason why you should be sent there." See ACUA, "Diary," June 10, 1917.
25. ACUA, "Diary," entry for Dec. 12, 1916.
26. *Ibid.*, entry for April 16, 1917.
27. The "Roman source" was the *Acta Apostolicae Sedis*, IX (March 22, 1917), 164 "*Cathedrali ecclesiae Montereyensis Angelorum, R.P.D. Petrum Jacobum Muldoon, hactenus Episcopum Rockfordiensen.*"
28. ACUA, "Diary," entry for May 23, 1917.
29. Despite the fact that Gross assured the bishop that "you have jurisdiction in Rockford until the day you leave for Los Angeles," Muldoon refused to open the circular tubes until Father Gross put the statement in writing. See AALA, Statement of the Right Reverend Henry W. Gross, Los Angeles, Nov. 26, 1963.
30. Edward L. McDonald, *Golden Jubilee History of the Diocese of Rockford* (Rockford, 1958), p. 59.
31. AALA, John Bonzano to Peter J. Muldoon, Washington, D.C., June 5, 1917. This was the last "recorded" time the Holy See acted without consulting the candidate, at least in the United States.
32. ACUA, "Diary," June 8, 1917.
33. David Francis Sweeney, O.F.M., *op. cit.*, p. 286. After his appointment to the bishopric, Muldoon was personally consecrated by the Apostolic Delegate to the United States, Archbishop Sebastiano Martinelli in "an effort to demonstrate to all that Muldoon had the strong support of the authorities of the Church." John Tracy Ellis, *The Life of James Cardinal Gibbons* (Milwaukee, 1952), II, p. 416.
34. James Ryan to Francesco Marchetti Salvaggiani, Alton, July 24, 1902, One writer felt that if Riordan had been alive, Muldoon's selection would probably have been shelved for in 1902, he had written the Sacred Congregation of Propaganda Fide with the charge that the auxiliary bishop "was concerned with but one purpose, namely to strengthen his own position." See David Francis Sweeney, *op. cit.*, p. 307.
35. Francis G. McManamin, *op. cit.*, p. 376, a remark attributed to the Very Reverend John F. Fenlon, S.S. By his refusal to return to the land of his birth, "Bishop Muldoon has the unique distinction of being both the first and second Bishop of the Rockford diocese." See Cornelius J. Kirkfleet, *The History of the Parishes of the Diocese of Rockford, Illinois* (Chicago, 1924), p. 40.
36. AALA, John Bonzano to Edward J. Hanna, Washington, D.C., Sept. 3, 1917.
37. AASF, Edward J. Hanna to John Bonzano, San Francisco, Sept. 22, 1917.
38. AALA, John Bonzano to John J. Cantwell, Washington, D.C., Sept. 16, 1917.
39. Los Angeles *Times*, October 14, 1917.

40. San Francisco *Examiner*, Sept. 19, 1917.
41. Quoted in the Los Angeles *Examiner*, Dec. 9, 1917.
42. *Ibid.*
43. San Francisco *Examiner*, Dec. 6, 1917.

15

This essay about the retirement years of James Francis Cardinal McIntyre was written by request for the *Los Angeles Times*. It appeared in the issue for August 2, 1970.

Quite probably, the obligations of no office in all the world are so minutely spelled out as those of the cardinalate. The select bishops chosen by the Pope for membership in the Sacred College receive a 485-page treatise outlining the duties, restrictions and privileges "de cardinalis."

One provision not anticipated by Roman canonists, however, was that of retirement, an almost unknown term in the ecclesiastical terminology of pre-Vatican II days. Only with the Church's 21st ecumenical council were provisions made whereby elderly prelates were "invited" to submit their resignations.

The Archbishop of Los Angeles was the first American in the College of Cardinals to retire from active duty. After providing for his orderly succession by the appointment of a coadjutor, James Francis Cardinal McIntyre asked Pope Paul VI for permission to put aside his burdensome duties as the Southland's second metropolitan archbishop.

That the New York-born prelate finds himself in a unique status, one without precedent, is quite in keeping with the adventuresome character of the man who ventured west for the first time in 1948, to take up the pastoral staff of the world's fastest growing archdiocese. This he did at an age when his contemporaries were anticipating the well-earned rest associated with a lifetime of active labor.

In addition to the irrevocable privilege of participating in papal elections, Cardinal McIntyre's only post-retirement obligations are the titular pastorate of Santa Anastasia Church in Rome and several post-conciliar commissions on which he retains a nominal seat. Though resigned from the administrative board of the U.S. Catholic Conference, the cardinal retains and intends to exercise, by virtue of his episcopal ordination, his voting membership in the semiannual meetings of the American hierarchy.

In retirement, the cardinal continues to reside in his small, modest quarters adjacent to St. Basil's Catholic Church near downtown Los Angeles. He neither has a rocking-chair nor any plans to acquire one. Though the orientation of his life has radically changed, his days are as crowded as ever with concern for the spiritual welfare of others.

Cardinal McIntyre cherishes the privilege of living in parochial surroundings as he did for the quarter-century he worked in New York as priest, bishop and archbishop. The opportunity of moving into a rectory presented itself only a few years ago when facilities were provided for that purpose at the new St. Basil's. Before that time, circumstances compelled the cardinal to live in the more commodious but isolated home of his predecessor in Fremont Place.

The 84-year-old prelate could hardly be considered "retired" by conventional standards. His daily horarium is crammed, in fact, with the normal demands associated with the parish minsitry. He rises early and is in the sacristy for Mass by 7:30 a.m. Unless impeded by other commitments, the cardinal offers a public Mass at 8:30 a.m. Sundays and holy days. Whenever possible, he exercises the recently inaugurated option of concelebrating with one of the other priests assigned in residence at the church.

On weekdays, His Eminence, dressed in a plain black cassock, spends several hours hearing confessions during the scheduled Masses. He enjoys the pastoral role of greeting the parishioners and visitors as they arrive and leave the handsome Wilshire Blvd. church.

The cardinal received his first "post-retirement" convert into the church on May 23. "It was a happy day," recalls the tall, slender prelate, "for I was also able to confer on him the Sacrament of Confirmation."

His appointment book does not, in any way, resemble that of a "retired" archbishop. The cardinal's 30 years as an active and provocative participant in proceedings of the National Catholic Welfare Conference partially accounts for the steady stream of cardinals, archbishops, bishops and priests who drop by his Kingsley Drive residence for a chat.

Though he has no secretarial staff, the cardinal responds personally to as much of his extensive correspondence as possible. The literal "avalanche" of good wishes following his retirement indicates the esteem held for the cardinal by the 1,727,161 Catholics whom he served for 22 hectic years as Archbishop of Los Angeles.

The cardinal has devoted a considerable amount of time to an oral history program whereby material has been recorded and preserved for an eventual biographer. All this public and personal correspondence and official papers have been consigned to and made accessible in the archdiocesan chancery archives.

Those who have visited the cardinal during this epilogue of his service to the church in the United States are impressed by the ease with which he has bridged this last of his many transitions in a long and productive life.

"To retire from a position of authority is one thing," says Cardinal McIntyre, "but to abdicate the care and concern of souls is something a priestly conscience could never endure."

16

This essay "From 'Father' Joe to Bishop" is taken from a special issue of *The Monitor* for March 19, 1966. It was republished in *The Catholic Herald* for April 20, 1987.

Joseph Thomas McGucken, the only son of Joseph A. McGucken and Mary Agnes Flynn, was born in a small residence near his grandfather's store at Seventh and Mateo Streets in Los Angeles.

Shortly after his birth, on March 13, 1902, the youngster was baptized in Saint Vibiana's Cathedral by Father Clement Molony, secretary to the Bishop of Monterey-Los Angeles, the Right Reverend George T. Montgomery.

Ireland figured prominently in the boy's background. His maternal forebears came from Castle-island, County Kerry, ancestral home of the Flynns. Not long after Joseph's father died his maternal grandfather moved the family from their home near the Fourth Street viaduct to more commodious surroundings at Wadsworth and 32nd Streets.

The youngster's early life was profoundly influenced by his Irish-born grandfather who transported the boy about town on his grocery wagon.

Joseph grew up in Saint Patrick's parish in Los Angeles under the watchful eye of Father Patrick O'Donohue who saw the young boy enrolled in the parochial school operated by the Sisters of Saint Joseph of Carondelet. After completion of his primary education, Joseph entered Los Angeles Polytechnic high school, at that time, the only institution in the southland offering courses in electrical engineering.

Intellectual opportunities widened four years later when he moved to the Vermont Avenue campus of the southern branch of the University of California.

In 1922, the collegian expressed his desire to study for the priesthood. Father Francis Ott gave him and Alden J. Bell, now the Bishop of Sacramento, private lessons in Latin and made arrangements for Joseph's entry to Saint Patrick's seminary at Menlo Park. As a student for the Diocese of Monterey-Los Angeles, Joseph enrolled in the fall for the first phase of priestly formation under the Sulpician Fathers. He was formally admitted to the clerical state on June 14, 1924, with the conferral of tonsure by Bishop Patrick Keane of Sacramento.

A short while later, at the recommendation of the Very Reverend Henry A. Ayrinhac, seminary rector, Bishop John J. Cantwell offered the seminarian the opportunity of completing his studies in Rome. After consulting his family he accepted the appointment to the eternal city. It was a time when Pope Pius XI, then in the early years of an eventful pontificate, was taking the first halting steps to restore papal freedom during the Mussolini regime. While in Rome he lived at the old North American College on the Via dell'Umilta under the rectorship of Msgr. Charles A. O'Hern and, later, Msgr. Eugene Burke.

Although the North American College is known for the high percentage of its graduates who subsequently become members of the hierarchy, only two of Joseph McGucken's class of 58 men achieved that distinction: Archbishop McGucken and the present Bishop of Oakland, Floyd L. Begin.

The Los Angeles seminarian attended formal classes at the Urban College of Propaganda Fide, at the time located in the Palacio on the Piazza di Spagna. There he studied under such scholars as Ernesto Ruffini and Gregory Agagianian, men later to win acclaim as outstanding members of the College of Cardinals.

Joseph McGucken was ordained in the Lateran Seminary chapel adjacent to Saint John Lateran Basilica in the early morning hours of January 15, 1928, by the Viceregent of Rome, the Most Reverend Giuseppe Palica, Titular Archbishop of Philippi.

The following July, Father McGucken was one of eighteen priests in his class to qualify for and obtain the doctorate in Sacred Theology. His final exam was taken in the former chapel of the Propaganda Palace where, seventy-five years earlier, Thaddeus Amat had been consecrated Bishop of Monterey.

Upon his return to Los Angeles, the newly ordained priest was named temporary administrator of Holy Trinity parish in Atwater park. In October of 1928, he assumed the duties of curate at Saint Vibiana's Cathedral where he stayed until being transferred to Cathedral Chapel parish on La Brea Avenue.

In November of 1929 Bishop Cantwell named Father McGucken his private secretary and for the next fifteen years he lived with the Southern California prelate in the intimacy of the episcopal residence at 100 Fremont Place. It was a mutually beneficial association for the young priest's innate sense of humor proved an ideal tonic for the heavily burdened bishop of a widely scattered flock. On the other hand, the mark of Cantwell's influence on his secretary during those formative years is plainly obvious even today and he is quick to affirm that "whatever of good I may be, he, after God, made me."

On October 31, 1938, a year after his creation as a papal chamberlain, Msgr. McGucken was named Chancellor of the Archdiodese of Los Angeles and in June of the following year, he was advanced to the domestic prelacy. Though each step involved greater duties, the monsignor maintained a keen interest in the historical setting and development of Catholic life in the west, and in 1940 he wrote an informative article, "The Golden Fields of California," which appeared in *Extension Magazine*. Some years later, he showed his sustained concern for the subject by becoming a charter member of the Academy of California Church History.

An important part of this history took place when the growing Los Angeles jurisdiction, since 1936 a metropolitan seat, necessitated the appointment of an auxiliary bishop. It was no surprise when Msgr. McGucken was named to the Titular See of Sanavo by Pope Pius XII, on February 4, 1941. The eighth native Californian named to the hierarchy was consecrated by Archbishop John J. Cantwell on the Feast of Saint Joseph in 1941.

By an interesting design of Divine Providence, the three prelates whom the new bishop would eventually succeed in Monterey-Fresno, Sacramento and San Francisco, were present in the sanctuary of Saint Vibiana's Cathedral on that Wednesday morning for the ceremony.

The added cares of the episcopate multiplied Bishop McGucken's activities considerably. The archbishop was advanced in years and anxious to turn over the more demanding tasks to his auxiliary. On February 19, 1944, Bishop McGucken was made pastor of Saint Andrew's church in Pasadena where, in addition to his other commitments, he immediately began taking an active part in the various parochial functions of the Crown City's mother church. He divided his parish into two sections, one for each of three assistants, supervised a census of the widespread area, and instructed the curate to spend several hours a day making house-to-house visitations.

Under his direction, enrollment in Confraternity classes was tripled and special attention given to the mission station of Our Lady of Guadalupe located within the parochial boundaries. The beautiful church begun by his predecessor was completed, and a new high school, grammar school and convent were built. Besides taking a personal interest in all these activities, Bishop McGucken participated in local civic affairs, even serving for a time as a director of the nearby Southwest Museum.

The multiple parish duties did not diminish the prelate's concern for other activities. As chancellor, and later as vicar general, the Los Angeles auxiliary was personally in charge of much of the planning for the two seminaries erected in the archdiocese, one at Camarillo in 1939, the other adjacent to Mission San Fernando in 1954. As bishop he was also involved with plans made in 1943 for a proposed new cathedral of Our Lady of the Angels on a block-long site along Wilshire Boulevard in Los Angeles.

Bishop McGucken has made broad use of those powers reserved to the episcopate. For example, he has acted as co-consecrator for a number of American prelates, and on October 15, 1946, he raised the Right Reverend Timothy Manning to the Titular See of Lesvi as Auxiliary of Los Angeles.

Because of the serious illness affecting Bishop Philip Scher of Monterey-Fresno, Pope Pius XII, on September 24, 1946, named Bishop McGucken apostolic administrator of the Central California diocese, a position he held for four months until plans were formalized for the appointment of a permanent coadjutor.

Possessing even from his early years a natural facility with languages, Bishop McGucken took every opportunity to perfect his lingual capabilities in the apostolate. In the summer of 1926, he and another Los Angeles student, Raymond O'Flaherty, traveled throughout Spain and spent a month in the home of a priest in San Sebastian where Bishop McGucken improved his fluency in Spanish. On the local scene he was active in the Church's multiphased program for the Mexican immigrants exiled by persecutions. Nationally, he was closely associated with the pioneers of the Bishop's Committee for Spanish-speaking Peoples.

Each year he participated in Pasadena's Italian observance honoring the Feast of Saint Sebastian, usually giving the principal address in flawless Italian.

During October of 1947, the Auxiliary Bishop of Los Angeles officially represented Francis Cardinal Spellman at the Marian congress in Buenos Aires, there joining 300,000 people from all parts of Latin America at the Shrine of Our Lady of Lujan. During his sojourn he spoke on the national radio network to all of Argentina.

While in Buenos Aires, Bishop McGucken was summoned to the deathbed of his beloved mentor, Archbishop John J. Cantwell, whom he eulogistically characterized as "one whom nature and grace, in generous conspiracy, had endowed above all the rest—a man marked to be an incomparable leader of the Golden Vale."

At the passing of this "incomparable leader" on October 30, 1947, the archdiocesan consultors selected Bishop McGucken, the senior auxiliary, as interim administrator of the Los Angeles jurisdiction. When the new metropolitan, The Most Reverend J. Francis A. McIntyre, was installed on March 19, 1948, Bishop McGucken was made vicar general, a post he shared for some years with the late Msgr. John J.Cawley.

Two years later in 1950, while in Rome for the Holy Year, Bishop McGucken witnessed the canonization of Blessed Anthony Claret, and later, in Spain, he assisted at the Ibero-American congress honoring Our Lady of Guadalupe. He again visited Latin America during the following year, this time as United States delegate to the National Eucharistic congress in the City of Nueva Guatamela de la Asumpcion.

While attending the cardinalatial investiture of Archbishop J. Francis A. McIntyre during January of 1953, the Auxiliary Bishop of Los Angeles quietly observed the silver jubilee of his ordination to the priesthood by offering the Holy Sacrifice at the tomb of Saint Peter where he had celebrated his first Mass.

Two years later, Bishop McGucken accompanied Cardinal Spellman and 329 pilgrims to the 36th International Eucharistic congress which convened at Rio de Janeiro. At the conclusion of the liturgical ceremonies, Bishop McGucken, representing the administrative board of the National Catholic Welfare Conference, attended the General Assembly of the Latin America episcopate called by Pius XII on July 25, 1955. At the request of the papal legate, Adeodate Cardinal Piazza, he spoke to the prelates on the advantages of closer inter-American collaboration in ecclesiastical affairs.

In the political sphere, the southland Auxiliary Bishop was active in the campaign to remove the tax burden from California's parochial schools. In addition to coordinating activities at the district level, he appeared a number of times before the Los Angeles board of supervisors on behalf of the educational program of the archdiocese.

On October 26, 1955, Bishop McGucken was sent to Sacramento as coadjutor to the ailing Robert Armstrong.

As he prepared to leave Los Angeles, the prelate could not "deny a sense of sadness in leaving the Archdiocese of Los Angeles, my native place, and the scene of many happy years in priestly work." But, he could take consolation in recalling the words he uttered a quarter of a century ago when he was first named to the episcopate: "It is no small privilege for me to be permitted to remain on these my native shores, in this land of promise, this California!"

17

"The California Bishops and Proposition 14" was published in *Front Line* III (Spring, 1965), 176-184.

Involvement of the hierarchy in political matters has a number of precedents in United States Catholic annals. Rarely, however, has such activity created as much attention as that aroused in California during 1964 when efforts were initiated to repeal by constitutional amendment certain provisions of the controversial Rumford Fair Housing Act. Even more outstanding than the campaign itself, was the *apparent* disagreement among the local bishops on the issue, a factor which, for practical purposes, dissipated their influence on the thorny subject.

Any discussion of the hotly-contested Proposition 14 must advert, at least in passing, to the question of whether the proposed amendment itself involved a moral judgment, for it was precisely that point which divided California's hierarchy. In a joint statement, issued during August of 1964, the eight residential bishops reasserted traditional Catholic teaching that "discrimination based solely on race, color, nationality, or religion cannot be reconciled with the truth that God has created all men with equal rights and equal dignity."[1] Three of the ordinaries, though not personally responsible for introducing the "moral" theme into the campaign, went a step further and put themselves on record as seeing such an issue at stake in the proposition in question.

Injection of the "moral" note into the controversy ultimately worked against the opponents of the constitutional amendment. Efforts to apply Pope John XXIII's statement that "every human being has the right to freedom of movement and residence"[2] were resented by certain Catholics familiar with *Pacem in terris* for, in its proper context, the phrase obviously has in mind the involuntary displacement of captive peoples in Iron Curtain areas, a situation hardly comparable even in that locale *Newsweek* recently labeled "The Mississipi of the U.S. Roman Catholic Church."[3] Proponents of Proposition 14 also had recourse to papal pronouncements and in defense of their position appealed to *Rerum novarum* and Leo XIII's remark that "it is precisely in [the] power of disposal that ownership consists, whether the property be land or movable goods."[4] In neither case could any positive note be attached to the actual selling or purchasing process since there is no absolute equation between the right to *acquire* property and the prior right to *hold* it.

While no conscientious Catholics openly disagreed with the national bishops' Statement of 1958 that "the heart of the race question is moral and religious," many saw the Rumford Fair Housing Act, part of which Proposition 14 sought to repeal, not so much as a case of moral discrimination as one of law-making about such practices. In most instances, the votes cast for the amendment by Catholics were not directed against any particular race or group but favored individual liberty for everyone equally.

The refusal of the Archbishop of Los Angeles to publicly commit himself on the question, though it was interpreted differently in various circles, apparently grew out of his recognition that Catholic principles of jurisprudence lie somewhere between rigidity in law and recklessness in liberty. This conviction, hardly a novel one, is held by a number of progressive writers who feel that "society cannot and does not admit that every claim to freedom of action based on an individual's or a group's conscientious beliefs is a natural right that must be satisfied."[5]

As the San Francisco *Monitor* noted after the campaign, the crux of the whole question was "whether this right over one's private property occasionally needs limitations and, if so, have we reached a point in California where it is necessary to limit this right by government regulation to avoid discrimination."[6] The electorate of California, 21% of it professedly Catholic, answered this question in the negative. While the democratic process itself is hardly the determinant of morality, the election outcome did indicate a grass-roots rejection by Catholics of episcopal involvement in questions, the moral quality of which is doubtful.

After almost a year's activity to induce an endorsement of the Rumford Fair Housing Act from the Archbishop of Los Angeles, Father William DuBay attempted to force the cardinal's hand by a widely publicized plea

to Pope Paul VI. In retrospect, it seems that this particular incident back-
fired for, as one journalist pointed out, "it is still true that the risks one
takes must be measured against the chances of success. Father DuBay
ignored that axiom to the detriment not only of himself but of the
Church and the Negro in Los Angeles as well."[7] Without any question,
the refusal of James Francis Cardinal McIntyre to formally answer the
charges of his recalcitrant cleric and the subsequent curtain of silence
which descended over the affair was interpreted by many people as an
endorsement of the amendment.

What the cardinal's actions might have been had the DuBay affair
never occurred, is another question. Except in the matter of taxation of
Catholic schools, where principles of strict justice were at stake,
McIntyre has consistently avoided commenting on political matters,
believing that "when an issue is submitted to the people for vote, it does
not behoove the Archbishop of Los Angeles to encourage the clergy to
presume to direct the faithful in the expression of their individual judgment and consequent vote."[8]

John Leo, whose earlier article in *Commonweal*, left little doubt about
his opinion of Southern California's archbishop,[9] noted later that the cardinal's position "cannot be condemned out of hand. Regardless of what
we think of Proposition 14, we must admit he is on to a great truth when
he says that Catholics do not want their bishops intervening in politics."
He further observed that "ironically, the very Catholics who brought
pressure to bear on the Cardinal to speak out are the ones who normally
could be expected to resist any attempt by a bishop to tell them how to
vote." Leo saw McIntyre as agreeing "that the political order belongs
essentially to the layman, and that in ordinary circumstances, bishops
should confine themselves to the teaching of principles for the layman to
apply in the natural order."[10]

Others, while failing to go along with the cardinal's alleged position on
the proposed amendment, expressed accord with his noninterference policy. H. F. Schilling of Pasadena wrote to the Los Angeles *Times* to repeat
an old German proverb: "speech is silver, silence is gold. Many of your
readers join me in commending Cardinal McIntyre for being on the gold
standard."[11] A Catholic laywoman, actively opposing the amendment,
decried "the whole effort to smear an aging man who was responsible for
the advent of the first Negro nuns to his archdiocese" and pointed out
that such energy and time could be better employed in other areas.[12]

Few voters were won to the "No" camp by the intemperate attacks of
certain extraterritorial journals which attempted to portray Southern

California under the merciless "tight control" of an archbishop who taps phone lines, passes out bumper stickers and personally censors all sermons on racial matters.[13] The most spectacular of the diatribes, launched by Edward Keating in *Ramparts*, can be best epitomized by the words *Sic semper tyrannus*[14] which he placed upon the cardinal's picture. Although slow to do so, the nation's Catholic press eventually reacted to this unwholesome procedure. The Georgia *Bulletin*, which saw "justification for disagreeing with some of the views and positions of Catholic leaders in the Los Angeles area," termed the Keating attack on McIntyre as "an unforgiveable piece of writing...more reminiscent of yellow journalism than Catholic culture."[15]

There were other departures. Commenting on an article by Dorothy Day in the *Catholic Worker*, the editor of *Ave Maria* noted that "too many people, like some of the laity in Los Angeles, wait for a Bishop or Cardinal to make everything safe and official before they will move." Observing Miss Day's personal attitude toward Church authority over the years, the writer confessed after reading her article that "we feel a little cleaner now, and a little surer, and somewhat ashamed."[16]

Probably a good number of undecided voters were influenced by the spectacle of a young priest attacking one of the nation's most dynamic prelates with the shaky charge of failing "to exercise moral leadership." This mood was expressed editorially by Hollywood's *Citizen News* which saw it as an unfortunate circumstance when a man of God whose life has been replete with good works for the benefit of man and his church gets caught in a maelstrom of circumstance wherein he can't emerge without losing."[17]

But did McIntyre lose? If he favored the amendment, as many have conjectured, he did not. Beyond the small group of people immediately surrounding the "angry priest," many of California's Catholics saw Father DuBay as one of those young clerics whom Pope Paul spoke of as "moved by the good intention of penetrating the masses or particular groups," somehow getting "mixed up with them instead of remaining apart, thus sacrificing the true efficacy of their apostolate to some sort of useless imitation."[18]

Nine of California's fourteen bishops made no comment on the issue, while five of the prelates openly endorsed a "No" vote on Proposition 14. Strongest of the statements was that of the Most Reverend Floyd Begin, Bishop of Oakland, who viewed the amendment as "of such a nature as to contradict what is clear and universal Catholic teaching on the rights and duties of those who own property."[19] The Archbishop of San Francisco originally opposed the measure on constitutional grounds alone, for which, admittedly, there is a strong case. Though he recognized "room for legitimate differences of opinion among Catholics regarding the legislation," McGucken issued a pastoral letter from Rome in late October defending the right of the Church "to speak out on the moral issues involved" and clearly, though not specifically, urging defeat of the amendment.

While Bishop Begin said unequivocally that Proposition 14 was a moral issue insofar as it concedes absolute rights to property owners with no reference to the rights of others," most of the prelates carefully skirted the "moral" aspect of the question, at least in their official statements. The Bishops of Sacramento and Santa Rosa joined other members of their province in opposing the amendment and Stockton's bishop, Hugh Donohoe, was among the three signatories of the opposition argument mailed to voters by the Secretary of State's office.

Reaction to the stand taken by the northern bishops was mixed. One commentator felt that "generally, the Catholic opposition was strong enough to make one realize that many Catholics simply did not accept the authority or the ability of bishops and clergy to speak on the moral implications of this political issue."[20] This view was heard in other quarters. The *National Catholic Reporter* agreed that "at the prudential level,…a priest or bishop is no more competent than the next man; and if he exceeds his competence by imposing his political judgments on the laity he may well be abusing his spiritual authority and keeping the laity in diapers."[21]

A committee of prominent Catholic laymen at Los Altos reacted to Archbishop McGucken's position in a manner almost as unparalleled in America's ecclesiastical history as the DuBay incident in Los Angeles. Their formation of a "Catholic Yes on Proposition 14" organization grew out of "mass indignation to the church becoming politically active in the anti-Proposition 14 battle."[22] Their full-page advertisement, appearing in the Bay City's newspapers on October 28, 1964, was a copy of a letter sent to McGucken:

> Many of your devoted subjects who have tried to live and think as good Catholics all their lives have suddenly found themselves at odds with some of their clergy. The bone of contention is Proposition 14.
>
> Many of our clergy believe and teach that our legislators will be precluded from passing housing legislation if Proposition 14 is adopted. This is untrue. Our legislators can pass any law they choose subject to approval by the people of the State by vote.

The Catholics of whom we speak are told that there is only one side to Proposition 14. Yet our reasoning, based on Catholic training, tells us that this is not true.[23]

The highly respected Thomas P. White, former state supreme court justice, spoke for countless other Catholics when he said, in defense of the silent Archbishop of Los Angeles, "we would resent and criticize our clergy if they undertook to advise us on our conduct at the ballot box."[24] That White's opinion was substantially correct was at least indicated at the polls on November 4th when the measure won a tremendous endorsement of almost 2 to 1. As one eastern paper reported: "Observers throughout the state said that the result of the balloting on Proposition 14 could not be described other than as a defeat for a great proportion of the state's clergymen."[25]

In a multiple interview carried by *The Commonweal* for its recent jubilee, one journalist chided those clamoring for more prelatial leadership in political matters and wondered "if liberals haven't consistently been playing the game both ways. If it is a measure they like, they ask the bishops to intervene. Otherwise they are quick to point out that political order belongs to laymen."[26]

It is hard to say whether McIntyre's silence or the northern bishops' open endorsement won more votes for proponents of the amendment. Only one of the state's fifty-eight counties disapproved of Proposition 14 and that by a narrow margin of nineteen votes.[27] Generally, Southern California recorded a higher percentage of affirmative ballots but much of that can be attributed to a traditionally conservative block of votes in that area. A definitive estimate of the hierarchy's influence and effectiveness (or lack thereof) must await further study for there were other powerful interests at work on both sides during the long struggle, such as the circular letter mailed to the state's Catholic clergy by the Theology Department of the University of San Francisco wherein it was stated categorically that "any Catholic who feels that he may vote for this measure has an erroneous conscience and is morally obliged to correct it in the light of Christian principles."[28] That these tactics were unappreciated seem obvious enough, but their real effect cannot yet be weighed.

This much can be said, that such comments as John O'Connors' that "incipient racism—shameful heritage of by-gone, ghettoed years, was behind the victory of Proposition 14"[29] are totally unfounded and indefensible. In the total analysis, it must be remembered, as a Negro minister in Los Angeles pointed out, that "in the West especially in the Southern California area, we have most of the provisions of civil rights justice on the books and in the attitudes of the people,"[30] a statement recalling Yves M. J. Congar's study for UNESCO in 1953 wherein the distinguished Dominican theologian concluded that "Negros in California suffer no discrimination."[31] The UNESCO survey was confirmed as late as November, 1964, by a report of the National Urban League which stated: "Living standards of Negro families in the Los Angeles area are the highest in the nation."[32]

While Los Angeles leads the nation in percentage of acceptable housing, both rental and owner-occupied, no one denies that there have been and are "pocketed inequalities" and efforts are being made to meet these problems. As the Archbishop of Los Angeles said after the campaign, "the approval of Proposition 14 does not repeal the serious moral obligation of all persons to avoid racial discrimination and segregation."[33]

The question remains, however, concerning the manner of remedying these serious ills in modern society. It would seem, from the incidents related above, that California's Catholics prefer to have their bishops remain aloof from politics, except in those rare cases where a specifically, *well-defined* issue of justice or morality is at stake. The Golden State's Catholics apparently want more emphasis placed on taking the slums out of the people than the people out of the slums. For then, and only then, do they see the Church and its collegially endowed episcopate empowered to speak. Today's Catholics respect the opinions of their bishops—but apparently only in areas of faith and morals. There alone do they see legitimate magisterial competency.

Notes to the Text

1. Los Angeles *Herald-Examiner,* August 24, 1964.
2. *Pacem in terris* (New York, 1963), § 25.
3. *Newsweek,* 65 (January 11, 1965), 57.
4. *Rerum novarum* (New York, 1939), § 6.
5. Francis Canavan, "Conscience and Pluralism," *America,* 110 (April 18, 1664), 539.
6. San Francisco *Monitor,* November 12, 1964.
7. Joseph R. Thomas in the Newark *Advocate,* July 9, 1964.
8. Los Angeles *Tidings,* July 31, 1964.
9. See. *The Commonweal,* 80 (July 10, 1964), 477-482.
10. *National Catholic Reporter,* November 18, 1964.
11. Los Angeles *Times,* June 28, 1964.
12. Alice Ogle in *National Catholic Reporter,* November 25, 1964.
13. Such accusations were actually made by A. V. Krebs, Jr., in, "A Church of Silence," *Commonweal,* 80 (July 10, 1964), 467-476.

14. In an advertisement in *The Reporter*, 31 (October 22. 1964), 55; the words are, of course, the slogan of John Wilkes Booth and the motto of the State of Virginia.
15. Georgia *Bulletin*, October 29, 1964.
16. *Ave Maria*, 100 (September 19, 1964), 16.
17. Hollywood *Citizen News*, June 17, 1964.
18. *Ecclesiam suam*.
19. San Francisco *Monitor*, June 26, 1964.
20. Niels J Anderson, "Proposition 14 and the Liturgy," *America*, 111 (November 21, 1964), 658.
21. *National Catholic Reporter*, November 4, 1964.
22. San Jose *Mercury*, September 10, 1964.
23. San Jose *News*, October 28, 1964.
24. Los Angeles *Herald-Examiner*, July 28, 1964.
25. Camden *Star Herald*, November 13, 1964.
26. *The Commonweal*, 90 (November 20, 1964), 266-267.
27. The verified count by the Secretary of State gave 4,526,460 votes in favor of the amendment and 2,395,747 against.
28. Statement of September 28, 1964, mailed out under the letterhead of the University of San Francisco Theological Faculty.
29. San Francisco *Monitor*, November 12,1964.
30. Statement of the Reverend Nathaniel Lacy quoted in the San Francisco *Monitor*, July 17, 1964.
31. *The Catholic Church and the Race Question* (Paris, 1953), p, 49.
32. According to the report, printed in the Los Angeles *Herald-Examiner* November 29, 1964, Los Angeles ranks with Gary (Ind.) at the bottom of the scale in a survey concerned with Negro families living on poverty incomes.
33. Los Angeles *Times*, November 7, 1964.

18

This address about the *"Real Patronato de Indias"* was given to the students of Mount Saint Mary's College in the Little Theatre, March 2, 1964. It was based on an essay that appeared in the *Historical Society of Southern California Quarterly* XLIII (June, 1961), 215-219.

In the History of Spanish America, and indeed in parts of our own country, no one feature is of greater interest, and perhaps of greater importance than the *Real Patronato de Indias*. Certainly none has been more influential in forming the pattern of ecclesiastical affairs in the republics of Latin America. The word *Patronato* means patronage which may be described as the "right" (*jus*) granted by competent ecclesiastical authority to a personage empowering him to take over the obligations of providing for the administration and maintainence of a religious benefice. This right was essentially exercised in the appointment or presentation of those in sacred orders who served the benefice. Since the patron was nearly always a layman, legal definition of his privileges was necessary, since he did not exercise it by virtue of an innate hierarchial character or office.

In principle, the concession of the right of patronage arose from the desire of the Church to publicly recognize the generosity of a benefactor and it was originally intended to be an expression of gratitude. A concession of this nature was, of course, regulated by ecclesiastical law and, in time, even by civil law in certain countries. In fact, it was rooted in the canonical practice of the church, in medieval custom, and in Germanic law. As the centuries passed, it became more common and for this reason is found in the Crusades and in other happenings of the Middle Ages. Donations and material support were held to be of the same general beneficiary character as defense of the Church's interests, and so should be, to some extent at least, similarly rewarded.

The exact meaning of the word *Jus* has not always been clear. It was often interpreted, by regalists, as the equivalent of "right," when "concession" or "privilege" would express its significance more correctly. This fact is well illustrated by the endless controversies attending the claims of the Seventeenth Century Gallicanism. At any rate, by that time the word *Jus* was often asserted to be any Privilege sanctioned by law, so that "right" does not accurately translate it.

The word "benefice" may be defined as any ecclesiastical office which afforded a living to its occupant, and at the same time, placed upon him the duty of the care of souls.

The *Real Patronato de Indias* was the exercise of the power of patronage on the part of the Kings of Spain in the ecclesiastical affairs of the New World, of the Philippines and other Spanish possessions in the Far East. It was the last of several concessions made in the final years of the Moorish Wars and early years of American discovery. Its immediate model was the patronage over the Church of Granada, granted to Ferdinand V and Isabella by Pope Innocent VIII in 1483. When King Ferdinand sought the same privileges for America, these were granted by Pope Julius II in the Bull *Universalis Ecclesiae* dated July 28, 1508.

It should be noted that these privileges were given as a personal favor to the sovereigns who had overthrown Moslem power in Spain, promoted salutary reforms and undertaken to promote the cause of religion in the New World. When Queen Isabella died in 1506, King Ferdinand became the beneficiary of the Pope's benevolence. The Holy Father had no intention whatsoever of creating patronage which would inhere in the Spanish Crown as the so-called *Regalistas* afterwards maintained. Indeed, they went a step further and held that the *Patronato* was a normal and natural attribute of sovereignty, which they maintained, was formally recognized in the Bull *Universalis Ecclesiae*, a view which is historically indefensible.

In any event, the *Patronato* was subsequently confirmed by the Popes to Ferdinand's successors because of their interest in the evangelization of America, and as a reward for their defense of the Holy See against the "reformers" of the Sixteenth Century.

Using the word "right" in its proper sense, the *Patronato* imposed definite duties as well as rights. These latter may be summarized: *first*, that no Cathedral, collegiate or prelatial churches were to be founded without formally expressed royal consent; *second*, that Bishops and other prelates, who were by custom nominated in Consistory, were not to be named by the Pope in this manner until their names were presented by the King; third, that nominations to lesser ecclesiastical dignities and benefices were to be made by royal presentation to the Ordinaries concerned. Thus the King could and did directly nominate the holders of ecclesiastical positions of all kinds, from Archbishops to sacristans.

In addition to these "rights" there were duties also. A very large one was the erection, furnishing and maintenance of churches. A second duty was the selection and support of missionaries. There were others, but these two were the most significant.

It must be pointed out that these duties were not neglected, however great the royal insistence upon their privileges. Philip II, for example, sent to the Indies 2,682 religious and 376 clerics. Nor was the King negligent in providing material support to the churches and missions. Hence it must be conceded that the *Patronato* played a large part in the prompt and successful organization of ecclesiastical life in the New World. Cathedrals, churches, schools and even universities came into existence in a relatively short time. By the middle of the Sixteenth Century, only sixty years after the discovery of America, all these were well organized and gave substance to the establishment of the viceroyalities and other civil divisions of the Americas.

On the other hand, it is equally undeniable, that the union of Church and State under this system was entirely too close. The civil officers were not always men of judgement and singleness of purpose and the military system often left very much to be desired. It was not a good thing to have ecclesiastical dignities dependent upon either civil or military rule. Also the ecclesiastical appointments were nearly always Spaniards and it was some time before Spanish-Americans attained any recognition. Unfortunately no encouragement was given to the formation of a native clergy. There was always a tendency on the part of the government to interfere in the works of the Church especially in the days of the Franciscan Missions.

In short, the system, whatever its advantageous merits may have been, threatened to enslave the Church and in the end it actually did so in many of the provinces of the Americas.

The answer to how this happened must be sought in the vicissitudes of Spanish political life at home. Before the death of Philip II in 1598, the decline of Spanish influence in Europe was well under way. Under Philip

II and Philip IV its tempo was accelerated and under Charles II involve-ment in all kinds of troubles brought matters to a crisis. This incompe-tent King reigned during the ecclesiastical and political troubles which beset France under Louis XIV. Without a direct heir, he was persuaded in the last years of his life, to settle the Spanish succession upon Philip of Anjou, grandson of Louis XIV and of María Luisa, daughter of Philip IV. When Charles died, on November 1, 1700, the successor-designate became King Philip V, first of the Spanish Bourbons, thus bringing to an end the rule of the House of Hapsburg in Spain.

With the change of dynasty, the undesirable characteristics of the *Patronato* increased. The evils of Gallican ideas came to the front, and the exercise of the royal power in ecclesiastical affairs soon became burden-some. The reign of Philip V was a long one, lasting forty-six years. Then came Ferdinand VI who, in turn, was succeeded by Charles III who occu-pied the Throne until 1788, the very eve of the French Revolution. Charles has been termed one of the "enlightened despots" of the Eighteenth Century. His ability and good intentions are evident in his efforts to reform the top-heavy character of colonial administration. Unfortunately this move came too late. On the religious side, he had the ideas characteristic of benevolent despotism. It was in his time that the Society of Jesus was suppressed in the Spanish realm. It was also during his rule that the Franciscan missions in California were first established, by the aid of the Pious Fund and not at all by the generosity of the royal treasury.

In those days the effects of the *Patronato* were certainly harmful. The writings of the French *philosophes* were widely read in Spain and the example of the absolutism of Louis XIV had borne fruit. The new king, Charles IV was not the man to cope with the difficulties of his time, and in another two decades insurrectionary outbreaks in the Americas grew to such proportions that a bare fifteen years later, Spain's vast empire melted away. Simon Bolivar drove the Spaniards from Caracas in 1813; Mexican Independence was a fact twelve years later.

The English colonies along the Atlantic Seaboard had meanwhile been set up as a Federal Republic. But, whereas these colonies had grown up in an atmosphere of self-government, the erstwhile Spanish dominions had no such experience. Hence, from the very beginning, the new Latin American states had to wrestle with unstable governments which succeed-ed one another in rapid fashion. There was little if any political stability. Yet upon one thing most of the Leaders agreed: they had succeeded to the *Real Patronato de Indias* as an integral part of the transfer of sovereignty from the Crown of Spain to the new republican order in the Americas.

For example, the California *Junta de Fomento* (1825-27) proposed a plan "for the better government of the Californias" which was submitted to Juan Francisco Azearate, President of the United Mexican States, on August 31, 1827. It provided for two lieutenant governors, one for each of the Californias" and according to Article Seven, these were to exercise the powers of the *Patronato*. Yet, the general provision in Mexico at the time called for the nomination of ecclesiastical officials by the president of the republic upon the nomination of the territorial governor. This is a definite example of how the new government supposed itself to have inherited, as a matter of right, the privileges of the *Patronato Real*.

So it was in other parts of the Americas, and so has it been since. There were, of course, men of affairs who did not support the theory that the *Patronato* was inherited by the rising republics. At Caracas, in 1811, a commission appointed by the constitutional convention or assembly, declared just the opposite. At Angostura in 1819, this view was again asserted and in 1821 at Cucuta, emphasis was placed on the "personal" character of the concession to the *Reyes Católicos*. This last convention insisted upon the establishment of direct relations with the Holy See.

This complex question can be summarized as follows: *Regalismo* had grown up in the days of the Austrian dynasty in Spain. Then, in the Eighteenth Century, there was a juncture of this dangerous Caesaropapism with the Gallican Theories of the relations of Church and State which had become acute in France under Louis XIV and which were bought into Spain by the Bourbons. These latter regarded the *Patronato*, not as a personal privilege, but as an inherent attribute of their sovereignty.

The church was thus virtually absorbed in, and became a part of, the machinery of government. In one form or another, and in varying degrees, this heresy has persisted ever since and has colored and vexed the relations of Church and State down to our own day.

Fortunately in recent years, there has been some improvement. This is evidenced by the creation of new metropolitan and episcopal Sees, and by a more vigorous catholic life in several countries.

The more dangerous theories of the *Patronato* have been modified by *concordats* between several of the Latin American Republics and the Holy See. With due recognition to the few benefits of the *Patronato*, it was always, but more especially after 1700, a grave source of potential and often active danger to the liberty of the church.

19

This essay about Father Johann Jacob Baegert appeared in the *Records of the American Catholic Historical Society* LXXXV (September-December, 1974), 141-143.

"The only comprehensive account written by an actual participant"[1] of experiences among the aboriginal inhabitants of the
rugged, sterile and uninspirational peninsula of Baja California is the
Nachrichten von der Amerikanischen Halbinsel Californien, compiled from
notes made by Johann Jacob Baegert (1717-1772) during his seventeen
years at San Luis Gonzaga.

Baegert's encyclopedic observations were published, according to one
authority,[2] to counteract "the illusory information that was currently
widespread"[3] regarding peninsular affairs that had appeared in such
works as Miguel Venegas'[4] three volume *Noticia de la California y de su
conquista temporal, y espiritual, hasta el Tiempo Presente* (Madrid, 1757).
Obviously, Father Baegert considered the more unattractive aspects of
the California apostolate as "the best weapon of defense in the controversy between the Jesuits and their sovereign."[5]

Though not generally esteemed an impressive record of missionary
accomplishments among the natives,[6] the *Nachrichten* contains "a good
account of their culture, languages, and distribution."[7] Indeed, the naively
objective compilation represents an abundant fund of anthropological
information as well as on-the-scene geographic and descriptive observations of considerable value to subsequent generations.

Baegert communicated "the feeling of the time, place, and people of which he wrote."[8] A sense of humor pervades the factual, literal, mathematical and realistic narrative as do occasional shafts of sarcasm. The author's descriptions of the area's geography, botany and zoology, while well done, reflect his personal distaste for Baja California and the hardships endured there by himself and his confreres. Bitter at seeing the Society of Jesus banished from New Spain, Baegert's scathing account of the treatment meted out to the Jesuits graphically reveals the "shocking conditions existing among the natives of Lower California, whom he considered but one step above the wild beasts that surrounded them."[9] He concluded his eye-witness journal on the note "that California is without exception the most miserable country under the sun, or, if an equally miserable or worse one was ever discovered by the Argonauts, then California was used by the Almighty Creator as a model for making it."[10]

The vigorous and amusing account[11] was completed by Father Baegert shortly after his return to Europe in 1769. The 358-page work was published anonymously in 1772,[12] by the Electoral Court and Academy at Mannheim as *Nachrichten von der Amerikanischen Halbinsel Californien: mit einem zweyfachen Anhang falscher Nachrichten*. A folding map bearing the description "*California per P. Ferdinandum Consak S.I. et alios*" facilitates the location of the Jesuit missionary foundations, showing as it does the routes along the west coast of Mexico over which Father Baegert travelled in 1751 and 1768. A second edition of the *Nachrichten* was issued the following year, containing only minor alterations with the same map and plates as the earlier imprint. An abstract of the work appeared in 1777 in the *Berlin'sche Litterarishe Wochenblatt*.[13]

In it annual report for 1863, the Smithsonian Institution published an English rendition by Charles Rau (1826-1887) of the initial four chapters of the *Nachrichten*, dealing with the life and customs of Baja California's native population, under the title, *An Account of the Aboriginal Inhabitants of the California Peninsula as given by Jacob Baegert, a German Jesuit Missionary, who lived there Seventeen Years during the Second Half of the Last Century*.[14] The remaining four chapters were issued by the Smithsonian Institution the following year.[15]

Rau's translation was reprinted as a monograph from the electrotyped plates of the annual Smithsonian reports and, in 1882, was included in an anthology of *Articles on Anthropological Subjects, Contributed to the Annual Reports of the Smithsonian Institution from 1863 to 1877* (Washington, 1882).

In 1942, Pedro R. Hendrich's 262-page Spanish translation of the entire *Nachrichten* was published at Mexico City by the Antigua Libreria Robredo do Jose Porrua y Hijos as *Noticias de la Peninsula Americana de California por el Rev. Padre Juan Jacobo Baegert*. Included in that edition was the brilliant thirty-page ethnographic study of Indian mores in the area by Paul Kirchhoff.

A wholly new annotated translation, based on the original German, was prepared by M. M. Brandenburg and Carl L. Baumann and published, in 1952, by the University of California Press. Issued as *Observations in Lower California by Johann Jacob Baegert, S.J.*, the 218-page treatise, with its nine illustrations and analytical index, faithfully rendered the author's stylistic peculiarities into readable and accurate English.

Johann Jacob Baegert has not fared well among the chroniclers, characterized as he has been as "arrogant" by one writer,[16] and a "career ecclesiastic" by another.[17] Plainly, the stalwart Jesuit missionary lacked much of the ardor, optimistic zeal and human sympathies of his predecessors in the peninsula. Nevertheless, even the critic can discern that Baegert recognized the disabilities of the natives as cultural, not inherent qualities. His overall observations confirm that "his heart was with his poor children of the wild among whom he had labored, for whom he had sacrificed, and toward whom he tried to be an instrument of eternal salvation."[18]

Notes to the Text

1. Homer Aschmann, "Book Review," *Hispanic American Historical Review* XXXII (August, 1952), 396.
2. See Carlos Sommervogel, S.J., *Bibliotheque de* la *Compagnie de Jesus* (Paris, 1890), I, 761.
3. Lazaro Lamadrid, O.F.M., "Book Review," *The Americas* X (October, 1953), 246.
4. Edited by Andres Marcoa Buriel.
5. Ursula Schaefer, "Father Baegert and His *Nachrichten*," *Mid-America* XX (July, 1938), 154.
6. See Gerard Decorme, S.J., *La Obra de Los Jesuitas Mexicanos durante La Epoca Colonial 1572-1767* (Mexico, 1941), I, 472.
7. Don Meadows, *Baja California 1533-1950* (Los Angeles, 1951), p. 2.
8. Maynard J Geiger, O.F.M., "Book Review," *Catholic Historical Review* XXXVIII (July, 1952), 193. The *Nachrichten* is divided into three parts: the first treating the topography, physical geography, geology and natural history of the peninsula; the second outlining the life and customs of the inhabitants; and the third sketching the history of missionary work in the area. Two appendices are devoted to "refuting earlier published accounts."
9. J. Gregg Layne, "Book Review," *Historical Society of Southern California Quarterly* XXXIV (March, 1952), 90.
10. Ursula Schaefer, *op. cit.*, 155.
11. Hubert Howe Bancroft, *History of the North Mexican States and Texas* (San Francisco, 1884), I, 478n.
12. Robert Streit, O.M.I. describes a 1771 edition he identified as belonging to the British Museum. No such volume bearing that date has yet been located, either at London or in any other of the major depositories. It is a reasonable presumption that Streit unconsciously transposed the 1772 date. See *Bibliotheca Missionum* III (Aachen, 1927), III, 265.

13. II, 625ff. See G.T.S., "Some Details in the Life of Johann Jacob Baegert," *Tlalocan* I (1944), 243-249.
14. *Annual Report of the Board of Regents of the Smithsonian Institution, Showing the Operations, Expenditures, and Conditions of the Institution for the Year 1863* (Washington, 1872), Pp. 352-369.
15. *Annual Report of the Board of Regents of the Smithsonian Institution, Showing the Operations, Expenditures, and Conditions of the Institution for the Year 1864* (Washington, 1865), Pp. 378-399.
16. Manuel P. Servin (Trans,), *The Apostolic Life of Fernando Consag, Explorer of Lower California, by Francisco Zevallos* (Los Angeles, 1968), p. 28.
17. Pablo L. Martinez, *Historia de Baja California* (Mexico City, 1956), p. 231.
18. Peter Masten Dunne, S.J., *Black Robes in Lower California* (Berkeley, 1952), p. 352.

20

This Dominican document from Baja California was published with an introduction under the title "The Church is beginning to crumble" in *California History* LVIII (Fall, 1979), 250-255.

Since founded in 1215 by Domingo de Guzmán, the Order of Preachers has diligently sought to make the world its cell and the ocean its cloister. Entering the New World in 1510, the Dominicans, as they are known, settled on Española, a small island in the Caribbean Sea, to begin an unparalleled humanitarian campaign on behalf of the region's native peoples. Pedro de Córdova, Antonio de Montesinos, Bartolomé de Las Casas, and Luis Cáncer are only a few who threw themselves whole-heartedly into the task of advancing the spiritual and material welfare of the Indian population.

In practically every corner of the two American continents penetrated by Spain, the Order of Preachers labored with distinction. As early as 1526, they moved from the Caribbean islands to preach the Gospel within the present borders of the continental United States, possibly with Ponce de León in 1513 and assuredly with Lucas Vázquez de Ayllón in 1526.

While never as influential in New Spain as the Franciscans, the Order of Preachers worked with singular success. Their missionary foundations in Oaxaca, for example, were considered outstanding models of evangelic accomplishment. The Dominicans were also the first group to gain a successful foothold in the Sierra Gorda region where, by the close of the seventeenth century, they maintained six flourishing missions.

On April 7, 1772, the Dominicans were officially entrusted with all the

Jesuit foundations in Peninsular California, as well as the recently-founded frontier establishment of San Fernando de Velicatá. Actual transfer of authority took place in mid-1773, when the last of the Franciscans departed for their new apostolate in Alta or Upper California. A territory of immense proportions, it included what one writer aptly called "the decadent area south of Velicatá and the virgin territory north."[1]

The Dominican presence in Baja California lasted for the next eighty years,[2] during which time the friars established eight new missions. Between 1772 and 1854, fourteen Dominicans occupied the office of *presidente*.[3]

After 1804, when the peninsula was politically severed from Alta California, the fortunes of missionary work in the area were irrevocably altered. Initially, the region's isolation beneficially insulated it from many of the vexations confronting the mainland, but time eventually caught up with Baja California and placed insurmountable obstacles in the path of the friars.

Very little is known and even less has been published about the ecclesial life of Peninsular California during the nineteenth century. According to Father Zephyrin Engelhardt, "The fault lies with the Dominicans themselves, who either failed to record interesting events and incidents, or allowed the documents to go astray."[4]

Materials unearthed in recent years, however, indicate that Father Engelhardt may have been unduly harsh on the Order of Preachers.

Recently emerging from the shadows is an archival treasure which sheds light on this subject. It is a packet of materials dated from 1808 to 1818 which found its way into the collection of Western Americana manuscripts gathered by the late Frederick W. Beinicke for the Yale University Library.[5] Among the documents is a fascinating and informative plea for financial assistance addressed to the prior and vicar general for the Order of Preachers, Father Alexander Fernández.[6] In the eleven page document written at Loreto on December 23, 1808, Father Ramon López,[7] president for the Dominican Missions in Baja California, provides a rare glimpse into the vicissitudes that plagued the peninsular outposts. It is herein translated and annotated for the first time.

Other correspondence in the packet indicates that the report was sent through the office of the Dominican procurator, Father Juan Rivas, to Fernández, who was residing at the Convento de Santo Domingo in Mexico City. Upon receiving the letter, the vicar general wrote a covering note[8] endorsing the proposal which he sent, along with the original plea, directly to Viceroy Pedro Garibay.[9] Unknown is the ultimate disposition of the request from the *presidente*, although it seemingly unleashed a raft of complaints and countercharges that continued for another decade.

While the Dominican missionary efforts in Peninsular California were considerably less productive and surely less dramatic than the padres' exploits in other areas of the New World, scant but emerging records show, as one historian has written, that the self-sacrificing friars "labored as effectually for the Indians, and accomplished as much good for religion, as either the Jesuits or the Franciscans. And these fruitful labors the friars of St. Dominic continued until they were deprived of all means of subsistence, and were forced to leave the country by the destructive secularization measures of the past century."[10]

Notes to the Text

1. Peveril Meigs, *The Dominican Mission Frontier of Lower California* (Berkeley, 1935), p. 5.
2. For an historical sketch of Dominican activity, see Francis J. Weber, *The Missions and Missionaries of Baja California* (Los Angeles, 1968), pp. 53-65.
3. The men were Vicente Mora (1773-1781), Miguel Hidalgo (1781-1790), Crisótomo Gomez (1790-1793), Cajetano Pallás (1793-1798), Vicente Belda (1798-1802), Rafaél Arviña (1802-1804), Miguel Gallego (1804-1808), Ramón López (1808-1816), Pedro González (1816-1819), Pablo Zácate (1819-1820), José Sanchez (1820-1822), Pedro González (1822-1825), Félix Caballero (1825-1840), and Gabriel González (1840-1854).
4. Zephyrin Engelhardt, *The Missions and Missionaries of California* (San Francisco, 1929), I:631.
5. The compiler thanks Dr. Archibald Hanna, curator of the Beinicke Rare Book and Manuscript Library, at Yale University, for permission to reproduce this precious document.
6. This entry is number 130 in Jeanne M. Goddard and Charles Kritzler, eds., *A Catalogue of the Frederick W. & Carrie S. Beinicke Collection of Western Americana* (New Haven 1975), I: 39-40.
7. Ramón López (c. 1775-1816) was a veteran missionary by the time of his appointment to the presidency in 1808. His longest previous term of service had been at San Vicente Ferrer, where he labored from 1797 to 1808. Father López was known to have visited Mission San Diego during November, 1798, in his quest for souls. He died on June 10, 1816.
8. Alexander Fernández, O.P., to Pedro Garibay, Mexico City, February 27, 1809, The Frederick W. & Carrie S. Beinicke Collection, Yale University.
9. Pedro Garibay (1727-1815) was among the more prominent of New Spain's viceroys.
10. Peter K. Guilday, "Notes and Comments," *Catholic Historical Review* III (January, 1918):495.

December 23, 1808
Loreto

Last November 7, I solemnly promised the Very Reverend Vicar General, Father Alexander Fernández, that I would send him by mail, through your kind offices, a plea on behalf of the Presidente *of the Missions in Peninsular California, who finds it impossible any longer to sustain himself at this Presidio of Loreto with the 300* pesos *he receives as support. I have hesitated only because of other pressing matters which demanded my immediate attention. Now, I briefly put aside all my other obligations long enough to make this presentation.*

There is no more effective manner in pleading my cause than to describe the status of the church and presbytery at this Presidio, as well as conditions in the other missionary foundations. It will be easy enough to see that it would be impractical to expect these buildings to be repaired with another 300 pesos, or even double that amount, as long as it is also necessary to support the Presidente *and his assistant priest from the same allocation.*

The situation here presently is thus: The entire church building,[1] the nave, chapel of the Holy Rosary, choirloft, sacristy, and tower are all badly worn, dilapidated and beginning to crumble on both the inside and the outside. The doors are in pieces. Only two of the six bells are usable. The altarpieces, five in the church and one in the chapel, are all broken, unglued and falling from their frames. Some of the altar tables are disintegrating too and everyone of them, except for the main altar, lacks such basic adornments for the worthy celebration of the Liturgy as antependia, altarcloths, crucifixes, candlesticks and bookstands. When Holy Mass is occasionally celebrated at any one of these altars, it is necessary to remove these items from the main altar, on which the Blessed Sacrament reposes. And that is surely disrespectful to the Lord. In the sacristy, only the clothespress is usable—probably because there is so little traffic there. Everything in the sacristy is in poor condition.

The rag-like copes can be somewhat repaired, except for their length. There are many chasubles and other vestments which should be burned. While there are enough vestments for offering Holy Mass, most all of them need considerable mending, especially the linens, most of which need replacement. There are two fairly new albs, but unfortunately, the lace on each is badly worn. The other albs are threadbare, but they should last for a while longer. The same is true for the amices, corporals, purificators and finger towels. There are quite a few of these last items, perhaps six complete sets. The altarcloths are virtually useless, as are the antependia. There are a few broken and ravelling cinctures, one of which is still used everyday. There are no hand towels, finger dishes or lecterns, to say nothing of the other instruments for the administration of the sacraments. There are enough sacred vessels, but even they need attention.

The sacristan of the church is retired from the Royal Navy. There are a few altar boys who enjoy participating in the liturgical ceremonies. Holy Mass is offered and certain other services are conducted for those wishing to attend.

The condition of the presbytery[2] is even more deplorable than the church. It is in a state of physical collapse and, in many places, unroofed. Those of us who live here are constantly in danger from falling tiles. Very little is functional, except for the doors, hinges and the like which I have repaired from my own personal funds. The furnishings consist of three or four paintings, two reasonably-good tables, a couple of old bookcases, some few books, a silver dish, one serving spoon and five utensils. There are a few chairs, some wardrobes and one or another small thing of scant value.

The rancho attached to the mission at Comondú, which my predecessor[3] acquired, should be of some worth. Formerly, it provided a bit of revenue, but in more recent times it has deteriorated and now needs a considerable investment to restore its productivity. Presently I can make no use of it, though I will hold title to it until an appraisal can be made.

This foundation owes the Royal Warehouse 716 pesos, four reales and a little more and there is a personal indebtedness of six pesos and four reales contracted by my predecessor. I feel these debts should be paid by the missions and in this I concur with my predecessor who considered these as legitimate expenses incurred in executing the office of Presidente.[3] These are some of the manifold problems which I have yet to resolve, with the help of God.

After mentioning the status of the church and presbytery here, let me now address myself to the other foundations. This I will do in cursory fashion, beginning with San Miguel, the northernmost mission and concluding with the outpost of San José del Cabo in the south.

Conditions at San Miguel[4] are not very good. While outwardly prosperous, its minister can barely provide the Presidente with twenty-five or thirty pesos annually. I know quite well that the priest there can hardly meet his own needs.

The Mission of Santo Tomás[5] is better off. Yet even though that foundation excels those on the frontier, when I look at the list of its current expenditures and then anticipate what is needed for the immediate future, I can see that there will be precious little left over. Hence that establishment must be classified with San Miguel.

The Mission of San Vicente[6] which, until recently, I administered for twelve years, remains much as when I departed. It is about the same as those already mentioned. It is not at all likely that my successor[7] there will be able to maintain the twenty-five or thirty pesos *formerly paid each year to the* Presidente.

The mission dedicated to our holy founder, Santo Domingo,[8] is in even worse condition financially than that of San Vicente. At most it is barely subsisting. Nevertheless, I will ask the minister there to at least try to meet a tax of twenty-five or thirty pesos *to the* Presidente.

The foundation of Santisimo Rosario[9] can contribute a little more. Though it has neither good ranches nor many cattle, the friars[10] have carefully managed in the past decade to support themselves and to put something aside.

The Mission of San Fernando[11] can give nothing because of a long series of unfortunate occurrences. It is akin to a very old man who lives on a day-to-day basis, until a lack of strength finally curtails his activity altogether.

The two missions in the hills, Santa Catalina[12] and San Pedro[13] cannot give what they don't have. The minister at Santa Catalina formerly was able to send something, but now he struggles just to make ends meet. San Pedro is good for little more and likely will always be that way. A lot more could be said about those missions in another context.

The Mission of San Borja[14] is anything but prosperous, but I would think the friar there could contribute a minimal sum to the support of the Presidente.

The same cannot be said for Santa Gertrudis,[15] which manages to exist solely through the kindness of Divine Providence.

The Mission of San Ignacio,[16] although it has seen hard times, now appears to be doing better. It can be grouped among those able to bear some taxation.

Mission La Purísima[17] can likewise be put in that category, since it is among the more stable foundations.

Nothing can realistically be expected from the Missions of Mulegé,[18] Comondú[19] and San Javier,[20] all of which are on their last breaths.

As for the southern missions of Todos Santos[21] and San Jose del Cabo[22] and the last one that belongs to the Dominicans,[23] I have only a limited acquaintance. But since they are still operational and are sur-

rounded by mining interests,[24] *I would assume they could manage some form of taxation for the maintenance of the* Presidente.

In this sad state of affairs, which relies entirely on Divine Providence for temporalities, I can only conclude, after a thorough examination of conscience and a great deal of reflection, that the only feasible way of carrying on the office of Presidente *is to have the Royal Treasury pay his salary. He would need 700* pesos *annually, over and beyond the 350* pesos *he receives as a minister. That amount, added to the 100* pesos *he may realize from taxation and what little comes as offerings and* stipendia, *would enable the* Presidente *to support himself and his companion and to make the more necessary repairs to the church and presbytery.*

This proposal should not be looked upon as unique or strange. The Presidio here numbers upwards of 700 souls between the militia, sailors, royal officials and neighbors. That estimate does not include prisoners or the many visitors that arrive here with ever-greater frequency. There is a real need for a parish church staffed with self-supported priests. Also, I feel that the already poverty-stricken missions should not be expected to bear the total or even predominate expenses of this foundation as its resident ministers.

If the Presidio here were located nearer to a mission, like those in Alta California, possibly other arrangements could be made for its temporalities.[25] *In that case, maybe one priest would suffice, if there were two in the adjoining mission. However, this foundation is eight leagues distant from the nearest mission and therefore unable to exist with a single minister.*

I have endeavored here to propose what is needed, along with sufficient evidence to prove its validity. This I do in eager anticipation of your favorable reaction.

May Our Lord continue to bless you.

The manuscript is reproduced through the courtesy of the Beinecke Rare Book Room and Manuscript Library, Yale University, New Haven.

Notes to the Text

1. Dating from 1793, the church at Loreto was once richly decorated.
2. It was a small house, which contained a *sala* or reception room and another larger room divided into several sections.
3. Father Miguel Gallego, the former vicar provincial and *Presidente*, had served at San Vicente Ferrer (1789-1794), San Francisco de Javier (1794), Nuestra Señora de Loreto (1795), and Santa Rosalia de Mulegé (1795-1798). He became *Presidente* in 1804. The venerable Dominican died at Loreto from a sudden illness on January 2, 1810.
4. Founded in 1787, Mission San Miguel Arcángel was located in an isolated area about fifty miles south of San Diego.
5. A new church had been completed at San Tomás de Aquino in 1801, along with a shelter for young girls and unmarried women. Its foundation in 1791 completed the projected line of communications between the two Californias.
6. Ideally situated on a large plain with abundant grass, marshes, water, and arable land, San Vicente Ferrer was the only Dominican mission not eventually relocated.
7. *Vg.* Father José Duro.
8. A severe epidemic in 1801 had killed many of the Indians at Santo Domingo.
9. Nuestra Señora del Santísimo Rosario, established in 1774, was the first Indian missionary outpost of the Dominicans in Baja California. Eventually it became the most stable and prosperous.
10. Father José Caulas was then stationed at the mission.
11. Situated along the thirtieth parallel at the northern limit of the San Borja desert, San Fernando de Velicatá was the only mission founded under Franciscan auspices in Peninsular California.
12. Santa Catalina, begun in 1797, was the last of the Dominican establishments in Baja California and the only one not built in a valley. Father Manuel de Aguila was the resident missionary.
13. A new church had been erected at the mile-high Mission of San Pedro Martir de Verona in 1801.
14. Established by the Society of Jesus in 1762, San Francisco de Borja had formerly been the most populous of the missions in Peninsular California.
15. Dating from 1752, the Mission of Santa Gertrudis was situated in an isolated ravine in the heart of a mountain area twenty-six miles from San Ignacio. The church was still in very good condition.
16. The origins of San Ignacio de Kadakaaman can be traced to 1727. It was one of the "mountain missions".
17. Purísima Concepción, founded in 1720, was located along the banks of the Cadegomó River.
18. The church at Santa Rosalia de Mulegé was in fairly good condition, but the rest of the buildings were rapidly disintegrating.
19. A stone church was located west of Loreto at San José de Comondú about midway between the gulf and the Pacific.
20. Father Gerónimo Soldevilla was then stationed at San Francisco de Javier.
21. Perched upon a high and picturesque mountain, Todos Santos also boasted a chapel, Our Lady of the Holy Rosary.
22. San José del Cabo was the first of the peninsular establishments begun in the south. It was located near an inlet anchorage frequented by foreign ships.
23. Presumably the reference is to Nuestra Señora de Guadalupe, which was actually an *estancia* or cattle ranch until 1834. Father Rafael Arviña was the resident priest.
24. Such mining towns were San Antonio, once the capital of Baja California, and El Triunfo, at one time the largest city in the southern part of the peninsula.
25. The questions of providing chaplains for the four presidios in Alta California was a constant source of friction between civil and religious leaders throughout the missionary era.

Report on Church in Baja California, 1808

The Peninsular California Missions in 1808
as described by Father Ramón López

Missionary Foundation	Order	Founded—Abandoned
Nuestra Señora de Loreto	Jesuit	1697-1822
San Miguel Arcángel	Dominican	1787-1834
San Tomás de Aquino	Dominican	1791-1849
San Vicente Ferrer	Dominican	1780-1833
Santo Domingo	Dominican	1775-1839
Nuestra Señora del Rosario	Dominican	1774-1832
San Fernando de Velicatá	Franciscan	1769-
Santa Catalina	Dominican	1797-1840
San Pedro Martir de Verona	Dominican	1794-1806
San Francisco de Borja	Jesuit	1762-1818
Santa Gertrudis	Jesuit	1752-1822
San Ignacio de Kadakaaman	Jesuit	1727-1840
Purísima Concepción de Cadegomó	Jesuit	1720-1822
Santa Rosalia de Mulegé	Jesuit	1705-1828
San José de Comondú	Jesuit	1708-1827
San Francisco de Javier	Jesuit	1699-1817
Todos Santos	Jesuit	1724-
San José del Cabo	Jesuit	1730-1840
Nuestra Señora de Guadalupe	Dominican	1834-1840

21

This annotated correspondence of Father John Baptist Camillus Imoda appeared in *Montana. The Magazine of Western History* XIX (Winter, 1969) under the title "Grant's Peace Policy: A Catholic Dissenter," 57-63.

Early in 1869, a delegation from Members of the Society of Friends called upon Ulysses S. Grant at the White House with a petition for "a more liberal and attentive consideration of the welfare of the Indians than had recently been given to the subject" by the President's immediate predecessors. The well-intentioned Chief Executive promised to have the matter thoroughly investigated, and on December 5, 1870, Grant informed Congress of plans to unite the Christian influence of the missionaries to that of the government by turning over the management of the Indian reservation to those religious denominations already established among the Indians and certain others willing to undertake the work on the same terms.

According to the Catholic Commissioner of Indian Affairs, had the program been properly administered, it would have brought "real and lasting peace and prosperity to the Indians" and would have given "to their Missions more power than any Christian Church has had in modern times in its efforts to evangelize heathen nations."

But while Grant's Indian policy had much to recommend it, the President's political naivete soon embroiled the project in all sorts of petty entanglements. There was considerable displeasure, for example, about the government's lopsided distribution system. Only eight of the

38 nominations to which they were entitled were given to Catholic missionaries, though the number of natives evangelized under Catholic auspices was about 100,000 as opposed to 15,000 for the Protestants. With the assignment of the other agencies to the spiritual and temporal control of the various Protestant denominations—most of them Methodist—80,000 Catholic Indians suddenly found themselves isolated from the Church to which they professed spiritual allegiance.

One outgrowth of the government's poor management of a "wise and humane" policy was the formation, in 1873, of the Bureau of Catholic Indian Missions at Washington. This agency was charged with the threefold task of administering the agencies already under Catholic direction, reclaiming as many others as possible from Protestant control, and protecting the spiritual interests of those Catholic Indians living outside the Church's sphere of influence. The Archbishop of Baltimore, James Roosevelt Bayley, appointed General Charles Ewing to act as commissioner on the part of the Catholic bishops, charging him to protect and further the temporal and spiritual interests of the Church's Indian missions scattered throughout the nation.

Contemporary correspondence of Catholic missionaries provides many insights into the complexities of complying with President Grant's program. An outstanding example of the inequities growing out of the new policy was graphically illustrated in a letter addressed to Father J. B. A. Brouillet, Director of the Bureau of Catholic Indian Missions, by the Jesuit John Baptist Camillus Imoda.

This cheerful, energetic Italian Jesuit was 45 years old and had been laboring in Montana's Indian mission field for a decade and a half when he wrote his analysis of the situation he and other Catholic missionaries now faced. Before we present the full text of his letter to Father Brouillet, it is interesting to note that his position already had strong secular support, support which eventually led to its official vindication. The question of alleged religious discrimination had come to the attention of the Weekly Rocky Mountain Gazette of Helena, whose editor decided to air the charges publicly.

According to the Gazette's account, dated November 26, 1873, the trouble began when the government agent for the Blackfoot Indians, Fletcher Ensign, arrived at his Helena assignment in the fall of 1872 to replace the interim appointee, Jesse Armitage. Despite the fact that he had been acting on behalf of the Methodist Church, Armitage had not interfered with the religious practices of the Indians.

146

Agent Ensign reversed the policy, however, by informing Father Imoda, early in 1873, that Catholic services would no longer be permitted on the reservation. Thereafter, the Jesuit missionary was compelled to dispense the sacraments furtively in a small cabin belonging to a half-breed and located several miles from the agency's headquarters.

Ensign's action was roundly criticized by the crusading newspaper printed each Wednesday morning at Helena "for the miner, farmer, merchant, mechanic and family circle." The *Gazette* charged that "none but a badhearted man could be guilty of debarring" Father Imoda from working among the people whom he had won over "in sixteen years of toil and devotion."

The editor showed no particular sympathy for the Indians themselves, who, he felt, were "a discredit rather than an honor to any church that claims them for members and converts;" nevertheless, he recalled that long before others took any interest in the matter, "the Reverend Father and his compeers worked bravely and faithfully to Christianize these most unthankful and uncompromising heathens."

He further reminded his readers that Father Imoda had gone among the Indians "when no other dared to do so," in order to nurse and care for them during the recent smallpox epidemic.

While the editor could see no reason why the government "should assume what is none of its proper business, the conversion of the Indians to Christianity," he did feel that no restrictions should be placed on the activities of "a priest who had devoted his life to the Indians; who had learned their language and preached in it before Montana had any white settlers."

A dash of unexpected color was added to the controversy when the *Troy Times* of New York disclosed that Fletcher Ensign had been appointed at the behest of Dr. John P. Newman, his brother-in-law, then pastor of the Metropolitan Memorial Church of Washington and spiritual advisor to President Ulysses S. Grant. In no small measure, it was due to the Montana newspaper that Ensign was dismissed as Indian agent and soon summoned before the Third Judicial Court of Montana in a civil action to recover $24,600 for "misapplication of annuity goods at the Blackfoot Agency." The indictment was subsequently dismissed for technical reasons but not before Ensign had been called before another district court to answer additional charges of mismanaging government funds.

Father Imoda's letter, written from Helena on January 30, 1874, now follows. It is reproduced from the Chancery Archives of the Archdiocese of Los Angeles through the kindness of James Francis Cardinal McIntyre.

In compliance with your desire, I send the following memoranda of the establishment and progress of the Catholic Mission among the Blackfeet, Blood, and Peigan [Piegan is the preferred spelling) Indians in Montana Territory, for the information and consideration of the Hon. Secretary of the Interior [Columbo Delano] as to the claims of the Catholic Church under the present religious denomination policy of the President in the control and management of the Indian Department.

Three years ago, the Hon. Commissioner of Indian Affairs [E. S. Parker] allotted the agency in question to the Catholic Church and appointed a Catholic agent; but within three months after the agency was given to the Methodist Episcopal Church, and an agent belonging to the denomination appointed named Mr. Jesse Armitage. Why, an agency, the Indians belonging to which, are in a considerable number Catholic, and among whom there is not a single Methodist or Protestant Indian of any denomination whatever, should be taken from our church and given to a denomination of which the Indians knew nothing, has always been a mystery to me. The Catholic agent may have been removed for personal reasons; but that should not be allowed to prejudice the claim of the Catholic Church. Our mission has not been dirilect [sic] or inattentive to its duties, and if it has not proven so eminently successful, as under more favorable circumstances might have been expected, the fault lies, rather in our limited means, than our endeavors.

As to the efficiency of our mission and the respect for, and confidence of these tribes in it, I beg to state that immediately after the fight between the U.S. troops under Col. [E. M.] Baker and the Peigan Indians during the winter of '69 & '70, I went to the Peigan camp on Belly River in the British Possessions and counseled them to make a lasting peace with the Government and citizens of the United States and had the honor to report to Gen. A[lfred] Sully, U.S.A., then Superintendent of Indian Affairs Montana (at his request) on the disposition of the Peigan camp, in regard to peaceful relations with our government and people under date of April 11th, 1870.

Our mission has always cheerfully aided and cooperated with the officers of the Government in the management and control of these Indians and our most earnest efforts have constantly been made to preserve peaceful relations between them and white citizens.

Mr. Wm. F[letcher] Ensign succeeded Mr. J. Armitage, as agent, and was also appointed through the influence of the Methodist Church.

On the fifth of January, 1873, Mr. Ensign refused me permission to hold Divine service in the agency buildings at the Blackfeet agency, stating he could not allow me to hold service there anymore as he was a Methodist appointee, and was afraid his doing so might reveal the fact in the East that the Blackfeet Indians are Catholics! He expressed himself, however, as personally sorry for giving the refusal.

This being the first interruption to my religious communication with these tribes since I came among them in the year 1859, I was surprised, and regretted it very much, as the Indians desired my presence and the celebration of our church service. All of these Indians who are christians, are Catholics, nor is there a single Indian belonging to any other christian denomination whatever. In support of this statement, I forward the enclosed protest signed by citizens (Protestant and Catholic) living in the vicinity of, and acquainted with these Indians for several years. They desired to express their disapproval of Mr. Ensign's' course, and to testify to the religious belief of these people. If any further proof be required, it will be found in the Treaty made between the United States Commissioner W. J. Cullen and the Blackfoot nation in the year 1868, wherein the Indians stipulated that: six hundred and forty acres of land shall be donated to our mission of St. Johns, so long as it maintains its religious and benevolent characteristics. This being an act of the entire Blackfeet Nation, the Hon. Secretary of the Interior cannot doubt their unanimity for the Catholic Faith.

The refusal of Mr. Ensign to permit a follower of the late Father [Pierre-Jean] DeSmet—to whose christian zeal for the spiritual welfare of the Indians, these, as well as many other tribes in the West are indebted for their knowledge of Christianity—to celebrate Divine service in accordance with the earnest wishes of these Indians; whose sole hope of salvation rests on the services and ministrations of our church, is, in my opinion a sad comment on the religious liberty vouchsafed to all under our noble Constitution; and is wholly at variance with the views of the President and the humane policy entertained by him in the administration of Indian Affairs.

Our mission among these tribes commenced in the year 1847, when they were visited by Father Nicholas Point, S. J., who baptized six hundred and sixty-seven at Fort Benton in the same year. There were visiting missionaries until the year 1859, when a permanent mission was formally opened on the Teton River, ten miles below the present location of the Blackfeet Agency buildings in the presence of A[lfred] J.

Vaughan, Indian agent and several other witnesses. I joined in conducting the mission in the same year. Every year since from two to three clergymen have been engaged in the mission work. I have participated in it every year since the permanent establishment of the mission.

Considering the nomadic habits of these Indians and the vast territory they traverse, the success of our mission is gratifying. There have been as many as five hundred and sixty-seven baptisms in one year since 1862, and in many other years our labors have produced good results. The number of Blackfeet baptized in the Catholic Church is over two thousand. The efforts of our church, in the work of christianizing these people, have been attended with many difficulties. I will omit further mention of them as I do not deem it essential. I pointed out only one instance, in which I endeavored to assist Gen. Sully because it may afford some evidence of the trust and confidence reposed in us by these people at a time when they were bitterly hostile to the Government and citizens of this country.

I may be allowed also to state that our mission maintained a school for the children of these tribes for a period of five years without any expense to or aid from the Government. Our means became limited, and we were reluctantly obliged to discontinue it.

From the fears expressed by agent W. F. Ensign, that it might become known in the East that the Blackfeet are Catholics, I am led to apprehend that there may have been some misrepresentation or suppression in this regard. If so, and additional evidence be required by the Hon. Secretary of the Interior, I beg he will refer to the Hon. Martin Maginnis, Delegate to Congress from Montana or, any gentleman acquainted with the religious belief of these tribes.

Trusting in the justice of our claim, and hoping the Blackfeet Agency may be restored to the spiritual supervision of the Catholic Church, I remain,

Your humble Servant in Christ,

J. C. IMODA, S. J.

Although Father Imoda's memorandum did not bring complete victory for the Catholic position in this difficult period, the Jesuit's lucid presentation confirms his position as one of the truly dedicated missionaries in the American West.

Father Imoda died at the residence of the Rt. Rev. John B. Brondel, Bishop of Helena, on the night of June 17, 1886. He had returned to

Helena in the fall of 1883 to assist with the increasing work of the Helena Diocese, then in the midst of building a new Episcopal residence.

No better source can be found on the death of Father Imoda, and for an appraisal of his accomplishments, than Chapter XXV of Father L. B. Palladino's *Indian and White in the Northwest* (Second Edition, 1922) which reads in part:

"...[Imoda's] health had been impaired by exposure and the many hardships he had endured on the Indian Missions and, as a consequence, for some years back he had become subject to occasional attacks of inflammatory rheumatism. These caused him at times intense pain, yet he never relented in the performance of duty and, notwithstanding his sufferings, he was always ready to indulge in an innocent joke.

"The Sunday that preceeded his death as he was the only priest at the Cathedral, he attended to all the services alone, that is, after hearing several confessions, he read the eight o'clock Mass and sang the late Mass at 10:30, preaching at both Masses. He presided at Sunday School, held from two to three in the afternoon and also gave an instruction to the children and officiated again at Vespers and Benediction in the evening. I WILL COME TO THEE AS A THIEF, AND THOU SHALT NOT KNOW AT WHAT HOUR I WILL COME TO THEE (Apoc. III, 3) was the text of his evening instruction, the fourth and last for the day, as well as the last of his life.

"The following Thursday, in the forenoon, he spent some hours with the architects and contractors of the new Episcopal residence, laying out the grounds, examining plans, etc., and attended in the afternoon to some business in town. Toward evening he appeared to be suffering more than usual. ...Later on, the same evening, he complained of his pain to Brother Megazzini, who made the remark, 'Father, it may strike the heart.' 'As God wills,' replied Father Imoda with a smile.

"He had retired to rest when Father Pauwelyn came to him shortly after 10 o'clock and the two Fathers were together for a while, hearing each other's confession. This was the last time he was seen alive.

"Knowing well that the Father needed rest, his not rising in the morning at the usual hour for Mass created no apprehension on the good Brother's mind. Later on, however, as repeated calls and knocks at the Father's door elicited no response, the Brother became alarmed. He now called the architect of the Bishop's House, who stood only a few yards off giving directions to the workmen and the two raised up the sash of the front window of the Father's room, the door being locked from the inside, to explore the situation. On first seeing the Father they thought he was sleeping, but he lay on his cot cold in death, though his countenance bore the peaceful expression of one asleep...

"The body was embalmed and lay in state in the Bishop's residence for several days. The Father's obsequies, held June 22, were attended by most of the clergy of the Diocese and by as many of the faithful as could crowd into the Cathedral. The remains were laid to rest in a brick vault in the rear of the church and over the one which contained the body of Father Philip Rappagliosi. Thus, these two missionaries of the Blackfeet Indians lie at rest in the same crypt beside each other, while two marble tablets on the east wall of the sacristy and just above them, perpetuate their memory along the living. [*The bodies of the two missionaries were later removed to the cemetery at Mt. St. Michael's, a Jesuit seminary near Spokane, Wash.*]

"We need not give any extended notice of Father C. Imoda....He was known throughout the length and breadth of Montana as one of the pioneers of the Northwest, his efficient missionary labors among the Indians and the whites having endeared him alike to both the former and the latter and gained him the reverence and love of everyone.

"Of a respectable family and one of several brothers, he was born in Turin, Italy, November 29, 1829, and entered the Society of Jesus, April 22, 1854, in which he had been preceded by his brother, Henry, at one time Superior of the Jesuit Missions in California. He made his novitiate at Massa-Carrara, in the Duchy of Modena, where we became first acquainted with him in 1855. Having asked to be sent to the Indian Missions of the Rocky Mountains, he left Italy soon after and rounding Cape Horn on a sailing vessel, landed in California after a six months' voyage. In 1859, he came into what is today the State of Montana and here he lived and toiled up to the moment that the Master bade him rest from his labors.

"Father C. Imoda was one of the few members of the human family of whom it is said: SORTITI SUNT ANIMAM BONAM. He was always in a cheerful frame of mind, while meekness of spirit and gentleness of manner appeared to be with him a second nature. In the many years we lived with him we never saw his remarkably calm temper ruffled by even as much as a ripple. But whilst meekness and cheerfulness appeared to be the characteristics of his happy disposition, his fidelity and constancy in the performance of duty, no less than exactness to the smallest detail in his every action, were admired even by worldly people. Father C. Imoda is gone to his rest, but he still lives among us in his work and the examples of his virtues."

22

This report about "Bishop Salpointe and the Indians" was published in the *Records of the American Catholic Historical Society* XC (March-December, 1979), 53-59.

In an earlier article on "Arizona Catholicism in 1878: A Report by John Baptiste Salpointe,"[1] this writer alluded to the Indian Peace Policy of President Ulysses S. Grant as "a dismal chapter in American history."[2] Although the well-intentioned program had much to recommend it, "the President's political naivete soon embroiled the project in all sorts of petty entanglements."[3]

Military forces and political corruption consistently took precedence over the claims of justice and the welfare of the natives. More basically, the whole approach to the Indian question was mis-orientated by those who felt it was possible to "pacify, humanize and civilize the aborigine without the moral influences of religion."[4]

The foundation for the Papago Indians at San Xavier, near present-day Tucson, is typically illustrative of the bureaucratic inefficiency built into the Grant policy. Early in 1873, Bishop Salpointe[5] had negotiated for the opening of the school with R. A. Wilbur, the Federal agent for the Papagoes. The institution was placed under the care of the Sisters of Saint Joseph of Carondelet.[6]

Though the earliest classes had to he taught through interpretors, the Sisters were soon able to surmount the language barrier. It was all the more promising an apostolate since the Papagoes, many of whom had been Catholics all their lives, already had a fair grasp of Christian principles.

According to one account of their involvement with the Papagoes, "the Sisters,worked hard to bring the young people to school, strove to learn their language, so that they might be the better fitted to teach them, visited them when they were sick, taught them how to work—especially the young women how to do housework—in short did everything possible to lead them into the ways of Christian civilization."[7]

As was the case with her sister-foundations, the school at San Xavier was carelessly provided for by its governmental administrators. On February 25, 1875, Bishop Salpointe wrote a seventeen page letter to Edward P. Smith,[8] complaining about the local agent, Mr. R. H. Wilbur, and asking for his removal.

The following transcript of that letter is based on microfilm prints in the Papers of William McDermott Hughes, on deposit at the Chancery Archives for the Archdiocese of Los Angeles. The lengthy letter, though signed by Salpointe, is not in his hand. It looks to be a revised copy, possibly a corrected version of a holograph manuscript in the Arizona State Museum Library.[9]

There is no record of an answer to Salpointe's intervention, at least in the Hughes Papers. Whether the withdrawal of the agent and the closing of the school, on April 1, 1876, was a result of the bishop's complaint cannot be determined from the papers available to this writer. In his own version of the incident, Salpointe attributes the discontinuance of the school "to the consolidation of the Papago agency with that of the Pimas."[10]

In a report which purposes to be a recapitulation of the official action, for a whole year, of an officer who has, according to his official statement, 6,000 Indians under his charge, one would naturally expect to find: 1st. a statement of some considerable amount of work having been done by the Agent; 2nd. Under the existing Peace Policy, we would also expect to find some indication, negative or positive, that the relations between the agent and the denomination under which he was working were harmonious, or, in case the Agent had complaints to make, that such complaints would be set forth in respectful, temperate language, and confined to specific charges of irregularity, accompanied with abundant proofs to sustain them.

I am glad to learn from your last Annual Report, that your official cooperation with religious bodies in the care and civilization of the Indian has been satisfactory to you, and that you are able to say, "that the relations of the Bureau to the several religious societies, in accordance with whose nominations its agents have been appointed, have been harmonious and, it is believed, mutually helpful"…; "and by no plan likely to be adopted, is it probable that better men can be secured for this service, than the several religious bodies offer in their nominations to the Government."

As a representative of one of the religious bodies referred to, I am happy to see that you find the plan adopted by the present administration working so well, and am greatly pleased, also, to find that you are able to give such an unqualified endorsement of our recommendations of agents to the Government.

But I am disappointed in so far as there are any exceptions to this endorsement, and am sorry that the Agency under my charge appeals to furnish one of those exceptions, although, strictly speaking, it is not one of those exceptions. You speak of difficulties between the religious societies and agents who have been appointed on the nomination of such societies. There has been a want of harmony between our religious society here and the Agent of this reservation, but the agent was not nominated by us. He was in possession of the agency, and had been for some time, when the care of the Indians was transferred to our Church. "Quickened by the sense of the responsibility imposed on me," as you so truly remark, I felt it my duty, in protecting the Indians, to look a little into the conduct of the Agent, and I soon found it very unsatisfactory; but when I undertook to remonstrate with him, he seemed to feel what was coming, and, in a very insulting letter to me, declined to hold any communication with me, and closed with the words: "And you are expecting more than you will receive, when you think I will extend to you very ordinary courteous association."

The Agent, Mr. R. H. Wilbur, in charge of the Papago Indians of Arizona, followed up his action by one of the most virulent, scandalous reports against our religious body here which has probably ever been forwarded to your Department, and I am sorry to find that this report appears in your Annual Report (See R. of C. of I. A., for 1874, p. 29).

The report of Agent Wilbur consisted of two things: 1st. A statement of his official action for the year preceding; and 2nd. A series of scurrilous charges against our religious society.

The greater part of his official action appears to consist in the fact, as he claims, that he had erected a large building for educational purposes during the past year," for which he, doubtless, credited himself in a large amount in his accounts with the Department. Now, when I tell you, as a fact, that no building of any kind, large or small, was erected by the U.S. during the past year, or in any other year, for educational purposes, on or for this Agency, you will appreciate the fact that, aside from personal feeling, it was not possible for me to act harmoniously with this Agent.

The most conclusive and appropriate reply to this scandalous report is the one you so promptly and justly made, long before I had an opportunity of seeing it, by removing the author from the official place that enabled him to breed discord in the affairs of your Bureau. I could not ask for any more complete refutation of his slanderous accusations, and, in behalf of the religious society which I represent, I return you my sincere thanks for this spontaneous and generous act of justice.

But as his report is officially published, and forms now a part of the public records of the country, I beg to make a brief statement of what was really done here, and trust that you will give it a place in your forthcoming report, in order that both of us may be heard in the matter, or, if it should not be in accordance with the policy of your Department, to publish such replies, I beg then that an investigation be ordered, so that the truth may be known; and if it can be shown that the report of this Agent, now made a part of the printed records of the Government, is false in its money accounts and slanderous in its vilifying charges, that there shall be some public record of the fact, to which access can be had when this official report of a Government Agent is hereafter at any time quoted against us.

I desire, first, to submit a statement of facts relative to the large building which, the Agent says, was erected during the past year for educational purposes.

Long years ago, generations before any of us were born, Catholic missionaries penetrated this remote region and labored with these Papago Indians. They were so successful in their efforts to inculcate principles of virtue and morality and habits of peace and order among them, that to this day the Papagoes are the only Indians in this Territory that have never broken the peace with our people; though a bold, warlike race who have not only never retreated before the terrible Apaches, but have often carried the war against them into their mountain fastnesses, and punished them severely when they have attempted to make inroads on the Papago country. They have never broken their faith with the whites. These principles of honor and fidelity are the result of the training of the early Catholic missionaries among them. Under the care of these missionaries they built the magnificent brick Church of San Xavier, which would attract admiration as an architectural ornament even from those familiar with the magnificent structures which adorn the capital of this country.

In connection with the Church, a long, broad room was built as a residence for the missionary fathers. A certain portion of the land around the mission had been reserved by the fathers, the products of which were devoted to their maintenance and the repairs of the Church and the buildings connected with it. When I came here, in February 1866, to take charge of the mission, I found the Church had been for many years without a priest, and in consequence the buildings were much dilapidated, and some of the garden grounds in the immediate vicinity of the Church were occupied by white people. The moment I informed them that I had come to take charge of the Church, and that I wished to have the possession of all the Church property, they gave up these grounds to me without objection. The larger tract, which had been broken up and cultivated by the fathers for over a century, and the proceeds of which were relied upon for improving the buildings and keeping them in repair, I found was occupied by some of the Indians for their exclusive benefit. I informed them that this tract belonged to the mission, and I asked them to return it, my intention being to devote it in the future, as it had been in the past, to the improvement of the Church and mission. The Indians have not given up the land, and consequently I have not been able to make any repairs on the mission buildings since I took possession of it. This is the only demand of any kind or nature in the way of any pecuniary benefit to myself or my church which I have ever made of these Indians, or any of them, since my coming here; and certainly this demand is a just one. If you will consent, as I hope you will, to order an investigation, you will find it proved beyond all reasonable doubt that the land I asked for is the property of the San Xavier Mission, and not of the. Indian reservation. The Agent characterizes this claim of mine as an unjust demand, I do not blame him for that; he may be honestly of the opinion, for I do not think he ever took the trouble to examine whether this old mission ever claimed and held any land as its own or not. This year the Agent took from one a part of the grounds of the old fathers, lying within a stone's throw of the Church, and gave them to the Indians. I cannot give him credit for sincerity of belief when he says he does not think the mission has any claim to those lands either. In this I claim that the mission has been wronged, and I ask that the action of the Agent be corrected. I claim there is no plea which can justify the withholding of either of these tracts of land from the mission, against its consent and without compensation.

As to the large building which the Agent says has been erected during the past year for the purposes of education. I have stated above that a large room, adjoining the Church, was erected during the last century for the residence of the missionary fathers. I have also explained why it was not kept in good repair, my sources of revenue for that purpose having been taken from me and given up entirely to the Indians. In this state of things the Agent came to me (before he had taken the lands away from the mission and before we had any difficulty) and told me he had an appropriation of $5,000 for school purposes, and asked me how it had better be expended. I was anxious to have as much of the money devoted directly to instruction as possible, and I suggested that he take this old residence of the fathers and repair it a little and use it for a school room, and that we (the priests) would content ourselves with a small room back of the Church, near the stable, for our residence, if he would fit it up a little. He agreed to this proposition, and asked me to superintend the work and he would pay the bill. I did so; I relaid the roof and made other necessary repairs. I kept an account of all my expenditures in a small blank book, and, to the best of my recollection, they amounted to about $1,900. The Agent furnished doors and windows and some furniture for the school and the teachers, the exact cost of which I, of course, cannot tell, having nothing to do with their purchase, but I think I make a very liberal estimate indeed in putting it at $1,500, or in all, $3,500. This is the whole story of the erection of the "large building for educational purposes" by the Agent. I must add, however, that he did not fit up the little room for the fathers as he had agreed. On this estimate I judged the Agent had still in hand about $1,500 for the use of the school, and as there were many other things lacking, I requested him to furnish them. He replied that he had already used up the $5,000 appropriation for the school. I protested that he had not expended any such amount for that purpose, and at this point our harmonious relations ceased. On looking for the book containing my memorandum of expenses, I found that it was missing, and I learned that the Agent had come to my house in my absence and asked the priest to let him have this book, saying he wished it to help make up his school accounts. The priest incautiously gave him the book, and he failed to return it. I sent a messenger asking for the return of the book, whereupon he addressed me the insolent letter to which I have referred, saying he had lost the book and that he would have no further intercourse with me; which letter you have in your office.

I think this is sufficient to show the animus of this Agent towards me. I do not think it necessary to go into a specific denial of his general outpouring of slander and abuse. Each and every material charge he makes is false, and I shall ask no greater punishment upon him than to have the Department institute an investigation, if it deems this abusive language worthy of a moment's consideration. I have no wish or desire to see any proceedings instituted against him, unless the Department should think any of his charges against the conduct of our Church here worthy of consideration, for reasons I will later in this letter explain.

He has appealed to the testimony of any truthful and unprejudiced traveler to support his utterances. There are many old and responsible citizens here, (better witnesses than travellers), who would like to have an opportunity of taking issue with him as to his boasted fidelity to his charge, and the prosperous condition of the Papagoes. They would like to have him show who is the doctor for the Indians for whom he has been drawing $1,200 per year, and who is the farmer for the Indians, who is charged to the Department at $1,000 a year, and to show that they performed their duties. They say, they would like to see how these personages, who look so well on paper and who help to balance accounts so nicely, appear in the flesh; they would like to know how he filled up those nine vouchers he got the Indians to sign in blank a short time since; they desire to know how a confessedly poor physician, notoriously without money or practice when he got this agency, and forbidden by law to practice while holding it, was able, nevertheless, in two years to build a magnificent home and furnish it with rich carpets and expensive furniture, with a family to support meanwhile, and all on a salary of $1,500 a year, without anybody hearing of any legacy being left him, any wealthy marriage contracted, or any successful speculation outside of his Agency happily terminated; and several other things which would make the proceedings very interesting, not only to the Agent, but to the other parties in this neighborhood. But I am not responsible for the shortcomings of this Agent; I did not nominate him, and all I want is to get rid of him, and have someone sent here in whom I can have some confidence, or who I can believe is acting honestly towards the poor Papagoes. Let those who nominated him, vindicate their nomination, or punish the man if he has betrayed them, if they desire.

I hope I have said enough to satisfy the Department that I have discharged the responsibility resting on one in this matter so far as calling attention to irregularities on the part of the Agent is concerned, and I will therefore, for the present, leave the subject with you.

Notes to the Text

1. *The Journal of Arizona History* IX (Autumn, 1968). 119-139.

2. *Ibid.*, 138, n. 51.

3. Francis J. Weber, "Grant's Peace Policy: A Catholic Dissenter," *Montana. The Magazine of Western History* XIX (Winter, 1969), 57.

4. Marc F. Vallette, "The Vicariate Apostolic of Arizona Forty Years Ago," *American Catholic Quarterly Review*, XLIV (October, 1919), 624.

5. John Baptiste Salpointe (1825-1898) served as Vicar Apostolic of Arizona from 1868 to 1884, when he became Coadjutor Archbishop of Santa Fe.

6. See Sister Dolorita Marie Dougherty, C.S.J., et al, *Sisters of St. Joseph of Carondelet* (Saint Louis, 1966), p. 333.

7. Lawrence F. Flick, "The Papago Indians and Their Church," *Records of the American Catholic Historical Society* V (1894), 413.

8. Smith, who represented the American Missionary Association, was named a commissioner in 1873.

9. The writer is grateful to Bernard L. Fontana, Ethnologist at Arizona State Museum for a xerox copy of the earlier manuscript.

10. *Soldiers of the Cross* (Banning, 1898), p. 264.

23

This report by John Baptiste Salpointe appeared as "Arizona Catholicism in 1878" in *The Journal of Arizona History* (Autumn, 1968), 119-139.

If and when the integrated and complete history of the Catholic Church in Arizona is written, the name of John Baptiste Salpointe (1825-1898) will occupy a place of unique importance. This French-born missionary, coming to the West eight years after his ordination, served as Vicar General of the Diocese of Santa Fe between 1859 and 1868. He was named to the newly-established Vicariate Apostolic of Arizona on September 25, 1868, and on the following June 20th was consecrated Titular Bishop of Dorylaeum at Clermont-Ferrand in France. In his subsequent efforts to stabilize the Church throughout the vast jurisdiction of his vicariate, Salpointe found it expedient to join the many other American prelates then taking advantage of the financial generosity exercised by the Society for the Propagation of the Faith in behalf of mission areas.[1]

The Société de la Propagation de la Foi was and is still an organization authorized by the Holy See "to promote the sowing of the seeds of faith in pagan lands..."[2] Founded at Lyons, France, on May 3, 1822, by two priests and ten laymen, the Society ultimately became a vital factor in developing ecclesiastical life in the United States. Structurally, the organization operates through two councils, one at Lyons, the other at Paris. Revenues are raised by private subscriptions of members, and the Society has neither investments nor permanent funds.

The following survey of Catholic activities in the Vicariate Apostolic of Arizona was discovered by this writer in the fall of 1962 while doing historical research in the Paris Council of the *Société de la Propagation de la Foi.* That the document, twenty-eight pages in length, in the archives of the Paris Council is a copy is due to the fact that all appeals were initially directed to the Lyons Committee. Only after that committee's examination was completed were the requests forwarded to Paris where they were approved, augmented, or reduced. Here, as in other cases, if the initial correspondence had not been submitted in duplicate, a certified copy was drawn up for the Paris Central Committee and the original retained in the archives at Lyons.[3] There is no record of a response to this particular appeal, although the worldwide missionary organization was exceedingly generous to Arizona over the years, distributing a total of $136,148 between 1869 and 1921.[4]

This report has never been published, but there is evidence that subsequent writers borrowed generously from its contents. Mark F. Vallette, for example, wrote an article in 1919 on the early days of the vicariate in which he recalled listening "with wrapt attention and the deepest interest to incidents related to me" by Monsignor Salpointe and others about their experiences "among the Mexicans, the Indians and the scattered English-speaking Catholics who settled in New Mexico and Arizona..." Though the author claimed that knowledge of the area had "been occupying cold-storage cells in my brain for some years,"[5] there is internal evidence to indicate that he defrosted the last six paragraphs of Salpointe's 1878 report for the early pages of his treatise. Whether he had access to a copy of the communication or personally consulted the archives of the *Société de la Propagation de la Foi* is a moot question.

Salpointe himself relied heavily on the report when, just a year before his death, he completed his *Soldiers of the Cross: Notes on the Ecclesiastical History of New Mexico, Arizona, and Colorado.* In that volume, the aged prelate revised and considerably expanded his earlier observations in order to place "before the general reader an account of those interesting events of which people at present have little more than a vague tradition."[6]

Even the casual reader will recognize that Bishop Salpointe's report to the Society for the Propagation of the Faith is noticeably more extensive than a mere statistical enumeration. Rather, this well-written and fascinating report, addressed to Francisque Des Garets,[7] vividly sketches the contemporary status of the Church's growth in Arizona against the colorful geographical and historical background of a region rich in Catholic heritage. After glancing at the bishop's chronicle, one would be inclined to agree with a newspaper editorial written at the time of his demise: "With the death of this man, the Right Reverend J. B. Salpointe,there passes away one of the most important figures in all the early history of Arizona."[8]

NOTES ON THE VICARIATE APOSTOLIC OF ARIZONA AND ITS MISSIONS

The Vicariate Apostolic of Arizona, erected on September 2, 1868,[9] encompasses the whole area of Arizona, plus that section of New Mexico known as Mesilla Valley, together with the counties of Grant, Doña Ana, and Paso (in Texas).[10]

Arizona

This territory, once a part of the State of Sonora, was ceded by the Mexican Government to the United States on December 30, 1853. It includes the area between the 31 st and 37th degrees latitude, and the 32nd and 37 1/2 th degrees longitude west of Washington. The boundaries are: northward, the territory of Utah; eastward, New Mexico; southward, Mexico; and westward, California, together with the territory of Nevada.[11] Most of the country is mountainous and arid. The extensive plains yield only cactus and uncultivated palm trees or shrubs, all of which appear thin and scraggy. On the other hand, those valleys irrigated by rivers are prodigiously rich. The main ones, bearing the name of the waterway crossing them, are: Gila, Salado, San Pedro, Verde, Colorado Chiquito, and Santa Cruz. In these valleys the vegetation is as plentiful as the trees are numerous. Along the rivers, people have settled down to cultivate the fields.

Products

The products of the territory are wheat, barley and corn. Potatoes grown in the north have a very good appearance and quality, but those produced in the south do not fare as well. Judging from what the early missionaries wrote, it seems that cotton was effectively cultivated by the Indians living in the Gila Valley, but nowadays it is no longer grown. To harvest a crop that can be consumed locally is more interesting than one which has to be transported large distances to realize a profit. In recent years, vineyards, fruit trees, and sugar cane have been cultivated rather extensively, and these items seem to have a promising future. The climate is good and the difference in temperature between the northern and southern parts of the territory results in the development of a wide variety of trees and plants.

The weather is also attractive to the area's inhabitants, although it can be tiresome during the summer months. Since the first missionaries came, severe fevers[12] have affected certain places, but this phenomenon has almost completely disappeared since 1869. Nobody ever thought of attributing this malady to climate factors, but rather to clearing the land or to some unknown cause. Winter, bringing snow to the mountains in the northern part of Arizona, is a rather pleasant season in the south.

In the last few years, which have been marked by less frequent hostilities with the Indians, animal herds have developed rapidly wherever there is sufficient drinking water. In addition to providing firewood and timber for the inhabitants, the mountain areas are rich in gold and silver. Only the lack of a railroad hampers more extensive exploitation of this area.[13]

Population

Presently, the population is made up of Mexicans, Indians and Americans. The latter, among whom are included all foreigners, are still only a minority but judging from what's in place, this element will soon predominate.[14] I shall not speak about the native population. Some narrators,[15] on the evidence of huge unexplained ruins and remnants of irrigating canals still evident in various parts of the territory, conjecture that before the arrival of the Spanish *conquistadores*, the country was inhabited by civilized people. This much is certain, that these relics of an earlier era already existed when the initial missionaries met the Indians of Gila. The priests visited the ruins and left us detailed descriptions, especially of those called *Casas Grandes*; but they recorded that nobody knew when or by whom the dwellings were built.[16] According to a prominent tradition among the Indians, the houses belonged to Montezuma and were to be approached with respect and trepidation. The buildings themselves, however, despite all the wonders visitors have claimed to find therein, have nothing extraordinary beyond their vast proportions. They consist of large walls erected along an old pattern still used in the territory, that is to say, with sundried bricks or with clay. As for their dimensions, they are about the same size as the homes of the Indian families presently inhabiting Taos and Picuries in New Mexico. The indications are that, at some uncertain date, several families or possibly a whole tribe lived in these ruins. It is fairly commonly held that before the arrival of civilized people, there was considerable intertribal conflict.

Such a view would account for the concentration of the natives in groups where they could defend themselves more easily from surprise attacks. All the large houses, which look like fortified castles from a distance, are only an aggregate of small huts arranged on a square pattern, with other dwellings superimposed on them up to the fourth and fifth story. These huts have a terrace as wide as one of the cabins for each ascending level. On the balconies peaceful Indians can be seen taking the air and resting idly in the sunshine. From those houses which are still inhabited, the residents can watch their fields of watermelons and corn on an elevated platform. It was from there that the natives formerly hurled arrows at attacking enemies. [17]

Another thing worth noting is that these houses are now, as in days past, without any opening other than the small entrance on the roof used for smoke exhaust. To reach the entrance, one must use ladders provided by every family. Probably for reasons of safety, these habitations have been built on slight elevations some distance from rivers and bushes. This explains the vestiges of aqueducts which are still visible.

Missions

At the outset of the colonial period in the New World, devoted missionaries came here with the Spanish *conquistadores* to dedicate themselves to the cause of evangelic preaching. The task provided herculean obstacles and several of the missionaries even sacrificed their lives.[18] The warrior came to win lands, while the minister of God came to gain souls for his Master. Both marched together but each with different weapons and views. One had a sword in hand to beat down and conquer the natives, the other, a cross to console the pagans and give them real freedom. Both the missionaries and the soldiers moved rapidly, for, within thirty years after the conquest by Cortés, all the missions of New Mexico had been established.[19] From Paso del Norte to Taos, that is to say, in practically all the territory, from the south as far north as the Río Grande, priests were caring for the spiritual needs of the natives.

Progress was slower along the western side of the Sierra Madre. Only in 1590, at the request of the Governor of new Biscaye,[20] did missionaries arrive in the Province of Sinaloa. It was almost another century before they appeared in the Province of Sonora, of which Arizona was then a part. The first mission established in the latter province was that of Dolores, founded by Father Eusebio Francisco Kino on May 13, 1687. Within three years that indefatigable Black Robe had inaugurated several other missions [21] which were visited in these years by Father Juan María Salvatierra, [22] who came as Inspector General. Wherever these two priests happened to go, reports a statistical study of the province, [23] Indians swarmed about asking for instruction about and admission to the religion of the Savior. It was about that time that the Sobaípuris, who lived about forty leagues to the north, came to these priests, knelt down with arms stretched crosswise, and asked spiritual assistance for their *rancherías* or villages, then located in a place called Guébavi. Their petition was granted and the missionaries launched among these Indians the mission that took the name of the place. That foundation, which has since been depopulated, was the proto-mission in present-day Arizona. In November, 1694, Father Kino visited a tribe of the Pimas living along the banks of the Gila, in the vicinity of the already-mentioned *Casas Grandes*. There he inaugurated two more missions, naming one for the Incarnation and the other after Saint Andrew. On February 7,1699, the same priest took another journey toward the Río Gila, this time visiting the Yumas and the Cocomaricopas. The Indians related details about neighboring tribes, *e.g.* the Iguanas, the Culganes, and the Alguedunes.[24] (These tribes have since disappeared or have lost their identity by being absorbed into others.) The missionaries ultimately extended their explorations to the western coast as far as the Gulf of California. Already the success of their ministry revealed how, in the short period of two years, these apostolic men had travelled throughout the vast province of Sonora, amid innumerable dangers and difficulties, everywhere building altars to the glory of Almighty God.

However, the persecutions which Our Savior foretold to His disciples, were not lacking in the New World. The Jesuits, already enumerating a goodly number of converted tribes, hoped to win an even greater number when, quite unexpectedly, the Pimas rebelled and killed the resident priest at the Caborca mission.[25] Shortly thereafter, the missions sustained another ordeal, equally as severe though beyond human control, and this was the death of Father Kino, who had been the driving force of the missions. The result of these unfortunate circumstances, according to reliable reports, was a generalized diminution in the overall program which perdured until the year 1727. At that time, however, the Bishop of Durango, Don Benito Crespo, whose jurisdiction then extended over almost all the Jesuit missions in New Spain, after having made a visitation to parts of the Sonora province,[26] sent a report to King Philip V. This action won the pecuniary assistance so badly needed to sustain further missionization. The author of the statistical report mentioned above declares that this royal favor made it possible for the missionaries to establish three new missions in 1731.

From that date until 1750, the only written documents I have seen regarding our missions are the incomplete books of the Church of San

Xavier, a mission of Indian Papagos, located nine miles (or three leagues) south of Tucson. These registers reveal that the mission was almost never without priests as far back as its foundation, which took place about the time the missionaries first came to the Sobaípuris, in the year 1620.[27] It can also be seen from the number of birth entries that this mission served a rather large population.

But hard times were not over yet. On November 21, 1751, the Pimas joined the Seris, *i.e.* all the Indians living in the northwest part of the province, in rebellion. According to the author of a book entitled *Rudo Ensayo o Descripción Geográfica de la Provincia de Sonora*, written in 1764,[28] the Indians of Pimería Alta were divided as follows: The Pimas, the Indians of Pueblos (those who lived in amalgamated clans), the Papagos or Papootam, and the Sobaípuris, together with the Pimas residing along on the banks of the Gila. This nation,continues the same writer,being new in the Faith and having daily communications with pagan tribes, was unsteady, rustic, stubborn, and extremely attached to superstitious practices.The revolution lasted over two years and resulted in the death of three missionaries.[29] The rest of the Fathers were obliged to leave their churches, thus allowing for the Indians to revert to their earlier abuses and vices.

Early in 1754, the missionaries resumed the apostolate in those foundations which had escaped total destruction, among which was San Xavier. The priest who returned there wrote in one of the record books: "On November 21, 1751, all the Pimas rebelled and this church was without a minister from that date until this year, 1754.[30]

The same priest cared for, beside the mission of San Xavier, the neophytes of Tucson, and Tumacácori. The latter was founded in the same year.[31] These missions were all located in the valley of Santa Clara[32] along a straight line of sixty miles (or twenty leagues) in length. Their populations can be approximated from the number of baptisms administered during pastoral visits, taking into consideration the period of time when there was no priest. The number of baptims was: for Tucson, 52; for Tubac and Tumacácori, 64; and for San Xavier, 61; or in total, 177.

With peace once again restored, the missions began to rise from their ruins. In 1762, the Jesuits operated twenty-nine missions for seventy-three *pueblos* of Christian Indians. The most important among these missions, located in that part of the province now known as Arizona were: San Xavier del Bac, Santa Gertrudis of Tubac, San José de Tumacácori, San Miguel de Sonoitag, Guebavi, Calabazas, and Santa Ana. If these missions were not forced to suffer at the hands of the Indians making up their population, the same cannot be said of the Apaches who inhabited practically the whole area of the northern frontier of the province, and who continuously carried on more-or-less disastrous raids. It is not surprising that we read in the writings of the missionaries their complaints about these savages, the losses of neophytes, the death of several priests and the extinction of the whole tribe of the Sobaípuris of San Pedro. Another point of difficulty was European intrigue which not only deprived the missionaries of practically all the support they were receiving from those who represented the Spanish government in the colonies but which eventually resulted in the expulsion of the Jesuits in 1767.[33]

The same year, the Marqués de Croix, Viceroy of Mexico,[34] carrying out a royal mandate, asked for twelve or fourteen Franciscan friars from the College of Santa Cruz de Querétaro.[35] The superior acquiesced and dispatched missionaries to assume direction of the Sonoran missions. It seems that Pimería Alta was the part of the province where the missions had suffered least since the departure of the Society of Jesus.[36] This is explained by the existence along the border of the military forts built when the Pimas first rebelled. It was in that same area, viz., at San Miguel de Ho[r]cacitas, that the Franciscan Fathers established their main headquarters. From there Father Francisco Garcés was sent to San Xavier where he ministered until 1781.[37] That priest, according to the book entitled *Crónica Seráfica y Apostólica del Colegio de Santa Cruz de Querétaro*,[38] several times travelled more than three hundred miles visiting the tribes along the banks of the Gila and Colorado. His overall knowledge of the country accounts for his appointment as guide of a military expedition, organized in 1774, to open a route between the missions of Sonora and those of California. The following year he was named to another expedition which pushed as far as the Port of San Francisco.[39] In both cases, after reaching the end of the journey, Father Garcés returned as quickly as possible to his Indians. From the various reports he left about the tribes visited on these trips, it appears that the Indians encountered numbered about 25,000. While returning from one of these tours, the dedicated missionary, encouraged by the good dispositions he found in the Yumas, asked his superiors for permission and personnel to establish permanent missions among these natives. Three additional priests were designated for that purpose, and placed under Father Garcés' direction; they were Fathers Juan Díaz, José Matías Moreno, and Juan Antonio Bereneche [*sic*]. With their help, he was able, in March of 1778, to make two foundations along the Colorado River. One of these, dedicated to the Immaculate Conception of Mary, was located near the junction of the Gila with the Colorado. The other, nine miles lower down the river, was placed under the invocation of the holy Apostles Peter and Paul. Both foundations were on the right bank of the Colorado.[40]

Though these missions had given great promise such expectations never came about. On Sunday, July 17, 1781, the Indians, aggravated about uncompensated damages to their harvests by the soldiers' horses, went to both churches during Holy Mass and slew the priests, the soldiers, and all the others present. It was this action which won for Father Garcés and the three priests the crown of martyrdom.[41]

That the missions progressed almost as well under the Franciscans as they had done during the Jesuit period is evidenced by the monuments left by the priests in the country, although the majority of these are no longer visible. I shall name only San Xavier, Tumacácori, El Pueblito [Tucson], and Caborca, places frequented by travelers of our times.

The Church of San Xavier, completed in 1797, was not the first church, at least according to a long-established tradition among the Papagos. It is a fine piece of Romanesque Byzantine architecture built with bricks and stones. Interiorly it is decorated with bas-relief and paintings in the chapels. More than forty statues can be counted, several of which could be considered outstanding. The most remarkable are those of the Apostles, placed in niches on both sides of the high altar. Practically all the others, apart from the figures of Our Lord and the Virgin Mary, represent Franciscan saints. The well-preserved church is still being used for divine worship. The churches at Tumacácori and Pueblito, although erected more recently, are now abandoned as far as liturgical functions are concerned.

The Franciscan Fathers administered the missions until December 2, 1827, when they too were expelled along with the rest of the Spaniards.[42]

A new era was beginning for Mexico. It was the Age of Independence, abounding in revolutions, most of them as disastrous to the country as they were fatal to the Indians, depriving them as it did of the priests who for over two centuries had toiled to bring them forth from barbarism. The missions which suffered the most from the departure of the missionaries were those along the farthest border of the new republic, since they were left defenseless against the unremitting attacks of their formidable foes, the Apaches. It is certain that the bishop in whose jurisdiction these missions were located[43] exhibited deep concern for his sheep, but there simply were not enough priests available to replace the friars after their sudden departure. Several of the missions were forced to remain without any spiritual assistance beyond a sporadic visitation. Such infrequent visits were all the more treacherous because of distance and the ever-present threat of the Apaches. As a result most of the buildings of the Arizona missions disappeared along with the effects of the long and arduous work of the evangelizers.

In 1859 that territory of Arizona, already belonging to the United States, was aggregated to the Diocese of Santa Fe, New Mexico, by the Holy See. In the same year, Bishop Lamy[44] deputized his Vicar General, Father Machebeuf,[45] presently the Vicar Apostolic of Colorado, to take possession of the territory. The bishop himself made an episcopal tour of the area early in 1864. The only church left standing in the whole territory was that of San Xavier. A hundred families of Papagos, all of that tribe which once made up the community of the mission, were still living around the church. The rest of the Catholic population, apart from the Pimas of Gila and other scattered tribes, consisted of a few Mexican families and some Americans - a collection of from 1,000 to 1,500 souls. The prelate did not leave that part of his diocese without priestly administration, and by Divine Providence and in spite of the difficulties and expenses, kept it equipped with resident priests who continued to provide for the spiritual needs of those people. But the humble Bishop of Santa Fe felt that the responsibility was too burdensome and asked the supreme pontiff for relief. It was this request that brought about the division of the jurisdiction and creation, in 1868, by Pope Pius IX, of the Vicariate Apostolic of Colorado and Arizona

Since 1866, the population of Arizona has increased daily in a noticeable manner. The agitation in Mexico was a contributing factor since those not wishing to be involved in the revolution came to the United States. It naturally followed that the territory was explored anew as fresh population centers sprang up and communications linked one place to another. Remarkably, all this growth took place in spite of the continued hostility of the Apaches. Several communities needed places of worship. The small town of Tucson was the first to have a House of Prayer, a decision due in part to the choice made by the priests to use that town as their base of operations. The good will of the inhabitants brought about the erection of a suitable church. Dedicated to Saint Augustine, the edifice was commenced in 1852 and finished sixteen years later.[46] Since then, other churches have been built in Yuma, Florence, Silver City, [and] La Mesa de Tularosa. In addition, chapels are located in San Lorenzo, San Isidro, Santo Tomás, San Miguel, Nuestra Señora de la Luz, to mention but a few. The present number of missions having priests, including those in the Counties of Paso, Grant, and Mesilla Valley,[47] is ten, with a total of thirteen missionaries.[48] The religious institutions of the vicariate include that of the Sisters of Loreto, established at Las Cruces in December of 1869 (and this has since become a novitiate of the same order), and the one operated by the Sisters of Saint Joseph, established at Tucson, in May of 1870 (with a house of novitiate begun on September 8, 1876).[49]

The nuns of these two orders presently have charge of three boarding and five parochial schools in Tucson, Yuma, and Las Cruces. The Saint Joseph Sisters also envision taking charge of the two new institutions being built at San Elzeario and La Isleta. There is a parochial school for boys in the town of Tucson under the direction of three lay teachers.[50] The building of these establishments, where more than five hundred students are under instruction annually, is due in no small measure to the assistance given the vicariate by the Society for the Propagation of the Faith. The population of the vicariate is estimated at thirty-eight thousand inhabitants, of whom about twenty thousand are Catholics. This figure excludes Indians.

The main tribes living in the territory are: the Apaches, the Papagos, the Pimas and Maricopas, the Yumas, the Mojaves, the Yavapai, and the Moquis. Although the number of people in these tribes has not been counted, it can be approximated at twenty thousand. Among these, the Papagos are the only ones among whom we have had much influence and to whom we can minister freely. The others have been cared for by ministers of the Reformed Church since the Grant administration.[51] Today these latter Indians are supposedly Protestants, though, in fact, they remain what they used to be, the only difference being that they daily become more degenerate and vicious through their relations with the whites. The unfortunate result of the government's so-called paternal policy is plain to the inhabitants of the country and acknowledged by the Indian agents in their official reports. It follows that it will be considerably more difficult in the future to convert the savages, supposing that the possibility one day presents itself. The Indians, however, and this is true of every tribe, would offer little resistance, at least that is what some of them have declared to me.

One of my priests had amicable relations with the Apaches, not as an appointed minister, but as the friend of the Catholic officer in command of the fort where these Indians live. Mass was occasionally offered for the men of the fort and the Apaches attended, mostly out of curiosity. A few months passed like this. Trying to instill in their minds some knowledge of the principal doctrines of our holy Faith, neither the priest nor the officer missed an occasion of speaking to the Indians through an interpreter. These lessons were appreciated as is evidenced by the exclamations sometimes bursting from the mouths of the listeners: "Dioch injou!" ("Good God!"). An old chieftain of the tribe one day told the priest: "It would be good if you could stay with us; you would ask God to keep dangers and diseases away from us, and your presence among my men would make us happy because it would be a warrant for peace." Unfortunately, the prolonged presence of a Catholic priest could have offended some persons and possibly have compromised the chief, so it was decided to wait for a more opportune time - which has yet to come.

May these few observations, directed to all the members of the Society of the Propagation of the Faith, inspire their fervent prayers for our vicariate and its poor Indian inhabitants!

Tucson, March 5, 1878
†J.B. Salpointe
Vicar Apostolic of Arizona

Notes to the text

1. Between 1822 and 1921 the Society sent $7,020,974.27 to the United States for missionary purposes. J. Freri, in *Annales de la Propagation de la Foi*, Vol. 85 (Paris, 1922), 68.
2. John F. Noll, "Relation of the Society for the Propagation of the Faith to the American Board of Catholic Missions," *American Ecclesiastical Review*, Vol. 91 (Oct., 1934), 337.
3. For an historical survey of the society, see Edward John Hickey, *The Society for the Propagation of the Faith* (Catholic University of America Press, 1922). The two councils, though functioning separately, operated in complete unanimity. The original of this document is no longer in Lyons, where the writer personally looked for it; many documents were moved from there to Fribourg, Switzerland around the turn of the century because of the possibility of their confiscation by anticlerical French government. Since the Paris copy is certified, there is no reason to doubt its authenticity.
4. Theodore Roemer, O.F.M., *Ten Decades of Alms* (St. Louis: B. Herder Book Co., 1942), 172. A newspaper noted in 1893 that "it is owing to the high esteem in which his [Salpointe's] merit is held in the church that the French Society of Propagation of the Faith has been sending from five to six thousand dollars, every year, to the Territory of Arizona, for the support of the Catholic clergy, the schools, and the churches." [Tucson] *Arizona Enterprise*, Dec. 21, 1893.
5. Mark F. Vallette, "The Vicariate Apostolic of Arizona Forty Years Ago," *American Catholic Quarterly Review*, Vol. 44 (October 1919), 616. Vallette at one time was editor of Philadelphia's Catholic Standard. The report was apparently unknown to Sister Edward Mary Zerwekh, a digest of whose M.A. thesis on Salpointe (done at the University of San Francisco in 1956) appeared in the *New Mexico Historical Review* under the title of "John Baptiste Salpointe, 1825–1894" in Vol. 37 (Jan., April, and July, 1962), 1–19, 132–54, 214–29.
6. John Baptiste Salpointe, *Soldiers of the Cross: Notes on the Ecclesiastical Hisory of New Mexico, Arizona, and Colorado* (Banning, Calif.: St. Boniface's Industrial School, 1898), vii. Cited hereafter as *Soldiers of the Cross*. A number of excerpts from Salpointe's earlier letters were published at Lyons in an article entitled "Etats-Unis. Vicariat Apostolique de l'Arizona," *Annales de la Propagation de la Foi*, Vol. 43 (1871), 265-74. Bishop Salpointe served as Vicar Apostolic in Arizona until February, 1885, when, in accordance with an appointment made the previous April, he became coadjutor to Archbishop John

Baptiste Lamy in Santa Fe. In July of the same year he was made Archbishop of the ancient See of Anazarba. The next month Lamy resigned his office and in November, Salpointe received the pallium as his successor. He served until January, 1894. Invested then with the titular archiepiscopal See of Tomi (Constantia in Scythia), he spend the last years of his life in Tucson, dying there on July 15, 1898. In the year before his death, Salpointe had the satisfaction of seeing a large part of his old Vicariate Apostolic achieve juridical autonomy as the Diocese of Tucson, created May 8, 1897. See Owen B. Corrigan, "Chronology of the Catholic Hierarchy in the United States," *Catholic Historical Review*, Vol. 3 (April, 1917), 31-32.

7. Des Garets was President of the Lyons Council from 1868 to 1898.

8. [Tucson] *Arizona Daily Citizen*, July 16, 1898.

9. The Vicariate Apostolic was created by Pius IX on September 25, 1868. Salpointe corrected his error in *Soldiers of the Cross*, 259.

10. Originally the jurisdiction comprised only the Territory of Arizona and the Parish of Las Cruces in New Mexico. Subsequently the Holy See transferred the Parish of Mesilla (in Doña Ana Co., New Mexico) and those of Isleta and San Elzeario (in El Paso Co., Texas) from the jurisdiction of Durango to that of the Vicariate Apostolic of Arizona. Donald F. Shearer, O.F.M., Cap., *Pontifica Americana: A Documentary History of the Catholic Church in the United States, 1784–1881* (Catholic University of America Press, 1933), 352.

11. Salpointe was of course incorrect in stating that all the territory of the Vicariate came to the United States through the Gadsden Purchase. Only the Mesilla Valley of New Mexico and that portion of present-day Arizona lying south of the Gila River were acquired by the Gadsden Treaty. Nevada achieved statehood on October 31, 1864. Richard B. Morris (ed.), *Encyclopedia of American History* (Rev. Ed., New York: Harper & Row. 1961), 216, 463.

12. *Saguaidodo*, or "yellow vomit," was an affliction probably brought on by the use of impure water.

13. The Southern Pacific reached the west bank of the Colorado River on May 23, 1877 and crossed into Arizona the following September 30th. It reached Tucson on March 20, 1880. David F. Myrick, "Railroads of Southern Arizona: An Approach to Tombstone," *The Journal of Arizona History*, Vol. 8 (Autumn, 1967), 155f.

14. The estimated Catholic population of the vicariate in 1878 was 40,000 whites and 20,000 Indians and non-caucasians. *Sadler's Catholic Directory* (New York, 1880), 418.

15. For further elaboration of the views of early writers, see Hubert Howe Bancroft, *History of Arizona and New Mexico* (San Francisco: The History Company, 1889), 4ff.

16. "In 1694 Father [Eusebio Francisco] Kino made a visit to the Pima Indians who lived on the Gila River in the vicinity of 'Casas Grandes,' [Casa Grande] the great house." *Soldiers of the Cross*, 130-31. For Kino's description of the ruins, see Herbert E. Bolton (trans. and ed.), *Kino's Historical Memoir of Pimería Alta* (2 Vols., Cleveland: Arthur H. Clark Co., 1919), I, 128-29. Cited hereafter as *Kino's Historical Memoir*.

17. Salpointe, in *Soldiers of the Cross*, 135f, gives his own description of Casa Grande, then adds: "the immense houses of the past must not be considered as a thing peculiar to Arizona. The ruins of such structures are found in Mexico, especially at Palenque, in the State of Chiapas…"

18. Frs. Juan de Padilla, Luis de Escalona, Juan de Santa María, and Francisco Lopez, among others. *Ibid.*, 41–45.

19. This statement is of course erroneous, since none of the missions established before the colonizing expedition of Juan de Oñate in 1598 was successful. Salpointe later corrected his error when he stated that by 1617 eleven churches and forty-six Christian *pueblos* had been established in New Mexico. *Ibid*, 52f.

20. Rodrigo del Rio y Losa served as *alcalde* at Guanajuato before assuming the governorship of Nueva Vizcaya.

21 Shortly after his arrival in Pimeria Alta on March 13, 1687, Kino established Mission Nuestra Señora de los Dolores. Later in the same year he founded San Ignacio and San José de Imuris, and then Nuestra Señora de los Remedios. "He kept alive the smouldering embers in the West, and started new fires in the North. He was indeed the 'Father of Missions.'…He was great as missionary, church-builder, explorer, ranchman, Indian diplomat, cartographer, and historian. He personally baptized more than four thousand Indians…" Herbert E. Bolton, *Rim of Christendom: A Biography of Eusebio Francisco Kino, Pacific Coast Pioneer* (New York: The Macmillan Company, 1936), 493, 587.

22. The fiery spiritual enthusiasm, cheerful energy, and unflagging perseverance of Juan Maria Salvatierra (1644-1717) was mainly responsible for the establishment of the Jesuit missions in Baja California.

23. Salpointe probably had in mind José Francisco Velasco's *Noticias Estatísticas del Estado de Sonora* (México, D. F.: 1850).

24. The three tribes all lived on the California side of the Colorado, though Fray Francisco Garcés found them "scattered on both sides of the river." Zephyrin Engelhardt, O. F. M., *The Franciscans in Arizona* (Harbor Springs, Michigan: Holy Childhood Indian School, 1899), 139. Cited hereafter as Engelhardt.

25. Fray Francisco Xavier Saeta, martyred on April 2, 1695. *Kino's Historical Memoir*, I, 141 ff.

26. The Diocese of Durango, erected on September 1, 1623 by Pope Urban VIII, included in its territory present-day New Mexico and Arizona. Crespo, the twelfth prelate to exercise jurisdiction on the area, visited El Paso in 1725 and again in 1730. He penetrated as far west as Arizona, the first bishop to enter that section. During his sojourn, he visited Suamca, Santa Maria, Guevavi,and San Xavier del Bac. For Crespo's report, see Edwin A. Ryan, "Ecclesiastical Jurisdiction in the Spanish Colonies," *Catholic Historical Review*, Vol. 5 (1919), 6ff.

27. Kino first visited the *ranchería* of San Xavier del Bac in August or September, 1692. *Kino's Historical Memoir*, 122. The first adobe building for use by a missionary was erected in 1697.

28. *Rudo Ensayo: Tentative de una Prevencional Descripción Geográfica de la Provincia de Sonora, sus Terminos y Confines*, written in 1763, is now known to have been the work of Fr. Juan Nentuig. It is an early account of that portion of Mexico lying north of the Yaqui River and west of the Sierra Madre Occidental, including the portion of Arizona south of the Gila River. The volume was first published by Buckingham Smith at Saint Augustine, Florida, in 1863. An English translation by Eusebio Guiteras appeared in the *Records of the American Catholic Historical Society*, Vol. 5 (1894), 112-264, and was reprinted by Arizona Silhouettes, Tucson, in 1951.

29. Fr. Tomás Tello was murdered on November 20, 1751 at Caborca, and Fr. Enrique Ruhen "and two others" at Soníta the next day. "More than one hundred persons perished...and the property of the victims had either been burned or carried away" within one week. Russell C. Ewing, "The Pima Outbreak in November, 1751," *New Mexico Historical Review*, Vol. 13 (Oct., 1938), 346.

30. The entry was signed by Fray Francisco Paner.

31. Salpointe's reference here is unclear. The *ranchería* of San Cayetano de Tumacácori was first visited by Kino in 1691. It became a *visita* of Mission Guevavi in 1701, and in 1757 reference was made to a Jesuit church there. For a brief history of the mission, see Earl Jackson, *Tumacacori's Yesterdays* (Santa Fe: National Park Service, 1951).

32. Salpointe meant Santa Cruz.

33. Peter Masten Dunne, S. J., "The Expulsion of the Jesuits from New Spain, 1767," *Mid-America*, Vol. 19 (Jan., 1937), 3-30.

34. Carlos Francisco de Croix (1730-1791), forty-fifth Viceroy, held office 1766-71. For a brief biographical sketch, see *Diccionario Porrua de Historia, Biografía y Geografía de México* (México, D. F.: Editorial Porrua, 1964), 397.

35. In addition to Fray Mariano Antonio de Buena y Alcalde (1717-1772), the number included Frs. Juan Crisostomo Gil de Bernave, Juan Díaz, José Maria Espinoza, Felipe Guillen, Francisco Garces, Martín Diego García, Antonio de los Reyes, Francisco Roche, José del Río, Estévan Salazar, Juan Sarobe, José Soler, and Francisco Zuñiga. Engelhardt, 31n. For background of the apostolic college, see Michael B. McCloskey, O. F. M., *The Formative Years of the Missionary College of Santa Cruz de Querétaro, 1683-1733* (Catholic University of America Press, 1955).

36. The missions taken over by the Franciscans were: San Ignacio, with the mission stations of Santa María Magdalena and San José de Imuris; Santa María de Suamca with the *visita* of Santiago de Cocóspera; Dolores de Saric with the *visita* of Santa Teresa; San Francisco de Ati with the *pueblo* of San Antonio Aquitoa; Purísima Concepción de Caborca with San Antonio Pitiquí and Nuestra Señora del Populo; Santos Angeles de Guevavi with the *visitas* of San José de Tumacácori, San Cayetano de Calabazas, and San Ignacio de Sonoitac; and San Xavier del Bac with the *visita* or *pueblo* of San José de Tucson. In the overall program, 3,011 Indians and 792 *gente de razón* were included. Engelhardt, 34f.

37. For a translation of Garcés' diary see Elliott Coues (trans. and ed.), *On the Trail of a Spanish Pioneer: The Diary and Itinerary of Francisco Garcés (Missionary Priest) in his Travels through Sonora, Arizona and California, 1775-1776* (New York: F. P. Harper, 1900). Salpointe was incorrect in asserting that Garcés remained at San Xavier until 1781; he led the expedition to found the Yuma missions in 1779 and in the same year was permanently transferred there. Engelhardt, 130; Bernard L. Fontana, "Biography of a Desert Church," *Smoke Signal* No. 3 (Rev. Ed., Tucson: The Tucson Corral of the Westerners, 1963), unpaged.

38. This treasury of Franciscan history was written by Juan Domingo Arricivita, O. F. M., and published in Mexico in 1792.

39. Garcés went with Anza only as far as the Yuma settlements, then made a long exploration in south-eastern California and northern Arizona before returning to San Xavier. For a full account of the journeys, see Herbert E. Bolton *Anza's California Expeditions* (5 Vols., University of California Press, 1930).

40. The missions were founded in 1779. It is now generally held that both were on the California side. Engelhardt, 138–41. A contrary thesis is advanced in Seward C. Simons, "Were the Colorado River Missions in California?" *Historical Society of Southern California Annual*, Vol. 15 (1933), 25ff.

41. The Yuma massacre actually took three days. Garcés and his fellow missionary, Fr. Barreneche, escaped the first onslaught by swimming the river. On the 19th they were martyred. Engelhardt, 142-45.

42. The Franciscans were not expelled all at once, as the Jesuits had been, but piecemeal, as they refused to take a second oath of allegiance to the Mexican national government. Engelhardt states: "What action the Fathers in Sonora took is not known; but it seems all declined to take the oath and were expelled, at least there is no mention of a Franciscan in Arizona or Pimería Alta after 1824." *Ibid.*, 199. San Xavier was abandoned in 1823. Cleve Hallenbeck, *Spanish Missions of the Old Southwest* (Garden City, N.Y.: Doubleday, Page & Co., 1926), 47. H. H. Bancroft says that "after 1827 there is nothing to show the existence of the Arizona [mission] establishments." *History of Arizona and New Mexico*, 406. The departure of the Franciscans was followed, in 1833 and 1834, by decrees of the Mexican government secularizing the missions. Roy H. Mattison, "The Tangled Web: The Controversy over the Tumacácori and Baca Land Grants," *The Journal of Arizona History*, Vol. 8 (Summer, 1967), 75.

43. Francisco Gabriel Olivares y Benito (1727–1812), Bishop of Durango from 1796 until his death.

44. John Baptiste Lamy (1814-1888) became Archbishop of Santa Fe on February 12, 1875, when that jurisdiction was raised to metropolitan status.

45. Joseph Projectus Machebeuf (1812-1889) had been Vicar Apostolic of Colorado and Utah since 1868. He was transferred to the newly-erected Diocese of Denver in 1887. For a short sketch of his life, see Frank C. Lockwood, *Life in Old Tucson* (Tucson:The Tucson Civic Committee, 1943), 193-99.

46. Salpointe was incorrect in his dating of the construction of St. Augustine's Church. Its cornerstone was laid by Fr. Donato Rogieri late in 1863, and the walls were begun in the same year. It was completed five years later. Rev. F. D. Rosettie, *St. Augustine's* (Tucson: St. Augustine's Cathedral, 1964), 26.

47. These missions were, respectively: Immaculate Conception, Assumption, Saint Vincent de Paul, Saint Francis de Paul, Nuestra Señora de Guadalupe, and Saint Albinus.

48. Frs. Peter Bourgade, John M. Chaucot, Julius Deraches, Andrew Escallier, Edward Gerard, John George, Antonio Jouvenceau, Francisco Jouvenceau, Peter Lassaigne, J. M. Leclerc, Augustine Morin, T, Rohault, and J. B. Stagnon.

49. These two schools were, respectively, Visitation Academy and Mount Saint Joseph.

50. At Yuma was located the Convent of the Sacred Heart; at San Elzeario, Saint Joseph's School; at Isleta, Nuestra Señora de Guadalupe; and at Tucson, Saint Augustine's Parochial School.

51. The Indian Peace Policy of President Ulysses S. Grant created American history. During his administration, military forces and political corruption took precedence over the claims of justice and the welfare of the Indians. See Peter J. Rahill, *The Catholic Indian Missions and Grant's Peace Policy, 1870–1884* (Catholic University of America Press, 1953).

24

This commentary on "Father Lawrence Scanlan's Report of Catholicism in Utah, 1880" appeared in the *Utah Historical Quarterly* XXXIV (Fall, 1966), 283-289. It later formed a chapter in William M. Kramer's *The American West and the Religious Experience* (Los Angeles, 1975).

A considerable amount of Catholic missionary extension work in the United States was aided by financial grants from the *Société de la Propagation de la Foi*, a charitable organization founded at Paris on May 3, 1822. Prelates in underprivileged areas submitted annual reports of their activities along with proposed programs they had outlined for the coming year. Though the Territory of Utah was juridically attached to the Metropolitan Province of San Francisco,[1] the vastness of its size prompted the vicar forane to send separate requests for funds as well as periodic sketches of his work in the Mormon stronghold. That the appeals were favorably received is evident, for the Society of the Propagation of the Faith supplied $16,400 to the jurisdiction between 1872 and 1887.

The report for 1880, like many others, was written by Father Lawrence Scanlan (1843-1915),[2] the Irish-born pastor of Salt Lake City, whose parish comprised the largest geographic unit in the United States.

It will be gratifying to you to learn that God still continues to bless our labors in this distant part of His vineyard. During the past year, we have not engaged in any new missionary enterprises, owing to a lack of funds and other causes; but, nevertheless, we have devoted our feeble energies to, perhaps, a more important matter, namely, the strengthening of those institutions already

177

established; and I am now happy to be able to report all these in a sound financial condition and finely rooted in the soil of Utah.

There are already in the territory six priests[3] and three good substantial churches[4] each having one or more resident priests. Besides, the churches we attend regularly about ten stations[5]—mining camps and Mormon settlements. These stations vary in distances from forty to one hundred miles from the residences of the priests who have to attend them. This renders missionary duty not only laborious, but often very expensive. Frequently, we have to leave the ninety-nine in the valley and climb the snow-clad peaks of the Rocky Mountains—1200 feet high—in search of the "lost one,"—thus, realizing the picture of the Good Shepherd in the gospel. Again, the voice of the dying calling for a priest is flashed over the electric wires to us, sometimes, from a distance of two hundred miles. Besides the suffering and anxiety attending the answering of sick calls—especially in winter, where we have to travel day and night in cold and comfortless stages over roads rough and sometimes almost impossible through snow—there is also a great expense, often amounting to forty dollars, and seldom we get any or but-little compensation. In answering those sick calls, we meet persons who had not confessed for twenty years; others who were married by a Justice of the Peace or a protestant minister and some again, who were living together without any form of marriage having been performed! Of course, we found the children of all unbaptized and in almost total ignorance of prayer and of the teachings of our holy Faith. In some instances, we have baptized whole families of such persons, with the exception of the father and mother who was baptized and raised a Catholic, but became lukewarm and indifferent until pressed by death.

But, notwithstanding all our labors and trials, we are not without consolation and encouragement. On all sides, we see our work bearing rich and abundant fruits not less visible than the sun in the heavens. Ten years ago, there was no permanently residing priest in this territory.[6] Now, there are six such priests! Ten years ago, there was not a church in the whole territory. Now, there are three good substantial ones with a good prospect of adding two more to the number before my next report![7] Ten years ago, there were in this city only about a half dozen regular attendants at the Holy Sacrifice of the Mass, and still less as regular communicants.

Now, there are one hundred in Salt Lake and as many more in Ogden and Silver Reef, besides those in the several missions, while there are over two hundred communicants in the whole territory! Six years ago, there was no Catholic school here, and few Catholic children could be found anywhere and even these were attending Mormon and Protestant schools where they were fast learning the religion of their masters and everything anti-Catholic; now, we have three of the best and most imposing school buildings in the territory,[8] wherein are being educated about one hundred and fifty Catholic and about two hundred and fifty non-Catholic children and not a Catholic child within reasonable distance of these schools is to be found in Mormon or other non-Catholic schools! Six years ago, there was no sister here; now, there are over forty and still they come![9] Six years ago, there was no hospital here, no place where the sick and dying Catholic could feel at home,—where he could be kindly and patiently nursed,—where his wounds could be tenderly dressed and where words of mercy and encouragement would fall on his ears in his last moments; now, there are two good comfortable hospitals conducted by the Sisters of the Holy Cross;[10] and it shall be known only on the last day how many poor sinners they have brought to penance and peace here, and heaven hereafter, by their kindness, sympathy and prayers!

Looking at all these fruits around us, and thinking of the many poor dying sinners to whom we have brought peace and hope, of the many on whom we have poured out the regenerating waters of Baptism, of the many strengthened in the Faith and practice of their holy religion and of the many young souls growing up in all the light and strength and knowledge of the Church, and who at no distant day will be its support and glory—reflecting on all these, I say, we cannot but feel encouraged and persuaded that God has been and is still with us in our work.

You, also, who have so materially aided us and to whom, in consequence, much of the glory and reward belongs, must feel encouraged to continue your noble assistance, being fully assured, that all you may be pleased to give us in the future, with God's blessing, will sanctify as abundantly as it did in the past. I do not think that there is any place in the world where your charity is more needed, and where it will be more certain to do good. In fact there is no obstacle to our progress here but lack of means.

Taking into consideration the means at our disposal, the material on which we had to work, the irreligious infidelity and open immorality that is everywhere rampant and the small beginning we had; the result, as already specified, must be, indeed, gratifying to every member of the Society—to every one who contributed even a mite of its funds, and I venture to say will compare favorably with any attained under like circumstances anywhere else.

It may not be uninteresting to you to know something about the workings of the Sects in this territory. Almost all the chief protestant sects, such as the Episcopalians, Methodists, Presbyterians, Congregationalists are vigorously and earnestly at work here, and I must say, on a far broader scale than we Catholics. Each of those sects has from ten to fifteen ministers, who have as many churches or "meeting houses." Besides these regular ministers, they have many Sunday-school teachers who are paid to teach the Catechism on Sundays, and to conduct a school during the week. All the aforesaid sects have free schools, to the extent that no child who cannot pay is refused admission. In Salt Lake City alone, they give free schooling to more than five hundred! They are enabled to do this by large sums of money given them every year by their respective "Missionary Fund Societies." The Episcopalians, for instance, receive for this territory, every year, for the support of their ministers, churches and schools over 20,000 dollars. This will give you an idea of their earnestness and extent of their work, as also, of the difficulty, on our part, to keep pace with them. What we lack in financial means, we must make up by energy and self-sacrifice. Our schools are the only self-sustaining ones in the territory.

We have now two great works in contemplation—the establishment of a boarding and day school to be conducted by the Christian Brothers,[11] and of a free school to be under the charge of the Sisters who have already acquired a name for themselves, as teachers of the young.[12] I have no doubt but both would be successful, but I fear that it will be some time before I can get sufficient means. I have already the promise of a sufficient number of competent brothers, whenever I am ready to receive them, and the sisters are ready at any time to conduct the free school, I am more in favor of schools here than of churches because the greater my experience, the more I am convinced that, if we would strike at the roots of the great evil prevailing here, we must do it, chiefly, if not entirely, through good schools, wherein the young minds shall be impressed, at least by example, by the truth and beauty of our holy Faith, before they are enslaved by passions and false teachings. Little, comparatively speaking, can be done with the adult portion of the Mormon people. Their training, the persecutions which they fancy they have suffered for the Lord; and their whole ecclesiastical system have made them fanatics and "set in their way"; and hence, there is no reasoning with them.[13] Those who apostasize from the Mormon faith are opposed to every form of religion and generally become spiritualists and down-right infidels. The Mormons, like their protestant progenitors, claim internal illumination by the Spirit; and hence, where pressed to give a reason for their faith, they answer by saying—"the Spirit tells me that I am right. I *know* that I am right, and whoever is baptized in the Mormon faith shall have the same spirit—the same assurance." Hence, you clearly see, that there is no use in reasoning with them, and that the best way to uproot the system is to begin with the young, and thus anticipate this spirit whatever it may be. Thanking you sincerely for your charity and generosity in the past and hoping that you will deem us deserving of a continuance of them in the future, I have the honor to remain

Your humble and obedient Servant in Christ,
L. Scanlan[14]

Salt Lake City November 8th, 1880

Notes To The Text

1. The Vicariate Apostolic of Colorado and Utah was erected on March 3, 1868. On the following August 16th, Joseph P. Macheboeuf was consecrated titular bishop of Epiphania and vicar apostolic of the new ecclesiastical jurisdiction. Three years later, the vicariate was divided and the area of Utah reverted to the Metropolitan Province of San Francisco. On January 23, 1887, the State of Utah and six counties of Nevada were formed into the Vicariate Apostolic of Utah. At that time Father Lawrence Scanlan was appointed to the titular bishopric of Laranda and placed in charge of the recently created district. When the region was advanced to diocesan status on January 27, 1891, Scanlan became bishop of Salt Lake. The Nevada section was dismembered and made into the Diocese of Reno on March 22, 1931, and two decades later, on March 30, 1951, the title of the original jurisdiction was changed to Salt Lake City.
2. Father Scanlan had worked in Utah since August of 1873. At the time of his appointment, the only Catholic place of worship in the 85,000 square-mile parish was the old church of St. Mary Magdalene in Salt Lake City.
3. Three of these priests, Fathers Denis Kiely, P.A. Foley and R. Beeker, lived with Scanlan at Salt Lake City. The others resided at Frisco (Reverend William Moloney), Ogden (Reverend Patrick Smith), and Silver Reef (Reverend P. O'Connor).

4. In addition to St. Mary Magdalene Church at Salt Lake City, there were permanent churches at Ogden (St. Joseph) and Silver Reef (St. John).

5. Among the mission stations were such places as Alta, Beaver, Corinne, Stockton, Ophir, and Park City.

6. One chronicler has noted that "the Catholic history of Utah, during the first two-thirds of the nineteenth century, is almost wholly a matter of the names of those who came, saw the land, and went their way." Robert J. Dwyer, "Pioneer Bishop: Lawrence Scanlan, 1843-1915," *Utah Historical Quarterly*, XX (April, 1952), 141.

The first Mass was celebrated at Independence Hall in Salt Lake City on June 4, 1866, by Father Edward Kelly, a priest attached to Marysville. Shortly after the erection of the Vicariate Apostolic of Colorado and Utah, Bishop Joseph P. Macheboeuf visited Salt Lake and met Brigham Young and other Mormon dignitaries. The vicar subsequently appointed Father James V. Foley to the city, but the priest remained only a few months. When the vicariate was divided and Utah placed in the Province of San Francisco, Archbishop Joseph Sadoc Alemany named Father Patrick Walsh parish priest of the vast area and it was he who built the original Church of St. Mary Magdalene at Salt Lake City.

7. In his report for the following year, Father Scanlan noted that churches were indeed built at Frisco (in the southern part of the territory) and at Park City (about 30 miles from Salt Lake). Cf. John B. McGloin, S.J., "Two Early Reports Concerning Roman Catholicism in Utah, 1876-1881," *U.H.Q.*, XXIX (October, 1961), 342.

8. There were schools at Salt Lake City (St. Mary's Academy), Ogden (Sacred Heart Academy), and Silver Reef.

9. Attempts to bring nuns to Utah materialized when the Sisters of the Holy Cross arrived at Salt Lake City in June of 1875.

10. Scanlan had supervised the opening of Holy Cross Hospital at Salt Lake City on October 26, 1875. Three years later a hospital was inaugurated at Silver Reef.

11. All Hallows College, named after Father Scanlan's Alma Mater at Dublin, was opened in 1886. It was later entrusted to the Marist Fathers.

12. In the spring of 1882, the sisters opened St. Joseph's School adjoining their academy in Salt Lake City.

13. Though Scanlan was obviously opposed to polygamy and other tenets of Mormonism, he usually confined his remarks to his own pulpit and "chose rather to cultivate amicable relations with individual Mormons, some of whom still recall his friendly spirit toward them during the periods of sharpest antagonism." Robert J. Dwyer, *The Gentile Comes to Utah* (Washington, 1941), 159.

It must be remembered that Scanlan here intended no reflection on his Mormon counterparts, whose enthusiasm for their own religious convictions equaled that of Scanlan for his. As a matter of fact, Father Scanlan always enjoyed cordial relations with his neighbors though, at that time, ecumenism may have been more a necessity than a virtue. One observer has noted that "Mr. Young and his successor in the presidency, indeed all of the Mormon officials, were ever friendly to the Catholic priest, and Bishop Scanlan has many times in conversation gratefully referred to this repeated manifestation of generous feeling towards himself and his predecessors." W. R. Harris, *The Catholic Church in Utah*...Salt Lake City, 1909), 332. A measure of this cordiality is seen in the offer by Mormon officials and by Scanlan's acceptance in 1879 to celebrate High Mass in the St. George Tabernacle with the Mormon Choir providing the chant.

14. As pastor and later bishop of Salt Lake, Lawrence Scanlan served the church in Utah for over four decades until his death on May 10, 1915. One obituary notice recorded that "he surely died the death of the just, and earned the crown of eternal bliss." *All Hallows Annual, 1914-1915* (Dublin, Ireland, 1915), 193.

25

This essay about "The Church in Utah, 1882. A Contemporary Account" is reproduced from the *Records of the American Catholic Historical Society* LXXXI (December, 1970), 199-208.

Catholic missionary activity has never been as effectively financed or centrally administered as that of its Mormon counterpart, either in Utah or anywhere else. In the Far West, expiration of the governmental assistance provided by the *Patronato Real*, confiscation of the Pious Fund of the Californias and suppression of the Society of Jesus were only three of the many factors demanding a total reorganization of Catholic missionary endeavors.

Providentially, there appeared on the scene in France, shortly after the turn of the 1800's, Pauline Jaricot, an extraordinary young girl, whose destiny it was to found the *Société de la Propagation de la Foi*. Originally composed of a small group of pious women-workers from the silk mills of Lyons, each pledging a cent a week toward the support of the foreign missions, the Society eventually became the most successful of the several organizations established during the nineteenth century to sustain the material needs of Catholic activities in the foreign missions.

Structurally, the *Société de la Propagation de la Foi* differed from similar Protestant organizations insofar as it took no part in selecting missionaries or in appointing them to their field of work. Its aim was solely that of financially underwriting those chosen, trained and sent forth to their respective posts by the usual Church authorities.

The effectiveness of the Society's work can be measured from a study of its expenditures, the figures for which have always been open to public inspection. Between 1822 and 1912, for example, $80,349,653.66 was distributed to over 300 dioceses, vicariates and prefectures throughout the world. Of that sum, missionary work in the United States accounted for $6,309,214.40.

Those wishing a share in the annual grants were required to submit a written request outlining the various endeavors sponsored by the Church in their particular regions. These carefully screened resumes were used as the basis for determining both the worthiness of a plea and the amount to be allocated.

Though juridically a part of the Archdiocese of San Francisco, the missionary complexities of Catholic interests in the Territory of Utah had qualified that vast area for special consideration by the Society since 1872, when the initial subsidy arrived from Paris. Apparently, pleas for additional grants were submitted each subsequent year, along with the customary report of existing circumstances in the predominantly Mormon territory.

During a tour of Europe in the Fall of 1962, this writer did considerable research in the archives of the Paris headquarters of the *Société de la Propagation de la Foi* at 128 rue du Bac. At that time, permission was obtained to reproduce the extensive report submitted from Salt Lake by Father Dennis Kiely (1848-1920) on November 15, 1882, on behalf of the pastor of Saint Mary Magdalen Church, Father Lawrence Scanlan.

The report is interesting for reasons other than its historical contents. It reveals, among other things, the personal attitudes of an Irish-born cleric struggling to assimilate the atmosphere of his newfound environment. Throughout the fourteen page document, Father Kiely exhibits a decided preference for his Mormon brethren over their Protestant neighbors, speaking perhaps with a frankness one would hesitate to employ in these more ecumenical times. In all fairness, however, it should be remembered that Father Kiely quite naturally couched his observations in those terms best calculated to trigger the generosity of his potential benefactors, few of whom had any experience or sympathy with the American tradition of a pluralistic society.

Portions of Father Kiely's letter were printed in the Society's annual report for 1883: *Annales de la Propagation de la Foi*, 55, 274-280, as were similar documents submitted by Father Scanlan in other years: *Annales*, 49 (1877), 292-295, and 59 (1887), 24-27. The observations contained in these rare volumes along with those that remain unpublished in the Society's archives make up a body of significant source material for the glory of early Catholicism in Utah. Two recent studies on this subject have been published in the *Utah Historical Quarterly:* John B. McGloin, S.J., "Two Early Reports Concerning Roman Catholicism in Utah, 1876-1881," volume 29 (1961), 322-344, and Francis J. Weber, "Father Lawrence Scanlan's Report on Catholicism in Utah, 1880," volume 34 (1966), 283-289. The same journal carried an article entitled "Pioneer Bishop: Lawrence Scanlan, 1843-1915," in volume 20 (1952), 135-158, by Robert J. Dwyer, who is the author of a pair of books on the Church in Utah: *The Gentile Comes to Utah* (Washington, 1941), and *The Story of the Cathedral of the Madeleine* (Salt Lake City, 1936). The standard surveys are the old work by W.R. Harris, *The Catholic Church in Utah* (Salt Lake City, 1909), and the more recent *One Hundred and Fifty Years of Catholicity in Utah*, by L.J. Fries (Salt Lake City, 1942).

FATHER KELLY'S OBSERVATIONS

As years pass by, it is a pleasure to be able to report more favorably, each succeeding year, the prosperity of the Church in this Territory. But a few years ago when making up our annual report for the "Society of the Propagation of the Faith," in a district embracing upwards of eighty thousand square miles, we could only report one Church in that wide-spread district. Those places, where a priest visited a few times each year, are today supplied with priests, who are aided in their missionary labors, by zealous, self sacrificing sisters, who have, in the missions thus far established, the pleasure of seeing their labors crowned with success.

Four years ago, the entire Territory of Utah formed one parish; today there are five parishes, all of which are under the immediate supervision of Very Rev. L[awrence] Scanlan.

To keep pace with the rapid growth of churches, schools, and hospitals in the Territory, his Grace, Archbishop [Joseph Sadoc] Alemany saw fit, that the jurisdiction of its Pastor, who saw the Church cradled in its infancy, and who labored zealously to bring it, and its noble institutions prominently before its very enemies should be extended, and in 1879, his Grace appointed Father Scanlan vicar forane of the Territory of Utah.

In 1873, when Very Rev. Father Scanlan received his appointment as Pastor, the Church was in its infancy, and the great work accomplished by him in those years is marvelous.

In 1874 when I received my obedience to come to Utah to aid him in the mission, he was alone. With a few Catholics to aid him in discharging a heavy debt, which then encumbered the Church, the only one at the time in the Territory, the future prospect of the Church was anything but encouraging; but the good seed of the Divine Word planted by him in those years has multiplied manifold, and to your noble, and generous society is due the gratitude of every Catholic in Utah; for to your generous aid may be traced the foundation of the churches, schools, and hospitals, which today are to be found throughout the Territory.

In 1874 though numerically as strong, as any one Protestant sect, in point of prominence, we fell far behind the least among them; because we lacked the public institutions which they had, and gave them prominence among the Mormon people. To this point, my attention was soon directed, by Very Rev. Father Scanlan, after arriving here. "We alone," he remarked "are without a school in Salt Lake, until this is done we will be in the background, the Church will not be fairly represented." "There is a tide in the affairs of men which, when taken at the flood, leads to fortune." "This," he remarked, "applies to the Church here at present." This was the all absorbing thought of his mind, when I first came to Utah, and his first gleam of hope was realized when in 1875 he received his Archbishop's sanction to found a day and boarding school for young ladies, and more than realized were his most sanguine anticipations, when through your generous assistance, aided by the voluntary contributions of charitably disposed persons, be saw his first great work crowned with success in its noble undertaking. The Sisters of the Holy Cross opened a school in a new three story brick building in Sep[tember] 1875. To the youth of Salt Lake the Sisters were at first an object of curiosity. More than once when passing along the streets, have I seen crowds of Mormon children following them; but their Christian example, aided by their effective work, soon dispelled the feelings entertained by them towards the Catholic Church, her institutions and noble band of workers.

The work begun by them in 1875 still continues to flourish, and with pleasure, do the few Catholics in Utah today look back, and contrast the Church of today, with that of eight years ago.

That prestige, which she has attained at present, and which gains for her the esteem, and admiration of all, is due principally to her schools and hospitals. Without these her light was hid under a bushel, through these like the early Church emerging from the catacombs, her beauty, and grandeur showed themselves in her great charity, and practical workings.

The very example of a procession of Sisters, going to church and wading through mud or snow in the cold winter season, was not without its effect on the Mormon people, who, though wandering in the mazes of error, are religiously inclined, and are, and have been so attracted on Sundays, that they would come to services. Eight years ago six Mormons would not enter our little church in twelve months. Today many attend regularly on Sundays. The impression existing in their minds regarding the Church, her services, and ceremonies is fast disappearing, and they no longer see her that terrible institution so much to be dreaded, as they were wont to regard her, nor are afraid to entrust their children to the charge of her schools. As a rule the Mormons are no more more bigoted against the Catholic, than against the Protestant, whatever bigotry they do possess is inherited by them from Protestant ancestary [*sic*] rather than taught to them by the Mormon Church.

Here in Salt Lake, with less pecuniary aid, and less influence, than any Protestant church, when once established, the Catholic Church has shown more vitality, than all other churches combined. In 1874 with our school or hospital in Salt Lake, the Protestant Episcopal Church (Church of England) had three schools, and one hospital with an annuity of over twenty thousand dollars a year for their support, and the influence of the richest of the non-Mormon residents of the place to back them up. The Methodist Episcopal society had the largest church, save the Mormon tabernacle, in Salt Lake, and a flourishing school with an annuity of over twelve thousand dollars a year for their support. The Presbyterians had their church and school with salaried elders, and teachers to carry on the mission. The Congregationalists enjoyed the same advantages. The Catholic Church alone was poor, depending on the voluntary contributions of a few poor Catholics, who were to be found travelling through the Territory or in the fastness of the mountains searching for their fortune.

To see the Church then as she really was, and contrast her with the Protestant, and let that contrast run along those years, that have marked the rise and growth of all non Mormon churches, one can not fail to perceive in that contrast the vitality of the

Catholic Church, in her vitality will be seen her strength, in her strength her truth. Her school, in Salt Lake today, is the finest and most flourishing in the city. Today she possesses the finest and grandest hospital, not in Utah, but within a radius of a thousand miles, and this hospital, it must be remembered, was founded at a time when no apparent means of support were to be had. St. Mark's Hospital under the auspices of the Protestant Episcopal Church was founded three years previous. The support, and influence of the non-Mormon population were on their side. They had possession of all that was worth possessing at the time, and the Sisters opening their hospital in 1875 had to depend solely on their own merits and ability to conduct an hospital. Once opened they had to engage in a fair contest, in an open field, with their more fortunate rivals, the Protestant Episcopalians. Public opinion, basing its judgment on the good accomplished by both institutions, was to decide which institution was superior. The work of the past seven years has decided the contest; for whilst the Protestant hospital has advanced but little, the Sisters' hospital has extended its salutary influence through Utah and the adjoining Territories. The former has nothing, save a small brick building, never intended for hospital use, to show the public as the result of its labor, and economy; the latter has succeeded in obtaining of a whole block of land (10 acres) in the healthiest part of the city, and within the past eighteen months, erected thereon the finest hospital, as already remarked, within a radius of a thousand miles. Protestants are wont to boast of their superiority over Catholics, but here in Salt Lake we apply the argument, from which there is no appeal, "*contra factum non datur argumentum.*"

In Salt Lake the Sisters' school is the most flourishing and prosperous in the city. Not only is it self sustaining, but they have been able to save sufficient, to enable them to commence, next spring, an addition to their already large building, a work much needed for the accommodation of its many, and constantly increasing boarders, and day pupils. Of all the mission schools in Salt Lake, it alone is self sustaining, as it grows older, it grows more in favor with the public. Here again can be seen how a Catholic institution can gain the ascendancy over Protestant institutions, even though the latter possess more advantages, which they do possess in Salt Lake City, first in pecuniary matters, and secondly and principally in not having to fight that prejudice entertained by infidels against the Catholic Church. The works, and workings of the Catholic Church we present to all non-Catholics, and say to them, "if you believe not our church believe her works." This argument is not without its effect upon the thinking, and unprejudiced public, and more than once have men of reason and intelligence, [remarked], "whatever truth, there is in religion, is to be found in the Catholic, and her institutions." I herewith send slips taken from papers published in this city, showing that greater praise is lavished on our schools by non-Catholics than I could bestow.

—Ogden—

The prosperous condition of the Salt Lake mission applies equally to Ogden, the second prominent city in Utah. The school conducted by the Sisters is in a flourishing condition, and receives pupils from points 400 and 500 miles from Ogden. In 1875 a three story frame building 50 ft. x 50 ft. was erected there. Very Rev. Scanlan, at the time, but little expected, that so large a building would not be more than sufficient for many years to accommodate all who would apply there for instruction. During the present years the numerous applicants as boarders was such, that the building was no longer sufficiently large, and a new two story building 50 ft. x 24 ft. was erected during the present year to make ample room for the accommodation of all applicants. As with Salt Lake, so also is it in Ogden. When contrasted with Protestant churches, her beauty, and grandeur, and superiority show themselves in her institutions. The last in the race, she is today the most prominent among the non-Mormon churches in Ogden.

In 1874, 75 and 76 when I visited Ogden monthly to say Mass, for a few poor Catholics, there was no church or school. Mass then was celebrated in a hall owned by the Spiritists. In this little hall Mass was celebrated for three years monthly, and during those years, often I did not have more than four persons in attendance, and the congregation never reached twenty persons. Catholics, long removed from Catholic influence were ashamed to identify themselves with the few Catholics then there, and not till the Church emerged from her nothingness, made her power and influence felt did they like the strayed sheep return to the flock, and today are good practical Catholics. The prominence, which the Church possess[es] today in Ogden, and the good, accomplished there during the past five years, are first traceable to your noble society, and to you gentlemen every Catholic in Ogden owe[s] a debt of gratitude for first helping them to secure a lot and build a church, which they themselves, no matter how freely they gave could [not] accomplish. From Ogden I pass to

—Silver Reef—

375 miles south east of Salt Lake is a little mining camp called Silver Reef. In 1877 Very Rev. Father Scanlan first visited this place. Being the first priest, who visited there, he was received with open arms by the Catholics of the place. Having sojourned there for two weeks, he found the people well disposed, and willing to aid him in any work he would undertake for the Church. He determined, after returning to Salt Lake, and arranging other missionary work, which was progressing at the time, to go back to Silver Reef, and commence the erection of a church. This he did in the early part of 1878, and very soon his labors were crowned with success; for in three months he succeeded in building a church and hospital. Since 1878 a priest and four Sisters have been in charge of the mission. In connection with the hospital, the Sisters have a school, where the Catholic children of the district are being educated.

Traveling from Silver Reef to Salt Lake over bleak mountains, and barren rolling land is to be met another mining camp, whose inbabitants are largely composed of Catholics. It is called

—Frisco—

In 1880 a little church was commenced and finished in this little town. Previous to its erection, the priest, who visited there occasionally, was subject to great inconveniences, trying to secure a suitable place to offer up the adorable sacrifice of the Mass, [or] hear confessions. On one occasion, the writer, when about to celebrate Mass, had to hear the confession of a good Catholic in the open air, for want of a more suitable place, the hall in which I was about to celebrate Mass, being filled with people, many of whom were non-Catholics. This inconvenience, thanks to God, no longer exists, and we have today in Frisco a nice church.

During a visit there last May, a prominent resident of the place, and a school trustee, asked if the Catholics would accept the public school of the place, and send Sisters to take charge of same.

I mention this fact to show that the good work being done by the Sisters in Salt Lake, Ogden and Silver Reef, is appreciated far beyond, the limits of these places, and to show also how their Christian example, and the moral and intellectual good accomplished by them in the past seven years are extending into the most remote and isolated parts of the Territory of Utah. Next in order is a thriving little town called

—Park City—

About 40 miles south east of Salt Lake at the foothills of the Wasatch Mountains is Park City with a population of 3000 inhabitants. Here within the past twelve months a new church with a parsonage has been erected. Last May Archbishop Alemany came from San Francisco, a distance of a thousand miles to dedicate the new church, and administer the sacrament of Confirmation. Notwithstanding the length of [the] journey and his fatigue, age and travelling, he felt that he was amply rewarded, and more than once expressed his surprise and agreeable disappointment to find in Utah, in the vastness of the mountains, so many Catholics. Hardy miners living in the mountains for years, and innured to hardship came to see the Archbishop. It was the first time in the history of the place, that a Catholic Bishop visited the place, and it was the first opportunity for years afforded many, to see a Bishop of the Catholic Church. Among the numbers who were attracted to come to see his Grace, were many who approached the sacraments, and who would not otherwise do so. On Sunday he administered the Sacrament of Confirmation to over thirty persons, many of whom were adults. Being pleased with the Catholic spirit manifested by the people, and having heard the expressed wish of some among them, that a Catholic school should be there, to help them to educate their children in the principles of the Catholic faith, his Grace promised that he would try and get the Sisters to come, and take charge of a school. Faithful to his promise, he succeeded, and a school was opened there in the middle of September which is largely patronized by non-Catholic children since its opening.

This is a brief recapitulation of the history of the Catholic Church in Utah during the past eight years. It shows what has been done. Much has been done. The many churches, schools, and hospitals which dot the territory today are an exemplification of the parable of the mustard seed. Though much has been done in the past, much yet remains to be done, and whilst it is gratifying to be able to report the great progress of the Catholic Church in Utah, as shown in her churches, schools and hospitals, it is the earnest wish of every priest in the mission, to see established in those same missions much needed Catholic institutions.

In Salt Lake City is one of the finest and most promising openings for a "brothers day and boarding school," that could be wished for. This institution established, the Salt Lake mission would be well provided for, and the priests' earnest wish would be no dream of life but a glad reality. Ogden offers, if not better, at least a good inducement for a similar institution.

Catholic parents wishing to send their boys to a Catholic boarding school, and young Catholic men who work during the summer and wish to attend school in the winter, (of this latter class many are to be found in the mining camps) have no means of satisfying their wishes in Utah, nor nearer than San Francisco in the West, and Omaha in the East. The result thus far bas been that many, who would gladly avail themselves of a Catholic school, go through necessity to the Protestant schools of this city. Protestants, realizing the great necessity of such schools, have made provisions for boarding as well as educating young men. We are last in the field, in this much needed institution, but we hope, D[eo] V[olente] with a little outside [assistance] to be able to report another flourishing institution for young men, and our Protestant competitors first in the race last at the goal. Notwithstanding the number of priests in the Territory and the number of miles travelled annually by each one of them, there are yet in this Territory places so far removed from civilization that a priest has never visited them; and strange yet true in those remote places are to be found Catholics, with grown families, over whose heads the regenerating water of Baptism was never poured. Only last week an instance of this kind came under my notice, whilst travelling in a wild unsettled district. At a small station a young man stepped into the car, in which I was seated. He looked at me for some time, evidently wishing to speak, but apparently afraid to do so. I said to him. "Well my boy are you belonging to this place?" He answered, "No I belong to the coal mines way up in the mountains. Are you a Catholic priest?" he asked. When I answered "yes" with a tear in his eye he said to me, "Well priest I am a Catholic. My mother always tells me [to] say I am a Roman Catholic, and I do say it, when the Mormons ask me to what Church I belong."

"Do you go to your duty?" I asked, and to my surprise the reply I got was: "What is that?" I next asked, "Do you go to the sacraments?" and here my surprise was still greater when he replied, "And what are these?" I said to him, "Why my boy did you not tell me you were a Catholic," and here he interupted [sic] me saying, "Yes, yes, I am and my mother always tells me [to] say I am a Catholic." "And you do not know what the sacraments are." He answered, "No"

"Baptism is a sacrament," I remarked, "you were baptized." He told me, "No." I asked his age. He said he was 17 years. His mother had always told him, when an opportunity offered be would be baptized, and as a proof that Catholic instinct was impressed on him poor boy, before parting with me said, "If I go to you tonight will you baptize me?"

This is one of the many cases that comes to our notice occasionally. It will show the necessity of establishing other missions, to increase the facilities of reaching the most distant places. All the missions, thus far established, are doing a good work, and others, which will do as much, [can] be established, as soon as circumstances and the means entrusted to the Very Rev. Father Scanlan's charge will permit.

For what has been done thus far pray accept the thanks, and gratitude of every Catholic in Utah, and a share in the prayers of your unworthy but ever grateful child in Jesus Christ.

26

"Buffalo Bill's Baptism" is the subject of this short essay which was published in the *Records of the American Catholic Historical Society* LXXIX (December, 1968), 243-244.

The initial meeting between Christopher V. Walsh (1877-1961) and William Frederick Cody (1846-1917) took place in Ireland during one of Buffalo Bill's tours with his Wild West Show. Walsh subsequently emigrated to Canada where he entered Montreal's Grand Seminaire as a clerical student for the Diocese of Denver. After his ordination in 1905. the young priest was sent to a mining area where he was forced to perfect his abilities as an outdoorsman.

It was on a hunting trip that Father Walsh again encountered Buffalo Bill. The two became close friends and spent many hours discussing religious views. On January 7, 1917, Father Walsh was summoned to a small bedroom at 2932 Lafayette Street in Colorado's capital. There he found the famous Indian scout hovering near death. Buffalo Bill requested and received the Sacrament of Baptism from the Irish-born priest and died three days later.

In the years that followed Father Walsh was besieged with questions about his noted convert and the circumstances surrounding his demise. Generally, he declined to comment. The following letter, probably composed at the behest of Bishop J. Henry Tihen, was written to T. F. Hughes on June 13, 1927, from Walsh's Church of Saint Louis in Denver. The original was presented to Monsignor John Tracy Ellis by Father Lamar J. Genovar on May 8, 1957. It is reproduced here through the courtesy of the Department of Archives and Manuscripts of the Catholic University of America.

The Rt. Rev. Bishop has turned over to me your letter of inquiry in regard to Wm. F. Cody (Buffalo Bill).

In answer to your question as to whether he was a Catholic during life and whether he died a Catholic I wish to state that the gentleman in question was not a Catholic—not even ever baptized untill [sic] I was called to his bed-side in his last illness and there administered the Catholic rite of Baptism and prepared him for a Catholic death. You further ask whether he was buried a Catholic! Yes, he was buried as a Catholic, but not with Catholic services. It was his expressed wish that his body be interred on *Top of Lookout Mountain,* near Denver, and overlooking the vast plains over which he had in life so often roamed.

The Elks (B.P.O.E.) had charge of his funeral services—also by his wish, tho [sic] the masons tried *hard* and *long* to claim they had charge, as they also tried too, to discredit his conversion to the Catholic Faith.

You know Buffalo was a unique character and the masons to whom he had belonged hated very much to lose [him] in death.

All this happened in the early part of 1917. At that time all the papers and other publications were just full of the happenings—and no doubt their *files* even now have the "clippings."

I am glad to send you these salient facts—tho [sic] brief—in regards to your request.

The Bishop referred your letter to me because I was the priest-friend of "Bill."

27

"The Development of Ecclesiastical Jurisdiction in the Californias" is the title of this essay which appeared in the *Records of the American Catholic Historical Society* LXXV (June, 1964.), 93-102

Ecclesiastical jurisdiction grants a licitly consecrated bishop "the right and the duty to govern his diocese both in spiritual and temporal affairs and to this end he possesses legislative, judicial and coercive power...."[1] As it developed in the Californias, episcopal jurisdiction was in no way connected with nor descended from the ecclesiastical organization set up in the eastern part of the nation when John Carroll was elevated to the episcopate at the hands of Charles Walmesley, O.S.B., Vicar Apostolic of England's Western District. Nor did the extensive French influence of Francis Montmorency Laval and his successors at Quebec have any casual relation with the jurisdiction vested in Francisco Garcia Diego y Moreno, O.F.M., named to the Diocese of Both Californias in 1840.

Traditionally, the Church has opposed establishment of hierarchies in areas where scarcity of people and poverty of means entail a lack of proper support for diocesan government. In the absence of such assurance, temporary measures are employed such as the erection of vicariates or prefectures apostolic, both of which are similar, in varying degrees, to the diocesan system. In some parts of the New World, however, a unique plan was devised whereby the normal powers of a bishop were delegated to an apostolic college. Historically, these foundations were an outgrowth of legislation issued by Leo X who, in 1521, gave broad faculties to the

Franciscans permitting them to preach, administer the sacraments, absolve from reserved sins and to settle practically all types of marriage cases in missionary fields, all independent of the diocesan system.

In Mexico, three apostolic colleges operated along these lines: Santa Cruz de Queretaro (1683), Nuestra Señora de Guadalupe at Zacatecas (1706) and San Fernando in Mexico City (1734), all subject directly to the Commissary General of the Indies. Each college was autonomous and functioned only in those missionary districts designated and approved by the Commissariate. It was understood that the special faculties given to the colleges were transitory, for the Holy See envisioned the eventual erection of normal diocesan curiae as soon as that became feasible. With an understanding of the system used in California, it is easy to understand why the lack of a bishop in the area did not become a matter of concern or even interest to the friars until governmental secularization undermined the collegial system and forced the friars to reappraise their whole concept of administration.

Vice Royalty of New Spain

It has long been a legend in the Franciscan Order that Fray Juan Perez,[2] the Prior of La Rabida, actually came with Columbus to the New World as chaplain on the first voyage in 1492.[3] However, legend it must remain since no evidence to substantiate the claim can be found either in the ships' journal or in any of the accounts written by contemporary chroniclers. A similar tradition among the Mercedarians relates how one of their number, a certain Juan de Solorazano de Aguilar, accompanied the "admiral of the ocean sea" on the maiden trip.[4] But here again, a search of Spanish archives fails to corroborate the tale.[5] A third priest is mentioned, one Pedro de Arenas, whose *Relacion del Venerable Sacerdote Pedro de Arenas que fue el Primer Sacerdote que digo la Primer Misa en las Indias accompanado a Colon* was discovered in the National Library at Madrid in 1891 by the Jesuit historian, Fidel Fita.[6] Current opinion among historians, however, is well stated by Samuel Eliot Morison who dismisses the subject by noting that "certain pious souls, worried by the absence of a priest, have tried to invent one."[7]

There is no question regarding the chaplains on Columbus' second voyage. The Spanish monarchs and Alexander VI

> took pains to provide missionary priests for the evangelization of the native races. Their choice of a leader for the band of preachers shows with what care the selection was made. A friend of St. Francis of Paula, the Benedictine Bernard Boyl, was the first apos-

tle of the New World. In the brief of 25th June, 1493, Alexander VI conferred upon this distinguished and in every way most competent man and his twelve companions, all the powers and privileges which they needed for their holy enterprise. Amongst his companions may be mentioned the celebrated Bartholomeo Las Casas, Fray Jorge, Commander of Knights of Santiago, and Pedro de Arenas, who is supposed to have said the first Mass ever celebrated on the newly discovered islands.[8]

It is clear from the papal brief, *Pius Fidelium*, that the new Vicariate Apostolic of the New World did not belong to or depend on the Metropolitan See of Seville but rather directly on Rome itself. In 1493 Boyl[9] came with Columbus to Hispanola where he put into operation the first canonically organized church in America. Boyl's tremendously broad jurisdiction extended to "those lands and islands which have been recently discovered…in the western regions and the oceanic sea, previously unknown to others as well as those that may yet be discovered."[10]

For some unknown reason, Boyl's mission proved wholly unsuccessful and late in 1494 he returned to Spain where he quickly dropped out of the annals of history. Another papal mandate was sought by King Ferdinand for a successor to Boyl but no action was taken during the next seventeen years, owing in part to friction over distributing emoluments accruing from the newly organized colonies. Religious activities, nonetheless, continued in the New World as is evidenced by a royal *capitulacion* issued on April 10, 1495 ordering "religious men to be sent over to administer the sacraments and to endeavor to convert the Indians."[11]

In the meantime, the power of the Spanish sovereigns over the ecclesiastical revenues and affairs continued to grow and by the early part of the 16th century, "…through usurpation, through custom, and finally through explicit papal recognition the crown had obtained an enormous power over the Church in (its) dominions, a power that came dangerously near to making the Church in Spain independent of Rome."[12] A long series of papal grants, beginning in 1482, gave the royal family effective control over all missionary appointments and disbursements.[13] Individual missionaries still had to receive jurisdiction either from the ordinary of their diocese of incardination or the major superior of the province to which they belonged, but all appointments came directly from the government.

METROPOLITAN PROVINCE OF SEVILLE
SUFFRAGAN DIOCESES IN THE VICE-ROYALTY OF NEW SPAIN
(1511-1545)

DIOCESE	PLACE	DATE	PONTIFICATE	PRELATE
Santo Domingo	Haiti	August 8, 1511	Julius II	Francisco Garcia de Padilla
Concepcio de la Vega	Haiti	August 8, 1511	Julius II	Pedro Suarez de Deza
San Juan	Puerto Rico	August 8, 1511	Julius II	Alonso Manso
Carolina*	Yukatan	January 24, 1519	Leo X	Julian de Garces
Baraçoa	Santiago	April 28, 1522	Hadrian VI	Juan de Umite
Tlaxcala	Puebla	October 13, 1525	Clement VII	Julian de Garces
Rio de las Palmas	Florida	1527	Clement VII	Juan Suarez
Mexico City	Mexico	September 2, 1530	Clement VII	Juan de Zumarraga
Comayagua	Honduras	1527†	Clement VII	Cristobal Pedraza
Leon	Nicaragua	February 25, 1531	Clement VII	Alvarez de Osorio
Coro	Venezuela	June 21, 1531	Clement VII	Roderigo de Bastidas
Santiago	Guatemala	January 18, 1534	Paul III	Francisco Marroquin
Antequer	Oaxaca	June 21, 1535	Paul III	Lopez de Zarate
Michoacan	Michoacan	August 18, 1536	Paul III	Vasco de Quiroga
Chiapas	Chiapas	April 14, 1538	Paul III	Juan de Artega

* Supressed. Julian de Garces was later appointed to Tlaxcala. In 1561 Pius IV
  appointed Francisco de Toral to the newly formed Diocese of Yucatan.
† Action confirmed by Paul III in 1531.

An abortive attempt was made by Pope Julius II in 1504 to establish an independent hierarchy for the New World. His bull, *Illius fulciti* of November 15th created the Metropolitan Province of Hispanola with the Archdiocese of Hyaguata and the two suffragan sees of Magna and Bayuna. But the unwise geographical choice of these areas and the obstinancy of the Spanish crown thwarted papal plans for several years and only on August 8, 1511, was an agreement reached whereby the three sees erected in 1504 were suppressed and those of Santo Domingo and Concepcion de la Vega in Hispanola and San Juan in Puerto Rico were erected and attached as suffragans to the Archdiocese of Seville.[14] With the consecration of the earlier named prelates, the history of ecclesiastical jurisdiction in the New World began.

The Vice Royalty of New Spain, established by Charles V in 1535, was divided into four *audiencias;* Hispanola, Mexico, Guatemala and Nueva Galicia. These districts were further portioned off into seventeen or eighteen provinces or states and it was around these latter areas that future ecclesiastical divisions took their delimitations.[15]

The *Audiencia* of Mexico is of special interest to the development of ecclesiastical jurisdiction in California. In 1524[16] it received its first vicar apostolic in the person of Father Martin de Valencia. The following year Pope Clement VII set up the Diocese of Tlaxcala and five years later that of Mexico City. By 1538 the chain of ecclesiastical centers in the *audiencia* was complete:

(1) Diocese of Tlaxcala[17] 1525
(2) Diocese of Mexico City 1530
(3) Diocese of Comayagua 1531
(4) Diocese of Leon 1531
(5) Diocese of Santiago..1534
(6) Diocese of Antequara...1535
(7) Diocese of Michoacan...1536
(8) Diocese of Chiapas...1539

Though second in point of foundation, Mexico City soon became the most important of all the sees created in New Spain. Located in the center of the old Aztec kingdom and surrounded by the remnants of an ancient culture, its magnificient new cathedral was to be the "mother church" of the Californias for the next 309 years. When, at the solicitation of Charles V, Pope Paul III separated the Mexican dioceses from the Province of Seville in 1545, erecting the metropolitan district of Mexico City, the suffragan dioceses of New Spain began to multiply so rapidly that by the end of the 16th century they included those of Guadalajara (1548), Verapaz in Guatemala (1556) and Manila in the Philippines (1581). At the close of the 18th century, all the sees outside Mexico had been withdrawn from the province, and other jurisdictions added, including those of Durango (1620), Linares or Monterrey (1777) and Sonora (1779).

Jurisdiction in California

Episcopal authority in Baja California dates from the mid-point of the 17th century, for by 1681 "spiritual jurisdiction over the Peninsula...was in dispute between Juan Garabito, Bishop of Guadalajara and Fray Bartolomew de Escanuela, Bishop of Durango."[18] Bartholomew contended that the area belonged to his Diocese of Nueva Viscaya and went so far as to delegate faculties to California-bound missionaries. He was later rebuked and told not to meddle in peninsular affairs. From that time onwards, Baja California was considered part of the Guadalajara jurisdiction.

As far as Alta California is concerned, there was no formal statement prior to 1779 that it belonged to any diocese.[19] However, on the grounds that unassigned territories could be claimed by the nearest bishop *(Por cercania)*, Bishop Marcarulla of Durango followed the pattern of his predecessor and sent a letter to Fray Junipero Serra in 1776 claiming authority over all future Spanish settlements in California.

Whatever be the validity of his contention, documentary evidences of episcopal jurisdiction in Alta California can only be traced from May 7, 1779, when Pius VI issued the bull *Innumera divinae* erecting the Diocese of Sonora, which at that time encompassed the states of Sinaloa and Sonora as well as the two Californias.[20] The new bishop, Antonio de los Reyes, O.F.M., a suffragan of Mexico City and his successors had the *de jure* responsibility of caring for the spiritual needs of California even though there are no indications that incumbents of that see ever visited the area. Nor should this lack of concern cause any wonderment since the bishops were aware of the missionary activity and considered it quite sufficient for the natives and what few white colonists were there. Several instances are recorded of bishops of Sonora sending broad faculties to the missionary *presidentes* who were frequently named Vicars General for California.[21]

With the approval of the Mexican Government's request for a separate diocesan curia in the Californias, the Holy See stipulated that "the said California Church thus constituted shall be of right subject to the Metropolitan Archbishop of Mexico enjoying all the faculties, exemptions and rights which belong to the other suffragans of the Metropolitan Mexican Church."[22] Hence, on April 27, 1840, the area comprising the Diocese of Both Californias was given canonical autonomy and removed from any adherence to the See of Sonora. The territorial limits of the new diocese was extensive in scope. Neither the first bishop, Francisco Garcia Diego y Moreno nor his Dominican successor, Joseph Sadoc Alemany, ever visited Baja California but the peninsula remained a part of the jurisdiction until 1853 when it reverted to the Metropolitan Province of Mexico City.[23]

The change of sovereignty in California in the late 1840's made reorganization of ecclesiastical boundaries necessary and a decree from the Sacred Congregation of Propaganda Fide, dated January 20, 1852, notified Bishop Alemany of the new arrangement:

> Since the Episcopal See of Monterey in the region of California in the United States of America is presently a suffragan of the Metropolitan See of Mexico, and because it now appears that the

region desires to participate in the synods which are held in the United States of America...the aforesaid See of Monterey is released from its attachment to its former Metropolitan See...[24]

On the following July 29th, acting on the advice of the First Council of Baltimore,[25] Rome erected a separate province in California "to provide for the orderly administration and the welfare of souls."[26] With this action, Alta California was divided into two jurisdictions,[27] the Archdiocese of San Francisco and the smaller suffragan Diocese of Monterey. Those parts of the archdiocese which later became separate sees were: Sacramento (1886)[28] Salt Lake City (1891),[29] Reno (1931), Oakland (1962), Santa Rosa (1962) and Stockton (1962). The southern jurisdiction of Monterey-Los Angeles[30] remained intact until 1922 when it was divided into the Dioceses of Monterey-Fresno and Los Angeles-San Diego. In 1936 California received its second province when Los Angeles was raised to archiepiscopal rank and given as its suffragans the Sees of Monterey-Fresno, San Diego and Tucson.

And so it is that within little more than a century, the original ecclesiastical jurisdiction grew from a single unit into twelve, the only state in the Union boasting of two distinct metropolitan districts. Already in January of 1953 when a member of the state's hierarchy became a Prince of the Church and member of the College of Cardinals, it could be said that "the Church in California had come of age!"

Notes to the Text

1. *Codex Juris Canonicis* (Rome, 1959), C. 335.
2. Juan Perez is credited with obtaining the backing of the royal court for Columbus' journey to the New World.
3. This legend dates from 1587. See J. I. Rodriguez. "The Friars in the West Indians," *American Catholic Quarterly Review* XVII (October, 1892), 797.
4. See Pedro de Nolasco, *Religiosos de la Merced que pasaron a la American Espanola* (Seville, 1923), I, 17.
5. See Rob. Streit, O.M.I. *Bibliotheca Missionum* [Americanische Missionsliteratur] (Aachen, 1924), II 1.
6. Reprinted in the *Boletin* de la Academia de la Historia XVIII (1891), 551-554.
7. *Admiral of the Ocean Sea* (Boston, 1942), II, 193.
8. Herman J. Heuser, "The Establishment of the First Vicariate in America, A.D. 1493," *Records of the American Catholic Historical Society* VII (1896), 147-154.
9. The identity of this man has been debated for centuries. His name is spelled in various ways, *viz.*, Boil, Boyl, Boyle, etc. and Spanish historians have discovered three contemporary ecclesiastics bearing the same name. There was Bernal Boyl, Abbot of Cuxa; Bernal Boyl, a Benedictine; and Bernal Boyl, a Minim, all of whom might have been the same person at different stages of his life. It has even been suggested that King Ferdinand might have altered the name in the original papal brief to another. See E. Ward Laoughran, "The First Vicar Apostolic of the New World," *American Ecclesiastical Review* LXXXII (January, 1930), 1-13.
10. Herman J. Heuser, *op. cit.*, 151.

11. Antonio de Herrera, *General History of the Vast Continent and Islands of America* (London, 1725), I, 156.
12. Edwin A. Ryan, "Diocesan Organization in the Spanish Colonies," *Catholic Historical Review II* (April, 1916), 149.
13. Collectively known as the *Patronato Real.*
14. The bishops appointed to the earlier suppressed sees were then given royal confirmation and told to take possession of the new jurisdictions
15. Herbert E. Bolton and T. M. Marshall, *The Colonization of North America* (New York, 1920), p. 75-76.
16. Mariano Cuevas, O.F.M., *Historia de la Iglesia en Mexico* (Texas, 1928), I, 165.
17. See Emeterio Valverde Tellez, *Bio-Bibliografia Eclesiastica Mexicana* (1821-1943), (Mexico, 1949).
18. Herbert E. Bolton, *Rim of Christendom*, (New York, 1960), p. 93.
19. Father Antonio de los Reyes, O.F.M., in a proposal to the Council of the Indies, June 30, 1777, stated his opinion that Texas, Coahuila and all of California belonged to Guadalajara. This view was shared by Felipe de Neve but Junipero Serra and the College of San Fernando thought that it belonged neither to Guadalajara nor to Durango but was pure mission territory outside any diocese.
20. Maynard J. Geiger, O.F.M. ventures the opinion that "Spain should have asked for a bishop for the Californias, considering the huge territory, even though churches were few and the income nothing. See *Life and Times of Junipero Serra* (Washington, 1959), II, 344.
21. On September 30, 1796, for example, Bishop Francisco Rouset granted broad faculties to Father *Presidente* Fermin Lasuen. See Frances J. Weber, *Pioneer Catholicism in the Californias* (Van Nuys, 1961), p. 32.
22. Archives of the Archdiocese of Los Angeles, Lambruschini to Garcia Diego, Rome, April 27, 1840.
23. *El Vicariato Apostolico de Baja California* (Mexico, 1938), p. 4.
24. Archives of the Archdiocese of San Francis, Fransoni to Alemany, Rome, January 20, 1852.
25. Peter K. Guilday, *History of the Councils of Baltimore* (New York, 1932), p. 188-189.
26. Santa Barbara Mission Archives, #III, 20, Papal Bull, Rome, July 29, 1853.
27. The earlier boundaries were Mexico on the south; the Colorado River on the east; the 42° of north latitude (Oregon boundary) and the Pacific Ocean on the west.
28. The Vicariate of Marysville was created in 1860. It was elevated to diocesan status under the title of Grass Valley in 1868.
29. The Vicariate of Utah dates from 1886.
30. Title of the see was changed to Monterey-Los Angeles in 1859.

28

This survey article on "California's Catholic Heritage Almost Reaches Second Century" is here taken from the *Central California Register* for December 14, 1967.

The beginnings of Catholicism in California date from the explorations of Juan Rodriquez Cabrillo in 1542 and Sebastian Vizcaino in 1602. These representatives of a Catholic power were accompanied by priests who celebrated Holy Mass on California shores over three centuries ago.

In a more proximate and particular sense, California's Catholic Heritage began with the establishment of Mission San Diego de Alcala by Fray Junipero Serra on July 16, 1769. During the ensuing fifty-four years, 98,055 Baptisms were recorded in the registers of California's missions and *asistencias*, an impressive figure if one recalls this was done for a people only a few generations removed from the Stone Age.

The decline of the missions was rapid, resulting as it did from "secularization," the legal process of removing the establishments from the administration of the Franciscan friars. From 1834 when a plan was inaugurated by the authorities for the "temporal welfare and spiritual interest of the Indians," lands and herds were expropriated by private parties, and even churches were sold or leased without sanction of law or justice.

Ecclesiastical jurisdiction in the Golden State stretches back to 1836 when the Mexican Congress enacted a formal resolution seeking canonical status for the California missions. Four years later, on April 27, 1840, the Holy See created the Diocese of Both Californias.

The newly created bishop, Francisco Garcia Diego y Moreno, succeeded in erecting a seminary at Santa Ines on land given to the Church by Governor Micheltorena but was able to do little else in his short episcopate. Worn out by efforts to better conditions in California, the Franciscan prelate died at Santa Barbara on April 30, 1846, at the relatively early age of sixty.

Administration of the vast diocese thereupon passed into the hands of Father Gonzalez Rubio, O.F.M. who for the next four and a half years ruled the jurisdiction as vicar capitular. Rubio witnessed a great change in the life and fortunes of California in that comparatively brief period for he had hardly begun his duties when war broke out between Mexico and the United States, a struggle which culminated in the raising of the stars and stripes at Monterey on July 7, 1846. With that act, a new chapter began and the part which the Catholic Church has played since has been nothing less than phenomenal.

An epochal event in 1848 brought on a new era in the economic and political character of California and greatly altered its historic future. Indeed, the discovery of gold at Coloma produced national excitement and news of the event spread to the farthest corners of the globe. So great was the resulting influx of fortune seekers and adventurers that the population of California swelled up past 100,000 within two years.

Unexpected and perplexing problems brought on by the emigration faced the leaders of the Church and demanded immediate action. The handful of clergy then in the diocese was far too sparse to care for the spiritual wants of so many people. And while the southern districts of the state were left substantially unaffected for a time, even that area required more care than could be given by Father Rubio.

In 1849, the diocese was re-designated Monterey and, in June of the following year, a new bishop was consecrated for California in the person of Joseph Sadoc Alemany. The Dominican prelate had been a missionary to scattered groups of Catholics in the rural districts of the east and midwest. Arriving in the Golden State shortly after its admission to the Union, Alemany's excellent executive ability was soon at work on the formidable tasks then facing the Church in California. Rubio had several religious orders working on the scene and the bishop continued his predecessor's policies in that regard.

One of the first permanent results of Alemany's plans was the establishment of Santa Clara College by the Society of Jesus in 1851 followed a few years later by the opening of Saint Ignatius in San Francisco. The bishop introduced several communities of nuns to California and a program of orphanages and academies for girls was inaugurated. Plans for the erection of hospitals were put forward to cope with the needs of the rapidly developing state.

It wasn't too long before important jurisdictional changes affected Bishop Alemany's activities. The peninsula of Baja California was withdrawn from his care since the Holy See recognized the complexities of ruling a diocese with area in two separate countries. The southern part of the state, notwithstanding a small migration of Americans, remained predominantly Spanish in language and custom.

Indians, scattered through the deserts and mountains, were often unruly and a partial answer to the question posed by these and other problems seemed to be a readjustment of diocesan boundaries, thus reducing the handicaps brought about by distance and poor communications. On July 29, 1853, the Diocese of Monterey was divided and a new province established at San Francisco with Alemany as metropolitan archbishop. To head the smaller Diocese of Monterey, the Sacred Congregation of Propaganda Fide appointed Father Thaddeus Amat, C.M. Like Alemany, a native of Catalonia, Amat's activities in the United States had been mostly in Louisiana, Missouri and Pennsylvania where he had toiled for fifteen years. He spoke English fluently and his knowledge of Spanish stood him in good stead for the apostolate in that part of California where the scattered Catholic population still clung to the Spanish language.

The "cow counties" of Southern California in the 1860's and 1870's were so designated, not in derision, but because that sobriquet actually described their chief source of wealth, cattle raising. There were horticultural interests too but everything depended on seasonal rainfall which was as inadequate as it was unpredictable. Hence it was only logical that the population increased slowly, isolated as that area was from outside influences. The surviving mission Indians, nearly all congregated in the south, became easy prey for exploiters whose intemperance they imitated.

This was the Southern California that faced Thaddeus Amat when he arrived in the fall of 1855. Fewer than a score of priests were serving those few churches managing to outlast the ruin of the missions. But to Amat there were unmistakable indications of better things. He had obtained several clerical students in Europe and within a few months some of these were ready for ordination. He brought the Daughters of

Charity to Los Angeles in 1856, and opened the first school and orphanage and two years later a hospital. In 1858, the tireless bishop went abroad to seek additional aid in Europe and again was able to acquire a fair number of recruits for the ministry.

The following year he asked for and was given authorization to move the episcopal seat to Los Angeles and to include that city's name in the official diocesan title. A seminary was high on the prelate's priority list but was thwarted for some additional decades. The bishop saw the opening of Saint Vincent's College at Los Angeles in 1865, an institution which continued for the next forty-six years as the nucleus of higher learning for Southern California.

At the conclusion of his first decade in the Golden State, Bishop Amat could point to the advancement of Catholic interests in a number of areas. The United States Land Commission, for instance, had confirmed the Church's claim to the missions and certain of their adjacent properties and as sixteen of the missions were within the limits of the Diocese of Monterey-Los Angeles. Amat became the principal beneficiary of this favorable decision. Even though some of the old institutions were in ruins, repair work made most of them serviceable and the venerable old churches once again became population centers of their day, stimulating the establishment of schools, hospitals and orphanages in the decades that followed.

There were perhaps 30,000 Catholics in the diocese in 1861, as compared to 125,000 in the Archdiocese of San Francisco and 30,000 in the Vicariate Apostolic of Marysville. The Civil War had little effect on Southern California in a military sense, although the old army posts set up after the conquest remained and continued to exert considerable economic influence in the region. In 1869, Archbishop Alemany, Bishop Amat and Bishop Eugene O'Connell set out for Rome and the First Vatican Council. Upon Amat's return he began a cathedral in Los Angeles and the edifice, dedicated to Saint Vibiana, was completed and consecrated in 1876.

The decade of the 1870's was a troubled one for Southern California. The disasterous drought of 1873-1874 ruined the cattle-raising economy and in 1876-1877 a second dry period virtually destroyed the sheep-raising business in many parts of the state. A financial crisis supervened in 1875, but within five years a process of slow recovery had set in and affairs gradually returned to their earlier status. A long illness forced Bishop Amat in 1883 to ask for a coadjutor in the person of Francis Mora, one of the priests who had come from Catalonia with Amat in

1855. The bishop's health continued to decline and he succumbed on May 12th, 1878. Bishop Mora immediately took up the reins of the diocese and proved to be a man of conservative and sound judgment. He presided over the jurisdiction during the crucial years that saw the first large population shift in Southern California.

By 1880, the state's population had reached 864,694 but there were only minor changes in the figures for the Diocese of Monterey-Los Angeles. There were, at the time, 11,183 inhabitants in the city of Los Angeles. Small as that figure was, it represented a doubling of the population since 1870 and marked a period of decided growth for the southland. The coming of the Santa Fe Railway was one of the signals for an increased migration, mostly from the Middle West and for a land boom which after 1886, reached staggering proportions only to subside as rapidly as it began in 1888 and 1889. Many people profited in the spirited financial speculation but in the end many more were wiped out. Nevertheless, permanent gains were discernible.

By 1890, there were obvious shifts in emphasis and Los Angeles' 50,395 persons accounted for the largest part of the state's growth from that time onward. The two Catholic churches in the city in 1880 had grown to five by 1890, and a fair start in the development of Catholic schools was well under way. In 1896, Bishop Francis Mora laid aside his mitre and retired to Barcelona where he lived out the remainder of his life in relative obscurity.

Although the financial panic of 1893 had a stifling effect on California's growth, Los Angeles maintained a high rate of expansion. Hard times in general, however, prevented the immediate realization of new enterprises and the decade of 1891-1900 was one of conservation rather than expansion. Bishop George T. Montgomery of Monterey-Los Angeles successfully opposed the intolerant spirit of the American Protective Association movement and by the turn of the century the Church in Southern California was plainly in a new era. 1901 saw the quickening of migration and chronologically, economically and industrially, better times were at hand. There were 42 parishes and 35 missions with 96 priests serving the Diocese of Monterey-Los Angeles. Eighteen parish schools and 19 academies enrolled 4,344 children out of a total Catholic population of 57,000.

The appointment of Bishop Montgomery to the coadjutorship of San Francisco in 1902, was a change deeply felt both in the northern and southern jurisdictions. The prelate was greatly admired by all classes of people and it was a reluctant diocese of Monterey-Los Angeles that saw its shepherd return to San Francisco. To Los Angeles came, as his successor, Bishop Thomas J. Conaty, recently retured from a term as Rector of The Catholic University of America. Bishop Conaty at once inaugurated a building program which carried forward well into the next decade. After only seven years in the diocese, Conaty could point to a growth from 102,479 people in 1900, to 319,198 in 1910. The six churches in Los Angeles now numbered 21 with the Catholic population maintaining a proportionate rate of increase.

Several churches and an orphanage were destroyed or badly damaged by the earthquake of April 18, 1906, but the losses were soon replaced with structures of more substantial character. The Diocese of Monterey-Los Angeles then listed 93 parishes and 65 missions with 188 priests serving a Catholic population of somewhat less than 100,000.

The next decade ushered in the First World War and saw curtailment of most building operations. Nonetheless, there were many changes. In Los Angeles, Saint Vincent's College was succeeded by Loyola College with the withdrawal of the Vincentian Fathers in favor of the Jesuits. Bishop Conaty died in 1915, and was replaced two years later by the Vicar General of the Archdiocese of San Francisco, John J. Cantwell. Cantwell was an organizer and a builder. Farsighted and possessing boundless energy, he had a rare gift of judgment in the choice of those selected to carry out his programs. Fortunately the Catholics of Los Angeles had the benefit of his leadership for more than three decades of spectacular growth. The bishop did noteworthy work to meet the spiritual and material needs of the men in the service of their country and entered very actively and successfully into the civic life of the community.

Statistically, by 1920, the Catholic Church in California was coming of age. The population of the state had risen to 3,246,861 with Los Angeles replacing San Francisco as the principal metropolis. Careful estimates place the count of Catholics in the Diocese of Monterey-Los Angeles at 214,000. Two hundred eighty-five priests were attending 126 parochial units and 116 missions. There were two colleges, four high schools, sixteen academies and sixty-three parish schools. Eight orphanages and an infant asylum were also in operation, as were three homes for the aged. Enrollment in the school system was placed at 14,313.

Plans for a separate ecclesiastical jurisdiction for that district in the old Diocese of Monterey-Los Angeles comprising Central California had been considered at various times since 1866. In a letter to a friend, Bishop Thaddeus Amat predicted that "within a few years another Bishop will certainly be established and form a new Diocese." No official action was taken at that time but early in 1889 Giovanni Cardinal Simeoni told Bishop Francis Mora that Roman officials found it difficult "to see how one person, however industrious, can effectively provide for the demands and necessities of the Church" in so extensive an area.

The matter was given serious attention and in September of that year Archbishop Patrick W. Riordan of San Francisco suggested to officials of the Sacred Congregation of Propaganda Fide the feasibility of a separate diocese at Monterey encompassing the six counties of San Luis Obispo, Monterey, San Benito, Tulare, Fresno, Inyo and those parts of Merced, Santa Cruz and Santa Clara not already attached to the Archdiocese of San Francisco.

Bishop Mora exhibited little enthusiasm for the proposal believing as he did that smaller units would not be financially viable. On February 24, 1890, the Archbishop of San Francisco reported that those he had consulted in the matter "were of the opinion that the line should be drawn north of Santa Barbara County and south of Kern County and south from San Bernardino."

Several additional reports were submitted to Rome later that year and circulated among the members of the congregation. In 1894, the cardinals endorsed Bishop Mora's views and voted to put aside the question of dividing the diocese in favor of appointing a coadjutor for California's southland.

Rumors of a division were revived after Bishop Thomas J. Conaty's death in 1915, by the long delay that ensued before the appointment of a successor. The territorial integrity of the Diocese of Monterey-Los Angeles remained intact, however, until 1922, when Bishop John J. Cantwell, acting on the advice of Gaetano Cardinal De Lai, petitioned Pope Pius XI to divide the unwieldy jurisdiction into more manageable units. Favorable response to the request came in June of 1922, with the announcement that the Holy Father had approved plans for removing the twelve northernmost counties from the Diocese of Monterey-Los Angeles and forming them into the separate ecclesiastical jurisdiction of Monterey-Fresno.

An estimated Catholic population of 50,000 souls were included in the new diocese whose geographical confines encompassed 43,714 square miles in the counties of Fresno, Kings, Tulare, San Luis Obispo, Kern, Inyo, Stanislaus, Merced, Santa Cruz, Madera, San Benito and Monterey. The boundary line between the new Diocese of Monterey-Fresno and the Archdiocese of San Francisco was adjusted to allow all of Santa Clara County to revert to the metropolitan see and all of Merced County to the newly erected diocese.

Archbishop Edward J. Hanna of San Francisco presided at the formal canonical ceremonies which were held in Fresno's newly designated Cathedral of Saint John the Baptist on December 3, 1922. Appointed by the Holy See as interim Apostolic Administrator of the diocese was Bishop John J. Cantwell who continued as Ordinary of the southern counties, now known as the Diocese of Los Angeles-San Diego. On March 27, 1924, Bishop John B. MacGinley of Nueva Caceres in the Philippines was chosen by Pope Pius XI as the first Ordinary of the Diocese of Monterey-Fresno. He was installed on July 31, 1924, by Dennis Cardinal Dougherty.

In the first statistical survey made of the area, it was reported that there were 53 priests maintaining 42 parishes and 21 mission stations to accommodate 51,265 faithful. The educational system was composed of four academies and seven elementary schools to care for 2,061 youngsters.

A long series of financial reverses, coupled with chronic illness, brought the retirement of Bishop MacGinley on September 26, 1932. Designated as second Ordinary of Monterey-Fresno was the diocesan vicar general, Father Philip G. Scher, who was elevated to the episcopate on June 29, 1933.

The great population shifts during and after World War II are reflected in the figures for 1950 which revealed 204 priests, 81 parishes, eight high schools, 31 elementary schools and seven hospitals to fill the needs of Central California's Catholic community which had grown, in a quarter century, to 214,615 souls.

During a four-month period in 1946-1947, the senior Auxiliary of Los Angeles, Bishop Joseph T. McGucken administered the Diocese of Monterey-Fresno with an apostolic indult. Late in 1946, the Holy See announced that Bishop Aloysius J. Willinger of Ponce had been transferred to the titular see of Bida and would function as coadjutor in the Monterey-Fresno jurisdiction. With Bishop Scher's death on January 3, 1953, after a long illness, his coadjutor automatically succeeded. Four years later, the diocese was given an Auxiliary in the person of Father Harry A. Clinch who was consecrated at Fresno as titular of Badiae on February 27, 1957.

Diocesan statistics, adjusted to 1966, indicated a Catholic population of 442,588 out of a total count of 1,653,900. The twelve counties were being served by 114 parishes, 12 high schools, 50 elementary schools and seven general hospitals. A diocesan minor seminary enrolled 87 students preparing to join the 290 priests already active in the apostolate.

The most recent adjustment of ecclesiastical boundaries affecting

Central California's twelve counties resulted in separate episcopal seats being established at Fresno and Monterey.

With the acceptance of 81-year old Bishop Aloysius Willinger's resignation and his assignment to the titular See of Tiguala, Pope Paul VI named the Auxiliary of the parent jurisdiction, Bishop Harry A. Clinch, as Ordinary of the Diocese of Monterey. Embracing an area of 8,475 square miles in the four counties of Santa Cruz, San Benito, Monterey and San Luis Obispo, the latter bishopric accounts for 133,000 Catholics in a population of 450,000.

29

"California Participation in the Spirit of 1776" is the topic of this essay which appeared in the *Southern California Quarterly* LVIII (Summer, 1976), 137-141. This article was selected to be included in the historical anthology issued in 1984 to mark the centennial of the historical Society of Southern California.

T he Declaration of Independence, certainly one of the most sublime assertions of human rights in recorded annals, triggered a series of social and political upheavals that eventually embroiled the whole of the civilized world. Though there was little more than a vast wilderness and a few French settlements between the Atlantic and Pacific Oceans in the late 1770s, the far-away Spanish province of California was not totally immune from the aftershocks unleashed by the "Spirit of 1776." A careful gleaning of the historical sources indicates that Californians played at least a participatory role in the establishment of the nation to which their descendants would one day join forces as the thirty-first commonwealth.

It all began on March 22, 1778, with an order from King Charles III directing Spanish possessions in the New World to observe strict neutrality in the hostilities that had erupted between France and England. Shortly thereafter, the order was reversed and local officials were instructed to disallow British vessels landing privileges. The change of policy is important for it brought California within the revolutionary ambit, inasmuch as its soil ceased to be neutral territory.

The king was playing a close hand. In virtue of the so-called "Family Pact" between the Bourbon crowns, Spain and France were pledged to mutual military assistance. Yet Charles III initially procrastinated in honoring that commitment, for fear of the influence that a cluster of "free colonies" might exert on his own nation's immense and valuable possessions in the New World.

England foolishly failed to exploit Iberian hesitancy by continuing to antagonize her historic foe with stepped-up attacks on and seizures of Spanish merchant ships. Finally, on June 23, 1779, the two nations went to war.

During the years that followed, "Spain's attitude towards the American Revolution changed with the political situations of the times. Although she kept on friendly terms with the Colonies, her own interests were always at stake."[1] The admittedly ambivalent Spanish policy served the crown well. For example, it was to King Charles' advantage to keep the Americans and their mother-country at sword's point, so as to divert English attention away from the attractive and vulnerable Spanish possessions on the continent. At the same time, officialdom at Madrid saw in the war a glorious opportunity for avenging past wrongs, acquiring fresh territories and crushing England's supremacy of the seaways.

News of the final rupture between Spain and England reached the Pacific Slope rather quickly. Fray Junípero Serra, the *Presidente* of the California Missions, learned about the ongoing hostilities during his second visit to San Francisco in the fall of 1779.

Confirmation came from Commandant General Teodoro de Croix who informed Serra on February 18, 1780, that on the previous June 24th, King Charles III, "inspired thereto by his sense of piety, and wishing above all things to implore the protection of the Almighty, on Whom depend the destinies of empires and the issues of wars, has given orders directing that, in all his possessions in Spain and America, public prayers be offered up for the prosperity of our Catholic armed forces." De Croix forwarded the full text of the royal directive "so that in conformity with His Majesty's command," the *Presidente* could "order public prayers to be offered" in the missions.[2]

The commandant general's letter reached the Franciscan *Presidente* on June 13. Serra immediately drafted a circular to the missionaries, outlining the king's wishes as spelled out by De Croix. He encouraged an unrestricted compliance because, as he pointed out, "we are in a special manner indebted here to the piety of our Catholic Monarch, who provides for us as his minister chaplains, and poor Franciscans, at his own expense, and, similarily, because we are interested in the success and victory of his Catholic armed forces, since by their means, especially are we to look for progress in our spiritual conquests here, which we have so much at heart."

Serra further asked each of the friars to be "most attentive in begging God to grant success to this public cause which is so favorable to our holy Catholic and Roman Church and is most pleasing in the sight of the same God Our Lord." Recalling the past two centuries of persecution against the Church in England, Serra reminded his confreres that "our Catholic Sovereign is at war with perfidious heretics. And when I have said that, I have said enough for all to join with His Majesty in the manner in which Heaven grants us to do so." The *Presidente* went on to say that "we should all be united in this purpose and display how we are one in spirit, an especial reason for offering to God our Lord our most pleasing if poor prayers."[3]

The Mallorcan-born friar then outlined the form of prayers to be followed in the missionary foundations then serving the Indians of California. As for the public orations, which were to begin June 24th, he directed that at the principal Mass on Sundays, the litany of the Blessed Mother or the Saints along with the psalm, verses and prayers prescribed by the *Rituale Romanum* for "time of war," be said. At the conclusion of the services, all were instructed to recite the *Credo* or Profession of Faith three times in order "to help to soften the pride of our enemies." Provisions were also made for private prayers on behalf of the Catholic sovereign.[4]

On the same day, the *Presidente* acknowledged De Croix's request for public prayers to hasten "the successful issue of His Catholic Majesty's undertakings in the present war" against England. Reporting that he had already circulated a letter to that effect, Serra assured De Croix that his orders would be carried out "to the last detail."[5]

On August 12, 1781, De Croix notified Serra that all of the "free vassals in America" were expected to make a contribution to the war effort. Every Indian was to contribute one *peso* apiece, while Spaniards and other residents in the area were obliged to twice that amount.[6] The commandant general expressed his hope that "Your Reverences will make them understand the importance of this small service which the king asks of all his faithful vassals, in order to help him to meet the extraordinary expenses which the present war against the enemies of religion and of the state calls forth, realizing that no other means were found to this end. They are light and sensible and can be met by the Indians. This they can do from their community assets in that proportion and at the same time the instruction provides."[7]

De Croix provided for those missions which might be poor and unable to comply with the royal directive noting that it was not the mind of the king to "burden" the Indians, though he did anticipate a minimal or token compliance wherever possible. The insistence on comformance with the royal directive was not lost in the delicacy of De Croix's terminology, for, as one commentator put it, "nominally the contribution was to be voluntary, but in reality was so managed as to leave no convenient methods of escape."[8]

Each of the friars was to draw up a *padrón* of all the Indians eighteen years and older within his jurisdiction, along with an account of the produce turned over to the governor and sold by him for cash.

Obviously the royal mandate could not be literally fulfilled in California, where the *peso* had not yet been introduced. It was ultimately decided by Governor Felipe de Neve that the missions themselves would pay the tax on behalf of the Indians.

Fray Junípero Serra was unhappy about the whole idea of a tax, for, as he related to the Guardian at the Apostolic College of San Fernando, Francisco Pangua, the natives could not "understand why *pesos* are necessary to wage a war for they have had frequent wars among themselves and for them no *pesos* were necessary. Much less could they understand why the king of Spain, our master, must ask them to give him a *peso* apiece."[9]

Though the resident friars at San Juan Capistrano and San Diego initially asked to be excluded from the tax, they ultimately joined the other missions in paying their assessment. This they did by pooling their Mass stipends and collecting debts owed by certain soldiers.

By the month of December 1782, California had contributed 4,216 *pesos* toward the expenses of Spain's war with England. The funds collected are thus recorded:[10]

Mission San Carlos Borromeo	106	Presidio of San Diego	515
Mission San Antonio de Padua	122	Presidio of Monterey	833
		Presidio of San Francisco	373
Mission San Gabriel	134	Mission San Luis Obispo (including Missions San Francisco and Santa Clara)	107
Missions San Juan Capistrano Presidio of Santa Barbara and San Diego	229	Presidio of Santa Barbara	249
		Pueblo Los Angeles	15

for a total of 2,683 *pesos*

Teodoro De Croix attributed the overpayment to Governor de Neve. The Franciscan chronicler, Father Zephyrin Engelhardt, stated that the added money "may account for the honors" subsequently bestowed upon the governor.[11]

The pittance of support for the crown's efforts came late, for the war between England and Spain was concluded by a treaty signed at Versailles in January 1783. Nonetheless, the record clearly shows that "if money constitutes the 'sinews of war,' the little towns of California make quite as good a showing as some of the older, richer cities of the Atlantic slope."[12]

Though their prayers and material contributions were negligible to the overall war effort, the Franciscan missionaries and their neophytes in California can be credited with sharing, at least nominally, a common cause with their contemporaries in the American colonies.

It may have been strictly fortuituous that Spain's conflicts with England reached fever-pitch at the precise moment as the War of American Independence. Yet the fact remains that during that struggle, "Spain and her colonies assisted the people of the United States in their gallant fight for freedom."[13]

Notes to the Text

1. William F. Mullaney, O.M.I., "Oliver Pollock, Catholic Patriot and Financier of the American Revolution," *Historical Records and Studies*, XXVIII (1937), 1f5.
2. Teodoro de Croix to Junípero Serra, Arispe, February 18, 1780, Santa Barbara Mission Archives (hereafter referred to as SBMA).
3. Junípero Serra — Circular Letter, Monterey, June 15, 1780, SBMA.
4. *Ibid.*
5. Junípero Serra to Teodoro de Croix, Monterey, June 15, 1780, SBMA.
6. Maynard J. Geiger, O.F.M., *The Life and Times of Fray Junípero Serra*, O.F.M. (2 vols.; Washington, D.C., 1959), II, 241.
7. Teodoro de Croix to Junípero Serra, Arispe, August 12, 1781, SBMA.
8. Hubert Howe Bancroft, *History of California* (7 vols.; San Francisco, 1884-1890), I, 427.
9. Junípero Serra to Francisco Pangua, Monterey, July 17, 1782, SBMA.
10. Antonine Tibesar, O.F.M., ed., *Writings of Junípero Serra* (4 vols.; Washington, D.C., 1955-1966), IV, 439-440. See also *The American Catholic Historical Researches* VII (October 1911), 366.
11. *The Missions and Missionaries of California* (4 vols.; San Francisco, 1912-1915), II, 390.
12. Margaret B. Harvey, "California in the Revolution," *American Monthly Magazine*, XXI (October 1902), 282.
13. Charles H. McCarthy, "The Attitude of Spain During the American Revolution," *Catholic Historical Review*, II (April 1916), 49.

30

This study on "Corporation Sole in California" is here taken from *The Jurist* XXV (July, 1965), 330-334.

Corporation Sole is a term applied to a person some of whose rights and liabilities are permitted by law to pass to his successors, in a particular office, rather than to his heirs, executors, or administrators. Such corporations are chiefly designed to insure the proper devolution of property pertaining to ecclesiastical establishments upon legitimate successors.

The process is one not common to the entire United States but regulated by individual state legislatures, some of whom "have leaned against it, believing that the church was asking for an undue privilege."[1] In other states no such legislation has been sought and bishops have hence been held not to possess corporate rights. In still other states, legal decisions have gone as far as creating quasi corporations sole without any express legislative authority.[2]

The first American provision for Corporation Sole, passed by the Maryland legislature on March 23, 1833, decreed:

> That it shall and may be lawful to, and for the trustees of any Roman Catholic Church, in whom the title to any lot or lots of ground, whereon any Roman Catholic Church is now erected, or which is used as a graveyard attached to any such church, to convey the same deed to be executed, acknowledged and recorded in the usual manner, to the Most Reverend James Whitfield, the present Archbishop of Baltimore, and his successors in the Archiepiscopal See of Baltimore, according to the discipline and

218

government of the Roman Catholic Church, forever; and it shall
and may be lawful to and for any person or persons or body corporate, to convey unto the Roman Catholic Archbishop of
Baltimore, for the time being, and his successors as aforesaid, forever, by deed as aforesaid, any lot piece or parcel of ground...[3]

Legal opinion, however, was not universally favorable to this arrangement and contentions were made in some quarters that Corporation Sole
is "somewhat of a contradiction in terms, and a useless feature of law."[4]
Hence, attempts to imitate the Maryland provisions in other areas of the
nation were often strenuously opposed, especially by proponents of
Nativism.

In 1844, the Bishop of Chicago, William Quarter, succeeded in obtaining
a charter from the legislature of Illinois empowering him and his successors
to hold property in trust for the diocese. A subsequent act provided that

gifts, grants, deeds, etc., heretofore made to any bishop shall be
construed as conveying the property to such person as the
Catholic Bishop of Chicago, and that title shall vest in this corporation sole.[5]

The formation of Corporations Sole by individual bishops was subsequently discussed by the American hierarchy at the Third Plenary
Council of Baltimore which met at the premier see on November 6,
1884. The prelates canonically approved such measures by decreeing that

In those states where a civil legal corporation of parishes or of
ecclesiastical congregations, in harmony with ecclesiastical laws,
does not exist, the bishop himself, by a law to be passed in the
assemblies, may become a public corporation or moral person
(Corporation Sole) to hold and administer the goods of the
entire diocese.[6]

According to the eminent historian, Peter K. Guilday, the action of the
bishops brought about "a quasi-compromise between the system of lay
trustees and that of fee-simple tenure on the part of bishops,"[7] but did
not assure the Church a safe system of legal protection on the national
level. In any event, the 1884 canonical legislation was confirmed, if not
strengthened, on July 29, 1911, when the Sacred Congregation of the
Council ruled that in those dioceses where

...the civil law precludes recognition of Parish Corporations in
the ownership and administration of Church property, the
method, hitherto in use in many dioceses, of constituting the

bishop a Corporation Sole is allowed, with the understanding that the Ordinary act with the advice, and, in important matters, with the consent of the diocesan consultors.[8]

This "permissive attitude" of the Church to Corporations Sole was not altered by the *Codex Iuris Canonici* in 1918.[9] Nonetheless, the Holy See plainly regards parish corporations as "preferable" to any other mode of holding property and prelates are still advised to "take steps to introduce this method...in their dioceses, if the civil law allows it."[10]

From a canonical point of view, Corporation Sole is frowned upon because it legally reserves the right to own property to the Ordinary, a prerogative which the Code grants also to parishes as moral persons. In addition, there has traditionally been a hesitance to localize as much authority in a single person as is the case when one prelate retains title to all parochial and chancery property in his jurisdiction.

It is also possible for bishops to visualize certain practical problems along these lines, since, even though Corporation Sole gives the local ordinary more latitude in governing his diocese than envisioned by the Code of Canon Law, the bishop, as incumbent for the Corporation Sole, is personally and directly responsible before the civil forum for all debts and liabilities contracted by his authorized agents in connection with Church holdings.

Prior to 1850, California legislation stipulated that real estate held by a religious body could not exceed two whole lots in a town, or twenty acres in the country. However, on May 12, 1853, the state removed the restriction and adopted into its statutes that "curious thing which we meet with in English law called a Corporation Sole."[11] The new law read, in part:

> Whenever the rules, regulations and discipline of any religious denomination, society or church require for the administration of the temporalities thereof, and the management of the estate and property thereof, it shall be lawful for the bishop, chief priest or presiding elder of such religious denomination, society or church to become a sole corporation...[12]

The measure went on to state that all property held by such bishop, chief priest or presiding elder, shall be in trust for the use, purpose and behalf of his religious denomination, society or church."

The State legislature restored the restrictive clause regarding property on May 13, 1854, and it was twenty-four years before the limitation was taken away[13] for the final time by a measure which gave Corporation Sole "the power to buy, sell, lease or mortgage property and in every way deal in real and personal property in the same manner that a natural person may."[14]

Essentially, the law for Corporations Sole in the State of California has remained intact for the last eight decades as indicated by the following historical chart:

Year Enacted	Canons	Year Repealed
1878	10002-10006	1947
1907	10007-10008	1947
1921	10010-10011	1947
1947	10000-10001	
	10009, 10012-10015	

In essence, the present law reads:

> A corporation sole may be formed hereunder by the bishop, chief priest, presiding elder or for the purpose of administering and managing the affairs and property of such religious organization…[15]

The Civil Code modified certain aspects of Corporation Sole common to English law. For example, the California legislation erects the ecclesiastical office itself into a Corporation Sole, thus making it possible for the incumbent to create an attorney of fact to survive his death and administer the Corporation Sole until a new appointee is named.[16]

Determination of the rightful incumbent is safeguarded by the law which directs that a vacancy in the office must "be filled by the rules, regulations or constitutions of the denomination, society or church" in question. The Corporation Sole has considerable power. It can sue and be sued; borrow money; make contracts; buy, sell or mortgage property; receive bequests; and appoint attorneys of fact. Although every Corporation Sole has perpetual existence, it may be dissolved and its affairs concluded voluntarily by filing with the state a declaration of dissolution signed and verified by the chief officer of the corporation.

Notes to the Text

1. Carl Zollmann, *American Church Law* (Saint Paul, 1933), p. 110. Approximately twenty-five ecclesiastical jurisdictions in the United States are Corporations Sole. Virginia and West Virginia forbid the incorporation of any church or religious denomination.

2. Apart from statute, Roman Catholic bishops are not generally recognized by Anglo-American law as Corporations Sole. *See* Wright vs Morgan, 191, U.S 55, 24, S.Ct. 6, 48 L.Ed. 89 (1903).

3. *Laws Made and Passed by the General Assembly of the State of Maryland* (Annapolis, 1833), Chapter 308.

4. F. W. Maitland, "The Corporation Sole," *The Law Quarterly Review* (England) XVI (1900), 353-354.

5. Quoted in Patrick J. Dignan, *A History of the Legal Incorporation of Catholic Church Property in the United States (1784-1932)* (New York, 1935), p. 179.

6. *Acta et Decreta Concilii Plenarii Baltimorensis III* (Baltimore, 1886), p. 153.

7. *A History of the Councils of Baltimore (1791-1884)* (New York, 1932), p.270.

8. *American Ecclesiastical Review* XLV (1911), 591.

9. The Code states that, as a rule, the pre-1918 discipline is retained except where specifically revoked or modified.

10. T. Lincoln Bouscaren, S.J., *The Canon Law Digest*, II (Milwaukee, 1943), 444-445.

11. Sir William Markby, *Elements of Law* (Oxford, 1885), p. 88.

12. *Compiled Laws of the State of California* (Boston, 1853), p. 310. [Stat. 1852, p. 168, *Civil Code*, sec. 602.]

13. The law was amended on March 30, 1878. *See* West's *Annotated California Codes* (Saint Paul, 1955), XXV, 43.

14. *The Statutes of California* (San Francisco, 1854) p. 163.

15. *Ibid.* (Sacramento, 1931), p. 1853.

16. Dale G. Vaughn, *El Obispo* (Los Angeles, 1929), p. 4.

31

This "Eulogy for a Country Graveyard" is here reprinted from the *Ventura County Historical Society Quarterly* XXVI (Fall, 1980), 13-25.

Just a century ago William E. Gladstone observed, "Show me the manner in which a nation or community cares for its dead and I will measure with mathematical exactness the tender sympathies of its people, their respect for the laws of the land and their loyalty to high ideals." The sentiments of that great British prime minister, if not his actual words, must have prompted the pastor and people of San Buenaventura Mission to look for a parcel of land on which to develop a new and more commodious burial ground for the historic old church.

The property for the parish cemetery, comprising a tract of land 400 feet by 400 feet, was acquired from George S. Wright, Henry Webb, Edmund L. Gould and Daniel C. Waterman in 1862. It was officially deeded to the Rt. Rev. Thaddeus Amat, Bishop the Diocese of Monterey-Los Angeles, on October 3 "for the use and purpose of a Catholic Burying Ground" at San Buenaventura.[1] Ynez Sanches was the first one to be interred in the "*cementerio nuevo*." She was buried by the Rev. Juan Comapla on October 21, 1862 in the grave purchased by her husband.[2] From an old subscription list, it would appear that only four lots were sold to Roman Catholics prior to 1882, the year the cemetery was divided into blocks.[3]

Responding to an invitation from the local Roman Catholic populace, Bishop Francis Mora dispatched his Vicar-General, Joachim Adam, to San Buenaventura where he solemnly blessed the parochial cemetery on

September 28, 1884, placing it under the patronage of Saint Mary.[4] Assisting at the ceremonies were the Revs. Juan Pujol and Cyprian Rubio.

Part of the Rancho Ex-Mission, the San Buenaventura cemetery was located on a hillside at the eastern edge of the townsite between Main and Poli Streets. When the city was incorporated in 1866, the burial plots were about 2000 feet outside its boundaries; an oversight only remedied a decade later.

In 1870 the San Buenaventura Commercial, Manufacturing and Mining Company, which owned most of the acreage in the original mission grant, deeded an adjacent section of property to the First Presbyterian Church for a "public" cemetery. [Although its Board of Trustees on October 28, 1876 "decided to grant to the Hebrew Society that of the graveyard east of the *barranca* (these appearing to be a debt of the Society)"[5] it was 1895 before a Jewish Cemetery was subdeeded to "L. Cerf, A. Bernheim, L. Hayfield, T. Wineman, all Trustees of the Jewish Church: Blocks nos. 2, 3, 4, 5, 42, 43, 44 and Lots nos. 7, 8, 9, 10, 11, 12 north of Block 2."[6] There may have been other ethnic sections since the Chinese names cluster close to Main Street. Although they set up a treasurer for the cemetery, the Presbyterians settled all claims against the account on October 1, 1878.][7] The City of San Buenaventura acquired the deed to these areas of the burial grounds in 1889.

[According to Austin Perley, Head of Ventura City Parks, the first caretaker was Joseph Richardson whose business and home were at the corner of Main and California Streets. De Moss Wilkin, a gardener, was next. In the end Frank Roby looked after those lots he was paid for; he was later hired by the city parks department, working two days of each week at the cemetery. The cobblestone retaining wall was built in 1934 on a WPA project. The two stones were engraved by a Myers of Ernie Frost's monument works.

The *Ventura city and county directories* list: J. M. Findley as sexton in 1910-11; L. T. Burdin in 1912-13; P. C. Kirkpatrick and Mrs. M. S. Burdin in 1914-15; F. H. Roby and Mrs. M. S. Burdin in 1916-17; and F. H. Roby in 1921-22.[8]

An item in the *Signal* one hundred years ago shows public interest in their cemetery: Two ladies of Ventura, Mrs. A. J. Snodgrass and Mrs. Charles Bergstrom, have taken on themselves the great task of getting money which will be used to put our cemetery on the hill in decent condition. They deserve credit for doing something that should have been done long ago by the town. We should all take a great interest in seeing to it that the last resting place of our relatives and friends is properly cared for. Our cemetery has long been like a wild field, overgrown with mustard. A vote of thanks to these ladies who, unaided, have shown a spirit in their enterprise that others would do well to emulate.[9]]

Inasmuch as the westernmost 110 feet or Saint Mary's Cemetery were never developed for interment purposes, it became customary for the various caretakers to utilize that area for gardening in return for looking after the graves in the cemetery proper. In 1922 Robert M. Sheridan, a prominent Ventura attorney, suggested to Bishop John J. Cantwell that "if the conditions contained in the original deed to Bishop Amat are of such a nature as would make possible a sale of that portion of the Catholic cemetery which has not been used for burials, a good price could doubtless be obtained for the property." Sheridan felt that such a transaction would "not only relieve the parish of the burdens of present and future taxes and assessments but would also give the parish a working fund for the upkeep and maintenance of the balance of the cemetery."[10] The bishop's secretary answered Sheridan's letter in a note to the Rev. Patrick J. Grogan, in which he expressed the view that the deed "would seem to prevent the consideration of the sale of any of this land for other purposes."[11]

In October of 1943 Archbishop John J. Cantwell contacted a descendant of the original donors of Saint Mary's Cemetery asking if the restriction that it be used "in its entirety exclusively for cemetery purposes" might be rescinded. The prelate noted that "because of the rapid growth of Ventura, the facilities at the old mission are no longer adequate and the Archdiocese of Los Angeles is "considering the building of a new church in Ventura to supplement the old mission." He felt that a "portion of the old cemetery property would provide an ideal site for a church." He concluded by asking for a quitclaim deed to the property, surrendering reversionary rights.[12] In 1945 the Rev. Daniel J. Hurley revived the earlier proposal that the undeveloped parcel of Saint Mary's Cemetery be used for building a church. Lawrence L. Otis, a counsel for the Title Insurance and Trust Company, rendered an opinion that "the erection and maintenance of a Catholic Church on a portion of the property" would not be a diversion of the original deed of gift.[13] By that time, however, the rapid growth of Ventura to the east had rendered Hurley's plan obsolete.

In September of 1949 the church deeded a ten foot frontage of the property to the city for the purpose of widening the streets. For its part, the city agreed to plant some hedges and install water lines.[14] On December 9, 1952 the Recreation Commission for the city outlined a "long-term plan for the development of a centrally-located site for a

Social-Cultural Recreation center" on the unused parcel of Saint Mary's Cemetery.[15] The following fall, the city completed arrangements to purchase the 110 feet from the Archdiocese of Los Angeles, with the understanding that it be used for recreational purposes. A check for $15,000 was drawn to James Francis Cardinal McIntyre on July 8, 1954 "in settlement of the condemnation action by the city of San Buenaventura for part of the old cemetery property."[16] It was further agreed that the city would assume responsibility for any general maintenance work in the Roman Catholic portion of the cemetery, for which the cost would be borne by the church.

Prior to 1917, Saint Mary's and its contiguous graveyard were the only burial area for the city and its environs. In October of that year George E. Hume and a group of developers[17] opened Ivy Lawn Cemetery, a factor that contributed to the diminishing use and importance of the older location. Although Ivy Lawn has always been privately owned and operated, provisions were made for Roman Catholic interments, a practice that perdured for many years. And in 1965 the parochial cemetery of Santa Clara was expanded to provide for burials of non-Oxnard inhabitants.

By the end of the 1930's the cemetery had become an object of neglect: weed-choked and cluttered with shattered tombstones, the area needed attention. A proposal was made by the city planning commission in December 1938 to convert the cemetery into a public park. Besides installing sidewalks along Main Street, no further action was taken on the suggestion. Eleven years later it authorized a feasibility study for using the property for multiple housing, a plan that was later put aside.

The final interments were made in 1943; one burial was made in each graveyard in January and March. In May of the following year an ordinance was passed prohibiting any further burials.[18] By law, a cemetery becomes legally abandoned five years after the last interment. The exact number of interments between 1862 and 1943 cannot be determined, mainly because a number of remains were subsequently removed to Ivy Lawn and other cemeteries. An approximation would read: 2,126 Protestants, 806 Roman Catholics and 48 Jews; a total of 2,980.

In 1963 the City of Ventura adopted a plan drafted by Charles Reiman calling for removal of curbs, slabs, vaults, headstones and bases. The Rev. Aubrey O'Reilly, Pastor of San Buenaventura Mission, suggested that small brass markers be set flush with the ground, with numbers keyed to a large monument whereon all the interments were enumerated. Letters were sent to heirs of all those buried in the tripartite cemetery, announcing the city's intention of removing the headstones and converting the

226

cemetery into a park. Families wishing to claim the approximately 600 headstones were told they could pick them up in Hall Canyon where they had been carefully stored, in alphabetical order, just inside a workyard operated by the Parks Department. After seven years they were taken to the Olivas Golf Course levee and buried in rubble. Only six bodies were actually moved, all of them originally interred above ground in lawn crypts; the remains were re-casketed and then buried directly beneath the earlier crypts. Eleven graves have been marked at the request of their descendants.

There were, of course, objections to the idea. For example, Mrs. Donald Lindsay was "quite horrified" at the whole concept; she maintained that the cemetery should be preserved "as an historical landmark" rather than dismantled and converted to a park area.[19] Others quite vociferously favored the program. Helen Emily Webster was "delighted with the plans now being carried forward". She noted that it was "gratifying to know that the space will remain an open greenbelt in the midst of the lively building activity in this part of the city."[20] Calm minds prevailed and the historic graveyard is now a beautiful memorial area overlooking the Pacific Ocean and the Channel Islands. Covered by trees, shrubs and thick lawns, the old cemetery has become a monument to those of earlier generations.

Notes to the Text

1. Santa Barbara Co., *Deeds*, A, 393.
2. *Libro de difuntos*, II (1824-1912), 1215.
3. *Plot book for Saint Mary's Cemetery, San Buenaventura, California* (1882-1921) in the Archives of the Archdiocese of Los Angeles (AALA).
4. *Libro de difuntos*, II (1824-1912), 1627.
5. First Presbyterian Church. Board of Trustees. *Minutes*, 1869-1883.
6. Zelma W. Wilcox, *Ventura-city cemetery record* (1966) 36.
7. *Op. cit.*, First Presbyterian Church.
8. *Ventura County directory*, 1896-.
9. March 27, 1880.
10. April 20 (AALA).
11. John J. Devlin on April 25, 1922 (AALA).
12. 21st (AALA).
13. To Ralph J. Bailey, Nov. 5, 1945 (AALA).
14. Daniel J. Hurley to James Francis Cardinal McIntyre, Sept. 24, 1949 (AALA).
15. Thor O. Olson to Robert M. Sheridan, Dec. 9, 1952 (AALA).
26. Memo to James Francis Cardinal McIntyre, July 8, 1954 (AALA.).
17. Others were Edgar Carne, David Darling and Joseph McGrath.
18. San Buenaventura, *Ordinances*, 600.
19. *Star-Free Press*, Dec. 3, 1964.
20. *Ibid.*, Dec. 20, 1964.

32

This essay, entitled "What Ever Happened to Saint Vincent's College," is here reproduced from *The Pacific Historian* XIV (Winter, 1970), 76-90. It was republished in *Vincentian Heritage* VI (1985), 67-85.

An aura of mystery has long surrounded the abrupt demise of Saint Vincent's College, the more so since it came at a time when that institution was the undisputed leader in the educational circles of Los Angeles, "the envy of the University of Southern California and Occidental College."[1] The topic takes on a particular relevance when one recalls the generally held view that "the history of this great old college is almost the history of early Los Angeles."[2]

Though the question has often been discussed, no effort has apparently ever been made to reconstruct, in chronological order, the chain of events which provoked the bewildering announcement, on July 30, 1910, that the Congregation of the Mission was retiring from its pedagogical endeavors in California's southland. Admittedly, the lacunae in the available evidence may forever militate against any "definitive" conclusions, but existing documentation, even if incomplete, does allow for a fairly balanced appraisal of the motives leading up to the closing of Saint Vincent's College.

Historical events cannot be properly evaluated if they are isolated from the framework in which they occur. For that reason careful attention must be given to the persuasive personality of Bishop Thomas J. Conaty (1847-1915), the dominating figure in the overall narrative of Catholic education in the Diocese of Monterey-Los Angeles during the years between 1902 and 1915. The Irish-born prelate was widely acclaimed as a natural leader of strong yet amiable character, and a pastor of singular devotedness and indefatigable zeal," honored and respected by all who knew him as an honest and upright man of God.³ Like many great personages, however, the bishop had his shortcomings. The key to understanding the prelate's relationship to Saint Vincent's College hinges on the recognition that Conaty was far from being an accomplished administrator, exhibiting as he often did neither talent in, nor concern for, the practical mundanities of daily life.

During the years immediately preceding his appointment as residential ordinary, Bishop Conaty occupied the rectorship of The Catholic University of America. At the time of his selection for that post, in 1896, it was generally thought that Conaty was an admirable choice. He was not a trained educator, but there were few among the American clergy who were. While achieving an enviable record during his years in the District of Columbia, Conaty's efforts, however, "did not resolve the growing complexity of the University difficulties" in a manner acceptable to the Board of Regents.⁴ Recognizing the general dissatisfaction with his administration, the bishop diplomatically withdrew his name from consideration for a second term.

Understandably, Conaty arrived in Los Angeles with something of an educational chip on his shoulder. Were he able to inaugurate a Catholic center of higher learning on the West Coast, the spectre of his failure at Washington would be effectively overshadowed. To the prelate, Saint Vincent's College, the area's leading Catholic educational institution, loomed prominently as the ideal launching pad for plummeting the Church into the more lofty atmosphere of graduate studies.

Bishop Conaty's appointment to the Diocese of Monterey-Los Angeles had been warmly applauded by the Vincentian Fathers who viewed his demonstrated enthusiasm for improving Catholic educational opportunities as a welcome contrast to the seemingly indifferent attitude of his two immediate predecessors toward anything beyond the limited primary and secondary parochial system enjoined by the Second Plenary Council of Baltimore. Initially, Father Joseph S. Glass and his Vincentian confreres were as elated as they were flattered by Conaty's overtures, made almost immediately after his installation, for expanding even further the influence of Southern California's most prominent institute of higher learning. At Conaty's suggestion, several lengthy meetings were scheduled between the bishop, Father Glass and community leaders to explore various ways of implementing their mutual objective.

The results of the discussions were made public in November, with announcement of the first in a series of projected steps to make St. Vincent's college "one of the largest institutions of learning in the United States."[5] The Vincentian Fathers disclosed the purchase, from E. J. Baldwin, of eighty-five acres of the Rancho La Cienega o Paso de la Tijera, southwest of the city limits on the Inglewood division of the Redondo electric line, as the projected site of a complexus of buildings with facilities to accommodate 1,000 students, or three times the existing enrollment.

As soon as the envisioned buildings were in operation, the masterplan called for converting the structures on Grand Avenue into a diocesan boys' school to allow for what one local newspaper called "perfection of the system of Catholic education for which plans were set on foot when he [Conaty] first came to the diocese."[6] In the meantime, a four-year secondary course, distinct from the college department, was to be inaugurated as a "feeder" for expanding the overall enrollment during the transition years.[7]

The unfortunate series of financial reverses that plagued business interests of Southern California in subsequent months were severe enough to incline Father Glass towards the logic of a less ambitious and more gradual expansionary program than originally outlined. The bishop's enthusiasm, on the other hand, was not so clearly curtailed, even after the Vincentian educator frankly told Conaty that the Congregation of the Mission, already overly extended at Holy Trinity College in Dallas, was unwilling to incur any additional indebtedness.

While remaining outwardly oblivious to the financial complexities entailed, Conaty continued publicly to recite the advantages that would accrue to Saint Vincent's College when it entered "that greater development which its interests on every side demand."[8] He declared on any number of occasions that "he would not be satisfied until the College had become a university."[9] Quite naturally the Vincentians resented the bishop's prodding, especially since his frequently repeated offers of aid and assistance stopped considerably short of the badly needed financial support.

It was generally known that during Conaty's years at The Catholic University of America, "he was wary of religious-order men on the teaching staff and no one was assigned to it in his time."[10] Nevertheless, the growing impatience of the Bishop of Monterey-Los Angeles over apparent Vincentian apathy partially accounts for Conaty's action, in mid-1908, of inviting the Society of Jesus, under whom he had been educated in Worcester, to assume the parochial activities of Our Lady of Sorrows Church in Santa Barbara. Though careful to elicit a pledge from the Jesuits that they would not open a college in the southland for at least ten years, and then only with the local ordinary's consent,[11] Bishop Conaty obviously reasoned that the presence of the Society, firmly ensconced in the mainstream of diocesan affairs, would pressure the Vincentians into taking measures to break what the prelate considered an educational logjam.

As a matter of fact, the opposite reaction took place. The constant badgering by the bishop induced Father Glass to bring the whole issue of expansion before the Vincentian provincial, the Very Reverend Thomas Finney. Noting Conaty's desire of having the college advanced to university status, Glass wondered if the Congregation of the Mission was adequately "prepared to enter upon such an enlargement and such development as that contemplated by the Bishop, and suggested by the great future in store for Southern California." While acknowledging that the prelate's encouragement and his frequent expressions of confidence in the faculty were "indeed most flattering," Father Glass felt that "honesty compels us to ask ourselves certain serious questions, and urges us to consider thoughtfully certain important facts" that can no longer be postponed.[12]

Meanwhile, Bishop Conaty's pressure tactics received a fortuitous impetus when, on December 28, 1909, a disastrous fire swept the central part of Santa Clara College, destroying the faculty building and severely damaging several other structures. Sentiment for relocating the college in Southern California, until that time voiced only in guarded tones, gradually emerged as more attractive than the previously projected sites of Manresa, Watsonville and Mountain View. The Jesuit provincial, Father Herman J. Goller, journeyed to Los Angeles where he discussed at some length the various alternatives open to the Society. Conaty advised against Los Angeles "for the present," though he left open the possibility of San Diego and Pasadena.[13]

The atmosphere at Los Angeles took on a wholly different tone when word of Goller's meeting with Conaty was leaked to Father Glass. The possibility of Jesuit interference had suddenly been advanced to the more tangible realm of probability. Sentiment among Vincentian officialdom crystallized rather quickly when Glass relayed assurances to his provincial that the forty-five years already invested in Southern California's Catholic higher education would be perpetuated. And so it was that the instrument originally envisioned by Bishop Conaty as a "pious threat" was the very one seized upon by the Vincentians as an escape clause from a situation they regarded as otherwise insoluble.

According to an entry in the Minute Book of the Vincentian General Council at Paris, dated May 2, 1910, Father Finney submitted the proposal to close Saint Vincent's College and to replace it with a house for missions. One of the chief reasons given for the request[14] was the possibility that "the Jesuits plan to open a Catholic College in this same city, which is not big enough for two institutions of the same kind." Finney was advised to submit the matter to his provincial council and to abide by that body's decision.[15]

In what local newspapers regarded as the most radical change of any that had occurred in Catholic circles of the Southwest in the past decade,[16] Father Glass issued a brief public announcement, on July 30, 1910, that the Congregation of the Mission had decided to retire completely from its educational commitments in California.[17] An excuse, if not a reason, for the action was given when the matter came before the diocesan Board of Consultors on September 11, 1910. There it was stated: "The General of [the] Vincentian [Fathers] forbids all college work and in [the] future the Fathers will devote themselves exclusively [to] the church's [missionary] work."[18]

On the day after disclosure of the Vincentian retirement, Father James P. Morrissey, a long-time advocate of moving Santa Clara to the south, was named president of that institution. Both Goller and Morrissey visited the as yet undeveloped La Cienega site and shortly thereafter, confident that the 319,000 population of Los Angeles augured well for the future, informed Bishop Conaty that the Jesuit institution would indeed move southward.

In the formal notification subsequently sent to Conaty by Vincentian authorities, the bishop was thanked for the "kindest consideration" and most gracious encouragement" he had exhibited for the work of the Vincentians in Los Angeles. Nonetheless, as the provincial stated, "teaching in colleges, except in the countries of the foreign missions, is a work not in accordance with our special vocation." Recognizing that facilities in California's southland would require an increased investment of funds and personnel, Father Thomas Finney felt that such would mean a further drifting away from their own special work, and the assuming of financial and other burdens which they were not prepared to bear.[19] Finney's letter was as loquacious for what it omitted as for what it stated. Even the casual observer would not be presumptuous in identifying the anxiety of the Jesuits for an establishment in Southern California with "the particular conditions and circumstances in Los Angeles" which the Vincentian provincial thought opportune "for beginning the execution of the purpose which we have before us."[20]

An attitude of utter dismay at the sudden turn of events was expressed in religious and educational circles. The diocesan newspaper stated that "Bishop Conaty had not the slightest intimation from any source whatever that such a determination had been reached..."[21] In his reply to the Vincentian provincial, Conaty reiterated that "the surprise which the message gave me was like a thunder-clap out of a clear sky. It had never occurred to me that your Fathers would be anxious to withdraw from a field of work in which they had been so successful." Then, quickly shifting moods, the prelate expressed his appreciation of the reasons outlined for the action, standing ready, as he said, to cooperate with the community in carrying out their plans.[22] "Thunder-clap" or no, what Conaty regarded as the chief obstacle to a Catholic university in Southern California had now been bridged!

For their part, the Vincentians, whether personally irritated at being "forced out" or elated at being "liberated," had earned the plaudits of a grateful community. The appreciation of one elderly resident was reproduced in the local Catholic press:

> It was a frontier life into which they [the Vincentians] entered, a voluntary exile, and they endured many privations in those early days of the *pueblo*. The story of their steadfast fidelity, whole hearted zeal, and exemplary lives can be truly appreciated only by the standards of eternity.
>
> The first priests were a superior band of men and since their day, their record has been ably upheld by their successors, who have at all times, been identified with the best progress of the city.
>
> For nearly fifty years, these priests have labored thus in Los Angeles, and the people owe them a debt of gratitude which it would be difficult to pay. The earnest cooperation of the people of the diocese will, without doubt, be theirs in all their undertakings, for the people can never fail to appreciate their presence here, and to beg God to give them long years of usefulness in their chosen Work.[23]

The transfer of collegial sovereignty came perilously close to being completely aborted in the aftermath of the confusion caused by the unexpected death, on November 5, 1910, of the forty-three year old Jesuit provincial, Father Herman Goller. Shortly after the appointment of his successor, Father James A. Rockliffe, Morrissey was called to Spokane where the question of the possible transfer of Santa Clara to Los Angeles was taken up as the best means of redeeming Goller's promise to Bishop

Thomas J. Conaty.[24] A questionnaire was secretly circulated among thirty-four Jesuits of the province about the advisability of transferring the college to the city or environs of the Southern California metropolis. Of those consulted, nineteen favored moving to Los Angeles, and fifteen preferred remaining at Santa Clara. Most of those responding expressed a sympathy for making the newly located institution a day school.

Gradually, however, with the removal of Father Goller, the most influential proponent of relocating Santa Clara College at Los Angeles, the apparently widespread opposition to such action among that institution's faculty emerged as the deciding factor against any further negotiations along those lines with the Bishop of Monterey-Los Angeles. In deference to the majority view of those most intimately concerned, the newly-named provincial avoided taking any action on the delicate issue until after circumstances forced the President of Santa Clara to proceed with an earlier announced program for rebuilding the gutted college structures at the existing campus. One writer has noted, almost by way of footnote, that "a person desirous of catching Father Morrissey's vision of Saint Vincent's on its Angelus Mesa campus can go to Santa Clara today fifty years afterwards, where the buildings he wished to grace View Park still flank Father McCoy's New Mission Church."[25]

The decision against moving Santa Clara to the Diocese of Monterey-Los Angeles necessitated a thorough reappraisal by the Jesuits of their firmly expressed commitments to California's southland. Even as early as August 7, 1910, Father Goller had notified Conaty that it would be "practically impossible" for the Society to take over the administration of Saint Vincent's College for at least another year.[26] Now, without the personnel from Santa Clara, prospects became even less promising.

As a temporary solution to the lack of available Jesuit educators, Father Rockliffe proposed suspending the collegiate division on an interim basis, and beginning with the initial two years of high school. An additional grade would then be added annually until the full-fledged college course could be restructured. To this outwardly acceptable suggestion, Bishop Conaty concurred, recognizing the difficulty involved in taking up the work at Saint Vincent's College as already initiated.[27] In the prelate's opinion, "The whole question resolved itself into the feasibility of purchasing a site and starting a day school for boys with a gradual and systematic development into a college."[28] Shortly afterwards, Rockliffe reported to the bishop, "The plan of commencing an educational work at Los Angeles with the lowest class of the High School and developing it on the lines usual in the Society meet the full and unqualified approval of my consultors."[29]

234

The Vincentian reaction to discontinuance of the college grades was predictably unfavorable. Father Glass reminded Conaty of the wishes expressed by the Congregation of the Mission that the only Catholic college in Los Angeles be perpetuated. Such a proposal as that advocated by the Jesuits would be a step backward. It was that concern that had motivated Glass's superiors to recommend that the community "be succeeded, in this special work, by a religious congregation, or society whose vocation is the direction of colleges..."[30]

The generally soft-spoken Vincentian, recalling his community's willingness to turn over its educational work in Los Angeles to any group able to broaden the existing prospectus, asked the bishop how a suggestion along the lines proposed by Rockliffe could achieve the prelate's plan of advancing the already established program. In addition, the President of Saint Vincent's felt that the general public would regard such a regression "as a crooked deal." Glass stated that he "most assuredly would never have approved, in any way whatsoever, the proposition to turn over Saint Vincent's to them," had he ever envisioned the course now outlined by the Society of Jesus. Seeing no advantage to the diocese, the cause of Catholic higher education or the college itself, Father Glass expressed the opinion that if the proposition to have merely a high school and modest college were acceptable to Conaty, he would favor a return to the relatively successful system followed in the pre-1905 years. Glass categorically stated that the Vincentian withdrawal would never have met with his community's approbation, had such action meant the doing away with Saint Vincent's College instead of its development into a greater school. Glass concluded by reminding Conaty that he was doing as well by his diocese in having Saint Vincent's as it is, as he would be "by approving the contemplated plans of the Jesuits."[31]

The vociferous protest of Glass caused the bishop confidentially to inform the Jesuit provincial that "the general understanding was that St. Vincent's would be continued" for at least a year so that justice might be done the pupils already studying there. Such an arrangement, the prelate pointed out, would relieve the Vincentians from any allegation that they had allowed "the change to be made without consideration for their students and Alumni."[32]

To Conaty's intervention, obviously intended as a compromise, Father Rockliffe responded that everywhere it had been the custom of the Society to begin its educational work on the lines of organic growth and gradual development. That procedure enabled the Jesuits to train the first students according to their own system, forming "newcomers year by year on the same lines by the example and traditions of the older boys." The provincial saw no merit in altering the tried and accepted pattern and felt that "surely the Catholics of Los Angeles will understand the temporary necessity of interrupting the High school and college course in the city."[33]

The bishop, Vincentians and Jesuits had obviously arrived at a physical impasse, inasmuch as the logic of Glass's observations was effectively counterbalanced by Rockliffe's inability to provide the necessary personnel to maintain the college. Ultimately a compromise of sorts was reached, whereby the Jesuits agreed to open the institution in the fall of 1911, with the full complement of high school classes.[34] Though the early catalogues of the Jesuit college stated it was "legally and in fact" a continuation of the earlier institution,[35] the three year suspension of collegiate courses plainly indicates that "there is no juridical succession"[36] between old Saint Vincent's and present-day Loyola University. Because of the unforeseen tribulations experienced in the overall transaction, one is inclined to agree with one Jesuit observer who said, "The hard fact of Garvanza is that the six religious[37] and one lay teacher[38] who began the Jesuit era with their jejune high school program...were not nearly what the press had given the people to expect."[39]

The question of a site for the Jesuit foundation in Los Angeles presented another problem of major proportions. Originally, the Society of Jesus had considered using the existing college buildings on Grand Avenue and to assume, in lieu of rent, the interest payments on the rather formidable debt already incurred by Saint Vincent's College. This arrangement, however, was vetoed by the Jesuit provincial consultors as financially prohibitive. Father Rockliffe also observed that since the Vincentians intended to retain their nearby parochial foundation, "it would be very painful...if our presence in the very midst of their fine parish would interfere in anyway with their good influence on their flock."[40]

When it became evident to Bishop Conaty that the Society of Jesus wanted a clean break from the Grand Avenue facilities, the prelate expressed his preference for a site in the Highland Park-Garvanza area of town. The Jesuits, on the contrary, favored the general vicinity decided upon when plans were first announced for expanding Saint Vincent's College in 1905. With a view towards implementing these designs, the Jesuits asked if they might be entrusted with the Parish of Saint Thomas, a centrally located parochial unit in a growing section of the city with adequate public transportation.[41]

Conaty replied that in earlier discussions "the matter of a parish had never been mentioned in any way." Moreover, the prelate countered, an offer of a parish in the Highland Park—Garvanza district was "the best we can do under the present circumstances." Conaty pointed out that there was no vacancy at St. Thomas and with the local pastor absent in Europe on diocesan business, "it would be most unseemly of me to think of giving the parish to anyone." The bishop regarded the Highland Park—Garvanza area, lying midway between Pasadena and Los Angeles, as a most suitable location for the Jesuit educational foundations and, therefore, parochial assignment. Railway facilities were readily available at the economical rate of five cents a ride. He recalled the success already enjoyed in the area by the Presbyterians at Occidental College.[42]

For his part the Jesuit provincial was not easily deterred. He observed that Father Goller had been a very sick man when the earlier negotiations took place and scarcely able to grasp the proposition in all its bearings. While anxious to comply with Bishop Conaty's expectations, Rockliffe emphasized his view and that of his consultors, "that a location on the West or Southwest is the most advantageous that could be chosen." He noted how sad it would be "to repeat the mistake in Los Angeles that has been made more than once elsewhere, and, after the price of property has advanced, to change the location of the college to the place that should have been selected from the very start."[43]

The inflexible attitude of Conaty finally triumphed, and the Society of Jesus purchased property on West Avenue 52 in Garvanza. With a minimum of remodelling, the three bungalows on the site were fashioned into classrooms, residence and faculty quarters. The northernmost section of Sacred Heart Parish was dismembered and formed into a juridical unit under the patronage of Saint Ignatius. On September 11, 1911, two Jesuit priests and four scholastics opened their institution in austere surroundings with an enrollment of eighty boys spread out through the four years of high school.

The name of the Garvanza foundation was also embroiled in a measure of confusion. As early as March 3, 1911, Bishop Conaty had requested "that the name 'St. Vincent's College' be retained in order that the splendid traditions of the past may continue unbroken."[44] To the prelate's suggestion, however, Father Rockliffe noted that "even if it were desirable for us to occupy the present premises of St. Vincent's College, it is clear that the Society would have to incorporate under a modified or under a new title in order to avoid any legal entanglements."[45] Rockliffe had been advised by an outstanding local attorney to be cautious about taking the old name, especially if it involved holding themselves out as the identical corporate institution.[46]

The logic of some title alteration was also shared by the institution's acting superior, Father Richard A. Gleeson: "Had we taken over St. Vincent's as at first arranged, and gone into the buildings of the Vincentians, and gone right ahead with their classes, it would be natural and most becoming to keep the old and honored name of St. Vincent."[47] Under existing circumstances, however, inaugurating a wholly new institution with, its own educational program, six miles from the earlier site, was reason enough, he thought, for changing the school's name.

In any event, the institution began operation as Los Angeles College. That name could not be long utilized for it was discovered that another private school was operating under the same title. For a brief period, the patronage of Saint Vincent was resumed, but since 1918, the foundation has been known in local annals as Loyola. In retrospect, allowing the origin title to die along with the college it designated, seems to have been a wise choice, inasmuch as the Jesuit institution, following neither the traditions nor the methods of its predecessor, has yet to regain the proportionate stature in Southland society enjoyed by old Saint Vincent's College.

If and when the history of the forty-six years of pedagogical work by the Congregation of the Mission in the Diocese of Monterey-Los Angeles is written, the removal of Saint Vincent's College from Southern California will loom in even greater perspective as the most unfortunate and needless turn of events in an episcopate otherwise remembered for its noble accomplishments. In addition to being "pained, shamed and humiliated"[48] by the retirement of the Vincentians, the uncompromising attitude of Bishop J. Conaty which provoked the action confirmed in substance, if not in extent, the dichotomy between recognized educational competency and undeniable administrative ineptitude which had earlier characterized the prelate's tumultuous years as Rector of The Catholic University of America.

The esteem for those who suffered most personally was well expressed in an unsigned editorial which appeared in the S.V.C. STUDENT for July of 1911:

> As educators, as teachers in Saint Vincent's College, they are no more, but as educators and teachers in the world of life they will ever hold an important place; wherever they go they will influence those with whom they come in contact to greater efforts in the cause of truth, to greater labors in the pursuit of justice, and by so doing will benefit not only individuals, but society as a whole.[49]

Notes to the Text

1. "Extension of Remarks of Hon. Gordon L. McDonough of California in the House of Representatives, Wednesday, June 28, 1961," *Congressional Record—Appendix* (July 10, 1961), p. A5091.
2. Harry Carr, *Los Angeles City of Dreams* (New York, 1935), p. 376.
3. *Ave Maria* II (October 2, 1915), 441.
4. Colman J. Barry, O.S.B., *The Catholic University of America*, 1903-1909 (Washington, 1950), p. 60.
5. Los Angeles *Times*, November 10, 1905.
6. Archives of the Archdiocese of Los Angeles (hereafter referred to as AALA), Unidentified news-clipping, November 10, 1905.
7. William E. North, *Catholic Education in Southern California* (Washington, 1936), p. 121.
8. AALA, Thomas J. Conaty to Joseph S. Glass, C.M., Los Angeles, November 11, 1908.
9. *The Tidings*, June 19, 1908.
10. Henry J. Browne, "Newly Published History of The Catholic University of America, *American Ecclesiastical Review* CXXI (November, 1949), 367.
11. AALA, George de la Motte, S.J. to Thomas J. Conaty, Santa Clara, August 2, 1908.
12. AALA, Joseph S. Glass, C.M. to Thomas Finney, C.M., Los Angeles, February 13, 1909.
13. AALA, Herman J. Goller, S. J., to Thomas J. Conaty, Santa Clara, March 23, 1910.
14. There is absolutely no available evidence to substantiate a persistent oral tradition that some sort of an accommodation had been reached between Conaty and Glass whereby the latter was assured of a bishopric if be could bring about an unobstrusive withdrawal by the Vincentians. That such a suggestion was ever seriously considered, probably derived from the resentment voiced by certain of Glass's confreres at his initiative in proposing that the Congregation of the Mission step aside for their Jesuit counterparts. The tradition seemingly arose after the appointment of Glass as Bishop of Salt Lake City as a convenient *post hoc, ergo propter* hoc explanation as to why Saint Vincent's College was closed. Bishop Conaty was in no position to make such a proposal, a fact that any episcopally-anxious candidate would have been the first to realize.
15. This information was graciously provided by the Very Reverend James A. Fisher, C.M., Visitor of the Western Province of the Vincentian Fathers. See AALA, James A. Fisher, C.M. to author, Saint Louis, November 8, 1968.
16. AALA, Unidentified news-clipping, late 1911.
17. *The Tidings*, March 3, 1911.
18. AALA, "Acts of Council of Diocese of Los Angeles-San Diego, 1893-1918," p. 55.
19. AALA, Thomas Finney, C.M. to Thomas J. Conaty, Perryville, September 12, 1910.
20. Ibid.
21. *The Tidings*, March 3, 1911.
22. AALA, Thomas J. Conaty to Thomas Finney, C.M., Los Angeles, February 24, 1911.
23. *The Tidings*, March 3, 1911.
24. This data was generously made available by the Reverend Leo Cullen, S.J. from the Archives of the Society of Jesus, Province of California (hereafter referred to as ASJC). See Richard A. Gleeson, S.J., Memoir, n.p., circa July 25, 1911.
25. Philip J. Connelly, S.J., "Santa Clara's Proposal to Come South," *The Loyola University Alumnus* (February, 1962), 10.
26. AALA, James Rockliffe, S.J. to Thomas J. Conaty, San Francisco, August 7, 1910.
27. AALA, Thomas J. Conaty to James Rockliffe, S.J., Los Angeles, March 20, 1911.
28. AALA, Thomas J. Conaty to n.n., Los Angeles. March 30, 1911.
29. AALA, James Rockliffe, S.J. to Thomas J. Conaty, San Jose, March 31, 1911.
30. AALA, Thomas Finney, C.M. to Thomas J. Conaty, Perryville, September 12, 1910.
31. AALA, Joseph S. Glass, C.M. to Thomas J. Conaty, Los Angeles, April 8, 191132.
32. AALA, Thomas J. Conaty to James Rockliffe, S.J., Los Angeles, April 5, 1911.

33. AALA, James Rockliffe, S.J. to Thomas J. Conaty, San Jose, April 13, 1911.

34. Alexander J. Cody, S.J., *A Memoir, Richard A. Gleeson*, S.J. 1861-1945 (San Francisco, 1950), p. 92.

35. *Second Annual Catalog of Los Angeles College*, 1912-1913 (Los Angeles, 1912), p. 4.

36. Archives of Loyola University (Los Angeles), Arthur D. Spearman, S.J. to Richard A. Trame, S.J., Santa Clara, January 30, 1958. The collegiate department was resumed only in 1914.

37. The new faculty replaced sixteen Vincentian Fathers and seven lay teachers.

38. The lay teacher, Charles C. Conroy, was the only faculty member retained from the earlier institution.

39. Philip J. Connelly, S.J., *op cit.*, 5.

40. AALA, James Rockliffe, S.J. to Thomas J. Conaty, San Jose, April 13, 1911.

41. AALA, James Rockliffe, S.J. to Thomas J. Conaty, San Jose, March 31, 1911.

42. AALA, Thomas J. Conaty to James Rockliffe, S.J., Los Angeles, April 5, 1911.

43. AALA, James A. Rockliffe, S.J. to Thomas J. Conaty, San Jose, April 13, 1911.

44. *The Tidings*, March 3, 1911.

45. AALA, James A. Rockliffe, S.J. to Thomas J. Conaty, San Jose, April 13, 1911.

46. ASJC, Francis S. Montgomery to James A. Rockliffe, S.J., Los Angeles, July 5, 1911.

47. AALA, Richard A. Gleeson, S.J. to Thomas J. Conaty, Los Angeles, July 16, 1911.

48. ASJC, Richard A. Gleeson, S.J., Memoir, n.p., circa July 25, 1911.

49. "The Vincentian Fathers," XIV (July, 1911), 365.

33

This sermon, preached on the hundredth anniversary of Saint Joseph's Cathedral, San Diego, appeared in the *Southern Cross* for March 28, 1974. It was entitled: "Where it all began for Christ along the Pacific Slope."

Among the Christian communities of this great nation, few if any have a greater claim to antiquity than the city and people bearing the hallowed and revered patronage of Saint Didacus.

Discovered by Rodriquez Cabrillo in 1542, named by Sebastian Vizcaino in 1602 and inaugurated by Junipero Serra in 1769, San Diego bears the added distinction of being the seat of the first bishopric for the Californias.

Indeed, this is where it all began for Christ along the Pacific Slope. Here, on America's western shores, was reared the first cross, was built the first church and was established the first modern city.

Here too sprang the first cultivated field, the first palm, the first vine and the first olive tree to blossom into fruitage. And most important of all, here the blood of the first martyr was poured out upon the ground as the seedling for Christianity.

From this missionary outpost, at the very edge of the known world, the gray-robed sons of Saint Francis pushed the Spanish frontier north to Sonoma, carving out of the wilderness that path later popularized in literature as the King's Highway.

Along that *Camino Real* went emissaries of the Spanish realm to claim and possess the land, to develop and harness its natural resources and to acquaint its inhabitants with the duties and privileges of citizenship.

Down that same roadway traveled the missionaries of Christ to proclaim and extend the Kingdom of Heaven, to evangelize and civilize its diverse peoples and to win a whole new race to the Christian way-of-life.

In this newest of the world's empires, Christ was King and the friars were his soldiers. They claimed this golden land in his name and possessed it for his glory-by living and practicing those Christ-like virtues of poverty, chastity and obedience.

Through the ministry of Fray Junipero Serra and his confreres, the Mission of San Diego de Alcala became the first tabernacle of God in Alta California. In this far-Western cradle of Christianity, the gospel message was brought first to the Indians and then to their multi-racial successors as God's people in this segment of his vineyard.

The Cathedral of Saint Joseph figures prominently into the historical montage of California's Catholic heritage. Though divine worship has been offered at this particular location for a mere hundred years, the parochial family of Saint Joseph legitimately claims lineal descent from nearby proto-missionary foundation on Presidio Hill.

On September 29. 1851, Father John C. Holbein laid the cornerstone for an adobe church in Old Town to succeed the disintegrating mission and *presidio*. Several years later, that never-completed edifice was abandoned in favor of a small chapel in the home of John Brown. Those facilities, dedicated to Our Lady's Immaculate Conception on November 21, 1858, served the spiritual needs of the local populace until the era of Father Anthony Ubach, the second founder of Catholicism in San Diego.

When that renowned cleric came to the area in 1866, he had only two parochial boundaries: the Pacific Ocean and the Colorado River. From the very outset of his Ministry in San Diego, Father Ubach determined to restore at least a portion of the dignity conferred on the city in 1840 by a Pope and withdrawn in 1842 by a bishop. If he could not make San Diego a diocese, he could build for the city a cathedral. And that he set out to do.

The first of his long-term plans was a magnificent celebration to commemorate the centennial of Mission San Diego on July 18, 1869. Ubach invited Bishop Thaddeus Amat to preach on that occasion and the Spanish-born prelate happily complied.

At the conclusion of the festivities, Bishop Amat set in place the cornerstone for the first church of Saint Joseph, in Old Town. Father Ubach's decision to invoke the patronage of that saint had considerable historical precedent, for it was through Saint Joseph's intercession that the abandonment of the whole San Diego enterprise was miraculously averted in 1770.

Work on the new church had not progressed very far, however, when the disastrous fire of April 20, 1872, totally destroyed the edifice. The conflagration was a sign to Father Ubach. He prayed and pondered and then decided to relocate the parish atop a *mesa* west of town, on a parcel of property at Third and Beech, donated to the Church by Alonzo Erastus Horton.

A frame church, the second dedicated to Saint Joseph, was erected in late 1874, and dedicated by Coadjutor Bishop Francis Mora the following January 31st. It is the centennial of that event which the people of God gratefully commemorate with today's liturgy.

The growth and development of the parish and the city in the next decade and a-half made possible the fulfillment of Father Ubach's dream for a "cathedral-like" church for San Diego.

By 1894, the walls of a handsome Gothic church were firmly etched onto the San Diego skyline. The brick structure was erected adjacent to the older frame building, which continued its service under the appropriate title of Junipero Serra Hall.

Bishop Mora returned to San Diego for the solemn dedication of the new Saint Joseph's church—that same house of worship in which we gather today. The bishop told a local reporter that "Father Ubach has not erected a church, but a cathedral."

That judgment was confirmed by the Catholic newspaper, which stated that Saint Joseph's "has no equal in church architecture in San Diego, and apart from the cathedral (of Saint Vibiana in Los Angeles), is said to be the most beautiful church in the diocese."

Father Ubach had indeed reared a "cathedral" for San Diego, though it would be another forty-two years before that title was officially bestowed. Yet, despite the fact that he had built a cathedral, Father Ubach would not be buried as a bishop. At his own insistence, the fabled priest laid in state in the old Junipero Serra Hall.

The fascinating story of this cathedral has yet to be fully told. Suffice to say that in 1936 San Diego received what was promised almost a century earlier, a residential bishopric. Restating the decree of his predecessor, five times removed, Pope Pius XI raised and elevated San Diego "to the honor and dignity of a cathedral city."

On that historic occasion, the Holy Father directed that "Saint Joseph's church be advanced to the rank of cathedral or mother church of the newly-proclaimed Diocese of San Diego."

In virtue of that distinction and the heritage it embodies, this cathedral certainly can hereafter be legitimately referred to in the annals as the "premier church of the Pacific Slope."

This community, though it be very old in years, is yet quite young in its destiny. With all their rich historical background, San Diegans do well to honor the past, but they would do poorly to worship it.

A backward glance into the dim and shadowy passage of 432 years serves contemporary Christians well only if it motivates them to renew their dedication to Him whose banner was first unfurled here, just 36 years after the earthly remains of Christopher Columbus were laid in the tomb.

Ours is a "pilgrim" Church and we are its heralds. As Junipero Serra said to the non-believers of his time, so must we proclaim in the 1970s: "Jesus Christ is our King, him alone do we serve. So be it. So may it ever be!"

34

"The Chapel in the Sea" is the title of this article which is taken from the *Records of the American Catholic Historical Society* LXXIX (September, 1968), 141-146.

There has always been an alluring yet inaccessible air about the four Channel Islands located off California's shoreline at Santa Barbara. Geographical isolation undoubtedly accounts for much of the mystery about the peaks of that ancient mountain range whose valleys have been inundated, since Pleistocene times, by waters of the Pacific Ocean.

On clear days, Santa Cruz, largest of the insular chain, stands out clearly on the horizon, about twenty miles due south of the coastline. The island's graceful, violet-hued peaks appear to float on the rim of the waterline, changing color tone with each successive alteration of the sun's descent. Limu, as the Indians called their home, a mountainous terrain approximately twenty-two miles long and five and a half miles in average breadth, has a superficial area of about 64,000 acres.

The aborigines inhabiting Santa Cruz, possibly a branch of the ancient Toltecs, were considerably superior to other California Indians in both physique and intelligence. Their earliest association with Christianity dates from the visit of Juan Rodríguez Cabrillo in 1542. An affidavit made eighteen years after that voyage testifies to the presence of a priest with the expedition, though neither in the document nor elsewhere is anything given concerning his identity. Periodical visitations by European adventurers in subsequent decades further ensconced the Christian tradition of that area which Sebastian Vizcaíno designated "*Isla de Gente Barbudo.*"

The island's current appellation seemingly originated with the Juan Pérez landing in 1769. It is related that a chaplain inadvertently left behind a staff with a cross on it. When the Indians returned it, the grateful cleric and his companions bestowed the Spanish equivalent of "Holy Cross" on the island to commemorate the incident.

From the earliest years of the mission era, the friars fully endorsed the Spanish government's policy of forbidding the forced removal from the Channel Islands of any Indians born there. At the same time, Fray Junípero Serra exhorted his confreres to exhibit every courtesy to the natives of that area during their occasional journeys to the mainland. In addition, Serra suggested to Teodoro DeCroix the usefulness of exploring the islands for possible sites of a future missionary foundation.

In his report for 1805, Father Estévan Tápis pursued his predecessor's thoughts about inaugurating a mission on Santa Cruz to accommodate inhabitants living in that island's ten *rancherias* as well as the seven on neighboring Santa Rosa, a population he estimated at 1,800. The Franciscan *presidente* noted that the naked and superstitious, though friendly, natives "were not disposed to join a mission on the mainland, yet caused friars trouble by their intercourse with the channel neophytes."

According to Tápis, the Indians were envious of the good fortune enjoyed by their counterparts on the mainland and had expressed a desire to have similar facilities in their own midst, unwilling as they naturally were to leave their insular habitat. Had such a project materialized, Tápis gave assurances that the residents of Santa Rosa would move to Santa Cruz.

The friar also pointed out that an insular mission would serve as an additional defense against the interloping otter hunters who even then were a cause of anxiety to civil authorities. The proposal was approved by Governor José Arrillaga, but before it could be implemented, a series of epidemics reduced the population beneath that necessary to support an autonomous foundation. From then onwards, religious instruction for the Indians was limited to that received on rare visits to the mainland and from neophytes occasionally journeying out to the islands.

The disintegration of the native race on Santa Cruz occurred more rapidly than it did on the mainland where the missions stood between the Indians and foreign rapacity. Depopulation of the islands accounts for the use of Santa Cruz as a penal colony in 1830. Thirty men, sent out with a supply of cattle and fish-hooks, were left to live as best they could. Most managed to escape within a few years on crude rafts built of hide-covered tree trunks insulated with asphaltum. Beyond a few unrelated facts, very little is known about the island's ecclesiastical history since the years when it was purchased by the late Justinian Caire.

The recent discovery of a memorandum in the Archives of the Archdiocese of Los Angeles helps to account for the continuance of the Christian tradition on Santa Cruz in the post mission years. The reason which prompted the writing of the five-page memorandum can be sketched by examining other related letters in the Archives. Apparently initial interest in the insular chapel was sparked by a request sent to the Chancery Office of the old Diocese of Los Angeles-San Diego by Father Charles Philipps. The pastor of Saint Sebastian's Church requested permission "to say Mass in the Private Chapel of Santa Cruz Island" where be planned to spend his annual vacation.[1]

Bishop John J. Cantwell granted the necessary authorization, provided that the Mass be open to anyone wishing to attend. The prelate admitted knowing nothing about a chapel on the island, though he recalled a visit several years earlier to Santa Cruz by a number of southland priests[2]. A subsequent letter from the bishop's secretary asked Father Philipps "to write us after your visit to Santa Cruz Island and tell us about the Private Chapel that exists there, that is, what it is like and by whom it is owned."[3]

Several months later, Father Philipps, by then pastor of Saint Mary's Church in Oakland, complied with the request. He consulted Miss Delphine A. Caire, daughter of the long-time owner of the island, and made arrangements for her to dictate "an accurate description of the building and of the events clustered around it."[4] That memorandum is the one here reproduced.

In acknowledging Miss Caire's typed recollections, the bishop's secretary thanked the Oakland priest for bringing the matter to the prelate's attention. "It is not often," said Father Joseph T. McGucken, "that a Chancery Office discovers a church within its jurisdiction that has been completely unknown to it."[5]

In reply to your inquiries concerning the origin and history of Holy Cross Chapel at Santa Cruz Island where occasionally we enjoy the great privilege of assisting at the Holy Sacrifice of the Mass, I beg to submit the following notes.

Although this small shrine was completed only in the year 1891, my father, Justinian Caire, must have had the project in mind for a long time. Near the site it occupies, there once stood a small adobe house, and it is probable that with its hilly background it reminded him of the chapels which in the last century still dotted the slopes of his own beloved

French Alps, also recalling to his memory the representations of the Nativity so dear to the Franciscans, to be found in the province of Liguria, Italy, where he spent a part of his young manhood. From the veranda of our island home, as his gaze rested on the simple little edifice on the opposite side of the valley, pointing to the lovely scene before our eyes, and combining two languages in one sentence as if to give expression to the double trend of his thoughts, he would say to me: "*Ne dirait-on pas un presepio?*"

When he had fully made up his mind as to the feasibility of his project, he decided that as a matter of courtesy or respect and *pour etre en règle,*" according to the sayings so dear to a Frenchman, it would be well to secure the approval of the bishop of the diocese of Los Angeles. Consequently a letter was addressed to Bishop [Francis] Mora, who, not understanding the circumstances of the case, approved the erection of a chapel provided the site and a right of way were deeded to the Church. These conditions could in nowise be complied with and we came near to abandoning all hope of ever seeing a chapel on this place which my father had grown to love so much.

But fortunately we found a friend when we most needed him. One day in the course of a conversation, I mentioned our difficulty to the beloved rector of old St. Mary's parish in Oakland, Reverend Father [Michael] King. This kind clergyman assured me that the answer of the bishop must have been the result of his misunderstanding our position, and he offered to settle the matter with the head of [the Monterey-]Los Angeles diocese. And he did.

All objections being thus removed, our men were put to work, and acquitted themselves of their divers tasks with courage and zeal. Practically all the building materials were produced on the Island itself. The bricks, from island clay, were baked by an expert Frenchman; the stone, quarried there, was worked by a very able Italian stone mason, while the lime used was burnt in a kiln which is still in existence. Even the wrought iron railing in the interior which, so to speak, separates the sanctuary from the nave, was the work of a Sicilian blacksmith, master of his craft.

The building, rectangular in shape, is of red brick, carved stone quoins decorating corners, ogival [sic] portal and windows, its shingled roof peaked, a small belfry for its mellow toned bell rising directly above the facade, surmounted by a cross. Outer dimensions are roughly twenty-seven by eighteen feet, side walls some thirteen feet high, facade and rear wall rising to a maximum of about twenty-three feet. My father insisted that above the door be carved the three initials D O M, such as they appear on so many Italian churches. Above these appears a carved cross. The same symbol is chiselled on every alternate slab of stone. Whether through design or by chance, I could not say, the chapel is properly oriented, the sanctuary being towards the rising sun, and it stands symbolically in a vineyard.

As may be guessed, its capacity is about twenty-five or thirty souls. Besides, a large open space in front of the building allows of doubling the congregation. The straight white plastered interior walls rise from the cement floor to a gently vaulted blue ceiling studded with stars. The four windows, of colored glass, are recessed a foot, three feet wide, those on the epistle side measuring about five feet high, those on the gospel side about half that dimension. The chairs for the congregation face a raised wooden altar of which the tabernacle is surmounted by a large ebony-hued cross. The iron altar rail has already been mentioned. So much for the material edifice.

When the building was completed, my brother Arthur visited the Jesuit Fathers in San Francisco (he had been a student at St. Ignatius College) to ascertain whether they could spare one of their number to preach a Mission to our men. My father judged this would be a fitting way of inaugurating worship in the chapel. Father [Gaspar] Genna, a Sicilian, then giving a retreat to the Sisters at St. Patrick's Church in Oakland, was designated for the task.

Now, once more the Rev. Father King came to our assistance. He obtained for us a consecrated stone from St. Mary's Cathedral and was kind enough to lend us a chalice with its paten, and a monstrance, each in its respective leather case, a censer, some incense and a supply of altar breads. The other requisites which could be handled by the laity were purchased. The altar linens were, of course, prepared by the "Marthas" of the family, and even comprised an alb sent from an aunt of ours living in Paris (her own handiwork). These different objects confided to my care reached the Island a short time previous to the arrival of the missionary who spent about ten days with us.

The good Father received a more cordial welcome than would ordinarily be expected from men who often boasted of their anticlericalism. He knew how to deal with these humble tillers of the soil, and my mother with exquisite tact paved the way to a better understanding between the shepherd and the flock. Exercising what I think may be called a feature of Catholic Action, she visited the men at their meals and urged them to follow the Mission which was given solely for their benefit.

During the days that Father Genna spent at the Island, we naturally assisted at an early Mass every morning. But after sunset, the chapel was closed to all but the ranch hands: sermon and prayers were intended for them exclusively. As Father Genna desired that we should have Benediction of the Blessed Sacrament, towards the close of the Mission, our little tabernacle had the great honor of harboring our Lord for a few hours. At the ceremony which appeals so strongly to Catholics and often to non-Catholics, besides the customary hymns, the zealous Jesuit Father insisted that my youngest sister Helene who had a fine contralto voice, should render the *Ave Maria* of Mercadante. Finally, on the last day, a large Mission cross was carried in procession to the accompaniment of hymns and prayers, and set up in the vineyard as a memorial of this great religious event.

How the zealous Franciscan Fathers who had gone to their heavenly reward must have thrilled with joy on knowing that after a lapse of eighty years, the praises of the Most High were sung over the land where they had hoped to establish a mission! The dream of Father [Estévan] Tápis had not been realized, of preaching the word of God to the poor ignorant island Indians whose honesty in restoring to Captain [Juan] Perez in 1769 a cross forgotten in their midst, won for ancient Limu the name of *Isla de la Santa Cruz*. But a number of men from the continent which had given birth to the intrepid missionaries of our own California and some in whose veins ran a strain of Indian blood were privileged to receive their God. The date of this Mission can be set about the year 1893.

On the return of the family to Oakland, I restored to the Rev. Father King all the objects he had so generously lent us and expressed as best I could the deep gratitude we felt for all his kindness.

For several years no priest visited the Island, and in 1897 we lost our beloved father who died after an illness which lasted about eighteen months.

At a date which I do not exactly recall, but which goes back to the first decade of the present century, nine clergymen obtained a permit to camp in one of the numerous little harbors on the northern shore of the Island. These worthy gentlemen came up to the *hacienda* on two consecutive Sundays, thus affording us an opportunity to comply with the first commandment of the Church. On the first Sunday, three Masses were celebrated; on the second, only one was said, but Father [Thomas] Kennedy added to the solemnity of the occasion by accompanying a part of the ceremony with the strains of a portable organ. Here are the names of the clergymen that my mother was very happy to entertain at dinner:

Monsignori [John] McCarthy and [John] Sullivan (the latter now of Mission Dolores), Dr. [John] Cotter, Reverend Fathers [Francis] Harvey, [John] Brockage, [Thomas] Kennedy, [Edward] Riordan, [Francis] Conaty and [Clement] Moloney.

Later, at a time that my brother Frederic and his family were summering at the ranch, three Franciscan Fathers of the Santa Barbara Mission spent several days at the Island, and as a matter of course offered up the Holy Sacrifice,—Fathers Turibius [Deaver], Modestus [Muennemann] and Francis [Redman]. With them was Rev. A[nthony] Serra of Montecito, the first "Archbishop of Santa Cruz Island."

After the death of my dear mother in 1924, vestments, altar linens and other things connected with the service of the altar were disposed of by being sent to poor churches. In April of 1925, I brought back to the Cathedral in San Francisco the altar stone which I delivered into the hands of Msgr. [Charles] Ramm.

1929 found the majority of the family planning to spend the Christmas holidays far from the confusion and bustle of civilization. But what about Mass and all the religious obligations incumbent on the faithful at this time of year? No priest attached to a parish could at such a solemn season absent himself from his church in order to satisfy the longings of less than a score of persons. All felt this keenly, but Divine Providence opened up a way for them to spend "*La Noel*" in a fitting manner. Father Thomas Sherman, son of the famous general of the Civil War, was then living in Santa Barbara and was easily prevailed upon to cross the channel to minister to the spiritual wants of the family. A vivid essay, entitled "Christmas on the Island," written by my niece, Helene, was published in the 1933 Jubilee Edition Christmas number of *The Monitor*.[6]

It is not for me to state how often in late years our Holy Cross Chapel has witnessed the offering of Mass, and that owing to the zeal and friendship of the Rev. Father Charles Philipps. But I cannot refrain from mentioning one thought that has impressed me strongly. Do you not think Rev. Father, that under Divine Providence, it is to St. Joan of Arc that we owe your ministrations at *la Isla de la Santa Cruz*? Was it not when a Triduum was held at St. Mary's Church in honor of the heroic young daughter of Lorraine that the Caire family became better acquainted with you? And I rejoice to think that it was while sojourning in this quiet spot, far removed from the mainland that you received your nomination as pastor to the church you had faithfully served as assistant. Allow me to assure you that as a former parishioner of St. Mary's for thirty years. I still nourish a deep affection for the Mother Church of the growing metropolis of the East Bay.

Hoping that for many years to come you will be spared to minister to its people, and that you will meet with great success in your projected work among the Mexicans of your parish.

Notes to the Text

1. Archives of the Archdiocese of Los Angeles (hereafter referred to as AALA), Charles Philipps to John J. Cantwell, Sebastopol, July 18, 1936.
2. AALA, John J. Cantwell to Charles Philipps, Los Angeles, July 20, 1936.
3. AALA, Joseph T. McGucken to Charles Philipps, Los Angeles, July 22, 1936.
4. AALA, Charles Philipps to John J. Cantwell, Oakland, November 27, 1936.
5. AALA, Joseph T. McGucken to Charles Philipps, Los Angeles, December 10, 1936.
6. *I.e.* the issue of December 16, 1933. The article was entitled "Christmas at a California-Island Hacienda."

35

This essay of how a "Museum Mirrors City's Past" was written for the July 3, 1977 issue of The *Los Angeles Times*.

Displays of historical items associated with the Ventura area are a tradition in the museum at the San Buenaventura Mission.

Special accommodations for that purpose were provided at least by the turn of the last century.

When President William McKinley visited San Buenaventura Mission on May 10, 1901, the *Star Press* reported that the nation's Chief Executive, Sen. Thomas R. Bard and other members of the official party "entered the historical old building and were shown its relics."

The earliest museum seems to have been located in or adjacent to the bell tower. In the late 1920s, a special building was provided on the eastern extremity of the patio "in order to preserve the treasures and relics of the past."

In *The Tidings* for Feb. 18, 1927, a writer noted that "recently a mission museum has been constructed near the entrance of the old church. There many curious and interesting relics are preserved. Old vestments and books, as well as samples of Indian handiwork, are gladly shown by an attendant." Cora McGonigle was the first person specifically charged with looking after the historical collection.

In an essay on San Buenaventura Mission written in April, 1930, Sol N. Sheridan reported that "the museum has been taken from the bell tower, and a new and attractive museum building has been built in the garden far from the church proper."

253

About five years after the purchase and refurbishment of the old Washington Hotel, the museum was moved to the rear section of the two-story edifice at 225 E. Main St., where it remanied until the closing weeks of 1975.

Early in the year of the nation's bicentennial, the museum was relocated in its earlier quarters, in the brick building on the east side of the mission patio. The display cases were rebuilt and outfitted with transparent frontices. Special lighting fixtures were installed, as well as carpeting.

A number of items unrelated to the collection were discarded, while other relics of earlier times were gathered from various sources. Most extensive of the new acquisitions are the artifacts amassed by Juan Camarillo II (1867-1936), which were formerly displayed at Saint Mary Magdalen Church. He was baptized at San Buenaventura Mission and spent much of his life within the shadows of the ninth and last of Father Junipero Serra's frontier outposts.

Another of the prominent displays is that of the liturgical vesture used in the provincial era at San Buenaventura. The 23 sets of vestments date from the earliest days of the mission. Several of the sets were fashioned from flowered-silk imported from China on the Manila galleons. There is evidence that some of the vestments were used earlier at one or another of the missions in peninsular California. For the most part they were brought to Alta California by the sea transports, which arrived twice a year at Santa Barbara from San Blas.

The books comprising the *Bibliotheca Sancti Bonaventurae* are exhibited in a case along the western wall of the museum. Almost half of the 146 tomes are printed in Spanish, with Latin, French, Italian and English following, in descending order. Of the titles still remaining in the *Bibliotheca*, 83 are bound in sheepskin or faded vellum, while 63 are encased in various kinds of less durable substances. Pieces of discarded manuscripts in many of the books indicate they were rebound at an earlier date. The ornamental printing is usually executed on a superb quality of paper which often bears identifiable watermarks. Most of the books were issued from such European cities as Madrid, Paris, Barcelona, London, Lyons and Venice. The preponderance of incomplete sets and series volumes in the library indicate that the largest percentage of the original books have been lost, borrowed or otherwise depleted.

The oldest book in the collection was published at Madrid in 1639. Ironically, 35 of the books bear the signature of Father Francisco Suner (1764-1831), who was blind for most of his years at San Buenaventura.

Several superb examples of Chumash basketry are exhibited in the museum. The baskets fashioned by the Indians attached to San Buenaventura were known for their fine workmanship, variety of forms and the extraordinary uses to which they were put. Probably, the most interesting of the baskets displayed is a small, deep jar, with a thin braid tied to loops for a handle. Its open-effect is achieved by twisting the material in each stitch. The basket is filled with large seeds.

The cases on the western wall contain a wide assortment of historical mementos associated with the history of San Buenaventura Mission, including the original sanctuary lamp for the first church. A host of farming implements are displayed, as well as such items as a barometer, compass and bellows.

A collection of items used at liturgical services is exhibited in the two freestanding glass cases. Included therein are such prized items as a monstrance used by Father Junipero Serra, an altar stone brought from Mexico City, in 1782, and an edition of the *Missale Romanum* published two years before the establishment of San Buenaventura.

Other noteworthy treasures include a Russian Cross modeled after the *Cruz Rosa de Cobre Esmaldo*, found on the *Rancho Canada Larga* by Marie Louise Canet, the writing set used by Father Juan Comapla (1824-1878) and a set of heirloom vases which belonged to the Olivas, one of the southland's oldest families.

36

The following essay was written for the fiftieth anniversary of Saint John's Seminary which occurred in 1989. Parts of it were published in the commemorative booklet issued for the occasion.

Among the papers at the Archival Center is a remnant of a sermon preached at Saint Victor's Church in West Hollywood for a memorial service marking the death of Archbishop John J. Cantwell:

"...he ordained numerous priests, received the vows of legions of nuns and brothers, confirmed thousands of people, joined the high and the mighty in wedlock, buried the famous, built hundreds of churches and schools, saw the number of his people doubled, tripled and quadrupled several times over, had his jurisdiction twice divided, administered an efficient archdiocese, inaugurated dozens of societies, attended myriads of events and lived to a biblical age. But nothing this man ever did was as important as the seminary he planned, built and brought to fulfillment at Camarillo. No bishop provides better for the Church's future than he who assures the continuity of its priests. That's what the Last Supper was all about and John J. Cantwell was there at that table for thirty years!"

It is now half a century since classes began at Saint John's Seminary and many of the Catholic priests in California's southland and elsewhere look fondly to Camarillo as their alma mater.

Saint John's Seminary is located on a terrace of the Rancho Calleguas Hills, about sixty miles northwest of Los Angeles, in the city of Camarillo.

Surrounded by orange and lemon groves and beautiful landscaping, the seminary looks out over fertile plains, with long highways stretching among orchards, cultivated fields and thriving towns.

The institution represents the fruit of many years' activity. As early as 1830 the Presidente of the California Mission, Fray Narciso Duran, suggested a seminary for the education of young men who heard a call to the priesthood. Six years later, the Franciscan *Comisario Prefecto* proposed establishing a college "to which all the youth of the Californias may flock, as well as many of the Indians of the various idioms, in order to receive the education and knowledge peculiar to their state." In his initial pastoral letter, Bishop Francisco Garcia Diego y Moreno announced to the faithful of the Diocese of Both Californias that, in compliance with the decrees of the Council of Trent, he would choose the building of a seminary as the object of his first episcopal endeavors. Shortly after arriving in the newly created diocese, the Franciscan prelate opened California's first seminary at Mission Santa Barbara. Located in the rear apartments off the corridors facing the patio, the earliest seminary functioned for about two years until the number of students and the lack of facilities demanded more spacious quarters.

Early in 1844, for the purpose of expansion, the bishop petitioned Governor Manuel Micheltorena for a grant of land adjacent to Mission Santa Ines, to be used for the building of a permanent seminary. Complying with this request, the governor authorized transfer to the Church of *Rancho Canada de los Pinos*, a parcel of land eventually amounting to 35,499 acres. On May 4th, Bishop Garcia Diego formally inaugurated the unfinished building, placing the state's first college under the patronage of Our Lady of Guadalupe. Although the school was moved in later years to San Isidro, it remained in operation until 1882.

The extreme poverty of the Church, the absence of an educational tradition, and the prevailing political and social unrest accounted for the uneven record of this pioneer seminary. The college functioned for as long as it did because it accepted students other than those preparing for the priesthood. Despite its humble beginnings and the many hardships facing the seminary, those early years of growth and development were important ones for the history of the Church in California. Zephyrin Engelhardt, the Franciscan chronicler, regarded the college as representative of "a transition period between the glorious days of old, when saintly and industrious friars reaped a harvest of souls, and the modern far-flung province that has passed its Second Spring."

In the 1850's Archbishop Joseph Sadoc Alemany moved those seminarians studying for San Francisco to Mission Dolores, while clerical students from the southland were sent either to Europe or to one of the educational institutions in the eastern part of the nation.

When Saint Vincent's College opened at Los Angeles in 1865, Bishop Thaddeus Amat reserved the right to educate seminarians for his diocese in the Vincentian staffed institution, although there is no evidence that the college ever had a formal seminary program. Subsequent Southern California prelates used the facilities of San Francisco's St. Patrick's Seminary, as well as those provided by Saint Thomas (Denver), Saint John's (Collegeville), Mount Saint Mary's (Emmitsburg), Saint Mary's (Baltimore), The Catholic University of America (Washington) and many foreign seminaries.

In 1924, Bishop John J. Cantwell revealed plans for a minor seminary and urged the southland's faithful to make the building of the seminary as the prayerful intention of their annual pre-Pentecost novena. Pointing out that such a preparatory school was an absolute necessity for the diocese, the bishop noted that only the generosity of the Catholic people could realize this dream.

In January 1926, Bishop Cantwell issued a pastoral letter concerning the seminary which he envisioned. He stated that "the soil is adapted to foster the growth of the old Faith, and although the harvest is plentiful, the children of the soil are not forthcoming to meet the demands for the laborers." The bishop observed that the See of Los Angeles-San Diego was no longer an infant diocese dependent on external material assistance; and since it was financially self-supporting, it should be also spiritually independent. Studies showed that the lack of vocations was due, in large measure, to the absence of a local program for recruiting and training priests. Both of these objectives could be accomplished better by building a minor seminary. Throughout the United States, experience had shown that candidates for the priesthood could be encouraged most effectively in those areas where preparatory schools had been established. In California, as elsewhere, the Church depended upon establishment of a local institution to train priests for its future growth.

In the same pastoral letter, the bishop observed: "The time has now arrived when, in obedience to the wishes of the Holy Father, and in duty to ourselves and posterity, it becomes necessary to raise funds for the immediate erection of a seminary." He went on to state that such an undertaking would admittedly require that, for a time, certain parochial activities be laid aside; however, the concentration of energy on the broader field of diocesan advancement was a worthwhile sacrifice.

A meeting of the lay and religious leaders of the diocese who gathered to inaugurate plans for a fund drive was held at the Olympic Auditorium of Los Angeles. Archbishop Edward J. Hanna came from San Francisco to address the largest meeting of Catholics ever held in the southland. Edward Laurence Doheny launched the campaign with a generous gift and, as General Chairman of the Junior Seminary Committee, directed letters and personal appeals to prominent Los Angeles civic leaders, among whom, he stated, were many "ever ready to assist any cause which brings to our country and our fellow citizens a contribution for betterment."

During the intensive three month drive, pastors exchanged pulpits and a speaker's bureau provided qualified laymen to address various groups throughout the diocese. The first door-to-door campaign ever conducted in the diocese was, by all standards, a tremendous success.

The bishop was so enthusiastic about the results of the drive that he remodeled temporary quarters on 21st Street, west of Grand Avenue, for students wishing to begin their seminary work in the fall of 1926. On September 7th, seventy seminarians registered in the new institution, staffed by the Fathers of the Congregation of the Mission (the Vincentians).

Since the new building on Detroit Street was ready for occupancy early in the new year, March 27th was chosen for the formal dedication and inauguration of Los Angeles College. On the occasion, a prominent attorney remarked that "the opening of the seminary commences a new era of instruction and religious advancement, the importance of which can scarcely be overestimated...To start a seminary in vision only, and in less than two years thereafter to produce a site, a great seminary building, furnished and equipped, an ample endowment fund, a school faculty, and sixty-five students, with everything in perfect functioning order, is a feat probably unparalleled in the history of such enterprises."

At the time of the dedication, Bishop Cantwell, stating that the building of a major seminary could not long be delayed, publicly acknowledged the gift made by Juan Camarillo to the diocese of a hundred acres of land near the town bearing his family name, to be used specifically for a theologate. It was the donor's intention that the new institution, to be named for his patron saint, would occupy the knoll formerly dividing the two historic *ranchos* of Calleguas and Las Posas.

Planning for the new institution, slowed by the economic stress of the depression years, stretched out over the next decade. On September 29, 1936, the Right Reverend John J. Cawley reminded the pastors of the diocese that "one of the obligations of the archbishop is to provide a new senior seminary for the education of young men for the priesthood." Not long afterward, Archbishop Cantwell explained the reasons why such an institution was necessary and what plans had been formulated for its construction. Noting that the preparatory seminary had occasioned a radical increase in the number of native vocations, the archbishop looked forward to the day when Los Angeles would be "practically self-sustaining in a spiritual and religious way as it is already in things material." He called attention to the fact that the creation of a new ecclesiastical jurisdiction in southern California was an "implied command" to erect those institutions found in the sister-provinces of the nation: "What better monument to record the creation of the Archbishopric of Los Angeles than the erection of a Major Seminary—a School of Philosophy and Theology that would bring to completion the work begun when the Junior Seminary was founded?"

Archbishop Cantwell stated that he had proceeded along such lines only after long deliberation and prayer. His decision rested upon the solid principle that "the needs of the diocese as an organic unit cannot be ignored by those who have the spirit of the universal Christ within them" Later, in an address to the Knights of Columbus, the archbishop called the campaign the greatest work for the permanency of religious life yet attempted in California.

The drive, begun on February 11, 1938, has been regarded as the most significant work ever undertaken to consolidate the apostolic labors of more than a century and a half of work by the Church in California. Those who gave generously of their time and energy to make the drive successful overlooked no possible means of communication: one group scheduled a series of radio talks; another conducted oratorical contests; the thirty thousand school children in sixteen parochial and high schools distributed circulars; a force of eight workers canvassed the 185 parishes of the archdiocese. Working diligently to increase the number of native California clergy, these volunteers responded to the archbishop's appeal on behalf of the proposed educational institution. Archbishop Cantwell's friends in the non-Catholic community also offered considerable support to the project.

By the time the campaign had drawn to a close in March, seventy-five percent of the goal had been subscribed. On the following May 10th, Monsignor John J. Cawley officiated at groundbreaking ceremonies at Camarillo, and from that time on weekly reports of the building progress were featured in the archdiocesan newspaper. When construction was virtually finished in the early part of the following year, the archbishop issued an invitation to the people of the archdiocese to participate in cornerstone-laying ceremonies on the feast of St. Joseph.

The first scholastic term began on September 12, 1939, when sixty-seven students presented themselves at the nearly completed seminary. The formal dedication took place on October 14, 1940, exactly a century after California's first bishop had been consecrated in the Basilica of Our Lady of Guadalupe. Fifty members of the hierarchy attended the event presided over by the Most Reverend Amleto Giovanni Cicognani, the Apostolic Delegate to the United States. The Archbishop of Mexico City, Luis Maria Martinez, celebrated the Pontifical Mass for the festive occasion.

During its first sixteen years, no major additions were made to the physical plant at St. John's Seminary. Early in 1955, in order to accommodate increasing enrollment, plans were completed for a third wing, together with an adjoining utility building at the eastern end of the seminary buildings. The Archdiocesan Youth Education Fund made this program possible.

On September 19, 1956, thirty-nine students occupied *Aedes Sancti Thomae* for the first time. His Eminence, James Francis Cardinal McIntyre, dedicated the new structures on October 2nd. Principal speaker for that occasion was the Very Reverend William P. Barr, the seminary's first rector. With great eloquence he thanked the Catholic populace of southern California for their "farsighted benevolence."

The new buildings, described by the Ventura County Building Commission as "the finest in the district," consisted of a two-story residence hall and a single story unit containing classrooms, a science laboratory, a radio station, a student canteen and recreational facilities.

In order to achieve the "highest standard of general education and learning" envisioned by Pope Pius XI and his successors, the Archdiocese of Los Angeles was among the first ecclesiastical jurisdictions in the United States to establish the three-unit system of seminary education. This program brought priestly training more in line with the prevailing American pattern of high school, college and graduate study.

Before 1961, St. John's College had been operated as two institutions, the first two years attached to the preparatory seminary at San Fernando, the last two years located at the theologate at Camarillo. In 1961, these were combined into a seminary college, occupying a single physical plant on property contiguous with the already existing major seminary, St. John's College offered courses in the liberal arts and was empowered to grant academic degrees.

Francis Cardinal Spellman dedicated the new institution on June 25, 1966, as part of celebrations honoring Cardinal MacIntyre on his 80th birthday. Assisting at the ceremonies were the Cardinal Archbishop of Guadalajara and numerous prelates from the western part of the nation.

While the first twenty-five years at St. John's can be described as brick-and-mortar years, the second quarter century was devoted primarily to internal development. With the seminary's physical structure firmly in place, the major thrust shifted to implementing the spiritual and academic programs mandated by the Second Vatican Council and, later, the Program of Priestly Formation. When the team of evaluators came to St. John's Seminary to conduct the papal visitation of American seminaries in 1984, they indicated in their report that St. John's was successfully implementing this program of priestly training in its curriculum and its other formational endeavors.

In fifty years of service to the church in southern California and elsewhere, St. John's Seminary, with its religious, diocesan and lay-staffed faculty, has sent forth 662 well-trained and pastorally-oriented bishops and priests to jurisdictions all over the western United States.

Historians need a greater perspective than fifty years to sort out the enrollment statistics, identify the growth patterns and appraise the administrative decisions that shaped the institution's direction in its first half century. But this much is clear from the hastiest glance: St. John's Seminary will be acknowledged as the most influential of many factors in bringing the message of salvation to one of the largest and most vibrant areas of the Lord's vineyard.

37

"We are God's Helpers" is the title of this essay which appeared in the *Sacred Heart Messenger* (October, 1964), 22-25.

The Lay Mission-Helpers Association was born into a world in which one-third of humanity had never heard the name of God. Founded by the Right Rev. Anthony J. Brouwers to help correct this universal tragedy, the organization was canonically erected as a Pious Association under the patronage of His Eminence, James Francis Cardinal McIntyre, Archbishop of Los Angeles. A constitution was drafted outlining the specific duties and obligations of the Mission-Helpers. Members receive no salary but are given an allowance of twenty dollars per month for food and clothing, enabling them to have the same standard of housing, board and medical care as do the local clergy. Their transportation is paid, but it is understood they will remain at their posts for a minimum period of three years. A contract is signed with the local Bishop stipulating the particular functions of each Mission-Helper. Men and women between twenty-five and thirty-five years of age are eligible and, beyond normal health, applicants are required to take the Minnesota Multiphasic Personality Inventory. Once accepted they take no Religious vows and wear no distinctive garb.

By September of 1956 there were already eight workers in Africa, where it was soon discovered that lay missionaries are frequently able to enter into the life of a community more completely than priests or nuns. So quickly did the organization develop that within a year after its establishment, a similiar group was set up by Bishop James A. McNulty of

Paterson under the title of the Association for International Development.

A staff of three priests conduct an intensive training program lasting an entire year and including such courses as ascetics, theology, Scripture, first aid and history of the area of assignment. Reports from members already in the field are carefully examined and scrutinized in seminar sessions. While college-trained applicants are preferable, others have been accepted. Teachers, doctors, mechanics, carpenters, electrical and metal workers, pressmen, journalists, social workers, pilots, radiomen and farmers are but a few of the skills and trades represented over the past seven years.

The training period emphasizes the spirit of personal mortification. Prospective members are acquainted with the climatic discomforts, transportation inconveniences, strange foods and pesty insects they may have to suffer. That these hurdles have not slackened interest is shown by the fact that well over 10,000 applications have been processed by Monsignor Brouwers' headquarters in Los Angeles.

The Lay Mission-Helpers and its sister organization the Mission Doctors Association are geared to provide skilled lay men and women to assume tasks that will advance the cause of Christianity on the mission frontiers. Members undertake no regular form of community life but they do follow a well-organized plan of spiritual practices. Daily Mass, regular prayers, reading of Scripture, obedience to authority, monthly reports and annual Retreats are their chief weapons and already it has been said that,

> Though they would be the first to disclaim it, they are minted coins of a treasure that is hidden behind the facade of American life. It is the treasure of a national heritage of religious belief, heroic sacrifices and generous concern for the poor and needy of the world.

Monsignor Brouwers' Lay Mission-Helpers antedated the papal volunteer program by several years and served as a "pilot system" for that world-wide organization set up by the late Pope John XXIII. Another proof of its effectiveness is seen by the fact that by 1960 there were seven separate diocesan groups on the national level paralleling the Los Angeles foundation and functioning in Brooklyn, Evanston, Paterson, Chicago, Washington, D.C., and Weston, Massachusetts.

As could be expected of any agency in the jurisdiction of James Francis Cardinal McIntyre, the Lay Mission-Helpers is an economically healthy organization. Compared to the cost for a three-year period of the Peace Corps (estimated as $27,000 per person) a Mission-Helper can be transported to and from his post and maintained for his tour of duty for approximately $3,000.

Files in the Los Angeles headquarters bulge with fascinating case histories. Mary Rose, for example, served as a social and parish worker in the capital city of Ghana's northern region. Her tasks varied from running a hostel to editing a mimeographed news-sheet. In her spare moments she taught Catechism and to her the people were "simple, warm and friendly." Veteran film executive Paul Smith served two terms and then returned to Hollywood to develop the 12,000 feet of film he took for the White Fathers. He later testified on conditions in Africa before the House Foreign Affairs Committee. William Wharton found time to write a text-book on the history of the Sudan, where he served as instructor at Khartoum's Comboru College. At least one alumna, Nora O'Mahony, went on to stardom on Broadway after her stint in the Association. She pledged forty-five per cent of her salary from one play to a mission station in Kenya.

Similiar case histories can be told from other fields. The Lay Mission-Helpers now work in Ecuador, Mexico, North Rhodesia, South Rhodesia, Sudan, Nyasaland, Kenya, Tanganyika, Nigeria, Ghana, and South Africa. The remarkably low percentage of failures over the years has been due, in great measure, to the 600-hour training and the extensive screening program insisted on by Monsignor Brouwers.

That isn't to say there haven't been unhappy moments. Ernest Ophuls, a veteran pilot in Ecuador, will never come back. He died at his post in Quito of a contagious virulent disease contracted from the natives. But before his death, he showed the fabric of the Lay Mission-Helpers when he wrote that "this time on my back gives me something to offer up for souls…and especially for the Lay Mission Helpers about to be assigned overseas."

On September 2, 1963, twenty-seven new members made their act of consecration before James Francis Cardinal McIntyre, bringing to 203 the number trained and sent to the missions since 1956. Imbedded in the minds of these dedicated soldiers of Christ was Pope Benedict XV's reminder that "missionary work surpasses all other works of charity."

38

"California's Debt to Ireland" was initially given as a homily on Saint Patrick's Day, March 17, 1966, at Saint Vibiana's Cathedral, Los Angeles. It later appeared in the *All Hallows Annual* XL (1967-1970), 29-32.

At the turn of the 19th century, some fifty years before the disastrous Irish famine, legend has it that a saintly Christian monk in the confines of Old Tunisia, beheld in a vision a great exodus from an island he knew only as Hibernia. A million bedraggled natives were seen leaving their thatched cabins on every mountain-side and moor, dragging their emaciated forms westward. From there, tall-masted ships bore them over the wide ocean to the great veldts of Southern Africa. After a brief spell mining diamonds, the exiles travelled on to the colonies of the South Seas. Others travelled to the far-away ports of New England, or even to Australia and New Zealand.

But on the western coast of North America, where "nature smiles the whole year through" and gold abounded in every hill, the monk could see a glorious new empire springing into existence. The valleys promised wealth to those who cultivated them and the inhabitants were blessed with freedom, contentment, and brotherly love. Here then the homeless children of Erin settled. And Almighty God, mindful of their fidelity, kept their Faith ever flourishing by sending a constant stream of new blood, inspired by the Holy Ghost and consecrated to His service, to break for them the Bread of Life and direct their souls in the paths of righteousness and Christian piety.

Whether this prophetic vision be fact or myth, such a migration really did take place during California's Gold Rush days. But however great the numbers were then, the great surge of *Esos Irlandeses* came almost a century after Irish influence had ruled in California. Indeed, the initial movement toward possession and settlement of this area was prompted by Irish-Spaniards and directed by a native of Dublin, the Conde Aleiandro O'Reilly. It was this Generalisimo of the Spanish Armies who gave an order that led eventually to the coming of Fray Junipero Serra and Gaspar de Portola in 1769.

Nor did Irish influence end there. When the Carson or Tahoe pass was discovered and the overland trail to California was opened, it was chiefly under the aid and direction of Thomas Fitzpatrick, a veteran trapper and guide. And when this route was menaced during the Civil War by possible action of the Southern Army and by Indian insurrection, the roadway was kept open and contact with the East maintained by Major Patrick E. Connor.

Thus California was saved for Mexico and subsequently for the United States, a trail was opened for the argonauts, and vital communications between East and West assured, through the efforts of three Irishmen. Apart from the Spaniards themselves, the only men appearing in the record of achievement by which the frontiers of New Spain were extended into the wilderness of *Las Californias* were Irish Spaniards. And it was fitting that those two great nations, Ireland and Spain, which had shared the Faith since penal days, should have cooperated so harmoniously in Christianizing California.

The Irish priesthood, too, has a long and noble heritage in the Golden State. But it has to be noted that even before her ministers came, the Faith carried over from Ireland was securely locked away in the hearts of a people who never forgot their religion, despite being deprived for many years of its priestly services,

There is something in the Irish character which readily takes up the call of the missions. As a playwright put it, the restless spirit of an Irishman "will never be content...with the mists and the winds of his native land. The Celt must wander; His youthful foot itches, and the mind and body are keen to follow!"

One historian of California, speaking of the Irish missionaries who followed Eugene O'Connell to Grass Valley, described the stream of the Emerald Isle's clergy who have so faithfully served this far-western apostolate:

> From the Apostolic colleges of Ireland, they came: from St. Kieran's in Kilkenny, from St. Patrick's in Carlow, from St. John's

in Waterford, from St. Patrick's in Thurles, and from All Hallows in Dublin. Nor were these messengers of peace all silver-haired divines who had borne the heat and burden of the day, but bright young clerics, just fresh from the anointing of the Bishop, fortified with the continence of the Virgin, the burning zeal of the Apostle, and the spirit and welfare of their fellowmen till death would meet them at the end of the trail.

That long list of Irish missioners perdures to our own day. In Southern California alone, 42% of the deceased secular priests and 39% of those presently serving in the Archdiocese of Los Angeles proudly claim the Emerald Isle as their place of birth.

This great state takes justifiable pride in the accomplishments of those who have been with her through the golden years since her infancy, those who have helped to make her name glorious in the eyes of the world. California is grateful to those argonauts and trail-blazers who assisted in pushing back the forces of ignorance and barbarism. She is mindful of those who, in the not-so-easy pioneering days, struggled, sometimes at the sacrifice of their own lives, to see that justice prevailed within her borders; of those who freely gave of their time, talent and resources that a stable government might be universally established. California is thankful for the men who have brought her honor and glory in the field of literature, arts and science. The Golden State, if she be highly respected today as a benevolent and godly commonwealth, a peaceful and desirable place to live, recognizes her great Irish builders as humble men of God, who by teaching and good example, added their share of knowledge, culture, courage and Faith to the state's development.

Pope Pius XI once said of the Irish: "They are everywhere, like the grace of God". Monuments of Ireland do, indeed, exist "everywhere", not monuments of cold marble or chilled stone but monuments of living nations whose Faith she has founded, fostered, or revived and whose manners she has purified, refined, and gilded with superb Christian wisdom. It would be difficult, indeed, to define the limits of the spiritual service of the Irish race in this or any other area, which may be why the Holy Father said they are "everywhere, like the grace of God".

That California is a beneficiary of the Irish spirit hardly needs emphasis. Here, the Sons of Erin have added much to the composite-American, made up as he is from various European, Asiatic and African stocks. The spiritual disciples of Saint Patrick, Co-Patron of the Archdiocese of Los Angeles, have softened California wit, added to its tenderness, increased the spirit of good fellowship, augmented our social graces, and increased our poetical imagination.

The Irish pioneers of California were great men and the reward of great men is that, long after they have died, one is not quite sure they are dead!

39

This address was delivered at the Century Plaza Hotel on October 22, 1971 for the centennial observances honoring the Sisters of the Immaculate Heart of Mary.

In his recent apostolic exhortation on the *Renewal of the Religious Life according to the Teaching of the Second Vatican Council*, Pope Paul VI recalled that the "Supreme rule of the religious life and its ultimate norm is that of following Christ according to the teaching of the Gospel." The pontiff concluded by opining that it was this preoccupation which, in the course of centuries, had "given rise in the Church to the demand for a life which is chaste, poor and obedient."

The Sisters of the Immaculate Heart of Mary, on the threshold of their second century of service along *El Camino Real*, personify the selfless dedication so carefully spelled out by the Vicar of Christ for those who give witness "through prayer and action, to the Good News of love, justice and peace."

The history of the *Congregación de las Hijas del Ssmo. e Inmado, Corazon de Maria* began at Olot, a picturesque Catalan village nestled in the foothills of the Pyrenees, where, on July 2, 1848, Canon Joaquin Masmitja, Augustinian archpriest of the Cathedral at Gerona, established a congregation of religious women dedicated to a way of life based on the rule of Saint Augustine and the modified constitution of the Servites. The initial community consisted of Teresa Terrada and six co-workers whose lives and talents were devoted to instructing youngsters in the fundamentals of the Catholic faith. Within three years after its foundation, the congregation received official authorization from the Royal Council of the Republic to formally engage in the teaching apostolate. Their constitution and rules were endorsed and canonically approved on April 18, 1861.

Bishop Thaddeus Amat, himself a native of Catalonia, was familiar with the work of the Sisters and eagerly hoped to extend their educational activities to the Diocese of Monterey Los Angeles. Enroute to Vatican Council I, the Vincentian prelate approached Canon Masmitja about the possibility of a California foundation for the nuns. Acting upon the recommendation of Archbishop Anthony Claret, whose intervention Amat had sought during conciliar proceedings at Rome, Masmitja agreed to allow ten of the nuns to begin preparation for the long journey to the Pacific Slope.

During the Franco-Prussian War of 1870, which delayed their departure for over a year, the Sisters studied English and acquainted themselves with other facets of American culture. In July, 1871, Father Francisco Mora, Vicar General for the Diocese of Monterey-Los Angeles, journeyed to Olot, where he finalized plans for bringing Mother Raimunda Cremadell and her companions to California. Their party set out from Gerona, on the Feast of Our Lady of the Angels. Upon arriving at Liverpool, Mora learned, to his annoyance, that the ship on which they were scheduled to sail, had already departed. The inconvenience and hardships involved in arranging subsequent passage were overshadowed by news that the earlier ship had been lost at sea! Father Mora, ten Sisters and seven clerical students finally reached California, on August 31, 1871, where they were met by Bishop Amat and Archbishop Joseph Sadoc Alemany of San Francisco.

Unforeseen developments necessitated an alteration in the initial plans for locating the Sisters at Los Angeles, and the tiny group of nuns was equally divided between the communities of Gilroy and San Juan Bautista. The weary, travel-stained missioners were greeted at Gilroy, on September 3, 1871, by abundant signs of affection from the local populace.

Meanwhile, the second contingency of nuns, under the superiorship of Sister Carmen Argelaga, re-opened, on September 11, 1871, facilities at San Juan Bautista previously maintained by the Daughters of Charity. Their work at the old mission was financed through contributions of money, food and clothing provided by local residents.

There had been a school functioning under Catholic auspices at San Luis Obispo, since 1872, on property donated to the diocese fifteen years earlier by Dolores Herrera. On August 12, 1876, the Immaculate Heart Sisters took charge of the institution and, two years later, moved their novitiate there. By virtue of one benefactor's generosity, the nuns were able to erect a lovely new community Chapel, in 1882. So generous was the support of the local inhabitants that, in 1885, the Sisters inaugurated a boys' school, in a small frame structure adjacent to the convent property.

Also about that time, Mrs. Catherine Quinn's munificence made it possible for the Sisters to extend their work to San Bernardino. They secured a residence and opened a parochial school which they fittingly placed under the spiritual patronage of Saint Catherine.

Five years later, the nuns finally secured a foothold in Los Angeles by assuming teaching responsibilities at the newly completed brick school which Bishop Mora had erected at Saint Vibiana's Cathedral. The handsome structure, located in one of the city's fashionable residential districts, opened its doors on January 4, 1886, to 250 pupils. In 1888, a high school department was added for students wishing to enter Los Angeles Normal School. On May 28, 1889, the bishop endorsed plans to remove the novitiate to a five acre section of the Schumacher tract purchased by Mother Raimunda in Pico Heights. The combination Immaculate Heart Academy-Novitiate, a fine, spacious brick building, was formally blessed on March 31, 1890.

Shortly after the turn of the century, the Sisters began formulating plans for moving their academy to an elevated site among the mustard fields of Hollywood. On April 24, 1905, ground was broken at the corner of Franklin and Western Avenue for a convent, high school and, eventually a college.

From 1908 onwards, the nuns teaching in the schools of Los Angeles lived in a community house at Eighth and Valencia Streets. The nucleus of privately-tutored children later evolved into an elementary school for the quasi-parish of Our Lady of Guadalupe (later Immaculate Conception). The next year, the Sisters took the initial step toward foundation of a central high school, by adding a ninth grade to existing facilities at Saint Vibiana's Cathedral. The high school received full accreditation by the State University, in 1912.

Father Patrick J. McGrath asked the Sisters to widen the ambit of their educational commitments to San Pedro, in the fall of 1914. The old, remodelled Church of Saint Mary, Star of the Sea, served as the initial building.

The Immaculate Heart Sisters began their work in Hollywood's Parish of the Blessed Sacrament, on February 1, 1915, with classes in the unpretentious frame building that had formerly served as parochial hall.

The California Institute of the Sisters of the Immaculate Heart of Mary, having entered a new era of expansion, was a potent force within the well-articulated school system operated by the Diocese of Monterey-Los Angeles. Eight of the sixteen parochial schools within the confines of Los Angeles were then conducted by the Sisters. The period of expansion to other areas of California that followed the 1924 papal decree severing the community's relationship with the parent Spanish foundation was made possible by the heroic devotion and sacrifice of noble, pioneering women, dedicated to God's service as reflected in the educational needs of His people. Involvement of the Immaculate Heart Sisters in the religious and societal interests of the Far West progressed another step during the second half century of their work along the Pacific Slope, when their apostolate was extended into the field of hospital care.

In the years during and immediately following the Second Vatican Council, the Sisters were provided with opportunities for re-defining their original concept of service in view of conciliar decrees and papal directives. Though the overall *aggiornamento* reduced the ranks of the Sisters drastically, the community rose from the ashes of heartbreak rejuvenated in spirit and confirmed in its determination to continue the educational apostolate on the California scene, recognizing all the while that it is only "through sacrifice and death that man attains true life."

Presently headquartered at Villa San Giuseppe, the fifty-nine professed Sisters, two novices and four postulants of the California Institute of the Sisters of the Most Holy and Immaculate Heart of the Blessed Virgin Mary staff two high schools, Mary Star of the Sea and Bishop Amat, a middle school, and eight grammar schools in the Archdiocese of Los Angeles. They are endeavoring to follow the papal norms about serving the needs of mankind by giving "an example of joyful, well-balanced austerity, by accepting the difficulties inherent in work and in social relationships and by bearing patiently the trials of life with its agonizing insecurity, as remunciations indispensable for the fullness of the Christian life."

40

This essay on "The Structure of Daily Life at the California Missions" is taken from *The Pacific Historian* XV (Spring, 1971), 13-24.

The old missions along *El Camino Real* are the most characteristic works of man in all of California. As for the friars who provided the aborigines with a whole new way of life at those historic foundations, few serious students would doubt "if a purer and more devoted set of men ever labored for the good of the heathen."[1]

The mission system as it evolved in Alta California, based on a routine "somewhere between the greater freedom and leisureliness of paganism and the full-day, full-week labor system of industrialism,"[2] endeavored to form Christian character by religious practice and instruction, ordered occupation and strict discipline. Precision was evident in all facets of the enterprise. For, example, the sequence of such communal activities as worship, labor, meals, sleep and recreation were regulated by the bell-ringer who carefully followed the latitudinal readings of the local sundial or *relojíto de sol*.

A basic daily pattern was strictly adhered to at each of the twenty-one missionary outposts. Sunrise heralded the beginning of the many chores. Following Mass and breakfast, assignments were announced in the patio, after which the Indians returned to their dwellings. They left for their jobs about an hour and a half later. At 11:15, work was discontinued for the noon meal. They resumed their tasks about two o'clock and toiled another hour and a half, or in some places, a while longer. After dinner, evenings were devoted to the enjoyable pursuits of games, music and dances. The *De Profundis* bell at eight o'clock warned that the main gate would be closed for the night in another sixty minutes. A slight variance of this schedule applied to those engaged in special activities, like sowing or harvesting which often required longer or shorter hours, depending on the season or the quantity of work at hand. There was an abundance of free time for everyone, except perhaps for the missionary. Besides Sundays and holy days, the Indians rarely labored on Saturdays, and occasionally, even Fridays were exempt. Including visits away from the central compound, an estimated ten or twelve weeks could be classified as "vacation" periods.

While the Franciscans came to California, not as schoolmen, but as apostles, educators they surely were if that term be construed as "character formation and an endeavor to fit one for the role he is to play in life."[3] In their catechetical endeavors, the friars adopted a variant of Bartolome Castaño's program used successfully in other areas of the New World. The Indians were taught the Sign of the Cross, Our Father, Hail Mary, Creed; Acts of Faith, Hope and Charity; the *Confiteor*, Ten Commandments, Six Precepts, Seven Sacraments, the Necessary Points of Faith and the Four Last Things. This summary of religious convictions and aspirations, known throughout Latin America as the *Doctrina Critiana*, provided the minimal requirement for those wishing to receive the Sacrament of Baptism.[4]

The *doctrina* was recited in common each day before Mass and again in the evening before retiring. With little exertion, even the dullest natives were able to absorb the basic tenets of the Christian Faith in a relatively short time. In their weekly sermons, the friars generally elaborated upon particular facets of the *doctrina*. Simple though the method was, it achieved surprising results among the California natives who "cared nothing for booklearning, nor for anything that taxed their mental faculties."[5]

The language barrier proved to be a formidable challenge to the *padres*, inasmuch as the terminology common to the six linguistic families among the mission Indians was literally devoid of philosophical concepts for anything incapable of being heard, touched, tasted or smelled. Scarcely a single foundation's population spoke the same language and the futility of learning local dialects was further complicated by the fact that one-fourth of all the separate lingual strains in North America were found in California, scene of "the greatest aboriginal linguistic diversity in the world."[6]

Despite royal directives, renewed as late as 1795, forbidding the missionaries to teach the neophytes in "their native tongue,"[7] there was no uniform practice among the friars in California. The younger ones, per-haps mindful of Saint Augustine's dictum that "men would prefer to be alone with their dogs than with a stranger whose language they do not understand,"[8] made heroic efforts to gain facility in the local tongues. For those further advanced in years, however, the possibility of achieving flu-ency in even one of the languages or dialects was not a realistic goal. Fray Junípero Serra tried to win over his listeners by "learning to talk with them in their own language,"[9] but the majority of the friars settled on the more practical expedient of teaching Spanish to the more gifted young-sters who then served as interpreters with the others.[10] The response of the natives to the Christian message expounded by the missionaries had to be a voluntary one. Throughout the region's history, no Indians were baptized without at least a moral assurance that they would thereafter lead lives in accordance with Christian ideals.[11] Even though Spanish and Mexican jurisprudence did not look upon rights derived from the natural law as totally unencumbered, the friars along the Pacific Slope consis-tently championed those traditions respecting an individual's inalienable religious responsibility. That no coercion was brought upon the aborigi-nals is confirmed by the greater number of Indians in such areas as Santa Barbara who decided against embracing the Christian way of life.

Once they had accepted the white man's religion, however, the neo-phytes were not free to reject it. The missionaries regarded such com-mitments as binding obligations subject to the restrictions and sanctions of any other public contracts, reasoning further that "one who forsook the Christian ranks was likely to be hostile and dangerous both to the Church and to the Spanish state."[12] On those occasions when a native ran away or failed to report after his monthly outing, other Christain Indians were sent out to fetch him. "On being returned he was reproached for failing to be at divine services on Sunday or holy day. He was warned that if he repeated the transgression he would be chastized. If he transgressed a second time he was put in stocks or given the lash. In certain cases even this was insufficient to effect a reform. Then he was placed in shackles and at the same time given work to do."[13]

The prominence of corporal punishment for such offenses as adultery, stealing and fighting was based on the friars' role as legal guardians of the natives. Directives from the Viceregal Council of War and Exchequer in 1773, defined the relationship of the missionaries to the baptized Indians as analogous to that occupied by the father of a family charged with the education and correction of his offspring.[14] For that reason, physical chastisement was looked upon as completely harmonious with the natural law concerning the raising of children, or in the case at hand, the natives for whom the missionaries acted in *loco parentis*.[15] Punishments were calculated to cause smarting pain and embarrassing ignominy, rather than protracted privation or abiding injury.

Possibly, "the most exquisite of all the gifts the Mission Fathers brought, save the boon of Christianity, was music."[16] Indeed it was a widely and effectively utilized pedagogical device in provincial times for catechizing the neophytes. The aborigines, whose natural music was in a primitive stage of monotonous rhythm, were fascinated by the tuneful Spanish melodies.[17] The *alabado*, a twenty-four stanza tribute to the Holy Trinity, Blessed Sacrament, Virgin Mary, saints and angels, was among the most familiar of the hymns sung daily by the friars, soldiers, colonists and Indians in church, at home, in the fields and on the trails.[18] That "music was fostered and developed all through the mission period"[19] is clearly evident from the impressions of such prominent observers as Robert Louis Stevenson who felt that God was served with more touching circumstances by the melodious renditions at San Carlos Borromeo "than in other temple under heaven."[20]

The plainsong comprising the greater portion of mission music was adapted, in large part, from the Gregorian chant of 18th century Spain and Mexico, much of it being arranged by the *padres* themselves.[21] Extant handbooks reveal a number of two and four part hymns and Masses. They were structurally simple; the two-part was usually sung in thirds, while the four-part compositions were homophonic. The music was written on a staff of four or six lines with notes in bold squares and diamonds, with and without tails, corresponding to present-day half, quarter and eighth notes. If there were two or more parts singing simultaneously, each group's notes was executed in different colors and each merely followed the designated sequence.[22] On festive occasions, the mission orchestra added its contribution with an assortment of violins, violas, violincellos, bases, viols, flutes, trumphets, horns, bandolas, guitars, drums and triangles.

The color, pomp and solemnity of religious pageantry deeply impressed the neophytes. Their eagerness to participate in the various liturgical functions was a major factor in assimilating Christianized civilization. So readily was the response that the friars were able to teach "the Indian boys and men to sing and chant the whole Office of the Church all the year round, and that, too, without organ accompaniment."[23]

The liturgical cycle permeated the entire year. In addition to the extensive ceremonials, observed at various seasons, were such numerous para-liturgical activities as *Las Posadas, La Pastorela, Casados y Velados, Benedición de las Animales* and the annual fiesta, all of which helped to integrate the Christian *modus vivendi* into the daily routine of mission life. Even the mundane sport of bull-fighting had its religious orientation, scheduled as it traditionally was for Easter Sunday and the yearly patron day. An unmistakable Marian tone was obvious from the very earliest times with the arrival at Monterey in 1770, of *La Conquistadora or Nuestra Señora de Belén*, a statue still venerated as California's oldest and most historic replica of the Blessed Mother.

The friars had a tolerable acquaintance with the practical arts. Besides the considerable expertise many had gained in the rough, mountainous Sierra Gorda region of Mexico, they imported previously trained Indians from Peninsular California to help instruct their northern counterparts in the basics of agricultural economy.

In the first days after a mission's inauguration, the *padres* concentrated on producing foodstuffs necessary for sustaining large numbers of Indians. Agriculture, the principal occupation in provincial time, involved clearing the land, plowing, planting, irrigating, harvesting and thrashing. Crude wooden ploughs, with sharp pieces of iron fitted between makeshift handles, were employed as were such affiliated implements as crowbars, hoes, axes, machetas and sickles.[24] Within a relatively brief span of time, the natives were making fantastic strides in their newly discovered way of existence.

As soon as the primary commodities of beans, corn and wheat were under cultivation, attention turned to such delicacies as cauliflower, lettuce, artichoke, onion, garlic, cantaloupe, watermelon, asparagus, cabbage, potato, turnip and rice. Steps were also taken to domesticate the vast natural gardens of herbs, roots, nuts, berries, wild vegetables and edible weeds already prolific in the area. Certain missions specialized in regional items which, among others, numbered chili peppers, melons, pumpkins, gourds and specific kinds of herbs. Freshly planted orchards and vineyards, fenced by adobe walls near the missions,[25] soon abounded in citrons, oranges, limes, apples, pears, peaches, apricots, cherries, plums, prunes, figs, almonds and walnuts. California's advantageously mild climate was especially conducive to the "mission grape," a large, tasty, reddish-black berry destined to become the cornerstone of California's viniculture empire.

Initially, the *padres* personally directed the various agricultural pursuits, but gradually specialists were trained and brought in to act as overseers. In subsequent years, the temporal management devolved upon the *may-*

ordomo, chief coordinator of mission activities. A tally of *inventarios* between 1783 and 1832 reveals that 41,137,625 bushels of grain of all types were harvested at the missions along *El Camino Real*,[26] a remarkable accomplishment when balanced against the primitive processes whereby those results were achieved.

Another of the chief occupations was that of caring for the diversified forms of livestock introduced by the friars. Cattle raising, eventually the greatest industry, required a fairly large quantity of personnel to guard, round-up, brand, count, slaughter and skin the ever-expanding herds. In addition to cattle, swine, goats and sheep were such beasts-of-burden as mules, horses and oxen without which the heavier chores would have been intolerable.

The "availability of grazing land was the most important factor governing the size of the herds,"[27] and as the numbers increased, they were moved to nearby *estancias* or ranches where pasturage and water were more abundant. The largest head-count of livestock at any of the twenty-one missionary establishments was recorded at San Luis Rey in 1823, where the number of cattle reached 27,500. Every mission and *estancia* had a *calaveras* where cattle and sheep were slaughtered by the Indian butchers. On Saturday mornings, the choicest animals were rounded up, and by night time their hides had been neatly stretched on the hillsides to dry.[28]

Work was underway in a myriad of other areas too. Mission life was structured to allow for "polytechnic schools, civic training grounds, and in general nurseries of civilized life, as well as paces of catechumenal indoctrination."[29] By sheer necessity, each foundation was a self-sustaining unit able to provide for practically all the basic needs of daily life.

Except for colorful baskets, the Indians of the Far West were not known for their handicrafts. Basketry, the single art in which they displayed outstanding skill, was cultivated by the women who were quite ingenious in weaving grass, sumac, splints, rushes, cedar, tule, yucca stems, kelp thread, willow roots and sea plants into mats, blankets and loin cloths.

The mortars and pestels, *metates* and *maños*, *canales* and carrying mats, burden baskets, seedbeaters, water bottles and storage jars of aboriginal times were effectively assimilated into the industrial routine of the missions. Where possible, the friars elaborated on the meager creative talents of the neophytes by instructing them in such crafts as woodworking and carpentry, wool drying and carding, tanning, metal forming and smeltering, loom production, hide, tallow and candle making, kiln-forming and whatever other natural arts proved helpful to their communal way of life.

It is hardly hyperbolic to observe that "the missionaries had to begin with the kitchen rather than the chapel in convincing the savages that Christianity was superior to barbarism."[30] For a host of reasons, the preparation of food was a matter of top priority for all concerned. Simple and functional utensils were used for cooking on stoves or bricks built over open fires. Adobe ovens were utilized for baking breadstuffs, cornmeal loaves, tortilla-like flat cakes and wheat bread.

There were three main meals in each day's schedule. On an average morning, the Indians partook of *atole*, a rich and nutritious gruel substance. At noon they lunched on *pozole*, a mush of thick soup of wheat, corn, beans and meat. To that basic diet was generally added a pottage and numerous wild seeds. *Atole* was served a second time at the evening meal. The sick were given special food consisting of *atole* or corn tortillas and a dish of veal beef or a combination of both. The overall fare was substantial and tasty. One missionary at San Luis Obispo reported that in a single year, in addition to 2,000 cattle, the entire harvest was consumed.[31]

The California missions, even in modern times, are "the finest relics in the United States,"[32] representing a unique and lasting contribution to American culture. Space was available, at each of those Spanish outposts, for the numerous social, religious, agricultural and industrial activities constituting the montage of provincial living. The architectural scheme, with living quarters for two friars as well as storehouses, workshops and dwellings for the natives, was as functional as it was protective. Most of the missions developed around an open-air patio. Understandably, the church, usually located in the northeast corner of the quadrangle, was the initial structure erected. Crude as were those early houses of worship, they were easily the most handsome of the mission buildings.

The earliest construction was supervised by the friars. In later times, however, the viceroys dispatched artisans, mechanics, masons, carpenters and others to direct and instruct the neophytes in the art of making and laying adobe bricks, felling trees, sawing and hewing lumber, preparing lime, mixing mortar and making roof and floor tiles. Simplicity, or lack of ornamentation, the distinctive charm of the California missions, was compensated by the frankness of proportions resulting from limitations of material. What little decorative work there was normally had to be imported, either from Spain or Mexico. Over the years a remarkably varied collection of sculpture and paintings accumulated, some of it quite artistic.

"Mission architecture," though related both to Spanish colonial in Mexico and that of the mother country, was comparatively unpolished. The more sturdy California version was generally fashioned around wood plastered with clay. Where timber was scarce, sundried bricks were utilized. Such distinctive features as gently slanting and burnt-tile roofs, thick adobe walls and extensive arcades were themes repeated from one mission to another.[33] Simple columns and pediments bespeak Moorish, Spanish-Roman and Renaissance motifs, although the style leaned more toward the neo-classic than the baroque. Among the obvious characteristics of the so-called "mission architecture" are massive walls and buttresses; arcaded corridors and arched colonnades; curved pediment gables; terraced bell-towers; pierced *companarios;* patios without fountains; wide, projecting eaves and low-pitched roofs.[34] The California missions are thought to be "unique among the Spanish buildings of the Americas, on account of their simplicity, often approaching in this respect the severity and the charm of the arcades and unbroken wall masses of the early Romans."[35]

The Iberian outposts have long been considered "the noblest architectural remains of former days to be found in the United States."[36] Probably no architectural style ever created so much with so little raw material to work with; so much that is warm and touching in its beautiful simplicity with so little creative experience to fall back on. One writer conjectured that "the priceless intrinsic ingredient that the *padres* put into their buildings was the very one that prompted them to venture into the wilderness in the first place. That ingredient was Faith."[37]

Every imaginable medical problem plagued the friars. Battle casualties and accidental wounds, coupled with the natural scourges of pneumonia, scurvy, consumption, typhoid, smallpox and cholera presented major obstacles to the missionary enterprise. Treatment was frequently crude and primitive, though, astonishingly, the Indians exhibited a remarkable facility at such difficult tasks as setting bones. Their native remedies revealed an extensive experimental knowledge about the value of many herbs, plants and roots. There was a hospital at San Gabriel which, by 1810, had more than 300 patients. Where similar facilities existed, they were built of thick, whitewashed adobe walls, with red tile floors and roofs and running water. Those foundations lacking such elaborate accomodations for the ill could at least boast of having apothecary shops. Admittedly, the friars were not as adept physicians of the body as they were of the soul. Nonetheless, they possessed medical knowledge enough to perform minor surgery and even, on occasions, more complicated operations. "They were really the medical Gibraltars in their establishments."[38]

This short "overview" of the many-faceted life at the California missions can be terminated by alluding to the words of the Golden State's poet laureate who observed that:

> These were the gifts the Franciscans brought with them to the Indians; Christianity, education, the joy of work, and music. It was an achievement scarcely paralleled in human history in so short a span of time—a little more than two generations.[39]

Notes to the Text

1. Henry W. Henshaw, "Missions and Mission Indians of California," *The Popular Science Monthly* XXXVII (August, 1890), 481.
2. Maynard J. Geiger, O.F.M., "Working Conditions of the Mission Indians," *Way* XX (December, 1964), 15.
3. William E. North, *Catholic Education in Southern California* (Washington, 1936), pp. 13-14.
4. As a rule, Indian adults would remain catechumens for as much as a year, though the period varied from place-to-place. No one was baptized until he or she had been sufficiently instructed and tried.
5. Zephyrin Engelhardt, O.F.M., *The Missions and Missionaries of California* (Santa Barbara, 1930), 11, 490.
6. A. L. Kroeber *Handbook of American Indians* (Washington, 1907), p. 191.
7. Finbar Kenneally O.F.M., (Trans.), *Writings of Fermín Francisco de Lasuén* (Washington, 1965), I, 329.
8. *De Civitate Dei*, Lib. XIX, Cap 7.
9. C. Scott Williams (Trans.), *Francisco Palóu's Life and Apostolic Labors of the Venerable Father Junípero Serra* (Pasadena, 1913), p. 124
10. Arthur L. Campa, "The Churchmen and the Indian Languages of New Spain," *Hispanic American Historical Review* XI (November 1929), 546.
11. Zephyrin Engelhardt, O.F.M. *San Diego Mission* (San Francisco, 1920), p. 31.
12. Daniel D. McGarry, "Educational Methods of the Franciscans in Spanish California," *The Americas* VI (January 1950), 355.
13. Maynard J. Geiger, O.F.M., *Mission Santa Barbara, 1782-1965* (Santa Barbara, 1965), p. 73.
14. Herbert Eugene Bolton (Trans.), *Historical Memoirs of New California*, (Berkeley, 1926), III, 50.
15. See James A. Burns, C.S.C., "Early Mission Schools of the Franciscans," *Catholic University Bulletin* XIII (January, 1907), 37.
16. John Steven McGroarty, "Foreword" to *Mission Music of California* (Los Angeles, 1941), p. ix.
17. Daniel D. McGarry, *op. cit.*, 352.
18. Herbert Eugene Bolton (Trans.), *Font's Complete Diary* (Berkeley, 1933), p. 25.
19. Maynard J. Geiger, O.F.M., *Mission Santa Barbara*, 1782-1965, p. 69.
20. *Across the Plains* (New York, 1901), p. 105.
21. Fray Narciso Duran's *Misa de Cataluña* was probably the most popular of these production. It was written during the years Duran served at Mission San Jose. Through the efforts of Father Edmond Venisse, the Mass subsequently became known in such a faraway place as Chile.
22. See Owen Francis Da Silva, O.F.M., *Mission Music of California* (Los Angeles, 1941), p. 13.
23. Zephyrin Engelhardt, O.F.M., "Catholic Educational Work in Early California," *Catholic Educational Association Bulletin* XV (November, 1918), 366.
24. Edith Webb, "Agriculture in the Days of the Early California Padres," *The Americas IV* (January 1948), 329.

25. Only Missions San Francisco, San Rafael and San Francisco Solano lacked orchards and vineyards and that because of their climate. See E. J. Wickson, "California Mission Fruits," *Overland Monthly* XI (May, 1888), 501.
26. Edith Webb, *Indian Life at the Old Missions* (Los Angeles, 1952) p. 59.
27. R. Louis Gentilcore, "Missions and Mission Lands of Alta California," *Annals of the Association of American Geographers* LI (March, 1961), 67.
28. See Guadalupe Vallejo, "Ranch and Mission Days in Alta California," *The Century Illustrated Monthly Magazine* XLI (December 1890), 190.
29. Daniel D. McGarry, *op. cit.*, 337.
30. Zephyrin Engelhardt, O.F.M., "Catholic Educational Work in Early California," p. 362.
31. Fray Luis Antonio Martínez, quoted in Edith Webb, *Indian Life at the Old Missions*, p. 40.
32. P.C.W. in the Los Angeles *Times*, January 24, 1896.
33. R. Louis Gentilcore, *op. cit.*, 60.
34. Rexford Newcomb, *The Old Mission Churches and Historical Houses of California*, (Philadelphia, 1925), p. 104ff.
35. Arthur B. Benton, "The California Mission and Its Influence upon Pacific Coast Architecture," *West Coast Magazine* IX (May, 1911), 146.
36. George W. Cole, "Missions and Mission Pictures: A Contribution toward an Iconography of the Franciscan Missions of California," *California Library Association Publication* XI (Sacramento, 1910), 47.
37. Kurt Baer, *Architecture of the California Missions* (Berkeley, 1958), p. 66.
38. George D. Lyman, "The Scalpel Under Three Flags in California," *California Historical Society Quarterly* IV (June, 1925), 149.
39. John Steven McGroarty as quoted in *Provincial Annals* XXIV (July, 1962), 143.

41

This essay on "The Editions of Palou's *Relación Histórica*, 1787-1958" is taken from the *Hoja Volante* #108 (May, 1972), 7-8.

There is always something fascinating about focusing attention on the printed sources from which the story of an area's pioneers is gleaned.

First place among materials pertaining to Junípero Serra must be given to the account written by his long-time companion and biographer, Fray Francisco Palou. Certainly no one was better qualified by opportunities and ability for such a task. The work takes on added significance inasmuch as most of the literature of secondary value which has been penned about Serra in subsequent years has been based on Palou's *Relacion Historica de la Vida y Apostolicas Tareas del Venerable Padre Fray Junípero Serra.*

Palou's monumental opus has other positive qualities. It has, for example, "the double distinction of being the earliest California biography and the best biography of California's most renowned character."[1] Even today, the work of the Mallorcan friar "remains the source into which essayists, preachers, orators, poets and playwrights have dipped their pens for their materials, and in this manner it enjoys an influence beyond the wildest dreams of its author."[2]

Though intended primarily "as a treatise for edification,"[3] the *Relacion Historica*, produced in 1787 at the printing shop of Felipe de Zuñiga y Ontiveros on Mexico City's Calle del Espíritu Santo, proved to be the "most vitally important work on the early years of the Spanish occupations of California."[4] Its sixty chapters, containing almost 100,000 words, occupy 344 pages of text.[5] Internal evidence indicates that the cost of publishing the first book written in California to find its way into print was borne jointly by the College of San Fernando and certain of its benefactors. Some copies read "*a expensas de Don Miguel González Calderon síndico de dicho apostólico colegio*" while others merely have "*a expensas de varios bienhechos.*" A few other discrepancies indicate at least two impressions, if not separate editions.

The frontispiece is significant in that it is the first purporting to be a portrait from life.[6] Clothed in the traditional Franciscan garb, Fray Junípero is depicted with a crucifix in his outstretched left hand and a large stone in the right hand with which he pounded his breast "as he exhorted his hearers to penance."[7] Surrounded by Indians, Serra stands on a slightly elevated piece of ground around which are scattered a number of symbolic designs. Beneath the 6-1/2-by-5-inch woodcut is the inscription: "*V.R. del V.F.E. Junípero Serra.*" There is no evidence to indicate what resemblance, if any, the print has to Serra, though it can reasonably be presumed that Fray Francisco Palou would have vetoed any outlandish alteration from Serra's earthly features. The woodcut was reproduced to exact scale in the *Land of Sunshine*, May of 1897.[8]

Another important feature of the "best original authority for the earliest period of mission history"[9] is Diego Froncoso's 10¼ by 13½ inch folding map "upon which for the first time are represented the missions of Nueva California."[10] There are two versions of the map, tipped in at the end of the book, one with, the other without the name "Mar Pacifico" lettered along the coastline.[11] One cartographer conjectured that the map was printed before the book, the earlier ones lacking the identifying words added in later editions.[12]

Though circulated widely, Palou's original work has never been in plentiful supply. In his preface to the first English edition, published in 1884, the Bishop of Monterey-Los Angeles, Francis Mora, observed that even then, "Fr. Serra's life by Palou is so scarce in the mother tongue that the few copies extant are estimated at the highest value."[13] The fortunate discovery, just after the turn of the century, by W. W. Blake, a bookseller in Mexico City, of fifty copies at the Apostolic College of Santa Cruz de Querétaro,[14] has greatly alleviated the demand of Western Americana enthusiasts, many of whom regard the treatise as the cornerstone of their collections.

The *Relacion Historica* was republished at Mexico City in 1852, as a supplement to Juan R. Navarro's edition of the *Historia de la Antiqua o*

Baja California. Obra Postuma del Padre Francisco Javier Clavijero.[15] Four years later, an edited version appeared serially in San Francisco's *El Estandarte* and, the following year, in *La Estrella* of Los Angeles.

In 1856, Roa Barcena published a lengthy five-part digest of the work under the caption *"Estudios Biográficas, El Padre Franciscano Serra"* in La Cruz.[16]

A truncated edition, the first in English, was translated in 1884, by Father Joachim Adam, and published by P. E. Dougherty, Book & Job Printers, 412 Clay St., San Francisco, as the *Life of Ven. Padre Junipero Serra Written by Very Rev. Francis Palou.* The late Henry Wagner regarded copies of this 156-page work as "even scarcer than the original."[17]

George Wharton James published a complete English version of the *Relacion Historica* at Pasadena in 1913. Unfortunately, a considerable number of inaccuracies in the textual rendition, under the English title *Francisco Palou's Life and Apostolic Labors of the Venerable Father Junipero Serra,* found their way into the 338-page translation by C. Scott Williams.

In 1944, another edition, this one in Spanish, was published as *Evangelista del Mar Pacifico* at Madrid under the editorship of M. Aguilar. The 317-page book, with a lengthy prologue by Lorenzo Riber, is regrettably marred by numerous typographical errors.

"The only truly scholarly edition in any language of the *Relacion Historica*"[18] was the translated and annotated version published in 1955 by the Academy of American Franciscan History under the title *Palou's Life of Fray Junipero Serra.* Rendered into a smooth and accurate style by the eminent Father Maynard Geiger, O.F.M., the "extremely valuable and pertinent editorial notations"[19] of the 547 page narrative go far "to correct some of Palou's misstatements and to clarify points hitherto obscure."[20]

An Original Leaf from Francisco Palou's Life of the Venerable Father Junipero Serra, 1787, assembled from a dismantled copy of the first edition, was tipped into each of the 177 copies of the bibliographical commentary on the *Relacion Historica* which David Magee published at San Francisco in 1958 for members of the Roxburghe and Zamorano Clubs.

Even those literary critics who would not rank the *Relacion Historica* as a serious historical opus by today's standards agree that "Palou's work will remain for just what it is,—the most valuable account ever published on early California history, though covering only a portion of that field."[21]

Notes to the Text

1. John Walton Caughey, *California* (Englewood Cliffs, New Jersey, 1964), p. 604.
2. Maynard Geiger, O.F.M., *Palou's Life of Fray Junipero Serra* (Washington, 1955), p. xii.
3. M. Aguilar (Ed.), *Evangelista del Mar Pacifico* (Madrid, 1944), p. 17.
4. Charles E. Chapman, *A History of California: the Spanish Period* (New York, 1923), p. 496.
5. Except for a small part of the last two chapters discovered at Orizaba, Mexico, the original manuscript has not been located.
6. Maynard Geiger, O.F.M., *Representations of Father Junipero Serra in Painting and Woodcut. Their History and Evaluation* (Santa Barbara, 1958), p. 5.
7. Zephyrin Englehardt, O.F.M., *The Franciscans in California* (Harbor Springs, 1897), p. 103.
8. VI, 241.
9. Hubert Howe Bancroft, *History of California* (San Francisco, 1884), I, 420.
10. George Watson Cole, "Missions and Mission Pictures: A Contribution towards an Iconography of the Franciscan Missions of California," *Publications of the California Library Association #11* (Sacramento, 1910), p. 45.
11. This map was reproduced, at one-fourth the scale, in *Land of Sunshine* VII (June, 1897), 12.
12. Henry Raup Wagner, *The Spanish Southwest*, 1542-1794 (Albuquerque, 1937), II, 479.
13. Joachim Adam (Trans.) *Life of Ven. Padre Junipero Serra Written by Very Rev. Francis Palou* (San Francisco, 1884), preface.
14. Henry Raup Wagner in *The Zamorano 80* (Los Angeles, 1945), pp. 47-48.
15. Pp. 125-252. The first part of this work contained the Spanish text of *Storia Della California Opera Postuma del Nob. Sig. Abate D. Francesco Saverio Clavigero* which originally appeared at Venice in 1789.
16. III (October 9, 1856), 303-309; III (October 23, 1856), 369-376, III (November 6, 1856), 432-437; III (November 27, 1856), 520-526 and III (December 11, 1856), 596-600.
17. *The Spanish Southwest* 1542-1794, II, 480.
18. David Magee, *An Original Leaf from Francisco Palou's Life of the Venerable Father Junipero Serra*, 1787 (San Francisco, 1958), no pagination.
19. A. P. Nasatir, "Book Review," *Hispanic American Historical Review* XXXVI (February, 1956), 112.
20. Donald C. Cutter, "Book Review," *Pacific Historical Review* XXIV (November, 1955), 402.
21. Charles E. Chapman, op. cit., p. 497.

42

This essay "A Postcard View of the Missions" is taken from *The Branding Iron* #158 (Spring, 1985).

In primitive times, pictures were drawn on rock faces, tree barks and animal hides. Then, in medieval days, wealthy nobles enhanced the bare walls of their castles with paintings and rich tapestries; industrious monks worked for years illuminating parchment books of hours. As far back as recorded history, people who loved beauty and the arts have collected depictions and portrayals. With the development of efficient reproduction processes, it became possible for such collecting to spread beyond the few who could afford originals. The 19th and 20th century saw the crude woodcut develop into the fine engraving, the photograph and the lithograph—forerunners of the modern halftone and gravure processes.

The postcard is an outgrowth of the universal love for pictorial art. As an accepted part of contemporary culture, it belongs to the interplanetary age just as surely as leisurely letters are now associated with the time of the stagecoach.

Inasmuch as postcards traditionally reflect the tastes, interests and sentiments of the areas where they originate, it is understandable that the California missions have been a favorite theme of westerners for almost seventy-five years. Possibly no other medium so vividly portrayed the provincial era. One authority claimed that, "as a record of local history they are valuable and bear a somewhat similar relation to the place represented as does its local newspaper."

The earliest known postcards date from 1861, when John P. Charlton of Philadelphia obtained a copyright for his privately issued "postal cards." These cards, decorated with a slight border pattern and labelled "Lipman's postal, patent applied for," were on sale for about a dozen years.

The origin of the "open postsheet" is generally attributed to Heinrich von Stephan, one-time Postmaster General of the Imperial German Empire, who in 1865, advocated the introduction of the *offenes postblatt* with "the dimensions of ordinary envelopes of the larger size" consisting of stiff paper. Von Stephan suggested that on the face of the card there might appear, at the top, the name of the district and perhaps a small device (the arms of the country, *etc.*). On the left hand would be space for the date stamp of the receiving office, offset on the other side by a previously impressed postage stamp. There would be additional room for the address and any other necessary printed notices. The reverse side of the card was reserved for the actual communication.

It was another four years, however, before the world's first authorized postcard came into existence. On October 1, 1869, the Austrian Postal Administration issued a group of thin buff-colored cards imprinted with a yellow 2 Kreuzer stamp. The popularity of the new medium was quickly acknowledged and within a few months, several million of the cards had been sold.

The United States Government issued its first "Postal Card," in May of 1873, but the innovation was not widely welcomed. One writer complained that "my grudge against the postal card is that it is gradually developing an affection of the eye—in others as well as myself—which I call heteropsis; that is, the tendency to read against your own will postal cards not addressed to yourself!"

Although common throughout less puritanical Europe in the 1890s, "the first picture postcards published in the United States of America—apart from some earlier advertising cards—were placed on sale at the World Columbia Exhibition in Chicago in May 1983." Congress officially sanctioned "Private Mailing Cards" and extended the same message privileges and rates then prevalent on the government-issued cards five years later.

New postal regulations, in 1901, spelled out a broader policy for "Post Cards" which were considered legally distinct from the official "Postal Cards." After 1907, further stipulations were made allowing messages on the reverse side of the pictorial postcards, provided a vertical dividing line set off the communication from the section reserved for the address.

Authorities considered the postcard as a medium of popular art, and there is some justification for the theory that the picture postcard was originally launched as a means of promoting taste and appreciation of art. The producers of postcards, whether they were artists, photographers or printers, shared in this unique form of folk-art. Their best examples resulted from the mingling of drawing and photography or from the one being superimposed on the other. Since the basic color tone could be modified considerably, a wide variety of depictions was possible and intervening issues portray effectively the changing public tastes in brightness of coloring and degrees of glossiness.

The character of the early postcards was limited by their shape, size, and thickness—all of which was carefully determined by the Universal Postal Union, when a thin piece of 5½" by 3½" cardboard was adopted as the official type.

In 1910, George Watson Cole reported "the most familiar form in which the old missions are presented to the eye at the present time is perhaps the postcard." Even a cursory glance at the volume of productions emitting from the various publishing houses lend credence to that assertion.

The largest western publisher of postcards was Edward H. Mitchell of San Francisco. His firm issued about 4,000 different scenes between 1898 and 1915, including thirty-two postcards depicting fourteen missions. In addition to an alternate series of scenes published on yellow or canary colored paper, Mitchell printed many cards distributed by other Californiana specialty houses.

The Detroit Publishing Company, originally known as the Photochrome Company, issued postcards from 1898 until 1919. Experts generally agree that the output of this firm was by far the most important in the American postcard field. It is estimated that approximately 15,000 different cards were published in their "photostint" process, 700 of which fell into the category of art and humor. An unspecified number of their twenty-nine views of twelve missions were printed in Switzerland.

Twelve views of five missions and one *asistencia* were published by the Cardinell-Vincent Company of Oakland. This firm was an outgrowth of Britten and Rey, early San Francisco lithographers.

M. Rieder of Los Angeles disseminated the greatest variety of specimens on the missions, representing all but San Jose. Among his 181 depictions are the only known views of Santa Ysabel and San Pascual. Printed in several places, mostly in Germany, then the center of the postcard industry, the Rieder line was purchased by George O. Restall about 1909.

There are 132 postcards distributed by the Oscar Newman Company of Los Angeles and San Francisco. The depictions of eighteen missions and two *capillas* were made in Germany prior to World War I and later in the United States. Adam Clark Vroman of Pasadena circulated thirty-six replica color prints of the missions. In addition to scenes of eighteen different missions and one *capilla*, was one outstanding postcard-map of *El Camino Real*, reproduced from the original used in the census of 1890.

Twenty different mission scenes were among the forty-four postcards published by the Paul C. Koeber Company of New York City. Included among the four scenes of *asistencias* is a rare view of Santa Margarita. The L.R. Severn firm of Los Angeles issued twenty-two views of six missions and two *capillas* on postcards printed in Germany. In later years the business was merged with Wood Publishers of Los Angeles and Leipzig.

The Pacific Novelty Company of San Francisco distributed fourteen views of seven missions and one *capilla*. Another Bay area firm, Richard Behrendt, circulated missions postcards between 1905 and 1909. N.H. Reed of Santa Barbara had a variety of 800 different California scenes. Among his photographic postcards were about 200 views of the missions, mostly of Santa Barbara. The Adolph Selige Publishing Company of Saint Louis offered nineteen views of four missions, while the Benham Indian Trading Company of Los Angeles made available fourteen views of four missions. Ghirardelli's Milk Chocolate Company furnished a set of fifteen missions which were never sold commercially.

Other less significant producers of mission postcards were: Tichnor Brothers, Inc. (Boston and Los Angeles), the Neuner Company (Los Angeles), Carlin Postcard Company (Los Angeles), Harold A. Taylor (Coronado), Frederick W. Martin (Pasadena), Souvenir Publishing Company (San Francisco and Los Angeles), California Sales Company (San Francisco), Bardell Art Printing Company (San Francisco), T.P. Getz (San Diego), Eno and Matteson (San Diego), Diederich-Schaefer Company (Milwaukee) and the Albertype Company (Brooklyn).

No period in human annals has been devoid of a medium to express its own particular beauty and fascination. When seen in their proper historical perspective, mission postcards certainly express the tone of California's provincial atmosphere more effectively than many other of the less ephemeral survivors of the era.

43

The following essay about "Ramblings at Pala" is taken from *The Journal of San Diego History* XXI (Fall, 1975), 38-42.

On March 15, 1866, Special Agent John Quincy Adams Stanly submitted a report to Washington, complaining about irregularities among the Indians then living at Temecula. He sent a copy of the charges to Charles Maltby, the Superintendent of Indian Affairs for California and, thirteen days later, Maltby left for the southland to make a personal investigation of the allegations.

After speaking at length with Stanly and meeting with concerned Indians and others, the Superintendent returned to San Francisco where, on April 13th, he dispatched a ten page, handwritten report to Dennis T. Cooley, the Commissioner of Indian Affairs.

The original manuscript of Maltby's report is now filed with other papers relating to the California Superintendency (1849-1880), in the Office of Indian Affairs, at the National Archives, Washington, D.C. A microprint of the report is among the many acquired some fifty years ago by the late Msgr. William McDermott Hughes, who served as Director for the Bureau of Catholic Indian Missions from 1921 to 1935. It is here reproduced from the Chancery Archives, Archdiocese of Los Angeles, with the permission of Cardinal Timothy Manning.

A number of such reports were published, at various times, by the Commissioner of Indian Affairs. Dr. Robert M. Kvasnicka, an official for the Natural Resources Branch, Civil Archives Division, informed this

292

writer, on November 30, 1974, that "to our knowledge this letter had not been published."

I have the honour to state that on the 28th ult. I left San Francisco for purpose of making a personal examination of the condition of the missions Indians in Southern California, and the causes of the troubles and difficulties amongst them as stated by Special Agent Stanly[1] in his report to this office a copy of which was forwarded to the Hon Comm. under date of March 15th ult. with my report for the month of February *ultimo*.

I arrived at Los Angeles on the 31st ult. and left there on the 2d inst for Temécula[2] with Special Agent Stanly where we arrived on the 3rd inst. On the next day we proceeded to the Old Mission of Pala,[3] a distance of 10 miles from Temécula over the mountains, in the valley of the San Luis River, the residence of Manuel Cota[4] the present-authorized Chief of the Indians in San Diego County. We made an examination of the old mission[5] and the lands in the vicinity and returned to Temécula the same day with Manuel Cota.

Information having been sent to the several *racharias (sic)* of my arrival with the request that the Indians meet the following morning at Temécula at which place a large number assembled. I ascertained that the opposition to Manual Cota, and the troubles and difficulties existing was caused by the dissatisfaction of a few lazy, vicious, and drunken Indians who would steal rather than work, led on and encouraged by low vicious white men[6] interfering with the efforts of Manuel Cota to prevent the selling liquors to the Indians,[7] and the selling of the squaws by the Indians to these degenerate white men for prostitution and further by the interfereance *(sic)* of a Lawyer in Los Angeles by the name of Howard[8] "who for a fee" and a few others had promised those disafected *(sic)* Indians that they would obtain the removal of Manual Cota from his appointment as Chief.

I told the Indians that I had continued Manuel Cota as Chief over them, that he was to have supervision for the settlement of their difficulties and the management of their affairs, and that he was authorized to arrest and take before the proper authorities of the County for punishment any or all Indians guilty of crimes and misconduct and that they was *(sic)* to be governed by him and pay respect to him as chief appointed by the proper authority. The Indians mostly stated that they were satisfied with Manuel Cota as their Chief and would be governed by him. A small number said that they had paid Howard of Los Angeles who told them that he would have Manuel Cota removed and if he now told them it could not be they would be satisfied and submit to his authority. I have reason to believe that now the disafected (sic) Indians being satisfied that they must submit to Manuel Cota as their Chief will cease all further opposition to his authority and that order and tranquility amongst them will be restored. I received on my arrival at Temécula a Petition signed by a large number of the citizens of San Diego County stating that they desired Manuel Cota should be retained in his position as Chief, that he was an Indian of good character, of extraordinary intelligence and energy and that he was labouring to improve the condition of his people[9] by preventing as far as possible the use of Spiritous Liquors by the Indians and inducing them by precept and example to be industrious and cultivate the lands they occupy for their support and subsistance. He is a remarkable Indian, perfectly temperate, uses no spiritous liquors, nor does he indulge in any of the vice so common amongst the Indians.

The Indians in San Diego County under his supervision number some three thousand, they have all been connected heretofore with the Catholic Missions, and are considerably advanced in civizitation (sic), but since the breaking up and abandonment of the missions they have scattered and located in various places in the vallies (sic) and on the streams, where water could be obtained for the irigation (sic) of the small patches of land they cultivate. Since they have passed from under the control and advice of the Padries (sic) or Priests they have to a considerable extent become demoralized indolent, lazy, fond of Liquors, and gambling, and other vices which has been the invariable result- in all cases in this state when the Indians have come in contact with that class of white population whose conduct and influance (sic) demoralizes and degrades instead of elivating (sic) the Indians.

Manuel Cota resides at the mission of Pala, he has a good adobe house and forty acres of land in cultivation, and owns a considerable number of horses, and cattle, and is highly esteemed by the citizens for his good character and influance (sic) with the Indians. His time is constantly employed in the supervision and management of the Indians, in the settlement of their difficulties and in maintaining order and discipline amongst them, and as their settlements embrace a large extent of country he has a large amount of traveling to perform in visiting their different settlements. I stated to him at Temécula that I would recommend to and ask of the Hon Comm. of Indian affairs that he be allowed fifty dollars per month for his services as chief.

The service of Special Agent Stanly who has had charge of these Indians will not be required after this date, and Manuel Cota having the entire charge and control of them, I believe it to be an act of justice, as well as economy that he should be allowed a small compensation for his services. It will be an inducement and stimulant for a more faithful discharge of his duties, and his position and authority will the more readily be recognized by the Indian as one employed and paid by the Government for his service. I would therefore respectfully recommend that he be allowed for his service fifty dollars per month, as I believe that this amount of money expended in payment of his services will be of much advantage to the Indian Service in this part of the State.

The Indians in San Diego County are residing mostly on Government lands, in some cases on lands held by individuals under Spanish or Mexican Grants, and they must as the country becomes settled by the whites give place to them. This has been and will be the result in all cases in this State, had all the Indians a perfect title to the lands they now occupy. Most of them as opportunity offered would be induced by the whites who desire a possession to sell them land for a few blankets or some trifling consideration, and then they would be turned over to the care of the Government, or on the community to obtain a subsistence as best they could.

This state of affairs existing, I believe now is the proper time for the Government to make some provisions for those Indians in providing for them a permanent location and future home. All they want is a tract of land suitable for cultivation on which they can locate and raise their subsistence, and be unmolested by the whites. A few farming implements and seeds they will require yearly—No expenses attending the establishment of a reservation will be required. Give them lands and protection, and they will provide for their own subsistence.

The old mission of Pala[10] located on the San Luis River embracing 25,000 acres valley and mountains lands would be the best location for those Indians in that part of the State. The lands in the valley adjoining the mission which could be irigated *(sic)* and made productive would subsist two thousand Indians as many as would ever require a home and lands at the hands of the Government. About 160 Indians reside here at present, and with this mission and land adjoining as above mentioned set apart by the Government for the Indians, their use and benefit, which I would recommend many of the Indians now without lands would come here and locate, and others as they will require to give place to the white would here find a home. The mission buildings here are in a fair state of preservation. The Indians here have recently repaired their Church, and enlarged their burying grounds by the advice and under the direction of Manuel Cota, and one of the Priests[11] formerly connected with the Missions, recently visited them, consecrated their burying ground, baptized their children, and married all those who were living together unmarried.

Most of those Indians understand and speak the Spanish language, and have great respect for the Priests, who have considerable influence and control over them. To protect and benefit this remnent *(sic)* of the natives of this State partially civalized *(sic)* and Christianized by the early missionaries "whose efforts and example are at present worthy of imitation," Government must assign them a tract of land expressly for their use and benefit and protect them in the occupation and use of the same from all aggressions and interference of the whites, and this should be done at an early day.

Spcial *(sic)* Agent Stanly has faithfully and efficiently discharged his duties as agent. He has been much anoyed *(sic)* and harrassed by the intereference of those evil disposed whites before mentioned. They have endeavoured to create discontent and discord amongst the Indians and to throw all the obsticles *(sic)* possible in his way which in the discharge of his duty they have proceeded so far as to commence a suit against him and Manuel Cota in the District Court of Los Angeles County for six thousand dollars, damages in favour of an Indian who was whipped for stealing by the order of Manuel Cota the chief with the assent of Agent Stanly, a custom and practice of punishment with the Indians.

The citizens of Los Angeles and San Diego Counties, with very few exceptions and those are and have been disloyal and opposed the Government since the commencement of the rebellion, approve and commend the manner in which Agent Stanly has discharged his duties, and say that no one could have done as well as he has under the difficulties in which he has been placed.

Under the present laws the Superintendent or Agent has but little power or authority outside the Indian Territory or reservation for preventing those abuses which arise from white persons interfering with the Indians, abusing their squaws, selling them Liquors, etc.

To attempt to prevent and punish offenders under the State laws would envolve (*sic*) expense, difficulties, and delays, which would produce no good results.

On the 5th we left Temécula for Los Angeles, where we arrived on the evening of the 6th. On the morning of the 7th I left Los Angeles for Wilmington where I took passage on Steamer and arrived at San Francisco on the 9th ult.

Notes to the Text

1. John Quincy Adams Stanly, approved as a Special Indian Agent on the previous May 8, was among the founders of the Historical Society of Southern California, on December 6, 1883. He was described by Helen Hunt Jackson as "a warm friend" of the Indians. See *Report on the Condition and Needs of the Mission Indians of California* (Washington, 1883). p. 32.
2. The Temécula Valley was part of the tract given to the San Luiseños by the Treaty of January 3, 1853.
3. The first mention of Pala in the annals dates from 1810. Six years later, a chapel was constructed and, by 1818. a town was beginning to take shape. San Antonio was sold, along with Mission San Luis Rey de Francia, on November 14, 1845, to José A. Cota and José A. Pico. Today, San Antonio de Pala is the only one of the California missionary establishments still serving the spiritual needs of an exclusively Indian population, the Palatinguas, moved there from Warner's Ranch by the United States Government.
4. Manuel Cota, known familiarly in the annals as Manuelito, was "a somewhat famous chief of several bands of the San Luiseños." See George Wharton James, *Picturesque Pala. The Story of the Mission Chapel of San Antonio de Padua* (Pasadena, 1916), p. 35.
5. Technically speaking, the outpost of San Antonio was not a mission but an *asistencia*, a term used to describe a foundation having all the requisites for a mission except a resident priest. Of the five *asistencias* in Provincial California, only San Rafael Arcángel achieved full mission status.
6. One such culprit is identified as Andrew Scott by Helen Hunt Jackson and Abbot Kinney in their *Report on the Condition and Needs of the Mission Indians of California*, p. 29.
7. This observation is confirmed by other sources too. See, for example, *Report of Chas. A. Wetmore* (Washington, 1875), p. 6.
8. This reference is likely to Colonel Jim (James G.) Howard, a highly successful but controversial southland criminal attorney.
9. According to one newspaper account, the Indians of the area were long "recognized as the most thrifty and industrious Indians in all California." See the San Diego *Union*, September 23, 1875.
10. See note number 5.
11. The priest here referred to is Father Anthony Ubach (1835-1907), who cared for the spiritualities of many Indians in the region. So great was his influence with the natives "that Ubach is credited with preventing a bloody reprisal from the Temécula Indians when they were forcibly ejected from their homes by unprincipled Anglo settlers." See Francis J. Weber, *Readings in California Catholic History* (Los Angeles, 1967), p. 157.

44

"The California Missions As Seen by Henry Chapman Ford" is the title of this essay taken from *The Pacific Historian* XIX (Summer, 1975), 101-102.

Among the most celebrated published works relating to the historic foundations of Fray Junipero Serra and his collaborators along *El Camino Real* must be Henry Chapman Ford's *Etchings of the Franciscan Missions of California*. The twenty-four proof etchings, measuring 17 x 22 inches on their mounts, were enclosed in a portfolio of two-tone linen. The prints, each signed by the artist, include duplicate views of Missions Santa Barbara and San Carlos Borromeo, together with a depiction of the abandoned ruins of the first La Purisma Concepcion. The handsome opus was printed, in 1883, at New York's Studio Press, in a limited edition of fifty sets.

The fifty-two year old, New York born artist had first visited the missions by covered wagon, in 1880-1881, and during that trek had made careful photographs which he later enlarged for use as models. From the very outset, Ford intended to produce the most elaborate work yet published on the subject. Upon completion of the oil portrayals, Mr. Ford journeyed to New York, where he personally supervised their transferral to copper plates. The freedom, delicacy and strength of the completed scenes amply testify to his success.

The publication of Ford's monumental opus was widely heralded. Archbishop Joseph Sadoc Alemany of San Francisco, recalling his own first tour of the missions, in 1851, found "the execution by Mr. Ford accurate." The Dominican prelate went on to say that the artist deserved "the special gratitude of the State of California for his zeal in preserving the glories of the Pioneers of its Christian civilization." Another foremost authority on the early missionary foundations, Father Joachim Adam, wrote from Los Angeles that he had carefully examined the etchings and considered "them not only exquisite as a work of art, but also a faithful representation" of provincial California.

A reviewer for the Los Angeles *Times* labelled the Ford etchings "an invaluable addition to the history of these earliest monuments of civilization in California" and hoped that folios would find their way into "every library and public institution of the State."

Newspapers from around the nation joined the chorus of praise. The Washington *National Republican* said that Ford's "work perpetuates on copper about the only interesting ruins to be seen in America." A writer in the Cleveland *Leader* called the etchings "not only beautiful and interesting as works of art" but also depictions of "great historical value." The Chicago *Times* ranked the portfolio as "one of the finest specimens of the 'art preservative' which has appeared in this country."

In its "Exposition Notes," the New Orleans *Times Democrat* declared that Ford's masterpiece showed "marked artistic talent, and admirable technique and perfect familiarity with the graver and acid bath." In Chicago's *Present Age*, Enoch Root wrote that the reproduction of the missions, from canvass to copper plates, demonstrated that the artist's "skill with the needle point equals his power in the use of the brush." Another prominent artist, Norton Bush of San Francisco, happily endorsed the etchings as being works of art of an exceedingly interesting character," while the Protestant Rector of Christ Church, Bridgeport, Connecticut, went even further and proclaimed them "the most ambitious work of the kind ever produced by an American."

When in 1961, many of the surviving sets were found to be soiled and battered, Mr. William A. Edwards made available his remarkably-clean portfolio for reproduction purposes to the Santa Barbara Historical Society. To the original twenty-four etchings, another dozen scenes, covering a variety of subjects, were added by Edward Selden Spaulding for his volume of Ford's *Etchings of California*.

Mr. Ford continued his interest in the missions and subsequently painted a number of other scenes, some of them in watercolor. At the time of his death, in 1894, the artist was busily working on the history of the early missionary foundations. A few of his isolated notes were published by the *California Historical Society Quarterly*, in 1961.

The assertion, by the San Francisco *Bulletin*, that the Ford portrayals would never be equalled "in truthfulness and artistic presentation," undoubtedly helped to sustain and augment the initial selling price of $50. The etchings have multiplied in value thirty-five times (!) in the past ninety years and a portfolio was recently offered for sale by Warren Howell at $1,750! Even a four page *Prospectus* for the *Etchings of the Franciscan Missions of California* was sold by Glen Dawson, in August, 1974, for $20!

Henry Chapman Ford's fascination for and reproduction of the California missions rank the artist among the truly great benefactors of Western Americana.

45

This essay is taken from the *Golden State Catholicism* (Los Angeles, 1990), pp. 78-80.

During the preparation of a book on the California *asistencias* or assistant missions, a rather significant memoir was unearthed about San Antonio de Pala. It was written in late 1913 by Father Peter Wallischeck, a Franciscan once described in the *Santa Barbara News Press* as "a kindly man with an ever ready smile and friendly greeting."

The friar was well-loved and highly-respected in Santa Barbara where, it is recorded, "his habit was silhouetted against the sidewalks of State Street for nearly 40 years."

Born in Weisloch, Germany, April 4, 1852, the youngster was brought to the United States where, in 1868, he entered Saint Joseph's College, Teutopolis, Illinois, as a candidate for the Order of Friars Minor.

The youthful priest taught for fifteen years in Illinois before affiliating himself to the Franciscan community at Santa Barbara. In 1896, he inaugurated Saint Anthony's Seminary and remained on as president until 1912.

In that latter year, Father Peter was made superior at San Luis Rey Mission and there he started a boarding school. Three years later, he returned to Santa Barbara, where he labored for the rest of his life.

The kindly old priest lived until May 28, 1936, by which time he had been a Franciscan for sixty-three years and a priest for fifty-six years. He is buried in the old mission cemetery.

Sometime in late 1913, Father Peter wrote the following memoir about the *asistencia* of San Antonio de Pala, probably at the behest of

Father Zephyrin Engelhardt. A transcript of that document was entrusted to the Archival Center, Archdiocese of Los Angeles, by the late Maynard J. Geiger, O.F.M.

Pala Mission, as it is now generally called, though it was never a mission properly speaking, is situated about twenty miles east of San Luis Rey in a very fertile valley. Low mountains surround this valley forming, as it were, a frame for the beautiful landscape.

In the mission days a great number of Indians lived in this valley. In order to christianize them, and to provide better for their spiritual wants, it was considered expedient to build a church for them.

Fr. Antonio Peyri, the superior of Mission San Luis Rey, therefore, decided that an "*asistencia*"—that is to say, a chapel with a visiting *padre*—should be erected at Pala.

Work on the church and residence was commenced in 1816, and the church placed under the patronage of St. Anthony of Padua, the Wonderworker of the world, as Charles Warren Stoddard calls this saint.

There is one feature that is unique in the construction of this church or chapel. The belfry or campanile is entirely separated from the main building. Two large mission bells are suspended in the openings, the sound of which is carred to a great distance, calling the Indians for divine service.

This mission, like the mother-mission, San Luis Rey, was prosperous from the beginning. Two years had hardly elapsed when the Baptismal Records showed a thousand names enrolled.

Fr. Peyri did not only have the spiritual welfare of his children at Pala at heart, he also provided for their material prosperity.

Seeing that some system of irrigation was imperative, he designed and constructed an aqueduct, or waterditch, which even now elicits the admiration of our modern surveyors. They admit that no better route could have been chosen.

The act of "secularization" also sounded the death-knell of the Pala *asistencia*. With the confiscation of the mission property and the departure of the *padre*, the Indian was without the necessary means of support, and without a friend and father, poverty and disease soon decimated their number, so that but few long survived this dreadful blow.

In 1902, the government of the United States decided to remove the Indians from Warner's Ranch to some other locality.

Much was done to select a proper place. Finally some property at Pala was purchased for this purpose.

The poor Indians were loath to leave their old homes: the place where their fathers and forefathers had lived and died, the, place where their mortal remains were buried. Many preferred death to a change of homes. The sad and sorrowful transportation took place in the spring of 1903.

Many a tear was shed, when the Indians bid a sad and last farewell to the graves of their ancestors; for the Indians retain a sacred memory for their deceased friends and relatives.

Owing to the efforts of Right Rev. Thomas J. Conaty, D.D., Bishop of Monterey-Los Angeles, the old chapel was partly restored and rededicated. Of late years the Rev. George Doyle, the present pastor of Pala Indian Reservation, has done much to improve both the interior and exterior of this old and venerable "*asistencia,*" the daughter of San Luis Rey.

As is the case with almost all of the old missions of California, it is not lack of zeal and energy of the present occupants, but a lack of funds that retards the restoration and preservation of the old landmarks. It is greatly to be feared that the people of California will realize too late that not good words, but good works—pecuniary assistance—are needed to enable the good work of restoration and preservation to go on.

The United States Government has repaired the old waterditch at Pala and installed a first class pumping plant. This provides the Indians of the reservation with an abundant supply of wholesome water for house and field.

On Monday June 2nd, 1913, the Pala Indians in festive attire celebrated the opening of this old waterditch, built by Fr. Peyri for his Indians almost a century ago.

The Indians from the surrounding reservations attended the ceremony of rededication. The schoolchildren of the reservation sang patriotic songs, and when a salute of three volleys was fired, the superior of San Luis Rey Mission pronounced a blessing upon the flowing waters.

Thus the good work of Fr. Peyri is continued. Let us hope that it may long continue and be productive of many blessings.

46

The following essay is from the *Branding Iron* of the Los Angeles Corral of Westerners (185), Fall, 1991.

Carillons are fairly uncommon in the United States. Only 129 true carillons and thirty-six electric-action carillons are known to experts in the field. San Fernando Mission is one of the nine places in California with such an instrument and its thirty-five electrically-operated bells are known to the 35,000 tourists who annually visit the seventeenth of the Golden State's missionary outposts.

According to the Guild of Carillonneurs in North America, a carillon is a musical instrument consisting of at least two octaves of bells arranged in chromatic series. A carillon is a cast, bronze, cup-shaped bell whose partial tones are in such harmonious relationship to each other as to permit many such bells to be sounded together, in various chords with a concordant effect.

The first carillon consisted of four to eight bells, operated by hand levers. About the 16th century, Belgian, Dutch and northern French carillons began to be built of about thirty-five bells.

The historical background of the carillon at San Fernando Mission, the only such instrument in a Catholic Church west of the Rockies, can be traced back almost sixty years.

Shortly after Msgr. Nicholas Connelly announced plans to build Santa Monica's Church in 1925, he was approached by Johanna Shanahan, an elderly Irish-born parishioner who had spent most of her life in the employ of Senator John P. Jones, founder of Santa Monica. Miss

Shanahan offered to give her life savings of $11,000 if the pastor would allow a carillon to be built and installed in the bell tower of the envisioned church.

It didn't take Connelly long to recognize that such a gift would impart a unique feature to his already fanciful designs. He immediately instructed his architect to make whatever modifications would be necessary to accommodate the carillon. (Carillon bells don't swing, they are mounted in a stationary position and provided with clappers inside and a hammer outside if there is an automatic player).

Connelly then did some research and decided on the carillon then being manufactured by Felix Van Aerschodt of Louvain. In mid 1927, Connelly contacted Father Thomas K. Gorman, a student priest attached to the Diocese of Monterey-Los Angeles then studying in Rome, and asked him to explore the possibilities of engaging Van Aerschodt for the project.

It was an ideal choice. The Van Aerschodt family name had been associated with bells for centuries. Felix had been at the helm of the business since 1898. Like his father, he was a metallic sculptor, having been educated in the studios of the famed Jef Lambeaux. His reputation was widespread enough to bring invitations to exhibit at the Universal Expositions in Paris (1898), Antwerp (1894), Brussels (1910), and Ghent (1913).

Felix was among the many outstanding residents of Louvain taken captive by the invading German forces in World War I. He later escaped and went to England, where the government entrusted him with the management of a munitions factory at Spitalfields (London). Unhappily, during Felix's absence from Louvain, his foundry was sacked and mostly destroyed. His ancient models and mortars, plans and mechanisms, mountings and bas-relief ornaments, inventories and archives were forever lost. Mr. Van Aerschodt returned to Louvain after the hostilities were ended and, by 1920 was again busily at work. Despite several economic mishaps, the foundry continued in operation. Felix had recently entered into a partnership with Marcel Michiels of Tournai and it was that latter gentleman who was deputized to draft the specifications for the Santa Monica carillon.

The casting of the thirty-five bells took several years. It was decided to use a combination of 78% copper and 22% tin. They were tuned to the chromatic scale, thus allowing music to be played in all keys. The biggest of the bells weighed in at half a ton, the smallest a mere twenty-two pounds.

Miss Shanahan insisted that Michiels accompany the instrument to the United States and personally supervise its installation. Unhappily, she died on October 14, 1931 and was unable to see the carillon operational.

Michiels and Gabriel Castelain spent several agonizing months uncrating and then hoisting the thirty-five bells into place. A five tiered iron frame was designed for that purpose inside the picturesque tower.

The bourdon-bell, weighing half a ton, is the largest of the group and was engineered to strike the hours, while a second large bell counted off the half hours. From the smallest bells on the top tier to the largest on the grand tier, they were designed to be tone perfect in their three octave range. The largest ones are made of iron and the smaller ones of soft metal. The tiniest are fashioned from hard steel, all of which imparted eveness of tone to the ensemble.

Aside from the clock driver, the bells were played by a mechanical baton in the loft with a wire leading to each bell. Directly under the bells, Michiels provided a huge iron drum which contained numerous perforations. Pegs were placed in the holes to correspond with the notes to be sounded. When the drum revolved, the bells would strike in succession against a mechanism which activated the bells in the proper sequence.

The carillon, which one newspaper account said was "unrivalled on the west coast, was solemnly dedicated by Bishop John J. Cantwell on December 22, 1931. Each of the bells had a sponsor for the ceremony and names were bestowed for each unit. While the bishop read the prayers, a priest climbed a ladder into the tower and sprinkled the bells with holy water. Marcel Michiels then gave a short concert. Three days later, Michiels also played carols at the Christmas Masses offered in the Church.

Since so few carillonneurs were available on the west coast, Msgr. Connelly investigated the possibility, in the mid 1930s, of engineering an electronic system whereby the bells could be operated from the keyboard of the church's pipe organ. Designed by L.M. Davis and installed by John Clevenger, the automatic device operated with solenoids which activated the bell clappers. It was a crude arrangement which, surprisingly, worked quite well.

In 1956, the whole system was dismantled, its metallic frame sandblasted and then repainted and placed back in service. During the following decade, however, the carillon was used only rarely, mostly because of its operational complexity. On at least one occasion, it went off accidentally during the night and upset the entire neighborhood before being shut off.

From the very outset, Michiels was concerned that the carillon would never achieve its maximum effect because the bells were sixty feet from the keyboard and thus not easily controlled by the over-extended wiring. And, partly due to the poor tuning and the repetitious melodies, the carillon became controversial among neighbors and others who outspokenly disliked its "noise." Connelly's dream became "Connelly's folly," and before long the irritated priest and his successors turned off the switch.

During the devastating earthquake of February 9, 1971, the bell tower at Santa Monica's Church suffered structural damage and was judged unsafe to support the massive weight of the carillon. The bells were taken down and placed in storage.

When plans were announced to rebuild the church at San Fernando Mission, mortally jolted during the same 1971 temblor, it was suggested that the carillon be installed in the newly constructed bell tower.

The instrument was crated and carefully moved the twenty-four miles to Mission Hills. Installation and rewiring of the massive system was supervised by Justin Kramer. After several months of diligent work, the carillon was ready for the re-dedication ceremonies which took place on December 4, 1974.

The carillon was programmed to play the *Cantica del Alba*, an ancient melody sung by the Fernandino Indians at the Old Mission. Once again the historic carillon pealed forth its beautiful tones for the glory of God.

47

"Chumash Indian Basketry at San Buenaventura" is the topic of this essay taken from the *Ventura County Historical Society Quarterly* XXIV (Fall, 1978), 17-25.

Excellence in the art of basketry has long been associated with the Indians of the Pacific Slope. Indeed, their outstanding skill in that handicraft prompted one authority to say that the baskets produced by the California Indians were far superior to those of any other people, in the fineness of weaving and beauty of decoration.

The basket industry was cultivated by the women who were ingenious in weaving grass, sumac, splints, rushes, cedar, tule, yucca stems, kelp thread, willow roots and sea plants into mats and baskets. Their finished products varied in sizes and shapes from flat, basin-shaped coiled weave bowls to the large pointed cones which the women carried on their backs when digging for roots, picking berries or gathering acorns.

The pliable baskets, some of which had lids, were woven (rather than coiled) from vegetable fibers often on a warp of willow strips. By adding pitch or some other resinous substance such as asphaltum, baskets were made waterproof. They could then be utilized for such purposes as cooking, trapping fish and carrying water. Moreover, basket-work was employed in fences, houses, shields and for harvesting.

It is generally agreed that the Chumash Indians were among the most sophisticated of all the native Californians, in terms of both their material and social culture. At the time of European penetration, there may have been between 10,000 and 15,000 Chumash living along the 6,500 square miles of coastline between present day San Luis Obispo and the Malibu.[2] If so, they constituted one of the largest groups of natives anywhere in western North America.

The early chroniclers expressed a particular fascination with the types of Indian basketry found at San Buenaventura Mission. Light, sturdy and attractive, the Chumash baskets were avidly sought out by the Europeans. Those fortunate enough to acquire baskets sent them back to New Spain, Peru and Spain. With the advent of the merchant ships, the baskets also found an eager market in London and Paris. At present the British Museum has one of the largest collections of Chumash baskets. Those baskets fashioned by the Ventureño Indians at San Buenaventura Mission were known for their fine workmanship, variety of forms and the manifold uses to which they were put.[3]

Observable regularities of techniques, form and decorative style make the design of Chumash baskets distinctive. This is partly due to the variegated rush materials from which they were woven. In addition to the established tradition of design, there were explicit rules of composition and space division in Chumash baskets. The principal band, for example, and its distance from the rim are generally the same width. Rim "ticks" are usual. The geometrical and symbolic designs in the body of the basket blend into a harmonious unity in the finished product.[4]

Ventureño women used a rush (*Juncus textilis*) for their baskets. After it was dried, the straightest stalks were split. The pitch was scraped out with the roughened edge of a clamshell and, finally, the strands were bundled according to need. Some were re-split, and others buried in the mud for color effect. After the initial "start" of shredded pieces was well stitched, whole *juncus* stalks were introduced, usually for a three-strand foundation. Stitching was aided by the use of a bone awl, and the stitches did not interlock with each other. It was necessary, of course, to keep the material damp while working with it.

Indian basket making was a skill that displayed patience, a sense of beauty and a feeling for symmetry and design. It was a highly symbolic means of expression, an art medium of considerable importance to the Indians themselves and to those who study their way of life.

There are 25 baskets on display in the Historical Museum at San Buenaventura Mission, some of which have been there for many years. The majority of the Chumash baskets originally belonged to Juan E. Camarillo (1867-1936) who was born in an adobe near what is now Main Street and Ventura Avenue.[5] Their provenance is interesting. Following the erection of Saint Mary Magdalen in the town of Camarillo,[6] Juan set up a small family museum in a wing adjacent to the church, where he proudly displayed the various mementos he had amassed in his tours around the world.

Chumash baskets were rare even in those early days and Juan E. Camarillo's outstanding collection received considerable attention as one of California's lost artforms. Of all his valued possessions, none was more carefully cared for than those treasures acquired in his youth from elderly Indians at San Buenaventura. There is an oral tradition that one or more of the Camarillo baskets were woven by the celebrated Juana Basilia,[7] a neophyte of the mission, an especially talented woman. Juana's basket, incorporating the royal arms of Spain, was made for José de la Cruz in 1822.[8]

In the spring of 1964 the departments of Art and Anthropology of the University of California sponsored an exhibit of Chumash artifacts at their Santa Barbara campus. The occasion resulted in bringing together from all parts of the country a major segment of the known 200 Chumash baskets. In the process of gathering together the 85 specimens, the Pastor of Saint Mary Magdalen Church was asked if the Camarillo baskets might be included in the exhibit. Msgr. Dennis Falvey readily acquiesced; and when the exhibit was dismantled, he agreed to extend the original loan agreement so as to allow them to remain for a while at Santa Barbara.

Unfortunately for his successors, he seemingly left no written memos on the subject. The archeology section of the university was equally neglectful. In the next decade the senior professor was changed three times; and but one member of the staff remained who knew of the exhibition.

In 1976, shortly after the historical artifacts in the Camarillo museum had been moved to San Buenaventura Mission for permanent display, Delee Marshall, a docent at the Ventura County Historical Museum, was asked to make a preliminary catalogue of the few baskets remaining in the collection. She then asked about the other Chumash baskets. It was a revelation for neither the present Pastor of Saint Mary Magdalen Church nor the writer knew there were others.

Fortunately the Camarillo treasures had been photographed while on exhibit in Santa Barbara. And in 1965 pictures and descriptions of nine appeared in print.[9] Enlisting the assistance of Director Richard Esparza of the Ventura County Historical Museum, Mrs. Marshall was able to determine that six baskets were still on display at Santa Barbara. This writer notified Donald E. Brown, Chairman of the Department of Anthropology, on December 8, 1976 that the loan agreement was now terminated. Dr. Brown referred the matter to Dr. Michael Glassow in archeology who made arrangements for returning the baskets. On January 20, 1977 Mrs. Marshall and the writer journeyed to Goleta and recovered the six baskets. They were temporarily stored in the vault of the Ventura County Historical Museum until adequate facilities could be provided for them at the mission.

During the summer Robert O. Browne and William Kirk began to build a specially outfitted display case in which all the baskets belonging to San Buenaventura Mission could be exhibited, a project that was completed in late November. Mrs. Marshall then arranged the 25 specimens in place, providing explanatory panels about the procedure, design and traditions of the basket weavers. New labels were made and the old ones updated. The exhibit was opened to the general public on January 22, 1978.

Notes to the Text

1. The writer wishes to thank Delee Marshall, a knowledgeable person on California Indian basketry, for her many useful and penetrating observations about this essay.
2. These figures are those of Allen G. Pastron and C. W. Clewlow, "The Chumash Indians of California" in *Pacific Discovery*, XXX, 1, 19.
3. See Eugene N. Anderson, Jr., *The Chumash Indians of Southern California* (Banning 1968) 9.
4. For an excellent treatment of Chumash baskets, see A. L. Kroeber, "Basket designs of the Mission Indians of California" in the *Anthropological Papers of the American Museum of Natural History*, XX, 177-183.
5. Juan's father came to Alta California with the Hijar-Padres Expedition in 1834. When San Buenaventura was incorporated as a city in 1866, he was a member of the first Board of Trustees. Nine years later the Camarillo family acquired title to the Rancho Calleguas, a land grant conveyed to José Ruiz in 1837.
6. Dedicated July 4, 1913, the church was built by Juan E. Camarillo as a memorial to his mother.
7. Juana Basilia (1782-1838) was a native of the Rancheria of Sumuahuahua. She was baptized at San Buenaventura Mission on February 7, 1806. See Zephyrin Engelhardt, *San Buenaventura, the Mission by the Sea* (Santa Barbara 1930) 154-160.
8. See Zelia Nuttall, "Two Remarkable California baskets" in the *California Historical Society Quarterly*, II, 341-343.
9. See Lawrence Dawson and James Deetz, "A Corpus of Chumash basketry" in the 1965 *Annual report of the University of California, Los Angeles, Department of Anthropology (Archaeological Survey*, 195-212, 24 plates).

48

This device for "Teaching Students About the Missions" was prepared for Network, a project of the *Los Angeles Times* III (October, 1983).

The approaching bicentennial of Fray Junipero Serra's demise provides an ideal incentive for studying and learning about the missionary outposts which he and his successors established along California's *El Camino Real*

While there have been hundreds of books, pamphlets and brochures written on the subject, there are relatively few which are both historically reliable and readily available. Some years ago, this writer compiled *A Select Bibliography of the California Missions 1765-1972* in which 500 titles were cited and described. More recently, an essay on "The Books of the California Missions" appeared in *Soundings*, a publication of the University of California, Santa Barbara. Many of the titles listed in those two works can be obtained at new or antiquarian bookshops or researched at libraries.

If the teacher wishes to go beyond the lecturing phase, some sort of project will be useful in acquainting youngsters with the subject. If an essay is required, restrict the subject by allowing each student to select a particular mission or aspect of mission life.

If the youngsters are not accustomed to essays, it may be helpful if the teacher provides them with a brief outline of what is expected in their completed work. Encourage hand-drawn illustrations, rather than those cut from books or pamphlets. Book reports can be highly educational too, if properly motivated. In addition to requiring a digest of the volume in question, the teacher can give the students a "directive page" with a dozen or so provocative suggestions. Overlook the horrendous grammar and punctuation, youngsters learn to write by writing.

This whole phase of California history can and should be a fun-event. Remember that teachers are learners also, so they must not feel intimidated being unable to answer specific questions. When a particularly difficult query is posed, simply suggest that "this is a good question and one which I think we can all share in answering. Tomorrow Mary Jane and Roger will assist me in responding."

Touring one of the California missions and studying its exhibits can also be a rewarding experience for youngsters, provided they are properly prepared and carefully supervised. (Last year 26,000 children from public, parochial and private schools visited San Fernando Mission.) Though most of the missions do not employ guides, some have part-time docents who are available for scheduled groups.

Teachers and others in charge of classes are encouraged to utilize the following guidelines as a means of maximizing the results of their outing: (1) call ahead for a reservation and make every attempt to be on time; (2) ask that a guidesheet be mailed ahead of the visit, study it and reproduce a copy for each member of the class; (3) prepare a questionnaire for youngsters to complete on the scene; (4) utilize the travel time on the bus for a brief explanation of what the children will encounter; (5) arrange for a couple of parents or helpers to rendezvous with the class at the mission to act as chaperons; (6) divide the class into manageable units of seven or eight; (7) keep the children busy so as to avoid their wandering off unaccompanied; (8) allow five or ten minutes for shopping in the Gift Shop, suggest they look for brochures and/or pamphlets about this particular mission or about the missions in general; (9) use the travel time returning to school for questions and discussions and (10) schedule a written report based on the questionnaire, observations and other sources to be finished within a week.

Youngsters can be impressed with the notion that visiting a mission is not just another casual outing, but a serious opportunity for expanding their knowledge bank. Proper preparation and adequate follow-up will allow both teachers and students to profit most fully from the experience.

As a 10 year veteran in the classroom, this writer is fully aware of the demands placed on teachers. But he can also testify to the advantageous results of motivating youngsters to read, write and discuss each new facet in their learning process.

49

This essay on "The Death of Fray Luis Jayme" which appeared in *The Journal of San Diego History* XXII (Winter, 1976) is based upon an address given on November 5, 1975, at San Diego de Alcala Mission. A Spanish version was published in *Fires I Festes a Sant Joan 1977*, Palma de Mallorca.

One of the brightest chapters in the history of humankind is that which relates the spiritual accomplishments of North America's Franciscan pioneers.

And perhaps the most glorious and long-lasting of the many contributions associated with the disciples of Saint Francis is the distinction of having provided the proto-martyrs for such areas of the New World as Mexico, Canada and the United States.

In North America alone, no fewer than 115 friars willingly underwent the supreme sacrifice in a saga of dauntless courage, inspiring heroism and wholehearted devotion unparalleled in ecclesiastical annals.

The Franciscans were especially lavish in bestowing their blood and virtue on the Church in California. Prominently etched onto the Golden State's martyrology are the names of six outstanding friars whose testimony for Christ is forever a monument to Christian endurance and bravery.

On the eve of the nation's bicentennial, the People of God gather at San Diego to honor the memory of Fray Luis Jayme, a cherished member of that Seraphic contingency who effected the initial triumph of religion and civilization in what was to become the thirty-first commonwealth of these United States. It was just two hundred years ago that the soil of the Pacific Slope was reddened by the blood of that youthful friar.

Sixteen of the Franciscans who carried the banner of Christ along *El Camino Real* hailed from Mallorca, the largest of the Balearic Islands, off the Spanish coast. Luis Jayme was one of those who bore in his temperament and exemplified in his demeanor the charm of that picturesque isle which writers have long referred to as the "spiritual god-mother" of California.

Melchor Jayme was born in the tranquil farming village of San Juan, about six miles west of Petra, on October 18, 1740. His earliest schooling was acquired from the local parish priest.

When their son reached his fifteenth birthday, the elder Jaymes brought him to Petra, the capital city of Mallorca, and enrolled him at the convent school of San Bernardino, where the famed Fray Junípero Serra had studied earlier.

On September 27, 1760, Melchor Jayme was invested with the Franciscan habit, in the Convento de Santa María de los Angeles de Jesús. Following a year of strict seclusion and rigorous discipline, Jayme solemnly promised to observe the rule of the Friars Minor for the rest of his earthly lifespan. From then onwards, he was known as Fray Luís.

The friar made his theological studies at the Convento de San Francisco, which then served as the motherhouse for the Franciscan Province of Mallorca. He was ordained to the priesthood on December 22, 1764. Upon completion of his courses, Fray Luís was appointed Lector of Philosophy, a position he occupied at San Francisco from 1765 to 1770.

It was during the year of Spanish penetration into Alta California that Luis Jayme determined to spend his remaining years as a missionary in the New World. He wrote for permission to the Commissary General of the Indies and was assigned to Mexico City's Apostolic College of San Fernando.

After a farewell visit to his native village of San Juan, Fray Luís left Palma early in 1770 for Cadíz. There an official for the Board of Trade provided the only extant description of the friar, recording that he was a "person with well proportioned physique, somewhat thin, and of a darkish complexion."

Jayme arrived in New Spain after a long and arduous trans-Atlantic voyage. There he began the special training course wherein soldiers of the Cross were conditioned to the privation, fatigue, mortification and penance encountered on the missionary frontier.

Finally, in October, Fray Luís and nine other priests set out for California, where they had volunteered to spend a minimum of ten years in winning over the hearts and souls of the primitive peoples then inhabiting the outer rim of the Spanish realm.

Jayme was happy when Fray Junípero Serra, the *Presidente* of the California Missions, appointed him to what would be his first and last assignment, Mission San Diego de Alcalá. That assignment had special significance for Fray Luís, since it was there that it had all begun for Christ in Alta California.

The Yuman Indians at San Diego were the most treacherous and uncooperative of all the tribes in the coastal areas. Generally described with such words as thievish, egocentric and untrustworthy, they consistently provided a formidable challenge to the evangelization endeavors of the Spanish missionaries.

A clever and talented friar, Jayme's earliest efforts at San Diego were devoted to mastering the complexities of the local native language. Once he had gained a facility with its vocabulary, he was able to compile a polyglot Christian catechism.

The extreme scarcity of water, combined with the proximity of the military personnel, induced Fray Luís to ask for and receive permission to move the mission from its original site, atop Presidio Hill, to the valley where it is presently situated.

The new location proved eminently more practical. Almost immediately there was a notable upsurge in the number of conversions which, by 1775, numbered 431. Such success obviously infuriated the devil who seems to have held the natives in bondage during aboriginal times. In any event, a plan was hatched by a handful of pagan sorcerers and others to rid the area of all traces of Hispanic influence.

At about 1:30, on the brilliantly-lit night of November 4, 1775, 600 or more warriors from some forty *rancherías* silently crept into the mission compound. After quietly plundering the chapel, they set fire to the other buildings. The crackling of flames soon awakened the two missionaries, the guards and the Christian neophytes.

Instead of running for shelter to the stockhold, Fray Luís Jayme resolutely walked toward the howling band of natives, uttering the traditional Franciscan greeting: "*Amar a Dios, hijos!*"

In a frenzied orgy of cruelty, the Indians seized him, stripped off his garments, shot eighteen arrows into his body and then pulverized his face with clubs and stones.

The attack on the mission was terminated when a well-aimed shot from a musket unnerved the Indians and caused them to flee in panic. Early the next morning, the body of the thirty-five year old missionary was recovered in the dry bed of a nearby creek. His face was so disfigured that he could only be recognized by the whiteness of his flesh under a thick crust of congealed blood.

The friar's mangled body was initially buried in the *presidio* chapel. When the new church at the mission was completed, it was re-interred in the sanctuary. There it rested until November 12, 1813, when it was transferred to the third and final church. Today the remains of Fray Luís Jayme repose in a common vault between the main and side altar.

The reaction of the Franciscan *Presidente* to the news of his confrere's death speaks volumes about the attitude of the early friars. Far from being saddened or disappointed, Fray Junípero Serra said: "Thanks be to God; now that the terrain has been watered by blood, the conversion of the San Diego Indians will take place." That proved to be a prophetic statement too, for by 1834, the number of baptisms at the mission reached 6,638.

Little else can be said about Fray Luís Jayme. There is a trinity of physical reminders of the Mallorcan friar: a concrete cross beside the *arroyo* where he died, a stone monument above the city hall of the village where he was born and a painting in the sacristy of the church where he was baptized.

It was only the mortal body of Fray Luís that was consumed in that November massacre two hundred years ago. His spirit and influence were born into eternity on that winter's night.

Fray Luís Jayme lives on in the affections of latter-day Californians as a noble pioneer who mortgaged his lifeblood to implant the principles of Christianity into California's landscape.

Through the centuries, martyrs have been regarded as objects of veneration, models of perfection and friends of God. Martyrdom was and is a praiseworthy ideal of all dedicated followers of the Nazarene for it is the ultimate proof of love and dedication to the Christian lifestyle.

Yet, two hundred years after the death of California's proto-martyr, those who trek along *El Camino Real* are reminded that death by the shedding of blood is far from being the only way whereby a Christian is transformed into the likeness of the Savior.

And were Fray Luís Jayme alive today, one strongly suspects that his message to the Christians of 1975 would echo the observation of Horace Mann that "it is often more difficult and calls for higher energies of soul, to live a martyr than to die one."

50

"An Appeal to Los Angeles" is here reproduced from *The Pacific Historian* XXI (Winter, 1977), 359-367.

I *n his first pastoral letter after arriving at Santa Barbara, Bishop Francisco García Diego y Moreno (1785-1846)[1] announced his intention of introducing "the system of collecting tithes"[2] throughout the newly-created Diocese of Both Californias.[3] The Franciscian prelate implemented the diézmos by a circular letter, on January 20, 1843, reminding his people of their obligation to support the Church and its ministers.[4] Therein he defined tithing as the setting aside of a tenth part from the products of the fields and orchards, the yearly increase of live-stock and from grapewine, brandy and olive oil, for the support of divine worship.*

Unfortunately, the program was never very successful and even the small amounts realized were "given grudgingly by most settlers, and denied altogether by not a few."[5] Even the bishop himself was forced to admit that the income was insignificant in comparison to the trouble involved in collecting the funds.[6]

With the prelate's death, on April 30, 1846, his close friend and secretary, Fray José María de Jesús González Rubio (1804-1875) became Administrator for the Diocese of Both Californias, "a post he held with distinction until the arrival of Bishop Joseph Sadoc Alemany in 1850."[7]

González Rubio "administered the diocese in a most difficult and trying period."[8] When conditions in the already-depleted jurisdiction worsened, the zealous friar desparately attempted to reactivate his predecessor's diézmos system. On July 14, 1848, he issued a seventeen page pastoral letter outlining the need for and use of tithing.[9]

An earlier version of that pastoral was recently acquired by the Chancery Archives for the Archdiocese of Los Angeles through the generosity of Msgr. Vincent Lloyd-Russell. Considerably shorter, the remarkably-preserved holograph was written on both sides of seven leaves (13 x 8-3/4). It was offered for sale by the late Robert Bennett, who had acquired it and numerous other early California ecclesial documents from the shadowy but ever-fascinating one-time cleric, Emile Valton (1873-1963). There's no way of determining anything more of the document's provenance except to say that it was unknown to all previous historians of the era.

Written at Santa Barbara, on June 20, 1848, the letter or "exhortation" was addressed to the residents of the Pueblo de Nuestra Señora de los Angeles. Its translation here confirms the observation of James Allen Hardie that Fray José María de Jesús González Rubio was "an enlightened and highly educated man, of more than ordinary talents."[10]

Reverend Friar José María de Jesús González Rubio, Preacher and Missionary Apostolic, of the Regular Observance of our Holy Father, Saint Francis, Vicar Capitular and Administrator of the Vacant Bishopric of Both Californias.

To all the residents of the Pueblo and Jurisdiction [of Nuestra Señora de] los Angeles, health and peace in Our Lord Jesus Christ.

With a grief-stricken heart we have observed, in recent years, that some are negligent in paying the tithes, that others pay them only grudingly and that many obstinately refuse to even acknowledge the obligation. My good people, this most serious attitude cannot be condoned. With this communication, our fatherly voice ever-so-gently seeks to inspire, instruct and recall your obligations, while pointing out the grevious consequences for those who refuse to comply.

As God is our witness, this paternal counsel is not in any way the desire for personal gain. Bound by religious vows, we are poor by profession. We are accustomed to all manner of privations and lack the slightest concern for our own comfort or welfare. And even if you persist in not paying the tithes, as you have until now, we are confident that Almighty God will somehow provide whatever is necessary to sustain our own temporal life. At the same time, those who ignore our plea are risking their salvation, for a likely result will be the gradual diminution of divine worship, along with a lessening number of priests empowered to absolve your sins at the hour of death. It is our fervent wish of avoiding such a misfortune that motivates this exhortation. Please listen attentively to it.

It is a religious obligation incumbent upon every creature to recognize God's supreme dominion. Failure to comply reduces a person to the level of mere beasts. Such individuals are worse off than savages who, in their own crude way, give universal testimony to the Deity. The just Abel and all the ancient patriarchs, guided only by the light of reason, complied with their innate craving to sacrifice the best of their earthly goods. It was the Lord himself who decreed: "Mine is the whole earth and everything that fills it. You will set aside the tenth part of all your fruits and cattle."

That precept, imposed on the People of God in the written law, indicated what percentage the Lord wanted for the support of divine worship. Now, in the new covenant of grace, in which mankind has been elevated to a much loftier dignity, can they be less obliged than their forebears in providing for religious services? Certainly not. Our obligation must correspond to the magnitude of His bounty. Recall that you are a holy people, redeemed by the Blood of the Savior and called to a higher level of perfection. Hence, your care in providing for divine worship must be proportionately more generous than that exhibited by the patriarchs of the Old Law. If you dare not listen to the dictates of reason, religion and conscience concerning these obligations, your attitude will surely place you in imminent danger of eternal punishment.

Beyond that, my good people of Nuestra Señora de los Angeles, you are aware that it was a legitimate use of divine authority that prompted the Church to legislate the payment of tithes. It is a universally recognized precept that Catholics attend Mass on Sundays and holy days, confess their mortal sins annually, receive the Holy Eucharist during the Easter season and fast at designated times. Also binding, under penalty of sin, is the mandate of tithing. Anything less would deny God the tribute due Him as Creator. Refusal to return a small part of His generous bounty bespeaks the worst kind of ingratitude. And, what is more, it would amount to cooperating in the destruction of religion, since the Church would not be able to provide the personnel and services necessary for divine worship.

These observations being what they are, one can only wonder why so many continue to offend God and endanger their souls, either by refusing to pay the tithes or doing so hesitatingly. The fact is, my good people, that many are so blinded by avarice, that they not only avoid giving their proper share, but even resort to fraud and injustice toward others. Those same individuals only satisfy their legitimate debts when forced to do so. And since there is, in this Diocese of Both Californias, no such enforcement personnel, they rarely, if ever, comply with the mandate of supporting the Church.

Certain persons are such slaves to vice as to never tithe. Though they have funds aplenty for gambling, dancing, partying, drunkeness and the like, they seemingly have nothing for God.

We observe still others who avoid such commonly degrading and gross vices as those mentioned above, but who are so corrupted by human pride that even worldly riches fail to bring them happiness. There is far too much expended on unnecessary and superfluous items like housing and furnishing. People are not justified in avoiding their spiritual obligations just because they are burdened with other expenses.

There may well be among us some whose reading of impious and anti-religious books has convinced them that tithing is unjust, cruel and ruinous to agriculture. With that pretense, they not only fail to tithe personally, but even encourage friends to follow their example.

What reason can there be for such an ill-advised refusal to support the Church? Do not those persons stain their souls with sin and thus expose themselves to eternal condemnation? For them, there appears to be no law greater than their own convictions.

Oh, my dear people, if there be such persons among those in the Pueblo de Nuestra Señora de Los Angeles, I would beg them, in the name of Our Lord's Precious Blood, to rectify their behavior. Give to God what is His, for only then will He bestow an abundance of graces and temporal blessings. And it is important that such actions be properly motivated. Recall the scriptural example about the two brothers, Abel and Cain. They were among the first to inhabit the world and although not as yet bound by evangelical perfection or the observance of ecclesiastical laws, they recognized their obligations of sacrificing to God the best of their fruits and cattle. Both brothers offered their gifts at the same time, but note the difference. Abel gave them willingly, and Cain with reluctance. For that, the one was blessed and the other turned away. Now, my beloved people, you are called to a greater perfection than Cain. Can you expect God's blessings if you refuse to give or do so unwillingly? On the contrary, such an attitude will incur the judgement of God.

It is not only the bad Christians who are failing to tithe. Many who boast about being good Catholics, virtuous persons and outstanding citizens rarely tithe or do so scantily. They apparently feel that tithing is a voluntary alms and hence they give it arbitrarily, whenever and wherever they like and without any remorse of conscience. And when they reduce their tithe, become delinquent or omit it altogether, they invariably forgive themselves on the grounds that poverty has befallen their family. I would have you know that such excuses were specifically invalidated by the eighth session of the Council of Constance.

My office obliges me to tell you that neither the most acceptable authors, nor the writings of the Fathers, nor those of the Roman Pontiffs nor the conciliar documents have ever equated tithes with alms. In fact, just the opposite is the case. It has been universally taught that tithing is a grevously-binding precept, a necessary obligation and an indispensable requisite for ecclesial worship. Without it or its equivalent, religion and divine worship must necessarily cease. That's why certain writers, even some saints, regard tithing as a divine precept. Whether it is a positive, divine or ecclesiastical law has yet to be clarified. But that factor is not relevant to the present sitution. Obliged to satisfy ecclesiastical as well as divine laws, it really makes little practical difference into which category the obligation fills.

My personal interpretation is that of the Angelic Doctor, Saint Thomas, who says that "paying tithes in the Old Law was partly natural and partly judicial precept." Reason dictates that those who care for public worship should receive whatever is necessary for sustenance, in much the same way as those who watch out for the civil realm receive their living. This is alluded to by the apostle, in his letter to the Church at Corinth: "Whoever wages war at his personal expense? Or who plants a vine and then doesn't eat its fruits?"

The theologian continues: "The determination of the share extended to ministers derives from divine positive law and should be proportionate to the condition of the people on whom the law is placed. Since the populace of the Old Testament were divided into twelve tribes, those of the last, the Levites, were completely consecrated to divine services. Lacking any provisions for support, it was agreed that the other tribes would set aside for the Levites a tenth of their produce so that they might live in an honorable manner."

Then the holy scribe treats the tithes established in the Christian era: "The determination of paying tithes was instituted by the Church, according to local practices, because the people of the New Law could not give less to God than was given by those of earlier times. If your justice does not surpass that of the scribes and pharisees, you won't enter the kingdom of heaven. The ministers of the New Covenant surely surpass, in dignity, those of the Old.

In another place, the Angelic Doctor says that the precept of paying tithes is a moral obligation, insofar as those who are dedicated to God's ministry should be supported in a way similar to those who serve the civil realm. Under this aspect it is proposed as a precept of the New Testament, for the Lord declared that a worker deserves his sustenance. The apostle wrote that the Lord wanted those who perform the Gospel and serve at the altar to be supported thereby. The actual percentage does not derive from the natural law or from a moral precept, but is ceremonial and judicial. It was a convenient determination for arriving at a figure for support. It pertains to both the New and the Old Law since each required ministers who, in return, needed a reasonable means of sustenance.

Any legislator must anchor positive laws to the natural law, for the former has no validity apart from the latter. The natural law dictates, for example, that a wrongdoer should be punished, but leaves the positive law with the task of determining how, when and to what extent the punishment is to be applied. Since the Church has the authority of creating laws pertaining to God's worship, it also possesses the right of stipulating the precise measure which its adherents ought to provide for ministers and services. And so there would be a uniformity of practice between the Old and New Covenants, the Church adopted the percentage used in the former.

While the teaching of Saint Thomas is really quite benevolent, yet the Angelic Doctor stresses that tithing is anything but a voluntary offering or an arbitrary alms. Rather, it is sacred and indispensable obligation, anchored to the natural and divine law, which demands that public worship be supported and its ministers decently maintained. Only the designation of the tenth part is ecclesial law and that determination can be increased, lessened or even held in abeyance as circumstances demand.

In those places where the Church has no outside income, as is the case in the Californias, tithing cannot be looked upon as an alms and thus left to the discretion of the giver. No, it is a sacred obligation, a serious precept whose fulfillment binds under pain of sin. And so fully does that obligation bind that the Church, in accordance with the decrees of many Roman Pontiffs and the canons of several conciliar councils, considers violators liable to the severe pain of excommunication. The Council of Trent, just to cite the most recent ecumenical body, said those who, by any means whatsoever, withhold their just tithes or fearlessly appropriate them to their personal use, sin gravely. Inasmuch as tithes are owed to God, those who default or encourage others to do so, take what is not theirs. Trent further stipulates that such offenders cannot be reconciled until they have made complete restitution.

This, my dear people, is a synopsis of tithing, along with the penalty for those who flaunt ecclesial legislation. Both the law and the punishment are imposed by the Church under the protection and guidance of the Holy Spirit. All believers, by express command of Jesus Christ, are obliged to obey the Church. Note, if you will, how the Council of Trent states that paying the tithes is owed to God. That has been the constant teaching of the Church. At an earlier council, the obligation was verbalized as if God were talking to the whole world:

> Oh men, the earth which you till belongs to Me. Mine are the grains that you plant, the animals you work and the sun that illuminates and warms you. And if all belongs to Me, one ought to take no more than a single share, leaving the other nine to Me. Yet, as is My prerogative, I leave nine for you and ask only one in return. But do give Me that tenth or I will take away the other nine. Be assured that if you satisfy this obligation, I will multiply what remains.

It is only good sense to see that everything comes from and belongs to God. If the earth gives sustenance, it comes not from man who only plants and waters. but from God who gives the increment. Yes, He alone makes the earth to support life; he alone allows the fruits to grow and ripen; He alone sends or takes away the rains; He alone multiplies the grain and the cattle. In fine, He is the only source from whose merciful hand man receives everything he needs. Consequently, to deny the Lord His tenth part is the grossest ingratitude, a grave crime and a serious sacrilege.

The Council of Trent also teaches that anyone who defaults on paying the tithes is taking another's property. And such a person is not only punished with excommunication, but is refused reconciliation until he makes complete restitution. Briefly, the tithe comes from God, who through the Church has destined it for the support of divine worship. Therefore, the tiller does not own the tenth part of his fruits and harvest - it belongs to the Church for whom it was destined and cannot be alienated.

I could write a lot more on this point, but already enough has been said to convince you that the payment of the tithes is not a voluntary offering, but a just tribute to the Deity. The tithe is not an arbitrary alms, but a rightful obligation and a most solemn precept couched in terms of the Law which commands it. Hence, the tithe must be paid exactly and promptly, without deducting expenses or costs. That tenth part applies to everything: the fruits of the gardens and vineyards and laborers who have looked after the herds of cattle.He who avoids this obligation in the future or he who fails to make restitution for his past failures is not only disgraced and unworthy of receiving final absolution, but must face God with his sins of disobedience, sacrilege, injustice and scandal, along with the grave crime of furthering the diminution of religion.

You will recall, my good people, that the religion of Jesus Christ was sown in this land by many zealous missionaries who, with God's help, banished the abominable practice of paganism, baptized many thousands and dedicated to divine worship more than twenty churches wherein Our Lord has been honored and glorified. And how was it all done, you may ask. The answer is obvious enough. Your forefathers witnessed what the missionaries accomplished with the assistance of the Pious Fund of the Californias. That monetary trust was established in Mexico by the sacrifice of those concerned with the conversion of the natives. Once the mission system had been firmly established, it was maintained mostly by the Indians who fulfilled their tasks of building and enriching churches and supporting their ministers on the part of the commonweal. Today circumstances have changed. The Pious Fund no longer exists and the Missions have been destroyed and the Indians de-populated and defrauded. Presently, the non-Indian population accounts for the major part of California's population. They are the ones who possess lands, vineyards, laborers, cattle, houses and goods. Consequently, just as times have changed, so must obligations.

All Christians, be they white, red or whatever, are obliged to make provisions for divine worship, but as long as the whites in California were few in number and poor in resources, the Church did not demand anything from them because there were Indians enough to provide whatever was needed. But today, that scene is totally reversed. There are only small clusters of Indians left. The majority of the population is white and many of them are rich or at least comfortable. The obligation then of looking after divine worship and its ministers has obviously shifted to them. And it behooves them to meet that challenge with dispatch.

Those who faithfully pay the tithes satisfy the precept that every Christian owes to God as His Creator, Redeemer and Sustainer. The Lord is generous in return and will bestow upon such persons all manner of temporal blessings. And with the payment of the tithes, the few remaining priests will be able to support themselves and begin providing facilities whereby young men of the next generation can be trained for the ministry. Finally, compliance will enable divine worship to be supplemented with decorum. God will be honored and glorified in our churches, zealous ministers will be available to perform the sacred liturgies and to instruct the populace in the truths of salvation.

If only all the Christians in this diocese might hear this plea. The Church in the Californias, formerly supported by the Pious Fund and the mission system, presently finds those means utterly depleted. It resembles a building without foundations or a column without a base. The whole structure is on the verge of collapse. Languished and impoverished, the Church is without resources, rents or adequate clergy. Lacking these things, it cries out for assistance like a dying mother pleading with her children for nourishment. Will you turn a deaf ear? I just can't believe that you would. I am persuaded that as good sons and daughters of the Church, you will come to the rescue. Your virtues of zeal, constancy and love will inspire you to pay up your tithes promptly.

Let me assure you that a continuance of the present situation will spell the ruin for Catholicism in the Californias. And then, woe to you and your children. Woe to a land without divine worship or religion. Its people will become like ignorant savages, lacking Church, altar, priests and religion. May Our Lord not allow such a thing to transpire! May He close my eyes in death before such a disgrace befalls this area!

My dear children, be faithful and fervent Christians. Honor God by the exact fulfillment of His laws, especially those which look to the maintenance of sacred religion. If you add to your sins the crime of letting the Church succumb here, of allowing religion to disappear from this country, of denying her the temporal goods needed to provide divine worship, support the clergy and establish schools, then surely the angry heavens will rain down all kinds of evils upon you. And then, after an unhappy existence, you may well suffer eternal death.

It is to forestall such a tragedy that I make this exhortation. As your spiritual Father, I will continue praying that God will fill you with the graces demanded for these perilous times.

Given at Santa Barbara, on this. the 20th day of June, 1848.

Notes to the Text

1. For a biographical sketch of the prelate, see Francis J. Weber, *Francisco Garcia Diego, California's Transition Bishop* (Los Angeles, 1972).
2. Zephyrin Engelhardt. O.F.M., *The Missions and Missionaries of California* (San Francisco, 1915), IV, 239.
3. Santa Barbara Mission Archives, Francisco García Diego, O.F.M., February 4, 1842, Santa Barbara.
4. Archives of the Archdiocese of Los Angeles (hereafter referred to as AALA), Francisco García Diego, O.F.M., - Circular Letter, Santa Barbara.
5. Zephyrin Engelhardt, O.F.M., *op. cit.*, IV, 391.
6. AALA, Francisco García Diego, O.F.M. to Minister of Justice, October 27, 1843, Santa Barbara.
7. Francis J. Weber, "Kidnapping the Vicar-General," *Front Line* VII (Summer, 1968).
8. Maynard J. Geiger. O.F.M., *Franciscan Missionaries In Hispanic California* 1769-1848 (San Marino. 1969), p. 115.
9. AALA. José Maria de Jesús Gonzalez Rubio, O.F.M. *Pastoral Letter*, Santa Barbara.
10. Francis J. Weber (ed.), "The Hardie Memorandum," *Southern California Quarterly* LIV (Winter, 1972), 348.

51

"A Report from California - 1851," appeared in the *U.S. Catholic Historian* I (Fall, 1981),133-140.

Edmond Venisse was born at Folligny (Manche) on September 9, 1823.[1] He joined the Congregation of the Sacred Hearts of Jesus and Mary (Picpus Fathers) on August 15, 1846. In July 1849, while still a seminarian, young Venisse was sent to Chile. There he continued his theological studies and, on March 15, 1851, was ordained to the subdiaconate.

Later that same month, Venisse was assigned to the Pueblo de Nuestra Señora de los Angeles, in Alta, California, where he was to teach in the recently opened school which Bishop Joseph Sadoc Alemany had entrusted to the Picpus Fathers. Recalling his work in that pioneering educational institution, Venisse noted that he had become a "real schoolmaster, teaching a little of everything to some poor chilren."[2]

The priestly candidate was also attached to the Pueblo Church of Nuestra Señora de los Angeles, as an associate to Father Anaclet Lestrade.[3] There he organized a choir of Indians for the great feasts. These Indians were the "survivors of those happy times when the talented Franciscan Fathers taught the arts with so much success." Venisse said that while he served in Los Angeles, he felt that he was "among the angels."[4]

In the spring of 1853, Venisse petitioned his superiors at Paris for advancement to the priesthood. The permission was granted and the usual dismissorial letters where dispatched to California. Alemany, the newly designated Archbishop of San Francisco, bestowed the priestly imprint on November 20.[5]

Enroute back to Los Angeles, Father Venisse stopped at Santa Barbara Mission, where Fray José María de Jesús Gonzáles Rubio insisted on having a grand ceremony honoring the recently ordained priest. He was lodged in the episcopal quarters once occupied by Bishop Francisco García Diego y Moreno and, on the Feast of Santa Barbara, offered his first Solemn High Mass.

Following the liturgy, everyone in the congregation came forward to greet the celebrant personally. Father Venisse spent some further days at Santa Ines Mission and then journeyed on to San Fernando Mission, which had been without a resident priest for some years.

The school operated by the Picpus Fathers at Los Angeles lasted until mid-1853, when Father Felix Migorel left the diocese. In the following months, Venisse toured California, assisting at various places in the administration of the sacraments.

In the summer of 1855, Venisse made a trip to Hawaii for his health.[6] But when he found the climate there no more conducive, he returned to California, arriving in time to witness the initial visit of Bishop Thaddeus Amat to the southland.[7]

The youthful priest, anxious to pursue his teaching apostolate, asked his superiors for an assignment more in keeping with his considerable talents. Some time later, he noted that since "the principal aim of our Congregation in this country has been the establishment of a college, and the time marked by Providence did not seem to have come, it was decided that I was to leave for Chile."[8]

Venisse departed early in 1856, arriving at Valparaiso on May 22. He was then sent to Copiapo, where the Picpus Fathers operated the thriving College of Our Lady of Mercy. He is last heard of on June 20, 1856, when he wrote a letter to his homeland, recalling his service to the Church in California. The date and place of his death are not presently known.

The following letter from Venisse to his priest brother was written from El Pueblo de Nuestra Señora de los Angeles on September 18, 1851. It was initially published in *Annales de la Propagation de la Foi* XXIV (Lyon, 1852), 405-415.

* * *

The letter you wrote last year reached me in Santiago, the capital of Chile. The one which I should have received two months later probably followed the same route as the first; it will have gone to Valparaiso, but not finding me there, it was probably forwarded somewhere. Who knows where it is now? Alas, perhaps it is at the bottom of the sea or a captive in a post office, waiting to be delivered. Provided this letter suffers a better fate, you wil know that I was ordained sub-deacon on March 15th of this year. On the 27th of that same month, another priest of our Congregation and I departed on a Dutch vessel. On May 16, after a pleasant passage of fifty-one days, I could repeat with the Latin poet, Inveni portum.

You must be impatient to know where I am. Patience! Not so fast, let us prolong the pleasure. You must try to guess the name of the port. Might it be Gambier? Oh! no doubt but I would have been happy to see again M. Henry, that young university professor who is so entirely devoted to the Mission and who is now teaching Latin and French to the young Mangarevians. His is not an enviable position in the eyes of most, but he is happy and God is preparing a magnificent reward for him. But, no, I have seen nothing of Gambier, except for a few shells that I sent you by the Captain of Esperance.

If it is not Gambier, might it be Tahiti to which I have come? If so, I should tell you something of Queen Pomaré and our old school friend, Pepin. Pepin I have not seen. He did write me recently that he was studing the local language and that Father Fouquest de St. Hilaire was doing much good in the island of Pomotou. So I am not in Tahiti.

Perhaps you might think I have left the south and returned north. Am I in the Sandwich Islands? There, you have guessed it! What is our cousin there doing, what has he to say? We did pass close to there, it is true, and for a moment I thought I might see Father Bouillon again and speak to him of his mother. And I could have tasted his poi, taro and sweet potatoes. But such was not our destination. Might the wind have carried us towards China and Japan? If so, I would have taken on Chinese dress, the skull cap and the pig tail. Have I then rejoined our old master of studies M. Gasset at the Abbaye-Blanche? In all parts of the world, we have our missionaries from Coutance. Well, I have seen some Chinese, but not China, much less Japan, Then where am I?

Okay, I will tell you since you cannot guess. I am in a country much spoken of in the world, a place which has turned the heads of quite a number with its promises of marvelous things. It is also an area that makes many people miserable. In a word, I am in the old country, Alta California. Yes, I am in California! Would you ever have guessed it? And what am I doing here? Have I put aside my cassock? Has the thirst for gold turned my head too? No, what I am doing in California, you will soon know.

I am in a place, that the early chronicles called Pueblo de los Angeles, that is to say, the City of the Angeles. Always such poetic names. A few months ago it was Valparaiso, the Valley of Paradise; now it is the City of the Angels! But is the Valley of Paradise much different from the City of Angels? No, the differ-

ence is negligible as far as temperature and terrain are concerned, but the people are as different as night and day. The Chileans are an amiable and obliging people of good faith. They are educated and see that their children are educated. They have high schools, a university, and so on. But in California, there is nothing of the sort. Here, young people know how to ride horseback and that is about all. Three of us are at Los Angeles to see if we can establish some sort of school The City of the Angels was, prior to the discovery of gold, among the more prominent areas of Alta California: there are today between four and five thousand souls. It is situated seven or eight leagues from the ocean. The port, which is inhabited solely by one Englishman, is called San Pedro; the name is fitting since before setting out for the City of the Angels, it is appropriate to address oneself to Saint Peter. It was he who opened the door of the area to us. We crossed, on foot, a plain of nine or ten leagues without encountering a single dwelling, or even a drop of water. Finally, toward evening, we beheld a green plain and the large community known as The City of the Angels. It is situated in a beautiful plain, bounded on the north and east by high mountains, and on the south and west by the ocean. It is traversed by the Rio San Gabriel and along this waterway are beautiful vines and gardens filled ,with fruit trees of different kinds, such as apple, pear, peach, apricot, fig, pomegranate, and orange. About three leagues east of the City of the Angels, one enters the community of the Archangels, which is the Mission of Saint Gabriel. I stayed there for a month. It was formerly one of the most beautiful frontier outposts in Alta California, but the buildings, except for the church and some of the rooms, are no more than ruins which the stranger must share with squirrels and owls. The same is true in most all of the missions. As this is the first time that I am writing from California, perhaps you would like to have some details about the country.

Discovered in 1548 [sic], by Spanish navigators, it was colonized by them. In 1768[sic], it was formed into a province of Mexico, which involved it in the consequences of the subsequent wars for independence and delivered it finally, in 1848, as a worthless appendage, to the United States. Such is, for the space of three centuries, its history. Let me add a word concerning the missions of Alta California. Those large foundations were established by apostolic men as a means of converting the native peoples. These Indians, says a famous mariner, Abel Aubert DuPetit Thouars, who formerly led a wild, vagabond existence, came under the paternal authority of the friars of Saint Francis. They were instructed by prudent lessons, their hands trained for useful work. Some were employed in agriculture, irrigation and the care of live-stock; others learned the craft of weavers, the trade of carpenters, and the skill of smiths.

Their children were given Christian upbringing within the religious atmosphere of the Church.

The missions of Alta California numbered twenty one: San Diego, the oldest, goes back to 1769; San Francisco de los Dolores dates from 1822. Each foundation had an administrator, a Franciscan who exercised full authority over the settlement. The later unrest in Mexico has been the cause of their decadence and ruin. Their downfall dates only from 1836. Most of the Indians who lived in these establishments have returned to their tribes in the interior of California. Only a small number has remained at the missions. That is the history of California until February 1848. Then it was that the cry went up from Sacramento. The news about the discovery of gold spread from valley to valley, from place to place, surprising even Europe in the midst of its turmoils. In the unnamed brooks and desert ravines of California, gold was found, handfulls of it. Then, from all points of the globe, people hastened to seek their fortune; laborers abandoned their fields, artisans their work-shops, merchants their counters, judges their tribunes and captains their ships. Oh, some were successful, but others were disappointed. Useless labors, vain privations, numerous assassinations and countless suicides! And all for a little gold! A person turns readily enough to crime when thinking to make a fortune in a matter of weeks. One hears them tell of enduring every kind of privation. And what other perils they have encountered? If someone does bring back some few pounds of gold, fifteen or twenty thousand piastres, more or less, what does he do? He often goes to a gambling house, picks up the cards and within an hour has nothing. If he is an American he will not be discouraged but will take up his sack and return to the mines; another will go and steal, while the Frenchman will blow his brains out or lose his sanity.

A word or two about San Francisco, where I spent several weeks. A fortnight before my arrival, half the city had been burned; a fortnight after my departure the other half suffered the same fate. In the first conflagration, fifteen hundred houses fell prey to the flames; the second was still more devastating than the first. It is said the like has never been seen. San Francisco, then, no longer exists? Not at all. A fortnight after the fire, there is little sign of the disaster. The houses are being rebuilt as though by enchantment so efficient are the Americans in their work! One has seen houses burned in the evening, rebuilt during the night by the light of the flames, and sold by the next morning. It is true that most of the homes are of wood, and even a few of metallic substances but nothing withstands the fire; these last have turned as red as an iron in the forge, and all their interior furnishings were destroyed. How many episodes I could tell about this place. The day after a fire, there were persons wandering about who were not able to save even their britches and shirts; some supposedly protected their belongs by hiding them in the mountains, but when they look for them, they likely do not find them. You might wonder if theses fires are started by accident. Not at all. Every day fires are started to make stealing easier.

A large part of San Francisco is built upon piles; not only are the houses fashioned from wood, but so also is a large part of the streets. There is even an entirely wood road of more than a league in length. Large numbers of houses are built over the water. Vessels are but a few steps from them and when the houses burn, so do the vessels.

The port is huge and the ships very numerous. Many are lacking seamen. They are moored to one another, surrounded by piles, as though they should never sail again, which well may be. They are deteriorating and no one attempts to repair them. What will become of them? Perhaps houses will be built on them, in which case part of the port could well become a city. The Pacific ocean is under the houses! If the pilings should fail, it wouldn't make too much difference for the city would go about its business as usual, already have been built on abandoned ships. What a port! What a city! What a population! French, English, Germans, Italians, Mexicans, Americans, Indians, Canadians and even Chinese; whites, blacks, yellows and browns; Christians, pagans, protestants, atheists, highwaymen, thieves, convicts, incendiarists and assassins. Little of good and much of bad–that is the population of San Francisco. It is the new Babylon, a city filled with crime, disorders, confusion and frightful noise. And who administers justice? On one day a malefactor is apprehended and the next day he is free. And what have law-abiding persons done about it? They have chosen from among their own number a certain number of judges and woe to those who fall into their hands! Here is what happened on the day before I left San Francisco: a thief was caught in the afternoon, at nine o'clock he appeared before the judges, at midnight he was sentenced and at one o'clock he was hanged. He didn't have time for supper. He was a Protestant convict from Sidney. On the day of my departure, there was another trial scheduled for three accused persons. The populace was waiting impatiently for the moment when the ropes would be put round their necks. But about that maybe I should draw the curtain. Let us speak of the monuments and the inhabitants of Alta California.

In San Francisco there is one poor little Catholic church, protected by God in an evident manner during the last fire. Otherwise it would have been necessary to rebuild it and churches are not as easily erected as houses.

One day I was coming back from downtown to Mission Dolores by a road used rarely except by the dead. I found myself in a small valley, solitary and silent, whose hills were covered with oaks in green, dense foliage. It was a vast cemetery. I looked closely, there was not a cross anywhere, so I concluded that I must have been in a Protestant cemetery. I decided to read the epitaphs. The first indicated that it had not been a year since the first interments were made, Yet the number of those waiting here for the day of resurrection had already risen to more than twelve hundred. Those epitaphs also revealed that most of these persons had departed in the flower of their youth, between their twenty-fifth and thirtieth years. I left with a feeling of melancholy, reflecting that the burial ground was more crowded than the placer-mines, and that this land had taken more lives than it had returned gold.

Speaking of monuments, Monterey, formerly the capital of Alta California and now the episcopal seat, does not possess any. I only saw it in passing, but it is a pretty little village, on the edge of the sea, surrounded by charming hills covered with pines and populated with wildlife.

As for humankind, one recognizes the two groupings, gente de razon *and* gente sin razon. *These last are the Indians. Disgusting in their filth, they are almost naked, lazy, careless, non-industrious, ungrateful, traitorous, hypocrites, thieves and drunkards. With only limited intelligence, these poor people, less than a century ago, willingly submitted themselves to the educational, spiritual and mechanical works of the missions. Among the* gente de razon *are the Americans, Mexicans and Californians, originating in Mexico. The American thinks, speaks and pursues only dollars. As for the Californians, they are different, being mostly orientated towards their horses. Such a one is content only when he feels a horse between his legs.*

Let me speak of the animal kingdom. The undomesticated animals of Alta California are the wild horse, bear, tiger, deer, roebuck, hare, a kind of dog-wolf who howls throughout the night and, at every step, a rabbit. Everywhere there are squirrels and partridge. In certain seasons the bays, rivers and lakes are filled with wild ducks and geese. Among the domestic animals there is only one called on to play a particularly distinguished role, and that is the hen who lays the golden eggs. Eggs are sold for as much as five or six piastres *a dozen. Thus, to make a profit, one need only have some good layers. Also it is interesting to observe how hens arrive at San Francisco from Chile, the Sandwich Isles and even Japan. Splendid provisions are provided for them. They have well-sanded courtyards and follow a regular routine. They arise at a specified hour and eat at a prescribed time. This is followed by a play-hour presided over by one or two overseers and then, they are taken to lay. In the establishment there is an infirmary and should a layer fall sick, a veterinarian will appear. The hens have doctors just as people do. The local attendant carefully follows everything ordered by the "doctors." It was a Frenchman who instituted this plan and he will no doubt carry it out. At the price for which eggs are sold, he will soon be as rich as Croesus.*

Let me conclude with some observations on the vegetable kingdom. Such items at San Francisco are very valuable. Gardeners really make a fortune. I shall cite only onion seed which is sold at the current price of twenty-five pias- tres. Imagine, one pound of onion seed for 500 francs! Who would believe that in Normandy?

And you, my dear brother, how are you doing? Oh! how I long to hear from you. You are already a priest and each day you must pray for me who aspires to that state. Pray also for our parents. Commend me to the Holy Virgin, Saint Joseph and my patron saint. If there is anxiety for this temporary separation, let us do everything to obviate such a state in the eternal order. I have been unmindful perhaps that a subdeacon does not have the right to preach! In your letters, tell me about our father, mother and brothers. It is pleasurable to hear of those we love. Adieu, I must end now. Embrace our relations and mutual friends. Your brother who loves you all.

Notes to the Text

1. Léonce Jore, "The Fathers of the Congregation fo the Sacred Hearts (called Picpus) in California," *Southern California Quarterly* XLVI (December, 1964), 313.
2. Francis J. Weber, *Documents of California Catholic History* (Los Angeles, 1965), p. 70.
3. Reginald Yzendoorn, S.S.C.C., *History of the Catholic Mission in the Hawaiian Islands*, (Honolulu, 1927), p. 191.
4. Brother V. Edmund, F.S.C., "A Los Angeles Picpus Father," *Academy Scrapbook* I (July, 1950-May, 1951), 313.
5. Zephyrin Engelhardt, O.F.M., *The Missions and Missionaries of California* (San Francisco, 1915), IV, 716.
6. It was Venisse who introduced the Misa Cataluña into the Hawaiian Isles. See *Academy Scrapbook* II (July, 1951), 59.
7. Francis J. Weber, *California's Reluctant Prelate* (Los Angeles, 1964), p. 41.
8. See *Annales de la Propagation de la Foi* XXX (Lyon, 1858), 63-68.

52

"Kidnapping the Vicar-General" is the title of this vignette taken from *Front Line* VII (Summer, 1968), 42-45.

According to the Santa Barbara correspondent for *El Clamor Publico*, there took place in that city, on January 22, 1856, "one of those events, rare in the history of towns, which will be remembered and transmitted down through generations."[1] The episode referred to, easily among the most effective examples of "lay interference" recorded in ecclesiastical annals, centered about the personage of Father González Rúbio (1804-1875) and his forceful abduction by a group of local citizens led by the city's mayor.

The Guadalajara-born friar, whose name still invokes expressions of esteem at Santa Barbara, was the last of California's great missionaries, one whom Hubert Howe Bancroft characterized as "respected and beloved by all from the beginning to the end of his career."[2] Rubio had been with that initial band of Zacatecan friars[3] arriving at Monterey in January of 1833, to replace the aged and infirm Fernandino Franciscans[4] in the northernmost of California's missions. The first decade of his priestly ministry was spent at the once-prosperous, but then rapidly declining Mission San José and while there he served a three-year term as his college's *presidente* or religious superior for the area. In 1842, he was recalled to Santa Barbara as secretary to the newly appointed Bishop of Both Californias, Francisco García Diego y Moreno.

Shortly before that prelate's death, in April of 1846, Father Rúbio was designated co-vicar-general of the diocese. The metropolitan chapter of

Mexico City appointed him administrator of the vacant jurisdiction the following year, a post he held with distinction until the arrival of Bishop Joseph Sadoc Alemany in 1850. Rúbio served two succeeding prelates as vicar-general and between the years 1858 and 1872, was pastor at Santa Barbara. His competency in matters of administration was widely recognized and prompted the submission of his name in mid-1851 as episcopal candidate for an envisioned vicariate apostolic in Baja California. Then, and again a few years later, the Zacatecan friar "declined both the honor and the burden" in deference to retaining his pastoral role in Santa Barbara.

The historian of Mission Santa Barbara has recorded of Rúbio that "the length of years given him, years that projected his personality deep into the modern era, the many and varied offices of trust bestowed upon him, the unanimous and unfailing love of the people of Santa Barbara for him, reveal him as a figure of magnitude in the period of transition between the Mexican regime and the initial American rule in California.[5] The esteem in which Rúbio was held is obvious from numerous other sources. One prominent visitor recalled his estimate of the friar as that of a "noble man, a true Christian, very much respected and beloved by his people, and by all who knew him."[6]

An understanding of the friar's stature at Santa Barbara helps to explain the resentment engendered when word arrived that Rúbio had been recalled from Santa Barbara to assume the superiorship of his apostolic college at Zacatecas. The archbishop of San Francisco was greatly disturbed by the transfer and wrote to Rúbio that "the people of this country will hardly believe us to be Roman, Catholic and Apostolic if they do not see us supported by you…"[7]

When Rúbio's resignation was denied, the friar, good religious that he was, prepared to leave for his new assignment. When the populace realized the archbishop's inability to effect any immediate reversal of the directive, they took matters into their own hands. Under the leadership of Antonio María de la Guerra, the beloved Franciscan "was detained without there being on anyone's part any innuendo, inducement or bribery or any other means except that of the spontaneous will of a people who take such measures to retain in its midst a person to whom it owes so much because of the religious and moral instruction it had received from him."[8]

The brazen action of the citizenry, described in the following account, was effective, for in April Father Rúbio was notified that his resignation had reluctantly been accepted. The gentle friar then resumed his routine at Santa Barbara, living on to observe his golden jubilee as a Franciscan. There, on November 2, 1875, "with the fame of uncommon virtues especially with that of prudence and exquisite tact in governing," Father Rúbio "peacefully surrendered his soul to his Creator."[9]

The Rev. Father González of the Franciscan Order, a member of the Missionary College of Our Lady of Guadalupe of Zacatecas, who at present, is in the charge of the parish of Santa Barbara and vicar general of this diocese, recently received an order to return to his college to preside there as guardian, to which office his brethren elected him.

In vain did he forward his resignation for a new election called him to the same office. Accompanying the news of his re-election was an order to present himself to the college. Despite his vehement desire to end his days among his parishioners, he resolved to obey the order of his superiors. On the 20th, after Mass, his eyes bathed in tears, and with a tender feeling of love in his heart towards his flock – a love that was reciprocated on the part of his audience - he made known the fatal order which was to separate him, perhaps, forever from them. He said farewell to all.

It is impossible to describe the great emotions this news engendered in the townspeople. The beautiful qualities of this worthy missionary have made him an object of veneration to all Catholics and of respect and esteem to all others in the city.

Thus as soon as his coming departure was noised abroad, the people agreed to make use of the most respected persons to persuade him not to depart, by recalling to him the enormous void that would be left in the parish for he would deprive them of his model, exemplary life and virtues and the College of Our Lady of Sorrows of this city, one of its principal supports. This was done, but in vain, for neither pleading, reasoning nor circumstantial remarks, succeeded in shattering his determination to obey his superiors and thus give an example of the obedience he had so frequently made the subject of his sermons.

Seeing that every method of persuasion failed, the people resolutely determined to prevent his departure. Fearing that he would leave without being seen, they appointed several fellow citizens to be on the *qui vive*. Finally, on the 22nd, at 10 o'clock, as soon as the smoke of the steamer on which he was to sail, was seen on the horizon, the worthy missionary went to the point of embarkation where a small boat was waiting to take him aboard. But alas, vain hope! When he arrived at the beach, the boat was already surrounded by fifteen or twenty men who had orders not to allow the *padre* to embark.

Almost at the same time that he arrived at the beach, there also arrived about 1000 persons of both sexes and of every nationality and creed, all moved, as if by instinct, by a common desire to detain this respectable gentleman. There they formed one body and surrounded his carriage. Don Francisco de la Guerra came up to him and in the name of all told him with all due respect, that the townspeople had determined to oppose his departure by every means and that it was useless for him to think of going away for it was impossible for him to move a step forward toward the ocean. De la Guerra pleaded with him to return to his abode. But the *padre* remained firm in his resolve. Yet to his every statement the answer came that the people were aware of his reasons for going but still remained determined to withhold their consent; furthermore it was impossible to persuade them to think otherwise.

Consequently, the order was given to the driver of the carriage to return the *padre* to his habitation. Afterwards representatives of the people were sent to Archbishop Alemany, in the absence of Bishop Amat, asking him to intercede with the superiors of Father Gonzalez to allow him to remain here. If necessary, the Archbishop was to intercede with the Holy Father. We hope that through so worthy an intercessor we shall obtain the object of our desires.

Notes to the Text

1. February 9, 1856. This interesting account appears in Francis J. Weber, *Documents of California Catholic History* (Los Angeles, 1965), pp. 76-78.
2. *History of California* (San Francisco, 1886), III, 760.
3. So designated after the Mexican city in which the apostolic college of Nuestra Señora de Guadalupe was located.
4. So named after the title of their apostolic college of San Fernando in Mexico City.
5. Maynard J. Geiger, in the Santa Barbara *News-Press*, October 3, 1948.
6. William Heath Davis, *Seventy-five Years in California* (San Francisco, 1967), p. 42.
7. Joseph Sadoc Alemany to González Rúbio, San Francisco, May 19, 1855, reproduced in Maynard J. Geiger, *Mission Santa Barbara*, 1782-1965 (Santa Barbara, 1965).
8. Archives of the Sacred Congregation of Propaganda Fide, Joaquin Carrillo to Cardinal Prefect, Santa Barbara, September 8, 1858.
9. Necrology entry of the Reverend José María Romo, reproduced in Maynard J. Geiger, "Biography of the Very Rev. José María de Jesus González Rúbio, O.F.M. (1804-1875)," *Provincial Annals*, 16 (1953), at 35.

53

This essay on "John J. Prendergast, Priest of the Church of San Francisco," is taken from *Front Line VI* (Summer, 1967), 34-38.

The honest and sincere Catholic cleric, who feels certain inclinations toward the episcopate, can take some solace in the scriptural dictum that anyone eager for the office of bishop desires a good work (1 Tm 3:1). Such praiseworthy ambitions are not universal, however, and one notable example of a priest who would have no part of the episcopate is John S. Prendergast (1834-1914) of San Francisco. Even during his own lifetime, it was recorded of this Irish-born priest that "he has refused the mitre more than once, a rare instance of humility in this selfish age." The writer of these words went on to state that Prendergast "desired no higher distinction in the Church than to be a priest at God's altar."[1] That such a distinction was even considered speaks well of the Dublin-trained priest who came to California at a time when that area was known chiefly to the gold hunter, the adventurer, and the speculator.

As early as 1864, only five years after Prendergast's ordination, the archbishop of San Francisco, Joseph Sadoc Alemany, referred to the young man as "a most promising Priest."[2] Later that very year Alemany included the cleric's name among four *episcopabili* submitted to Rome's Sacred Congregation of Propaganda Fide.[3]

Shortly after Prendergast was appointed vicar general of San Francisco on August 23, 1874, and apparently without his knowledge, his name was proposed for the coadjutorship of the suffragan diocese of Grass Valley.[4] The appropriate bulls were drawn up and in a document dated August

20,. the pastor of San Francisco's cathedral parish was informed by a papal rescript of his appointment to the titular see of Serbia. Prendergast immediately informed Alessandro Cardinal Franchi of his respectful but firm refusal[5] of the nomination preferring as one writer put it, "to remain with the flock which he had so long and lovingly tended."[6] By the time the Archbishop of San Francisco submitted Prendergast's name on a list of candidates for his own successor, officials of Propaganda Fide were obliged to disqualify the terna on the grounds that all of its recommended priests had "already declined other episcopal appointments."[7]

Shortly after his silver episcopal jubilee in 1875, Archbishop Alemany again petitioned for a coadjutor. The usual terna of candidates was drafted and this time the name of San Francisco's vicar general was listed in the third place. In an accompanying letter, the Dominican prelate described Prendergast as "very able, learned, eloquent and attentive to his duties." However, because the Bishop of Monterey-Los Angeles, Thaddeus Amat, felt that Prendergast was of a "noncommunicative" nature, the metropolitan suggested that if the nod went to Prendergast, it be without the right of succession.[8] No action was taken and the matter of Alemany's retirement was temporarily shelved.

Six years later, in August of 1881, a petition was circulated among the clergy of San Francisco favoring the episcopal candidacy of the popular Bay City priest. In their spontaneous statement, the signatories noted:

We the undersigned secular and regular Clergy of the Archdiocese of San Francisco, California, having learned that a Coadjutor is to be appointed to our Venerable Archbishop most respectfully submit to Your Eminence for the consideration of the Sovereign Pontiff the following statement:

That among the names forwarded to His Holiness occurs, as we understand, that of the Very Rev. John Prendergast, Vicar General of this Diocese. That his name should have been so submitted has caused us much gratification, but no surprise, for mentally, morally and phisically [sic] we regard him as possessing the qualifications requisite for so important a position, and that in so eminent a degree that we have felt impelled to manifest in this rather unusual manner the unanimity of the Clergy in favor of Father Prendergast, as may be seen from the signatures hereunto appended. His faithful services during the past twenty years, his intimate knowledge of the wants of the Diocese and the experience received from his position of Vicar General seem to us to render his appointment particularly appropriate. Therefore, in as much as we believe Father Prendergast possesses every requisite, learning, piety, zeal, prudence, we sincerely trust that the Sovereign Pontiff will be graciously pleased to listen to our petition for which act of Sovereign Clemency we shall be profoundly grateful.[9]

Prendergast later wrote to a friend that on hearing of the petition, "I took advice with wise, experienced men, conversant with the religious wants of this state; and I have concluded to decline the honor if tendered." The vicar general emphasized that his reluctance should not be interpreted, in any way, as a lack of affection for Alemany whom he regarded as "one of the most holy, laborious, indefatigable, and self-sacrificing bishops in the Church."[10]

For his part, while unequivocally endorsing the petition, Alemany informed the prefect of Propaganda Fide that Prendergast would most assuredly decline the appointment unless the Holy Father personally intervened. The archbishop reminded Giovanni Cardinal Simeoni of Prendergast's refusal some years earlier, of the mitre of Grass Valley, a decision he seemed not to regret.[11]

In response to a personal request of Prendergast to Propaganda Fide *"ad honorem episcopalem declinandum,"*[12] the prefect dispatched a letter to the candidate expressing the favorable reaction of Rome to the communiqué of San Francisco's clergy which was looked upon as a positive sign of Prendergast's true worth. Simeoni exhorted the vicar general "to do nothing to frustrate the proposal of your name to the Holy Father," noting that such recommendations were not lightly made.[13] Prendergast was unmoved at the cardinal's extraordinarily kind letter and reiterated his already expressed reluctance. This view he also communicated to the archbishop who apparently made no further attempts to have him named to the bishopric.[14]

John Prendergast was no less esteemed among the laity than he was among his fellow clerics. One contemporary correspondent is on record as saying, "there is not a more retiring, a more modest priest on the entire Pacific Coast than Monsignor Prendergast, nor one who has done half as much for the spread of religion and the diffusion of knowledge."[15] While there is no evidence to substantiate the veracity of its allegation, an interesting letter unearthed by this writer some years ago further attests to the respect Prendergast enjoyed among the lay people. It dealt with the vicar general's nomination to a proposed new diocese:

I hear that the name of the Very Revd. John Prendergast Vicar General has been sent to Rome for Bishop of Oakland. As a layman I do not presume to interfere in clerical matters, but as one who has the welfare of the Church in California at heart, I entreat of you to have this most worthy man appointed for Oakland. He has labored here faithfully and arduosly [sic] for the past twenty-five years, and by his zeal, piety, learning, and eloquence will be an acquisition and an ornament to the episcopacy.[16]

The reluctance of Prendergast to accept the episcopacy must be understood in its proper context. As he remarked to a friend in 1881, "Candidly, I am not obstinately wedded to my own opinion and judgment in this matter of episcopal promotion. Neither am I averse [sic] on principle and *a priori* to assuming the responsibilities of a ruler in the Church. My reasons are practical, prudential, local, and approve themselves, as I have intimated, to better minds than my own."[17] There is every reason to believe that had the appointment been imposed as a matter of obedience, San Francisco's vicar general would have accepted. He merely believed that, "We should always be perfectly frank with our superiors. If they ordain anything, we must submit humbly and respectfully; but if they ask our opinion we must be frank."[18] It was in this spirit that Prendergast accepted the unsolicited and totally honorary papal distinction of the domestic prelacy, bestowed at the request of Archbishop Patrick W. Riordan on the occasion of the vicar general's golden jubilee in the priesthood.

The personal philosophy of this great churchman, characterized by his archbishop as "a true Catholic priest...faithful in his work, zealous for the Church, solicitous for his flock,"[19] was voiced by Prendergast himself as he glanced backward over a half century of dedicated apostolic work in California: "After all my experience and much thought, I have come to the unalterable conclusion that, no matter where God has placed us—in the church, in the hermit's solitude, in community life or in the bosom of the family—the only way to true peace is to see Christ in everything."[20]

Notes to the Text

1. Hugh Quigley, *The Irish Race in California, and on the Pacific Coast* (San Francisco, 1878), 423.
2. Archives of the Archdiocese of Baltimore, Joseph Sadoc Alemany, O.P., to Martin J. Spalding; San Francisco, September 4, 1864.
3. Archives of the Sacred Congregation of Propaganda Fide, Joseph Sadoc Alemany, O.P., to Alessandro Cardinal Barnabo; San Francisco, December 26, 1864.
4. For the interesting background of this appointment, see Archives of the Archdiocese of Los Angeles, Thaddeus Amat, C.M., to Alessandro Franchi; Los Angeles, November 26, 1868.
5. *Ibid.*, John J. Prendergast to Alessandro Cardinal Franchi; San Francisco, October 9, 1875.
6. Dennis J. Kavanagh. *The Holy Family Sisters* (San Francisco, 1922), p. 229.
7. James P. Gaffey, *The Life of the Most Reverend Patrick William Riordan, Second Archbishop of San Francisco, 1841-1914* (Washington, 1965), p. 106; unpublished dissertation.
8. Archives of the Archdiocese of Los Angeles, Joseph Sadoc Alemany, O.P., to Napoleon J. Perche; San Francisco, August 8, 1875.
9. Quoted in John B. McGloin, *California's First Archbishop* (New York, 1966), pp. 302-03.
10. Archives of the Archdiocese of Los Angeles, John J. Prendergast to William Fortune; San Francisco, November 21, 1881.
11. Archives of the Sacred Congregation of Propaganda Fide, Joseph Sadoc Alemany, O.P., to Giovanni Cardinal Simeoni; San Francisco, August 22, 1881.
12. *Ibid.* John J. Prendergast to Giovanni Cardinal Simeoni; San Francisco, July 7, 1881.
13. Giovanni Cardinal Simeoni, quoted in McGloin, *op. cit.*, p. 304.
14. Prendergast's name did appear again on a terna dated March 7, 1882, but this time only as an alternate.
15. *All Hallows Annual* (Dublin, 1911-1912), 95.
16. Archives of the Archdiocese of Los Angeles, D.J. Olivero to Giovanni Cardinal Simeoni; San Francisco, June 9, 1884.
17. Archives of the Archdiocese of Los Angeles, John Prendergast to William Fortune; San Francisco, November 21, 1881.
18. Quoted in Kavanagh, *op. cit.*, p. 220.
19. The *Monitor* (San Francisco), July 3, 1909.
20. Quoted in Kavanagh, *op. cit.*, p. 218.

54

This essay about the beloved "Joaquin Adam y Tous" was published in the *Southern California Quarterly* LXVII (Summer, 1985), 135-152.

No other city or region in the world provided more priests for the west coast of America during and after the Mission Era than the Principality of Catalonia,[1] described by Cervantes as a fountain of courtesy, a refuge for foreigners, an asylum for the poor, a home for the courageous and a revenge for the offended.

One of California's most intriguing and gifted clergymen, Joaquin Adam y Tous,[2] was born in that cradle of catholicity on October 12, 1837,[3] the Feast of Our Lady of Pilar. His father was a machinist and the principal foreman for his grandfather who owned and operated an important factory in Barcelona.[4] Little could Adam's parents have imagined that their son's imprint on the spiritual and cultural development of faraway California would have few parallels in the New World's ecclesial annals.

Early in childhood, Adam made the acquaintance of Francisco Mora y Borrell (1827-1905), a friendship that would endure a lifetime. Adam's decision to study for the ministry was suggested and encouraged by Mora who would eventually become Bishop of Monterey-Los Angeles and a trusted confidant.

Having heard from returning missionaries that there were thousands of "untutored children of the forest"[5] still waiting evangelization in California, Adam responded favorably to Bishop Thaddeus Amat's invitation to become a clerical aspirant for the Vincentian prelate's newly-established diocese in western America.

Recognizing the exceptional talents of his fellow countryman, Amat made arrangements for Adam to enroll at Rome's Urban College of Propaganda Fide in 1855. Adam's studies in the Eternal City stretched over the next seven years and culminated with his ordination to the priesthood on June 14, 1862, by Constantine Cardinal Patrizi, in the Basilica of Saint John Lateran.[6] His studies were completed the following January.

Following a brief visit to his homeland, prolonged by order of his physician, Adam and Father Peter Sastre[7] set out for the long trek to the Pacific Slope on September 1st, 1864.[8] Upon their arrival at Los Angeles, just prior to Christmas, they were enthusiastically greeted by the local Catholic populace. After several months of intensive orientation, during which Father Adam developed an easy facility with English, he was appointed, on August 11, 1865, as assistant to Father Daniel Dade, Nativity Church in Visalia, a parish then encompassing the whole of Tulare county.[9]

A local newspaper writer reminisced about Adam's surprise when he arrived in Visalia, from the grand, glorious and gorgeous Saint Peter's to the stable chapel in Visalia; from his beautiful Castilian home to his rural quarters in California. "His willingness to endure all things for Christ overcame the natural repugnance which springs up in a delicate and sensitive soul. What would have discouraged and disheartened a stronger man was to him a grand opportunity for putting in practice the lessons he received in the long and arduous training which a priest has to go through."[10]

One of the few recorded events associated with Adam's short tenure in Visalia was that of assisting at the execution of José Stanner, a young man of eighteen who had killed and robbed two sheepmen, brothers named Williams, while they were herding their flocks on the west side of Tulare Lake.[11]

Adam later recalled that soon after his arrival in Visalia, he had written the legendary Father José María de Jesús Gonzales Rúbio at Mission Santa Barbara asking for information about the Indians in his area. Rúbio responded on September 22, 1864.[12] Later Adam made that answer public in order to provide an insight into the missions under the guidance of the Franciscan Fathers.[13]

In 1865 Adam was transferred to Pajaro Valley as an associate to Father Apollinarius Roussel, Pastor of Immaculate Heart of Mary Parish.[14] During those years, Adam would occasionally journey to Mission San Antonio where he became a close friend of Father Doroteo Ambris who was the only Mexican secular clergyman in the diocese.

Adam later wrote admiringly of Ambris and how the first parish priest in California wished "only to live and die amid the ruins of San Antonio."[15]

Bishop Amat asked Adam to pursue his ministry at Santa Barbara, in April 1868, at Our Lady of Sorrows Parish. Six months later, he was moved again, this time to Santa Cruz as pastor.[16] Father Adam found the Catholic people at Santa Cruz spread out in almost every direction. By that time, the curtain had fallen on the Spanish-Mexican scene and the relatively few Anglo parishioners were scattered widely around the countryside.

The natural setting was certainly attractive. Grace Greenwood visited Santa Cruz during Adam's time and later mentioned in a letter published in New York that "Santa Cruz is a beautiful city, seated on the knees of pleasant terraces, with her feet in the sea."[17] Masses and other liturgical functions were conducted in a wooden church erected after the earlier edifice had collapsed from weathering and lack of maintenance. Mary Hallock Foote's sketch of Father Adam praying his breviary in the Old Mission garden during November 1877 was among several that appeared in *Scribner's Magazine*.[18]

The years at Santa Cruz heightened Father Adam's interest in Fray Junípero Serra and the California missions. In addition to reading extensively, he used every opportunity to know and visit pioneers whose pedigree stretched back to 1769 and the European penetration into Alta California. He subsequently recalled his acquaintance with Ramón Rodríquez, who had served as a soldier during the time the mission system was in its vigor.

> He told me that the so-called *conquesta* consisted in sending during the summer a few soldiers and some christianized Indians to the Tulares to try to induce those roaming Indians to come to the mission and see what a happy life their companions were enjoying there. Some would follow them, others would refuse, but none were forced to go. It is true that after an Indian had once been received into the mission fold, he was not free to go back to his former life. The same rule is observed in the present reservation method of the United States; and cannot be different; otherwise, one or two ringleaders would cause mutiny and a general uprising.[19]

On another occasion, he remembered that:

> while at Santa Cruz I collected from the attic of his house some papers of the old missions, and from them could see that each missionary was obliged every year to send a report to his superior

in Mexico of the temporal and spiritual state of his missions. Boxes were filled with these reports in the convent of San Fernando, Mexico. When I visited the capital ten years ago and asked the one venerable Franciscan left to take care of the church to show me some of those papers, with a sigh he said they exist no more. 'The government confiscated our convent and opened a street through our property, seized all papers and, thinking them not worth keeping, burned them.' Many things we might know of the dealings of the Fathers in missionary times if our modern vandals had spared these documents. As it is, they should be gathered up from the different missions for safe keeping; otherwise in a few years nothing will be known of them, as to my own knowledge in our time they have been used to light the fire in some places.[20]

Early in 1875, Adam began writing "a series of short letters or notes, in which all the information" he had obtained from various sources could be preserved. He admitted that "the writing of these notes will in some measure assuage the pain I feel at seeing before me the remains of numerous tribes, now impoverished and many of them degraded, for whom we can do nothing but pray."[21]

At the suggestion of several friends, Adam's observations were sent off to the editor of *Ave Maria* who agreed to publish them serially as "A Sketch of the Catholic Church in Upper California."[22] The response was so favorable that the articles were corrected and edited for reissuance three years later in the *Annals of Our Lady of the Angels*. Plans for further expanding the treatment into monograph form were apparently never realized and in the November 26, 1898 issue of *The Tidings* it was announced that "the publication of the proposed history of Montery-Los Angeles has, for good and sufficient reasons, been indefinitely postponed."[23]

It was during his latter years at Santa Cruz, that Father Adam began the herculean task of translating Fray Francisco Palou's *Relación Histórica de la Vida y Apostólicas Tareas del Venerable Padre Fray Junípero Serra* into English. According to an early advertisement, the book was occasioned by the finding of Serra's remains on July 3, 1882.[24] Its central purpose was "to perpetuate the memory of a poor Franciscan, who left home, relatives and friends, to spend his life in laboring for the conversion of the aborigines of Alta California." Adam submitted his manuscript to the San Francisco publishing house of P. E. Dougherty where it was received with considerable enthusiasm. This first English edition of the *Relación Histórica*, released as the *Life of Ven. Padre Junípero Serra Written by Very*

Rev. Francis Palou, was an immediate success and very shortly it went out of print. One outstanding bibliographer noted that this 156-page edition eventually became "even scarcer than the original."[25] In his preface to the book, Bishop Francis Mora noted that 1884 was the centennial year of Serra's falling asleep in the Lord, an ideal time to recall "the glories of the founder of the Missions in Upper California."

Father Adam took a keen interest in whatever pertained to the spiritualities of his parish. On May 7, 1873, he wrote that "the image of Our Lady has been venerated in this place for more than fifty years, first in the Old Mission Church, now in ruins, and since July 4, 1858, in the new frame church, on the main altar. In 1870 I built a nice side-chapel in one of the towers of the Church, and the image was taken in solemn procession from the main altar to the new chapel, March 25, 1870, where it has been venerated since, with great devotion, by people of every condition in life."[26] Not only a well-read and cultured man, Adam also knew something about artistic expression. Once, after being asked to give his judgement concerning Henry Chapman Ford's etchings, he said that they were "not only exquisite as a work of art, but also a faithful representation" of Provincial California.[27]

The pastor of Santa Cruz was popular on the lecture circuit too. On January 15, 1876, for example, he spoke at a benefit for the local public library on "California in the Eighteenth Century."[28] In that address he traced the Portolá Expedition of 1769 to San Diego and then on to Monterey. It was one of the many addresses subsequently published by the Historical Society of Southern California.

Father Adam served the Santa Cruz parish uninterruptedly for almost fifteen years, except for part of 1877 when he returned to Spain on business. On November 23, 1877, he was named Vicar Forane for the northern area of the diocese, a position in which he served as episcopal overseer for the parishes not easily accessible to Bishop Francis Mora.

The scarcity of Catholics in and about Santa Cruz, coupled with a fairly widespread indifference to the accomplishments of an earlier era, accounts for Father Adam's inability to restore the buildings of the Old Mission. Not long after his departure, an article in the San Francisco *Chronicle* noted that:

> The Old Mission Church of Santa Cruz is in an entire state of ruin and stands in the yard of the present church. The mission buildings have long since disappeared. The side walls of the church are still standing, the front walls having fallen in 1857.

The part of the roof that still remains is shingled. An old adobe stairway is still extant, which must have led up to a gallery within the church. The traces of a wine-cellar can yet be seen, and in the garden hidden under a thicket of roses can be found one of the old church bells.[29]

When Bishop Thaddeus Amat decided to build a cathedral in Los Angeles, he borrowed the design from San Miguel del Mar in the *puerto* district of Barcelona, a church which was well known to Father Adam. When the new Cathedral of Saint Vibiana was consecrated in 1876, it was Adam who was chosen by the bishop to conclude the services with a memorable address in English.[30]

On February 28, 1883, Bishop Mora named Father Adam to the rectorship of Saint Vibiana's Cathedral. Among the new rector's first priorities was Catholic education. A building fund was begun in the fall of 1885 and work inaugurated on a three-story schoolhouse, which was ready for occupancy by Christmas. Facing the alley that was to become Los Angeles Street, the commodious building provided five classrooms, a parlor, a chapel and several dormitories. The old frame stables formerly used by the bishop were converted into kitchen and dining quarters. The Sisters of the Immaculate Heart of Mary assumed charge of the school and classes commenced with 250 pupils on January 4, 1886. Two days later the handsome, red brick building was dedicated by Bishop Mora as the first parochial school in the city of Los Angeles.[31]

In 1885 Adam enlarged the rectory to provide additional room for the curia of the far-flung diocese. In 1888-1889, when Second Street was extended east from Main, Father Adam erected a three-story parsonage facing the new thoroughfare. Bishops Mora, George T. Montgomery and Thomas J. Conaty lived in that edifice which served the three-fold function of parochial rectory, episcopal residence and chancery office. For many years, the Cathedral rectory also housed the diocesan library. In the early 1880s, Bishop Mora had moved the *Biblioteca Montereyensis-Angelorum Dioceseos*[32] into several rooms of the earlier house and when the new quarters were completed, the valuable book collection was stored on specially designed shelves off a tunnelway connecting the rectory with the church tower.

The first major internal change of the Cathedral itself was made under Father Adam's direction in 1893, when the permanent high altar of Parian Carrara marble and Mexican onyx was installed. It was consecrated on February 24, 1894.[33]

Lighting and other electrical facilities replaced the earlier gas lamps in 1898. A circle of fifteen frosted globes was added around the arch of the sanctuary to illuminate the sky-blue field of silver stars with a soft white light. Father Adam had a stained-glass window, with an etched figure of a dove, placed atop the dome to represent the Holy Spirit. According to one source, "the radiant rays coming from this dove upon the relics in the shrine and down upon the altar, are of rare beauty and infuse into the soul a happy thought of the world beyond the stars."[34] The seating capacity was considerably enlarged by replacing the antiquated benches with freshly-hewn, wooden pews. In place of the original fixed pulpit, a portable lectern was rolled into the sanctuary in the late summer of 1898.

At the same time he was appointed rector of the Cathedral, Adam was also entrusted with the title of vicar general, a canonical position in which he served as the bishop's *alter ego*. In that capacity, the Catalan priest moved around the diocese assisting in the many outreach programs inaugurated for the Catholics of southern California. That he was successful in that role is evident in many quarters. It was recorded in the annals of the Mercy Sisters, to cite one example, that Adam was "an invaluable friend, and a saintly director."[35] Tributes of that kind were repeated in many hearts and souls.

An entertaining and erudite speaker, Father Adam was a favorite lecturer on religious and historical topics throughout the state. Though now mostly obsolete because of subsequent discoveries, Adam's research was amazingly extensive given his lack of professional training and the communication difficulties of his time.[36] Many of his addresses were published by the Historical Society of Southern California and *The Tidings*, official newspaper for the Diocese of Monterey-Los Angeles.

In 1890 Father Adam acquiesced to a request that he prepare a condensation of a larger work in which he outlined the "History of the Catholic Church in Los Angeles County."[37] The original manuscript, if it is ever located, will be a treasure of first-hand information from one who knew personally most of California's transitional clergymen and pioneers.

In an address which he labelled "A Defense of the Missionary Establishments of Alta California," Father Adam "indicates how ignorant have been the obscure 'historians' against whom was necessary any defense of a noble and wonderfully able missionary program."

While acknowledging that "there is no institution on earth, no matter how beneficent in its purpose, or how divine its principles, that can escape the criticisms and prejudices of the multitude,"[38] the Vicar General decried the continuance of such behavior in the society of his time.

One of Adam's more outstanding contributions was a two-part treatise on the development of devotion to Our Lady of Guadalupe which appeared in the April 1889 issues of *Ave Maria*. His study was based on findings which he discovered while on a tour to Tepeyac.

In April 1893, Father Adam delivered a lecture at a public gathering of the Historical Society of Southern California on the "Destruction of the Catholic Missions on the Rio Colorado in 1781."[39] Data for that informative essay was gathered from descendants of the natives involved who were attached to the school operated by the Sisters of Saint Joseph of Carondelet at Fort Yuma. Adam journeyed to Yuma and spent some days roaming the hills in search of the ruins of San Pedro y San Pablo. He noted that "after one hundred years, you can yet notice signs of the building, having been burned down to the ground."

Adam's "Notes on the Mission San Gabriel" was an address based on excerpts he had made over the years from the register books at San Gabriel, tomes which confirmed a continuity stretching back to the 1770s.[40] One of the few early accounts of the old *Biblioteca Montereyensis-Angelorum Dioceseos* is that which Father Adam gave before several southern California audiences. The revealing lecture about the books assembled in mission times was published by the Historical Society of Southern California as "Rare Old Books in the Bishop's Library."[41]

Another of Adam's more prominent lectures dealt with "The Pious Fund" and efforts by Bishop Thaddeus Amat, his predecessors and successors, to settle this complicated legal case which eventually was decided by the International Court of Arbitration at the Hague.[42]

On numerous occasions the Historical Society of Southern California met at the Cathedral rectory, 118 East Second Street. In an account of one of these gatherings, it was noted that "the number of old portraits of the Catholic Fathers that outlined the walls of the large audience room added a unique as well as historical setting for the meeting." Father Adam amusingly pointed out that Mrs. M. Burton Williamson, president of the Society was "the first woman to occupy the Bishop's Chair at Saint Vibiana during a meeting."[43]

At the 1889 centenary celebration of the nation's oldest ecclesial jurisdiction at Baltimore, Archbishop Francis Janssens of New Orleans and his suffragans held a meeting concerning the long vacant vicariate Apostolic of Brownsville, Texas. Janssens requested Bishop Mora of Monterey-Los Angeles to submit a list of candidates for the Texas jurisdiction.[44] Mora complied, drafting a *terna* of names with that of Father Joaquín Adam in the first place. After the usual scrutiny process, Adam was asked by

Roman officials, if he would accept the position. On January 5, 1887, he declined for reasons of poor health.[45] The appointment ultimately went to the second candidate on the terna, Father Peter Verdaguer, pastor of the Plaza Church of Nuestra Señora de Los Angeles.

As early as 1882, shortly after sustaining a serious carriage accident injury during a pastoral visitation, Bishop Francis Mora began thinking about the feasibility of asking the Holy See for episcopal assistance. Six years later, Archbishop Patrick W. Riordan of San Francisco informed the Sacred Congregation of Propaganda Fide that division of the diocese or at least the appointment of a coadjutor for the ailing Mora would alleviate the more pressing problems then facing the Diocese of Monterey-Los Angeles. A few months later, the Holy See advised Mora that "your diocese is too large and the number of inhabitants increases daily, so that it is extremely difficult to see how one person, however industrious, can effectively provide for the demands and necessities of the Church."[46]

The Bishop of Monterey-Los Angeles welcomed the proposal for a coadjutor and immediately suggested for the position his Vicar General, Father Joaquín Adam. Giovanni Cardinal Simeoni, the Prefect of Propaganda Fide, then wrote to Archbishop Riordan for the metropolitan's appraisal of the candidate asking why Adam had been proposed, given his earlier self-proclaimed health problems. In his response, Riordan acknowledged that the priests of the southern jurisdiction, if consulted, "would overwhelmingly prefer Adam," but he felt that, in many ways, the Vicar General was "wholly unfit to be made a Bishop." He enumerated the advantages of appointing a man "rather young in age but endowed with talent, energy and strength of character so as to be able to infuse vitality into that diocese which is presently weak and infirm." In the archbishop's opinion, a "strong, active, energetic Bishop, who has good use of the English language" was needed in the southland.[47]

The cardinal then directed Mora to submit the formal terna of candidates. Such a list was drafted by the diocesan consultors and listed in order: Fathers Joaquín Adam, Polydore Stockman and Laurence Serda. These names were forwarded to San Francisco where the four bishops of the province, in September of 1889, put aside the last two names and substituted Fathers Edward Dunne[48] and George T. Montgomery. Riordan agreed to leave Adam's name at the head of the list, apparently as a concession to induce Bishop Mora to allow his jurisdiction to be split into smaller sections.

Upon receipt of the terna in Rome, the cardinal prefect decided to appoint a commission to examine the entire question. After a diligent investigation, Father Aloysius Meyer, C.M., recommended immediate appointment of a coadjutor. On the other hand, Father Kilian Schloesser, O.F.M., advised against both a coadjutor and a division of the diocese. After weighing the evidence, the Roman officials of the Sacred Congregation of Propaganda Fide sided with Schloesser and ruled on February 23, 1891, to abide by the geographical *status quo* in the Diocese of Monterey-Los Angeles.[49]

Riordan's hesitation about Adam's candidacy eventually prevailed and, in 1894, Father George T. Montgomery was named coadjutor to the ailing Bishop Mora.

Through Riordan effectively blocked the vicar general's being named coadjutor, Adam himself was clearly responsible for the initial refusal. And, likely, had he been asked, Adam would also have declined the subsequent appointment. A casual observation made some years later is probably as correct as any, that Adam's "continued ill health…alone, in all probability, prevented his elevation to the Episcopacy."[50]

Adam's deteriorating physical condition compelled him to resign in the midsummer of 1899. At the city-wide "Farewell Banquet" held in honor of the vicar general at Saint Vincent's College on August 1st, Bishop George Montgomery likened Adam to the Cedars of Lebanon.[51]

Joaquín Adam had decided to live out his remaining years with his family in Spain, near Bishop Francis Mora in the Barcelona suburb of Sarria. Though a prodigious writer, only a handful of his letters have survived. From the few that were printed from time to time in *The Tidings*, one can piece together some details of his retirement.

On August 11, 1899, Adam wrote from New York noting that he would depart the next day "for sunny Spain, to meet old friends—but I will not forget my friends in California who love me yet." While in New York, Adam paid a courtesy call on Archbishop Michael Corrigan. Upon his departure he asked the prelate's blessing after which Corrigan embraced him "as when school boys used to embrace one another in college on parting for the Missions." Recalling that the archbishop wished to visit him in Barcelona, Adam said that "if everyone that has promised to see me in my city keeps his word, I will have to open a hotel, and it will pay me if they lodge with me, but I fear that one-half will fail to accomplish their good wishes. Let them come, one and all; my city is large enough for a whole army."[52]

In a subsequent letter Adam related the details of his seven-day voyage across the Atlantic. At Gibraltar he noted with satisfaction the many cannons and sentries peeping through the rocks and deemed the best plan for him was to keep quiet and not attempt to rescue Gibraltar from the English and give it back to his native country. After another sea voyage from Algeciras to Barcelona, during which he suffered a painful seige of swollen ankles, Adam finally spied Montjerich, the famed landmark of his native city.[53]

Following a quick visit to his family home, Father Adam went to see Bishop Francis Mora, only to find the retired ordinary out of town on a confirmation tour for the vacant bishopric of Barcelona. Several days later Adam and a sister journeyed to Viladran, famous for its pure mountain air and refreshing mineral water.

A month later, on September 30, 1899, Adam wrote John Bodkin from Pobla de Claramunt, noting that it was "thirty years ago today I landed at New York, and set my foot for the first time on American soil." In a reminiscent mood, he said that "when I look back on those years of my missionary life I perceive many ups and downs, many recollections that cheer me up, but at the same time many shadowy and blackspots, good deeds that might and should have been done, but were neglected." He concluded by thanking God "that my retired life gives me time to bewail my shortcomings."

Remarking that Bishop Mora had journeyed to Pobla de Claramunt with him, Adam told Bodkin that "you may imagine our conversation turns often on the same subject, our pioneer days in the Far West. The barber shaving me this morning wanted to know if Venezuela was in California; but this is not so bad as that girl near San Luis Obispo that asked me if Mexico was close to Spain."[54]

Six months later Adam wrote again, this time from Alicante, where he had gone to observe the total eclipse of the sun. After describing the event, Adam said he anticipated seeing a number of Angelinos this year. "Thank God my health is good and I grow stronger day by day. I hope to live to see the total eclipse of 1905, but I am not anxious to remain for the next after that, which will not come along until about the end of the century."[55]

Adam kept up a busy correspondence during his years of retirement. Once, after receiving a copy of the Historical Society of Southern California's *Annual Publication* with an article about Santa Catalina, he wrote that "some of the happiest days of my life have been spent on that Island."[56]

Adam enjoyed his retirement and utilized his time visiting many areas of Spain and the adjoining countries. He journeyed to the sulphur baths of Bagneres de Luchon, the shrine of Our Lady at Lourdes, and the mountain villages of the Pyrennes.[57]

In May 1905, he made a pilgrimage to the Holy Land, his second visit. He told about his travels in a journal sent to Los Angeles, portions of which were printed in *The Tidings* for July 28, 1905. The venerable priest fell and hurt his leg rather severely in a chapel which was once the workshop for Saint Joseph. Though lame for a few days, he recovered enough to continue with the group with whom he was traveling. Two years later, Mrs. Josephine R. Lecouvreur and several friends visited Father Adam in Barcelona. She found him "in bed, and suffering acute pain." Yet she remarked that in spite of his illness, he received them most cordially. She noted that "Father had a store of letters awaiting us; and we spent the afternoon communing with the dear friends away off in the land of God's blessed sunshine and happiness."

Mrs. Lecouvreur and her companions were entertained several times in Barcelona by Adam's family. She recalled that "his health was rather delicate-as happens every winter. He certainly misses the warm sun and genial clime of California; but particularly longs for the company of his friends, of the olden times, and for the old home where his youth and manhood were spent, and where the best that was in him was devoted to the salvation of souls." She concluded with the observation that the Catalan "missionaries of early days have left a bright and shining example which the young should delight in copying, and which parents should inculcate in their children."[58]

Another of the prominent visitors who found his way to Sarría was Bishop Thomas J. Conaty who stopped to see Adam enroute to Rome for his *ad limina* visit early in 1906. The Bishop of Monterey-Los Angeles spent a week with him in his own home. Conaty later said that during that time he "realized the great sympathy, the great spirit of loving obedience which prompted him, under considerable strain to travel over four hundred miles to bid me greeting and to assure me of the affection he felt toward the Bishop of the Diocese."[59]

When Conaty arrived in Rome, he petitioned Pope Pius X to bestow upon Father Adam the honor of Papal Chamberlain with the title of monsignor. In those days such a distinction was rare indeed and, in fact, only once before had it been conferred on a California priest. Bishop Conaty recalled that "one of the pleasantest memories of my life is in the thought that I was able to obtain from our Holy Father the dignity of the Monsignorate which made him feel how much we loved and respected him."[60]

Shortly after receiving word that he had been named a monsignor, Adam decided to make a final trip to California to personally thank

Bishop Conaty for requesting that distinction from the Holy Father. Adam journeyed first to Lourdes and then on to London, where he visited friends in the Vincentian Seminary at Strawberry Hill. Then he set out for Liverpool to catch a steamer on which his old friend Father Patrick Hawe was also booked.[61] Enroute he fell ill and was taken to Mercy Hospital, London, where he was treated for cardiac insufficiency. He lingered for several days, during which time he received a cablegram from Raphael Cardinal Merry del Val with the Holy Father's personal blessing. The venerable priest succumbed on July 30, 1907. Several days later, Adam's remains were removed to Sarría for interment near those of Bishop Francis Mora.[62]

On Monday, August 12, 1907, Bishop Thomas J. Conaty offered a Solemn Pontifical Requiem Mass in Saint Vibiana's Cathedral for the one-time rector. In his masterful homily the bishop noted that throughout Adam's life of "active service among the poor, among the sick, he preached the Gospel of Christ, urged sinners to repentance, gave the cheering word of encouragement, brought the light of faith to many who had never possessed it, brought out of sin into the grace of God many who had forgotten their duty." Conaty remarked that Adam's "disinterestedness, his devotedness, and his self sacrifice have been to his brother priests a subject of praise and an object of imitation." The prelate concluded by saying:

> ... the tenderest, sweetest memory to us is that desire of his to return to this Diocese before he died, to visit his brother priests, to come back and witness, as he said in more than one of his letters to me, 'the growth and development of the Catholic religion in this Diocese,' to come and be again with the people he loved and who loved him, and perhaps to pass his remaining years here where so much of his life had been spent in faithful service and it was a strange thing that when he was between the old home and the new home, journeying toward this home that possessed so much affection for him and from him, he should be called to his reward. His heart was with the priests of this Diocese and its people and his affection for its work never changed. The same spirit that bade him leave his father's house, the same spirit that bade him seek for a mission in California, was the spirit that was with him when he left that same home to travel back to the places made sacred by his ministrations.[63]

There were numerous eulogistic sentiments expressed by those who had known and admired Msgr. Adam during his many years of active ministry on the southern California scene. Henry D. Barrows spoke for the Historical Society of Southern California and others when he wrote to the Los Angeles *Evening Express*, August 3, that:

> ...the news of the sudden death of good Father Joaquin Adam in London this week, brought a pang to many a heart in Los Angeles. The reverent–truly revered–cleric, had long been a resident of our city, and his good deeds and gentle courtly ways had endeared him to many of our people outside of his own communion. He was a prominent and active member of the Historical Society during the latter years of his residence here, and members contemplated giving him a warm and hearty welcome on the occasion of his contemplated visit, which, unfortunately, was prevented by his sudden sickness and death after he had started for Los Angeles.

Barrows concluded by saying that the "Friends of Father Adam are never to see him again in the flesh, but they will, so long as they live, retain a warm place for him in their memories."[64]

Though Joaquín Adam certainly deserves better than this cursory memorial, even a hurried glimpse into his life affirms a statement made eighty-seven years ago that "few priests in California ever so endeared themselves to their flocks."[65]

Notes to the Text

1. See Francis J. Weber, ed., *Sacerdotal Necrology for the Archdiocese of Los Angeles 1840-1965* (Los Angeles, 1966).
2. Adam's given name has always presented a problem to chroniclers. Throughout his life it appears alternately as "Joachim" and "Joaquin" or simply as "J. Adam." In the Chancery Record, 1855-1923, Bishop Thaddeus Amat used "Joachim." And Adam is listed in the first book of Baptisms in Watsonville as "Joachim." In a letter to *The Tidings*, August 31, 1899, the priest signed his hame "Joachim." Near the end of his life, however, Adam seems to prefer "Joaquin" and that name appears on his printed stationery.
3. *Chancery Record* 1855-1923, I, 86, Archives of the Archdiocese of Los Angeles (hereafter referred to as AALA).
4. *The Monitor* (San Francisco), August 5, 1899.
5. J. Adam, "A Sketch of the Catholic Church in Upper California," *Ave Maria*, X (September 25, 1875), 622.
6. This would appear to be the more likely date. Several others are given.
7. Father Sastre (1832-1901) was also journeying to California for the first time.
8. *The Tidings* (Los Angeles), July 29, 1899.
9. Father Dade was one of the pioneer priests of the San Joaquin Valley.

10. Visalia *Daily Times*, May 12, 1905.
11. Sister Mary Thomas, O.P., *Apostle of the Valley* (Fresno, 1947), p. 62.
12. *The Tidings*, July 29, 1899.
13. See Francis J. Weber, Comp. and ed., *Documents of California Catholic History* (Los Angeles, 1965), pp. 33-36.
14. See the Los Angeles *Times*, January 28, 1891.
15. Francis J. Weber, *California's Catholic Heritage* (Los Angeles, 1974), p. 49.
16. *The Tidings*, August 2, 1907.
17. Quoted in Francis J. Weber, comp. and ed., *Holy Cross Mission. A Documentary History of Santa Cruz* (Los Angeles, 1984), p. 59.
18. Issue for August 1878.
19. J. Adam, "A Defense of the Missionary Establishments of Alta California" *Annual Publication Historical Society of Southern California* (hereinafter *APHSSC*, IV (1898), 156.
20. J. Adam, "Rare Old Books in the Bishop's Library," *APHSSC*, IV (1898), 156.
21. J. Adam, "A Sketch of the Catholic Church in Upper California," *Ave Maria*, X (September 25, 1875), 623.
22. The series appeared between September and December 1875.
23. See issue for September 17, 1898.
24. *Academy Scrapbook*, II (July 1951), 61.
25. Henry Raup Wagner, *The Spanish Southwest* 1542-1794 (2 vols., Albuquerque, 1951), II: 480.
26. Quoted in Francis J. Weber, *Catholic Footprints in California* (Newhall, Calif., 1970), p. 215.
27. Quoted in Francis J. Weber, *California Catholicity* (Los Angeles, 1979), p. 82.
28. *APHSSC*, I (1886), 14-22.
29. August 28, 1884.
30. Francis J. Weber, *California's Reluctant Prelate* (Los Angeles, 1964), p. 169.
31. Francis J. Weber, *Saint Vibiana's Cathedral, A Centennial History* (Los Angeles, 1976), p. 55.
32. See Francis J. Weber, *A Bibliophilic Odyssey* (Los Angeles, 1969) pp. 13-15.
33. *The Tidings*, May 28, 1926.
34. *Ibid.*, September 3, 1898.
35. Sr. Mary Athanasius Sheridan, *...And Some Fell on Good Ground* (New York, 1982), p. 185.
36. In an anonymously edited collection of memoirs, the late Msgr. John McCarthy is on record as saying that "Father Adam spoke terrible English." If quoted correctly, one must question the validity of McCarthy's observation, especially in view of Adam's widespread popularity as a preacher and public speaker. See, *Academy Scrapbook*, I (1950-1951), 165.
37. *APHSSC*, I (1890), 22-26.
38. *Ibid.*, III (1896), 35.
39. *Ibid.*, III (1893), 36-40.
40. *Ibid.*, IV (1898), 131-133.
41. *Ibid.*, IV (1898), 154-156.
42. *Ibid.*, IV (1899), 228-233.
43. *Ibid.*, XI (1919), 86.
44. Weber, *Catholic Footprints in California*, p. 36.
45. Giovanni Simeoni to Francis Mora, Rome, February 18, 1889, AALA.
46. Francis J. Weber, *Francis Mora, Last of the Catalans* (Los Angeles, 1967) p. 34.
47. Patrick W. Riordan to Giovanni Simeoni, San Francisco, June 1, 1889, AALA.
48. Interestingly enough, Dunne was a cousin of Archbishop Riordan, then serving as pastor of All Saints church, Chicago.
49. For an excellent survey of Riordan's intervention, see James F. Gaffey, *Citizen of No Mean City. Archbishop Patrick Riordan of San Francisco* (Wilmington, 1976), pp. 128ff.
50. *The Monitor*, August 5, 1899.
51. The program for that event is a treasured item in the Historical Museum, Archival Center, Archdiocese of Los Angeles.
52. *The Monitor*, August 27, 1899.

53. *The Tidings*, September 23, 1899.
54. *Ibid.*, October 28, 1899.
55. *Ibid.*, June 23, 1900.
56. Quoted in the *APHSSC*, XI (1919), 87.
57. *The Tidings*, October 4, 1902.
58. *Ibid.*, July 15, 1907.
59. *Ibid.*, August 16, 1907.
60. *Ibid.*
61. Father Hawe had been assistant to Adam in Santa Cruz.
62. *The Tidings*, August 2, 1907.
63. *Ibid.*, August 16, 1907.
64. *APHSSC*, (1906), 47.
65. *The Tidings*, July 29, 1899.

55

This essay on "A Nobel Churchman" is taken from *The Priest* (December, 1967), 1006-1010.

Charles Adolph Ramm, a man "endowed by God with exceptional qualities of mind and will and heart," was born into a Lutheran family of eight children near Camptonville, California, on August 4, 1863.

Young Ramm entered the University of California upon graduation from the Berkeley Gymnasium in 1880. There he took courses in the College of Engineering, and on May 28, 1884, was given his degree along with a special award as "the most distinguished graduate of the year."

Soon after completing his studies, Ramm was received into the Catholic Church by his long-time friend, Father John Prendergast. He later authored a pamphlet on "Why I Became a Catholic," wherein he attributed the grace of his conversion to James Bouchard, S.J., the famed Indian priest, whose "eloquent sermons helped me along the path to the Church of Christ."

Ramm stayed on at Berkeley as Recorder of the University until 1888, when he applied for admission to Saint Mary's Seminary in Baltimore as a clerical student for the Archdiocese of San Francisco. He was ordained in the premier see by James Cardinal Gibbons on September 24, 1892.

At the suggestion of Archbishop Patrick W. Riordan, Father Ramm remained in Baltimore an additional two years as a graduate student at Johns Hopkins University. He returned to the Bay City in 1895 to become a curate at Saint Mary of the Assumption Cathedral. Ramm's association with the mother-church of San Francisco became legendary even in his own lifetime. He had watched as a non-Catholic when the church was erected on the sand dunes of Van Ness Avenue. There he was baptized and there he spent the greatest part of his priestly life.

The most remarkable part of this long association, related by Coadjutor Archbishop George T. Montgomery, centers around the time Father Ramm saved the cathedral from the devastating fire of 1906. According to the prelate, great portions of the city were already in ashes as the flames raged toward Saint Mary's. The fire department "made a final determined stand at our cathedral feeling as everyone else did that if the cathedral went, the western portion (of the city) was doomed." Just as success seemed imminent, the archbishop noted, "it was observed that the cross of the cathedral was burning. Since the firemen were worn out, a call came for volunteers." Ramm was among the spectators watching the flaming inferno swallow up the nearby Richelieu Hotel. A small boy ran up to the priest and tugged at his cassock, excitedly gesturing toward the tower of the cathedral.

"Look, Father, the church is burning," said the youngster.

By that time smoke was already fanning from the tower beneath the cross. While the flames leaped across the street, most of the surrounding district was lost in a maze of smoke. The golden cross was now reflecting the conflagration. Gradually it grew brighter and flames were discernible at the very pinnacle of the tower. The fire was too high to be combatted from the street.

Father Ramm quickly recruited another priest, Father Philip 0. Ryan, two young boys and a sailor and led the small group up the perpendicular ladders, a dangerous undertaking since the massive copper bell hung in a perilous position over their heads. Though the dead weight of the hose streaming with water was unbearably heavy, Father Ramm somehow reached the top of the tower and after considerable effort successfully extinguished the flames. Meanwhile additional hoses were trained on the church with the result that firemen, bystanders and priests united in a singular battle against the forces of nature.

It was a turning point in the struggle to save San Francisco, and Archbishop Montgomery was quite right when he noted that the quick action of the five brave men had saved not only the cathedral but "with it the rest of the city."

Father Ramm's knowledge of history, his literary ability and deep spirituality were virtues not easily concealed. Already by 1902 his famous "Address Before A Marriage Ceremony" had an established place in Catholic rituals throughout the English speaking world. Even today the old formula is preferred by many couples beginning their married life.

My Dear Friends: You are about to enter into a union which is most sacred and most serious…That future…its hopes and disappointments, its successes and its failures, its pleasures and its pains, its joys and its sorrows, are all hidden from your eyes.

And so you begin your married life by the voluntary and complete surrender of your individual lives in the interests of that deeper and wider life which you are to have in common. Henceforth, you will belong wholly to each other; you will be one in mind, one in heart and one in affection.

The rest is in God's hands. Nor will He be wanting to your needs; He will pledge you the lifelong support of His graces by the Holy Sacrament which you are now to receive.

Almost as widely known was Father Ramm's prayer for "An Old Man Seriously Ill."

O God, it is toward evening and the day of my life is far spent. Not so long ago, I did not even exist, but in your mysterious way You have given me length of days. All along the way You have let your blessings rain upon me. And as for me–a humble last word when my hour comes, I commend my spirit into your merciful hands.

Father Ramm accompanied Archbishop Riordan to the Hague in 1902 when the International Arbitral Court heard the plea of California's hierarchy for a settlement to the long-pending Pious Fund Case. Two years later, Ramm became the prelate's secretary, a position he occupied until 1914, when he returned to the cathedral as pastor.

The widely known and highly respected priest held a number of positions in the ensuing decades. He served as Regent for the University of California from 1912 until 1944 and for many years was a member of the State Department of Social Welfare.

Creation as a Domestic Prelate by Pope Benedict XV in 1919 did not diminish the occasions which called for Monsignor Ramm's public utterances. Among his more noteworthy were dedicatory addresses for both the Golden Gate Bridge and the San Francisco-Oakland span and the opening of the Golden Gate International Exposition in 1936. Monsignor Ramm's memorable life ended in 1951.

56

"William McDermott Hughes: A Latter-Day Missionary" is the title of this essay taken from the *Records of the American Catholic Historical Society* LXXXV (September-December, 1974) 198-204.

The late historian, William R. Harris. once observed that "the life of a missionary priest is never written, nor can it be. He has no Boswell. His biographer may recount the churches he erected, the schools he founded, the works of religion and charity he inaugurated and fostered, the sermons he preached, the children he catechized, the converts he received into the fold; and this is already a great deal, but it only touches upon the surface of that devoted life. There is no memoir of his private daily life of usefulness and of his sacred and confidential relations with his flock; all this is hidden with Christ in God, and is registered only by his recording angel."[1]

One of those "missionary" priests was born on January 9, 1880, the son of Owen and Catherine Ellen (McDermott) Hughes.[2] Quite early in life William McDermott Hughes "was marked by those traits of earnestness and thoughtfulness"[3] which he so admirably developed in later years.

He attended the public schools of Sacramento and the Christian Brothers College. Subsequently, William enrolled at Saint Mary's College, Oakland, where he received his Bachelor's degree in 1900. Then he went to Washington, D.C., for a three-year course in philosophy and science at Saint Thomas College, the Paulist school at The Catholic University of America. In 1903, he entered Saint Joseph's Seminary, Dunwoodie, as a clerical candidate for the Diocese of Monterey-Los Angeles.

After successfully completing his theological studies at Yonkers, William returned to Los Angeles, where he was advanced to priestly orders by Bishop Thomas J. Conaty, on August 15, 1905. Five days later, he journeyed to Sacramento for his first Solemn Mass which "was attended by a great concourse of worshipers." The newly anointed clergyman, the first native son of the capitol city ordained to the priesthood, obviously had "a wide circle of warm friends" who took "a deep interest in this great event in his religious life.."[4] The "youthful and eloquent"[5] priest was named curate at Saint Agnes Parish in Los Angeles, a position he occupied until the early months of 1907, when he was transferred to Pasadena. Though he served at the latter post for little more than a year, Father Hughes "endeared himself to the people of St. Andrew's parish" in such a way that his departure was greatly regretted."[6]

From his earliest years, William McDermott Hughes had exhibited a fondness and kinship for the Indians. As a young lad, he had "lived among them, passing many an hour riding across the fields of Sacramento in northern California...and fishing in the streams with them."[7] It came, then, as no surprise that early in 1908, Father Hughes asked Bishop Conaty if he could devote his ministry to looking after the remnants of the California mission Indians, whose once vast numbers had dwindled to less than 3,000 souls. With the prelate's endorsement, the youthful priest journeyed to Mexico for an intensive program of mastering the Spanish language and assimilating the Hispanic way of life.

Upon arriving back in Los Angeles, Father Hughes was assigned to San Jacinto, a small mountain town close to the southern end of the Sierra Nevada, as a missionary to the Soboba, Cahuilla and Coyote Indians. He was also entrusted with the spiritual care of the Catholics residing in Murietta, Temecula and Perris. The tireless cleric was eminently proficient in his apostolate to the Indians. In short order, "Father Hughes won the confidence and love of his Indian charges through speaking their own language and thus eliminating the use of an interpreter."[8]

Much of his success with the natives can be attributed to Father Hughes' respect and appreciation for Indian traditions and customs. He often "baptized" local practices, noting that in California natives had "an instinctive reverence for God" whom they saw "reflected in the mountains and woods." This, he said, made them "apt pupils in spiritual and religious things."[9]

Though he suffered many hardships in his lonely 5,000 square mile parish, Father Hughes reckoned it of little importance "compared to what hundreds of priests, in early California days, underwent."[10] The inconveniences of his far-flung apostolate gave Hughes "an encouraging feeling of kinship with those truly heroic men on whom first fell the trials and to whom is now accorded the glory of the greatness of the fine work of religion in the United States, the Indian missions of California."[11] The indefatigable missionary once recorded the vicissitudes of a tour through his parish, a portion of which is reproduced here:

> The first mission is five hours by horse over the shortest trail. At the summit, where the trail divides, the two demons, Darkness and Fog, overtook me, covering my eyes (as the Indians would say) from both the little traveled trail and the mountain peaks, which serve as landmarks.
>
> Fully realizing that I had hopelessly lost my way, I calmly cast about in the fast-falling darkness and fog, to find a spot on which to rest my weary body. The poor pony was supperless. So was I. He might be hobbled, but the grass was short, even here in the mesa, at the head of the trail, which furnishes Cahuilla all of the pasturage for its cattle.
>
> A likely place was found for a camp. A fire was soon kindled with *manzanita* wood torn by hand from the river bank. The sandy bed of the river-it was an *arroyo seco* was as dry as the desert. Here a hole, long and wide enough for a bed, and six inches deep, was made, and a fire built in it. When the wood was reduced to coals, it was covered with a layer of sand deep enough to retain the heat and yet not to burn. The device is a familiar one among the Indians. Reclining upon this improvised bed, I placed over me the saddle blankets, now thoroughly dried by the fire.
>
> With the saddle as a pillow, a good night's rest was enjoyed. In the morning it was not hard to get one's bearings and to reach Cahuilla in time to say Mass for the waiting Indians.[12]

Among the proudest of his visible achievements for the natives was the construction of a beautiful mission-style chapel on the Soboba Reservation. When Bishop Conaty dedicated the concrete edifice, on May 11, 1910, the diocesan newspaper reported that countless Indians, their faces alive with "the refining and elevating influence of the Christian religion," gathered about the prelate.[13]

The talents and skill of Father Hughes eventually "attracted the attention of (James) Cardinal Gibbons of Baltimore"[14] and the Board of Trustees for the Bureau of Catholic Indian Missions invited the

California priest to join the staff of that nationwide agency[15] in what was described by the local press as "a recognition of the splendid work done by Father Hughes among the Indians of Southern California."[16] The appointment was well received in all quarters. One journalist character-ized the clergyman as "a clear-eyed, clean-skinned and bright-brained young priest...who is the type that any church, Catholic, Methodist or what not, should be glad to have carrying its banner."[17]

During his first years with the Bureau, Father Hughes travelled widely throughout the nation speaking "on the platform and in the pulpit of every city and town where the Indian Missions have sympathizers."[18] In announcing his affiliation with the Bureau of Catholic Indian Missions, the official journal of that agency admitted that "few men have ever brought to any cause more ability and energy and self-sacrifice than Father Hughes brought to ours."[19]

His lectures were as informative as they were popular. With "a vivid style...and easy familiarity in manner, together with a fund of numerous experiences and ready information,"[20] Father Hughes further enhanced his presentations with numerous stereopticon views gathered during his own days as a missionary. It was true that no one was "better qualified than the lecturer by study, temperament and personal contact, to present in graphic story the conditions, customs and needs of the Indians."[21] Another observer lauded Hughes for telling the "romantic history of the Mission Indians, once possessors of the entire coast with none to dispute their sovereign rights, but now driven from their original haunts by civi-lization far back into the mountain recesses."[22]

On April 17, 1912, just two years after his arrival in Washington, Father Hughes was made assistant director for the Bureau. Under the able supervision of the Reverend William H. Ketchum, the California priest continued his apostolate for the Indians until October, 1915, when he was recalled to the Diocese of Monterey-Los Angeles as Pastor of Saint Paul's Parish, in Coalinga.

Shortly after the outbreak of World War I, Father Hughes volunteered for a chaplaincy in the United States Army. He was commissioned a First Lieutenant, on November 27, 1917, and assigned to the 335th Field Artillery, 87th Division. He ministered to American troops in France and Germany and was later associated with various functions of the Occupation Army. By the time of his retirement from active duty, on June 4, 1919, Father Hughes had become "one of the most popular chap-lains in the service."[23] He retained his status and rank and, some years later, was named a Lieutenant in the Chaplain Corps Reserve.

Following his departure from the Army, Father Hughes was named *interim* Pastor of Saint Patrick's Parish in Watsonville, where he quickly "made a splendid impression by his forceful and forthright" personality.[24] He remained in the Pajaro Valley until November, 1919, when he was recalled to Los Angeles and appointed founding pastor for the newly-created Parish of Saint Basil. During his sojourn in the northern part of the diocese, Father Hughes "endeared himself to all with whom he came in contact...He started to put the parish on a self-sustaining basis, and was succeeding admirably when called away."[25]

Local newspaper accounts attributed the transferral to the southland "as a reward for his services to church, and country." In terms more fanciful than realistic, the reports described his new parish as having "a beautiful new church" and being "located in the finest residential section of Wilshire Boulevard." The facts were considerably less pretentious and the pastor of "Wilshire Boulevard Heights" soon discovered that he had little more than a vague set of geographical boundaries within which to organize a new community of Catholic worshippers.[26]

Father Hughes took up his duties on December 4, 1919, and immediately began looking for a site on which to erect a church. He divided the parish into guilds and made each responsible for some particular aspect of the projected plans. Property was acquired on the southeastern corner of Seventh and Catalina Streets, about a block from the handsome and popular California Hotel. The building itself was completed in the allotted seventy-five working days. The Liturgy was offered, for the first time, on October 10, 1920. By the standards of the time, the wooden frame edifice was something of an architectural feat. All the modern innovations were incorporated, including an unusual ventilation system borrowed from the pastor's war experiences. When the formal dedication for the "artistically constructed and apportioned"[27] church was held, on November 21, Bishop John J. Cantwell publicly congratulated the pastor and his flock for the taste and industry with which they had erected a worthy dwelling place for the Lord.

During the remaining months of Father Hughes' pastorate, the pace of events at Saint Basil's never slackened. Inaugurated, for example, was the practice of special religious observances for Armistice Day, at which the governor, mayor and other civil dignitaries participated.

On December 1, 1921, Cardinal Dennis Dougherty of Philadelphia nominated Father Hughes to be National Director for the Bureau of Catholic Indian Missions. It was a prestigious appointment, described by a reporter as "one of the most important national positions in the Catholic Church."[28]

As Director of the Bureau, Hughes immediately began promoting more friendly relations and cooperation between the Catholic missionaries and governmental agencies. "His genuine interest in Indians, his understanding of their problems, his personal uprightness and singleness of purpose, his friendliness, his sense of justice and his good judgment won him the abiding confidence and respect of Congressmen and officials in the Indian Service."[29] Hughes' own years of hardship as a missionary not only gave him sympathy with those engaged in the Indian apostolate, but also "led him to emulate them in the simplicity of his own personal life."[30]

On September 13, 1924, at the instigation of Bishop Cantwell, Father Hughes was honored by Pope Pius XI, with the title of Domestic Prelate.[31] It was also in the mid 1920s, that Monsignor Hughes' name was mentioned prominently for several episcopal vacancies. In a letter to Archbishop Bonaventure Cerretti, the Papal Nuncio to France, Hughes acknowledged that he had been "considered for the diocese of Tucson, Arizona." The Director said that he "was not at all disappointed" when the official nod went to Father Daniel J. Gercke. He admitted that he "would have welcomed" the position "for the hard work as well as the honor, and because of the nearness to my own California." Hughes confided to the nuncio his willingness to accept the episcopal seat at Oregon City, were it offered.[32] Apparently it never was.

In 1931, the Director for the Bureau of Catholic Indian Missions was able to report that the Catholic Church was ministering to Indians in thirty-three dioceses and twenty-one states, and to Indians and Eskimos in the Territory and Vicariate of Alaska. The Bureau was operating nearly 400 mission chapels attended by 200 priests, as well as maintaining eighty-eight Catholic missionary and boarding schools. A host of miscellaneous missionary activities were functioning on the reservations scattered around the United States and Alaska.[33]

Throughout his relatively short life, Father Hughes was a prodigious writer. In addition to numerous articles for *The Tidings*, the Catholic newspaper for the Diocese of Monterey-Los Angeles, he wrote for *Commonweal*, *The Catholic World* and *Ave Maria*. He edited *The Indian Sentinel* from 1922 to 1935 and during his years as Director for the Bureau of Catholic Indian Missions, Hughes published numerous pamphlets and brochures of various phases of Indian lore and history. His vast collection of typed transcripts from the Bureau, now arranged in six separate volumes, together with several hundred individually dated microprints, is available to researchers in the Chancery Archives, Archdiocese of Los Angeles.

Hughes remained at the helm of the Bureau for fourteen years and his successor reported that the monsignor's resignation, in June 1935, "caused deep regret to his superiors and to countless friends among the missionaries."[34] Shortly after returning to California's southland, Hughes was appointed Pastor of Saint Catherine's Parish on Santa Catalina Island. Ten months later, he was transferred to Laguna Beach, where he served until his demise, on May 6, 1939.

William McDermott Hughes was ever the pastor of souls. It was his intense love of the poor and unfortunate, his zeal for the Church, and his love of Christ that kindled his seemingly endless efforts on behalf of the natives of California.[35]

He was a missionary worthy of a place in the historical annals.

Notes to the Text

1. *The Catholic Church in Utah* (Salt Lake City, 1909), p. 338.
2. There were five other children, *viz.*, Eugenia, Luke, Jennie, John and Charles.
3. Sacramento *Union*, August 4, 1905.
4. *Ibid.*,
5. *Ibid.*, January 1. 1906.
6. *The Tidings*, May 29, 1908.
7. Worcester *Telegram*, June 3, 1912.
8. Los Angeles *Herald*. November 13, 1910.
9. Denver *Catholic Register*, September 21, 1911.
10. William McDermott Hughes, "Mission Indians of Today," *The Indian Sentinel* (Annual, 1910), p. 36.
11. Francis J. Weber, "Halo of Hardship Crowned Work Among the Indians," *The Tidings*, June 5. 1970.
12. Quoted by Francis J. Weber. *The Pilgrim Church in California* (Los Angeles, 1973), p. 61.
13. *The Tidings*, May 20, 1910.
14. Sacramento *Bee*, June 27, 1910.
15. The office of Catholic Commissioner for Indian Missions was established on January 2, 1874. It was merged into the Bureau Of Catholic Indian Missions, in 1879.
16. *The Tidings*, May 13, 1910.
17. *The Spectator*, September 3, 1910.
18. *The Tidings*. October 21, 1910.
19. *The Indian Sentinel* I (Annual, 1916), 25.
20. Niagara Falls *Journal*, October 13, 1911.
21. Riverside *Press*, November 5, 1910.
22. Los Angeles *Herald*, November 13, 1910.
23. Sacramento *Herald*, September 14, 1918.
24. Watsonville *Pajaroian*, July 7, 1919.
25. *Ibid.*, November 28, 1919.
26. See Francis J. Weber, *Christ on Wilshire Boulevard* (Los Angeles, 1969), p. llff.
27. Los Angeles *Times*, November 22, 1920.
28. Sacramento Bee, December 30, 1921.
29. J.B. Tenneally, S. S., "In Memoriam," *The Indian Sentinel* XIX (June, 1939), p. llff
30. *Ibid.*

31. *The Tidings*, June 28, 1935.
32. Archives of the Archdiocese of Los Angeles, William McDermott Hughes to Bonaventure Cerretti, Washington, D.C., December 30, 1924.
33. William McDermott Hughes, *Opportunities for Service by Catholics among American Indians* (Washington, 1931), p. 7.
34. J.B. Tenneally, S.S., *op. cit.*, p. 95.
35. Francis J. Weber, *Catholic Footprints in California* (Newhall, 1970), p. 161.

57

This "obituary" on the famed Franciscan historian, Father Maynard J. Geiger, is taken from "Notes and Comments" in the *Catholic Historical Review* LXIII (July, 1977), 498-499.

Maynard Joseph Geiger, O.F.M., long-time archivist and historian at Santa Barbara Mission, died on May 13, 1977. At his funeral his successor, Francis Guest, O.F.M., preached the eulogy, and the Archbishop of Los Angeles, Cardinal Timothy Manning, presided. Born in Lancaster, Pennsylvania, on August 24, 1901, Joseph went to Los Angeles with his parents at the age of twelve. In 1919 he entered St. Anthony's Preparatory Seminary in Santa Barbara; at the time of his clothing with the Franciscan habit four years later he was given the name "Maynard." Upon completion of his philosophical and theological studies at St. Elizabeth's Seminary in Oakland, he was ordained to the priesthood on June 9, 1929, at Mission Santa Barbara. Between 1933 and 1937 he pursued graduate studies in history at the Catholic University of America. His doctoral dissertation, published in 1937, was entitled *The Franciscan Conquest of Florida* (1573-1618) and has been called "the best single specialized volume on Spanish Florida." Three years later he brought out his Biographical Dictionary of the Franciscans in *Spanish Florida and Cuba (1528-1814)*. His contributions to the history of Spanish Florida were recognized by the Hispanic Institute, which conferred its Cervantes Medal Award on him in 1947.

Soon after returning to Santa Barbara, Father Geiger was appointed mission archivist. In that position he organized and augmented the vast number of manuscripts that his predecessors had collected over the decades. The first tangible result of his labors was his *Calendar of Documents in the Santa Barbara Mission Archives* (1947). As archivist he tripled the holdings of that depository, adding 8,000 pages of transcripts related to the cause of beatification of Junípero Serra alone.

Father Geiger devoted the most productive years of his professional career to the study of Serra's life. Between 1941 and 1958 he traveled 100,000 miles in the United States, Mexico, and Europe, locating and copying documents in 150 public and private libraries and archives for the beatification process. He translated and annotated Palou's Life of Fray Junípero Serra (1955) and finally brought out his own definitive biography, *The Life and Times of Fray Junípero Serra, O.F.M.*, in two volumes (1959), for which he was awarded the American Catholic Historical Association's John Gilmary Shea Prize of 1960. The subtitle of this work, "The Man Who Never Turned Back," also characterizes the energetic author who spent many hours seven days a week in his bare-walled cell, patiently and accurately gathering the records of his order's spiritual conquest along the Pacific Coast. In 1969 he published *Franciscan Missionaries in Hispanic California, 1769-1848: A Biographical Dictionary*. His articles that appeared in learned journals and encyclopedias are too numerous to mention. His last major accomplishment was to translate the reports written by the Franciscan missionaries in 1813-1815 on the life and customs of the California Indians and to compose a historical introduction and notes for a book entitled *As the Padres Saw Them* (1976), for which a coeditor prepared the anthropological commentary and notes.

The scholarly works of this humble friar and member of the American Catholic Historical Association will continue to be read and utilized by all who wish to study the missions of the Spanish Franciscans in the present -day confines of the United States. Characterized by the late W. W. Robinson as one who "writes as he talks, with clarity, ease, and frankness," Father Maynard's "carefully researched publications have won him the respect and admiration of the profession by reason of the thoroughness of his research, his unceasing labor, and the high integrity with which he has told the story of his religious family." In fact, not even his personal involvement in the Serra cause compromised the impartiality and objectivity of his treatment of the subject. His kindliness and charity will also long be remembered by those who knew him.

58

"Father John B. Thom - A Memoir" is the title of this essay which appeared in Emmanuel LXXVII (June, 1972), 256-259.

The priestly vocation is sublime in its dignity, but frightening in its challenge. Its dignity lies in conforming to Christ through a perpetual and intimate fellowship with His chief representative in the community, the local bishop; its challenge in living the victimhood of apostolic charity demanded by such conformity. Christ loved the Church and gave Himself for it. The diocesan priest is worthy of his calling only inasmuch as he does, or is willing to do, the same.

The dignity and challenge of the sacerdotal calling is eminently discernible in the brief six years that Father John B. Thom (1933-1965) wore the priestly mantle. His tragic and untimely death, on July 23, 1965, was an indictment of all the unleashed hatred rampant within the human family. Totally devoid of personal ambition, Father Thom's greatest consolation, and very likely his most lasting contribution, during the short span of his ministry, was the hour he daily spent hidden away before his Eucharistic Lord.

John Thom was born at Minneapolis, on February 14, 1933, the son of Al and Elizabeth (King) Thom. His earliest education was obtained at primary schools in Montana and Minnesota. It was during his years at Polytechnic High School, in Long Beach, California, that John was offered a $50,000 contract with the Cleveland Indians, a tempting offer to any teenager, especially one with John's athletic potential. Acting upon the advice of his spiritual counselor, Msgr. Bernard Dolan, John opted for the seminary, where he directed his energies towards the work of priestly formation with all the vigor and determination that had brought success on the diamond.

He enrolled in the preparatory seminary, in 1951, as a clerical aspirant for the Archdiocese of Los Angeles. Two years later, he entered Saint John's Seminary, at Camarillo, for studies in philosophy and theology. Always highly respected among his peers, John served as President of the Associated Students during the academic year, 1957-1958, and, in the course of his term, introduced a number of innovative improvements. A measure of the esteem held for John is evident from the seminary publication which spoke of his "growing reputation for doing exceptionally well with wood in his hand, whether the lumber happened to be in the shape of a baseball bat or a gavel." It was during his days at Camarillo that John began the daily holy hour, a practice he continued, without exception, to the day of his death.

John was advanced to the priestly office by James Francis Cardinal McIntyre, on April 30, 1959, at Saint Vibiana's Cathedral. Shortly after ordination, he was appointed curate for the newly-established Parish of Saint Anthony, in Oxnard, California, a small farming community some sixty miles north of Los Angeles. There, in addition to his parochial duties, the young priest taught a full schedule of courses at the nearby Santa Clara High School.

On May 14, 1962, he was named assistant secretary to Cardinal McIntyre, a position incorporating a host of duties at the Los Angeles Chancery Office. Father Thom's previous classroom experience, together with his obvious intellectual acumen, brought about his appointment, early in 1964, to The Catholic University of America, where he entered Divinity College as a candidate for the doctorate in Sacred Theology. His dissertation, published posthumously, was a detailed examination of "The Formal Object of Faith" as it had developed prior to Vatican Council I. Upon completion of his studies, in the summer of 1965, Father Thom returned to Los Angeles. Inasmuch as his assignment to the theology faculty at Saint John's Seminary did not become effective until the following September, he had agreed to fill in as a summer replacement for various chancery officials and it was in that capacity that he was functioning on that fateful day of July 25, 1965. Aside from the obviously delicate memories it evokes, the historical record requires that the "extraordinary and deplorable catastrophe" that snuffed out the youthful priest's life on that day be dwelt upon in some detail.

A few minutes before two o'clock in the afternoon, a neatly-groomed lady presented herself to the receptionist of the Los Angeles Chancery

Office, Miss Mary Sinclair, for an appointment with Father Thom, who was serving as interim secretary to James Francis Cardinal McIntyre.

Shortly after arriving back at the office from luncheon at the episcopal residence, Father Thom greeted the auburn-haired visitor, who identified herself as Mrs. Dorothy M. Brassie. When she asked to speak privately, the priest ushered her into the adjoining conference room.

At approximately 2:10, two muffled shots were heard from the chamber, after which Father Thom opened the door into the lobby, fell across the threshold, gasping: "My God, I have been shot...I have been shot!"

The fatally-wounded priest, struck by twin bullets from a 32 calibre derringer, sustained two wounds; one in the head which perforated the carotid artery, the other in the chest which pierced the right lung and heart, causing massive internal hemorrhaging.

In the few seconds it took this writer, who was standing just outside the lateral entrance-way of the conference room, to dash into the chamber, Mrs. Brassie placed the two-barreled pistol on the table, and then calmly and unobstrusively seated herself in a corner of the room.

After instructing Miss Sinclair to summon an ambulance, this writer rushed to his car in the adjoining parking lot for the holy oils. By the time he had returned and administered the last rites, an interval of about four or five minutes, Father Thom was in the throes of his death agony. Though muscular action continued for some additional moments, the victim apparently succumbed within ten minutes after being struck down.

The ambulance attendants arrived soon, and though there was evidence of vital signs, they made no attempt to administer oxygen or in any other way to sustain life. Msgr. Edward Wade accompanied the ambulance to nearby Central Receiving Hospital, where Father Thom was pronounced dead-on-arrival.

At 2:34, this writer telephoned the cardinal from the hospital with official word that the stricken priest had expired. He and Msgrs. Edward Wade and Edward Maddox then returned to the Chancery Office to begin preparations for the news conference which the press had requested for later that afternoon.

Meanwhile, the fifty-five year old assailant, a resident of 3856 1/2 Valley Brink Road in the Atwater District of Los Angeles, had been taken into custody and booked on suspicion of murder at Sybil Brand Institute.

Subsequent investigation disclosed that Mrs. Brassie, who had disappeared from her Saint Louis home three years earlier, had previously contacted a prominent local detective, William R. Colligan for "help against the Catholic conspiracy." The detective later recalled suggesting that the distraught woman "see a psychiatrist to get herself certified insane."

In her subsequent trial, Mrs. Brassie admitted having called the Chancery Office three times on July 19 in an unsuccessful attempt to secure a personal interview with the cardinal. On the following day, however, she did make an appointment, under an assumed name, to see Father Thom, on July 23.

During the course of her short interview with the priest, Mrs. Brassie, overcome with frustration at her "inability to obtain a personal interview with James Francis Cardinal McIntyre," pulled from her purse the gun she had purchased six weeks before at a Hollywood artillery store.

Several "rambling, almost incoherent typed letters" were discovered in which Mrs. Brassie, a nurse who had been dismissed from her previous position "because of emotional instability," expressed "acute anguish" at being "tormented by Catholics and their collaborators" in her "home, on the street, at work, in business shops etc. twenty-four hours a day, every day of the year, for four years." In a letter unearthed in the Chancery Archives written December 4, 1964, she asserted that her persecutors had "concealed microphones and remote controlled relay switches that set off loud noises...monitored by persons in the immediate neighborhood."

On August 4, Mrs. Brassie was bound over for Superior Court trial on charges of murder. She was subsequently convicted of second degree murder, by Judge Herbert V. Walker, in a non-jury trial. Found innocent by reason of insanity, she was sentenced to Patton State Hospital, on December 15, 1965.

Aside from a twenty-six hour period, in April, 1967, when she absented herself from the hospital without authorization, Mrs. Brassie was a model inmate at the institution, until, apparently cured, she was released.

In his eulogy for the slain priest, Auxiliary Bishop Timothy Manning noted that when "this priest fell there was something in his falling that was purposeful and willed by our providential God. It was not solely the consummation of a personal life consecrated to His service, but it had also a social and a priestly implication, a lesson needful for the healing of our present ills."

Indeed, Father Thom was chosen by God for sacrifice. He was not only a priest, but a victim as well. He was innocent, guiltless and unassociated with the tags of hatred attached to others. His sacrifice was a clean oblation in fulfillment of God's plan.

"He was a gentle priest. The meekness within him somehow suggested a conquest. One sensed beneath it a masculinity that was tamed and brought to minister to a higher and nobler order of his nature. It was supernaturalized. It might have been released in a great athletic career or in legitimate human affection. But in the primacy of his manhood there was a measured and decisive surrender of these potencies for a holier cause."

Father Thom "walked out of the Gospel story-the Lord looked upon him and loved him. In return he merited a great integrity and a love of wisdom. These he pursued as a lover might one beloved. It transcended love of father and mother, counted no cost in service, and only death in its defense could adequately express it."

Bishop Manning pointed out that "Wisdom itself writes his final epitaph":

> The just man, though he die early, shall be at rest. For the age that is honorable comes not with the passing of time nor can it be measured in terms of years. He who pleased God was loved; he who lived among sinners was snatched away lest wickedness pervert his mind or deceit beguile his soul. Having become perfect in a short while, he reached the fullness of a long career, for his soul was pleasing to the Lord.

59

This essay on the Los Angeles "Bicentennial 1781-1981" appeared in *Westways* LXXII (December, 1980), 51-53.

This essay about the unreligious founding of Los Angeles is presented to the readers of *Westways* with apologies to Harry Carr who once complained that "some ruthless historian always comes alone to kick the romance out of all the best stories."

Ironic it surely is that the largest metropolis in Western America must be historically arrayed without the colorful framework of dramatic circumstances normally associated with the birth of a city or nation.

But try as one might, the contemporary researcher cannot improve on the conclusion made 50 years ago by Phil Townsend Hanna, the editor of this journal's predecessor, *Touring Topics*, that the genesis of El Pueblo de Nuestra Señora la Reina de Los Angeles "is almost as obscure as the legendary beginnings of Venus, who, the myths recount with brevity and a sad lack of detail, sprang full-blown from the sea."

Regrettably, the absence of eyewitness accounts of the founding of Los Angeles has been no deterrent to its many graphic descriptions. One commentator, noting the high incidence of pure fantasy and romance surrounding the event in the imaginative writings of certain chroniclers, wryly concluded that "no respectable author passes through our *pueblo* and touches his pen to its history without describing that historic day when [Felipe] de Neve marched over from San Gabriel, with the white banner of the Virgin carried in front-the chanting priests-the procession of soldiers in leather armor..."

379

Keenly interested as Felipe de Neve was in the foundation of the *pueblo*, his biographer, Edwin A. Beilharz, confirms that the governor was not on hand for the event. Nor is there the slightest shred of evidence that Fray Francisco Miguel Sanchez, the resident priest at San Gabriel, accompanied the colonists.

Disconcerting as it may be, the facts are that the founding, on September 4, 1781, did not involve processions, speeches, fanfare or music even among a ceremony-loving people. Rather it consisted of 44 tired, dusty, sweaty people unpacking their mules and getting temporarily settled.

One must remember that Franciscans were opposed in principle to the founding of Los Angeles. Fray Junípero Serra and other friars felt that the establishment of Spanish towns was still premature. He worried, and rightly so, that they would prove prejudicial to Indian and Mission rights.

It should also be borne in mind that the founding of a California *pueblo* did not demand processions, speeches or music. Nor did it call for the presence of governor, priests or pageantry. Henry Raup Wagner based his reservations about any formalities on the fact that "the other *pueblo*, San Jose, which was authorized at the same time as Los Angeles, seems to have come into existence without any of the accustomed ceremonies."

The earliest of the "mythological" accounts about the founding of Los Angeles was by Helen Hunt Jackson. In December 1883, she wrote a lengthy essay for *The Century Illustrated Monthly Magazine* (successor to the old *Scribners*) in which she canonized the "pomp and ceremony" tale of Antonio Coronel.

In the first "historical" account of Los Angeles as distinct from its surrounding area, Charles Dwight Willard pictured the panoply of the foundation as probably the most extensive and impressive ever held for the founding of an American city:

> As they neared the selected spot a procession was formed, made up of the soldiers, with the governor at their head, the priests from San Gabriel, accompanied by their Indian acolytes, then the male settlers, and, lastly, women and the children, the former bearing a large banner of the Virgin Mary painted upon it...Prayers and a benediction from the *padres* concluded the ceremony.

Events were further described even more dramatically three years later when Genevieve Solon credited the governor with delivering a formal speech to the settlers, possibly of glowing prophecy for the *pueblo's* future. Elaborating upon Willard's imaginative notion that the ceremony "was probably the most impressive that was ever held over the founding of an American city," the author added her equally unfounded opinion that "not more than half-a-dozen American cities ever enjoyed the distinction of being really founded."

In yet another description of the procession encircling the *plaza*, Dana W. Barlett somehow concluded there was a parade three times around it, as if to inject some vague sociological overtone into the celebration. In her account of the foundation, Alice Mary Philips conjured up a scene of "curious Indians from Yang-Nasaw" gazing in bewilderment at the strange happenings unfolding before their eyes.

Most ornate of all the descriptive accounts was surely that of Harrie Rebecca Piper Forbes. The "picturesque caravan" that she portrayed as leaving Mission San Gabriel at dawn on the morning of September 4, 1781, was quite appropriate for an age when "every act of importance was carried out with all the pomp and ceremony possible for the leaders to provide."

> The civil and military officers were grand in their uniforms brought from Spain; the guards were businesslike in their leather jackets and defensive arms; the *padres* were attended by Indian acolytes and the settlers brought their women and children in the picturesque *carreta* along with the household goods. The party arrived at the banks of the Rio de Los Angeles de Porciúncula as the sun began to cast long shadows.

Then, with her imagination running at full speed, Mrs. Forbes described the procession of characters, even to the extent of locating each personage in line. Her conclusion would do justice to the Parousia:

> Approaching the arbor where an altar had been erected, Mass was said, speeches made and finally each man was allotted his home plot of ground, the guard was stationed and camp for the night was made. Thus was the City of the Angels ushered into existence, amid old country pomp and aboriginal simplicity.

William A. Spalding's version of the historic day continued in the same romantic vein:

> A procession was formed, headed by Governor de Neve, with a detachment of soldiers carrying the banner of Spain...As the march from San Gabriel was nearly completed a formal procession was established which included the Governor and his escorts, the priests from San Gabriel accompanied by their Indian acolytes, and the male settlers, and lastly the women and children.

The women carried that famous banner with the Virgin Mary painted on it, which had enchanted the Indians aforetime.

Spalding's conclusion was as colorful as that of Mrs. Forbes:

The procession marched around the *Plaza*, assembling finally under booths where Governor Felipe de Neve delivered a speech, and the ceremonies were concluded by prayers and a benediction from the Fathers.

The nine-mile trek from San Gabriel Mission was dramatically described by Morrow Mayo in his characteristically flippant style:

It was a colorful procession that marched at sunrise, September 4, 1781, from the Angel Gabriel Mission. The Governor led the parade on horseback, followed by a detachment of cavalry. Next came several sandalshod Franciscan priests, trudging along in their skullcaps and corded robes, attended by Christianized Digger Indian acolytes...

Mayo's version added the liturgical footnote that "candles were lighted" and the "*Te Deum* was sung." The grand finale was capped off when the "soldiers fired three volleys of musketry."

California's beloved poet laureate John Steven McGroarty in his 1911 account added to the "music and singing by the Indian choruses and the firing of a volley of musketry" details of the Forbes version, then appended his own epilogue to what must have been an eventful day:

The parade countermarched in a circle when it came three leagues that were designated and then drew up in front of a prepared altar of twigs and bows where the Mass was celebrated. The proclamation of the King was read, a *Te Deum* sung, a volley of musketry fired and the deed was done.

By 1959, such writers as Ed Ainsworth were taking a closer look at the meager sources. He was the first to admit that "fierce arguments" had begun as to "whether Governor de Neve was present at the founding of Los Angeles, whether there was an elaborate ceremony, whether there was a large crowd of visiting onlookers."

Louis Adamic's contention that "the explanation for the city's present unmistakably Christian character, its prosperity and all-around greatness, should be sought in its auspicious beginning" may tickle the ears of high-minded and well-intentioned enthusiasts.

But this "ruthless historian" must point out, as his contribution to the bicentennial observance for El Pueblo de Nuestra Señora de Los

Angeles, there just isn't any corroborative evidence whatsoever to substantiate that noble thought.

While nearly every religion in the world is represented in the 1980s by a place of worship in Los Angeles, it all began two centuries ago, as a very "unreligious" affair for which the Lord will certainly forgive the *pobladores*.

60

This essay about "California"s Negro Heritage" is here taken from the *Negro Digest* XVI (February, 1967), 87-88.

Romanticists are wont to think that the Pueblo de Nuestra de Senora de los Angeles was settled by Spanish grandees and *caballeros*, sophisticated descendants of the *conquistadores*.

A close look at the record reveals, however, that the original founders or *pobladores* were "a motley lot, there was not a full-blooded white family among them, but they were pioneer stock" and with three exceptions they stayed and built the town we know today as Los Angeles.

When plans were completed for the envisioned *pueblo*, Fernando de Rivera y Moncada journeyed to Mexico to recruit settlers for the town. There, after a whole year of persuading, he succeeded in interesting only 12 families, or 46 people and, of that number, only 11 families, or 44 people, actually made the trek.

The outfitting of the settlers took place at Alamos, a small town on the Mexican mainland not far from the Gulf of California. Seven of the families enlisted at Rosario, three at Sinaloa and one at Alamos. The small group, accompanied by an army contingent, set out for their new home on Feb. 2, 1781.

Though it is not widely known or emphasized, the overwhelming majority of the founders of the Pueblo de Nuestra Senora de los Angeles were Catholics of Negro racial strain.

Of those 44 *pobladores* ultimately arriving at the projected site, "the only people of unmixed Caucasian race in the whole community were two Spanish men." The settlers, who represented a mixture of Indian and Negro with, here and there, a trace of Spanish, can be broken down into four racial strains:

> 3 Indian families..8 people
> 2 Indian-Caucasian families.................................8 people
> 4 Negro families...15 people
> 2 Negro-Caucasian families.................................13 people

Intermarriage among the Latin American natives and Europeans produced a multitude of castes. Children of an Indian mother (in an Indian-Caucasian union) are considered mestizos; whereas those of a Negro mother (in a Negro-Indian union) are classified as mulattos. By this enumeration, the 44 founders of Los Angeles were:

> Caucasian 2
> Indian 16
> Negro. 26

Using the hyphenated system for the children of all mixed marriages, the classification would be:

> Caucasian 2
> Indian 12
> Indian-Caucasian 4
> Negro 17
> Negro-Indian 9

If these statistics prove nothing else, at least they dispel any notion that there were any "blue-blooded Spanish Dons" among the Catholics who pioneered the City of the Angels.

Quite the contrary is the case, for "there were more Negroes among the founders of Los Angeles than any other racial group" and a realization of this factor, useful for the social historian, confirms that these noble *pobladores* "sprang from hardy stock, and the blood of true pioneers coursed through their veins."

61

"California Catholicity in 1848. A Layman's Appraisal" is here taken from *The Pacific Historian* XVII (Fall, 1973), 48-56.

The decline of the missions, coupled with the Mexican Government's disdain for the diocesan system of ecclesial administration, all but destroyed the Catholic Church in California during the latter part of the 1840s. Three years before he died, the area's proto-bishop, Fray Francisco Garcia Diego y Moreno, warned Mexico City's officialdom that its failure to comply with the obligations voluntarily assumed in the original petition to the Holy See[1] would surely militate against the immediate appointment of his successor.[2] The prelate pointed out that it had long been the policy of the Sacred Consistorial Congregation to demand certain minimal requirements prior to advancing a territory to episcopal status, few of which, though promised, had been fulfilled in the Californias. For this and other prudential reasons, the message to the Minister of Justice announcing the bishop's death discreetly suggested that intervention with the holy See, at the presidential level, might be a useful means of prodding Rome into naming a new shepherd for the orphaned church.[3]

Fortuitously, Mexico City's Metropolitan See was also vacant, as Archbishop Manuel Posada y Guarduño had died on April 30, 1846, the same day as Francisco Garcia Diego. It was only on October 7, 1847, that the Chapter officially designated Father José María Gonzáles Rúbio,[4] a long-time associate of the deceased bishop, as Administrator for the Diocese of Both Californias.[5]

Contemporary accounts of those years reveal that the state was "Catholic at heart." One account said there were "Catholics scattered in every town and village, up every mountain and valley." Since many had grown careless and indifferent about their commitments, the area possessd "a people whose conversion would be a great triumph to the Church, as well as an inestimable blessing to the recipient of the graces and consolations following their conversion."[6]

The discovery of gold, on January 24, 1848, in the south fork of the American River, some miles from Sacramento, provoked a whole new range of challenges for the struggling Church in California. The subsequent influx of peoples from various parts of the nation and world called for considerably more clerical personnel than the orphaned diocese could muster. The 100,000 immigrants that swarmed into the state by the end of the following year represented a migration "so stupendous as to outrank in point of numbers anything of its kind in the nation's history, and to stand on equal footing with some of the great world movements of population."[7]

Though a fair proportion of the new arrivals were Catholic, a headcount of available clergy indicates that there were only seven Franciscans and five secular priests, all Spaniards or Mexicans, most of them unfamiliar or ill-at-ease with the English language, to serve their needs. The indefatigable Administrator's intensified efforts to provide additional clerics is reflected in a pastoral letter, on May 30, 1848, in which he outlined the necessity for more "evangelical workers...who by their sound doctrine, edifying conduct and apostolic spirit, can bravely uphold in this diocese of the Californias the noble edifice of the religion of Jesus Christ."[8] Father González Rúbio confided that the Church in California was entirely destitute of means, noting that even the sources which it formerly possessed in the mission system and the aid derived from the Pious Fund[8] and similar sources had all disappeared.[9]

A measure of the concern exhibited for the shepherdless diocese can be gleaned from a cross-section of correspondence exchanged with outside churches. Early in 1848, for example, Edward H. Harrison, asked a friend to inform Archbishop Samuel Eccleston[10] that the 200 Catholics in San Francisco desparately desired an English-speaking priest to look after their spiritual wants.[11] A similar plea was addressed to the Archbishop of Baltimore by Jonathan D. Stevenson, a prominent non-Catholic military official, who reported that the handful of priests in Southern California, most of them either aged or infirm, had "forfeited the respect of their parishioners" by their careless way-of-life.[12] Eccleston forwarded Stevenson's letter to the Sacred Congregation of Propaganda Fide, along with some personal suggestions about prompt remedial action.[13]

A memorandum from James Hardie, an army lieutenant, described how California's once-prosperous Church beheld itself "at this moment without even the most necessary ailment and seems to appeal in vain to her children for that support without which she must even cease to exist."[14] Further evidence came to Eccleston's attention six months later from Frederick Chatard, an officer in the United States Navy, who reported that San Francisco's religious complexion was composed of "a wild motley set of all nations & creeds" where "the Golden Calf alone is worshipped." It was his contention that of the available priests, none was really "suitable for the present population emigrating to Upper California."[15]

Concern for the ecclesial plight of the Far West was shared by other members of the American hierarchy. When Bishop John Hughes of New York solicited the view of Jose De la Guerra, an outstanding Santa Barbara layman,[16] he was bluntly told that the area required a Spanish-speaking prelate to coordinate and expand the work inaugurated by the existing, but wholly inadequate clerical recruits.[17] Hughes had already proposed that the Holy See be apprised about the importance of appointing one or more Bishops for that and other recently acquired portions of United States territory."[18]

It was within this context that Joseph Warren Revere (1812-1880),[19] a grandson of the famous hero of revolutionary times,[20] figures into the ecclesial picture of transitional California. An educated and practicing Catholic, Revere wrote to Archbishop Eccleston, on October 29, 1848,[21] with his appraisal of the problems facing the struggling People of God along the Pacific Slope. It is that eleven page missive, mailed from New York City that is here presented.

Notes to the Text

1. For the text of the petition, see Francis J. Weber, *Francisco Garcia Diego. California's Transition Bishop* (Los Angeles, 1972), Pp. 29-30.
2. Archives of the Archdiocese of Los Angeles (hereafter referred to as AALA), Francisco Garcia Diego, O.F.M. to Minister of Economic Affairs, Santa Barbara, October 27, 1843.
3. AALA, *Libro Borrador*, Entry for May 1, 1846.
4. For a biographical sketch of González Rúbio, see Francis J. Weber, "Kidnapping the Vicar-General," *Front Line* VII (Summer, 1968), 42-45.

5. AALA, *Libro Borrador,* Entry for February 4, 1848.

6. Francis J. Weber, *Catholic Footprints in California* (Newhall, 1970), p. 199.

7. Robert Glass Cleland, *History of California: The American Period* (New York, 1927), p. 232,

8. For a background of this intriguing financial arrangement, see Francis J. Weber, *The United States Versus Mexico-The Final Settlement of the Californias* (Los Angeles, 1969).

9. Santa Barbara Mission Archives, José Maria Gonzales Rúbio, O.F.M., *Pastoral Letter,* Santa Barbara.

10. As Archbishop of the Premier See of Baltimore, Eccleston was the ranking member of the American hierarchy.

11. Archives of the Archdiocese of Baltimore (hereafter referred to as AAB), Edward H. Harrison to Francis Lucas, San Francisco, March 16, 1848.

12. AALA, Jonathan D. Stevenson to Samuel Eccleston, Los Angeles, May 1, 1848. For the full text of Stevenson's letter, see Willard E. Wight, "An Appeal from California in 1848," *Pacific Historical Review* XXVI (August, 1957), 289-292.

13. AAB, Samuel Eccleston to Giacomo Cardinel Franzoni, Baltimore, September 4, 1848.

14. AAB, James Hardie Memorandum, San Francisco, November 23, 1848.

15. AAB, Frederick Chatard to Samuel Eccleston, San Francisco, November 23, 1848.

16. For a brief biographical sketch of California's El Gran Capitan, see Francis J. Weber, *Readings in California Catholic History* (Los Angeles, 1967), pp. 167-168.

17. See Joseph A. Thompson, O.F.M. *El Gran Capitan. José De la Guerra* (Los Angeles, 1961), pp. 221-225.

18. AAB, John Hughes to Samuel Eccleston, New York, December 23, 1848.

19. Born in Boston, May 17, 1812, Joseph entered the Navy as a midshipman and, in 1828, sailed on his first visit to California. He returned to Monterey, aboard the USS Portsmouth, under the command of Captain John Montgomery, in April, 1846, where he was able to "watch over the rapid developments immediately preceding the war with Mexico." See Russell E. Belous, "A Revere in California," *Museum Association Quarterly* XVII (Spring, 1961), 5. In the absence of army personnel, Revere personally lowered the Bear Flag and unfurled the American standard, at Sonoma, on July 9, 1846. He remained there for about six months, establishing the usual routine of patrons and scouts. Revere was also able to make numerous excursions, during which he visited all the parts of the district subject to his jurisdiction. In October, 1846, Lieutenant Revere acquired the estate of San Geronimo, about five miles from San Rafael. Shortly thereafter, he was transferred to San Diego. He participated in hoisting the stars and stripes at La Paz, thus having the honor of raising the American flag at the most northerly and southerly points of the Californias. After the war, Revere returned by ship to Boston, but was ordered back to California as agent for the protection of live oak and other naval timber lands. In 1850, he resigned from the Navy and entered business as a merchant seaman. He purchased part interest in a clipper ship in partnership with Sandy McGregor. Revere served briefly as an instructor in artillery for the Mexican Government. He returned to the United States, in 1853, and in later years functioned as a military consultant to various European governments. He associated himself with the United States Army, in 1861, where he eventually rose to the rank of Brigadier General.

20. Revere was indeed a "grandson" and not a "nephew," as reported in John B. McGloin, S.J., *California's First Archbishop. The Life of Joseph Sadoc Alemany, O.P. 1814-1888* (New York, 1966), p. 68.

21. In the footnote to a peculiarly-distorted six line excerpt from this letter, one author compounds carelessness with inaccuracy by citing the letter as "undated, no place of composition indicated." See "The California Catholic Church, 1840-1849: A Report on Religion," *Records of the American Catholic Historical Society* LX (December, 1949), 219.

Although I have not the honor of a personal acquaintance, I am emboldened by the widely spread reputation you enjoy for affability of character,[1] to address you a few lines on a subject which concerns the welfare of the Church, of which you are so influential a dignitary, and of a whole people; by the operation of recent events; become interesting to their Roman Catholic brethren of the United States.

I allude to the population of the territory of Upper California now forming an integral portion of the Republic of one of the finest districts of which I had the command,[2] during the first military occupation of that territory by the military and naval forces of the U. S.

During my sojourn among this interesting people, I made many promises to represent their earnest desire to have sent to them from the Atlantic states the spiritual aid, of which they stand in so much need; on my return here, and I now beg to be permitted to reciprocate the hospitality I received, by adding my humble prayer to theirs in behalf of so noble an enterprise as a mission to that country.

The fertile and beautiful province of Upper California recently acquired by treaty with Mexico, borders on the Pacific ocean for ten degrees of latitude North of the parallel (sic) of 32°, and that portion of which I am personally acquainted, lying west of the Sierra Nevada, possesses a delightful and balmy climate, unsurpassed fertility of soil, and scenery totally different from any in our eastern states and of the same character with that of Southwestern Europe, divided into lofty mountains, and well timbered uplands, spreading into lovely valleys, where the grape and the olive, and other productions of Italy and Spain flourish in their greatest luxuriance.

Excepting the great alluvial valleys of the San Joaquin and the Sacramento, there are no valley regions where periodical overflows take place, as in the great valleys of the Mississippi and Ohio, etc. and consequently, in no other portions is the settler exposed to the malaria engendered by the decomposition of vegetable matter and the train of diseases it brings with it.

The commercial advantages of this fine country are also unequalled and its maritime littoral is indented with the very best harbours, which can be justly called the best in the Pacific.

It would far exceed the limits of this letter, indeed, would also probably add to its tediousness, to recapitulate all the advantages of this noble territory, destined at no distant day to be the seat of an empire on the Pacific, for a large emigration may be confidently expected.

The white population of this country, at present, does not exceed ten thousand and of whom about eight thousand are of Mexican descent and two or three thousand Americans and Europeans of various nations. There are also some eight or ten thousand "Christians," - Indians converted by the fathers of the missions - and, to conclude with this slight estimate of the population - at the least computation, fifty thousand "Gentiles," or unconverted wild Indians live in their "Rancherias" or villages in different parts of the territory, but mostly in the gorges of the Sierra Nevada.

The first - those of Mexican descent - are all professing Roman Catholics, and have been brought up in that faith. The Americans and other emigrants number also many of the Catholic faith, particular those from the valley of the Mississippi, where the labors of the missionaries of the Church - as is well known to you - have been crowned with a great success. The "Christianos" or Christian Indians have nearly relapsed into a state of barbarism, since the secularization of the Missions by the Mexican government in 1832, and the consequent abandonment of them by the good fathers.

These Indians have also carried with them among their "Gentile" brethren most of the vices and few of the virtues of civilization.

The California Indians are however a docile and indolent race, and although not professing the warlike character of the aborigines of the eastern part of this continent, still possess sufficient intelligence to reward the efforts of the religious philanthropists.

It will thus be seen that by far the greater portion of Californians are by belief, and principle Roman Catholics, and I can add with the firmest conviction, that they are strongly attached to that Church, to which they feel the deepest affection, and raise their children in the same belief, having known none other up to the present time.

In all that country, at the time of my departure in the summer of the past year, not, one single Catholic clergyman of education, intelligence, or superior virtue, existed. The whole clerical function of the entire province was in the hands of four Mexican priests, three of whom were either full blooded or three quarter Indians, one a Spaniard and none possessing the respect of the population, apart from their clerical character, for reasons which - notorious as they were in the country - I should hesitate to name from respect to so virtuous and elevated a prelate as him I have now the honor of addressing.

These four being the only persons bearing the clerical character in so widely spread a country - the population being chiefly engaged in pastoral pursuits and widely separated from each other - I have known the dead to remain unburied and the dying often departing without any of the usual consolations of the church, and in the village of Sonoma, the centre of a population of two thousand whites and an equal number of Indians, I have only known Mass to be performed twice in the course of six months.

The property of the Church is great in value and needs supervision by some authorized agent deputed for that purpose, the condition of things having changed by the political change within country and change of government.

The landed property belonging to the different missions was formerly very large and immense herds grazed upon it yielding (sic) a handsome income to the mission, which was employed by the good fathers in converting the Indian and other purposes, erecting buildings, drains, fencing and otherwise improving land, etc.

When the missions were deprived of their property and the good fathers driven forth from their missions, the improvements fell to ruin, the fields remained "unturned and the entire splendid establishment fell to ruin, and I know of no more melancholy sight than one of these deserted missions at the present time.

Large tracts in the immediate vicinity of the mission buildings however were set aside for the maintenance of the establishment and selected as these were in the first forming of these "presidios," by the priests and government officers, they now form some of the most valuable landed property in California. These lands I say, were reserved for the Church, and to that Church it still must belong, but as the existence of a regular congregation does not now seem apparent, owing to the absence of regular clergymen, etc, hence the necessity of forming one, which can only be done by a clergyman of that denomination, of which the Californians form part. Under the Mexican government the Church and State being united, the priests were salaried, and supported by the government. True, the salary was not regularly paid, but the principle of the State being obliged to support the priest existed and the authority of the State was often called to aid the Church in collecting contributions.

The Population being presumed all *Catholics the Church as a corporate body might hold property as such.*

Now, it will readily be seen, the same state of things exist, for the American Government not acknowledging any preference in religion, has already discontinued the priests salaries,[3] *and would probably acknowledge the title to the property, were it questioned, to be settled in the courts of law, either to settlers in the land by pre-emption, or did a protestant religious society form so numerously as to make itself master of the church, and land in its vicinity, to keep possession.*

The mission buildings are of great value although many of them are in ruins and might be easily repaired, among the latter class I might mention that of San Luis Rey, and that of Santa Barbara.

This state of things calls for prompt action on the part of the Church and early attention to many details concerning the property of the Church, might prevent future litigation to a great extent.

It is highly probable that the priests have already left California in obedience to the orders of their temporal and spiritual superiors, the diocese of Sonora, or

Sinaloa in Mexico.[4]

I think, from the most ample opportunities of personal observation there is not in the world at present so ample and glorious a field for the operations of the devout Roman Catholic missionary than is opened in this climate and country, with the advantages of education and virtuous aspirations. The previous attachment already deeply rooted in the hearts of this neglected, simple hearted and friendly people towards the Ancient Church, the beauty of the country, the advantages of a good form of Government, now introduced among them, and the independence and wealth of the inhabitants, all combine to make it one of the most attractive areas to which a clergyman of generous aspirations could aspire to.

Any one of education and personal dignity of character, appearing as a priest of the Roman Catholic Church, no matter what his country, or language, would be warmly received, more particularly if the great cause of education was combined with that of our holy Religion.

I am about to go out to that country myself and if I could carry back the assurance to the many anxious inquiries I am sure there will be, that they are remembered, with the sanction of yourself most reverend sir, I shall be most happy to receive a line in answer to this, I fear, lengthy and tedious epistle.[5]

You will, I am sure, give me credit for the sincerity of my wish to do all in my humble means to benefit the great cause of restoring the lost sheep to the fold in that distant though most interesting country.

With an apology for taxing your time and patience through so long a letter,[6] *and with the hope that the objects for which it was written will meet with your approval and support I have the honor to be, most reverend sir, with the deepest respect,*

Your obt. servt,
J. W. Revere
Lieut. U.S. Navy

Notes to the Text

1. Samuel Eccleston (1801-1851), the Archbishop of Baltimore, was the Maryland-born Sulpician who had headed the nation's premier jurisdiction since 1834.
2. Revere's command encompassed the district on the north side of San Francisco Bay, garrisoned by Company B, California Battalion Mounted Riflemen.
3. This statement is misleading inasmuch as the "salaries" of the friars had long since been suspended.
4. The whole concept of secularization embodied the notion of replacing religious with secular clergy. In California, however, that actuality was never realized, since the Diocese of Sonora had a critical personnel shortage of its own and could ill afford to dispatch priests into the missionary frontiers.

5. Apparently Revere's letter to Archbishop Eccleston brought a response, for the Boston-born seaman wrote again, some months later, acknowledging "your kind letter in answer to the communication which I had the honor of addressing you in behalf of the Catholics of this country." See AAB, Joseph Revere to Samuel Eccleston, San Francisco, April 29, 1849.

6. Revere's name is remembered by bibliographers as the author of *A Tour of Duty in California* (New York, 1849) and *Keel and Saddle: A Retrospect of Forty Years of Military and Naval Service* (Boston, 1872). That Revere was far-sighted is indicated by the following sentiment on the last page of the former volume:

"Perhaps a hundred years hence some curious book-worm...will be tempted to find out what was said and predicted of California at the eventful period of her annexation to the United States...The poor Indians will then have passed away; the *rancheros* will be remembered only as the ancient proprietors of broad lands...the Grizzly Bear will live only in books and tradition...and California...will she have become populous and enlightened, the seat of arts and learning, the generous rival of her elder sisters in all that is lively and of good report among men? Will not her arts of peace flourish beyond example, and the majestic tread of man still press onwards towards a yet more glorious Destiny?"

62

"The Hardie Memorandum" here reproduced is taken from the *Southern California Quarterly* LIV (Winter, 1972), 343-352.

Though it was firmly established, carefully administered and materially productive during the provincial era of California's history, the spiritually-orientated missionary system found itself in desperate straits by the mid-1840s. Premature secularization, governmental harrassment and personnel shortages were among the factors that practically negated the overall influence of the Catholic Church along the Pacific Slope.

The final blow occurred on April 30, 1846, with the passing, at Mission Santa Barbara, of Fray Francisco Garcia Diego y Moreno, the first Bishop of Both Californias. With the Franciscan prelate's death, "the whole mission structure collapsed and buried him in its dust."[1]

One of the most graphic and knowledgeable portrayals of Catholic life in California during the troublesome years immediately after Garcia Diego's demise was that of James Allen Hardie (1823-1876),[2] a plain, frugal and remarkably industrious career-soldier who was acting as the chief military assistant to Colonel Jonathan D. Stevenson.[3]

The fourteen-page memorandum, which is herein reproduced, addressed to Frederick Chatard, a captain aboard the U.S.S. *Lexington*, at Sausalito, was written at San Francisco and dated November 23, 1848. Chatard forwarded the information-laden missive to Archbishop Samuel Eccleston, who, as the occupant of the Premier See of Baltimore, functioned as the titular head of the American hierarchy. In his accompanying observations, Chatard explained that Lieutenant Hardie was seriously concerned over "the spiritual state of affairs in this country and hopes to see them ameliorated through the help of some pious and enlightened clergy." Chatard maintained that the Hardie memorandum was based on first-hand knowledge. He joined his own voice to that of Hardie in hoping that the intervention might "be productive of good to this portion of the church..."[4]

The Hardie memorandum is presented here in its textual integrity, without any alteration of style, punctuation or grammar. For permission to use this treatise, first discovered by the editor a decade ago in the Baltimore Cathedral Archives, grateful acknowledgement is made to the Reverend John J. Tierney, Archivist for the Archdiocese of Baltimore.

* * *

From the conversation I had with you, a few days since upon the condition of the Catholic Church in California and particularly of the wants of the Catholic population of San Francisco, I am induced to believe that the interest you manifested upon the occasion, would lead you upon your arrival in the United States to make such representations in valuable quarters, and to use such endeavors as would make known the real condition of Catholic matters here and would tend to apply a remedy to what you believed to be existing evils.

Though the shortness of the time before your departure and the nature of my occupations do not permit me to enter into the subject to any length, or my want of experience or judgment to discuss it with justice, I am constrained to say a few words to you, uniting my humble testimony with yours concerning the deplorable condition of the Church in this country and the necessity of prompt and vigorous action to sustain it even on its present footing.

Once rich and powerful and growing, yet more so by the judicious and correct management of the means at her control, the Californian Church beholds herself at this moment[5] without even the most necessary aliment and seems to appeal in vain to her children for that support without which she declares (Padre González's[6] late Circular)[7] she must even cease to exist! When we take into consideration that by the persevering toil and the self-sacrificing zeal of the earlier missionaries, California was reclaimed from the savage wilderness-that under their guidance the Indian, made to forsake his wild life and taught the arts of peace and the practices of christianity, laid the foundations for a great and prosperous country in bringing vast tracts of land under cultivation, in erecting splendid piles of buildings, in the exercise, in fine, of all the useful arts, while he lived happily under the peaceful government of the Church, we cannot but wonder at the beauty of the plan and the magnificence of an enterprise which making the savage practically acquainted with the advantages of civi-

lization from the moment of his conversion, and teaching him to be virtuous and to be useful, might with justice have aimed at the reclamation of a large portion of the Indians of the American Continent. And when we see that the fruits of all these pious labours-all this beauty and skill of planning, all this perseverance in execution have been snatched from the Church at a period she was beginning to need them most, we are at a loss how sufficiently to explore the causes which have produced so lamentable a result. The destruction of the Missions, the ornament of California and the pride of the Church, threw loose upon the country multitudes of converted Indians, who loosed from the restraints of civilised life, deprived of their homes and protection and cast abroad to seek their subsistence where best they might, speedily forgot the good lessons they had been taught-and impelled by want and unchristianized by association with wild Indians, relapsed into their former mode of life, rendered tenfold more vicious and barbarous than before. These form now the predatory bands of thieves who infest the borders of California and who not infrequently make descents upon farms, pillaging and devastating all within their reach.

So saddening is the spectacle of the ruins of these missions and the scattering and retrocession of their numerous dependents so absurd the pretexts of the tyranny and wickedness of the clergy and the demands of the political necessities of the country, urged by scheming enemies-and so notorious the disposition of the spoils-that one is almost tempted to believe that California has been the scene of a Protestant Reformation similar to that which visited England, and the devastations of which had been so forcibly described by Cobbett[8]-[The springs of action, the objects to be gained and the results of the two movements were the same, varying only in extent-but Protestantism was in California no agent in secularizing (as it was termed) these missions. It was the work of Catholics-unnatural' children who have fattened upon the plundering of their parent.]

It would be useless to detail the intrigues, the plans and the various revolutions which were antecedent to the accomplishments of the grand objects of secularization. Suffice it to say that in general the same characters were conspicuous in all the scenes of the drama; and most unfortunately, some of the most intelligent individuals of the country are embraced in the number of those tainted with the sacrilege.

But these things are now accomplished; another state of things has succeeded the former anarchy or misrule, and all must rejoice in the stability and justice of the government of a great and enlightened nation. The Catholic Church must appeal to the government of the United States to know if the illegal and most unjust seizure of the mission property by the Government in California (it is difficult to tell whether it was Californian or Mexican) is to be sanctioned; and whether so wise and just a nation will take advantage of the iniquity of

*those who preceded her, in witholding those poor remains of land from the
Church which now constitute all that sacrilege and fraud have left of her former wealth unconverted to private uses. By the right of conquest, the United
States acquired all rights the Mexican Government had in these establishments, which was really none at all. This might be asserted, had the Mexican
authorities decreed or even approved the steps which the Californian provisional
or revolutionary government had taken in the matter. The matter was accomplished without the consent of the central Mexican government in the first
place-the greater part of the lands were divided among the spoilers as grants
from the Government for "pay for services" rendered in the second place-and
yet the Government had as yet not been consulted. I am informed that the secularization was officially disapproved in Mexico, but the same authority, himself
a holder of mission property, added that when the news arrived in California,
"it was too late"-all had been done: and to finish the work with perfection
defrauders of smaller importance have absorbed most of the remaining property
that is moveable. "The Government" remained at the time of the hoisting of
the Flag of the United States in this country in possession of but the shell of the
missions, while its zealous advocates had rifled the fruits.*

*This miserable remains is however now of importance to the Californian
Church-it is her all. Deprived of this, she must be sustained by assistance from
abroad and appeal to the charity of the Catholic world. Restored to her, this her
just right, a restoration which can present no difficulties, she will have with
careful and judicious management in time a comfortable support.*

*Is there not a necessity then my dear Sir, for prompt and powerful action on
this subject on the part of the Church in the United States? Is it now the time
for the voice of justice to make itself heard and for the friends of the church
under authority to be active? I commend these questions to your particular
attention.*

*As I have above stated, some of the worst enemies of the Church in
California are to be found within her communion. Not it is true that they have
become open and avowed enemies of the Catholic Religion, but their affections
centered upon their possessions and their jealousy always awake, they would
view with alarm any measure promising justice to the Church; and cannot be
relied on in general for contributing to its support or favoring the successful
management of its interests in the country. Unfortunately these people are of
the most intelligent in California; their influence is in consequence great, and
their example pernicious.*

*The Churches gone into decay or rapidly decaying-the pastors few and scat-
tered-their support miserable-their congregations thinned by the baneful influences I have mentioned, causing a growing neglect of religious duties-the entire*

absence it may be said of education among the youth-the new directions given to attention by the change of prospects in California-together with the influence of Protestant principles which of course are daily being introduced with emigrations; how long, my dear Sir, unless God prevent, will it be, before the religion planted at the expense of so much toil, hardship, and pious devotedness will be uprooted and even forgotten?

Reflect too upon the influence which the luxury and fashionable manners and customs of the new inhabitants of California is to have upon the simple habits of the people, and how strong that influence is made to bear upon youth, where they can hardly learn to read (there being but one Catholic school I believe in the country)[10] without imbibing Protestant principles. Will not all in the change that is to take place, be tempted to leave off their religion with their old fashioned customs, and be as ashamed to be thought Catholics as to be thought ignorant rancheros? *But you can better imagine what the effects of the various influences under which the Catholics in this country will be brought under the change of Flag will be, than I can describe them.*

This then being the state of affairs, nothing but extraordinary energy and great skill will succeed in struggling with the difficulties which beset the Church in this country. The spirit of the age has made changes everywhere, and nowhere is the [   ] greater than in California. A knowledge of this spirit and of its workings is necessary for the management of every important interest in this era of the world. It is impossible to stem the current; old fashioned systems of action must be vivified with a spirit of energy-and new difficulties must be overcome with new means.

How unprepared for such a struggle as is now necessary, are the clergy of the old simple times of California! A change has taken place which but few of them can understand-time and experience will be needed by them to make them comprehend the genius of the nation of which they now form a part and under which they have to manage the interests of the Church. In the meantime, who can calculate the losses that may insue [sic] to Catholic interests for the want of prompt, skillful, and opportune measures? The superior of the Clergy in California, Padre I. M. González[11] is an enlightened and highly educated man, of more than ordinary talents, of apostolic character, beloved, admired and respected by all. Were all the clergy like him I could not hope for a better state of things than would ensue among the Spanish population particularly. But as there are few men, in any circle, of the stamp of Padre González when compared with the rest, so it is no injustice to say that few of his fellow clergymen equal him in ability and perhaps in enlightened zeal, and it is truth to say, some, there are who are far from imitating his purity and unreproachable morality-(These exercise a most baneful influence at this moment particularly and their profligacy must be a source of deep regret to every Catholic.) Thus, more laborers and those of energy and zeal and skill are needed for the gathering of the harvest; it is in danger of being lost with the feeble resources at hand now. A new language is now heard in all parts of the country, and there are many Catholics recently emigrated who cannot speak the old language of California; thus a necessity is created for assistance from America and England. Schools are to be established, religious education is to be diffused, the churches built up, the congregations to be gathered and kept together, and the evil practices in which the faithful have fallen to be removed.

How urgently then does the Californian Church need the attention and care of her authorities in the United States-There only can she find redress for her grievances, and relief in her distress-there she must appeal for succour in the hour of need.

Commending these views by our notice, I beg to add a few remarks upon the wants of the Catholic population of the town of San Francisco. You are too well acquainted with the position and growing importance of San Francisco to need any reference to them here. Already of no considerable size, a few years will behold it a large and flourishing city.[12] Yet, although there is a Protestant minister here whose congregation afford him a liberal support, the Catholic population of the town (among whom there are some Americans of standing) and of the whole district of San Francisco including all the families of a large space of country, have to divide their pastor with two other large parishes on the other side of the Bay of San Francisco and he in the exercise of his functions of pastor of this flock, in visiting them in cases of sickness or necessity, and in journeying from parish to parish has to spend a large portion of each month in the saddle! And when the the priest celebrates Mass in San Francisco, he does so at the mission three miles from the town, there being no chapel in the town-So that during the rainy season (and in fact during the whole year for the poor) it is a matter of difficulty to get to Church even when Mass is celebrated. And for all his labor and devotion to his duty our pastor receives a most miserable support. The system of tithes (diezano) which is now existing does not seem to have the effect which the method of supporting the Church in the United States produces. Whatever be its advantages or its former results, it now appears to be unsuited to the condition of matters in this epoch. The burden of the support of the Church, by the system of tithes, falls pretty much upon the agricultural interest, which is now less than any other perhaps in California, able to afford subsistence in support to the Church, but where the tithes are not paid in and the claims of the Church disregarded as they are from the inimical spirit of the large land and cattle owners, the influential and intelligent farmers of the country-this subsistence must entirely fail and resort must be had to some other means. A strong appeal has just been made upon this subject to the Catholic population of California by Padre González;[13] a short time will suffice to show what will be the result. At all events our pastor[14] receives but a sorry support, and those who are best able to contribute, are not called upon (he informs me) by the requirements of the Church to do so. The merchants and professional men are exempt from this contribution, and they comprise the wealthy class of San Francisco. As the greater part of the population of the town is American (or rather speaking the English language) I think an American priest of energy would unite a large flock in the town and its vicinity of Catholics who are now scattered without a guide, while the effect upon the Catholics of the country would be most excellent. I am confident that you must agree with me upon this point from what you have yourself observed. A church is to be built and means for it are to be raised,[15] I have no doubt but that the ground and the money could be secured were a proper person to undertake it. A good clergyman, in the state of public feeling incident to the general prosperity might I should think easily procure the means for building a chapel suited to our present wants without departing from the town for subscribers. How long this state of affairs will last, I cannot say, but it is all important on every account that the present moment be improved.

Time does not permit my pursuing the subjects of this letter to any further length, or even my reviewing patiently what I have written. I have endeavored to put you in possession of information merely upon the state of the Church here; and have to hope that the attention of Catholics at home being awakened to the necessitous condition of their brethren in California such means for their relief shall be afforded as in judgment and prudence shall deem most fit. Upon your representations at home much may depend, and if this hurried letter shall assist you in communicating upon the subjects of it with whom [you] think proper, for the purpose of carrying out the interests we are both, I am confident desirous of serving-you are quite welcome to make whatever use of it may seem best to you.

Wish you a safe and pleasant voyage home, and happiness and prosperity through life,

I am, Dear Sir,
Yours Very Respectfully,

JAMES ALLEN HARDIE.

Notes to the Text

1. For a biographical sketch of the prelate, see Francis J. Weber, *Francisco Garcia Diego, California's Transitional Bishop*, (Los Angeles, 1972).

2. The eldest of eight children born to Allen and Caroline Cox Hardie, James studied at Western Collegiate Institute, Pittsburgh College and Poughkeepsie Collegiate School prior to his appointment, in 1839, to West Point Academy. During his years at the Academy, the the youthful cadet was a quiet, diligent and studious individual, popular with his professors and esteemed by his fellow scholars. Shortly after graduation, he returned to West Point as assistant professor of geography, history and ethics. In 1846, Hardie journeyed to California with Colonel Jonathan D. Stevenson. His position proved to be both arduous and delicate, inasmuch as it involved dealing with turbulent volunteers, anxious for the field and impatient at the restraints of garrison life. Hardie was also expected to watch over the discontented and sullen natives, along with the motley assortment of adventurers then pouring into the area from all over the world. Well-founded fears of an uprising against the American occupation served to keep the commanding officers in a constant state of watchfulness and anxiety about the inhabitants, that they might not move against the troops by surprise, and the soliders that they might be ever prepared to march or fight. It was while visiting Oregon to solicit additional recruits that Major Hardie affiliated himself with the Roman Catholic Church, towards which he had long been tending, and within whose communion he remained as devoted, sincere and active a member as its laity ever boasted. He was baptized at San Francisco's Mission Dolores, in mid 1848. Hardie's embracing of Catholicism took place only after he had thoroughly satisfied his mind and conscience about the wisdom and righteousness of that commitment. Hardie's biographer states the "it is probable that among the influences that contributed to the bringing in of General Hardie to the Catholic fold was his personal experience and observation of the piety, zeal, and devotion of the missionary priests who had been for so many decades laborers and even martyrs among the Indian tribes of the Northwest." As for the California missionary establishments, the same writer noted that "the silent voice of those interesting remains of the…early missionaries no doubt induced him to study a subject of which he knew before." Hardie married Margaret Hunter, in 1851, a union blessed by eight children. In the years after his departure from California, Hardie continued his advance within the military ranks, until early 1863, when he became judge advocate general of the Army of the Potomac. Until the time of his demise, Hardie was a brigadier general.

3. In 1877, the year after Hardie's demise, the assistant adjutant general of the United States, Thomas M. Vincent, outlined the major accomplishments of his New York-born confrere to the anonymously-edited, seventy-nine page *Memoir of James Allen Hardie, Inspector-General, United States Army.*

4. Archives of the Archdiocese of Los Angeles, Frederick Chatard to Samuel Eccleston, San Francisco. November 29, 1848. Portions of this letter are quoted in John B. McGloin, S.J., "The California Catholic Church, 1840-1849: A Report on Religion," *Records of the American Catholic Historical Society*, LX (December 1949), 217-218.

5. For a brief treatise outlining the problems faced by the Church, see Francis J. Weber, *Catholic Footprints in California* (Newhall, 1970), pp. 199-200.

6. José María González Rúbio, O.F.M. (1804-1875) was the Administrator of the vacant Diocese of Both Californias. For a sketch of his life, see Francis J. Weber, "Fr. González Rubio, The Last Missionary," *The Tidings*, July 16, 1971.

7. The pastoral letter was issued on May 30, 1848. See Maynard J. Geiger, O.F.M., *Calendar of Documents in the Santa Barbara Mission Archives* (Washington, 1947), p. 173.

8. V.g., William Cobbett, *History of the Protestant Reformation in England and Ireland* (London, 1824).

9. The term "unnatural" here means disloyal or unfaithful.

10. The reference here is not clear. Actually there were several educational facilities then available, though their designation as "schools" could be questioned.

11. See *note 6*, above.
12. By the beginning of 1849, the population of San Francisco had reached 2,000. See Zephyrin Engelhardt, O.F.M., *San Francisco or Mission Dolores* (Chicago, 1924), p. 310.
13. See *note 7*, above.
14. Father Prudencio Santillan served at Mission San Francisco from January 1846 to February 1850.
15. And so it was. According to William Gleeson, *History of the Catholic Church in California* (2, vols., San Francisco, 1872), II, 201-202, "the first Catholic church erected in the city of San Francisco for the use of the immigrants, was a petty wooden shanty, built in the early part of 1849, on the site of the present substantial church of St. Francis, Vallejo Street." Gleason goes on to record that "Mass had been previously celebrated in a room gotten up for the purpose, by the kindness of lieutenant, now inspector-general, Hardy [*sic*], of the United States service, who was a convert to our holy religion."

63

"Edward Vischer's Pictorial of California" is the title of this essay taken from the *Californian Librarian* XXXIII (April-July, 1971), 140-141

E dward Vischer (1809-1878) saw the world through the eyes of an educated man familiar with the highest cultural accomplishments of Europe. His depictions of California plainly reflect the dual sense of artist and author. Though forced by circumstances to devote a majority of his time to commercial pursuits, the Bavarian-born illustrator's talents for drawing and appreciation for the picturesque naturally inclined him to sketch scenes and objects wherever his business activities led him. The quality of those works earned for the versatile genius the honor of being "pre-eminently the greatest artist in the early history of our state."[1] While solidly ensconced in the annals "as a pioneer merchant and artist during the years following the gold rush,"[2] the name of Edward Vischer is not widely known in present times.

In an effort to provide a permanent record of "the natural characteristics of California, the life and movement of the changes coming over them, and the elements of commerce and industry,"[3] Vischer conceived the idea of publishing a collection of the scenes he had sketched between 1858 and 1867. "He had his drawings photographed and mounted the prints on cards or in albums, obtaining in this way great flexibility in quantities and varieties of editions."[4] The subjects were divided into five general categories; one each for landscapes, trees and forests, Franciscan missions, rural life and mining areas. Early in 1870, the San Francisco printing firm of Joseph Winterburn and Company released *Vischer's*

Pictorial of California. Landscape, Trees and Forest Scenes. Grand Features of California Scenery, Life, Traffic and Customs. Upwards of 150 views comprised the volume which was accompanied by a separate 132-page descriptive text.[5] The favorable public response is echoed in the San Francisco *Examiner* which labelled the publication as "a comprehensive birdseye view of California life, traffic and scenery, the landscape views being enlivened with groupings such as only could be derived from happy observation, deep study of, or familiarity with, California's historical transitions and the divers elements composing its population."[6]

Vischer exhibited a special interest in and concern for the California missions and his sketches of those venerable foundations are of particular value to historians inasmuch as they were made before the institutions "were greatly overtaken by the earlier period of decay or the later process of restoration."[7] It was undoubtedly Vischer's self-assumed task of trying to preserve the missions "in faithful pictures for the edification of future generations"[8] that motivated his issuance of a "supplement" to the pictorial work devoted exclusively to the Franciscan establishments. That subsequent publication, considerably more rare than its earlier counterparts, has been overlooked by many of California's bibliographers.

Apparently, it was Vischer's original intention to publish the supplementary volume as the final installment of a trilogy. This writer possess two red and gold trial-title-pages, both bearing the date 1870, one reading *Mission Ruins. And Reminiscences of the Patriarchal and Pastoral Era of California*, the other *Mission Ruins and Renovated Mission Churches of Upper California.*[9] *De facto*, it was two years before Joseph Winterburn and Company actually released *Missions of Upper California, 1872,*[10] which it advertised as "a supplementary to *Vischer's Pictorial of California.*" According to one authority, the forty-four page supplement appeared in several sizes and styles of typography. A few album-views were also reportedly made.[11]

The photographic detail of his pencil drawings testify to Edward Vischer's artistic talent and explain how he came to be known for the fidelity and delicacy of his work. In the case of the descriptive notes on the *Missions of Upper California, 1872,* Vischer extended his talents to the written page, hoping thereby to preserve from oblivion those fast-fading relics of zealous missionary labor. Such was altogether fitting for "he, more than any other, loved the Old Missions, the work of a generation anterior to his, for themselves and for what they represented."[12]

Notes to the Text

1. C.C. Pierce, "VISCHER—Young California's Foremost Artist," *Touring Topics*, XXV (April, 1933), 18.
2. Erwin Gustav Gudde (Trans. and Ed.), "Edward Vischer's First Visit to California," *California Historical Society Quarterly*, XIX (September, 1940), 193.
3. Francis Peloubet Farquhar, "Camels in the Sketches of Edward Vischer," *California Historical Society Quarterly*, IX (December, 1930, 332.
4. Francis Peloubet Farquhar, *Edward Vischer and His "Pictorial of California"* (San Francisco, 1932), pp. 7-8.
5. According to Robert Ernest Cowan, "another volume was also published in which 110 photographs are in miniature, for his friends who were abroad, or at a distance where the folio volume could not readily be sent. Few copies contain precisely the same number of plates." See *A Bibliography of the History of California, 1510-1930* (San Francisco, 1933), p. 662.
6. June 17, 1870.
7. Robert Ernest Cowan, *A Bibliography of the History of California and the Pacific West, 1510-1906* (Columbus, 1952), p. 241.
8. C.C. Pierce, *op cit.*, 19.
9. This page also carries the subtitle, *Repertoire of Photographs from Different Galleries, Representing Some of the Franciscan Mission Churches, in Different Stages of Decay or Reconstruction in or about the Year 1870.*
10. The title on the protective wrapper reads: *The Mission Era. California and Mexico. Reminiscences of Thirty Years Ago.*
11. Francis Peloubet Farquhar, *Yosemite. The Big Trees and The High Sierras. A Selective Bibliography* (Berkeley, 1948), p. 27.
12. Charles Beebe Turrill, "Early Photographers of the Missions," *The Redwood*, XIX (February, 1920), 187.

64

This essay about "The Oak Autograph Album" appeared in *The Branding Iron* #771 (Spring, 1988), 13-16.

One of the truly great treasures at the Archival Center, Archdiocese of Los Angeles, is an album entitled Autographs of California Pioneers. This book measuring 17x14 inches and about 5-inches thick, contains more than 1,600 autographs (covering 1,150 individuals) of Californians and visitors to the area prior to 1849. The material is skillfully mounted on thin sheets inlaid atop the original leaves of the album. Appended to most of the entries are printed biographical sketches which the compiler excised from newspaper accounts or other early printed sources.

The individuals represented by the autographs were all pioneers in the early life of the Golden State. They were men and women who had come to California by ship (around the Horn), on foot or horseback across uncharted deserts, or by dangerous and tiresome trails in an oxcart or wagon of pre-Gold Rush vintage. Friar and scout, captain and sailor, author and adventurer, trapper and *alcalde*, lawyer and merchant, all are part of a unique collection in our western annals.

For many years, the fascinating scrapbook belonged to Ora Oak, a one-time employee of A.L. Bancroft & Company of San Francisco. She sold the album to Ernest Dawson about 1927. Charles Yale, then an employee of Dawson's Book Shop, was asked to write a comprehensive description of the album in order to enhance its saleability. In so doing, he leaned heavily on the biographical insertions for the essay which he and his assistant, Eleanor Reed, prepared for publication in Catalogue No. 53 issued by Dawson's Book Shop in January 1928. A copy of that now-rare catalogue was given to this writer by Glen Dawson, along with permission to quote liberally from its contents.

Yale concluded his lengthy description of the album by noting that, since duplication of such a work would be an impossibility, it was being "moderately priced" at $6,000. There was no dearth of interest in the book, but prospective buyers were not breaking down the door for a glance at the prized item, all due in part to the cost even in pre-Depression times. Finally, one year later, "father" Dawson had to reduce his price. Carrie Estelle Doheny purchased the album as the centerpiece of her Western Americana Collection.

In 1940, the album became part of the Estelle Doheny Collection of Books, Manuscripts and Works of Art and, as such, was presented to Saint John's Seminary in Camarillo. There it remained, a cherished historical jewel, until 1987. At that time it was moved to the Archival Center, at Mission Hills, and formed a part of the newly-constituted Estelle Doheny Collection of California.

The compiler of the album was Henry Oak (1844-1905), a native of Maine who had come to California in 1866. On his arrival he took a position as a clerk in charge of a grain warehouse in Petaluma. He later taught briefly at the Napa Collegiate Institute and then joined the staff of the San Francisco *Occident*.

In 1869, Oak became associated with Hubert Howe Bancroft's library in San Francisco, where he labored for 18 years. While there he spent much of his time writing and editing at least 10 of the 39 volumes that eventually comprised *The Works of Hubert Howe Bancroft*. Unhappily, the role of Oak in the monumental Bancroft publishing century was never adequately acknowledged by Bancroft, a factor which deeply embittered his long-time New England collaborator.

Oak was an avid autograph collector. During his tour of the California missions in 1874, for example, he interviewed a number of prominent personages such as Benjamin Hayes, Cornelius Coe, Alfred Robinson, Andres Pico, B.D. Wilson and J.J. Warner. And, in every case, he sought and was given either an autograph, a document, or a letter for his personal files. Later on, whenever an important individual came to the library, he left behind something for the Oak collection. It can easily be seen how a man of this diligence came to acquire such a varied and exquisite collection. Everything about this volume indicates the methodology of its compiler. The contents are neatly mounted, carefully cross-indexed and minutely researched. The sketches, mounted next to the autographs, sub-sequently became the basis for the pioneer register and index which began appearing under the name of Hubert Howe Bancroft in 1885.

Oak divided his 266 page album into categories. The first entries are those of the earliest settlers in California. Twelve pages are devoted to men who came to the area between 1814 and 1830. Among this distin-guished group was John Gilroy (born Cameron, who took the name Gilroy to avoid arrest and the possibility of being sent back to Scotland), an honest, good-natured sailor-*ranchero*, one who proved to be as powerless in the hands of the land-lawyers as were the natives them-selves. He lost all his property and cattle, but lived on to see his *ranchero* become the site of the flourishing town bearing his adopted name.

Another of this group was William E.P. Hartnell, a man of affairs whose generosity and openheartedness kept him in financial difficulties. Arriving in 1822, this outstanding figure was a rancher, custom collector, educator, visitor of the missions, interpretor and translator.

Then there were Robert Livermore, William A. Gale, Daniel Hill, John R. Cooper, David Spence and James McKinley - to enumerate but a few of the many whose names awaken memories of pioneering times.

The missionaries also occupy a prominent section in the album. *Primer inter pares* would be Fray Junípero Serra (1713-1784), founder and *Presidente* of the California missions. Actually there are two Serra auto-graphs, one clearly dated at San Carlos de Monte-Rey, July 17, 1774. Others included in this section are Fermin Francisco de Lasuén, Estevan Tápis, Jose Séñan, Vicente de Sarría, Mariano Payeras, Jose Sánchez and Francisco Garcia Diego y Moreno who later became the proto Bishop for the Diocese of both Californias.

There are eleven pages in the album concerned with the other mis-sionaries, three devoted to the friars who came to California from the Apostolic College of Nuestra Señora de Guadalupe at Zacatecas. Priests, clergymen and chaplains are next considered and among them are Walter Colton and John Nobile, the founder of Santa Clara College.

A listing of California's Spanish, Mexican and military governors begins on page 34, a notable assemblage from Jose Joaquin Arrillaga to Richard B. Mason. Evidence of Oak's meticulous care is shown in his sec-tion covering pioneers living in 1855, for whom he made careful cross references to the native Californians, the pioneers of 1825-1829, 1830-1840 and each succeeding year to 1848. He thus provided an index to those whose autographs are found elsewhere in the album.

The Graham Affair (1840), the Bear Flag men, the Hijar and Padres expedition, Stevenson's regiment, the Mormon colony (with Sam Brannan as its prime leader), the Constitutional Convention, the Donner party and the Hudson's Bay Company, each with its full complement of important signatures, ably depict instances of diplomacy, intrigue and bravery in the history of the Golden West.

Placed under the heading "Episodes of California History" are signatures which bring to mind such incidents as John C. Fremont's ride, the discovery of gold by Francisco Lopez (1842), the *Star of the West*, smuggling and the historical background of Bret Harte's *Story of a Mine*.

Seven pages are given over to autographs and biographical sketches of early authors who recorded California's history, heroes and scenic wonders. This listing would of course include Fray Geronimo Boscana, who wrote about the Indians at San Juan Capistrano Mission; Alfred Robinson whose *Life in California* (1846) was issued with Boscana's work; Walter Colton, author of *Three Years in California* who was an interesting figure as *alcalde* of Monterey; Joseph Revere, a young lieutenant whose adventures and observations gave him material for his *Tour of Duty*; Eugene Duflot de Mofras, the young French diplomat whose varied experiences occasioned *Exploration* (1844), together with Edward Vischer, William Dane Phelps, William Thomas, William Taylor, Samuel Ward and Felix Paul Wierzbicki whose literary work made them outstanding figures in western history.

Among the hunters, trappers and explorers whose names are recorded in the album are Christopher (Kit) Carson, his brother Moses, James Clyman, lsaac Graham, Ewing Young and George C. Yount. There are remembrances of over 75 Spanish, Mexican and foreign traders who visited the Pacific Slope. Outstanding of these are Alpheus, Francis and Joseph Thompson, John Parrott, Fred Macondray, Thomas Larkin, William Gale, William Leidesdorff, Jose Bandini and Jose Aguirre.

The autographs of vessel masters, super-cargoes and agents, sailor-visitors and naval settlers occupy 14 full pages. There were such personages as John Cooper, the trade rival of Hartnell & Company, who made many trips up and down the coast; Edward McIntosh, who came with Cooper on his trip to California in 1823, Lansford Hastings of the *Tasso*; James Hedge of the *Monmouth*; Mariano Malarin of the *Senoriano* and Henry Mellus, agent for Appleton & Company are just a sampling,

Physicians, lawyers, journalists, printers, secretaries, surveyors and lumbermen are assigned 13 pages in the album. In the first group are such names as John Griffin, who came to California with Stephen

Kearney and was later in charge of the military hospital at Los Angeles; John Marsh, a misunderstood and somewhat maligned fellow whose chief interest appears to have been that of seeing California brought into the federal union and James L. Ord, who arrived in about 1847 as a surgeon with the Third United States Artillery unit.

Among the lawyers were George Hyde, *alcalde* of San Francisco, Charles T. Botts, member of a leading law firm and a delegate to the 1849 Constitutional Convention, together with Lewis Dent, a well-known jurist in the Bay Area.

Among the prominent names in the state's printing history was Agustin V. Zamorano, publisher of many imprints emanating from the Spanish Press of California; Walter Colton and Robert Semple of the *Californian*, the first newspaper and E.P. Jones and Edward C. Kemble of the Los Angeles *Star*.

Spanish and Mexican officials are well represented. They include the Arguello family—Jose Dario (father), Luis, Antonio, Gervasio and Santiago (sons); the Carrillo family—Jose Raimundo (father), Anastasio (son) and Raimundo (grandson), together with Joaquin (cousin) and the Estrada brothers—Jose Mariano and Jose Raimundo.

Remembered for his romantic "march to the sea," William Tecumseh Sherman also had a claim to fame in California history, as well as a place in this album. Bancroft felt that Sherman "reached a higher position than any other pioneer named in this register." With him in this section of the album is Edward O.C. Ord, known for surveying the area that became metropolitan Los Angeles. Those prominent in the state's political affairs are such legendary figures as James Alexander Forbes, Manuel Castro and Gabriel Torre.

The pages devoted to capitalists and those connected with islandic affairs can be passed over with scant notice, but the next section is important because it deals with pioneer women of California. Among the first of them is Mary Kinlock (wife of George), who came from Scotland before 1830. Her autograph, beautifully written, is one of several including Josefa and Mary Carson, wives of Kit and Moses B. Carson. Others are Rachel Larkin (wife of Thomas O.) and Mary Paty (wife of John).

United States and Mexican naval commanders are featured as well, attesting to the part played by men of the sea in those times. Montgomery and Page, Lavalette and Stribling, Thorburn and Watson for the Americans; Milatin, Araujo and Narvaez for the Mexicans are indicative of the officers whose names appear.

John Bidwell stands tall among the migrants to California, as do his three companions R.H. Thomas, George Henshaw and Michael Nye. Practically all those who joined what was later known as the Bartleson Company are represented in this album. Examples are Josiah Belden, David Chandler, Henry Brolaski and Joseph B. Chiles.

Those whose names adorn valleys and mountains, lakes and rivers, towns and countrysides and streets and avenues were avidly sought out by Henry L. Oak. Among them are Juan Alvarado, Edward Kern, Pio Pico, Jonathan Stevenson, Robert Stockton, John Temple, Ignacio Martinez, and Jaspar O'Farrell.

German, French, Irish, Italian, Scotch, Russian and English pioneers occupy seven well-filled pages, each recalling the cosmopolitan character of the population in those early days. Those names read like a modern telephone directory - Alder, Behn, Bolcof, Douglas, Ehrenberg, Fleury, Prudon, Rubidoux, Sainsevain, Wrangel - men of diverse nationalities who, through their military connections, their love of adventure and their search for new fields of commercial enterprise, visited these shores and played a role in the establishment of new communities.

Of the native Californians, there are autographs of practically every important family...the Guerras, Lugos, Estudillos, Picos, Pachecos, Ortegas, Sepulvedas and Vallejos. From page 201 onwards to the end of the album, the arrangement is totally geographical - first the San Diego military officers, friars and citizens; the Los Angeles merchants and officials; then representatives from Santa Barbara, Purisima, San Luis Obispo, Monterey, Santa Cruz and, finally, San Francisco. Thus completely and amply are the centers of population from the missions of the south to the cities of the north systematically played out.

Covering the outlying *ranchos* of the interior, the last pages of the album contain autographs and sketches of men notable in the annals of pastoral California. Chief among these is John Augustus Sutter, the German-Swiss trader who changed the face of California by his discovery of gold.

They are all here in this magnificent album-those valiant men and women who came from all parts of America and from many foreign countries to lift California high upon the crest of worldwide acclaim. They came to be part of the American dream.

65

The following article on"Antonio F. Coronel and the Serra Centenary" is excerpted from *The Branding Iron* #118 (June, 1975), 7-10, 16.

In the annals of the history of Los Angeles, few if any individuals have occupied as many positions of public trust as Antonio F. Coronel. Born at Mexico City, on October 21, 1817, into a family long associated with and accomplished in jurisprudence, Antonio came to California in 1834, in the trifold role of merchant, rancher and educator.

During his sixty years in the southland, Coronel had the good fortune of participating in the transitional phase of the area's history. "He witnessed the gradual development of its resources and the remarkable expansion of its interests, contributing much thereto by his sagacity, enterprise and thorough familiarity with local conditions."[1]

His training in medicine, which Coronel seems never to have utilized in California, admirably qualified him for the various positions of trust to which he was called. The "popular, clever and sprightly" pioneer served as justice of the peace, member of the city council and county assessor.[2]

In 1873, Antonio married Mariana Williamson, the daughter of a prominent New England family. A highly intelligent and affable lady, Mariana was of invaluable assistance to her husband in the many public roles he occupied in succeeding years.

Coronel's name was well known throughout California. He was state Treasurer for several years as well as a member of the California Legislature. He established the first Department of Public Works at Los Angeles, and was the city's Mayor from 1851 to 1853. During his tenure in the latter office, "it was the practice of the citizenry to gather in the Plaza at the sound of a gong and vote on general matters by raising of hands."[3]

Through his association with the old Franciscan friars, Coronel, a devout Catholic, became a staunch champion of the defenseless Mission Indians of Southern California, addressing countless interventions on their behalf to federal, state and local officialdom. He gave most generously of his time when the *padres* sought his assistance in business matters.

Coronel exhibited a deep appreciation of the need for preserving the evidences of the Golden State's early heritage. He was an organizer of the Historical Society of Southern California and the one most responsible for the celebration marking the centennial of Fray Junípero Serra's death. Antonio's close friendship with Helen Hunt Jackson was acknowledged by that versatile writer in her historical works.[4]

During the course of many years, Coronel gathered "the largest and most valuable collection of historical materials relating to this section and to this coast, in the country."[5] After his death, Mariana Coronel presented the extensive holdings to the City of Los Angeles. They were displayed in the Chamber of Commerce Building until 1922, when they were transferred to the Los Angeles County Museum of History, Science and Art. The Coronel Collection can still be viewed by appointment. Catalogued as No. A.110.58, the vast assortment of documents, paintings, photographs, costuming and other memorabilia forms a vital link with the transitional years of California's heritage.[6]

The kind-hearted Coronel was essentially "a man of the people and for the people, and, having for so many years generously aided in public and private enterprises, Los Angeles owes him much indeed!"[7]

In 1884, Coronel journeyed to Carmel, where he participated in the celebrations marking the hundredth anniversary of Fray Junípero Serra's demise. The essay he wrote for that occasion, published in several of the state's newspapers,[8] indicates a close familiarity with Fray Francisco Palóu's *Relación Histórica*.[9]

Notes to the Introduction

1. James Miller Guinn, *Historical and Biographical Record of Los Angeles and Vicinity* (Chicago, 1901), p. 509.
2. "Benjamin David Wilson's Observations on Early Days in California and New Mexico," *Historical Society of Southern California* XVI (Annual, 1934), p. 148.
3. *Mayors of Los Angeles*, (Los Angeles, 1965), p. 12.

4. For Coronel's part as the "villain" who launched the "pomp and ceremony" tale about the beginnings of Los Angeles, see Francis J. Weber, *The Founding of the Pueblo de Nuestra Senora de Los Angeles. A Study in Historiography* (Los Angeles, 1970), pp. 3ff.

5. Henry Dwight Barrows, "Antonio F. Coronel," *Historical Society of Southern California* V (Annual, 1900), p. 82.

6. See *The Antonio F. Coronel Collection* (Los Angeles, 1906).

7. James Miller Guinn, *op. cit.*, p. 510.

8. The particular version is taken from an unidentified newspaper clipping mounted in the first of the four scrapbooks acquired by the Huntington Library from the Episcopal Church Home of Los Angeles. The volumes in question contain miscellaneous Californiana clippings gathered by Georgie Truman. The writer wishes to thank Mr. Carey Bliss, Curator of Rare Books, for permission to publish this excerpt.

9. For the background of that famous work, see Francis J. Weber, "Cornerstone of Western Americana," *Quarterly Newsletter of the Book Club of California* XXXIV (Spring, 1969), pp. 36-39.

A great sentiment, one more elevated than that of honoring the virtue which even on this fragile earthly mantle cannot be shaken off, is that of remembering the dead, of placing a flower where lie those who have passed into eternity. That sentiment moves me to-day 28th of August, 1884, at the hundredth year of the death of Rev. Father Junípero, a man who by his services and sacrifices, gave days of glory to his country, honor to religion, and to his descendants a rich inheritance. At the present time, when illustration is producing such advantageous and healthy fruits, leaving aside all prejudice that originates passions, one can duly qualify properly the merits of those worthy of praise and acknowledgment. The voices from all the towns of this State should be raised to-day to repeat the praises of the first founder of morality and civilization. But this being a proper occasion, I shall relate some of them, which by their nature possess an estimable worth.

He was born[1] one of those beings endowed with intelligence. His earliest desire was to become a priest. At the age of sixteen he entered the Franciscan Order,[2] and before he was eighteen he had taken the final vows.[3] In this vocation his most ardent desires were to labor among the Indians of the western shores of the New World, but to his disappointment these desires were not realized, until nineteen years after having become a priest, when he was sent to Mexico.[4] There he was kept at work founding Missions, preaching, taking care of the sick in the jails and hospitals, exposing his own life.[5]; this country[6] being threatened by the English and Russians.

The Spanish Government sent an expedition to secure their just rights. Father Junípero Serra joined it as President of all the California Missions, which important position he performed with ability and great patience. The voyage from the port of Vera Cruz to the City of Mexico,[7] and from there to the port of San Blas, he made on foot.[8] The same he did from La Paz (Lower California) to San Diego (Upper California). These voyages caused an ulcer to form on his leg, from which he suffered all the rest of his life.[9] Those who know how rough and unhealthy these places are, can imagine what he must have endured. At the founding of the first Mission,[10] which they called San Diego,[11] the arduous fatigues, the scarcity of provisions, and exposure, caused a pestilent disease[12] through all that colony, the majority of them dying, and those who survived were left so weak that they could not even make the graves for their unfortunate friends. Father Junípero and the engineer,[13] although sick, had to perform this operation with their own hands, besides taking care of the sick and feeding them seeds and herbs, which they obtained from the Indians.

In this critical situation, the few remaining who had not caught the disease and the convalescent ones, afraid of yielding to this crisis, urged Governor [Gaspar de] Portalá [sic] to abandon such a rash undertaking and put them on safer land. Partalá [sic][14] not being able to refuse such just complaints and taking into consideration his own life, fixed the 20th of March, 1770, for their departure.

Father Junípero, on learning of this determination, looked low-spirited, for he considered that all the efforts and expense would be buried forever, and above all California would be lost to Spain.[15] The 19th was St. Joseph's Day. On the morning of it, Father Junípero, who had been praying night and day for weeks, celebrated to St. Joseph a High Mass with special invocations for relief. Before noon, a sail was seen on the horizon. There were some who scoffed at it as a mere apparition, but Portalá [sic] believed and waited, and four days later, in came the ship San Antonio, *bringing bountiful stores of all that was needed.[16] No time was lost in organizing expeditions to go in search of Monterey,[17] and possession was taken of the place, and the peaceful and perfect occupation of the new country was accomplished; which had been of so much expense to the court of Spain and the great conqueror [Fernando] Cortéz.*

Portalá [sic] and his people, ashamed of their weakness, had to pay greater homage to that heroic man.

It is seen that through that effort this garden of gardens was won by Spain, or now we would not be enjoying its great advantages nor our institutions. In 1772, when perplexities seemed inextricably thickened, and supplies had fallen so short that starvation threatened the Missions, Father Junípero, not wishing to trust any one with such an important affair, took ship to San Blas, with no other companion except an Indian boy.[18] He toiled on foot from

SAN BLAS TO GUADALAJARA,

Two hundred and forty miles. Here they both fell ill of fever, and sank so low that they were supposed to be dying, and the Holy Viaticum was administered to them. But they recovered, and while partly convalescent pushed on again, reaching the City of Mexico in February, 1773. The Viceroy of Mexico[19] at first manifested some difficulty, but who could refuse the prayers of an aged man who had given such proofs as this of his earnestness and devotion. The difficulties were cleared up, money and supplies obtained,[20] and Father Junípero returned to his post with a joyful heart. Before leaving he kissed the feet of the Friars in the College[21] and asked their blessing, saying that they would never behold him more. Father Junípero's insatiable passion was baptizing Indians, thus saving souls from death, filling him with unspeakable joy. The transports into which Father Junípero was thrown by the beginning of a new mission are graphically written by the man[22] who went with him to establish the mission, with his little train of soldiers and mules. Laden with a few weeks' supplies, he wandered off into the unexplored wilderness. As soon as he would see a beautiful oak-shaded plain he ordered a halt, would seize the bell, tie it to a tree and ring on till the echo was heard by some of the Indians, who, moved by curiosity, would appear at the place. As soon as Father Junípero saw them he would call them. They had for guard and help a few soldiers, and sometimes a few already partly civilized Indians; several head of cattle, some tools and seeds and holy vessels for the church service, which completed their store of weapons, spiritual and secular, offensive and defensive, with which to conquer the wilderness and its savages. There needs no work of the imagination to help this picture. Taken in its sternest realism, it is vivid and thrilling, contrasting the wretched poverty of these single-handed beginnings with the final splendor and riches attained. The result seems well-nigh miraculous. From the rough booths of boughs and reeds of 1770 to the pillars, arched corridors and domes of the stately stone churches of a half century later, is a change only a degree less wonderful than the change in the Indian from the naked savage with his one-stone tool, grinding acorn meal in a rock bowl, to the industrious tiller of the soil, weaver of cloth, worker in metals and singer of sacred hymns. Alexander Humboldt, after having visited this country in 1802,[23] speaking out in his historical essay, says, "That of all the missions of New Spain, those of California represented the most rapid progress and notable civilization, and that all this was owing to the good management of the missionaries."

Father Junípero possessed the wonderful instinct of going in search of the unfortunate. He distinguished himself in everything for the sake of charity. It was wonderful to see this man animated by motives so different from those that distinguish actions that are purely human. He left his country, his parents, and his friends forever, to dedicate himself for life to sow the seed of faith and moral principles in the hearts of a people of a country who had never known it, exposing himself to all danger and suffering. In this saintly priest,[24] interest toward humanity was identified by the most grave religious and political questions. He was a practical agriculturist, a great moralist and good director. Witnesses of all this were the beautiful and productive towns[25] *which he established in such a short time and with such small resources, the thousands of savages he converted into useful men, the communications he sent to*

THE KING OF SPAIN

And to the superior authorities of Mexico and the Superiors of his Convent, which show the tedious examination he made of this country, and of its great elements and resources, prognosticating what is now being realized. The history of his last hours and of his death written by his faithful friend and partner, Palon [sic], *is a quaint and touching narrative.*[26] *Up to the day before his death, his indomitable will upholding the failing strength of his dying body, Father Junípero had read in the church of San Carlos, Monterey,*[27] *the canonical offices of each day, a service requiring an hour and a half of time. The evening before his death he walked alone to the church to receive the last sacraments. The church was crowded to overflowing with Indians and whites, many crying aloud in uncontrollable grief. Father Junípero knelt before the altar with great fervor of manner, while Father Palon* [sic] *with tears rolling down his cheeks, read the services for the dying, gave him absolution and administered the Holy Viaticum. Then rose from choked and tremulous voices the strains of the grand hymn,* "Tantum Ergo." *A startled thrill ran through the church as Father Junípero's own voice, high and strong as ever, joined in the hymn. One by one the voices of his people broke down, stifled by sobs, until at last the dying man's voice almost alone finished the hymn. After this he gave thanks and returning to his cell-like room, spent the whole of the night in listening to penitential psalms and litanies, and giving thanks to God, all the time kneeling or sitting on the ground, supported by the loving, faithful Palon* [sic].

In the morning early he asked for plenary indulgence, for which he again knelt, and confessed again. At noon he was visited by the principal persons and authorities of the place.[28] *He welcomed them, and after making a few remarks, bid them good-bye. After they took their leave, he asked Palon* [sic] *to read to him again the recommendations of the soul. At its conclusion he responded earnestly, in as clear a voice as in health,* "Thank God I am now without fear." *Then with a firm step he walked to the kitchen, saying that he would like a cup of broth. As soon as he had taken the broth he exclaimed,* "I feel better now. I will rest," *and lying down he closed his eyes, and without another word or sign of struggle or pain, ceased to breathe, entering indeed into a rest of which his last words had been solemnly prophetic.*

Behold here a rapid tribute to the merits and virtues of that illustrious man and venerable patriarch. Let the descendants remember when the town meets in some place to bless the memory of that great apostle, as long as we cannot place upon his brow the unfading wreath to which his deeds make him worthy. But Father Junípero is not dead. He still lives immortal in the just pages of history, and in the memory of those who know of his important services in California that he so much loved.

What has occurred in this country in the hundred years past is astonishing to the eye of the keen observer. It has absorbed all elements that comprise modern civilization in its most elevated scale, considering its geographical situation, its vast elements and resources, which contain a population of several millions of inhabitants, being now in its infancy. It is easily foreseen that our fortunate descendants, protected by the Divine hand in the hundred years to come, will reach the perfect step of moral and physical intellect, which the rapid progress of the age affords. Hoping they may continue paying the debt which is due to the man to whom I yield this small tribute, since it seems so ordained by human events.

Notes to the Text

1. Miguel José Serra was born at Petra, Mallorca, Spain, on November 24, 1713,
2. Serra was admitted as a novice at the Convento de Jesús, outside the walls of Palma, on September 14, 1730.
3. It was on the occasion of his profession as a Franciscan, on September 15, 1731, that Serra chose the name Junípero, in memory of the brother companion of Saint Francis.
4. It was on April 13, 1749 that Fray Junípero Serra and his former pupil, Fray Francisco Palóu, sailed from Palma for America by way of Málaga and Cádiz.
5. Serra's earliest years in New Spain were spent in the missions of the Sierra Gorda region of northern Mexico.
6. The reference here is to Alta California.
7. The writer back-tracks here to Serra's pre-California days. Fray Junípero and an unnamed companion walked the distance of 250 miles from Vera Cruz to Mexico City.
8. There were seventeen years between these two journeys.
9. Though he appears to have a fundamentally robust constitution, Fray Junípero suffered greatly from mosquito bites sutained on his trek from Vera Cruz to Mexico City. Scratching caused such varicose ulcers as to occasionally impede his walking.
10. Serra had previously established the Mission of San Fernando de Velicatá, on May 14, 1769, in Peninsular California.
11. The mission named for San Diego de Alcalá was formally established on July 16, 1769.
12. The illness was scurvy.
13. Possibly a reference to Captain Juan Pérez.
14. Gaspár de Portolá served as Military Commander or Governor in 1769-1770.
15. Serra and his companion, Fray Juan Crespí, had decided to stay behind in the event that the governor decided to abandon the establishment.
16. Apparently weather conditions delayed the "bringing in" of the ship, until March 24th.
17. The *San Antonio* set sail for Monterey on April 16th. Actually Monterey had already been "discovered" the previous year by Portolá. Perhaps the author is inadvertently thinking about the Bay of Monterey.
18. The Indian's name was Juan Evangelista whom Serra had baptized on March 19, 1771. Juan received Confirmation in Mexico City, the first Indian of Alta California to receive that sacrament. He died at Carmel in 1778.

19. Viceroy Antonio María Bucareli y Ursua was an honest, self-sacrificing and qualified public official.
20. After the meeting, the Franciscan *Presidente* had no more loyal and consistent friend than Bucareli.
21. Serra was attached to the Apostolic College of San Fernando, in Mexico City.
22. *Viz.*, Fray Francisco Palóu (1773-1789), the biographer of Serra on his *pro-tempore* successor as *Presidente* of the California missions.
23. The reference is to the four volume work, *Political Essay on the Kingdom of New Spain*, published at London, in 1811.
24. Fray Junípero Serra's cause for beatification was opened in 1934.
25. A better term is "mission" for Serra felt that it was premature to establish *pueblos* in California during his lifetime.
26. See Maynard J. Geiger, O.F.M. (trans.), *Palóu's Life of Fray Junípero Serra* (Washington, 1955), pp. 243ff.
27. Not so. Serra resided at Carmel's Mission San Carlos Borromeo.
28. Among the visitors were José Cañizares and the royal chaplain, Cristóbal Díaz.

66

"California's Gold Discovery. The Record Set Straight" is the title of this study which appeared in *The Pacific Historian* XVIII (Fall, 1974), 16-19.

Accounts of California's gold rush traditionally associate the person of James W. Marshall with that discovery in terms effectively overshadowing any presence of the precious substance prior to January 24, 1848. That such an impression is historically indefensible becomes obvious from remarks of Richard Henry Dana who reported that he had "heard rumors of gold discoveries" at least a dozen years before.[1] The number of claims and counter-claims are legion. Among the more persuasive is that of the itinerant trapper, W. F. Thompson, who supposedly found gold in the Downey River in Sierra County sometime in 1839.[2] The San Fernando Mission district in Southern California, however, bears the distinction of having supplied the world with the first documented instance of California gold, six years before Marshall found the glittering nuggets in Sutter's millrace near the south branch of the American River.

As early as 1840, Andres Castillero,[3] a renowned Mexican mineralogist, reported finding, in the vicinity of San Fernando, *tepate* (water-worn pebbles of iron Pyrite), a substance which, he claimed, indicated the likelihood of placer gold in the area. Eugene Duflot de Mofras visited San Fernando in the 1840s, and in his description of the once proud frontier outpost, the French traveller commented on the *estancias* or mission ranches of Las Virgenes, La Amorga, La Huerga, San Francisquito, noting that "at this last *rancho*, gold was discovered."[4]

The incident alluded to is the earliest for which a definite date and probable location can be authenticated. Credit for finding the elusive metal goes to Francisco Lopez,[5] the *mayordomo* of the mission, who unearthed the precious substance on March 9, 1842, in present-day Placerita Canyon, near Castaic.[6] The discovery was made near a ranch house on a parcel of land granted by Governor Juan Bautista Alvarado to Antonio del Valle on January 22, 1839. The epochal event was described by Abel Stearns:

> Lopez, with a companion while in search of some stray horses, about midday stopped under some trees and tied their horses to feed. While resting in the shade, Lopez with his sheath knife dug up some wild onions, and in the dirt discovered a piece of gold. Searching further he found more. On his return to town he showed the pieces to his friends, who at once declared there must be a placer of gold there.[7]

Subsequent investigations indicated that auriferous fields extended "from a point on the Santa Clara River about fifteen or twenty miles above its mouth over all the country drained by its upper waters and thence easterly to Mount San Bernardino."[8]

It is related how "news of the discovery soon spread among the inhabitant, from Santa Barbara to Los Angeles, and in a few weeks hundreds of people were engaged in washing and winnowing the sands and earth of these gold fields."[9] Though the ensuing rush to California was modest in comparison to the one following the Mother Lode find in 1848, Hubert Howe Bancroft recorded that a goodly number of prospectors soon filled the area, many of them from as far away as Sonora. Within a few weeks after Lopez's discovery, "the dirt, with a scanty supply of water, was paying two dollars per day to each man engaged in mining."[10] A second placer was found the next year in San Feliciano Canyon on the same ranch, about eight miles west of Newhall. Christian baptism of this first authenticated finding of gold in California took place in the spring of 1843, when Father Blas Ordaz offered Holy Mass at the site on an altar built under a rustic bower."[11]

The actual amount of gold taken from the area has never been accurately determined although one writer told of a prospector who realized $80,000 from precious metal.[12] The quality was good, as Stearns later testified.

> I find by referring to my old account books that November 22nd, 1842, I sent Alfred Robinson, Esq., twenty ounces,

California weight,[13] of placer gold to be forwarded by him to the United States Mint at Philadelphia for assay.[14]

The gold bullion, deposited by Robinson on July 8, 1843, was evaluated at $344.75 or $19 per ounce.[15]

Excitement abounded for the next four years though scarcity of water and crude extracting methods made efficient mining extremely difficult. With the development of the Mother Lode Country, interest in the small San Fernando deposits gradually abated and soon died out.

There were those who believed that the *padres* at the nearby mission had hidden away great quantities of gold for their private use. Theodore T. Johnson's treatise accounted for "the rigid silence as to the existence of gold in the country, maintained for more than a century" by charging that the missionaries realized that "the day of their supremacy and influence in California had gone by never to return" and were planning well for the years ahead.[16]

A visitor to the mission in 1904 saw huge gaping holes dug into the soil within the Church itself. Even before the main altar were vestiges of a disappointed prospector.[17] As late as 1915, vandals were reported "searching for the holy treasures that were buried in the bosoms of the dead monks"[18] interred within the confines of the ruined mission church. Though the friars could scarcely have profited from a discovery made a generation after secularization, "the Fates would have been inconsiderate if they had not granted the Franciscan missions at least a minor role in that momentous drama of the discovery of gold in California."[19]

If it is true that prior to Marshall's fortuitous discovery the great treasure of the California mountains remained unsuspected by foreign visitor and native resident alike, one can understand the relative silence of the annals for pre-1848 prospecting activities in the Golden State. In all fairness, however, this writer endorses a view expressed quite forcibly forty-five years ago:

> Let Mr. Marshall yield up the laurel of fame as the first pioneer discoverer of gold in California to the brow of Don Francisco Lopez, to whom it justly belongs!

Notes to the Text

1. *Two Years Before the Mast* (Los Angeles, 1964), I, 167.
2. Richard H. Dillon, "The Gold Rush Came Late," *Westways* LVIII (October, 1966), 23.
3. Castillero later discovered the New Almaden quicksilver mine in Santa Clara County.
4. *Exploration du Territoire de l'Oregon, des Californies et de la Mer Vermeille* (Paris, 1844), II, 360-361.
5. Also known as "Cuso" Lopez in the annals. The association of the discovery with Jean Baptiste Rouelle by John Bidwell cannot be accepted.
6. J. N. Bowman, "The First Authentic Placer Mine in California," *Historical Society of Southern California Quarterly XXXI* (September, 1949), 229.
7. Quoted in J. M. Quinn, "The Gold Placers of Los Angeles," *Land of Sunshine V* (July, 1896), 61.
8. Theodore Hittell, *History of California* (San Francisco, 1898), II, 313.
9. J. J. Warner, Benjamin Hayes and J. P. Widney, *An Historical Sketch of Los Angeles County California* (Los Angeles, 1936), p. 19.
10. *History of California* (San Francisco, 1886), IV, 297.
11. *The Tidings*, May 1, 1914.
12. William Heath Davis, *Seventy-Five Years in California* (San Francisco, 1929), p. 159.
13. The actual amount was 18.34 ounces.
14. Quoted in Charles J. Prudhomme, "Gold Discovery in California," *Historical Society of Southern California Annual XII* (1922), 20.
15. Shortly after the discovery of gold, Templeton Reid, a goldsmith and assayer from Georgia, moved his coining equipment to California. There he issued territorial gold coins in denominations of ten and twenty-five dollars. The only known specimen of his 1849 twenty-five dollar coin, stolen from the Cabinet of the United States Mint on August 16, 1858, was reportedly made from the dust of the San Fernando placer mine.
16. *Sights in the Gold Region* (Dublin, 1850), p. 135.
17. See Joseph B. Roure, *History of the Mission San Fernando, Rey de España* (San Fernando, 1922), p. 9.
18. Los Angeles *Times*, February 14, 1915.
19. John A. Berger, *The Franciscan Missions of California* (New York, 1948), p. 168.

67

This article about the "Paul Revere of the Cuban Crisis" was written especially for the *Twin Circle Magazine*, August 16, 1970.

One of Southern California's most active and colorful Catholic laymen, a multi-talented individual conversant in three tongues and accomplished in a host of professional roles, was once a "shoot-him-on-sight" target of Fidel Castro's henchmen in Communist Cuba. Today, José Norman places that "distinction" at the top of his impressive *curriculum vitae*.

José and his family went to Cuba, in 1949, to manage a 450-acre parcel of land that his wife, the granddaughter of patriot Calixto Garcia Iñiquez, had inherited in the foothills of the Sierra Maestra region of Oriente province. There, by introducing new agricultural methods and offering work to many otherwise-unemployed mountain folk, he was able to convert a portion of the dense, tropical jungle into a thriving coffee plantation.

Myriad of Pursuits

In Havana, José also delved into a myriad of other pursuits. He was a columnist for the Havana *Post* and its rival, the *Times*, as well as a principal music arranger for CMQ-TV studios, one of Latin America's most modernly equipped radio and television stations.

In June of 1958, during the guerrilla skirmishes preceding the Castro takeover, Communist agitators harassed local land owners and eventually provoked the looting and burning of the Norman home, and its adjacent plantation buildings. When José appealed for redress, he was assured that the structures would be restored. A lengthy interview ensued with the Castro High Command during which José was offered (and refused) the directorship of chemical warfare. When his attitude toward the revolutionary ideology remained adamant, José, his wife and son, were imprisoned and falsely accused of murder.

Politically, José was in a dilemma. He had already been arrested by the Batista regime for allegedly possessing unauthorized weapons. José admits that the Batista government did bring a measure of prosperity to the Caribbean nation. He also amusingly notes that Castro did something for Batista that even the Church could not do-"made him a saint by comparison."

José's entry into politics was more accidental than premeditated. He already was, by temperament, training and reputation, a well-known classical pianist, composer and orchestra leader in his native England where he introduced the rumba, in 1930. His "Cuban Pete," which Art Linkletter ranks as "one of the most popular rumbas ever written," became Desi Arnaz's signature tune for many years and inspired a film by the same title at Universal Pictures.

Norman's staunch Catholicism and outspoken political views made him a *persona non grata* in Cuba. With his life and those of his family in the balance, José fled to the United States, in 1960. He had vowed, while in prison, to dedicate the remainder of his days to telling the world about the atrocities of Cuban misrule, Church oppression and the contagious effect such a movement would surely have on other American countries.

Relentless Fighter

Referred to by *Time* as Castro's "most publicized confiscation victim," José has relentlessly toured the United States, the Caribbean and Central and Latin America for the past decade explaining the chaos which Communists have prepared for the Free World. He has appeared on numerous television "talk shows," and for a number of years his daily newspaper column was syndicated around the country.

Known as the "Paul Revere of the Cuban crisis," José Norman won wide acclaim for publicly disclosing the location and number of the island's 30 Russian-built missile bases prior to the announcement by President John F. Kennedy. Even now, José is privy to "leaks" from Cuba that fascinate government agencies like the Central Intelligence Agency. Presently, Norman is warning of a contemplated Russian naval base in Cuba.

Though he doubts if Castro was initially a Soviet puppet, Norman says that the Cuban revolutionary's affiliation with the Marxist cause was long-ago confided to the members of a select group of guerrilla rebels living near Bayamo.

Regrets Sympathy

José regrets the sympathy given to Castro by certain churchmen in the early days, but he feels that their positions were more a reaction to the existing Batista regime than an endorsement of the aims and purposes of the "infidel" Castro.

An outspoken member of the West Hollywood community, José recently startled his fellow parishioners at Saint Victor's Church by jumping up, in an unguarded moment, to challenge what he considered to be the "fuzzy" thinking of the Sunday homilist. He later apologetically confided to Danny Thomas, who was ushering at that Mass, that wounds inflicted for one's faith heal slowly.

The 64-year-old Norman, a native of Liverpool, hopes soon to become an American citizen. A more dedicated patriot this nation could hardly find!

68

This survey on "The 'High Spots' of Californiana Historical Literature to 1835" is taken from the *California Librarian* XXIX (July, 1968) 198-203.

The study of a people's literature is far more than an analysis of words and the manner of their arrangement. Rightly conducted, "it is a probing into the inner self of the man who used the words, an investigation into his thoughts, feelings, emotions, environment, social and political life, religion, aspirations."[1] What may be said of the printed word in general can surely be predicated of those writings pertaining to the Golden State for the "pursuit of books, and more pointedly, books on California, is in truth, a consuming passion. It has opened vistas of new worlds, liberally sprinkled with deeds of courage, adventure, fortitude and heroism, to a growing company of readers. Those whose sons, husbands or brothers may have fallen victim to it, and who are wont to voice petulant criticism, may reflect that it is a gentle–aye a genteel–vice after all, and has kept many a weak and erring soul from the arms of strumpets, and the iniquities of the brothel."[2]

Any worthwhile list of "high spots" necessarily reflects the personal tastes and prejudices of the compiler. In the present case, an attempt has been made to enumerate, in narrative form, a handy checklist of volumes which scholars generally regard as historically significant to the overall development of California literature. Antiquity, or the mere ability of the printed page to survive the passage of time, obviously cannot be the sole determinant factor of a book's real worth, yet that characteristic remains a dominant influence in any attempt to amass a representative collection of titles pertaining to the literary growth of a given area.

It is only fair to point out that the historian's judgment in assaying the classical qualities of a book must be weighed against his professional inclination to identify a work's importance with its usefulness as a factual source. While exhibiting some zeal for preservation, the historian usually avoids any tendency to equate importance with rarity. In defense of such a position, he might well plead that all too frequently the rare book is the one that failed, a publisher's mistake, a book that need not have been so elaborately multiplied.[3] Though aware that "very generally when a man begins to accumulate books he ceases to make any use of them,"[4] the historian does, for practical reasons, amass books relevant to the field of his particular interest. Even then, however, he seldom falls into the category of a "bibliophile" properly so-called, for his pragmatic attitude normally insulates him from any undue concern for such items as edition number, quality of printing and physical condition.

Available evidence indicates that the term "California" first appeared in *Las Sergas de Esplandian*, a book published at Seville in 1510.[5] If one accepts the plausible theory that this work of García Ordóñes de Montalvo directly influenced Hernando Cortez to undertake his voyage to peninsular California in 1535, then this volume has a justifiable claim to be the cornerstone of any collection of Western Americana.

From a strictly chronological point of view, the first printed tomes brought to California were undoubtedly the missal and breviary used by the chaplain(s) attached to the Juan Rodrígues Cabrillo expedition of 1542-1543. No mention is made of any religious rites performed when the commander died on San Miguel Island, but it may be presumed that he was given a Christian burial with ceremonials contained in the *Missale Romanum*.[6]

As far as the official record is concerned, the Bible belonging to Francis Fletcher, chaplain of the Sir Francis Drake party in 1579, is the first book specifically mentioned in the chronicles. The account of the voyage relates that "prayers, singing of psalms, and reading of certain chapters in the Bible" made up the religious ceremonies held at various times during the thirty-nine-day sojourn on California soil.[7] While no allusion is made concerning the version of the Scriptures used, one commentator logically suggests that it "was very probably the Geneva Edition of 1560 rather than the bulky Bishop's Bible of 1568."[8] According to another widely recognized authority, the *Voyages de l'Empereur de la Chine dans la Tartarie* was the first separately printed account of California to appear.[9] This tome was published at Paris in 1685. The earliest known work since Juan de Torquemada's *Monarchia Indiana* to include information regarding what is now known as Upper California,[10] was the *Estracto de Noticias del Puerto de Monterey* of Pedro Fages. Issued in pamphlet form by the Mexican government in 1770, the small treatise contains the first announced results of the Portolá expedition to California in 1769 and 1770."[11]

The thirty-two *diarios* now in print for the explorations on land in or toward California will charm readers as long as the epic of the Golden State's birth is recalled.[12] Though the manuscript was published only in 1857, the initial literary work actually written in California was the first of the seven *diarios* of Fray Juan Crespi who accompanied the Fernando de Rivera expeditionary force in early 1769.[13] The minute observations recorded by the chaplain to that courageous caravan of men who ventured across the perilous desert between Velicata and San Diego are "carved deep in the palimpsest of North America."[14] Apart from their chronological prominence, the Crespi diaries merit for their compiler an unparalleled place among the famous explorers of the New World. One historian felt that Crespi "deserves even more than Fray Francisco Garcés to be considered the great explorer of the Southwest in the eighteenth century."[15]

The first book relating exclusively to California, the territory so designated today,[16] was Miguel Costanso's *Diario histórico de los viages de mar, y tierra hechos al norte de la California*. Printed at Mexico City in October of 1770, this succinct narrative, covering the period between July 14, 1769 and January 4, 1770, is very likely "the most valuable of all the documents relating to the expedition" of Gaspár de Portolá.[17]

Though not set to type until 1930, the *Diario que formo el Padre Predicador Apostólico Fray Pedro Font* was considered by Herbert Eugene Bolton as one of the best in all Western Hemisphere history.[18] Certainly the most illuminating description of the times, these notes have earned a coveted place in the literature of New World explorations.[19]

Closely related to the *diaries* are the writings of Fray Francisco Palou. In the opinion of an early bibliographer, of all works on California history, first place must be accorded to *Noticias de las Californias*.[20] The documentary character of this classical opus is enhanced by the many original materials incorporated wholly or in part into the text. Palou's *Relación histórica de la vida y apostólicas tareas del venerable Padre Junípero Serra*, printed at Mexico City in 1787, "enjoys the double distinction of being the earliest California biography and the best biography of California's most renowned character."[21] As the major compendium of primary material covering the first dozen years of Spanish occupancy, the *Vida* is "the very first book upon which our knowledge of the history of the state depends."[22]

To Carlos Antonio Carrillo is attributed the first production of a native Californian printed in book form.[23] *His Exposición dirigida á la Cámara de Diputados del Congreso de la Union* appeared at Mexico City in 1831. Unhappily, as one commentator put it, the small tome "proved to be of passing conservative influence in an historic process which moved inevitably toward liberalism, the disintegration of Mexico, and the regime of the Yankee in California."[24] The earliest known piece of printing in California is a letterhead for the *"Comisaria Subalterna, y Aduana Maritima Provicionales del Puerto de Monterrey"* on a document written August 25, 1830,[25] and now in the Bancroft Library at Berkeley. The first printed broadside, dating from January 16, 1833,[26] announces the new governor's arrival. Located in 1919, it has since disappeared.

Probably the first booklet printed in the continental Western United States was the *Reglamento Provicional para el gobierno interior de la Ecma. Diputación territorial de la Alta California*, issued at Monterey in 1834.[27] Aside from its chronological importance, the *Reglamento* is doubtless the rarest of the imprints of the Spanish press.[28] A facsimile edition was published at San Francisco in 1954. Robert Ernest Cowan regarded José Figueroa's *Manifiesto [sic] a la república Mejicana* as "the most important of the early books printed in California on the Spanish press."[29]

The published accounts of Provincial California's early visitors are vitally important for a well-balanced view of the area's historical development. Generally regarded as superior to any of its kind, the description gained in 1791-1792 by George Vancouver has been considered "the chiefest source of authority of that period."[30]

Auguste Bernard Duhaut-Cilly "was the first outlander to become intimately acquainted with, and describe"[31] the thriving Spanish California of 1827. That French visitor is also credited with penning the most extensive contemporary account of California's missions and settlements in provincial times.[32] The first printed account of an overland journey to California was *The Personal Narrative of James O. Pattie, of Kentucky.*[33] Despite its semi-fictional qualities, the work of this itinerant vaccinator "remains the epic of the mountain men, perhaps more truly representing their attitudes, their experiences, and their adventures than any other book which has appeared on the subject."[34] That Richard Henry Dana's *Two Years Before the Mast* continues to be the most popular work on

California written,[35] is confirmed by the no fewer than ninety-one printings which have appeared in the United States since the initial edition was issued at New York. The account is a literary masterpiece-the first in the annals of California literature.[36]

Related to the foregoing, though perhaps only accidentally, is Captain Frederick Marryat's *Narrative of Travels and Adventures of Monsieur Violet in California, Sonora and Western Texas*. Authorities exhibit little enthusiasm for this "proto" fictionalization which is so full of plagiarisms that even the Library of Congress saw fit to enumerate certain examples.[37] The book merits inclusion in this survey if for no other reason than its being "the worst novel that anyone ever wrote."[38]

The study of literature in any era reveals the continuously evolving procession of ideas and ideals characteristic of a given people. Through the medium of the printed page, the great thought, no matter where or when uttered, need not be allowed to die. "It does not perish amid the snows of mountains, or the floods of rivers, or in the depths of valleys. For a time it may seemingly be forgotten, but it is somewhere embalmed in memory, and after awhile reappears on the horizon like a long-gone star returning on its unchanging orbit, and on its way around the endless circle of eternity."[39]

Notes to the Text

1. George Wharton James, *The Influence of the Climate of California upon its Literature* (n.p.: privately printed, 1912), p. 1.

2. Phil Townsend Hanna in *Libros Californianos* (Los Angeles: Zeitlin and Ver Brugge, 1958),p. 62.

3. John Walton Caughey, "Rare Books and Research in History," in *Rare Books and Research* (Los Angeles: University of California Library, 1951), p. 34.

4. J.J. Peatfield, "The Bancroft Library," *Overland Monthly*, XXV (March 1894), 274.

5. "The Queen of California," *The Atlantic Monthly*, XIII (March 1864), 266.

6. Henry Raup Wagner, *Juan Rodrigues Cabrillo* (San Francisco: California Historical Society, 1941), p. 55.

7. Francis Drake, *The World Encompassed* (London: Hakluyt Society, 1854), pp. 124, 222.

8. J.N. Bowman, "Libraries in Provincial California," *Historical Society of Southern California Quarterly*, XLIII (December 1961), 427.

9. Henry Raup Wagner, "The Descent on California in 1683," *California Historical Society Quarterly*, XXVI (December 1947), 310.

10. Henry Raup Wagner, in *The Zamorano 80* (Los Angeles: The Zamorano Club, 1945), p. 27.

11. Frederick J. Teggart, ed., *The Official Account of the Portolá Expedition of 1769-1770* (Berkeley: University of California Press, 1909), p. 17.

12. Charles J.G. Piette, O.F.M., "The *Diarios* of Early California, 1769-1784," *The Americas*, II (April 1946),409.

13. For the interesting story behind these famous diaries, see Alan K. Brown, "The Various Journals of Juan Crespi,"*The Americas*, XXI (April 1965), 375-398.

14. Herbert Eugene Bolton, *Fray Juan Crespi, Missionary Explorer on the Pacific Coast, 1769-1774* (Berkeley: University of California Press, 1927), p. xvii.

15. Charles J.G. Piette, O.F.M., "An Unpublished Diary of Fray Juan Crespi, O.F.M." *The Americas,* III (July 1946), 102.

16. Adolph van Hembert-Engert and Frederick J. Teggart, eds., *The Narrative of the Portolá Expedition of 1769-1770 by Miguel Costanso* (Berkeley: University of California Press, 1910) p. 93.

17. Henry Raup Wagner, in *The Zamorano 80,* p. 17.

18. Herbert Eugene Bolton, *Anza's California Expeditions* (Berkeley: University of California Press, 1930), IV, vi.

19. Phil Townsend Hanna, "The Heritage of a Californian," *Historical Society of Southern California,* XXX (December 1958), 281.

20. Henry L. Oak, "Some Rare Books about California," *Overland Monthly,* XII (June 1874), 567,

21. John Walton Caughey, *California* (Englewood Cliffs, N.J.: Prentice-Hall, Inc., 1964), p. 604.

22. George Wharton James, ed., *Francisco Palou's Life and Apostolic Labors of the Venerable Father Junipero Serra* (Pasadena: George Wharton James, 1913), p. xi.

23. Hubert Howe Bancroft, *History of California* (San Francisco: The History Company, 1885), II, 743n.

24. Herbert Ingram Priestley, *Exposition Addressed to the Chamber of Deputies of the Congress of the Union by Señor Don Carlos Antonio Carrillo...* (San Francisco: John Henry Nash, 1938), p. xiv.

25. George L. Harding, "A Census of California Spanish Imprints," *California Historical Society Quarterly,* XII (June 1933), 8.

26. Doyce B. Nunis, *Books in Their Sea Chest* (Berkeley: California Library Association, 1964), p. 25.

27. Robert Greenwood, ed., *California Imprints, 1833-1862, A Bibliography* (Los Gatos: The Talisman Press, 1961), p. 38.

28. Robert Ernest Cowan in *Libros Californianos,* p. 21.

29. *A Bibliography of the Spanish Press of California, 1833-1845* (San Francisco: Robert Ernest Cowan, 1919), p. 13.

30. Robert Ernest Cowan, *A Bibliography of the History of California and the Pacific West, 1510-1906* (Columbus: Long's College Book Company, 1952), p. 236.

31. Phil Townsend Hanna in *The Zamorano 80,* p. 24.

32. Wright Howes, *U.S. Iana* (New York: The Newberry Library, 1963), p. 175.

33. Gregg Layne in *The Zamorano 80,* p. 48.

34. Franklin Walker, *A Literary History of Southern California* (Berkeley: University of California Press, 1950), p. 13.

35. Charles E. Chapman, *A History of California: The Spanish Period* (New York: The Macmillan Company, 1923), p. 495.

36. Dorothy Bowen, *A Century of California Literature* (San Marino: The Huntington Library, 1950), p. 2.

37. John Swingle, "Collecting California Fiction," *Quarterly News Letter of the Book Club of California,* XXVI (Fall 1961). 86. Though it was published only in 1845, there is reason to believe the manuscript of this work was written considerably earlier.

38. George R. Stewart, Jr., "Dumas's Gil Blas en California," *California Historical Society Quarterly,* XIV (June 1935), 137.

39. Quoted in Ella Sterling Cummins, *The Story of the Files* (San Francisco: The World's Fair Commission of California, 1893), keynote page.

69

This essay on "The Rare Book. Some Objective Criteria" is here reprinted from *Coranto* VII (1971), 20-26.

An historian once observed that books, like steaks, can be classified as rare, medium rare, and well done. He went on to point out that the rare book is often the one that failed.

It is a publisher's mistake, a book that did not need to be so elaborately multiplied. The chances are that it did not sell very well in the first place. Or it is a book that most owners thought so dull, so worthless, so insignificant that they took no pains to preserve it.[1]

"Rarity" can be an ambiguous term when applied to books and the bibliophile is well advised to be "a little curious about what constitutes a rare book."[2] By its very etymology, the word encompasses only those items valued for their scarcity and/or character. Determining in particular cases the rarity and consequently the worth of a volume can involve a rather wide spectrum of considerations, depending on a particular person's hierarchy of values.

The collecting of books is the *summum bonum* of man's acquisitive desire.[3] According to one rather severe commentator, the collector "makes a fetish of 'condition' and judges any volume that may come to hand from its 'points,' that is, its physical state: the absence or presence of its original binding, whether or not its pages have been trimmed to eliminate worm-holes, foxing, or torn edges."[4] In any event, to the dedicated collector, amassing books "involves the excitements of the hunt, the pleasures of competition, and the triumph of winning over [his] competitors, or even, rarer yet, over the dealers."[5]

On the other hand, the student's attitude toward rare books is often a programmed reaction to the oft-repeated and untrue dictum that "when a man begins to accumulate books he ceases to make any use of them."[6] His pragmatic esteem for books and their value is based almost exclusively on

> their contents - the wisdom of their philosophy, the cadence of their prose, the music of their verse, the pertinency of their ideas, or the sagacity of their composers. The pursuit is a mad and bitter quest for knowledge. It matters not to these folk if a book be a first edition or a fourth, so long as it is the best edition.[7]

It really isn't true, as Henry Raup Wagner so boldly stated, that dealers "declare books to be rare simply to attract buyers."[8] In fact, the commercial measuring-rod is nothing more than the basic economic law of supply and demand. While the dealer recognizes that "when a book becomes part of a collection its value increases, just as the collection itself is worth a great deal more than its component parts,"[9] he is also aware that unless a given book appreciates in value at a minimum rate of five percent a year, it is not an overly wise long-term investment.

Apart from the penchants of particular collectors, there are a number of very valid "ground rules" by which truly rare books can be identified and their objective worth rather accurately gauged.

Inclusion of a volume in one of the recognized select listings invariably inflates its attractiveness. Collectors are ever attuned to obtaining first or later editions of titles appearing in such compilations as Merle Johnson's "High Spots of American Literature," the Grolier Club's "One Hundred Books Famous in English Literature" or that elite group of distinguished California books known as the "Zamorano 80." Even the appearance of a book in such bibliographies as Wright Howes's *U.S.iana* (New York, 1963),with its 11,620 entries of "uncommon and significant books relating to the Continental Portion of the United States," is enough to guarantee the title in question a place of distinction on the bookshelves of the nation's private and public libraries and centers of learning.

The extent of the original press run, where that can be determined, along with the number of known copies, is a vitally important consideration. Limited editions are more apt to be in scarce supply, especially in those cases where copies are individually numbered. Presentation copies are preferred, as are volumes personally autographed by the author or ones into which a signed letter of the author has been tipped. Complete copies of Brother Antoninus' *Novum Psalterium PII XII* (Los Angeles, 1955), for instance, are known to total forty-eight. Of those, nineteen were numbered and inscribed with the name of the recipient. The careful records kept of both the inscribed volumes and those distributed in subsequent years should make it relatively easy to locate the entire press run of this exquisitely printed work.

If an edition has been recalled, suppressed, or destroyed, escaping volumes are highly prized. Copies of John Thomas Doyle's *In the International Arbitral Court of the Hague. The Case of the Pious Fund of California* (San Francisco, 1906)[10] were so effectively sought out by the author's heirs that the work eluded even the careful bibliographical eyes of Robert E. Cowan. The book, dealing with a controversy between Doyle and Archbishop Patrick W Riordan concerning legal fees, reproduced the correspondence exchanged by the two disputants, much to the chagrin of the parties concerned.[11] *The Poetical Works and Biographical Remarks of the Rev. Joseph Phelan, with Album Scraps and Catholic Poems* (San Francisco, 1902), "a collection of some of the most appalling doggerel ever committed to writing and set in type,"[12] was immediately interdicted after its release by Father Phelan's religious superiors for fear that its circulation would occasion unnecessary scandal and disgrace. The ravages of fire can bring about rarity too. William Gleeson's two volume *History of the Catholic Church in California* (San Francisco, 1872), a nondescript series of lectures delivered at St. Mary's College, is valuable only because of its scarcity. Initial enthusiasm for the work was minimal and few copies had been sold by April 28, 1886, when the largely intact press run was destroyed during a conflagration in Albert L. Bancroft's publishing firm at 723 Market Street in San Francisco.[13]

A fair scattering of generally accepted rare books has achieved that distinction for a number of reasons, any one of which would have more than sufficed. The classic example, of course, is the *Biblia Latina*. In addition to its being the first book printed with movable type, Johann Gutenberg's masterpiece is still regarded as the most beautiful version of the scriptures ever printed. It is also significant that only forty-seven of the originally printed 185 copies have been located.[14]

Antiquity, or the mere ability of the printed page to survive the passage of time, obviously cannot be the sole determining factor of a book's real worth.[15] Even with today's inflated prices, a copy of the *Supplementum Chronicarum*, published at Venice 1490 by James Philip Forrest, was recently offered for sale at the relatively reasonable sum of $95.[16] Nor is scarcity an infallible criterion. If there is no demand for a book, its value can remain totally unaffected by its paucity. Bishop John England's *The Roman Missal Translated into the English Lanquage for the Use of the Laity*

(New York, 1822) was the nation's first vernacular edition.[17] Though only six registered copies of the work could be located in the United States, this proto-American missal has become a collector's item only since the fairly recent revival of interest in liturgical studies. As late as 1955 a copy sold for the paltry sum of $5.[18]

A book's claim to rarity is notably enhanced when its provenance can be determined through bookplates, inscriptions, or other internal or external evidence. One of the several copies of the *Biblia Sacra* in the *Bibliotheca Montereyensis-Angelorum Dioceseos* can be traced from the time of its publication at Cologne in 1765. It bears the signature of Father Pedro González, O.P.,who came to the missions of Baja California prior to 1804. A further notation states: *"Mision Sti. Ygnatii de Loyola en Baja California, 1812."* The book was known to be at Santa Ines by 1845, which indicates that it was probably sent in response to Bishop Francisco Garcia Diego's plea for volumes to fill out the library of his newly inaugurated seminary.

The place and circumstances of publication can be crucial in fixing the value of a printed volume. Books bearing a Los Angeles imprint prior to 1853, for example, are exceedingly scarce, as are tomes published by short-lived firms which, for various reasons, occasionally released books under fictitious imprints.

When a book has been issued in several editions, such as Richard Henry Dana's popular *Two Years Before the Mast*, usually the first is the most desirable in terms of rarity. For instance, four hundred copies of Douglas S.Watson's *The Expedition into California of the Venerable Padre Fray Junípero Serra and His Companions in the Year 1769 as Told by Fray Francisco Palou* were printed, numbered, and signed as the initial publication of the Nueva California Press. A few minor alterations were made and then another thousand copies were run through the press, without the facsimile letters, and published as *The Founding of the First California Missions under the Spiritual Guidance of the Venerable Padre Fray Junípero Serra.*

There is an obvious distinction between the rare book and the fine one; though the terms can occasionally be predicated of the same volume, as is the case with certain publications issued by the private presses "in which all the elements in design, craftsmanship, and materials are beautiful in their own right and are combined harmoniously" in a production of surpassing artistry.[19]

A number of books are esteemed exclusively for their artistic embellishments. One much sought-after contributor to such works is Bernhardt Wall (1872-1956), whose individually signed etchings appear in a wide variety of titles published in the years after 1919. Locating his works and those of certain others is hampered because the books they adorn are invariably indexed under the author's name rather than that of the artist. An even more intricate artistic device is the fore-edge painting, a graphic art that flourished in England between 1775 and 1850. Tiny scenes, done mostly in watercolor, are applied to the front edges of a book while its leaves are secured in a fanned position. (The ultimate decoration, the "double" fore-edge painting, is today a completely lost art.)

Although the quality of a book's binding can increase its worth, most bibliophiles prefer an original in poor condition to an elaborately-tooled replacement. While the excellence of bindings is not usually a primary concern, even that feature cannot be dismissed as irrelevant inasmuch as the lack of a permanent cover often restricts the circulation of an otherwise valuable work. Very few libraries are equipped to provide for paper-covered or pamphletized publications.

Such features as the author's reputation, style, and competency, the tenor of his reviews, and the quality of his printed works often figure in the rarity of a volume. It has happened that books became rare for "reverse reasons," as is evident with Frederick Marryat's *Narrative Of Travels and Adventures of Monsieur Violet in California, Sonora and Western Texas*. The first edition of this fictionalized account is scarce despite the book's reputation for being "the worst novel that anyone ever wrote."[20]

Works dealing with popular themes, especially if they are issued in series form, are generally desirable. A complete set of Glen Dawson's *Early California Travel Series* is seldom seen on the market and same will be true of his current *Baja Travel Series*. It is worth noting that the initial volume in the latter series was issued in a press run of five hundred copies, while at least one other volume was printed in a quantity of 900. Those attempting to piece together a complete set in future years will probably find that the first volume has turned out to be the rarest of the series.[21]

Apart from their worth or rarity, books give man the choice of living islanded in his own personality or being free to examine the limitless horizons of time and space. Makers and sellers of books are his chief benefactors; the library is his servant and sampling-field. Borrowing, for the biblioplile, does not suffice. An anonymous writer long ago conceded that

> books that strike deep chords of response demand personal ownership with its sense of proprietorship in excellence. The presence of these books upon his shelves creates an agreeable, immediate weather for his spirit and at the same time acclimatizes him to the universe.

Notes to the Text

1. John Walton Caughey, "Rare Books and Research in History," *Rare Books and Research* (Los Angeles, 1951), p.34.
2. Henry Raup Wagner, "Remarks on Rare Books," *Rare Books and Research*, p. 14.
3. Lawrence Clark Powell, "Book Collectors and California Libraries," *California Library Bulletin*, XI (June, 1950), 163.
4. Phil Townsend Hanna, *Libros Californianos* (Los Angeles, 1958), p. 12.
5. James D. Hart, "Rare Books in the Public Library," *Quarterly News-Letter*, The Book Club of California, XXX (Winter, 1964), 7.
6. J.J. Peatfield, "The Bancroft Library," *Overland Monthly*, XXV (March, 1895), 274.
7. Phil Townsend Hanna as cited in Allen R. Ottley, "Collecting Californiana," *Quarterly News-Letter*, The Book Club of California, XXX (Spring, 1965), 35.
8. *One Rare Book* (Los Angeles, 1956), p. 3.
9. Wagner, *Sixty Years of Book Collecting* (Los Angeles, 1952), p. 48.
10. Also bound with this treatise was Doyle's The *Pious Fund Case. In the Matter of the Distribution of the Award. Fees of Counsel* (San Mateo, 1904).
11. See Francis J. Weber, "John Thomas Doyle, Pious Fund Historiographer," *Southern California Quarterly*, XLIX (September, 1967), 297-303.
12. Robert Dwyer, "Poet's Justice," *The Tidings* (Los Angeles), September 5, 1969.
13. Wagner "Albert Little Bancroft. His Diaries, Account Books, Card String of Events and Other Papers," *California Historical Society Quarterly*, XXIX (March, 1950), 99.
14. Twelve of the extant copies are printed on vellum, thirty-five on paper. See Weber, "Camarillo's Gutenberg Bible," *Catholic Library World* XL (October, 1968), 110-11.
15. Weber, "The High Spots of Californiana Historical Literature to 1835" *California Librarian*, XXIX (July, 1968), 198.
16. R. J. Hyland (Cataloguer), *Bennett & Marshall Catalogue No. 7. A Selection* (Los Angeles, 1968) p. 5, no. 28.
17. See Weber, "America's First Vernacular Missal," *American Ecclesiastical Review*, CLXI (July, 1969), 33-39.
18. Edward Lazare, *American Book-Prices. Current Index, 1950-1955* (New York, 1956), p. 993.
19. Robert 0. Schad, *Beauty in Books* (Los Angeles, 1935), no pagin.
20. George R. Stewart, "Dumas's *Gil Blas en Californie*," *California Historical Society Quarterly*, XIV (June, 1935), 137.
21. Actually, according to Mr. Dawson, this writer's own *Missions and Missionaries of Baja California* (1968), no. XI in the series, is now the most elusive of the lot.

70

This essay about the *Biblioteca Montereyensis-Angelorum Dioceseos* appeared in various forms. It is here reproduced from *The Book Collector* XX (Winter, 1971), 496-503.

Speaking about the Golden State's good fortune in having 'truly pious, excellent men' as "the original founders of Christianity in California", Alfred Robinson added the observation that their successors, generally, have endeavoured to sustain that honourable character.[1] What was true in the spiritual order, is no less demonstrable in the intellectual domain as can be seen in the fascinating story of a truly unique and significant library, gathered from the ashes of the mission era to rekindle the torch of learning for yet other generations.

Though it is essentially hybrid in origin. the *Bibliotheca Montereyensis-Angelorum Dioceseos*, amassed from existing missionary holdings in the early 1840s, once represented the foremost collection of California provincial tomes in existence. The books forming the nucleus of the library were those collected by Francisco Garcia Diego y Moreno for the seminary he initiated in several rooms of Mission Santa Barbara shortly after his arrival in the Channel City as Bishop of Both Californias.[2] Most of the tomes had been in the area for some time, but it was only in the years after 1842 that they found their way into the bishop's newly assembled theological library. The collection was moved from Santa Barbara in 1844, to quarters at close-by Santa Ines for the autonomous Seminary of Our Lady of Refuge.[3]

During its four decades at Santa Ines, the *Bibliotheca* was housed in a large room near the central part of the old mission building not far from

440

the two-story adobe occupied by the seminary.[4] When the institution's prospectus was broadened to include non-clerical students, the college was moved to another site about a mile and a half away on the vast 36,000 acre College Ranch. Students continued to have access to the books but the *Bibliotheca* was never transferred to the new location.[5] Undoubtedly many of the missing volumes were alienated during those years when distance militated against the effective management of the collection.

No descriptive check-list of the *Bibliotheca* has yet been discovered, though an inventory drawn up in 1853, fixes at 744 the number of volumes then belonging to the library.[6] Twenty one years later, the eminent historian, Hubert Howe Bancroft, visited Santa Ines and recorded seeing about 600 tomes in the collection[7] "among which were many sermons and a good stock of dictionaries."[8] In neither case was any distinction made between the books bound in vellum and those in leather and other materials.

During the 86 years after 1882, the *Bibliotheca* was placed in storage, first in Los Angeles and, later, at the archdiocesan major seminary, about 65 miles north-west of the Southern California metropolis. On 7 February 1968, this writer was authorized to re-activate the *Bibliotheca* and make it available to competent researchers. The tomes were removed to San Fernando and temporarily assembled in an unused room at Queen of Angels Seminary. Those volumes needing attention were cleaned, repaired and categorized, prior to being placed on permanent display in recently refurbished quarters of the adjacent San Fernando Mission.[9] Each volume was individually catalogued as to author, title, publication date and place, publisher, pagination, language, size and provenance. A code number was assigned to each entry, based respectively on tier, shelf and location, a system which allows researchers to locate items quickly while, at the same time, avoiding the necessity of defacing the spines with unbecoming call-letters.

The 875 distinct titles among the 1760 books of the *Bibliotheca Montereyensis-Angelorum Dioceseos* indicate a preponderance of sets and series-volumes. Unfortunately, what was once the largest and most complete library of mission-era tomes has suffered extensively from alienation and ill-care. Several dozen volumes were so broken and defaced that they had to be discarded altogether. A fair share of the others exhibit effects of water damage, probably traceable to their sojourn at 241 South Detroit Street in Los Angeles. About a hundred of the less scarred books wsre restored through the craftsmanship of Mr. Robert G. Cowan.

Considering their various backgrounds, the books have a remarkable similarity in format. Of the tomes presently associated with the

Bibliotheca, 613 are bound in sheepskin or faded vellum, while 1154 are encased in various kinds of less durable substances. Pieces of discarded manuscripts are in evidence in many of the books re-bound at an earlier date in California. The ornamental printing is usually executed on a superb quality of paper which often bears identifiable watermarks.

According to one authority, "the books the padres brought with them were understandably necessary or useful ones, professional in nature and utilitarian in purpose."[10] The wide range of subject matter emphasizes the need in provincial times for books encompassing a broad spectrum. Some dealt with Scripture, theology and homiletics, while others touched on history, music, medicine, agriculture, geography and architecture. Hence, thc books have been arranged into the ten categories commonly used by the 18th century librarians.[11] Thus divided, the 875 titles clearly form a well-rounded collection: 144 fall into Category A *(Asceticos, Místicos, Espirituales);* 109 into Category B *(Biblia, Sus Expositores y Concordancias);* 58 into Category D *(Derecho Canónigo, Civil y Regular);* 64 into Category F *(Filosofía, Matemáticas y Medicina);* 72 into Category H*(Historia Eclesíastica y Profana);* 86 into Category L *(Letras Humanas, Varia Educación);* 72 into Category M *(Moral, Casuístas);* 104 into Category P *(Predicables, Catequistas y Retórica);* 39 into Category S *(Los Santos Padres)* and 127 into Category T *(Teología Dogmática y Escolástica).*

By far, the largest number of the tomes bear publication dates in the 1700s. About a third were printed in the 1800s, while an even 100 were scattered between 1500 and 1699. Only 38 of the entries have no dates, this being due either to missing title-pages or lack of imprint.

The contrast in educational background between the friars trained in multilingual Europe and their confréres in the New World is highlighted from a scrutiny of the predominant languages represented. The hybrid nature of the library, for example, can be explained by noting that Bishop Francisco García Diego, born and reared in Mexico, obviously gravitated towards books printed in Spanish and Latin, the two languages with which he had personal familiarity. Over two-thirds of the collection fall into that category. French, Italian and English, in that order, account for only 251 of the 875 titles. Most of the books were issued from such European cities as Madrid, Barcelona, Rome, Paris, Cologne and Antwerp.

The obvious lacunae in the *Bibliotheca Montereyensis-Angelorum Dioceseos* would indicate to any knowledgeable bibliophile that at some time in its long and harrowing history, the library was relieved of its more precious tomes. The extreme measure of removing those titles which Father Joachim Adam claimed had 'no duplicates in existence'[12] might even be regarded as a *felix culpa* in the light of general neglect endured by the *Bibliotheca* at various times.

While the library may lack any volumes of excessive monetary worth, a random glance at the recently completed index indicates that it is rewarding in other ways. Take, for example, the historical value of inscriptions. A copy of the *Biblia Sacra*, printed at Cologne in 1765, bearing the signature of the Dominican, Father Pedro Gonzalez, and the further notation, *"Misión Sti. Ygnatii de Loyola en Baja California, 1812"*, confirms the reasonable assumption that many of the books brought to California came from the earlier established peninsular foundations. So also, inscriptions can be used to determine the date of a book's accession to the collection. A considerable number of tomes, though bearing imprints early enough to qualify them as charter additions to the *Bibliotheca*, were obviously assimilated in later decades. One such set is the 13-volume *Histoire Generale de L'Église* by the fiery French Ultramontane, Mathieu Richard-August Henrion (1805-62). This handsomely bound edition, published at Paris in 1841, bears a note indicating it was presented to the newly-consecrated Bishop of Monterey in late April of 1854:

> A Monseigneur Taddee Amat, Eveque de Monterey en Amerique. Offre ce petit souvenir, Son admirateur et ami Joachim Zluck, Carme Miss. Ap.,Prieur d l'Hopitil de Barcelona et nomme Regent de la Paroisse de St. Michel a Notre Dame de la Medir dans meme ville.

Another book, more noteworthy for its inscription than its contents, is Zacharia Laselue's *Annus Apostolicus*, published at Venice in 1755. Written across the title-page, in the hand of Fray Junípero Serra, is the notation: *'De la Misión de Sn. Carlos de Monte-Rey'*. Of the estimated 50 volumes on Carmel's shelves at the time of Serra's death, only about half bear the handwriting of the man who founded the California missions.[13]

The impressive *Monasticon Anglicanum* represents almost a lifetime of antiquarian research by William Dugdale (1605-86). It was 1655, 16 years after his initial commission by Sir Christopher Hatton, before the author was able to publish the first of his eight volumes of drafts and records about the monuments in the principal churches of the British Isles. Another of the relatively few English books is a 1782 edition of Lemtuel Gulliver's *Travels into several remote Nations of the World*, printed at Edinburgh. Evidence is strong that this book was one of the first tomes associated with the *Bibliotheca*.

A seven-volume theological treatise, probably used by Bishop Francis Mora in his seminary days, is *Divi Thomae Aquinatis Doctoris angelici praedicatorium summa Theologica*. Inside the opening page of Volume VII of this Madrid-published set is the note: *"Del Seminario Tridentino de Vich"*. Apparently, the originator of the *Bibliotheca Montereyensis-Angelorum Dioceseos* added his own books to the collection. One obvious example is Joseph Ignatius Claus's *Spicilegium Catechetico Concinatorium* (Venice 1773). The prelate personally wrote, *'Del simple uso del P. García Diego.'* Interestingly enough, a rubber-stamp bearing the words, "Cathedral of St. Vibiana", is also on the title-page.

That libraries of provincial times had circulation problems is indicated in a set of *Theologia moralis universa* by Paul-Gabriel Antoine (1679-1743). According to a notation in the first volume of the set, *"Este libro se halla en Cádiz en la libraría de Juan Ravet, Calle de San Francisco, Casa N. 69"*. How this vellum-bound set found its way to California cannot be determined, although the signature of Padre Francisco José Arróitia (d. 1821) may indicate that the friar brought the book with him when he came to the west in 1876. Another fugitive, *Conduite des Confesseurs* (Toulouse 1787), carries the label of the *Bibliotheca Selecta de Buenos Libros*, Valparaiso.

Easily the most precious item in the *Bibliotheca* is an incunabula written by Nicolaus de Ausmo, O.F.M. (d. 1453) and published by Leonardus Wild at Venice in 1479. The *Supplementum Summae Pisanellae*, a revised and increased edition of the 'Summa' of Bartholomew of San Concordio, pre-dates by a decade the tome previously considered 'the oldest published book as far as mission holdings go'.[14]

One cannot long work with and study the books associated with the libraries of provincial times without acquiring a deep-seated appreciation of the area's initial pioneers. Perhaps it was such a realization that prompted John F. Davis to note that "every Californian as he turns the pages of the early history of his State feels at times that he can hear the echo of the *Angelus* bell of the missions that are long dead and gone".[15]

Specific Characteristics of the Bibliotheca Montereyensis-Angelorum Dioceseos

LANGUAGES

(SHELF)	Fr.	Sp.	Lat.	Eng.	It.	Others	Total Titles	Total Vols
(1)	25	30	17	5	11	0	88	339
(2)	24	30	33	4	7	0	98	317
vellum (3)	0	59	78	0	10	0	147	268
vellum (4)	3	83	76	0	22	0	184	281
(5)	53	75	63	15	28	3	237	335
(6)	0	19	14	3	0	0	36	105
vellum (7)	28	5	10	1	1	0	45	64
vellum (8)	3	19	10	0	8	0	40	51
Totals	136	320	301	28	87	3	875	1760

CATEGORIES

(SHELF)	A	B	D	F	H	L	M	P	S	T	Total Titles	Total Vols
(1)	14	13	2	4	17	9	5	11	4	9	88	339
(2)	15	7	10	11	11	9	9	8	1	17	98	317
vellum (3)	17	5	14	5	7	13	20	23	6	37	147	268
vellum (4)	36	11	12	11	14	17	17	24	15	27	184	281
(5)	39	23	15	28	18	33	18	22	12	28	237	335
(6)	0	17	2	2	0	2	0	13	0	0	36	105
vellum (7)	3	27	1	2	2	3	1	1	0	5	45	64
vellum (8)	20	6	2	1	3	0	2	2	1	3	40	51
Totals	144	109	58	64	72	86	72	104	39	127	875	1760

Specific Characteristics of the Bibliotheca Montereyensis-Angelorum Dioceseos

PUBLICATION DATES

SHELF	n.d. Unk.	1500s	1600s	1700s	1800s	Total Titles	Total Vols
(1)	1	31	4	42	40	88	339
(2)	4	1	5	46	42	98	317
vellum (3)	4	6	30	98	9	147	268
vellum (4)	7	3	20	138	16	184	281
(5)	12	1	15	88	121	237	335
(6)	1	0	6	12	17	36	105
vellum (7)	2	1	2	31	9	45	64
vellum (8)	7	0	5	22	6	40	51
Totals	38	13	87	477	260	875	1760

Notes to the Text

1. *Life in California* (Oakland 1947), p. 47.
2. For the story of California's first seminary, see Francis J. Weber, *California's Reluctant Prelate* (Los Angeles 1964), pp. 139-47.
3. The name of the institution was changed in 1854 to the Seminary of Our Lady of Guadalupe.
4. Kurt Baer, *The Treasures of Mission Santa Ines* (Fresno 1956), p. 93.
5. William E. North, *Catholic Education in Southern California* (Washington 1936),p. 100.
6. J.N. Bowman, "Libraries in Provincial California" *Historical Society Of Southern California Quarterly* XLIII (December 1961), 432.
7. It was conjectured that another library of considerable importance, the *Bibliotheca Sancti Francisci Archdioceseos*, housed at St. Patrick's Seminary in Menlo Park, might have been part of the Santa Ines collection. A careful examination of the tomes at Menlo Park fails to substantiate that theory, however. Indications are that Archbishop Joseph Sadoc Alemany kept the Bay Area library completely separate from either the mission tomes at San Carlo Borromeo or the *Bibliotheca Montereyensis-Angelorum Dioceseos*.
8. 'Personal Observations,' p. 79. Access to this typewritten manuscript was graciously granted by the Bancroft Library at the University of California, Berkeley.
9. The books have no traceable relationship to the mission itself, though a number may well have belonged to San Fernando in earlier days. There was a *librería* of 191 volumes at the mission in 1835, valued at $417. Subsequent inventories indicate 50 volumes for 1838, and 216 in 1849. No evidence has been unearthed as to the fate of the library in post-secularization times.
10. Maynard J. Geiger, O.F.M., *The Story of California's First Libraries* (Santa Barbara 1964). p. 4.
11. See Maynard J. Geiger, O.F.M., "The Library of the Apostolic College of San Fernando, Mexico, in the Eighteenth and Nineteenth Centuries," *The Americas VII* (April 1951), 430-3.
12. "Rare Old Books in the Bishop's Library", *Historical Society of Southern California Annual IV* (1899), 155.
13. James Culleton, "California's First Library", *Central California Register* (Annual Review 1933), pp. 3-5.
14. Doyce B. Nunis, Jr., *Books in their Sea Chests: Readings Along the Early California Coast* (n.p., 1964), p. 23.
15. "Sources of California History", *Transactions of the Commonwealth Club of California VIII* (July 1913), 315.

71

The story of *"The Biblioteca Sancti Francisci Archdioceseos"* is here taken from the *California Librarian* XXX (January, 1969), 28-29.

One of the most intriguing book collections in California, long housed at Saint Patrick's Seminary in Menlo Park, has recently been catalogued and made available to competent researchers.[1] Though not associated with the mission period of the Golden State's history, many of the tomes predate that era by well over two centuries.

In a description of the *Bibliotheca Sancti Francisci Archdioeceseos* made in 1878, Flora Haines Apponyi noted that "in the library of J. S. Alemany, Archbishop of California, at San Francisco, there are two thousand seven hundred and fifty volumes, consisting principally of various versions and editions of the holy bible, commentaries on the same, the writings of the fathers and doctors of the church, bullarisms, canon law, theology, history, liturgy and the classics."[2] There are presently 1612 tomes in the *Bibliotheca* under 621 separate titles. In addition to an undisclosed number of volumes accessioned into the active seminary library, a fair proportion of the books have been lost, borrowed and otherwise alienated in the ninety years since the appearance of the Apponyi treatise.

The origin of the library can be traced to August 8, 1850, when Bishop Joseph Sadoc Alemany, newly appointed to the See of Monterey, recorded in his diary that he had shipped a large parcel of his personal books from Marseilles to California.[3] Indications are that the prelate kept the volumes at his residence in Monterey until 1853, when he moved to San Francisco as the area's first metropolitan archbishop.

Whether the tomes were placed at Mission Dolores, where the archbishop opened Saint Thomas Seminary, is only a conjecture. In any case, clerical aspirants surely had access to the valuable library during their years of training in the Bay City. Sometime after January 15, 1883, the *Bibliotheca Sancti Francisci Archdioceseos* was moved to the seminary inaugurated at Mission San Jose. There it remained until the opening in Menlo Park of Saint Patrick's shortly before the turn of the century. A brochure issued in 1898 notes that "the shelves of our Library already contained a few thousand volumes–the greater number purchased; the remainder coming from the Old Seminary at Mission San Jose, or donated by His Grace the Most Reverend Archbishop."

While some of the more basic volumes were integrated into the general students' library, the *Bibliotheca* seems to have remained a seldom-used, autonomous collection. With the passage of the decades, it gradually became more of an historical oddity than a useful source of information. Most recently, upon the completion of the McKeon Memorial Library at Saint Patrick's, the *Bibliotheca* was placed in its present location, in two caged-compartments on the upper level of the stack area.

This writer, with the assistance of Mr. Paul Kelly, has completed cataloguing the old library, many of whose volumes bear the inscription, "Joseph Sadoc Alemany, O.P." or *"Diocesis Sancti Francisci"* in the archbishop's own hand. Books were classified into a series of ten categories based on subject matter. Each volume was assigned a code number, based respectively on tier, shelf and location. The system allows researchers to locate titles quickly, while at the same time, avoiding the necessity of defacing the spines with unbecoming call-letters.

History, theology, and humane letters, in that order, account for the greatest number of titles. Well over a third of books were printed in Latin, with French, Italian, English, and Spanish following in descending order. The oldest book in the *Bibliotheca* is a *SACRATISSIMA*, printed at Venice in 1514. Of the 621 titles, 187 bear publication dates in the 1800's, 296 in the 1700's, 94 in the 1600's, and 25 in the 1500's. The year of publication cannot be determined in nineteen instances. About a third of the collection is bound in faded, but fairly well-preserved vellum.

By making the *Bibliotheca Sancti Francisci Archdioceseos* once again accessible to scholars, the seminary authorities affirm John Henry Newman's dictum that "it is our duty to live among books."

Biblioteca Sancti Francisci Archdioceseos

Notes to the Text

1. See J.N. Bowman, "Libraries in Provincial California," *Historical Society of Southern California Quarterly*, XLIII (December 1961), 433.
2. Flora Haines Apponyi, *The Libraries of California* (San Francisco: A. L. Bancroft Company, 1878), p. 228.
3. Francis J. Weber, ed., "The Long Lost Ecclesiastical Diary of Archbishop Alemany," *California Historical Society Quarterly* XLVI (December 1964), 321.

72

This essay about "A Governor's Literary Legacy" is taken from *Coranto* IX (1973), 32-34.

Carlos Antonio Carrillo (1783-1852) belonged to that family which "must be considered in several respects the leading one in California, by reason of the number and prominence of its members and of their connection by marriage with so many of the best families, both native and pioneer."[1] Though a man of many distinctions, Carlos Antonio is chiefly remembered by bibliophiles for his authorship of "the first work issued in printed form of any native Californian."[2] The story behind that now-rare treatise is worth recalling.

During his years of service in the military, Carrillo achieved the enviable rank of *soldado distinguido*. It came as no surprise when this brother-in-law of José de la Guerra entered the political arena as a member of the *diputación*, or departmental assembly, in 1827. His election to the Mexican Congress three years later brought to the Distrito Federal an ardent defender of provincial interests.

Shortly after arriving at his new post, Carrillo plunged into the heated debate raging in the Chamber of Deputies about proposals to dispose of the properties belonging to the Pious Fund of the Californias. Revenues had dwindled to practically nothing in the years since 1811, and sentiment was strong to sell the holdings and turn the proceeds over to the public treasury. Carrillo argued convincingly that Mexico was obligated in justice not only to perpetuate the wishes of the original donors towards support and extension of the missions, but to increase the productivity of the trust estate.

In an impassioned speech delivered before the chamber on September 15, 1831, Carlos Antonio exerted all his considerable influence and eloquence towards forestalling any deviation from the traditional aims of the Pious Fund. Sensing the mentality of the moment, the gifted orator reminded his listeners that even had the missions done no more than prepare the savage tribes for civilization, they would have achieved their primary purpose. He pointed out the vast dichotomy discernible between the natives of California's interior regions and those attached to the Franciscan missions.

Carrillo also drew attention to the obvious fact that California, already coveted by other nations, could not be held indefinitely without greater governmental concern for those missionary institutions which had made possible the initial opening of "that faraway province." His address "developed into a veritable panegyric which, though richly deserved, must have appeared a strange novelty where, as among the bawling Californians, denunciation of friars had been the fashion."[3]

The talented legislator's observations were so well received that he consented to have his argument "permanized" for future reference by members of the various congressional delegations. The text was set into type in the establishment of C. Alejandro Valdés and released near the end of 1831 as *Exposición Dirigida á la Cámara de Diputados del Congreso de la Union por el Sr. D. Carlos Antonio Carrillo, Diputado por la Alta California, sobre Arreglo y Administración del Fondo Piadoso.* That the sixteen-page monograph, measuring eighteen centimeters by fifteen, was effective became obvious when thirteen of its proposals were incorporated into the Law of May 25, 1832.[4] By the provisions of that measure, the estates of the Pious Fund were to be rented for terms not exceeding seven years, and the revenues devoted exclusively to the missions.

Unfortunately, as Hubert Howe Bancroft observed, "the victory was a barren one, for the missions derived little or no benefits" from the legislation.[5] Carrillo ultimately proved to be "of passing conservative influence in an historic process which moved inevitably toward liberalism, the disintegration of Mexico, and the regime of the Yankee in California."[6]

Copies of Carrillo's intervention were apparently never very plentiful, and by 1931 Robert E. Cowan regarded *the Exposición* as one of the "twenty rarest and most important books dealing with the history of California."[7] The work was also included in the *Zamorano 80.*[8]

In 1938, Herbert Ingram Priestley translated the *Exposición* into English and issued it, together with his own lengthy and enlightening historical introduction, as the *Exposition Addressed to the Chamber of*

Deputies of the Congress of the Union by Señor Don Carlos Antonio Carrillo, Deputy for Alta California Concerning the Regulation and Administration of the Pious Fund. Six hundred and fifty copies of the fifteen-page opus, artistically embellished by William F. Rauschnabel, were printed at San Francisco by John Henry Nash.

Glancing at this most prominent of his literary contributions,[9] one is inclined to recall the wish with which the Governor of California concluded his inaugural address in 1837: that "some day over my sepulchre you will shed a tear to the memory of your friend and fellow citizen, Carlos Antonio Carrillo."[10]

Notes to the Text

1. Hubert Howe Bancroft as quoted by Brian McGinty, "The Carrillos of San Diego: A Historic Spanish Family of California," *Historical Society of Southern California Quarterly*, XXXIX (March, 1957),3-4.
2. Robert Ernest Cowan, *A Bibliography of the History of California and the Pacific West, 1510-1906* (San Francisco, 1914), p. 42.
3. Zephyrin Engelhardt, O.F.M., *The Missions and Missionaries of California* (San Francisco, 1913), III, 404.
4. See *Ley y Reglamento Aprobado de la Junta Directiva y Economica del Fondo Piadoso de Californias* (México, 1833).
5. *History of California* (San Francisco, 1886), III, 313.
6. Herbert Ingram Priestley (trans. and ed.), *Exposition Addressed to the Chamber of Deputies of the Congress of the Union by Señor Don Carlos Antonio Carrillo, Deputy for Alta California Concerning the Regulation and Administration of the Pious Fund* (San Francisco, 1938), p. xiv.
7. "The Twenty Rarest and Most Important Works Dealing with the History of California," *California Historical Society Quarterly*, X (March, 1931), 82.
8. Published by the Zamorano Club (Los Angeles, 1945), pp. 11-12.
9. Carrillo also authored the even rarer (three known extant copies!) *Exposición que el Diputado de la Alta California Ciudadano Carlos Antonio Carrillo Hace á la Cámara de Diputados...para su Administración de Justicia* (México, 1831) wherein he attempted to convince the Mexican Congress to provide California with its own judiciary. This intervention, an essential source for comprehending early Mexican California's maladministration of justice, is reproduced in *The Coming of Justice to California: Three Documents* (San Francisco, 1963).
10. Quoted in Robert Glass Cleland, *From Wilderness to Empire* (New York, 1954), p.118.

73

This study on "John Thomas Doyle [Pious Fund Historiographer]" is here reproduced from the *Southern California Quarterly* XLIX (September, 1967), 297-303.

Rarely in California annals does one run across a more "successful and happy combination of a tenacious and expert lawyer, an astute business man, a scholar of the classics and of history, and a family man"[1] than in the person of John Thomas Doyle.

Doyle was born on November 26, 1819, at the family's residence atop his father's bookstore, 237 Broadway, New York City. Not long after, the youngster was taken by his parents, John and Frances (Glinden) Doyle, to Ireland where he was subsequently enrolled at Burrell Hall, a fashionable academy in Kilkenny.

After returning to the United States, John pursued his studies at Columbia Grammar School and Georgetown College, graduating as valedictorian from the latter institution in 1838. Doyle practiced law in New York between 1842 and 1851, when he chanced to meet Cornelius Vanderbilt during a trip to Nicaragua. When the commodore offered Doyle a position in his Atlantic and Pacific Company, the youthful lawyer moved to Central America. While in Nicaragua, Doyle built the transit road from the lake to the Pacific and organized the trans-Atlantic service between the two oceans.

In the winter of 1852-53, Doyle emigrated to San Francisco and resumed his legal career. There he married Antonia Pons[2] and plunged himself into the mainstream of California activities. In the Golden State,

453

"the eminence of John T. Doyle as a lawyer and a public spirited and most valuable citizen of his time is generously conceded by historians, and also by official records!"[3]

After helping to lay the legal foundation for the government of the University of California, Doyle accepted a position on the institution's first Board of Regents. He also served as trustee of the San Francisco Law Library for thirty years and, for a brief period, in 1877-78, was a State Commissioner of Transportation.

The interests of the New York-born jurist were not reserved to the local level. He was, for example, deeply interested in Irish affairs and publicly expressed misgivings about the wisdom of absolute independence for the Emerald Isle. In this area, as in others, Doyle exhibited his typically epigrammatic approach, noting that Ireland had done more than her part in building up the British Empire and was fully entitled to a proportionate share in the benefits reaped therefrom.

Though he was often formidably antagonistic in his legal career, Doyle preferred the simple life he enjoyed in the seclusion of his family at Menlo Park. The historian, Hubert Howe Bancroft, noted that this gentleman "has been, since the early days of this state, a very conspicuous and reputable jurist; recognized not only among the ablest lawyers of the coast, but as one who can be depended upon to maintain the honor and dignity of the bar; and withal, a scholar of rare culture and refinement."[4]

John Doyle was, indeed, a man of considerable intellectual attainment. This fact is attested to by another contemporary who recorded that Doyle had a "keen appreciation of the very best of everything. His library is a wonderful repository of varied lore. In the rarity and beauty as well as the value of its volumes, it has few parallels."[5] Doyle's books have been acknowledged as the first notable, outstanding collection of materials on the prestate history of California, particularly regarding the missions.[6] The noted jurist was not only a reader of history; he was generally considered pre-eminent among early California historians. One observer felt "there was no man in California better informed on the early history of the State than he."[7]

It was his keen sense of the importance and value of original documents that prompted Doyle's call[8] for the formation of "a California or Pacific Historical Society, whose object it shall be to collect, preserve, and from time to time make public the interesting records of our early colonial history."[9] Soon thereafter, Doyle's advice was heeded and the California Historical Society was organized[10] with the advocate as its first president. During his tenure, Doyle encouraged the publication of several important tomes. In 1874, he personally edited Father Francisco Palóu's *Noticias*[11] and a while later the *Reglamento para el Gobierno de la Provincia de California.*[12]

In his later years, Mr. Doyle became a respected authority in viniculture, spending much time at the Cupertino vineyards in Santa Clara County, where he experimented on a disease-resistant type of grapevine. John Thomas Doyle died on December 23, 1906, "leaving a large family, to whom he bequeathed a comfortable independence, an an unblemished record of a long and an honorable life."[13]

* * *

The Pious Fund

When Doyle arrived in San Francisco, he came at a time when Anglo-Americans were eagerly taking advantage of the unsettled conditions resulting from the recent transfer of sovereignty from Mexico to the United States. Since he had "preserved his familiarity with the Latin classics" and had "acquired after leaving school, the French and Spanish languages, with a reading knowledge of Italian,"[14] he was eagerly sought as an adviser in complicated land cases. His competence was further enhanced from his years in Nicaragua where he had done considerable research on Spanish colonial history.[15]

Though his talents spread over a wide range of activities,[16] John Doyle's importance to students of the Golden State's historiography center mostly around his position as legal counselor to Archbishops Joseph Sadoc Alemany and Patrick William Riordan on the famous case of the Pious Fund of the Californias.[17] During the fifty years he worked on the case, Doyle wrote any number of historical accounts about the complicated litigation he initiated to affect a settlement between the Catholic Church and the Republic of Mexico.

A glance over the titles listed below serves to confirm the statement that "without John Thomas Doyle there would have been no Pious Fund Case."[18] Seldom have a man and a cause been so closely associated.

1. *THE ARCHBISHOP AND BISHOPS OF THE R. C. CHURCH OF CALIFORNIA, JOSEPH S. ALEMANY, ET AL. VS. THE REPUBLIC OF MEXICO* (San Francisco, July 12, 1875). 38 pp.
Presents the arguments on behalf of the plaintiffs before the umpire.

2. *AS TO THE DIVISION OF THE FEES IN THE PIOUS FUND CASE* (n.p., 1878). 55 pp.
Only twenty copies were printed of this treatise outlining the author's disagreement with Eugene Casserly.

3. *BEFORE THE PERMANENT ARBITRAL COURT UNDER THE HAGUE CONVENTION. THE CASE OF THE PIOUS FUND OF THE CALIFORNIAS. POINTS SUBMITTED BY COUNSEL FOR THE PRELATES* (Menlo Park, August, 1902). 28 pp.
This presentation is mostly an elaboration on the favorable decision handed down by the Mixed Land Commission on November 11, 1875. It was drawn up in collaboration with W.T. Sherman Doyle and later re-printed in Jackson H. Ralston, *Foreign Relations of the United States, 1902, Appendix II* (Washington, 1903), pp. 262-281.

4. *BRIEF HISTORY OF THE "PIOUS FUND" OF CALIFORNIA* (San Francisco, 1870). 20 pp.
This digest version, apparently prepared as background for the initial hearings of the Mixed Land Commission, was reprinted with minor variations in the *Woodstock Letters*, XXXI (October, 1902), 223-234.

5. *DEPOSITION OF MR. JOHN T. DOYLE WITH EXHIBITS* (San Mateo, August 26, 1902). 24 pp.
This resume of the author's long-time association with the case appears also in Jackson H. Ralston, *ut supra*, pp. 399-421.

6. *"HISTORY OF THE PIOUS FUND OF CALIFORNIA" Papers of the California Historical Society, I* (1887), 41-60.
A corrected version of the author's earlier *BRIEF HISTORY OF THE "PIOUS FUND" OF CALIFORNIA* (q.v.), this treatise was issued also in monograph form by Bosqui Engraving and Printing Co. (San Francisco, 1887).

7. *IN THE INTERNATIONAL ARBITRAL COURT OF THE HAGUE. THE CASE OF THE PIOUS FUND OF CALIFORNIA* (San Francisco, 1906), Geo. F. Spaulding and Co., Printers. 106 pp.
The Doyle family rigidly suppressed this book because of its generally unfavorable treatment of Archbishop Patrick W Riordan.

8. *MEMORANDUM FOR HON. ASSISTANT SECRETARY OF STATE, AS TO THE CLAIM OF THE R. C. CHURCH OF CALIFORNIA AGAINST THE REPUBLIC OF MEXICO, FOR ARREARS OF INTEREST, OR THE PROCEEDS OF THE PIOUS FUND OF CALIFORNIA* (Menlo Park, October 2, 1897). 6 pp.
This work subsequently appeared in *Diplomatic Correspondence Between the United States and the Republic of Mexico Relative to the "Pious Fund of the Californias"* (Washington, 1902), pp. 18-21.

9. *MEMORIAL....AGAINST THE REPUBLIC OF MEXICO, ON BEHALF OF THE ROMAN CATHOLIC CHURCH OF THE STATE OF CALIFORNIA, AND OF ITS CLERGY AND LAITY AND ALL PERSONS ACTUALLY OR POTENTIALLY WITHIN ITS FOLD AND ENTITLED TO ITS MINISTRATION, AND ALL OTHERS BENEFICIALLY INTERESTED IN THE TRUST ESTATE HEREINAFTER MENTIONED AND REFERRED TO* (San Francisco, December 28, 1870). 14 pp.
This treatise, prepared partly by Nathaniel Wilson, was later reissued in the *Transcript of Record of Proceedings before the Mexican and American Mixed Claims Commission with Relation to "The Pious Fund of the Californias"* (Washington, 1902), pp.9-15.

10. *MEMORIAL OF THE CLAIM OF THE UNITED STATES OF AMERICA AGAINST THE REPUBLIC OF MEXICO* (n.p., n.d.). 13 pp.
This resume of the claim, drawn up in conjunction with W. T. Sherman Doyle, also appeared in Jackson H. Ralston, *ut supra, pp.* 21-29. A Spanish version was later released in *Reclamacion del Gobierno de los Estados Unidos de America Contra Mexico Respeto del Fondo Piadoso de las Californias* (Mexico, 1903), pp. 10-23.

11. *OBSERVATIONS ON THE ANSWER OF MEXICO TO THE MEMORIAL OF THE UNITED STATES* (San Francisco, September 18, 1902). 11 pp.
W. T. Sherman Doyle collaborated in writing this treatise which was reproduced in Jackson H. Ralston, *ut supra*, pp. 335-340.

12. *OBSERVATIONS ON THE LETTER OF HIS EXCELLENCY DON IGNACIO MARISCAL, TO HON. POWELL CLAYTON, UNITED STATES AMBASSADOR TO MEXICO, DATED DECEMBER 14, 1900* (Menlo Park, February 22, 1901). 12 pp.

This rejoinder, co-authored by W.T. Sherman Doyle, was subsequently incorporated in *Diplomatic Correspondence, ut supra, pp.* 58-66.

13. *OBSERVATIONS ON THE REPLY OF HIS EXCELLENCY, DON IGNACIO MARISCAL, MINISTER OF FOREIGN AFFAIRS OF THE MEXICAN REPUBLIC, TO THE NOTE OF HON. POWELL CLAYTON, U.S. MINISTER AT MEXICO, OF SEPTEMBER 1st, 1897, RELATING TO THE CLAIM OF THE CATHOLIC CHURCH OF CALIFORNIA AGAINST THE MEXICAN REPUBLIC FOR ARREARS OF INTEREST ON THE PIOUS FUND OF THE CALIFORNIAS* (Menlo Park, December, 1897). 8 pp.

14. *THE PIOUS FUND CASE. IN THE MATTER OF THE DISTRIBUTION OF THE AWARD. FEES OF COUNSEL* (San Mateo, February 12, 1904). 67 pp.
    This book was bound into certain copies of the author's *IN THE INTERNATIONAL ARBITRAL COURT OF THE HAGUE. THE CASE OF THE PIOUS FUND OF CALIFORNIA (q.v.).*

15. *"THE PIOUS FUND OF CALIFORNIA," The Overland Monthly,* XVI (September, 1890), 232-242.
    An almost identical reprint of the 1887 article in *Papers of the California Historical Society, (q.v.).*

16. *"RECOVERY OF THE PIOUS FUND," History of the Bench and Bar of California* (Los Angeles, 1901), The Commercial Printing House, pp. 81-91.
    One of a group of treatises released under the editorship of Oscar T Shuck.

17. *THE R. C. ARCHBISHOP AND BISHOPS OF CALIFORNIA, JOSEPH S. ALEMANY, ET AL. VS. THE MEXICAN REPUBLIC* (San Francisco, January 2, 1872). 41 pp.
    Presents the arguments against the motion to dismiss the case. This defense is reproduced in *Transcript, ut supra,* pp.80-99.

18. *THE R.C. ARCHBISHOP AND BISHOPS OF CALIFORNIA, JOSEPH S. ALEMANY, ET AL. VS. THE MEXICAN REPUBLIC* (San Francisco, January 1, 1875). 32 pp.
    The plaintant's reply was included in *Transcript, ut supra,* pp. 462-477

19. *SOME ACCOUNT OF THE PIOUS FUND OF CALIFORNIA AND THE LITIGATION TO RECOVER IT* (San Francisco, 1880), Edward Bosqui and Co., Printers.

A compilation by the editor of "as many copies of the printed papers, as my materials afforded–from twenty-five to forty in all, some more some less complete–for deposit in public libraries." Probably less than twenty sets were actually issued.

Notes to the Text

1. Kenneth M. Johnson, *The Pious Fund* (Los Angeles, 1963), p. 30.
2. Antonia (1836-1910) was a native of Lyons, France.
3. Thomas F. Prendergast, *Forgotten Pioneers* (San Francisco, 1942), p. 194.
4. *History of California* (7 vols., San Francisco, 1884-1890), VII, 177.
5. Oscar T. Shuck, *Bench and Bar in California* (San Francisco, 1889), p. 121.
6. See John T Doyle, "The Missions of Alta California," *The Century Illustrated Monthly Magazine*, XLI (January, 1891), 389-402. This opus was subsequently reprinted at San Francisco in 1893 as *The California Missions.*
7. Richard C. O'Connor, "John T Doyle," *The Journal of the American Irish Historical Society*, XI (1912), 148.
8. Occasion was a speech delivered on August 9, 1870. *Cf.* John T Doyle, *Address Delivered at the Inauguration of the New Hall of Santa Clara College* (San Francisco, 1870).
9. "California Historical Society, 1852-1922," *California Historical Society Quarterly*, (July, 1922), 11.
10. The present California Historical Society traces its beginnings only to 1922.
11. The four volumes, issued in one hundred numbered sets, carried the title *Noticias de la Nueva California.* Doyle wrote the foreword to this now-rare edition.
12. There were only 150 copies published at Santa Clara in 1874 and most of them were subsequently destroyed by fire. *See Papers of the California Historical Society*, I (1887), xxi.
13. *The Monitor,* January 27, 1902.
14. Oscar T. Shuck, *History of the Bench and Bar of California* (Los Angeles, 1901), p. 519.
15. It was while in Nicaragua that Doyle pointed out the similarity between the constitution of the Venetian Court and that of Nicaragua. This he did in an article entitled "Shakespeare's Law–the Case of Shylock," in the *Overland Monthly*, VIII (July, 1886), 83-87.
16. Doyle was something of a pamphleteer. Among his writings are *A Letter to the President of the United States* (New York, 1860) and *Railroad Policy of California* (San Francisco, 1873). An interesting address he delivered to the American Antiquarian Society in October of 1873 was later published as *Memorandum As to the Discovery of the Bay of San Francisco* (Worcester, 1874).
17. Long recognized as the most outstanding legal case in the Golden State's annals, the Pious Fund was a charitable trust formed by generous Catholics anxious to further the conversion and civilization of Indians in the Californias. In 1842, the holdings of the Fund were secularized by the Mexican Government and incorporated into the national treasury. It was John Thomas Doyle who gathered and prepared the evidence used in the two successful court battles by the Church to gain yearly annuities from Mexico. A definitive solution to the ninety-two-year-old litigation was finally reached in August of 1967 whereby the United States Secretary of State, acting on behalf of the Archbishop of San Francisco and those parties he represented, waived perpetuity in exchange for a lump sum payment.
18. Johnson, *The Pious Fund*, p. 23.

74

"John Steven McGroarty" is the title of this essay taken from *The Journal of San Diego History* XX (Fall, 1974), 33-37.

In a eulogy for John Steven McGroarty, delivered on the floor of the United States House of Representatives, Congressman Jerry Voorhis said that "no man has caught the spirit of California from the beginning…of the Spanish *padres* down to the present time and gathered it together into one continuous thread such as this great man has done."

John Steven McGroarty was born near Wilkes-Barre, in Foster Township, Pennsylvania, on August 20, 1862, just a month before the issuance of Abraham Lincoln's Emancipation Proclamation. He took great pride in his ancestry and often recalled that the McGroartys of Donegal were kinsmen of Columbkille. John's father, Hugh McGroarty, was a grand-nephew of Richard Montgomery, one of George Washington's generals who died in the ill-fated Quebec Expedition of 1776.

Upon completion of elementary courses in the parochial and public schools of Wilkes-Barre, John taught for two years. As soon as he was financially solvent, he completed his education at the Harry Hillman Academy. His erudition and native talents won for young McGroarty a teacher's credential before he had reached his seventeenth birthday. Following his graduation from the Hillman Academy, where he took advanced studies in journalism, John joined the staff of the Wilkes-Barre *Evening Leader,* and quickly advanced to the managing editorship.

On November 19, 1890, shortly after a successful campaign for Treasurer of Luzerne County, John married his childhood sweetheart,

Ida Caroline Lubrecht (1866-1940). Three years later, he became, again by popular suffrage, Justice of the Peace, the youngest man ever to occupy that post in Pennsylvania. It was also in 1893 that the thirty-one year old McGroarty began reading law. He was admitted to the State Bar in 1894. Just before the turn of the century, the McGroartys journeyed to Butte, Montana, where John served on the legal staff of the nation's "Copper King," Marcus Daly, at the Anaconda Mining Company. McGroarty neither excelled in nor cared for the legal profession, and upon Daly's death, he resumed his journalistic career.

When, in 1901, John was offered employment with the San Francisco *Chronicle,* the McGroartys decided to dispose of their possessions and begin life anew in faraway California. Providentially, they stopped enroute in Los Angeles, just at the time that Friedrich Alfred Krupp, the munitionsmaker, had passed away. John expressed his reactions to that event in verse and, at the insistence of his wife, he submitted the poem to the city editor of the Los Angeles *Times.* Those poetic lines. which proved to be the changing point in his life, appeared in the next day's edition of the paper:

Dead! and the belching thunder
   Of the guns on sea and shore
Though they rend the world asunder,
   Can break on his ears no more.

Forth from his hands he sent them,
   Wherever men met as foes;
And wherever strong hands unbent them,
   The cry of the wounded rose.

The groans of the maimed and dying,
   The moans of the ebbing heart
On the fields of the dead, low lying,
   Were praise of his master art.

Wherever the ocean's billows
   The ships of the fleet have sped,
Deep over the coral pillows.
   Where the wild seas keep their dead.

Wherever, in rush or rally,
   Man crashed in the strife with man.
In Paardeberg's war-strewn valley,
   Or the red heights of Sedan.

Death and blood and disaster
  Spoke his great name in dread;
And now in his shroud, the master
  That fashioned the guns, lies dead.

The day after the poem appeared, General Harrison Gray Otis summoned the surprised McGroarty to his office and offered him a permanent position on the editorial staff of *The Times*. Though his political views differed widely from those of his publisher, John Steven McGroarty became the "whitehaired boy" of *The Times*. During most of his more than forty years of association with that newspaper, he wrote a daily column "From the Green Verdugo Hills."

Always a dedicated man of principles, McGroarty considered journalism among the most vital and necessary forces within society. He once noted that in a newspaper, "there is a dignity which is its grandeur; the sincerity which is its truth; the thoroughness which is its massive substance; the sterling principle which is its force; the virtue which is its purity; the scholarship, mind, humor, taste, versatile aptitude of simulation and beautiful grace of method which are its powerful and delightful faculties and attributes."

Late in 1904, shortly after purchasing *The Tidings* and making it the official Catholic newspaper for the Diocese of Monterey-Los Angeles, Bishop Thomas J. Conaty offered the editorship to McGroarty. The journalist declined the position, telling the bishop that "Catholic journalists could do more for their religion as contributors to secular papers."

Demanding as he made it, journalism failed to exhaust McGroarty's potential and his manifold talents found abundant expression in a host of other literary enterprises. Timely articles under his signature began appearing in such prominent journals as *The Southwest Magazine*. Between 1906 and 1914, John edited the *West Coast Magazine* for the Grafton Publishing Company. In addition to an impressive array of historical and poetical publications, the industrious McGroarty composed numerous promotional books and magazines, some of which are now highly-prized "fugitives" among collectors and librarians of Western Americana.

Though his volume *California, Its History and Romance* went through ten editions in only thirteen years, McGroarty was not and never claimed to be a serious historian or an original scholar. His style was "folksy" and concentrated on the pageantry and glamor associated with the discovery, colonization and early development of the far west.

It was beneath the shadow of the cross erected in memory of Fray Junípero Serra, atop Mount Rubidoux, that McGroarty thought out and set to words his immortal *Mission Play*, in 1912. That fascinating portrayal about the inauguration of Christianity on the western shores of America was, according to Vice President Thomas R. Marshall, a classical blending of historical accuracy with dramatic imagination. It went through 3,268 performances and was seen by more than 200,000 persons. The acid-tongued Lady Gregory, co-founder of the Abbey Theatre, saw the play and remarked that it was "the only thing I have seen in America worth remembering!"

In 1923, John and Ida built their home, Rancho Chupa Rosa, in the solitude of the Verdugo Hills. Characteristically, McGroarty hung three portraits in his study, bearing the likenesses of Bishop John J. Cantwell, George Washington and Robert Louis Stevenson. "Those pictures," he once said, "symbolize my ideals of the spiritual and political and literary."

McGroarty long harbored plans for establishing, for his own century, a missionary outpost patterned after those of the Franciscan friars in earlier times. His "twenty-second" mission was to have been located in a glen at the foot of the Verdugos. Developer N.V. Hartranft set aside an acre of Oak Grove Park as the site of the proposed foundation and announced plans for its construction in the Tujunga *Record-Ledger*, in 1923.

In its tenth anniversary edition, the newspaper proclaimed that "the plan of the author of the Mission Play to add a new Franciscan mission to the great chain that was founded by Fray Junípero Serra and his brown-robed priests and to build it this summer at Tujunga may be properly classed as a non-sectarian project, for men and women of all creeds and faiths are rallying to his aid with offers of assistance." The account went on to say that "the ceremonies attending its founding will be a reproduction of the great and colorful pageants that marked the founding of the old missions in the days of the Spanish occupation."

For reasons yet-to-be-explored, the high hopes and elaborate plans for San Juan Evangelista, once envisioned as the capstone of the California missions, never materialized. Had things gone differently, the entire economic, cultural and social climate of the Valley very likely would have been changed, no doubt for the better.

In 1934, McGroarty decided that he could more effectively serve the general public, whose poet laureate he had been since May 15, 1933, in the legislative halls of the nation's capital. Running as a Townsendite Democrat, McGroarty handily won election to the 74th and 75th Congress, for California's eleventh district. For a brief moment,

McGroarty cast a fond glance at the White House. According to a news-story in the Los Angeles *Times*, McGroarty "tossed his fedora in the ring" as a full-fledged candidate for the United States Presidency, on February 15, 1936, as a candidate for the Townsendite Party.

California's poet laureate served in the House of Representatives from 1935 to 1939, when he retired from public service. At the time of McGroarty's departure from Washington, John E. King, editor of the Hemet *News* lauded him "as author of the Mission Play, as friend and comforter to the Indians, as almoner to the weak and weary of every race and clime, as friend and guide to the oppressed and the downtrod-den." King went on to say that "we think of his work in the halls of Congress; of his efforts for the silent masses of the downcast and dis-couraged, too often without a friend in the courts of the mighty. In all his varied labors he has given the strength of a great enthusiasm, the charm of a great idealism. From his endeavors has come little of materi-al wealth, but in the hearts of his countrymen there is the gold of love and esteem, of sincere appreciation."

The retired Congressman returned to the Verdugo Hills, where he rejoiced at being "alive and well from aches and pains, busy with the day's work, still fit to earn a living, and no fault to find with the way Fate has dealt with me."

John Steven McGroarty was honored many times during his long life. He was especially pleased when Pope Pius XI created him a Knight of Saint George in recognition of his editorial campaigns to restore the Golden State's missionary foundations. King Alfonso XIII of Spain also cited McGroarty for that work, naming him a Commander of Isabela Católica.

The esteemed California author, poet, lawyer, statesman, educator, dramatist and journalist went home to God on August 7, 1944. The night before he died, the ever-gracious McGroarty answered a query about his health in the lines of his last poem:

When I have had my little day,
My chance at toil, my fling at play,
And in the starry silence fall
With broken staff against the wall,
May someone pass, God grant, that way,
And, as he bends above me, say:

Goodnight, dear comrade, sleep you well,
Deep are the daisies where you fell,
I fold your empty hands that shared
Their little all with them that fared
Beside you in the rain and sun-
Goodnight, your little day is done.

Though he belonged to all of California, John Steven McGroarty exhibited a discernible proclivity to San Diego. In a special, undated issue of *The Kingdom of the Sun*, a beautifully-illustrated quarterly magazine published by Lillian D. Gregory of Oro Grande, McGroarty described the city as "the Place of First things, where California began."

In his long essay, prepared especially for the San Diego County Board of Supervisors, McGroarty declared that it is no "wonder that San Diego lures the wanderer and the traveler from every land, as well by the charm of her wondrous beauty and her gateways to opportunity as by the glamor and fascination of a past rich in romance as a lover's dream. For it was upon the glinting waters of San Diego's Harbor of the Sun, and upon her shining hills, that our California of today drew its first breath of life and ventured its first uncertain footstep on the long road to power and fame and greatness."

He concluded his treatise with the prediction that "in the days to come–and that are coming thick and fast–San Diego will rank among the great cities of the world; no doubt of that. God made much land and still more sea, but He did not make many harbors that man can use handily. And when the engineer draws his calipers upon the maps it is seen that what harbors there are have been placed where they ought to be."

And now as time advances the work of man to meet his needs, the Bay of San Diego comes to its own. Behind it lie the fertile hills, the great plains and the limitless desert made opulent by the irrigation ditch and canal. From these, even now, come teeming the wealth of farm and orchard and forest to find outlet and the waiting barter on the shores of the great ocean. Where rail and sail meet is the gateway of San Diego. The day when she depended on men to make her great is past, and the day has come when men depend on her to make them great.

The San Diego of tomorrow will be a place of crowding domes that will stretch upon the wide-flung uplands everywhere that the eye can see. Ships shall come and go ceaselessly into her wondrous harbor, and she shall match the glory of Carthage and of Tyre that was of old.

Then, as now, men will journey far across many lands and many waters to look upon her beauty. Then, as now, men will come to her for peace or gain, each as his needs may be. Nor shall her beauty fade or her glory vanish. What she has wrought and what she has won shall still be hers through all the centuries to be–the place where Padre Serra knelt; the Place of First Things that guards the Harbor of the Sun.

A McGroarty Bibliography

California,. Its History and Romance (Los Angeles: Grafton Publishing Company, 1924), Originally published in 1911, this popular treatise went through many editions.

California of the South. A History (Chicago: S.J. Clarke Publishing Co. 1933). 5 vols. Presents the story of "a conquered desert, of an arid land, immemorially desolate, yet with a wild beauty, that was made to bloom and emerge from age-old loneliness to life and gladness."

The California Plutarch (Los Angeles: J.R. Finnell. c. 1935). This portrayal of the great figures of the historic past, together with those who followed in their footsteps, was the first in a projected but never completed series.

The Endless Miracle of California (Chula Vista: Denrich Press, c. 1922). An essay on Rancho Santa Fe.

Five Wander Songs (South Pasadena: W.A. Abbott, 1918). A collection of poetic verses.

Fresno County (Fresno: Fresno County Expositions Commission, 1915). An expository essay on the geographical hub of the Golden State.

History of Los Angeles County (Chicago: American Historical Society, 1923), 3 vols. To the initial volume, devoted to a complete history and description of the area, are added two strictly biographical tomes.

"Just California" and Other Poems (Los Angeles: The Times-Mirror Press, 1933). A popular collection of the author's verses.

Just California and Songs Along the Way (Los Angeles: The Times-Mirror Company, 1903). A volume of the author's essays "from memory's crowded closet-place."

The King's Highway (Los Angeles: The Grafton Publishing Co., 1909). A poem graphically illustrated by Langdon Smith.

The Life Story of Fred Lind Alles (Los Angeles, 1938). This short essay is excerpted from *The California Plutarch, q.v.*

Little Flowers of Saint Francis (Los Angeles: The U.S. Library Association, Inc., c. 1932). Translated from the Italian, this work is handsomely illustrated by Al. Wach.

Los Angeles-A Maritime City (Los Angeles: Los Angeles Chamber of Commerce, 1912). This equation of the city's development to its seaway and railroad communications was prepared with the assistance of Edwin Schallert.

Los Angeles from the Mountains to the Sea (Los Angeles: The American Historical Society, 1921). 2 vols. The first of these volumes is devoted to an historical treatise, while the second contains selected biographies of witnesses to the period of growth and achievement. A few copies of a "Special limited edition" omit the historical section in Volume I in favor of 200 biographies.

The Mass (Los Angeles: Michael J. O'Halloran Publishing Co., 1932). This layman's appreciation gives ample evidence of the faith which illuminated the author's life.

Mission Memories (Los Angeles: Neuner Corporation, 1929). An attractively-prepared book by California's poet laureate with twenty-two pages of handsome illustrations by the talented Frederick V. Carpenter.

The Pioneer (Los Angeles: Press Publishing Co., 1925). An essay on Herman W. and Isaias William Hellman.

Poets and Poetry of Wyoming Valley (Wilkes-Barre: R. Lambert, 1886). A selection of forty-eight "samples" from the poetical literature of the area.

Santa Barbara, California (N.p., 1925). A history of the Channel City illustrated with photographs by Samuel Adelstein.

Silver Jubilee All Souls Parish (Los Angeles: Denton's, 1938). California's poet laureate reflects on parochial activities in the suburb of Alhambra.

Southern California (San Diego: Southern California Panama Expositions Commission, 1914). Historical sketches of Imperial, Los Angeles, Orange, Riverside, San Bernardino, San Diego and Ventura counties.

The Story of the Missions (South Pasadena: Walter A. Abbott, 1918). A minuscule portrayal of the famous California frontier outposts reprinted from the author's *California, Its History and Romance. q.v.*

The Vale of Monte Vista (Los Angeles, 1910). This reflection of a visit to Monte Vista State Park was excerpted from *West Coast Magazine* VII (August, 1910), 373-378.

The Valley of Our Lady (Los Angeles, 1909). This romantic history of Los Angeles and the San Gabriel Valley is reproduced as a reprint from the *West Coast Magazine* VI (July, 1909), 3-19.

Wander Songs (Los Angeles: Grafton Publishing Company, 1908). A moving volume dedicated to the author's mother "from whose heart of song these rhymes are but the echoes."

A Year and a Day:Westwood Village, Westwood Hills (Los Angeles: Westwood Hills Press, 193-?). A promotional essay on a now-prominent suburban community.

75

"Peter Guilday: American Church Historian" is the topic of this bibliographic essay which is taken from the *American Ecclesiastical Review* CXLVII (September, 1962), 145-154.

"The heritage of the past is the seed that brings forth the harvest of the future."[1] This was the creed of Peter Guilday, the "*gran maestro* of historians of the Catholic Church in the United States."[2] The author recently examined Monsignor Guilday's papers, scrapbooks, diaries and journals in the Archives of The Catholic University of America and this article has been prepared to give readers of another generation an overview of the major accomplishments of one of the truly great churchmen of our century.[3]

Peter Keenan Guilday was born in Chester, Pennsylvania, on March 25, 1884. At the conclusion of his early education, he was admitted to Saint Charles Seminary at Overbrook where he was eventually awarded a scholarship to the University of Louvain. He was ordained there along with three other Americans on July 11th, 1909, by Henry Gabriels, Bishop of Ogdensburg. Then began five years of research in preparation for his career in the academic world where he was convinced that "the Church herself will be judged by the standard of intellect."[4] Young Father Guilday matriculated with honors from the graduate school of Louvain after three years of intensive work. From there he went on for special courses at Rome and at the University of Bonn during which time he came to know several internationally known members in his chosen field of Church history. Undoubtedly the greatest influence on his scholarly development, however, was exerted by Alfred Canon Cauchie, founder of the *Revue d'Histoire Ecclesiastique* under whom Guilday trained as a student. Upon finishing the required course work, the budding historian spent two years at Saint Mary of the Angels Church in Bayswater, London, while preparing the final draft of his doctoral dissertation on *The English Catholic Refugees on the Continent, 1558-1795* (London, 1914). Some years later he published a "Guide to the Materials for American Church History in the Westminster Archives, 1675-1798"[5] which he compiled during his stay in London. Soon after his thesis was accepted by the history faculty at Louvain, Father Guilday was given the coveted *Docteur en Sciences Historiques*. His long and pleasant association with the "Athens of Belgium" is reflected in his "History of Louvain University"[6] in which he gives ample praise to European traditions of education.

It was while doing research for his dissertation that Guilday's attention was attracted to the field of American Church history, an area full of untapped riches. And soon after his energies became cemented in that direction he began his career at The Catholic University of America where he came as assistant to the late Dr. Patrick J. Healy in the fall of 1914. The beginnings of a department of historical sciences had been made by Thomas J. Shahan shortly after his arrival at the University in 1891, but with his designation as rector in 1909, the work had been interrupted. Shahan, then the recently named titular Bishop of Germanicopolis, quickly sought to have Father Guilday released from his diocesan duties and appointed permanently to the nation's Pontifical University.

Almost immediately, Guilday set out to establish a national Catholic journal patterned after the *Revue d'Histoire Ecclesiastique* and devoted exclusively to American Catholic Church history on a scale corresponding to the importance which Catholicism was assuming in the life of the country. Hence it was that the first number of the *Catholic Historical Review* appeared in April of 1915. As editor of the quarterly, Guilday enlisted nation-wide interest in the study of Catholic history, a program that received his continued support even after financial problems necessitated a broader scope for the *Review* in later years. Nor did Guilday's activities as secretary of the National Catholic War Council[7] in 1917 and 1918 lessen his zeal for historical work; it merely delayed temporarily his next project, that of founding the American Catholic Historical Association. From the earliest days of its inauguration in Cleveland, on December 30, 1919,[8] Father Guilday gave the Association his ceaseless attention. "He has nursed it through a long period of infancy and adolescence; he has encouraged younger historians in their first steps on the public stage; he has been a master in procuring publicity and a hard-working organizer amid the thankless drudgery behind the scenes; he has lent the prestige of his own scholarly achievement to the Association. No other leader could have done the things he has done, nor done them so well. The Association is his monument."[9] Guilday saw to it that the annual sessions of the organization received papers on vital historical topics prepared and delivered by reputable scholars. Three volumes of essays given at the annual meetings were edited and published by Guilday under the titles: *Church Historians* (New York, 1926), *The Catholic Church in Contemporary Europe* (New York, 1932) and the *Catholic Philosophy of History* (New York, 1936). Most of the major addresses also found their way into the *Catholic Historical Review*[10] which was subsequently moved to Washington as the official organ of the American Catholic Historical Association.

Guilday's personality as a professor, linked with a genuine interest in the work of his graduate students, awakened in them much of the zeal that he himself carried into the classroom. He believed that the most important function of The Catholic University of America was the training of leaders in the various sacred sciences and with this in mind he published his booklet on *Graduate Studies* (Washington, 1924) which defined the principles of research that should characterize Catholic graduate work. In this brief monograph of 118 pages, he elaborated on the original ideals in the minds of the founders of the University.

> To work for the Church and for America, by doing what men
> can do to create a University, which shall radiate light and love, be
> a center of union and peace, and a nursery of the higher life.

The seminar was the focal point of Professor Guilday's work during the thirty-three years he spent at Catholic University. And in connection with the seminar, he published his *Outlines of American Church History* (Cleveland, 1915), *American Church History Seminar Publications* (n.p., 1915-1922) and *Studies in American Church History* (Washington, 1922). Besides his own publications, over forty printed doctoral dissertations were written under his guidance as well as three times that number of Master's essays, many of which found their way into various historical journals. In the middle 1930s, when the University published its *Dissertations on American Church History, 1889-1932* (Washington, 1933), the great majority of entries had already appeared in print in one form or another.

Constantly on the alert for fresh material useful to his students as well as to himself, Guilday unhesitatingly made available to his classes the results of his own research and study. An example of this historical detective work is "Recent Studies in American Church History."[11] Those fortunate enough to have studied under Guilday recall that he came to class laden down with multitudinous assortments of books for his students to evaluate. His own appraisals were evident enough and the students were quick to acquire that same critical appreciation. This author has seen no fewer than one hundred book reviews written by Father Guilday and these in themselves are a testimony of his close contact with the rapidly developing events in the historical world. And somewhere among all his other duties, he managed to find time for articles in standard reference-works such as the *Catholic Encyclopedia* which he served as joint-editor, the *Dictionary of American Biography* and various other encyclopediae, and for prefaces and introductions to new books, and for sermons or addresses on occasions of historical importance.

Guilday's correspondence reveals the respect in which be was held by the hierarchy. This esteem was due, in no small measure, to his interest in the problems of the episcopate as evidenced by his many works on or about various members of that assemblage. "John Cardinal Farley, 1842-1918"[12] was the subject of Guilday's pen as were "Four Early Ecclesiastical Observers in America."[13] In 1935, shortly before his appointment to the domestic prelacy, Father Guilday wrote a masterful treatment of the "Historians in the American Hierarchy."[14] Other walks of life were singled out for his attention too, among them "Father John McKenna, A Loyalist Catholic Priest,"[15] "Arthur O'Leary,"[16] and "Lambing, Historian of Pittsburgh,"[17] all of whom were considered by Guilday as significant contributors to Catholic Americana.

One author has noted that "a remarkable coincidence designates May 30 as a significant day in his career as a speaker"[18] since four of Guilday's greatest addresses were delivered on that day. In 1932 it was *George Washington: His Catholic Friends and Allies* (Washington, 1932) delivered at the bicentennial of Washington's birth. Two years later came *Three Centuries of American Catholicism* (Washington, 1934) on the occasion of the tercentenary celebration in Baltimore's Stadium. In 1937 it was *America's Greatest Catholic Layman* (n.p., 1937) given at Doughoregan Manor to commemorate the two hundredth anniversary of Charles Carroll's birth. And in 1939 it was Guilday's address on the sesquicentennial of the creation of Baltimore as a diocese.

"Peter Guilday the priest was never lost sight of as he rose to eminence as the professional historian."[19] This is nowhere more obvious than in his sermons for the *Three Hours Agony of Our Lord Jesus Christ* (New York, 1917) given at the Church of Our Lady of Lourdes in New York City. His deep-seated appreciation for his vocation is echoed in "The Priesthood of Colonial Maryland, 1634-1773."[20] These sentiments are also revealed in his penetrating treatment of the "Immaculate Conception"[21] which he wrote to commemorate Our Lady's appearances at Rue de Bac.

Monsignor Guilday's impact on Catholic historiography in the United States has awakened interest in the preparation of diocesan, parochial and institutional histories and has called attention to the need of gathering archival material for such undertakings. Many of his articles such as the "Guide to the Biographical Sources of the American Hierarchy,"[22] "Our Earliest Printed History of the Church in the United States,"[23] "The Church in the United States (1870-1920): A Retrospect of Fifty Years"[24] and "Catholic Lay Writers of American Catholic History"[25] were and are challenges to Catholic America and the need for a wider interest in her historical beginnings. The "Dean of American Catholic Historians" steadily but surely created a consciousness of our historical wealth, never failing to direct and improve methods for its utilization. One can only stand in amazement that a single man could have found the time for all these activities, especially in the light of his now famous biographical tomes.

His insistence on the importance of method, as an historical device, resulted in *An Introduction to Church History* (Saint Louis, 1925) as well as the booklet *Graduate Studies in American Church History* (Washington, 1922). The former volume was an elaboration of his prior *Outline of an Introduction to the Study of American Church History* (Washington, 1919), issued privately some years earlier. All of these books were intended to help the student orientate himself and become familiar with what source material was available. *An Introduction* could almost be called biographical, revealing as it does the author's own long and fruitful labors pointing out avenues of interest in the intriguing field of Church history and defining in succinct terms its various meanings, scopes and values.

An endeavor toward developing a national Catholic historical center prompted Guilday's highly constructive treatise On *the Creation of an Institute for American Church History* (Washington, 1924) which commemorated the centenary of John Gilmary Shea's birth. His plan envisioned a permanent center of Catholic scholarship encompassing three broad aspects: the preservation and classification of a national Catholic archives, formation of a national Catholic library and establishment of an institute for training reputable historians. Unhappily, however, the plea went unheard and the Catholic Church in the United States still finds itself struggling with the instruments of another era to record its priceless heritage. Two years later, the first comprehensive biography of *John Gilmary Shea, Father of American Catholic History, 18241892 (New* York, 1926) was published by his distinguished successor who wrote sympathetically and appreciatively of the great pioneer and the "debt that the Church in America owes to Shea…"

Within one five-year period, Father Guilday released his two scholarly biographical studies, *The Life and Times of John Carroll* (New York, 1922) and *The Life and Times of John England* (New York, 1927). The Carroll biography, now superseded by a later study, followed by two years his article on "The Appointment of Father John Carroll as Prefect-Apostolic of the Church in the New Republic, 1783-1785."[26] The two volumes on Baltimore's first bishop are elaborately documented and yet quite readable. Over two decades after its release, it was re-issued in a single volume with only minor alterations. The life of Bishop England grew out of Guilday's "Church Reconstruction under Bishop England, 1822-1842"[27] and shows greater research than the earlier study on Carroll. Guilday builds up the image of England piece-by-piece, deftly sketching in the background of the often misunderstood prelate against the panoramic interpretation of the times. The Reverend Antonine Tibesar, O.F.M., a student of Guilday and now Associate Professor of History at The Catholic University, recalls how Guilday had a small scale model of Bishop England's residence made which he studied thoroughly before beginning to fill in the details of his life.

In *The Catholic Church in Virginia, 1815-1822* (New York, 1924) Guilday outlined a practical procedure for historians of the American Church and one which he himself used in writing his two great biographies. This was "to center around the great figures in our Church the story of their times with the hope that, as the years pass, our documentary knowledge will be increased and the institutional factors of our Catholic life become more salient and tangible." Another of his major contributions was his study on *Trusteeism* (New York, 1928)[28] made from first-hand documents which he painstakingly investigated and collected from the various chancery archives in those areas where the problem was at its worse.

Another milestone was passed with the appearance of *The History of the Councils of Baltimore, 1791-1884* (New York, 1932). This is a valuable study insofar as it represents a consecutive narrative of Church law in the United States expressed in the legislation of the various Baltimore councils. Far from being a dull chronicle of ecclesiastical juridical development, the treatise is one of Guilday's most attractive books. His earlier volume on *The National Pastorals of the American Hierarchy, 1792-1919* (Washington, 1923) was no less attractively presented and has gone through several editions. In 1946 Guilday wrote "Les Conciles de Baltimore, 1791-1884"[29] which he condensed from his earlier works.

Father Guilday had no hesitation in putting into practice those precious words of Eugenio Cardinal Pacelli that "after the priesthood of the altar there is none greater than the priesthood of truth"[30] and with this sentiment in mind he constantly encouraged others to interest themselves in his own chosen field of endeavor. When his work on "The Writing of Parish Histories"[31] appeared in 1935, he had it reprinted and distributed on a nationwide basis in an attempt to stimulate those on the local level to help advance the "priesthood of truth." In his own words, Guilday believed that:

> The pages of Catholic life need to be opened anew to men of good will, that they may see written therein that the truth of Christianity and civilization go hand in hand, that social culture and social progress are unthinkable apart from the doctrine of Christ, that all intellectual advancement which breaks with Christian theology is doomed to lead to moral obliquity of vision, that the religious aspirations of the individual as well as the nation can never be fully developed outside the warmth and glow of Catholic devotional life, and that, beyond all these, in the fearsome uncertainty which hangs over the world, no durable peace is possible unless it be hedged about by the international authority of the Prince of Peter, the Vicar of Jesus Christ on earth.[32]

Frequently in demand as a speaker, Father Guilday amassed hundreds of speeches and addresses which are neatly filed away in the Archives of The Catholic University of America. Of the dozens that were later printed, one of the more prominent includes discourses on *The Teaching Order of Saint Dominic* (Washington, 1916) prepared for the celebration of the seventh centenary of the Order of Preachers. The "Address at the Dedication of the Mullen Library"[33] was an outstanding example of

Guilday's oratory as was *The Sacred Gateway* (Pennsylvania, 1937), a sermon delivered at the sesquicentennial of the Church of the Sacred Heart, Conewago, Pennsylvania, in which he gives credit for the "grassroots" element of the American Church.

While his primary interest centered about American Church history, Guilday never lost sight of the universality of Catholicism. His penetrating treatise on "The Sacred Congregation de Propaganda Fide, 1622-1922"[34] is ample evidence of that point. Equally penetrating were his studies of "Francis Aidan Cardinal Gasquet"[35] and "Greenland's Catholic Priest."[36] Even "The Church in Liberia"[37] fell into Guilday's ambit as did the "Studies and Research in the Field of Canadian Catholic History."[38] Nonetheless, despite his occasional forays into other areas, such as *Loss and Gain in the Medieval Revival* (Boston, 1932) Guilday confined his interest to his own country. He was given the unique honor of being the first contributor to *Thought* with his sesquicentennial essay on "The Catholic Church in the United States, 1776-1926"[39] and three years later he wrote "A Catholic Chapter in United States History"[40] for his own *Review.*

Born of Irish parents, Guilday harbored a very special love for the *Supernatural Value in Irish History* (Washington, 1917) and rarely did the feast of Saint Patrick pass without an address or article on the *Echoes of Erin* (New York, 1918). Among the many sermons later printed was the one on *The United States* (n.p., 1925) delivered at the 154th annual banquet of the Society of the Friendly Sons of Saint Patrick in the presence of Calvin Coolidge.

Other publications, to mention but a few, include "En Route" and "Church Music,"[41] "Magna Charta's Centenary,"[42] and "Gaetano Bedini,"[43] an episode in the life of Archbishop John Hughes of New York. In addition to the numerous periodical contributions herein listed, Monsignor Guilday's scrapbooks contain numberless articles of a shorter length in such journals as the *Rosary, Historical Bulletin, Voice, Torch, Preservation of the Faith* and others, to say nothing of his newspaper columns.

The sentiments of Guilday's friends, students and admirers were echoed by Pope Pius XI on the occasion of his investiture as a Domestic Prelate on March 7, 1935, in the Crypt Church of the National Shrine of the Immaculate Conception. Despite his personal wishes, the papal brief was read aloud and affirmed that the honor had been conferred

...in recognition of your scientific attainments shown in the works on history which you have published and which have won on all sides the highest appreciation of your productive scholarship.[44]

Peter Guilday died on July 31, 1947, after a long and painful illness. His funeral was, by his own desire, devoid of any solemnity. And as we of another generation look back now over the past fifteen years since his death, we could hardly sum up his career in more appropriate words than those found at the tomb of a great Persian ruler... "*si monumentum quaeris, circumspice*. If you look for his monument, you need merely look around!"

Notes to the Text

1. Inscription on the National Archives Building, Washington, D.C.
2. Patrick J. Dignan, *A History of the Legal Incorporation of Catholic Church Property in the United States, 1784-1932* (Washington, 1933), p. vi.
3. A debt of gratitude is due to the Reverend Robert Trisco, Archivist of The Catholic University of America, for his kindness in allowing us to study the papers of Monsignor Guilday.
4. John Ireland, *The Church and Modern Society* (St. Paul, 1905), I, 92.
5. *Catholic Historical Review*, V (January, 1920), 382-401. Hereafter referred to as *CHR*.
6. *CHR*, XIII (January, 1928), 563-567.
7. Presently known as the National Catholic Welfare Conference.
8. See Peter Guilday, "The American Catholic Historical Association," *The Catholic Mind*, XVIII (June, 1920), 227.
9. *The Historical Bulletin*, XIX (March, 1941), 56.
10. See *CHR*, VI (April, 1920), 3-14; VII (April, 1921), 16-19; XIII (April, 1927), 18-28.
11. *American Ecclesiastical Review*, LXXXIV (May, 1931), 528-546. Hereafter referred to as *AER*.
12. *Catholic World*, CVIII (November, 1918), 183-193.
13. *AER*, LXXXV (September, 1931), 236-254.
14. *AER*, XCII (February, 1935), 113-123.
15. *Catholic World*, CXXXIII (April, 1931), 21-27.
16. *CHR*, VIII (January, 1923), 530-545.
17. *America*, L (December, 1933), 251-252.
18. James J. Kortendick, S.S., "Monsignor Peter K. Guilday, Historian of the American Church," *Catholic Library World*, XII (May, 1941), 266.
19. John Tracy Ellis, "Peter Guilday," *CHR*, XXXIII (October, 1947), 266.
20. *AER*, XC (January, 1934), 14-31.
21. *Catholic World*, CXXXX (December, 1934), 284-289.
22. *CHR*, V (April, 1919) thru VII (January, 1921).
23. *CHR*, VI (October, 1920), 343-357.
24. *CHR*, VI (January, 1921), 533-547.
25. *CHR*, XXIII (April, 1937), 45-62.
26. *CHR*, VI (July, 1920), 204-248.
27. *AER*, LXVIII (February, 1923), 135-147.
28. Reprinted from *Historical Records and Studies*, XVIII (March, 1928).
29. *Miscellanea Historica Alberti De Meyer* (Louvain, 1946), 1203-1216.
30. Ellis, *op. cit.*, p. 268.

31. *AER*, XCIII (September, 1935), 236-257.
32. Peter Guilday, *An Introduction to Church History* (Saint Louis, 1925), p. 291.
33. *CHR*, II (July, 1925), 291-297.
34. *CHR*, VI (October, 1920), 478-494.
35. *Catholic World*, CXV (May, 1922), 210-216.
36. *Baltimore Catholic Review* (August, 1934), 13.
37. *Commonweal*, XIII (February, 1931), 380-381.
38. *CHR*, XIX (April, 1933), 59-61.
39. (June, 1926), 3-20.
40. *CHR*, XV (April, 1929), 14-18.
41. *American Catholic Quarterly Review*, XXXIX (April, 1914), 303-317.
42. *Catholic Mind*, XIII (June, 1915), 291-306.
43. *Historical Records and Studies*, XXIII (1933), 87-170.
44. *Commonweal*, XXI (March, 1935), 599.

76

The following essay on "Zephyrin Engelhardt, O.F.M. Dean of California Mission Historians," is taken from the *Southern California Quarterly* XLVII (September, 1965), 235-244.

It has been said the "the historical alertness and productivity of a people are true indices of their culture. If they perceive their traditions, if they take a family pride in the achievements of their forebears, if they delight in the tales of romance and sorrow in the lives of men and women who made their commonwealth, such folks have their roots deep in the native soil and they bear a definite stamp and character in their way of living. This spirit must have been alive in California."[1]

Among the greatest contributors to this "spirit" was Zephyrin Engelhardt, O.F.M., the Dean of California Mission Historians. Born at Bilshausen, Hanover, Germany, on November 13, 1851, Charles Anthony was brought to America the next year and spent the following eighty-two years in his adopted country. The youngster's studies were made at St. Mary's in Covington, Kentucky. He entered the Order of Friars Minor at Cincinnati and became attached to the Province of the Sacred Heart on September 22, 1872. After studying philosophy at Quincy, Illinois, and theology at St. Louis, Missouri, he was ordained on June 18, 1878, by the Right Reverend Patrick Ryan, Coadjutor Bishop of St. Louis.

Upon completion of his final year of theology, Father Engelhardt was appointed to teach at St. Joseph's College in Cleveland. The next year he was sent to the Menominee Indians in Wisconsin, and before long was adept enough in the cumbersome language to translate the *Guide to Heaven* into the colorful Indian dialect under the title of *Kachkenohamatwon Kesekoch* (St. Louis, 1882).

In 1885, the tireless missionary was transferred to Superior, where he supervised the building of a small church. He was subsequently given a term on the Commissariate of the Holy Land with headquarters at New York, and while in the Empire State reorganized the monthly *Pilgrim of Palestine* into the weekly publication later known as *The Crusader's Almanac.* After expiration of his tour of duty in New York, Engelhardt came to California as a missionary to the Pomo Indians in Mendocino County. His next assignment placed him in charge of the Indian Boarding School at Harbor Springs, Michigan. Here, among the Ottawan Indians, the friar installed a printing press and published a four-page life of the saintly Indian maiden, Katherine Tegawatha. It was also in 1896 that he initiated *Anishinabe Enamiad* (Praying Indian) on his own hand printing press.

Nineteen hundred saw Engelhardt's return to California. He labored at Banning's Indian Boarding School until his transfer to Mission Santa Barbara and the resumption of his literary activities. Except for a five-year stint at Watsonville, Engelhardt spent the rest of his life in the Channel City. In addition to his numerous publications,[2] he organized and added to the now famous historical collections in the Santa Barbara Mission Archives. His notes from the United States General Land Grants Office in San Francisco included many of the 2,000 original letters, reports, and orders written by missionaries, governors, and viceroys, which were subsequently destroyed by fire. His experience as an Indian missionary gave him "a second sight in studying the old mission documents and claims for himself a place in the annals of later day missions."[3]

California's *Lector Jubilatus,* thus proclaimed by the Franciscan Minister General on the occasion of his golden sacerdotal jubilee, lived on at Santa Barbara until his death on April 27, 1934. It was a grateful city that proclaimed its famous resident among the nation's "most distinguished citizens and also one of the outstanding men not only in his order but in the field of present-day historical research and record."[4]

Among the first works published by Father Zephyrin Engelhardt on the press at Harbor Springs Indian School was his *Franciscans in California,* which appeared on October 2, 1897. This slender volume subsequently served as the ground plan for the set of *Missions and Missionaries of California.* The latter work "is not to be taken as a history of California; it occupies a field entirely apart from such books as

Bancroft and Hittell, and it is just in this characteristic that its distinctive importance resides."[5]

Undoubtedly, *Missions and Missionaries of California* was the greatest and most valuable work of Engelhardt, and in those four books, the author "in simple but eloquent language [allows] these entertaining volumes to plead the cause of the missions against their many calumniators," establishing a heritage whereby no man "will have the daring to assert that these missions were a failure..."[6] The set was issued between 1908 and 1915, and rated from one reviewer the comment that "from many points of view...Father Engelhardt is the most indispensable of all the historians of California."[7] It was an altogether justified statement, for the publication of these volumes had "won the respect of non-Catholic scholars by [their] loyalty to truth, meticulous accuracy and untiring labor..."[8] In 1929, after the publication of the diaries of Cabrillo and Vizcaíno by Herbert Bolton,[9] the need arose to expand certain of Engelhardt's earlier chapters, and a revised edition of volume one was released.

Volume two revealed that "the historian is not afraid to discuss the scandals which occurred...but he placed the blame where it belongs, namely on the interference of the civil authorities."[10] Its style was described[11] as "exact and clear rather than elegant, the mechanical work is neatly and substantially done; the illustrations are unusually good and numerous."[12] In structure, the third volume seems to have been "marred by a lack of chapter unity and by an incoherent choice of material entailed by intimate knowledge of the field, to the detriment of perspective. Where it is not annalistic, the style is controversial."[13] Nonetheless, its fullness of detailed presentation makes the volume a valuable contribution to Californiana. One reviewer felt impelled to observe that "one cannot be too grateful to the zealous friar...for having undertaken the task of correcting the errors of such writers as Bancroft and Hittell and vindicating his brethren from the many accusations brought against them."[14] The final volume of 817 pages closes the series on the general history of the missions. That these four books were a notable contribution to American Catholic history is indicated in the acceptance accorded them by reputable scholars in the field. "To glance through [these works], even hurriedly, is to realize that in painstaking research, in thorough and scholarly documentation, the execution is not beyond the level of view with which it was undertaken, at least when its full and final inspiration came to the author."[15] An *Index* to volumes two, three and four was issued in 1916, greatly facilitating their use by researchers.

In 1899, Engelhardt brought out *Franciscans in Arizona*, also published at Harbor Springs, a study which up to that time had never been adequately treated because of the lack of reliable material and the inability on the part of writers to appreciate the ideals and motives which activated the Spanish missionary pioneers.

A small book on *The Holy Man of Santa Clara* appeared during 1909 in connection with the opening of beatification proceedings for Father Magin Catalá, for whom Engelhardt was vice postulator. It was translated into Spanish by Fray Pedro Sanahuja, O.F.M., and was published in Barcelona in 1924 under the title *Vida del Padre Catalá*. "Here we have an account of the life, of which, apparently, very little is known, and of the virtues of one of the Franciscans of California who labored in the neighborhood of Santa Clara…"[16]

In the years after 1920, Father Engelhardt began issuing monographs on the individual missions which he wrote "with a view to historical accuracy of fact rather than to attractiveness of style and method."[17] In the first and perhaps the best of these sixteen local volumes, *San Diego Mission* (San Francisco, 1920), the author assures his readers that they "may confidently rely on the statements made in this work, since they are based on official documents and other trustworthy authorities." Particularly interesting are those sections "describing how capably the resources of the mission were developed. To force the hard earth to yield the poor Indian a livelihood, the Franciscans became skilled engineers and constructed a tile aqueduct three miles long…"[18]

In 279 pages, Engelhardt tells the story of *San Juan Capistrano* (Los Angeles, 1922), published under the patronage of the Bishop of Monterey-Los Angeles, the Right Reverend John J. Cantwell. "The story itself unfolds pleasantly yet most accurately …through days of stress and strain, of earthquake wreckage and of pinching poverty until Divine services were interrupted in the old adobe church in 1891."[19] *San Gabriel Mission* (San Gabriel, 1927) relates the background of the northernmost of the four Indian missionary establishments under the military jurisdiction of the *presidio* at San Diego. "Its story is adventurous and thrilling though often saddening, for the episodes that make it up include as many reverses as triumphs."[20]

San Francisco or Mission Dolores (Chicago, 1924) was the first permanent settlement established on the peninsula. This attractive volume, sponsored by Archbishop Edward J. Hanna, "Gives a detailed account of the history of the mission of St. Francis from the discovery of the bay in 1595 to the appointment of José Sadoc Alemany as Archbishop of San

Francisco in 1854. The history is well documented and portions of it are exceedingly interesting."[21] The author acknowledges in his preface to *San Buenaventura* (Santa Barbara, 1930) that "the publication of this little volume...is due to the energetic action of several public spirited citizens of Ventura." It has been described by one reviewer as substantially "a story of the Padres' devotion to an ideal and to the Indians, of labors hampered by greedy government officials and avaricious soldiers..."[22]

The monograph *Mission Santa Ines* (Santa Barbara, 1932) was delayed for some time, as Engelhardt noted in his preface. "The manuscript, containing its local history, was completed nearly a decade ago." In any event, the next year saw the publication of *Mission San Luis Obispo* (Santa Barbara, 1933), the story of a mission bearing the distinction of having been among those founded by Fray Junípero Serra himself. This volume "is done with all the apparatus of scholarship, amply supplied with translated documents and sets of tables worked out in biographical, economic and social divisions."[23]

"Old age with accompanying ailments, even serious illness, could not lessen the solicitude of this distinguished scholar of history. When it became apparent that his life's course was nearly run, his thoughts turned once more to the book on *Mission San Carlos* (Santa Barbara, 1934) which he wanted so eagerly to finish..."[24] And "the book is typical of the long list of productions which the Santa Barbara historian has given to Catholic historiography."[25]

Other volumes from the pen of this Dean of California Mission Historians include: *San Luis Rey* (San Francisco, 1921), *Santa Barbara* (Santa Barbara, 1923), *San Fernando Rey* (Chicago, 1927), *San Antonio de Padua* (Santa Barbara, 1929), *Mission Nuestra Señora de la Soledad* (Santa Barbara, 1929), *San Miguel Arcangel* (Santa Barbara, 1929) and *Mission San Juan Bautista* (Santa Barbara, 1931).

In addition to his books on missionary activity, Engelhardt was a frequent contributor to periodical journals, both under his own signature and under his two pen names, "Der Bergmann" and "Esperanza." Three of his more prominent articles include "The First Ecclesiastical Synod of California," a revealing treatment of the pioneer assemblage of clergy in the old Diocese of Monterey, called in 1852 by Bishop Joseph Sadoc Alemany.[26] Therein the author included a copy of the decrees of the synod, produced from a certified copy unearthed in the Santa Barbara Mission Archives. He also wrote an interesting essay under the caption, "Florida's First Bishop" dealing with the questionability of Juan Juarez's consecration.[27] Finally, there was his *"Interrogatorio y Respuestas of Fr. José*

Señan," wherein Engelhardt lists statistics of race, origin, language, education, etc., of the typical California Indians.[28] The renowned old chronicler also contributed to the following journals, among others too numerous to mention: *Katlische Missionen, California Volksfreund, St. Josephsbaltt, Church Progress, Franziskus Bots, Franciscan Tertiary* and *St. Anthony Messenger*. His articles in the *Catholic Encyclopedia* number twenty-three, covering with detailed accuracy the activities and vicissitudes of the Franciscans in the West.[29]

"This dean of California historians was anything but a retiring, colorless compiler of records. Ever a crusader, he labored to spread a broad knowledge of the place of the missions in the building of the Far West, all the while pitting his forces against ignorance and the occasional hostility that would smother the glory of the missions and their indefatigable *Padres*."[30]

There are many features about Engelhardt's work which influence its objective value and determine, to a great extent, its place in the over-all field of Californiana. His works represent an exhaustive study of the activity of the friars on the mission frontier, despite the fact the "the historian is frequently displaced by the zealot."[31] Although Engelhardt had an inordinate passion for truth and accuracy, it is undeniable that he tended to spread his own religious ardor over the pages of his works. It would seem, too, that his judgment of evidence occasionally fell victim to his enthusiastic faith. "His volumes are, nevertheless, a thorough, honest and scholarly contribution to the literature of California history. Indeed, it is as a great chronological source-book of mission history, as a kind of Franciscan Bancroft, that Father Engelhardt's work is primarily important."[32]

In the opinion of Francis Borgia Steck, O.F.M., an occasional collaborator of the venerable historian, Engelhardt "was of the old school, in the matter of scientific method and universal outlook, while in the matter of critical research and approach he somewhat approximated and certainly enriched and influenced the new school."[33]

One could hardly deny that "some reservations must be made with regard to brevity and clearness...the narrative lacks clear continuity and there are parts where the paragraphs become a mere chronicle of events."[34] In replying to this observation on the volume on *Mission Dolores*, it should be pointed out that Engelhardt never really considered himself a professional historian. He worked diligently on his assignments, "meanwhile nourishing fond hope that some day a writer, more artistically inclined and qualified [than he, would] take up his volumes and with them as a basis tell the story of the California missions in a manner not only accurate but also readable ... a term Engelhardt [did] not care to have applied to his historical writings."[35]

There have been other criticisms of Engelhardt. Herbert Bolton rightly claimed that he was "too hard on the Spanish monarchs. Their pious professions were not pure hypocrisy. They were truly desirous of spreading the Faith. But they were terribly 'hard up' and they had little means to support the religious projects unless they served both political and religious ends."[36] One final dissenter claims that Engelhardt did not, "in any instance, investigate the political reasons for the explorations and settlements with which his history deals." He "appears unconscious of the many problems presented by the authorities upon which he relies."[37] Perhaps this criticism, valid though it be, is counterbalanced by Engelhardt's "innate talent for historical research...fortified by an unyielding passion for historical truth and accuracy, [which] on the one hand supplied in large measure [for] his lack of scientific training in his chosen field, and on the other hand secured for his writings those qualities of historical scholarship that ensure reliability and create confidence."[38] And while Engelhardt lacked the niceties of historical methodology, "there is everywhere seen and felt the true instinct and handiwork of a genuine historian whose sole aim, as the writer says, 'is to dig out the facts, arrange them in connected as well as chronological order, and present them, truthfully, clearly and briefly!'"[39]

In summary, it must be said that, with all their shortcomings, the encyclopedic value of Engelhardt's works remains unchallenged, even in the 1960s. And yet, "each dead hand relinquishes a light; each living hand carries it on,"[40] and every new study dealing with the California scene diminishes, to a greater or lesser extent, the relative importance of the Engelhardt volumes.

This writer does not feel that the cause of scholarship is being furthered by reprinting certain of Father Zephyrin's volumes. The kindly old friar would probably be the first to point out that nothing so impedes intellectual growth as the indiscriminate reproducing of outdated research. Zephyrin Engelhardt made available a wealth of previously inaccessible details in his carefully documented tomes. Now the factual chronicler, his reputation secure, must step aside for the interpretative historian.

Notes to the Text

1. *Thought*, X (September 1935), 313-314.
2. This survey concerns itself primarily with Engelhardt's writings on the Missions of California. For a more complete listing of his works, *See* Maynard J. Geiger, O.F.M., "A Bibliography of Fr. Zephyrin's Writings," *Provincial Annals*, VI (April 1944), 19-28.
3. William Hughes, "Zephyrin Engelhardt, O.F.M.," *Indian Sentinel* (October 1921).
4. Santa Barbara *Daily News*, April 28, 1934
5. Frederick J. Teggart, *American Historical Review*, XVIII (April 1913), 599.
6. *Catholic World*, CIII (March 1916), 829-830.
7. *Commonweal*, X (September 1929), 513.
8. *Catholic World*, CXXXII (September 1930), 756-757.
9. *Viz., Spanish Explorations in the Southwest* (New York, 1916).
10. *America*, VII (July 1912), 331.
11. The reviewer mentions that the "Bancroft Library was destroyed in the San Francisco fire...," an obviously erroneous statement.
12. *Catholic World*, XCVI (October 1912), 98-99.
13. *American Historical Review*, XIX (April 1914), 694.
14. *America*, IX (May 1913), 116.
15. *Ibid.*, XIII (October 1915), 619.
16. *Ibid.*, II (November 1909), l01.
17. *Catholic Historical Review*, XX (April 1934), 99.
18. *America*, XXV (August 1921), 380-381.
19. *Ibid.*, XXVIII (February 1923), 379.
20. *Ibid.*, XXXVII (June 1927), 214.
21. *Ibid.*, XXXII (January 1925), 356.
22. *Ibid.*, XXXV (August 1931), 406.
23. *Thought*, X (September 1935), 314.
24. Felix Pudlowski, O.F.M., in the preface.
25. *Thought*, XI (September 1936), 339.
26. *Catholic Historical Review*, I (April 1915), 30-37.
27. *Ibid.*, IV (January 1919), 479-485.
28. *Ibid.*, V (April 1919), 55-66.
29. *Makers of the Catholic Encyclopedia* (New York, 1917), p. 53.
30. *Thought*, X (September 1935), 313-314.
31. Robert G. Cleland, *From Wilderness to Empire* (New York, 1954), p. 380.
32. Charles E. Chapman, *A History of California* (New York, 1921), p. 502.
33. "Father Zephyrin Engelhardt," *Commonweal*, XX (June 29, 1934), 237.
34. America, XXXII (January 1925), 356.
35. *Catholic Historical Review*, XX (April 1934), 98.
36. Herbert E. Bolton, "The Mission as a Frontier Institution in the Spanish American Colonies," American *Historical Review*, XXIII (October 1917), 42-61.
37. *American Historical Review*, XVIII (April 1913), 599.
38. *Catholic Historical Review*, XX (July 1934), 203.
39. *America*, XIII (October 1915), 619.
40. Carlos E. Castañeda, *Our Catholic Heritage* (Austin, 1936), dedication page.

77

This bibliographic tribute to "John Tracy Ellis, Historian of American Catholicism" is taken from *The American Benedictine Review* XVII (Winter, 1966), 467-478.

John Tracy Ellis, "a historian who is sacramentally united to the oldest tradition of the Western world,"[1] is one of those rare scholars with the gift of making dull, dusty and unappealing events of the past live again. He combines the tools of an expert historian with those of a flawless grammarian in such a way as to make the reading of his volumes a genuine treat.

Ellis was born at Seneca, Illinois, on July 30, 1905, the son of Elmer L. Ellis and Ida C. Murphy.[2] After obtaining his bachelor's degree from Saint Viator College in 1927, Ellis entered The Catholic University of America on a Knights of Columbus scholarship. He received his doctorate[3] and then returned to Saint Viator as Chairman of the Department of History. During the two years prior to entering the seminary, Professor Ellis taught at the College of Saint Teresa. In 1934 he became a divinity student for the Diocese of Winona, Minnesota.[4] He was ordained to the priesthood at Winona on June 5, 1938, and that fall became a full-time instructor of history in The Catholic University of America.

Father Ellis became associated with the *Catholic Historical Review* in 1939 and was made editor of the journal two years later, a post he occupied for the next twenty-one years. In 1941 he took over most of the duties of the ailing Monsignor Peter K. Guilday[5] in the field of American Catholic history, in the University's Graduate School of Arts and

Sciences. To round out his own background, Ellis spent most of the 1941-1942 academic year at Harvard auditing courses in American Social history and surveying the printed and archival *fontes* of the Catholic Church's development in the United States.

Shortly after returning to Washington, Ellis and his seminar students compiled a forty-nine page "Select Bibliography of American Church History (1492-1942)," which was enlarged four years later into *A Select Bibliography of the History of the Catholic Church in the United States.*[6] Father Ellis spoke of the publication as "a convenient work-list by which teachers and students in universities, seminaries and high schools may more readily make their way through the growing literature on the Catholic Church in the United States." In 1959 the work was further expanded and brought up to date in *A Guide to American Catholic History.*[7] Even though he modestly disclaimed any attempt at exhausting the field, "an examination of the biliographies of the best monographs will show that nothing consequential has been omitted."[8]

The first attempt to draw together into a single volume a sampling of the original sources underlying the nation's Catholic history was *Documents of American Catholic History*[9] first published by Ellis in 1956. A perusal of this work makes it "possible to gain a very fair and balanced picture of the Church in the United States at the various stages of her history."[10] A year later it was revised and enlarged, the volume of *Documents* had the distinction of being selected for the White House Library.

Those familiar with John Tracy Ellis' affection for the nation's pontifical university can fully appreciate the personal reluctance with which he left there in 1964 for the University of San Francisco. A long-time campaigner for his *alma mater*,[11] Ellis had outlined as early as 1932 "the accomplishments and contributions made by that University to the world of scholarship...,"[12] and fourteen years later released his now scarce volume on *The Formative Years of The Catholic University of America*. The study was not a mere laudatory essay but a strictly historical monograph written from the sources which had been "investigated thoroughly and evaluated soundly."[13]

The *opus magnum* of John Tracy Ellis is his biography of James Cardinal Gibbons.[14] In addition to the research he did in the major ecclesiastical archives of the country, Ellis read and studied his way through more than a hundred thick file boxes in the Archives of the Archdiocese of Baltimore. The results of his seven-year saga were intensely rewarding, for as one commentator noted, the work "is important because it gives us not only the life of the greatest American churchman of the late nineteenth and early twentieth centuries, but also the history of the American Church from 1877 to 1921..."[15]

Reviewers of the 1442 printed pages were mostly commendatory, one of them stating that "when a definitive history of the American Church is written, there will be but little to add for the first two centuries that is not found in Guilday and Ellis."[16] In his remarks on the Gibbons' biography, Shane Leslie hopefully expressed the desire that since the materials of the Cardinal's life had been wonderfully edited and compressed, it might soon be possible to draw out the character of the archbishop "within a hundred pages or less..."[17] Though it somewhat exceeded Leslie's limitations, such a volume actually did appear in 1963, in Francis L. Broderick's abridged edition, *The Life of James Gibbons*.[18] Based on Ellis' research, the digest version was awarded the first National Catholic Book Award.

Ellis performed a number of useful services to historiography while working on the Gibbons volumes. "A Guide to the Baltimore Cathedral Archives"[19] surveyed the holdings of that vital depository of source materials for American Catholic history. He also edited "Some Newman Letters from the Baltimore Cathedral Archives"[20] dealing with the legal proceedings lodged against Newman by the apostate Dominican, Giacinto Achilli. Two years later Father Ellis published an interesting item on "Cardinal Gibbons' Assistance to Pastor's History of the Popes."[21] Two regional studies on Baltimore's Archbishop, "Cardinal Gibbons and Philadelphia"[22] and "Cardinal Gibbons and New York"[23] highlighted the work of the eminent churchman in local affairs. One final item worthy of mention is "The Centennial of the First Plenary Council of Baltimore"[24] which was issued in 1952.

Since Ellis had long nourished an interest in the activities of John Lancaster Spalding, the research on the history of The Catholic University of America only increased his admiration for the one-time Bishop of Peoria. In 1944 he made known a desire "to publish an article in some future issue of the *Catholic Historical Review* on Spalding and the University" and asked those with materials on Spalding to "inform him of such so that at sometime in the not-too-distant future a critical biography of the great American bishop may be written."[25]

His own fascination for Spalding reached its fulfillment on October 25, 1960, when the indefatigable historian addressed the annual meeting of the School Superintendents of the National Catholic Educational Association at Peoria. The printed version of this Gabriel Richard Lecture was subsequently enlarged into a slender monograph on *John Lancaster Spalding, First Bishop of Peoria, American Educator.*[26] Though the study added "little to our knowledge of this master of epigrams,"[27] it did reach "a high level of objectivity"[28] while remaining warmly human in its depiction.

The small volume on *American Catholicism,*[29] enabled its readers "to interpret within the scope of a very limited volume the reasons which underlie the providential expanse"[30] of the Catholic Church in the United States. Originally issued as part of the Chicago History of American Civilization Series, the collected essays afforded "a significant account of the Catholic story in American history in a way that will be serviceable not only to those who concentrate on the political aspects of American history but also to those who want an introduction to specialized Catholic history."[31]

In 1956, soon after beginning work on a proposed single volume narrative on the Church's development in the United States, Ellis wrote a series of articles on "Catholics in Colonial America."[32] Eight years later these articles were expanded as *Catholics in Colonial America.*[33]

In a paper delivered at Rosary College in June of 1960, on "The Present Position of Catholicism in America,"[34] Ellis pointed up the challenges and responsibilities facing a faith that had grown from a ghetto minority to impressive stature within the confines of a pluralistic society. The Monsignor exhorted his co-religionists "to seek the transformation of public opinion toward the Church, and in so doing, to take our share in the ultimate liquidation of the accumulated animosity of more than four centuries..." Ellis has an unusual ability of relating historical events to currently topical subjects. For example, when discussion first arose about using English in certain liturgical ceremonies, he wrote a short treatise on "Archbishop Carroll and the Liturgy in the Vernacular,"[35] outlining the views held by the father of the American hierarchy on the subject. Some years later, when asked to contribute a descriptive essay on American Catholicism, Ellis wrote "A Letter from Washington"[36] wherein he outlined how the Catholic Church in the United States was "keeping pace with the tremendous growth of population" in the urban areas. Again, in the early days of the Second Vatican Council, when that ecumenical gathering was the source of wide speculation, Ellis delivered an extremely succinct and lucid lecture on "The Church Faces the Modern World: The Vatican Council, 1869-1870,"[37] in the series of lectures sponsored by The Catholic University of America on ecumenical councils.

Ellis' interest in Catholic higher education was shown as early as 1936, when he made a comparative analysis of the nation's schools of higher learning as rated by regional accrediting agencies."[38] Some years later, he expressed concern about the apparent lack of interest in his own academic specialty, pointing out that "the history of the Catholic Church of the United States is one of the most neglected subjects in the curricula of American Catholic institutions through high school, college, seminary and university levels."[39] At that time, The Catholic University of America was the only place in the country offering a graduate program in American Catholic history.[40] Another survey was published by Ellis in 1959, on the changes that had transpired in Catholic education in the United States, in which he briefly outlined the position of the laity in the development of higher education.

Another facet of education to which Ellis has devoted considerable attention is that of seminary training. Since he had taught for three years as a layman and again for the final three years of his theology course at the Sulpician Seminary attached to The Catholic University,[41] Ellis was thoroughly familiar with the field. In stressing a need for deepening the intellectual virtues, Ellis observed that "like every human enterprise, the Tridentine seminary, too, has grown old, and in the judgment of many prudent and respected churchmen and laymen it now stands in need of change."[42] It was this view that prompted the Monsignor to contribute an "excellent two-part historical survey"[43] to the collection of essays on *Seminary Education in a Time of Change*.[44]

Surely "the future will show that John Tracy Ellis has not only written about American Catholic history, but that he has himself helped to make it by exerting upon current problems of the Church today the influence of his own intellect."[45] Ellis has anything but a retiring personality. He has been described as "one of the 'characters' of the Church, at its present stage in history, for he has been at the hurricane's eye of controversy because of his search for truth and his courageous expression of the truth as he sees it."[46] Never has he hesitated to express himself on matters of national or international concern, especially when they have been related to the Church. As early as 1933, for example, he was stressing "the duty of every Catholic to work for the establishment of the genuine moral principles necessary to international peace."[47] When the matter of President Franklin D. Roosevelt's diplomatic representation at the Vatican arose with the appointment of Myron C. Taylor, Ellis took up his pen to record the mostly unfavorable reaction and its precedents in United States history.[48]

There were several areas, however, where Ellis himself initiated controversies. One of these was the heated reaction to his address given on

May 14, 1955, at Maryville College of the Sacred Heart in Saint Louis. Speaking on "American Catholics and the Intellectual Life,"[49] Monsignor Ellis began "the great debate" on the educational standards and attainments of American Catholics. One authority commented, "Very seldom during the lifetime of this generation have we encountered a rather brief article which has aroused intense interest from the very moment of its publication, and which has continued to be the center of lively and valuable discussion over a long period."[50]

Basically, Ellis maintained that the Catholic system of education in this country was failing in its efforts to develop a strong intellectual life among students. This "perpetuation of mediocrity," as he called it, constituted a scandal for the Church. Reaction was quick and sharp on both sides, and for several years the matter was a prime center of debate at meetings of Catholic educators. Ellis disclaimed any intention of purposely stirring up the controversy, although he does admit, in retrospect, that the whole affair did cause a long needed re-examination of the criteria previously used to evaluate Catholic intellectual goals. According to a later address which he based on the replies sent him personally, there had been "substantial agreement" with his overall views on the matter.[51] It would be wrong to take the Monsignor's views as a blanket denial of the positive accomplishments of parochial education, for he noted that when Catholicism reached its maturity in the United States there would be ample proof "that while the Church of this Republic has by no means occupied a leading role in actual accomplishments during the past sixty years, its contributions have not been altogether negligible."[52]

Another of the controversies centering around Ellis grew out of a talk he gave on May 27, 1962, at the commencement of Carroll College in Helena, Montana. The Catholic University of America's professor of Church history warned his listeners on this occasion about "a note of strain in clerical-lay relations,"[53] which he discerned in certain areas of the nation. Early the next month, Ellis enlarged on the theme at Saint Mary's College, by pleading for more "freedom in the numerous and varied avenues of contemporary Catholic life and action where the prudent layman can and should be allowed to travel with as much warrant and right as the priest and bishop."[54] In a later evaluation, Ellis wrote, "The Helena address—and the commencement address delivered at St. Mary's College at Moraga, Calif., on June 9 were devoted to an examination, in the light of the history of Catholicism in this country, of what I sincerely believe are some current strains in clerical-lay relations…"[55] Without any doubt, to quote the eminent historian himself, "an astonishing number of inaccurate and misleading statements arose as a consequence of that address.[56] In all fairness, it must be said that the idea was not a new one for Ellis, for some years earlier like John Courtney Murray, S.J., he too had detected faint clouds of anti-clericalism on the horizon,[57] in certain letters he received on the intellectual climate of America's Catholics.

The Monsignor's attitude on freedom is a logical development of his views on historical truth. His opus on "Church and State: An American Catholic Tradition,"[58] published late in November of 1953, treated the matter in the words of the nation's hierarchy. Ellis went a step further, however, for he felt that "there is no aspect of Catholic teaching that is more in need of clarification for future good relations between Catholics and those outside the Church than that of religious freedom."[59]

Later, Ellis wrote more extensively on the relations of religious freedom to Roman Catholics in the United States observing that even in modern times, "perhaps, the most universally held bias of the American people"[60] is a prejudice of what the Church really is and what it stands for. A strong supporter of Vatican Council II's attempt to speak out on religious freedom, Ellis felt that it was "the most important single subject to which Catholics can, and should, address themselves in relation to those who do not share their religious faith," feeling as he did, that it is the "duty of every man to follow his conscience as the final and determining guide in arriving at his religious commitment."[61]

While he championed freedom, Monsignor Ellis has given no encouragement to abuses. He said, for example, that "bishops are not free, even if they should so desire, to permit in their diocese publications bearing a Catholic name to speak and act as though they had no responsibility to the local ecclesiastical authority."[62] Further, in a comment about critics of the hierarchy, Ellis cautioned that "above all else the criticism one offers must be polite, free from the sting that has of late appeared here and there in the writings of a few laymen."

However they view him, few ignore John Tracy Ellis. This is why, to cite one instance, his address on the occasion of the diamond jubilee of Saint Paul's College, Washington, in January of 1965, had such an effect. The Monsignor noted that "at the time when a few of the Church's more restive sons would seem to have become a trifle intoxicated by the heady wine of the new-found freedom within her fold," there was a calling into question of authority itself.[63] The warning was picked up almost immediately and one well-known writer commented that "as one who risked much for the Catholic intellectual in America, long ago when the road was uphill, Monsignor Ellis deserves serious attention."[64] Whatever one may think of America's foremost Catholic ecclesiastical historian, few can deny that "perhaps more than any other man, save Pope John himself, Monsignor Ellis inspired the cleansing climate of self-scrutiny now beginning to infiltrate every level of American Catholicism."[65]

John Tracy Ellis' overriding motivation has been to cultivate a deep and genuine respect for history as an academic discipline because of "its special merit as a source of guidance and enlightenment for men," and in view of "the reassurance and meaningful record it unfolds of the people of God who constitute His Church."[66] The Monsignor has consistently maintained that in the field of historical research, there should be no dread of what can be unearthed about the defective members of the Church for the cockle often grows with the wheat or, as John Lancaster Spalding phrased it, "what God bas permitted to happen, man may be permitted to know..."[67] Ellis is fond of recalling what Pope Leo XIII once told Cardinal Manning: "If the historians of the last century had written the Gospels...we might never have heard of the fall of Peter, or of the treachery of Judas."[68]

"It is the business of the ecclesiastical historian," according to Ellis, "to record all the significant facts, the losses as well as the gains, the failures as well as the triumphs,"[69] and it is for that reason that the Monsignor has never exhibited any sympathy for the apologetic value of history. To Ellis, the Catholic's relationship to history is aptly summed up in the words of the English Benedictine, Dom David Knowles:

> However wide his scientific knowledge or his philosophical out-look, however great his understanding of physics or his contempt for metaphysics, he cannot neglect history, for it is part—nay, it is the essence—of his faith that the transcendent Creator of the universe, on a certain day and at a certain place, and at an ascertainable conjuncture of the world's history, came upon the earth to teach and to save the human race, and to endow the sons of his election with the inheritance of divine life.[70]

The Monsignor regards Pope Leo XIII's memorable letter on historical studies as the *vade mecum*[71] of the Catholic historian, for Ellis has consistently maintained that "nothing is gained by denying what is palatably true."[72] In the Pontiff's judgment, according to Monsignor Ellis, "the ecclesiastical historian was all the better equipped to bring out the Church's divine origins the more loyally he refrained from extenuation of the trials which the faults of her children, and at times even of her ministers, have brought upon the Spouse of Christ during the course of the centuries."[73]

An essay such as this could hardly be more fittingly concluded than with remarks penned by Ellis himself, for they sum up his concept of the goals that historians in general, and of the Church in particular, should seek in their research:

> The pursuit of truth - in whatever form it takes through writing - can be an immensely thrilling and rewarding experience. Personally, I find the discovery of new truths in the history of American Catholicism through the medium of original research an experience of this kind, and for that reason I feel the impulse to share these truths with others by writing them down in a permanent form. And there is no better way, it seems to me, for a person who has the aptitude, taste and training for the intellectual life to further the advancement of the Church than through this means.[74]

Notes to the Text

1. Paul Horgan, "An Open Letter to John Tracy Ellis," *Catholic Mind* LXIV (January, 1966), 32.
2. For an autobiographical sketch, see Walter Romig, *The Book of Catholic Authors* (Michigan, n.d.), V, 81-88.
3. Ellis' doctoral thesis was published under the title, *Anti-Papal Legislation* in *Medieval England, (1066-1377)* (Washington, 1930). The dissertation treated parliamentary activities between William the Conqueror and Edward III to limit the ecclesiastical and temporal power of the papacy.
4. In May of 1947, Ellis transferred to the Archdiocese of Washington, D.C.
5. *See* John Tracy Ellis, "Peter Guilday," Catholic Historical Review XXXIII (October, 1947), 257-268.
6. (New York, 1947).
7. (Milwaukee, 1959).
8. Maurice B. McCloskey, O.F.M. "Book Review," *The Americas* XVI (April, 1960), 431.
9. (Milwaukee, 1956).
10. Robert J. Dwyer, Book Review, *Catholic Historical Review* XLIII (April, 1957), 64.
11. *See* "Light and Freedom in the University," *Way* XX (July-August, 1964).
12. "Some Catholic Research of 1932," *Catholic World* CXXXVI (January, 1933), 427.
13. James H. Ryan, Book Review, *Catholic Historical Review* XXXII (October, 1946), 369.
14. *The Life of James Cardinal Gibbons, Archbishop of Baltimore, 1834-1921* (Milwaukee, 1952).
15. Lawrence J. Shehan, Book Review, *Catholic Historical Review* XXXVIII (January, 1953), 531.
16. Victor Mills, O.F.M., Book Review, *The Americas* X (October, 1953), 246.
17. Book Review, London *Tablet* CCII (October 10, 1953), 345.
18. (Milwaukee, 1963).
19. *Catholic Historical Review* XXXII (October, 1946),341-360.
20. *Ibid., XXXI* (January, 1946), 438-445.
21. *Ibid.,* XXXIV (October, 1948), 306-318.
22. *Records of the American Catholic Historical Society* LVIII (March, 1947), 87-102.
23. *Historical Records and Studies* XXXIX (New York, 1952), 5-32.
24. *American Ecclesiastical Review,* CXXVI (May, 1952), 321-350.
25. "Some Select Letters of John Lancaster Spalding," *Catholic Historical Review* XXIX (January, 1944), 510-516.

26. (Milwaukee, 1961).
27. Thomas T. McAvoy, C.S.C., Book Review, *Review of Politics* XXV (July, 1963), 400.
28. Merle Curti, Book Review, *Catholic Historical Review* XLIX (April, 1963), 131.
29. (Chicago, 1956).
30. Paul Sullivan, Book Review, *Homiletic and Pastoral Review* LVII (September, 1957), 1162.
31. Thomas T. McAvoy, C.S.C., Book Review, *Catholic Historical Review* XLIII (April, 1957),65.
32. *American Ecclesiastical Review* CXXXVI (January, 1957), 11-27; CXXXVI (February, 1957), 100-119; CXXXVI (March, 1957), 184-196; CXXXVI (April, 1957), 100-119; CXXXVI (May, 1957), 304-321.
33. (Benedictine Studies, III; Baltimore, 1965).
34. *The American Benedictine Review* XI (March-June, 1960), 1-20. The treatise was subsequently republished under the title *Perspectives in American Catholicism.* (Benedictine Studies, V; Baltimore, 1963).
35. *Worship* XXVI (November, 1952), 545-552.
36. *Dublin Review* CCXXXII (Winter, 1958-59), 363-371.
37. This address was later included by William J. McDonald in his volume on *The General Council* (Washington, 1962), 113-145.
38. "Accreditation and the Catholic College," *Catholic Educational Review* XXXIV (December, 1936), 589-597.
39. "Teaching American Catholic History in Our Schools," *Bulletin*-National Catholic Educational Association XLVIII (May, 1952), 8.
40. "The American Catholic College, 1939-1959, Contrasts and Prospects," *Delta Epsilon Sigma Bulletin* II (June, 1959), 3.
41. In that regard, *See* "A Seminary Jubilee," *Chicago Studies* IV (Summer, 1965), 115-136, an address given by John Tracy Ellis for the golden jubilee of Saint Paul's College in Washington, D.C.
42. "A School for the Lord's Service," *The American Benedictine Review* XV (September, 1964), 307.
43. Francis J. Weber, Book Review, *Homiletic and Pastoral Review* LXX (August, 1965), 973.
44. Edited by James Michael Lee and Louis J. Putz, C.S.C. (Notre Dame, 1965).
45. John J. Meng, Book Review, *Catholic Historical Review* L (October, 1964), 405.
46. John O'Conner, editorial in the *Delmarva Dialog*, December 3, 1965.
47. "Catholic Action for Peace," *Commonweal* XVII (March 29, 1933), 602.
48. See "Our Envoy to the Vatican," *Catholic World* CLI (August, 1940), 573-581.
49. *Thought* XXX (Autumn, 1955), 351-388. The treatise was published in book form in 1956.
50. Joseph Clifford Fenton, "Intellectual Standards among American Catholics," *American Ecclesiastical Review* CXXXV (November, 1956), 323.
51. "No Complacency," *America* XCV (April 7, 1956), 25.
52. "The Sixtieth Birthday of the American Ecclesiastical Review," *American Ecclesiastical Review* CXXI (October, 1949), 279-280.
53. "The Catholic Layman in America Today," *Commonweal* LXXVI (June 22, 1962), 320. For an excellent digest of this article, *See* the London *Tablet*, June 2, 1962,532.
54. "The American Catholic Laity," *Way* XVIII (September, 1962), 16.
55. "Letter to Editor," *America* CVII (July 7, 1962), 451.
56. "Correspondence," *Commonweal* LXXXI (February 19, 1965), 651.
57. "No Complacency," *America* XCV (April 7, 1956), 25.
58. *Catholic Mind* LII (April, 1954), 209-216. This article first appeared in *Harpers* CCVII (November, 1953), 63-67.
59. "Correspondence," *America* CII (February 6, 1960), 541-542.
60. "Religious Freedom and American Catholicism," *Cross Currents* XIII (Winter, 1963), 4.
61. "Conscience and Religious Commitment," *Catholic Mind* LXII (June, 1964), 32.
62. "The Catholic Press: Reflections on Past and Present," *American Benedictine Review* XIV (March, 1963), 57.
63. "A Seminary Jubilee," *Chicago Studies* IV (Summer, 1965), 125.
64. Robert A. Graham, "John Tracy Ellis on the Pathetic Blackout," *America* CXII (March 6, 1965), 305.

65. Edward R.F. Sheehan, "American Catholicism, Not Peace but the Sword," *Saturday Evening Post* CCXXXVII (November 28, 1964), 26.
66. "Reflections of an Ex-Editor," *Catholic Historical Review* L (January, 1965), 473.
67. John Lancaster Spalding, *op cit.*, p. 75.
68. *The Ambassador of Christ* (Baltimore, 1896), p. 252.
69. "A New Church History Series," *American Ecclesiastical Review* CLIII (September, 1965), 149.
70. "The Need for Catholic Historical Scholarship," *Dublin Review* CCXXXII (Summer, 1958), 122.
71. *See* "Another Anniversary," *Commonweal* XIX (February 2, 1934), 378-380.
72. John Tracy Ellis as quoted in *Newsweek* LXIII (February 10, 1964), 55.
73. *Perspectives in American Catholicism* (Baltimore, 1963), p. 193.
74. Walter Romig, *op. cit.*, V, 87-88.

78

This bibliographical survey about "Thomas T. McAvoy, C.S.C.: Historian of American Catholicism," appeared in the *Indiana Magazine of History* LXIV (March, 1968), 16-24.

It is the firm conviction of Father Thomas T. McAvoy, archivist and professor of history at the University of Notre Dame, that "The divorce between government and religious institutions, especially outside the thirteen original states, and the tendency to write history from governmental sources has resulted in an underwriting and even an ignoring of religious history in the United States."[1] In his own capacity as a nationally recognized authority on American Catholic history, McAvoy has devoted his intellectual talents to reversing the trend which traditionally has placed such study among "the most neglected subjects in the curricula of American Catholic institutions through high school, college, seminary and university levels."[2]

Thomas Timothy McAvoy was born at Tipton, Indiana, on September 12, 1903. There he acquired his earliest education at Saint John's School from the Sisters of Saint Joseph. After completing courses at Tipton Public High School, McAvoy entered Holy Cross, one of the theological colleges affiliated with The Catholic University of America in Washington. Shortly after his ordination to the priesthood on June 24, 1929, the young priest was assigned to organize the uncataloged historical collections which had been amassed at the University of Notre Dame by the late Professor James F. Edwards. Six years later he enrolled at Columbia University as a doctoral candidate in the field of American history. Upon his return to South Bend in 1938, Father McAvoy became chairman of Notre Dame's department of history, a position he occupied with considerable success for the next twenty one years. Since 1942 he has been co-managing editor of the university's highly respected *Review of Politics.*

As a long-time professor of the cultural and social history of the United States, McAvoy has been committed to the theory that the study of history "will lead the student into the real world and teach him patience, precision, and humility in the face of truth"; and this, he points out, "is no mean element in any liberal education."[3] In his own historical research the widely read historian has avoided the label of "popularizer." Although admitting the usefulness of constantly engaging in controversy about the character of the past,[4] McAvoy regards the desire to philosophize inimical to historical understanding and exposition and "a fundamental cause of American Catholic failure not only in the field of history but in most of the fields of the liberal arts."[5] The tenor of his own writing veers away from generalizations, which he considers valid only if founded "in the facts of the past and not imposed from without."[6]

The cultural enrichment that a broad knowledge of history in a pluralistic society gives to priests is extremely profitable; and in this vein, McAvoy notes, few studies offer a safer antidote for any preconceived notion of economic determinism regarding the theory of man.[7] The Notre Dame historian has long advocated a deeper appreciation of history's place in seminary programs, pointing out that "if the Catholic clergyman is to function properly as pastor and teacher he must not be dependent upon the weekly pictorial magazines or the partisan press for his information about the past."[8]

As guardian now for almost four decades of the historical collections at Notre Dame, Father McAvoy has repeatedly reminded his confreres about the advantages of becoming more thoroughly manuscript-conscious. By calling attention to the "need for a concerted effort by those who appreciate these personal, family, society, and group records to see that they are preserved,"[9] McAvoy has placed new emphasis on the scientific techniques for eliminating myth from fact that grows out of carefully investigating the records of man's achievements.[10]

Researchers have always been welcome at South Bend. For those unable personally to journey to Notre Dame, McAvoy has published excerpts from some of the most important of the university's holdings. In 1933 he edited a number of "The War Letters of Father Peter Paul Cooney of the Congregation of the Holy Cross" from the unpublished correspondence and service records of Catholic chaplains in the Union and Confederate armies.[11] Another fascinating item reproduced from documents in the archives of the University of Notre Dame is "Brownson's Ontologism," which is based on an exchange of letters between the famous English apologist and Father Henry S. McMurdie concerning man's cognitive ability to know the Supreme Being.[12] "Bishop Bruté's Report to Rome in 1836," a valuable combination of theoretical ideas and practical missionary experience on the condition of the Catholic church in the United States, was published by McAvoy as an example of the value he places on contemporary observations. McAvoy claims, however, that such historical documents must always be evaluated in light of "the competence of the observer and his intention to give the benefit of his knowledge" to others.[13]

Notre Dame's archivist has no hesitation in proclaiming that "all research that does not lead ultimately to a greater knowledge of the Divine plan has lost its true purpose."[14] This attitude has motivated the publishing of such ecclesiastically important documents as "Bishop Flaget's Pastoral to the People of Detroit," which remains among the more interesting statements made by a member of the American hierarchy.[15]

McAvoy described the historical background of the archives at Notre Dame, with the 500,000 items gathered prior to 1951, in a survey on "Manuscript Collections Among American Catholics"[16] in 1951. To the dedicated researcher history without documents is simply rhetoric;[17] and as the country's leading Catholic archivist, Father McAvoy has tirelessly added to the university's holdings over the past quarter century. In 1961 he personally filmed thousands of items in the Paris and Lyons offices of the *Société de la Propagation de la Foi* and in Rome's Sacred Congregation of Propaganda Fide.[18] The acquisition of this extensive microfilm collection is surely McAvoy's greatest contribution to the archives at Notre Dame and, possibly, to United States Catholic scholarship in general. Making this valuable series of letters from American missionaries accessible to interpretative historians may eventually reshape much of the overall thinking about the Church's development on the national scene.

Father McAvoy has exhibited special competence in writing about historical developments in the American midwest. His doctoral dissertation, published under the title *The Catholic Church in Indiana, 1789-1834,*[19] wove together "a very readable narrative of the Church's work in Indiana,"[20] depicting as it did the transition between the French missions and diocesan organization. He returned to a more localized aspect of this subject in a lecture given thirteen years later and subsequently published as *The History of the Catholic Church in the South Bend Area.* A paper which

McAvoy read at the meeting of the Mississippi Valley Historical Association in April of 1946 appeared in print as "The Abbé Rivet at Vincennes." A contrast between the English and French frontiers forms the central theme of his work on "The Old French Frontier in the Central Great Lakes Region," a study which included Cadillac's description of Point Saint Ignace on the Mackinac Straits.[21]

Quite naturally, the University of Notre Dame figures prominently in McAvoy's writings. His first such article dealt extensively with Father Stephen Badin, a pioneer Holy Cross priest, who "in many ways typifies the transition period in the history of the Catholic missions in the west...," being as he was a Canadian cleric working as the first missionary from Baltimore on a whole new frontier.[22] In 1953 McAvoy published a personal evaluation of Father John F. O'Hara in light of his work at South Bend. This study was later expanded into a full-length biography, *Father O'Hara of Notre Dame: The Cardinal Archbishop of Philadelphia.*[23] The pre-O'Hara years at Notre Dame received attention too as did the magazine *Ave Maria*, which observed the centennial of its establishment at the university in 1965.[24]

On the national level it was his concern about "the lack of balanced textbooks and the bias of those who are rushing in to take care of the job"[25] that occasioned McAvoy's collaboration with four other scholars in *A History of the United States*, a widely-used college text.[26] McAvoy also edited a collection of essays, *Roman Catholicism and the American Way of Life*, in 1960 and the following year published his treatise, "What Is the Midwestern Mind?" as one of a series gathered under the title *Midwest: Myth or Reality?*[27] Possibly Father McAvoy's three most outstanding survey articles are his essays on "The Catholic Church in the United States Between Two Wars," "The Catholic Church in the United States," and "This American Catholicism."[28]

Though his historical interests have generally been confined to Catholic areas, McAvoy is a respected authority in the secular field. His article, "Roosevelt: A Modern Jefferson," was widely hailed for its keen observation that "what is common to both and what is peculiarly American is the fact that despite superficial changes each made more secure the established American tradition of political democracy."[29] Perhaps McAvoy's willingness to delve into the nation's strictly secular history grew out of his conviction that "the reading of official documents and the study of the lives of our American leaders offer sound proofs that recent secularist and antireligious attacks on American institutions are contrary to the American tradition."[30]

The McAvoy prognosis is an optimistic one, for he is convinced that "American Catholicism is just coming of age, forming a spirit of its own, with a tradition of its own and facing problems that do not exist anywhere else in the Western World."[31] He is quick to point out, however, the successes of the past, noting that

> the emergence of the Catholic layman in the United States which has been heralded so frequently since the opening of the Second Vatican Council has tended to do a grave injustice to the American Catholic laymen of earlier generations…The number of prominent Catholic laymen and laywomen of the nineteenth century is large as can be seen in the mere listing of the galaxy that participated in the two lay Catholic Congresses in Baltimore in 1889 and Chicago in 1893.[32]

Father McAvoy contends that in most of the historical accounts of the Catholic body in the United States the cultural composition of the group has generally been misunderstood.[33] It is perhaps this contention which accounts for his interest in the elements that have created the present Catholicity patterns of the nation.[34] A goodly portion of his writing has centered on the history of the relations between the Catholic minority and the dominant culture of the country. While he admits a proportionate lack of Catholic influence on the national level, McAvoy has criticized the bitter accusations made against the church's leadership as "mostly cries of anguish and definitely not intelligent attempts to analyze the real position of the Catholic minority with a view to the better use of its meager resources."[35]

In his many writings the Notre Dame historian has traced the Catholic minority through the various stages of its growth in American society. He has demonstrated that the essential characteristics of this religious group were established during the thirty years between John Carroll's arrival from England as first bishop and Ambrose Marechal's return from Rome in 1821.[36] In evaluating these patterns he has relied on the so-called "Le Bras Method," which endeavors to work out an analytical formula for the religious activities of a people in any given period of their history based on the contemporary social, political, and economic factors involved.[37]

One interesting phenomenon that stands out clearly in McAvoy's treatises is the freedom discernible among Catholics in the United States. The American hierarchy, for example, is seen to be freer and more self-sustained than any other hierarchy in the English-speaking world.[38]

Diversity is another unexpected characteristic. McAvoy shows that "if there is one note that is forever absent in the story of Catholicity in the United States it is unity in either political or social activities."[39] If there is a Catholic vote, it is only such in the sense that a good Catholic should always seek justice and public honesty in every phase of American government and vote accordingly.[40] The Notre Dame historian does not overstate his position when he affirms that "in the Catholic Church in the United States one can detect with differences of proportion, almost all the elements which go to make up this great democracy of ours."[41] The divergent opinions among Catholics and between themselves and their neighbors about politics and business and social positions are just part of the American way of life which would be suppressed only in a totalitarian state.[42]

Father McAvoy regrets that Catholics of the last century failed to heed the advice of John Lancaster Spalding about the proper development of the Catholic minority and especially about Spalding's concept of the nature and work of truly intellectual endeavors. Had the ideas of the Bishop of Peoria been accepted, "the Catholic answer to the great social problems of the age would be more clearly defined in American literature and Catholic higher education would be far better equipped to withstand the materialistic pragmatism which is eating away at the very essence of true humanism in American life."[43]

As an expert in the American phase of Catholic development, McAvoy has noted that there has never been a real heresy during the three centuries and more of Catholic life within the boundaries of the present United States.[44] There have been "phantom heresies," however, and the shrewd observer can easily see how certain tendencies in the American Catholicism of the 1890s were wrongly rationalized by Europeans into a New World brand of Modernism. McAvoy has long considered this phenomenon one of the most interesting in all of American Catholic history. According to him, there were no theological overtones in the cultural conflict between "Americanism Reviewed by Abbé Felix Klein."[45] Then, in 1957, he published insofar as the conservative groups were trying to accuse the Americanizing groups of the condemned liberal Catholicism of the Syllabus of Pope Pius IX."[46] His essay, "Americanism, Fact and Fiction," gives "in an admirable way the general background of the conflicting personalities and the incidents which occasioned most of the troubles. It also treats of the European aspects that were expressed in the newspaper controversies in France and Italy" and the theological and political productions that were mainly responsible for the ultimate declaration of Pope Leo XIII.[47]

McAvoy's views were restated in an excellent, concise outline form in "Americanism Revised by Abbé Felix Klein."[48] Then, in 1957, he published the standard reference work on the subject, *The Great Crisis in American Catholic History, 1895-1900*.[49] This book had the honor of being selected for inclusion in the White House Library.

After World War II, McAvoy noticed some of the misunderstandings condemned by Leo XIII again in evidence.[50] This time, he noted, a "false Americanism is offered as an improvement of Catholicism in the United States by those who do not seem to understand the reasons for its present prosperity."[51] This movement McAvoy decried, reminding his readers that the tendency for Europeans to misjudge American Catholicism had always existed and need not be given any serious consideration. Perhaps the most unfortunate result of the whole Americanism issue was the sad effect it had on historical writing, for as Father McAvoy says, "There has been a too great reluctance to discuss the accomplishments of those energetic leaders of Catholicism at the turn of the century, whose zeal led them into the controversy but did not keep them from working tirelessly in the service of the Church in America."[52]

To the dismay of current educators, Father McAvoy points out that nearly every phase of present-day arguments about the Catholic school was discussed in the period between 1870 and 1900. Far from being an episcopal "imposition," the noted historian recalls that the Instruction of 1875 establishing Catholic schools at the parish level was championed by the laity who were unwilling to accept the more modest proposals of the nation's hierarchy.[53]

As an educator himself, McAvoy recognizes the need for certain changes in the contemporary Catholic approach to learning, though he is wont to suspect that "the basic reason for the lack of intellectual leaders among American Catholics is closely connected with a too great attachment of Catholic families to this world's comforts."[54] Considering the cultural background of worldly poverty and limited resources available to Catholics, McAvoy feels that Catholic higher education has not failed.[55] In his own analysis of the shortcomings discernible in the field, he observes that the seminary curriculum, which originally formed the basis of Catholic collegiate courses, failed to take properly into consideration that most of the students had chosen secular professions.

If there is a failure on the part of Thomistic philosophy to meet current problems, then McAvoy attributes that failure to the philosophers themselves, not to Scholasticism. He goes a step further by suggesting that "the historian of Catholic education in the United States has some justification for questioning the dominance of philosophers in our Catholic colleges and universities," since these scholars have generally failed to create a living, relevant, and influential Catholic philosophy.[56]

McAvoy concedes that there are no shortcuts to the educational process. His years in the classroom have convinced him that "true learning seldom appeals directly to the emotions."[57] Rather, he has said, education is the work of the student "and there is no magical book or teacher who can change the dullard or slothful youth into a wise and learned youth!"[58]

In a survey article such as this it is impossible to more than mention McAvoy's more prominent works. This outstanding scholar's prodigious writings, dating from his teen years when he wrote extensively for the Tipton *Times*, encompass now a half century's collection of outstanding literary and historical productions. He has contributed learned articles to the *Encyclopedia of Religion*, the *Dictionary of American Biography*, the *Indiana Magazine of History*, *Grolier's Encyclopedia*, the *Catholic Encyclopedia*, the *Catholic Encyclopedia for School and Home*, and the *Dictionnaire D'Histoire et de Geographie Ecclesiastiques*. His concise book reviews have appeared in dozens of journals, to say nothing of the many articles carried under his by-line in *Notre Dame*, *Our Sunday Visitor*, and other Catholic publications.

What the silvery-haired Holy Cross priest once wrote about the ideal historian surely applies to himself: "To sift evidence patiently, to avoid the clamor of the daily press for flashy items, to bring to one's writings the weight of learning and skill, require talent and labor in every step of the process."[59]

Notes to the Text

1. Thomas T. McAvoy, "The La Bras Approach to the History of the Diocese of Fort Wayne," *Indiana Magazine of History*, LII (December, 1956), 369.
2. John Tracy Ellis, "Teaching American Catholic History in Our Schools," National Catholic Educational Association *Bulletin*, XLVIII (May, 1952), 8.
3. Thomas T. McAvoy. "The Role of History in the Catholic Liberal College," *The Catholic Educational Review*, XLVIII (October, 1950), 515. This article also appeared in the Bulletin of the Educational Conference of the Priests of the Holy Cross, XVIII (May, 1951), 22-29.
4. Thomas T. McAvoy, "American Catholics: Tradition and Controversy," *Thought*, XXXV (Winter, 1960), 583. Father McAvoy's article was republished as "American Catholics: History of a Minority," *Catholic Mind*, LIX (March-April, 1961), 125-34.
5. Thomas T. McAvoy, "The Cult of Philosophism," *The Catholic Educational Review*, LVIII (December, 1960), 595.

6. Thomas T. McAvoy, "The American Priest Discovers American History," *American Ecclesiastical Review*, CXXXI (September, 1954), 181.

7. Thomas T. McAvoy, "The Image of the Catholic College Graduate of 1961," *The Catholic Educational Review*, LIX (November, 1961), 508.

8. Thomas T. McAvoy, "The Study of History and Clerical Education," *American Ecclesiastical Review*, CXXVII (July, 1952), 19.

9. Thomas T. McAvoy, "Manuscript Collections among American Catholics," *Catholic Historical Review*, XXXVII (October, 1951), 284.

10. Thomas T. McAvoy, "Fact versus Abstractions: A Rejoinder," *The Catholic Educational Review*, XLIX (April, 1951), 257-59.

11. Thomas T. McAvoy (ed.), "The War Letters of Father Peter Paul Cooney of the Congregation of the Holy Cross," *Records of the American Catholic Historical Society*, XLIV (March, 1933), 47-69; *ibid.*, XLIV (June, 1933), 151-69; and *ibid.*, XLIV (September, 1933), 200-37. Just a year earlier McAvoy published a biographical study of the chaplain of Indiana's Irish Regiment, the Thirty-fifth Infantry. See Thomas T. McAvoy (ed.), "Peter Paul Cooney," *The Journal of the American Irish Historical Society*, XXX (January, 1932), 97-102.

12. Thomas T. McAvoy, "Brownson's Ontologism," *Catholic Historical Review*, XXVIII (October, 1942), 376-81. McAvoy subsequently explained how the great political theorist changed his notion of the role played by the Catholic church in America with the passage of time. See Thomas T. McAvoy, "Orestes A. Brownson and American History," *Catholic Historical Review*, XL (October, 1954), 257-68.

13. Thomas T. McAvoy, "Bishop Bruté's Report to Rome in 1836," *ibid.*, XXIX (July, 1943), 177.

14. Thomas T. McAvoy, "The Apostolate of Research," *Ave Maria*, LXXIII (January 20, 1951), 71.

15. Thomas T. McAvoy, "Bishop Flaget's Pastoral to the People of Detroit," *Catholic Historical Review*, XXX (April, 1944), 28-40.

16. McAvoy, "Manuscript Collections among American Catholics," 281-95.

17. McAvoy, "The Study of History and Clerical Education," 22.

18. For the interesting background of this program, see Thomas T. McAvoy, "Catholic Archives and Manuscript Collections," *The American Archivist*, XXIV (October, 1961), 409-14.

19. Thomas T. McAvoy, *The Catholic Church in Indiana, 1789-1834* (New York, 1940).

20. See book review by Fintan G. Walker, *Catholic Historical Review*, XXVII (April, 1941), 92.

21. Thomas T. McAvoy, *The History of the Catholic Church in the South Bend Area* (South Bend, 1953); Thomas T. McAvoy, "The Abbé Rivet at Vincennes," *Mid-America: An Historical* Quarterly, XXIX (January, 1947), 24-33; Thomas T. McAvoy, "The Old French Frontier in the Central Great Lakes Region," *Records of the American Catholic Historical Society*, LXV (December, 1954), 230-39.

22. Thomas T. McAvoy, "Father Badin Comes to Notre Dame," *Indiana Magazine of History*, XXIX (March, 1933), 7-16.

23. Thomas T. McAvoy, "John F. O'Hara, C.S.C., and Notre Dame," *Records of the American Catholic Historical Society*, LXIV (March, 1953), 3-21; Thomas T. McAvoy, *Father O'Hara of Notre Dame: The Cardinal Archbishop of Philadelphia* (Notre Dame, Ind., 1967).

24. Thomas T. McAvoy, "Notre Dame 1919-1922: The Burns Revolution," *The Review of Politics*, XXV (October, 1963), 431-50; Thomas T. McAvoy, "The *Ave Maria* After 100 Years," *Ave Maria*, CI (May 1, 1965), 6-9, 21.

25. Thomas T. McAvoy, "The American Clergy and History," *Ave Maria*, LVIII (September 25, 1953), 391.

26. Aaron I. Abell *et al.*, *A History of the United States* (New York, 1951).

27. Thomas T. McAvoy (ed.), *Roman Catholicism and the American Way of Life* (Notre Dame, Ind., 1960); Thomas T. McAvoy *et al.*, *Midwest: Myth or Reality?* (Notre Dame, Ind., 1961), 53-72.

28. Thomas T. McAvoy, "The Catholic Church in the United States Between Two Wars," *The Review of Politics*, IV (October, 1942), 409-31; Thomas T. McAvoy, "The Catholic Church in the United States," in Waldemar Gurian and M.A. Fitzsimons (eds.), *The Catholic Church in World Affairs* (Notre Dame, Ind., 1953), 358-76: Thomas T. McAvoy, "This American Catholicism," *The Catholic World*, CXC (November, 1959), 117-23.

29. Thomas T. McAvoy, "Roosevelt: A Modern Jefferson," *The Review of Politics*, VII (July, 1945), 279.

30. McAvoy, "The Study of History and Clerical Education," 21.

31. Thomas T. McAvoy, "American Catholicism and World Catholicism," *The Review of Politics*, XXVIII (July, 1966), 388.

32. Thomas T. McAvoy, "Public Schools vs. Catholic Schools and James McMasters," *ibid.*, XXVIII (January, 1966), 19.

33. Thomas T. McAvoy. "The Formation of the Catholic Minority in the United States, 1820-1860," *ibid.*, X (January, 1948), 15.

34. Thomas T. McAvoy, "The Catholic Minority in Early Pittsburgh," *Records of the American Catholic Historical Society*, LXXII (September-December, 1961), 67.

35. Thomas T. McAvoy, "The Anguish of the Catholic Minority," *American Ecclesiastical Review*, CXXI (November, 1949), 382.

36. Thomas T. McAvoy, "The Catholic Minority in the United States, 1789-1821," *Historical Records and Studies*, XXXIX-XL (1952), 50.

37. McAvoy, "The Le Bras Approach," 370.

38. McAvoy, "The Catholic Minority in the United States," 33.

39. Thomas T. McAvoy, "The Background of American Catholic Unity," *American Ecclesiastical Review*, CLV (December, 1966), 384.

40. Thomas T. McAvoy, "Where is the Catholic Vote?" *Ave Maria*, LXXXIII (June 16, 1956), 16.

41. McAvoy, "The Catholic Church in the United States Between Two Wars," 409.

42. Thomas T. McAvoy, "American Catholics and the Second World War," *The Review of Politics*, VI (April, 1944), 150.

43. Thomas T. McAvoy, "Bishop John Lancaster Spalding and the Catholic Minority (1877-1908)," *ibid.*, XII (January, 1950), 19. Father McAvoy's article was republished in M. A. Fitzsimons, Thomas T. McAvoy, and Frank O'Malley (eds.), *The Image of Man* (Notre Dame, Ind., 1959), 392-406.

44. McAvoy, "The Formation of the Catholic Minority in the United States," 13.

45. Quoted in Walter Romig, *The Book of Catholic Authors* (6th series, Grosse Point, Mich., n.d.), 261.

46. Thomas T. McAvoy, "The Catholic Minority after the Americanist Controversy, 1899-1917: A Survey," *The Review of Politics*, XXI (January, 1959), 55.

47. Thomas T. McAvoy, "Americanism, Fact and Fiction," *Catholic Historical Review*, XXXI (July, 1945), 133-53; Peter E. Hogan, S.S.J., *The Catholic University of America, 1896-1903* (Washington, 1949), 138n.

48. Thomas T. McAvoy, "Americanism Reviewed by Abbé Felix Klein," *American Ecclesiastical Review*, CXXII (May, 1950), 355-63.

49. Thomas T. McAvoy, *The Great Crisis in American Catholic History, 1895-1900* (Chicago, 1957). The work was reissued in paperback form as *The Americanist Heresy in Roman Catholicism, 1895-1900* (Notre Dame, Ind., 1963).

50. For McAvoy's assessment of this pontiff, see Thomas T. McAvoy, "Leo XIII and America," in Edward T. Gargan (ed.), *Leo XIII and the Modern World* (New York, 1961), 157-78; and Thomas T. McAvoy, "Pope Leo XIII's Condemnation of Pragmatism," *Ave Maria*, LXXI (June 3, 1950), 679-81.

51. Thomas T. McAvoy, "New Traces of False Americanism," *Ave Maria*, LXIII (January 26, 1946), 103.

52. Thomas T. McAvoy, "Americanism and Frontier Catholicism," *The Review of Politics*, V (July, 1943), 301.

53. McAvoy, "Public Schools vs. Catholic Schools and James McMasters," 20.

54. Thomas T. McAvoy, "Do American Catholics Need Reform?" *Ave Maria*, LXXXVII (May 31, 1958), 6.

55. McAvoy, "The Anguish of the Catholic Minority," 383.

56. Thomas T. McAvoy, "The Philosophers and American Catholic Education," *The Catholic Educational Review*, XLVII (November, 1949), 583.

57. Thomas T. McAvoy, "The Role of the Good Teacher," *ibid.*, LVII (October, 1959), 477.

58. Thomas T. McAvoy, "The Myth of the Great Teacher," *ibid.*, LVI (September, 1958), 361.

59. McAvoy, "The American Clergy and History," 394.

79

This essay on "Chancery Archives" is taken from the *American Archivist* XXVIII (April, 1965), 255-260.

According to legislation enacted by the Third Plenary Council of Baltimore, the care of the Chancery Archives "should be entrusted to the chancellor whose sedulous labor will be of great value in conducting the business of the diocese accurately and promptly." Frequently, in the larger jurisdictions, the chancellor has neither the training nor the time for such duties, and in some cases he has delegated this obligation to an officially appointed archivist.

Organizational procedure is rather uniform in American curiae. The table on the next page lists the major divisional units and internal organization of a particular set of Chancery Archives, those of the Archdiocese of Los Angeles. Smaller jurisdictions can add or omit units depending on local needs.

Quantity and quality of holdings will dictate the manner in which early correspondence should be filed. In the Chancery Archives of the Archdiocese of Los Angeles, all materials before 1903 (drawers 3-30) are placed in individual folders with the seal of the archives embossed on each document. In accordance with Canon 375, an accompanying 4"x6" slip is typed to serve both as a permanent inventory entry and as a card file for researchers. The slip bears at the top the seal and printed name of the Diocesan Archives and at the left, in a column, printed words to indicate the information to be typed in—"Correspondents: Date: Place of Origin: [and] Digest: ."

Drawer Numbers	Subjects	Arrangement
31-44	Defunct Diocesan Priests	alphabetical
45	Priestly Faculties	chronological
46	Priests' Retreats	chronological
	Chaplains	alphabetical by institution
47-52	Inactive Extern Priests	chronological
53-64	Religious Men—Priests	alphabetical by order
65,66	Religious Men—Brothers	alphabetical by order
67-85	Religious Women	alphabetical by order
86-88	Diocesan Seminaries	alphabetical by name
89	American Seminaries	alphabetical by name
90,91	European Seminaries	alphabetical by name
92,93	Ex Seminarians	alphabetical
94	Ordinations	chronological
95	Catholic University	chronological
96,97	Indian Matters	by subject
98-106	Auxiliary Bishops	chronological
107	Apostolic Delegation	chronological
108	Roman File	by congregation
109-112	Macdonald Legal File	alphabetical
113,114	Junipero Serra File	chronological
115-120	Cemetery File	alphabetical by subject
121-123	Details on Worksheets	alphabetical
124	Psycho-Ceramics	chronological
125-139	Parishes Inside City	by diocesan directory
140	Mission Restoration	by subject
141-168	Parishes Outside City	by diocesan directory
169, 170	Parochial Monographs	by diocesan directory
171	Other Calif. Monographs	alphabetical
172	Misc. Hist. Monographs	alphabetical
173-176	Insurance	by subject
177-180	Education	by subject
181-184	Catholic Societies	alphabetical
185-187	Chancery Properties	alphabetical
188	Motion Picture Industry	by subject
189-207	General File	alphabetical
208	American Hierarchy	alphabetical
209-220	Misc. Correspondence	varied

When all the documents have been cataloged, an index of names, places, and incidents can be made to further facilitate quick reference. More recent correspondence (drawers 209-220) is arranged chronologically by year and then alphabetized. A record series may begin and end with a change of episcopal incumbents. As a general principle, all material not assigned to one or another of the classes mentioned above goes into this Miscellaneous Correspondence series.

Although the material in the Chancery Archives is "retired," there is frequent need to consult some of the documents. If there is basic uniformity between the current filing system and that used in the Archives, the procedure for finding particular items is greatly simplified. It is suggested that the drawers of the filing cabinets in the Chancery Archives be numbered as above. A chart of the overall holdings can then be made and given to other offices of the curia. In addition the labels on the drawers of the active records can carry the typed notation: "Corresponds to Drawers _____—_____ in the Chancery Archives." If this system is used, however, it is vitally important that the archivist allow generous room for expansion of the records, for he should not have to remake the charts more often than once in a decade.

The archivist is often confronted with materials that do not fit conveniently into filing cabinets or boxes because of their peculiar size. Maps, souvenir folders, mementos, undated manuscripts, and the like can be handily stored in a multidrawer all-steel functional unit. Most common is the 30-drawer case measuring 9 1/4 × 3 1/8 × 11 3/4'. Again, particular circumstances will dictate the divisional units although most of the following titles can be put to good use:

Archival	Hospitals	Photos
Cathedral	Indians	Plates
Circulars	Legal Matters	Propaganda Fide
Clergy	Local Prelates	Properties
Confraternity	Maps	*Relationes*
Deeds	Missions	Reprints
Displays	Nearby Dioceses	Seals
Education	Newspaper	Seminaries
Financial	Official	Societies
Forms	Ordinations	Synod
Grants	Parochial	Taxation
Hierarchy	Pastorals	Undated Material

It is also helpful to have a large press cabinet made to accommodate oversize books, newspapers, and pictures. Papal bulls, neatly wrapped in tubes, fit nicely into such a press. The upper part can contain several rows of shelves to house bound copies of diocesan publications, circular letters, synodal decrees, *relationes*, statutes, and diocesan directories.

Press clippings are best stored in boxes unless there are few enough for a scrapbook. If the services of a clipping agency have been used, it is not always advantageous or economical to buy scrap-books because the material is generally repetitive in content. The storing of blueprints, wrapped securely on rolls, will over the years save the diocese considerable expense because most parishes have no provision for retaining such bulky items. Firms doing business with a diocese can be informed that the bishop expects a duplicate set of all building specifications for the records. Pigeonholes built along a wall of the archives serve as useful containers.

According to the Code, all qualified scholars have the right to be admitted to the Chancery Archives and should not be barred if they comply with the ordinary's regulations. As a record for the archivist and a precaution against alienation, however, each applicant should be asked to fill in a questionnaire somewhat like the "Permission Request" illustrated here.

Minute regulations regarding the use of the Chancery Archives spell out what is expected of visiting researchers and eliminate requests for special favors. A copy of the rules, approved by the chancellor, can be handed to anyone seeking access to the archives; and exceptions to normal procedure can easily be referred to higher authority, thus freeing the archivist from responsibility for damage or alienation. The set of regulations given below was drawn up in accordance with Canon 377 and approved for use in the Chancery Archives for the Archdiocese of Los Angeles.

1. Permission to use the CHANCERY ARCHIVES must be obtained from the Chancellor or his duly deputized Archivist. All persons admitted to the ARCHIVES will be accompanied either by the Chancellor or the Archivist. At no time will a person be allowed to remain alone in the ARCHIVES.

2. The CHANCERY ARCHIVES are not intended to serve the general public, and only those having a legitimate interest in their content will be afforded admission. Among those whose requests will be favorably considered are members of the ecclesiastical tribunal and duly recognized historians.

3. Permission to use the CHANCERY ARCHIVES is not to be construed as authorization to quote *verbatim* from materials contained therein.

4. Every researcher or visitor will fill out a registration card noting thereon the purpose of his work and the materials he wishes to consult.

5. No book, document or manuscript shall be removed from the ARCHIVES except for the purpose of repair or to be photo copied, and then only by the Archivist.

6. Should certified copies of any document be required, the Archivist will arrange to have the pertinent material photographed. It is understood that the cost of this process is to be borne by the interested party. Microfilmed or photo copied documents, when used, must acknowledge the Archives of the Archdiocese of Los Angeles (AALA) as their source.

7. No marking of any kind shall ever be placed on any book or document in the CHANCERY ARCHIVES.

8. No smoking is allowed while examining or working with documents.

9. Any violation of the above regulations will be construed as malicious.

Questions sometimes arise about what actually is to be found in the Chancery Archives beyond the obvious documents of diocesan business. Frequently the answer rests with the archivist alone, and he quickly learns that the archives attract unwanted materials from all quarters. All records of the Chancery Archives itself should be carefully filed away in chronological order. At the end of each calendar year, these materials can be numbered and indexed by subject or correspondent and then bound together in a tome entitled "Archival Activities—1963." Among the items kept therein are the monthly reports to the chancellor, listing of purchases, visitors' forms, inquiries, and documents relating to any other business transacted by the archivist.

Records that are security-classified can be stored in a vault or metal cabinet with a combination lock. The chancellor and the archivist can formulate a policy on what records should be placed in this file, and it is understood that researchers are never allowed to use these documents without a special mandate of the bishop.

A final word might be said about two areas of curial business that do not usually fall to the archivist's care, the matrimonial archives and records pertaining to the financial dealings of the diocese. Experience has shown that these two areas are better served by maintaining the pertinent materials in records-storage centers separate from the Chancery Archives.

It has been said that the historical alertness and productivity of a people are true indexes of their culture. If they know their traditions, if they take a family pride in the achievements of their forebears, if they delight

in the tales of romance and sorrow in the lives of the men and women who made their history, such folk have their roots deep in the native soil, and they bear a definite stamp and character in their way of living. But without well-organized archives there can be no documents, and without documents there can be no history.

80

This study on the "Roman Archives of Propaganda Fide" is taken from the *Records of the American Catholic Historical Society* LXXVI (December, 1965), 245-248.

As recently as 1946, a prominent Catholic historiographer noted that "despite the substantial quantity of foreign material now available in transcript and authentic copy in American depositories, the researcher in many fields of American Catholic history must still have recourse to archives beyond our borders."[1] Chief among such collections are the Roman Archives of the Sacred Congregation of Propaganda Fide which Peter K. Guilday considered "the most valuable in the world for the American Catholic historian."[2]

Propaganda itself has a long and notable history. It was founded on January 5, 1622 by Pope Gregory XV as a congregation of thirteen cardinals, two prelates and a secretary, to which was committed the work of propagating the Catholic Faith. The territory over which the new congregation held authority was immense, embracing all areas of the world where the Gospel had not yet been preached or where a hierarchy had yet to be established. Since practically all dealings between the Catholic Church and America after 1622 were channeled through this agency of the Holy See, it is understandable how Carl Russell Fish could classify the Archives of Propaganda as "more important than all others taken together"[3] for a study of this nation's ecclesiastical history.

The archives are as old as the congregation. In 1627, Pope Urban VIII provided space for Propaganda's documents in the Vatican Palace and in later years they were housed in the Apostolic Chancery. From 1660 onwards, there was an officially appointed archivist and, except for the peregrination to Paris during the time of Napoleon,[4] the documents have been kept in the Eternal City's Palace of Propaganda Fide on the Piazza di Spagna.

Reorganization of the Roman curia by Pope Pius X in 1908 narrowed the influence of Propaganda Fide by removing from its jurisdiction those countries no longer considered missionary. Such areas were Ireland, England, Scotland, Holland, Luxembourg, Canada, Newfoundland and the United States.[5]

As an historical collection, the Archives of Propaganda Fide have been open sporadically to scholars only since 1863 when the present filing system was given permanence. Though Pope Leo XIII decreed, on August 18, 1883, that "our archives shall be accessible, so as to promote, as much as possible, religious and serious studies,"[6] Charles Haskins noted thirteen years later that Propaganda's archives "for some years open to the public, are now closed, as their constant use by investigators was found to interfere with the current business of the congregation."[7] Gerolamo Cardinal Gotti attempted to explain away his restrictive policy by telling one American Church historian that the congregation's holdings were "not primarily historical documents but the *family* archives of the Church, and as such do not fall within the expressed wish of Leo XIII."[8] Fortunately, in recent times, there has been considerably more freedom at Propaganda and duly accredited historians can usually gain admission to the archives upon presenting a written request to the Cardinal Prefect.[9]

As is the case with all archival centers, a knowledge of the parent agency's working procedure is imperative to a proper understanding of its record system. Like the other sacred congregations, the functions of Propaganda Fide are administrative and disciplinary, not legislative or judicial. Quite naturally, the archives have followed the physical structure of the congregation down through the centuries. The basic operational program of the congregation has remained rather constant. It is composed of a body of cardinals presided over by a prefect. Next in authority is the secretary who is aided by *minutanti* and advised by specially appointed consultors. The historical collection is cared for by an archivist[10] who works directly under the Cardinal Prefect. The actual administrative process can be seen by a close examination of the following documents which have been singled out for their special significance to students of American Catholicism.[11]

(i) *Scritture riferite nei congressi.* (1622-1892)   1346 vols.
   (abbreviated *Congressi*)
      The ordinary and routine incoming letters from church offi-
   cials subject to Propaganda Fide make up the thickly bound volumes of this series which is neither indexed or calendared.
   Tomes are arranged by geographical subdivision. The following
   have special interest for American ecclesiastical history:[12]
      a. *America Antille* (1634-1892)   11 vols.
         Islands adjacent to the continent.
      b. *American Settentrionale* (1668-1892)   32 vols.
         Canada, Labrador and Newfoundland.
      c. *America Centrale* (1673-1893)   59 vols.
         Areas between Canada and the Isthmus of Panama
      d. *America Meridionale* (1649-1892)   15 vols.
         Countries south of Mexico
      e. *America Misc.* (1673-1893)   4 vols.
         Latin America, Mexico and parts of Canada.

(ii) *Acta Sacrae Congregationis.* (1622-1892)   328 vols.
   (abbreviated *Acta*)
      Protocols of the plenary sessions of the cardinals form this
   valuable collection of resumes *(ristretto)*[13] and rescripts *(riscritti)*.
   Obviously compiled from a strictly administrative point of view,
   these tomes more-or-less repeat the data contained more fully in
   the following category.

(iii) *Scritture originali riferite nelle Congregazioni Generali.*
   (1622-1892)   1041 vols.
         (abbreviated *Cong. Gen.)*
      Matters subject to papal approval and discussed in plenary ses-
   sions, at which all the cardinals who form the congregation
   meet, fall under this classification. Tomes 256 thru 260 relate to
   America. The first 417 volumes were arranged geographically.
   From 1699 onwards, materials were filed chronologically and
   references to Catholicism in the New World must be sought
   through a system of cross references. This series touches on such
   pivotal matters as the erection of dioceses, appointment of bishops and church discipline.

(vi) *Udienze di Nostro Signore.* (1666-1895)   252 vols.
      (abbreviated *Udienze*)
      Minutes of the bi-monthly papal audiences are filed in this record series. Those matters requiring the pontiff's approval, such as marriage dispensations and special local privileges, etc., were usually presented in formal petition. The decision is noted at the bottom or on the reverse side of the written request. Arranged chronologically and alphabetically by jurisdiction, it not infrequently happens that "one comes on original letters inserted after the official notation...containing items of considerable importance."[14]

(v) *Lettere della S. Congregazione.* (1622-1892)   388 vols.
      (abbreviated *Lettere)*
      Decisions reached by the Cardinal Prefect alone, in plenary session or by papal audience, along with their necessary implementation make up this well-indexed series. The recipient's name and his ecclesiastical status are attached to the documents, many of which are digests of longer and more formal decrees or bulls.

In addition to these major records series, there are a number of less spectacular but equally useful categories. For example, the seven volumes of *Instruzioni* (1623-1808) contain vitally important resumes of instructions addressed to nuncios, bishops and vicars on matters of church discipline. Another interesting series is *Brevi a Bolle* (1795-1952), eleven volumes of the more important papal decisions on particular matters such as creation of ecclesiastical provinces and nominations of bishops. These are issued as briefs or bulls.

This cursory glance at one aspect of the vast holdings of the Archives of the Sacred Congregation of Propaganda Fide forces agreement with Peter K. Guilday's observation that this historical collection is "the pride of Rome and the delight of all who have had the privilege of working therein."[15]

Notes to the Text

1. Thomas F. O'Connor, "Catholic Archives of the United States," *Catholic Historical Review* XXXXI (January, 1946), 427.

2. *On the Creation of An Institute for American Church History* (Washington, 1924), p. 29

3. *Guide to the Materials for American History in Roman and other Italian Archives* (Washington, 1911), Pp. 121-122.

4. Several large record series from the Archives of the Sacred Congregation of Propaganda Fide are still housed in the Bibliotheque Nationale di Paris. For a list of these holdings, *Cf.* Fernand Combaluzier, C.M., *Un Inventaire des Archives de la Propaganda* (Suisse, 1947).

5. In America, Propaganda Fide continues to govern ecclesiastical matters in the Polar regions, a prefecture in Newfoundland and certain districts of Latin America.

6. "Saepenumero," *Epistola-Acta Leonis XIII Pontificis Maximi* III (Rome, 1884), 270.

7. "The Vatican Archives," *Catholic University Bulletin* III (April, 1897), 179.

8. Peter K. Guilday, "Sacred Congregation de Propaganda Fide, 1622-1922," *Catholic Historical Review* VI (January, 1921), 491.

9. The present Prefect is Peter Cardinal Agagianian. Permission to use materials in the Archives of the Sacred Congregation of Propaganda Fide is restricted and, when given, rarely extends beyond one complete century from the present calendar year. The archives are open from October to the end of July and researchers are admitted between 9 and 1 P.M. on Mondays thru Saturdays.

10. Currently, the archivist is Father Nicola Kowalsky, O.M.I.

11. For the past twelve years, Mr. Anthony Debevec has been cataloging and summarizing all the historical documents in the Archives of Propaganda Fide dealing with Catholicism in the New World prior to 1865. The work has been subsidized by the Academy of American Franciscan History in Washington which plans to publish a catalogue of the materials in several annotated tomes. All the calendared papers have been microfilmed for the Archives of the University of Notre Dame.

12. Researchers will encounter a great multiplicity of languages. Reports, letters and other documents are received in Latin, English, German, French and Italian according to the ability of the writer. The replies were usually done in Latin or, more rarely, in Italian. In practically every case, the volumes herein enumerated contain from 600 to 1000 sheets, foliated (and not paginated) by stamped numbers in pen and ink.

13. From 1817 onwards, the cases *(ponenze)* were printed.

14. John B. McGloin, S.J., "The Roman Propaganda Fide Archives: An Overflow and Assessment," *Church History* XXXIII (March, 1964), 89.

15. Peter K. Guilday, *op. cit.*, 490.

81

The following study on "The Catholic University of America Archives" originally appeared in the Records of the *American Catholic Historical Society* LXXVII (March, 1966), 50-59.

In a survey of ecclesiastical archives in the United States, the late Thomas F. O'Connor recorded that "Monsignor Peter Guilday, Professor of American church history at The Catholic University of America, has during the last three decades assembled at that institution an unusually significant collection of transcripts and photostats, gathered from throughout Europe and America, pertaining to the Catholic history of the United States from the eighteenth to the twentieth centuries."[1] Guilday proposed, as far back as 1924, the formation at Washington of an Institute for American Church History which would "bring together into one place the results of all the historical activities which have been part of our intellectual Catholic life from the earliest days to the present."[2]

Actual establishment of an autonomous archives at The Catholic University of America ultimately grew out of the combined efforts of officials representing the John K. Mullen Library and the University's Department of History. A Committee on Archives and Manuscripts, authorized by the rector on September 14, 1948, recommended and won approval for administrative recognition of a duly designated university archivist. In addition, the following regulations were drawn up to guide the activities of the newly created Department of Archives and Manuscripts:

ADMINISTRATION:

1. The Department of Archives and Manuscripts will have for its purpose the concentration, custodianship and servicing of the official records of the University, as well as of special collections of historical manuscripts.

2. The Department will be a separate unit of the University under the immediate jurisdiction of the Rector and it will have a separate budget which will be submitted annually to the administration.

3. The Department, however, will also be responsible for the historical manuscripts of the general library, and will work with the staff of the general library in the utilization of equipment for photostating and microfilming.

4. The Archivist as official records officer of the University will be designed as having power under the Rector directly to acquire and administer non-current records.

5. The Archivist shall be a priest who has training in American Church History and archival administration, and ordinarily shall be associated with the Department of History.

6. The work of the Department is detailed under the following headings:

COLLECTION (ARCHIVES):

1. Official records of any University office, school or department are the property of the institution, and therefore are not to be destroyed or removed without authorization

2. Such records include the following types produced in any office, school or department.

    a) files of letters sent or received

    b) record copies of mimeographed material; ledgers; cash books; etc.

    c) record copies of any matter printed for official use

    d) record copies of printed publications, e.g. doctoral dissertations, reprints of faculty articles, etc.

3. The existing material of enduring value in the various vaults and other up to now official depositories shall be unified in the archives.

4. The archivist, in consultation with the Committee on Archives and Manuscripts and with the heads of the record creating agencies of the University, will develop

a) a University records management program, aimed at facilitating the disposal of useless records and the transfer of permanently valuable records to the Department of Archives and Manuscripts.

b) a University-wide program for the disposal of records that do not have enduring value, and

c) a program for the accessioning of records of enduring value by the Department of Archives and Manuscripts, and, in his capacity as records officer of the University will submit these programs to the Rector of the University for his approval.

5. The archivist will be ready to receive and will seek such semi-official records of the University's life, as unpublished speeches or papers given at University functions, programs of University affairs not supplied by some official, campus publications of a popular nature, records of clubs and classes, pertinent pictures and cuts or scrapbooks, the private papers of members of the faculty or administration (except they constitute collections of historical manuscripts not pertaining to themselves).

COLLECTION (HISTORICAL MANUSCRIPTS):

1. These collections should contain non-printed documents pertaining to the history of the Catholic Church, especially in the United States. They may be of any of the following types:

a) the letters, diaries, notebooks, *etc.*, of Catholic clerics or laymen, whose papers pertain to the official records of no existing institution or to one unable to care for them,

b) the records of any Catholic organization presently defunct or wishing to dispose of the obsolete material,

c) microfilm, photostats, or copies of material in other archives relating to the history of the Church in the United States, and particularly of The Catholic University of America.

2. Gifts of such material will be sought by the archivist through personal contacts, and through the interest and help of the staff of the University as well as of its alumni and friends. No collection or part of a collection will be purchased or acquired by gift without a previous decision of the Committee on Archives and Manuscripts on its importance and value. If possible, gift collections should be received with the understanding that the University will have full control over them. In certain cases the Committee may decide to take manuscript collections in the nature of a temporary deposit.

PRESERVATION:

1. Both archival and manuscript material will be housed in Room 33 of the Mullen Library which has been made safe against theft, fire, insects and dampness. All such documents will there be treated in the same manner, except that the Archives proper will be separated by a wire screen partition across the far end of the room.

2. After assembling both types of material the archivist will make provisions when necessary for the repair of documents, and then undertake the shelving of them and the preparation of finding aids. Part of the room will necessarily have to be set aside for this processing work.

3. In time a guide to the collections of historical manuscripts should be prepared.

UTILIZATION:

1. Different regulations should be followed for the use of archives and manuscripts due to the diverse natures of the material. All searchers, however, should be made to register their name and address, the date, and the object of their search. Part of the depository room will be set aside as working space for them, and no material will be worked on outside of the archives. In time a small group of books might be brought together in the archives for the ready reference of searchers. The archivist will be in attendance and assist all those using the departments facilities. Mail inquiries, including requests for photographic duplications, will be answered according to the judgment of the archivist.

2. Archives:

    a) The agency producing the records will have access to their own records at any time. Lesser inquiries will be answered by the archivist over the telephone.

    b) Other members of the University will need the permission of the archivist and the head of the office whose records are to be consulted.

    c) Investigators, whether they are from within the university or not, who wish to do historical research will need permission of the Committee on Archives and Manuscripts, and of the heads of the offices whose records they wish to consult.

3. Historical Manuscripts:

    a) These collections may be used with permission of the director of the library and the archivist.

    b) The staff and students of the University are to be encouraged to use them for research and publication purposes.

    c) Primary utilization of historical manuscripts may be limited to the University body since the University has expended its efforts and money in the acquisition of them. In conformity with general university practice, however, a liberal policy will be followed regarding the admission of *bona fide* research students from other institutions.[3]

The newly inaugurated Department of Manuscripts and Archives at The Catholic University of America was blessed and formally made available to researchers at ceremonies presided over by the university's chancellor, Archbishop Patrick A. O'Boyle of Washington, on December 8, 1949, the patronal feast of the institution.[4]

In subsequent years several notable additions have been made to the original holdings. Twenty linear inches of manuscript records on the Fenian movement were added in 1952 and it was also at that time that Bishop William O. Brady "presented thirty-one documents, personal papers of Thomas O'Gorman, professor of church history at the university from 1890 to 1896 and Bishop of Sioux Falls from 1896 to 1921."[5]

Several years later, it was announced that the collection of papers pertaining to the nation's first bishop, gathered by John Tracy Ellis and Henry J. Browne during 1952-1955, would be augmented by copies of nearly 700 letters written by Archbishop John Carroll "in photostat form or on film."[6] In 1963, the papers of John Brophy, former special representative for the Industrial Union Department of the AFL-CIO, were "deposited by his family in the Department of Archives and Manuscripts of The Catholic University of America."[7]

Those interested in preserving materials relevant to the historical development of Catholicism in the United States are anxious to see the already impressive collection of documentary materials at The Catholic University enhanced by further contributions of public and/or private papers of outstanding American pioneers.

The following survey of the archival holdings now on file will be a convenient check-list for those engaged in research on some aspect of American Catholic history.

THE LABOR COLLECTIONS:
    1. John Brophy Papers, 1917-1963
            40 Boxes — Miscellaneous Correspondence
            1 Box   — Miscellaneous Speeches, *etc.*
            6 Scrapbooks

2. Congress of Industrial Organizations Papers, 1937-1955
    83 Boxes — Correspondence, *etc.*
    12 Boxes — Central Office
3. John W. Hayes Papers, 1885-1910
    35 Boxes — Correspondence
    24 Boxes — Personal Correspondence
    1 Box   — Letters from Terence V. Powderly
    3 Boxes — Membership Materiels
    1 Box   — G.E.B. Minutes
    1 Box   — Miscellaneous, Knights of Labor
4. Mary Harris Jones Papers, 1885-1925
    1 Box   — Clippings
5. John Mitchell Papers, 1889-1919
    45 Boxes — General Correspondence
    11 Boxes — American Federation of Labor
    13 Boxes — Correspondence, 1914-1919
    1 Box   — United Mine Workers Journal, 1900-1902
    2 Boxes — Strike Correspondence, 1901-1902
    3 Boxes — American Federation of Labor, 1912-1914
    152 Boxes — Miscellaneous (Correspondence, Clippings, Pictures, *etc.)*
6. Philip Murray Papers, 1943-1952
    137 Boxes — Miscellaneous Papers
7. Terence Vincent Powderly Papers, 1869-1924
    100 Boxes — Materials filed by weeks, 1869-1901
    50 Boxes — Letter Books, 1887-1907
    28 Miscellaneous Scrapbooks
    24 Newspaper Scrapbooks
    83 Boxes — Miscellaneous Materials, filed by title
    7 Volumes of Proceedings of the General Assembly, Knights of Labor
8. Miscellaneous Materials
    77 Scrapbooks pertaining to Labor Activities
    Miscellaneous Collection of Source Books on Local Labor Activities

THE FACULTY COLLECTIONS:
1. Thomas Bouquillon Papers
    1 Box   — Materials, 1873-1902

2. Romanus Butin Papers
   1 Box   — Miscellaneous clippings, 1900-1921
3. John Montgomery Cooper Papers
   16 Boxes — Papers, 1898-1949
4. George F. Dougherty Papers
   2 Boxes   — Papers, 1900-1925
5. John Tracy Ellis Papers
   3 Boxes   — Historical notes, n.d.
6. Philip J. Garrigan Papers
   1 Box   — Papers, 1896-1901
7. John J. Griffin Papers
   1 Folder — Professional Certificates, n.d.
8. Peter K. Guilday Papers
   105 Boxes — Historical Materials, 1914-1947
   8 Scrapbooks — clippings
9. Francis J. Haas Papers
   28 Boxes — Papers, 1919-1952
10. Patrick J. Healy Papers
   8 Boxes   — Writings and Notes, n.d.
11. Edward B. Jordan Papers
   10 Boxes — Papers, 1930-1948
12. Henry Hyvernat Papers
   3 Boxes   — Papers, 1890-1939
13. William J. Kerby Papers
   8 Boxes   — Papers, 1887-1936
14. Thomas Simm Lee Papers
   1 Box   — Correspondence, 1860-1898
15. Charles H. McCarthy Papers
   9 Boxes   — Papers, 1900-1920
16. Patrick J. McCormick Papers
   2 Boxes   — Personal Papers, 1914-1935
17. Martin R. P. McGuire Papers
   2 Boxes   — Committee service materials, 1945-1955
18. Bernard McKenna Papers
   1 Box   — Papers, 1920-1935
19. Donald A. MacLean Papers
   3 Boxes   — Writings, Correspondence, 1935-1950
20. Charles P. Neill Papers
   5 Boxes   — Papers, 1895-1900

21. Thomas O'Gorman Papers
       1 Box   — Papers, 1895-1900
22. Edward A. Pace Papers
       9 Boxes — Personal and semi-official materials, 1890-1925
23. Richard J. Purcell Papers
       1 Box   — Writings, 1939
24. William T. Russell Papers
       4 Boxes — Clippings and Correspondence, 1925-1945
25. John A. Ryan Papers
       6 Boxes — Papers, 1909-1945
       20 Scrapbooks
26. Thomas J. Shahan Papers
       25 Boxes — Personal Papers, 1909-1928
27. Fulton J. Sheen Papers
       1 Box   — Notes and Writings, n.d.
28. Ignatius Smith, O.P. Papers
       1 Box   — Writings and Miscellaneous, n.d.
29. John Spensley Papers
       2 Boxes — Papers, 1903-1915
30. Leo F. Stock Papers
       6 Boxes — Papers, 1925-1945
31. Charles Warren Stoddard and Joseph Schroeder Papers
       1 Box   — Parts of original diaries, c. 1895

THE NON-FACULTY COLLECTIONS:

1. John Carroll Papers
       9 Boxes — Photostats, 1764-1814
2. Patrick Cudmore Papers
       1 Box   — Manuscript writings on Irish history, n.d.
3. Charles Warren Currier Papers
       17 Boxes — Writings and Correspondence, 1890-1920
4. Richard L. Deverall Papers
       125 Bound volumes on labor matters, 1936-1959
5. Charles Ewing Papers
       1 Box   — Correspondence, 1875-1890
6. Lawrence F. Flick Papers
       43 Boxes — Papers, 1875-1938
       146 Bound volumes of correspondence

7. Louis Aloysius Lambert Papers
      1 Box   — Papers, 1863-1909
8. Eli Washington Lindesmith Papers
      24 Boxes — Papers, 1860-1920
9. William Montavon Papers
      12 Boxes — Papers, 1925-1954
10. John Gilmary Shea Papers
      1 Box   — Clippings and Scrapbooks, 1891
11. John Talbot Smith Papers
      4 Boxes — Papers, 1895-1900
12. Edward J. Wallace Papers
      2 Boxes — Papers, 1816-1835
13. Joseph A. Weber Papers
      3 Boxes — Genealogies and Statistical lists, *etc.*, 1920-1935

INSTITUTIONAL COLLECTIONS:
1. American Catholic Historical Association Papers
      100 Boxes — Archives, Records and Correspondence, 1919-1960
2. The Catholic Encyclopedia Papers
      6 Boxes - Statements and Correspondence, 1905-1930
3. Committee on the Revision of the New Testament Papers
      2 Boxes - Records, 1936-1944
4. National Federation of Catholic College Students Papers
      5 Boxes — Miscellaneous Literature, Brochures and Bulletin,
1930-1950
5. International Federation of Catholic Alumnae Papers
      6 Boxes — Correspondence, 1914-1935
6. The Fenian Brotherhood Papers
      3 Boxes — Correspondence, 1865-1880
7. The National Catholic War Council Papers, (1917-1932)
      16 Boxes — Executive Secretary
      23 Boxes — Reconstruction
      4 Boxes — Employment Files
      4 Boxes — Motion Picture Committee
      1 Box   — Raymond O'Grady
      5 Boxes — Index Files
      11 Boxes — Men and Women's Committees
      15 Boxes — War Drive Files
      29 Boxes — G.I. Files

17 Boxes — Men's Committee
1 Box   — Historical War Materials
16 Boxes — Overseas Data
20 Boxes — Women's Committees
4 Boxes — Visitor's Houses
10 Boxes — Historical Material

MICROFILM HOLDINGS:

1. Archdiocese of New York Materials
   3 Rolls   — Data from the Archives of the Sacred
   Congregation of Propaganda Fide relating to
   Bishop John Hughes, 1785-1866
2. Diocese of Richmond Materials
   14 Rolls   — Data from the diocesan archives, including the
   Roman correspondence of Denis J. O'Connell,
   1855-1926
3. Archives of the Sacred Congregation of Propaganda Fide
   10 Rolls   — Data pertaining to America, 1600-1850
4. Archbishop John Carroll Materials
   11 Rolls   — Data, n.d.
5. Abbot Bernard Smith Materials
   15 Rolls   — Correspondence relative to America, n.d.
6. Henry Edward Cardinal Manning Materials
   1 Roll   — Correspondence with American prelates
7. Archbishop Martin J. Spalding Materials
   1 Roll   — Journal, 1860-1864
8. Bishop Peter J. Muldoon Materials
   3 Rolls   — Diary, 1901-1926
9. Hammond-Kehoe Materials
   1 Roll   — Correspondence, 1860-1883
10. Archives of the Irish College at Rome
    1 Roll   — American materials, 1832-1849
11. Franklin D. Roosevelt Materials
    3 Rolls   — Correspondence regarding Catholic Matters
12. Charles P. Neill Materials
    1 Roll   — Scrapbook, 1904-1923
13. Knights of Labor Materials
    4 Rolls   — Proceedings of the General Assemblies
14. Terrence Vincent Powderly Materials
    3 Rolls - Letterbooks, 1878-1887

Notes to the Text

The author wishes to acknowledge the kindness of the Reverend Michael Hall, O.S.B., archivist of The Catholic University of America, who, in addition to opening the archives for our inspection on a university holiday, provided a convenient overview inventory upon which this check-list was based.

1. "Catholic Archives of the United States," *Catholic Historical Review XXXI* (January, 1946). 425.
2. *On the Creation of an Institute for American Church History* (Washington, 1924), p. 35.
3. *See* Henry J. Browne, "A Plan of Organization for a University Archives," *American Archivist* XII (October, 1949), 355-358.
4. "Notes and Comments," *Catholic Historical Review* XXXV (January, 1950), 477.
5. *Ibid.*, XXXVII (January, 1952), 482.
6. William D. Hoyt, Jr., "Miscellany," *Catholic Historical Review* XLV (April, 1959), 28. See also Henry J. Browne, "A New Historical Project: Editing the Papers of Archbishop John Carroll," *American Ecclesiastical Review* CXXVII November, 1952), 341-350.
7. "Notes and Comments," *Catholic Historical Review* XLIX (July, 1963) 306-307.

82

"Printed Guides to Archival Centers for American Catholic History" is the title of this study from *The American Archivist* XXXII (October, 1969), 349-356.

The generally flagrant lack of concern by Catholics for the documentary evidence of their early history in the United States is a sin of omission for which there can be no adequate reparation. So careless, in fact, were certain pioneers that Archbishop Michael Corrigan of New York complained that "in too many cases old papers have been regarded as good only to burn or sell for waste."[1] The seriousness of this disregard for past accomplishments is further underscored by the realization that preservation of the contemporary chronicles concerning the growth and development of the church within the wholly new concept of a pluralistic society could well have formed the basis for one of the most interesting and edifying chapters in all of ecclesiastical annals.[2]

Without question the paucity of primary sources has been the chief contributing factor for the disjointed manner in which the story of Catholicism in this country has so far been related. It may be hoped that the discovery of new evidence, along with the more effective utilization of existing data, will eventually bring about an integrated and reliable narrative consistent with the best standards of professional historiography. Paradoxically, though they are widely scattered, poorly organized, and dreadfully incomplete, there are numerous documents available whose contents have yet to be exploited. That published guides do not exist for some of the more prominent ecclesiastical holding agencies can be considered one of the unfortunate corollaries to the neglect of prior generations. This brief sketch is restricted to those primary *fontes* of Catholic Americana for which at least some kind of printed finding device has been prepared.

The archival status of United States Catholicism was the dominating theme of a trilogy of general surveys written in a 15-year period. The first, published early in 1946, was Thomas F. O'Connor's analytical overview of those ecclesiastical, institutional, and religious archives which, by reason of antiquity, range, and integrity offer the richest opportunities to qualified researchers.[3] Also included in that well-balanced treatise are the canonical precedents for current legislation on archival management. In addition to updating the O'Connor article, Henry J. Browne's informative essay, "The American Catholic Archival Tradition,"[4] concentrated on the distortion and frustration unleashed into the public record as a result of the arbitrary attitude taken about retention of chronicles by many of the Nation's earliest churchmen. The New York priest also dwelt on the obvious breach between the notion of archives as treasure chests in which only historians and antiquarians are interested and the more complete concept of their prior role as tools of administration. He concluded by exhorting his fellow historians to make "the self-denying admission that the archivists whom they have for the most part begotten are meant to be more than the servants of the servants of historical truth." Browne felt that the time had arrived for recognizing documentary custodians, in a wider sense, as "the servants of the servants of God." In the last of the general surveys, Thomas T. McAvoy approached the subject from his vantage point as long-time archivist at the University of Notre Dame. Having personally encountered most of the technical difficulties in the science, McAvoy astutely advised against generalizing about what historians of the future might seek in record centers, in favor of a greater concentration on more effective means of preserving the evidence as it becomes available.[5]

Several relevant biblio-archival essays have also appeared in recent years. Forty of the entries compiled by Edmund L. Binsfeld for the Church Records Committee of the Society of American Archivists pertain exclusively to Catholic holdings.[6] An entire section of John Tracy Ellis' *Guide to American Catholic History*[7] is devoted to 23 ecclesiastical "Manuscript Depositories" located in the United States. Finally, in 1963, August R. Suelflow prepared an expanded edition of the *Directory of Religious Archival and Historical Depositories in America*,[8] listing 162 separate Catholic archival centers.

Of all the holding agencies, "the most valuable in the world for the American Catholic historian" is unquestionably the Roman Archives of Propaganda Fide.[9] Before 1908 practically all the correspondence between churchmen in the United States and officials at the Vatican was channeled through the headquarters of the Sacred Congregation of Propaganda Fide on the Piazza de Spagna. Two descriptive overviews of the vast quantity of documentation in this pivotal depository, one by John B. McGloin,[10] the other by this writer,[11] are useful as general guides for researchers of Catholic Americana. Since 1955 the Academy of American Franciscan History has been sponsoring the compilation of an index to Propaganda Fide's holdings in collaboration with Anton Debevec, a leading European cataloger. The two volumes, calendaring an extended series that has already appeared under the competent editorship of Finbar Kenneally, O.F.M.,[12] are indispensable reference works for ecclesiastical historians.[13]

Other archival centers on the Continent abound in materials not fully utilized by American Catholic scholars. An excellent survey of the more useful private holding agencies, most of them religious, is outlined by William L. Davis in "Some Neglected Archives of Europe."[14] Another valuable guide, extra-territorial in scope and not restricted to Americana, is Arthur G. Doughty's "Sources for the History of the Catholic Church in the Public Archives of Canada."[15]

If the foremost among the historical treasure houses of the Catholic Church in the United States are the Archives of the Archdiocese of Baltimore, it is because the incumbents of that episcopal seat, erected in 1789, initially exercised jurisdiction over the entire country. With the subsequent divisions of the vast metropolitan district, the premier see remained the ecclesiastical capital of Catholic America. Even today, a "pre-eminence of place" accords the residential ordinary of Baltimore precedence over all non cardinalatial members of the Nation's hierarchy. When Martin I. J. Griffin arrived at 1886 in Baltimore to do historical research, he found the archival materials there wrapped "in bundles in book closets" at the archbishop's residence. Little care was given the collection until it was almost destroyed by a conflagration in 1904. After that James Cardinal Gibbons entrusted J. Frederic Weltry with the task of arranging the documents in a logical sequence and relocating them in safer quarters near the cathedral crypt.[16] The actual cataloging was begun two decades later by George W. White and carried on sporadically by succeeding enthusiasts. In 1948 Archbishop Michael J. Curley placed the Baltimore Cathedral archives in a fireproof vault in the chancery office and appointed a part-time archivist to look after the collection. During the years he was working on his monumental biography of Cardinal Gibbons, John Tracy Ellis prepared a highly useful and succinct guide to the archives, giving a brief description of the different series along with such information as terminal dates, number of file boxes or drawers, some notion of their content, and a few words on their general arrangement. Also included were a list of newspaper files, Catholic directories, reference books, registers, ledgers, and scrapbooks housed in the archives.[17]

A brief overview of the 7,000 manuscripts and 35,000 volumes amassed by the American Catholic Historical Society during the first three decades of its existence at Philadelphia was published by William L. Lallou in 1915.[18] The short treatise also shed a "flash of light" on the extensive collection of Catholic newspapers, rare pamphlets, sermons, lectures, and biographical sketches that had been collected by the Nation's oldest Catholic historical society.

It was during the 1880's that James Farnham Edwards,[19] librarian at the University of Notre Dame, "first conceived the idea of collecting in one place the documents and other priceless papers referring principally to the history of the Catholic Church in America."[20] Edwards' systematic endeavor to gather, from a wide array of sources, any and all kinds of relevant material into his envisioned Catholic Archives of America[21] eventually culminated in the largest single collection of its kind in the country. Thomas T. McAvoy compiled an outline of the major categories in the rich archival center in 1952, along with pertinent excerpts from Edwards' unpublished diary concerning some of the obstacles he encountered in his zealous pursuits.[22]

Except in isolated cases, very little was done towards preserving the records of Catholic activities in the decades immediately following Edwards' death in 1911. The eminent ecclesiastical historian, Peter K. Guilday of The Catholic University of America, attempted to enkindle new interest in the project by calling for the establishment in 1924 of a national Catholic historical center honoring the centenary of John Gilmary Shea's birth.[23] "His plan envisioned a permanent center of Catholic scholarship encompassing three broad aspects: the preservation and classification of a national Catholic archives, formation of a national Catholic library, and establishment of an institute for training reputable historians."[24] Even Guilday's persuasive plea, however, was buried beneath the indifference of those without whose support such a program could not succeed.

Agitation for setting up an archival depository at The Catholic University of America was an outgrowth of joint efforts by library officials and members of the history staff.[25] Nucleus of the collection, organized as an autonomous department of the university in 1949, was the outstanding array of transcripts and photostats gathered by Peter K. Guilday during his three decades at Washington as professor of American Church history. Subsequent designation of the Archives "as a repository for the papers of any prominent Catholic who has made a significant contribution to the Church or to the Nation and whose papers would have no other fitting means of proper provision for scholarly use"[26] has resulted in a widely diversified assortment of materials of vital interest to students of Catholic Americana. The major categorical divisions of the holdings are spelled out by this writer in a descriptive checklist, "The Catholic University of America Archives."[27]

An extensive microfilm collection of documentary sources for activities of the Society of Jesus in the New World during the colonial period has been amassed at Saint Louis by Fathers Lowrie J. Daly and Ernest J. Burrus. The materials, drawn mainly from Spanish, Roman, Mexican, and German archives, are broadly described by John Francis Bannon in his essay, "The Saint Louis University Collection of Jesuitica Americana."[28] Also located at that university are the chancery archives for the Archdiocese of Saint Louis. Some idea of those holdings can be ascertained from examining the general description and partial catalog prepared a half-century ago by Frederick G. Holweck.[29]

Surely the most ambitious accomplishment of its kind yet to appear in the United States is the 283-page calendar, *The Archives of the Archdiocese of Santa Fe, 1678-1900*, issued by the Academy of American Franciscan History in 1957. The extensive assortment of loose documents, books of patents, accounts, baptisms, marriages, and burials was assembled by the late Archbishop Rudolph A. Gerken in the mid 1930s. Although the vast majority of materials pertain to missionary work in New Mexico, the relatively small group of papers encompassing the pre-1900 archdiocesan era is also recorded in the calendar, which was prepared as an "extracurricular" project by the meticulously accurate Angelico Chavez, O.F.M.[30]

Similar in coverage, if not in thoroughness, to the Santa Fe calendar is Sister M. Claude Lane's short but well-ordered survey, *The Catholic Archives of Texas: History and Preliminary Inventory*, published by Sacred Heart Dominican College.[31] This 14-page compilation, intended "to make known the work of a group of men who collected and preserved the early records of the Catholic Church in Texas,"[32] extended Paul J. Foik's earlier "Survey of Source Materials for the Catholic History of the Southwest."[33]

Included in the extensive archival calendaring program of the Historical Records Survey of the Work Projects Administration, launched by Presidential order in 1936, were several valuable inventories of select ecclesiastical centers.[34] Each of the mimeographed volumes benefited from the collaboration of a large corps of generally competent and careful researchers and compilers.

The ecclesiastical record centers in California have received proportionately more attention than those of any other State in the Union. A section on "Archival Depositories" in this writer's *A Select Guide to California Catholic History*[35] enumerates and locates 8 curial holding, agencies and 11 nondiocesan archival centers in which materials relating to the Golden State's Catholic heritage can be located.

To the scholarly world the *Calendar of Documents in the Santa Barbara Mission Archives* (Washington, 1947), prepared by Maynard Geiger, O.F.M., and published by the Academy of American Franciscan History, is "an outstanding contribution to the study of California mission history"[36] as well as "a distinct service to archivology."[37] In the calendar, 2,842 items are specifically enumerated and described, exclusive of reports, statistics, tables, lists, and a considerable number of documents not belonging to the Californiana collection. Now that the archives have been reassembled in a specially constructed annex off the central corridor at Santa Barbara Mission, Father Geiger hopes to publish a revised and much enlarged edition of this valuable finding device. The interesting story behind the amassing of material pertinent to the beatification process of Fray Junípero Serra is told in Geiger's article, "In Quest of Serrana."[38]

Students of western Americana are quick to recognize the importance of the Chancery Archives of the Archdiocese of San Francisco, inasmuch as the incumbents of that metropolitan seat have traditionally occupied a pivotal position in furthering Catholic interest in the State of California. The appointment of a chancellor for the archdiocese, as early as 1878, conferred a measure of permanency on the ecclesiastical archives not widely shared by other American jurisdictions. Basically, the organizational structure has not deviated from that initiated by Father Charles Ramm, who cataloged the more obviously valuable materials shortly after the turn of the century. This writer examined the holdings late in 1963, and subsequently issued a survey article, "The San Francisco Chancery Archives,"[39] based on the format used by John Tracy Ellis for the Baltimore Cathedral Archives.

Closely akin to the Bay City's curial collection, but differing essentially in structure and content, are the Chancery Archives of the Archdiocese of Los Angeles.[40] Much of the documentation has been assembled since July 8, 1963, when, on the ground level of the newly constructed chancery annex, James Francis Cardinal McIntyre formally blessed and inaugurated what one local newspaper predicted would eventually constitute the largest concentration of ecclesiastical documents in the Western United States.[41] The numerous materials acquired in recent years render obsolete the brief overview, "The Los Angeles Chancery Archives,"[42] issued in 1965, wherein specific items were classified within general categories. The more outstanding accessions are enumerated in a special section of the annual edition of the archdiocesan directory issued by *The Tidings.*

In 1961 John B. McGloin published a descriptive account of a tour he had made 3 years earlier, to photograph materials from European ecclesiastical archives pertaining to the American period of Catholic development in California.[43] Items mentioned by the Jesuit historian are now in the Gleeson Library at the University of San Francisco.

Of vital necessity to any program of record retention is an understanding of the "archival mechanics" associated with collecting Catholic Americana. The excellent essay by Thomas T. McAvoy "Catholic Archives and Their Preservation,"[44] superbly outlines procedures for calendaring materials and schedules for retiring and/or disposing of outdated records, both in diocesan and institutional offices. The doctoral thesis of William F. Louis, *Diocesan Archives,*[45] in addition to tracing their canonical history, treats such practical items as the care, custody, and accessibility of documents normally associated with day-to-day activities of chancery offices in the United States. Charles A. Kekumano's opus, *The Secret Archives of the Diocesan Curiae,*[46] also written as a dissertation at The Catholic University of America, focuses attention on the creation, contents, and use of those ecclesiastical records that are rarely examined by historical researchers. This writer's essay, "Chancery Archives,"[47] based on the organizational structures used in the Archdiocese of Los Angeles, was prepared specifically as a guide for American curiae interested in adopting a workable yet simple solution for cataloging their holdings. A considerable amount of useful information for classifying materials associated with religious orders is obtainable in Sister M. Paschalia's account of the records and archives of the Dominican Sisters housed at Santa Clara Convent in Sinsinawa, Wis.[48] Additional data can be gleaned from the "Trial Draft" of *Archives Management,* issued by the Generalate of the Sisters of Mercy.[49]

A former Assistant Chief of the Manuscript Divison at the Library of Congress once noted that "the Catholic Church, though firm in her reliance upon something higher than humanity, can nevertheless ill afford to be neglectful towards the record of her human activities."[50] Fortunately, evidence points to a more intensified archival consciousness on the part of the Nation's ecclesiastical administrators in recent years, both among curial officials and directors of institutional activities. It is hoped that this archival *aggiornamento* will bring about the realization that even the "most highly significant and valuable collection amounts to no more than a warehouse of waste paper unless finding aids and retrieval systems are available.[51]

Notes to the Text

1. "Introductory," in *United States Catholic Historical Magazine*, 1:1 (Jan. 1887).
2. Lawrence P. Flick, "Preservation of Catholic Documents," in American Catholic Historical Society, *Records*, 26:105 (June 1915).
3. "Catholic Archives of the United States," in *Catholic Historical Review*, 36:414-430 (Jan, 1946). This article also appeared as "Historical and Archival Activities of the Roman Catholic Church in the United States" in *Church Archives and History*, p. 287-304 (Raleigh, N,C., 1946).
4. *American Archivist*, 14:127-139 (Apr. 1951).
5. "Catholic Archives and Manuscript Collections," in *American Archivist*, 24:409-414 (Oct. 1961).
6. "Church Archives in the United States and Canada; a Bibliography," in *American Archivist*, 21:311-316 (July 1958).
7. (Milwaukee, 1959), p. 7-12.
8. Issued by the Society of American Archivists.
9. Peter K. Guilday, *On the Creation of an Institute for American Church History* (Washington, 1924), p. 29.
10. "The Roman Propaganda Fide Archives: An Overview and Assessment," in *Church History*, 33:84-91 (Mar. 1964).
11. "Roman Archives of Propaganda Fide," in American Catholic Historical Society, *Records*, 76:245-248 (Dec. 1965).
12. *United States Documents in the Propaganda Fide Archives. A Calendar* (2 vols., Washington, 1966, 1988) 2,278 entries are listed, identified, dated, and cataloged in the first volume and 2,127 in the second.
13. The Archives of the University of Notre Dame has a complete microfilm collection of all documents enumerated in the Academy's calendars.
14. *Mid-America*, 38:15-37 (Jan. 1956).
15. *Catholic Historical Review*, 19:148-166 (July 1933).
16. "The Archives at Baltimore," in American Catholic Historical Society, *Records*, 21:85-95 (June 1910).
17. "A Guide to the Baltimore Cathedral Archives," *Catholic Historical Review*, 32:341-360 (Oct. 1946).
18. "The Archives of the American Catholic Historical Society (Philadelphia)," in *Catholic Historical Review*, 1:193-195 (July 1915).
19. For a biographical sketch, see Sr. Damien Tambola, O.S.B., "James F. Edwards, Pioneer Archivist of Catholic Church History of America," in American Catholic Historical Society, *Records*, 72:3-32 (Mar.-June 1961).
20. Paul J. Foik, C.S.C., "Catholic Archives of America," in *Catholic Historical Review*, 1:63 (Apr. 1915).

21. Because of the legislation in the Code of Canon Law, promulgated in 1918, the notion of a national agency was discarded. The title was changed by Thomas T. McAvoy to the Archives of the University of Notre Dame.
22. Manuscript Collections Among American Catholics," in *Catholic Historical Review*, 37:281-295 (Oct. 1951). For another interesting account of the archives, see *Library Occurant*, 11:177-178 (Apr.-June 1934), a reprint from the South Bend *News-Times*. A final descriptive article on the holdings of the Notre Dame Archives is Ralph Wright's "Something for Historians," which appeared in the *Catholic Educational Review*, 47:380-383 (June 1949).
23. *On the Creation of an Institute for American Church History* (Washington, 1924).
24. Francis J. Weber, "Peter Guilday: American Church Historian," in *American Ecclesiastical Review*, 147:150-151 (Sept. 1962).
25. Henry J. Browne, "A Plan of Organization for a University Archives," in *American Archivist*, 12:355 (Oct. 1949).
26. Michael Hall, O.S.B., "The Department of Archives and Manuscripts," in Catholic University of America, *Bulletin*, 1:3 (Nov. 1967).
27. American Catholic Historical Society, *Records*, 77:50-59 (Mar. 1966).
28. *Hispanic American Historical Review*, 37:82-88 (Feb. 1957).
29. "The Historical Archives of the Archdiocese of St. Louis," in *St. Louis Catholic Historical Review*, 1:24-39 (Oct 1918).
30. Both the Utah Genealogical Society and the Huntington Library at San Marino have microfilmed reproductions of the contents in the Santa Fe Chancery Archives.
31. (Houston, 1961).
32. Review by Bernard Doyon, in *Catholic Historical Review*, 48:298 (July 1962).
33. *Ibid.*, 15:275-2811 (Oct. 1929).
34. "These included: *Guide to Depositories of Manuscript Collections in New York State* (Albany, 1941); *Inventory of the Church Archives of Michigan, the Roman Catholic Church, Archdiocese of Detroit* (Detroit, 1941); *Inventory of the Church Archives of Nevada, Roman Catholic Church* (Reno, 1939); *Inventory of the Church Archives of New York City, Roman Catholic Church, Archdiocese of New York* (New York, 1941); *Inventory of the Church Archives of Wisconsin, Roman Catholic Church, Diocese of La Crosse* (Madison, 1942); *Inventory of the Roman Catholic Church Records in New Hampshire, Diocese of Manchester* (Manchester, 1938); *Preprint of Inventory of Records of St. Patrick's Church and School* (Washington, D.C., 1941); *and Translation and Transcription of Church Archives of Florida, Roman Catholic Records, St. Augustine Parish, White Baptisms, 1784-1799* (Tallahassee, 1941).
35. Pp. 157-162 (Los Angeles, 1966).
36. Review by Mathias Kieman, O.F.M., in *Franciscan Studies*, 8:205 (June 1948).
37. Review by Roscoe R. Hill, in *American Archivist*, 11:69 (Jan. 1948).
38. *The Americas*, 1:97-103 (July 1944).
39. *Ibid.*, 20:313-321 (Jan. 1964).
40. For the historical background, see Francis J. Weber, "California's Catholic Heritage," in *American Ecclesiastical Review*, 113:9-18 (July 1965).
41. Los Angeles *Times*, July 20, 1963.
42. *The Americas*, 21:410-420 (Apr. 1965).
43. "European Archival Resources for the Study of California Catholic History," in *Church History*, 30:1-3 (Mar. 1961).
44. David Martin, C.S.C., *ed.*, *Catholic Library Practice*, 2:87-99 (Portland, 1950).
45. (Washington, 1941).
46. (Washington, 1954).
47. *American Archivist*, 28:255-260 (Apr. 1965).
48. "Preluding History," in *Illinois Libraries*, 26:238-244 (June 1944).
59. (Washington, 1962).
50. John C. Fitzpatrick, "The Preservation of Ecclesiastical Documents," in *Catholic Historical Review*, 1:390 (Jan. 1916).
51. August R. Suelflow, "The Stewardship of the Institute," in *Concordia Institute Quarterly*, 38:119 (Oct. 1965).

83

"Ecclesiastical Archives" is the topic of this article taken from the *Catholic Library World* XXXXV (February, 1974), 330.

The collecting and preserving of ecclesial documents exemplifies the ageless dictum that "each dead hand relinquishes a light and each living one carries it on." Inasmuch as the history of the Catholic Church is the saga of mankind from the dawn of the Christian era, ecclesiastical archives are indispensable for adequately understanding the march of civilization.

Pope Clement I, the fourth of the Roman pontiffs, is known to have made provisions for retaining the *Acts of The Martyrs* through appointment of a number of notaries. That Clement's concern and that of his successors was heeded is evident from a host of patristic sources, including Saints Augustine and Jerome. A papal archives was operative by the close of the fourth century, as were parallel repositories in a number of patriarchates, archbishoprics, bishoprics and parishes throughout the Christian world.

Present-day legislation for ecclesial archives dates from Pius V's constitution, *Muneris Nostri*, issued on March 1, 1571, wherein, a local bishop was instructed, as he foresaw death approaching, to commit the crucial documents to his confessor or a monastery until a successor was appointed.

The legislation was applied to the Church in the United States, for the first time, in 1884, by the Third Plenary Council of Baltimore. After referring to Pope Benedict XIII's *Maxima Vigilantia*, on the traditional anxiety of the Holy See for archival holdings, the American hierarchy directed that diocesan tabularies be established, in safe and convenient places, for retention of the temporal and spiritual instruments and writings of local curial offices. They further entrusted the chancellor with the duty of looking after and preserving the archives in such a manner as to insure the accurate and prompt conducting of diocesan business.

Existing custodial obligations were codified and expanded in coverage by the promulgation of the *Codex Juris Canonicis*, in 1917. Canons 375-384 call for indexing and/or cataloguing archival holdings and inquiries about (and hopefully recovering) lost documents. In addition to spelling out a number of procedural regulations regarding accessibility and accountability, the code also touched upon the need for record-management at the parochial and institutional levels.

At the present time, the chief sources of manuscript materials and records for the Catholic Church in the United States are the Roman Archives of Propaganda Fide, Notre Dame's Catholic Archives of America and the Baltimore Cathedral Archives.

Among other prominent repositories, at the regional level, are the Chancery Archives for the Archdiocese of Los Angeles, the Santa Barbara Mission Archives and the Archives of the Archdiocese of Santa Fe. Additional worthwhile documentary collections are on deposit at the American Historical Society of Philadelphia and in the libraries attached to Georgetown University, the University of Saint Louis and The Catholic University of America.

The administrative machinery of an (arch)diocese, religious community or church-affiliated institution confirms that no factor is of greater importance as an index of ecclesial growth or decline, than the care extended to the records and documents of Church government and administration.

84

This study on "The Los Angeles Chancery Archives" appeared in *The Americas* XXI (April, 1965), 410-420.

Some years ago this author was commissioned by His Eminence, James Francis Cardinal McIntyre, to write a history of the Catholic Church in the southern part of California. The first and undoubtedly most important step in the program was a complete re-organization of the Chancery Archives of the Archdiocese of Los Angeles,[1]. for it was realized that "history to be above evasion, must stand on documents, not on opinion."[2] This proved to be a formidable task since southern California's early prelates were far too busy making history to care about recording it. Hence it was that several months were spent in the major archival centers of Europe and the United States photostating and microfilming the early correspondence and reports emanating from the jurisdiction's pioneer bishops.

Through the foresight of the Right Reverend Benjamin G. Hawkes, Chancellor for the Archdiocese of Los Angeles, one complete floor of the new curia annex was set aside for the archives, and in April of 1963 it became possible to separate the historical materials into a distinct collection. On July 8, Cardinal McIntyre blessed and formally inaugurated the Chancery Archives, which the Los Angeles *Times* opined would "eventually constitute the largest collection of ecclesiastical documents in the Western United States."[3]

Since that time, an effort has been made to classify the contents of the Chancery Archives and it is hoped that one day a published catalogue can be issued containing a brief description of those documents of particular worth.

Prior to 1962, the most valuable collection of documents pertaining to the diocesan phase of California's Catholic heritage was that housed in the San Francisco Chancery Archives.[4] Even today, the Bay City's holdings far surpass in quantity the Los Angeles collection, although their lack of organization renders them a difficult tool indeed.

Much of the documentation in the Los Angeles archival collection predating 1903 has been added within the last few years. Only since the turn of the century has there been an organized curia, and what little survived succeeding decades is due to the solicitude of the jurisdiction's several chancellors:

1898-1914	Very Reverend Polydore Stockman
1915-1918	Reverend Francis J. Conaty
1918-1924	Very Reverend John J. Cawley
1924-1938	Right Reverend Bernard J. Dolan
1938-1948	Most Reverend Joseph T. McGucken
1948-1956	Most Reverend Timothy Manning
1956-1962	Most Reverend Alden J. Bell
1962-1970	Right Reverend Benjamin G. Hawkes

This following guide mentions only those files pertaining directly to the historical development of California Catholicism. No effort has been made, for example, to survey the vast collection of matrimonial and departmental archives which, while they are of utmost importance, seldom contribute to the formation of an historical image.

I. THE MISSION PERIOD (1769-1840)

Mission Registers. 9 vols.

Most of the Register books of the California missions are retained by the institutions in question.[5] The Chancery Archives of the Archdiocese of Los Angeles possesses the following original volumes:

a) Mission *Santiago de las Coras* (Baja California).
    Register of Baptisms, 1739 thru 1768.   1 vol.

b) Mission *Santa Rosa or Todos Santos* (Baja California).
    Register of Marriages, 1768 thru 1862.   1 vol.

c) Mission *San Buenaventura*.
    Register of Patents, 1806 thru 1833.   1 vol.

d) Mission *San Diego de Alcala*.
    Register of Patents, 1806 thru 1842.   1 vol.

e)   Mission *San Fernando, Rey de España.*
        Register of Patents and Inventories,
            1806 thru 1847   1 vol.
        Register of Marriages, 1798 thru 1854.   1 vol.
        Register of Baptisms, 1797 thru 1855.   1 vol.
        Register of Deaths, 1797 thru 1852.   1 vol.
f)   *Gobierno de las Misiones de Baja California.*
        Certified typed copy of the original blotter
        book of the Church in Peninsular California,
        1840 thru 1872.   1 vol.

II. THE DIOCESAN PERIOD (1840 - onwards)

Historical Collection - I (1840-1903)

The documents in this section are filed in individual folders with the seal of the archives embossed on each page. In accordance with the Code of Canon Law,[6] a separate index file is maintained wherein the correspondents, date, place of origin, language, number of pages, and brief digest of all documents serves both as a permanent inventory and a card file for researchers.

   2.   Pre-Diocesan Materials
   3.   Right Reverend Francisco García Diego y Moreno, O.F.M. (1840-1846)
   4.   Right Reverend Joseph Sadoc Alemany, O.P. (1850-1853)[7]
   5-6. Right Reverend Thaddeus Amat, C.M. (1854-1878)
   7-8. Right Reverend Francis Mora (1878-1896)[8]
   9.   Right Reverend George Thomas Montgomery (1896-1903)[9]

Historical Collection - II (1903-1947)

The documents in this section are filed chronologically and then alphabetically with the seal of the archives embossed on each page.

   10 thru 12. Right Reverend Thomas James Conaty (1903-1915)[10]
   13 thru 18. Most Reverend John Joseph Cantwell (1917-1947)[11]

Historical Collection - III (1948 - onwards)

The documents in this section are provisionally filed by subject headings.

   19 thru 30. James Francis Cardinal McIntyre (1948 - onwards)[12]

General File

While the material in this section is officially "retired," it is correlated with the active files in such a way that each drawer carries the number of its corresponding cabinet along with a brief description of contents.

45. Priests' Faculties
Arranged chronologically in folders, 1927 thru 1961. One file marked alphabetically, 1948 thru 1956 and 1957 thru 1961.

46. Chaplains
Arranged chronologically in folders, 1917 thru 1960. Additional folders marked *Military Chaplains, Military Ordinariate, Chaplains Outside/Inside, Prison Chaplains,* and *Hospital Chaplains.*

47. Spiritual Retreats
Arranged chronologically, 1921 thru 1962. Additional folder marked *Clergy Conferences.*

48. thru 50. Extern Priests
Arranged alphabetically and then chronologically, 1904 thru 1936.

51. Extern Priests
1. *Mexican Priests during Persecution* - arranged alphabetically;
2. *Miscellaneous Personal Records* - arranged alphabetically;
3. *Temporary Faculties* - arranged alphabetically;
4. *Extern Priests*-arranged in folders alphabetically.

52. Extern Priests
Priests' Applications arranged alphabetically, 1946 thru 1960.

53. Religious Men
Miscellaneous Communities

54. thru 66. Religious Men
Arranged alphabetically by community's legal title

67. Religious Women
Miscellaneous Sisterhoods arranged chronologically, pre-1926; 1926 thru 1958. Additional folder marked Canonical Visitations.

68. thru 85.
Miscellaneous Communities arranged alphabetically by community's legal title.

86. thru 88. Diocesan Seminaries
1. *Los Angeles College* (1927-1954);
2. *Saint John's Seminary* (1939-   );
3. *Queen of Angels Seminary* (1954-   );
4. *Seminary Applications*;
5. *Seminarian Reports*

89. American Seminaries
    1. *Saint Mary's Seminary* (Baltimore);
    2. *Saint Thomas Seminary* (Denver);
    3. *Mount Saint Mary's Seminary* (Emmitsburg);
    4. *Saint Joseph's Seminary* (Mountain View);
    5. *Saint Patrick's Seminary* (Menlo Park);
    6. *Holy Cross Seminary* (Worcester);
    7. *Saint Paul's Seminary* (Saint Paul);
    8. *Saint Bernard's Seminary* (Rochester);
    9. *Mexican Seminary* (Montezuma);
    10. *Kenrick Seminary* (Webster Groves);
    11. *Saint Francis Seminary* (Loretto);
    12. *Outside Seminaries* - Miscellaneous.

90. thru 91. European Seminaries
    1. *Saint Patrick's Seminary* (Carlow);
    2. *All Hallows Seminary* (Dublin);
    3. *Saint Kieran's Seminary* (Kilkenny);
    4. *Mungret College* (Limerick);
    5. *Saint Patrick's College* (Thurles);
    6. *Saint Patrick's College* (Maynooth);
    7. *Mount Melleray Seminary* (Waterford);
    8. *Saint Peter's College* (Wexford);
    9. *Collegio Irlandese* (Rome);
    10. *North American College* (Rome);
    11. *Capranica College* (Rome);
    12. *Beda College* (Rome);
    13. *Albertinum* (Fribourg);
    14. *Colegio de Nobles Irlandese* (Salamanca);
    15. *American College* (Louvain);
    16. *Collége des Irlandais (Paris)*;
    17. *Collegium Canisianum* (Innsbruck);
    18. *Seminario Patriarcal de Cristo Rei* (Lisbon);
    19. *Montpelier Grand Seminaire* (Herault);
    20. *Ushaw College* (England);
    21. *Seminario Español Extranjero* (Burgos).

92. thru 93. Former Seminarians
    Arranged alphabetically in individual folders.

94. Ordinations
    1. *Testimonials*, 1951 onwards;
    2. *Ordinations*, recorded by year.

95. Catholic University
    1. *General Correspondence;*
    2. Monographs of *Minutes* of the Meetings of the Board of Trustees, 1936 onwards.

96. thru 97. Indian Affairs (William Hughes Collection)
    1. Transcripts of documents from the Bureau of Catholic Indian Missions;
    2. Private Scrapbooks of the Right Reverend William Hughes;
    3. Fifteen packets of photostats from the Archives of the Archdiocese of Santa Fe.

98. Archbishop Joseph T. McGucken[13]
    Personal file arranged topically and chronologically.

99. thru 105. Bishop Timothy Manning[14]
    Personal file arranged topically and chronologically.

107. Apostolic Delegation
    Arranged chronologically, 1905 onwards.

108. Roman File
    Arranged by Congregation and subject.

109. thru 112. J. Wiseman Macdonald Collection[15]
    Legal papers, arranged alphabetically.

113. Serra Collection[16]
    Photostatic documents filed chronologically.

115. Cemetary File
    1. Operational Reports arranged chronologically, 1954 onwards;
    2. General Account Reports arranged chronologically, 1927 onwards.

116. Cemetery File
    Financial Reports arranged chronologically, 1953 onwards.

117. thru 120. Cemetery File
    1. *Calvary Cemetery and Mausoleum*
    2. *Holy Cross Cemetery*, etc. according to entries in the diocesan directory;
    3. Miscellaneous Folders arranged by subject;
    4. General Correspondence, arranged alphabetically.

121. thru 123. Details on Worksheets
    Arranged by school concerned.

125. Parishes Inside City
    1. *Parish Boundaries,*
    2. *Miscellaneous Parochial Files.*

126. thru 139. Parishes Inside City
Arranged alphabetically as they appear in the archdiocesan directory.

140. Parishes Outside City
    1. *Miscellaneous Parochial Files;*
    2. *Mission Restoration;*
    3. *Installation of Pastors;*
    4. *Deaneries;*
    5. *Extra-Territorial Parishes.*

141. thru 168. Parishes Outside City
Arranged alphabetically as they appear in the archdiocesan directory.

169. Parochial Monographs - Inside City
Arranged alphabetically by parish.

170. Parochial Monographs - Outside City
Arranged alphabetically by city.

171. Monographs - Miscellaneous
    1. *Educational;*
    2. *Extra-Diocesan;*
    3. *Religious Communities;*
    4. *Missions;*
    5. *Miscellaneous.*

172. Unpublished Parochial Histories
Arranged alphabetically by parish.

173. thru 176. Insurance
Arranged by subject headings.

177. thru 180. Educational Materials
Arranged by subject titles.

181. thru 184. Catholic Societies
Arranged alphabetically by society title.

185. thru 187. Chancery Properties
Arranged chronologically from 1923, inside and outside city.

188. Motion Picture Industry
    1. *Archbishop John T. McNicholas correspondence;*
    2. *Reverend John J. Devlin correspondence;*

3. *Legion of Decency;*
4. *Motion Picture Industry,* arranged alphabetically;
5. *Material for American Ecclesiastical Review article;*
6. *Private Papers of John J. Devlin* - arranged alphabetically.

189. thru 207. General File
Arranged by subject, alphabetically.

208. American Hierarchy
Arranged alphabetically.

209. thru 220. Miscellaneous Correspondence
Arranged chronologically and then alphabetically from 1948 onward.

Curial Collection. 50 vols.
These volumes represent the major part of the official curial holdings for those years prior to the formal organization of the archives.

a) *Libro Borrador,*[17] *1840-1882. 1 vol.*
The invaluable "Day Book" contains drafts or blotters of all the letters issued from the office of the first Bishop of Both Californias and his successors. (Zerox copy)

b) *Libro Gobierno, 1840-1929. 1 vol.*
Companion volume to the *Libro Borrador.* This book was given to the southern jurisdiction when the Diocese of Both Californias (later Monterey) was separated in 1853.

c) *Libro Primero de Decretos y Dispensias, 1840-1899.* 1 vol.
Contains record of matrimonial dispensations and declarations of nullity, etc.

d) *Libro Segundo de Gobierno, 1851-1889.* 1 vol.
Parallels preceding entry.

e) *Ristretto Con Summario, 1860,* 1 vol.
Encompasses letters and briefs filed at Rome by the Right Reverend Thaddeus Amat, C. M., in his case against the Franciscans at Mission Santa Barbara.

f) *Roman Documents, Decrees and Faculties, 1840-1896.* 1 vol.
Contains encyclicals, briefs, instructions, dispensations, excom- munications, and faculties granted by the Sacred Congregation of Propaganda Fide to the southern jurisdiction.

g) *Book of Buildings, 1861-1898.* 1 vol.
Lists diocesan edifices and gives limited descriptions of holdings.

h) *Journal Book, 1896-1897.* 1 vol.
Contains entries in the hand of the Right Reverend George T. Montgomery.

i) *Registrum Confraternitatis Sacerdotalis Adorationis Sanctissimi Sacramenti, 1897-1922.* 1 vol.
Membership is divided into deaneries.

j) *Letter Extracts, 1877-1885.* 1 vol.
A partial "blotter book" in the hand of the Right Reverend Francis Mora.

k) *Church Property References, 1874-1896.* 1 vol.
Incomplete listing of diocesan holdings in the hand of the Right Reverend Francis Mora.

l) *Abstract of Title,* n.d. 1 vol.
Records of the Los Angeles Vineyard Society.

m) *Convent of the Immaculate Heart,* n. d. 1 vol.
A deed and property book on the Schumecher Tract in Pico Heights.

n) *Daily Journal Books, 1918-1923 and 1925-1943.* 25 vols.
Desk record of the Most Reverend John J. Cantwell. Very sketchy.

o) *History of Monterey,* n.d. 1 vol.
Handwritten account of the historical development of Monterey, California, 327 pp.

p) *Biographical Sketch-Right Reverend Francisco García Diego y Moreno, 0. F. M.* 1 vol.
Manuscript in the hand of Father Theodore Arentz, O. F. M.

q) *Biographical Sketch - Very Reverend Gonzales Rubio, O. F. M.* 1 vol.[18]
Manuscript in the hand of Father Theodore Arentz, O. F. M.

r) *Seminarians Memoranda, 1888-1893.* 1 vol.
Account of diocesan seminarians.

s) *Seminarians - Diocese of Monterey-Los Angeles, 1900-1907.* 1 vol.
Continuation of preceding entry.

t) *Acts of Council,* 1893-1918. 1 vol.
Contains council minutes and decrees for the Diocese of Monterey-Los Angeles.

u)   Chancery Office Diary, 1918-1924. 1 vol.
     This 112 page book is mostly in the hand of the Right Reverend
     John J. Cawley.

v)   *Chancery Record, 1855-1923; 1918-1931; 1931-1947; 1947-1961;
     1961 onwards.* 5 vols.
     Contains clerical biographies for the Diocese of Both Californias
     and its successive jurisdictions.

Miscellaneous Data Filed by Subject. 120 trays

Individual drawers are labeled. The titles below read from top to bottom, left to right.

1.	Bishop Francisco García Diego, O.F.M.	22.	Bishop Timothy Manning
2.	Bishop Joseph Sadoc Alemany, O.P.	23.	Bishop Robert J. Armstrong
3-4.	Bishop Thaddeus Amat, C.M.	24.	Bishop Laurence Scanlan
5.	Bishop Francis Mora	25.	Bishop James T. O'Dowd
6-7.	Bishop George T. Montgomery	26.	Bishop Harry A. Clinch
8-9.	Bishop Thomas J. Conaty	27.	Bishop John B. MacGinley
10-11.	Archbishop John J. Cantwell	28.	Bishop Patrick Manogue
12-15.	James Francis Cardinal McIntyre	29.	Bishop Eugene O'Connell
16.	(vacant)	30.	Bishop Floyd L. Begin
17.	Archbishop Patrick W. Riordan	32.	Bishop Merlin J. Guilfoyle
18.	Archbishop Edward J. Hanna	33.	Bishop Aloysius Willinger, C.Ss.R.
19.	Archbishop John J. Mitty	34.	Bishop Charles F. Buddy
20.	Archbishop Joseph T. McGucken	35.	Bishop Leo T. Maher
21.	(vacant)		

36.	Bishop Alden J. Bell	65.	Legion of Decency
37.	Bishop John J. McCort	66.	*Patronato Real*
		67.	Pious Fund
38.	Bishop Peter J. Muldoon	68-69.	Reprints
		70.	Property File
39.	Bishop Hugh A. Donohoe	71.	Papal File
40.	Bishop John J. Ward	72.	Archives
41-42.	Junípero Serra	73.	Archives - Applications
43-44.	California Missions	74.	Archives - Regulations
45.	Archdiocese of San Francisco	75.	Plates
		76.	Circular Letters
46.	Diocese of Sacramento	77-78.	Photographs
		79.	Weber Notes
47.	Diocese of San Diego	80.	Conroy Notes
48.	Diocese of Monterey-Fresno	81-83.	(vacant)
		84.	Parochial materials
49.	California Prelates	85.	Irish seminaries
50.	Hierarchy	86.	Diocesan seminaries
51.	California Catholicism	87.	Newspapers
52.	Lay Mission Helpers	88-89.	Saint Vibiana Cathedral
53-54.	Archdiocesan Clergy		
55.	(vacant)	90.	Saint Vibiana
56.	United States Indians	91.	City of Los Angeles
57.	California Indians	92.	Financial
58.	William Hughes Collection	93.	Catholic Welfare Bureau
59.	(vacant)	94.	Display materials
60.	Santa Ines	95.	*Relationes*
61.	Undated Materials	96.	Synodal materials
62.	Materials to be filed	97.	Pastoral Letters
63.	Propaganda Fide data	98.	(vacant)
64.	Maps, charts	99.	Ordinations

100.	Legal file.	111.	Franciscans
101.	Joseph Scott	112.	Jesuits
102.	Saint Vincent's College	113.	Immaculate Heart Sisters
103.	Edward L. Doheny	114.	Daughters of Charity
104.	Doheny Libraries	115.	Religious Orders
105-106.	Education	116.	Stamp Set
107.	José Alamany	117.	Taxation
108.	Queen of Angels	118.	C. Y. O.
109-110.	(vacant)	119-120.	C. C. D.

Miscellaneous Chancery Records.

1. *Transcripts of Letters in the Archives of the Bureau of Catholic Indian Affairs.* 2 vols.

2. Translation of Selected entries of:

   a) *Libro de Difuntos* (Mission San Fernando)

   b) *Libro Primero de Bautismos* (Mission San Femando)

   c) *Libro de Matrimonios* (Mission San Fernando)

3. *Taxation of Catholic Schools in the State of California,* 1919-1961. 10 vols.

4. *Relationes,* 1905 thru 1964, one complete set and several odd numbers.

5. *Announcement Books, Sacred Heart Church, Worcester, Massachusetts,* 1885 thru 1888; 1888-1891; 1891 thru 1895; and 1896 thru 1899.[19]

6. *Annuario Pontificio,* 1938, 1944 thru 1945, 1948, 1950 onwards.

7. *Catholic Directories* (national), 1833 thru 1834, 1836 thru 1837; 1840 thru 1844, 1846 thru 1847, 1849, 1864, 1871 thru 1872, 1875, 1877 thru 1878, 1880 thru 1896, 1903, 1905 thru 1915, 1917, 1919, 1921 thru 1923, 1925 onwards.

8. *Catholic Directories* (archdiocesan), 1953 onwards.

9. *Circular Letters* - bound 1903 thru 1926, 1927 thru 1931, 1932 thru 1935, 1936 thru 1940, 1941 thru 1943, 1944 thru 1947, 1948 thru 1950, 1951 onwards annually.

10. *Educational Department Circulars,* 1937 thru 1942.

11. *Clergy Appointments* - bound 1952 thru 1957, 1958 thru 1962.

12. *Synodal Decrees*, 1852 thru 1962. Two bound sets, bound in one volume and separately.

13. *Register Book - Archives* - bound 1963, 1964 onwards bi-annually.

14. *Catholic Charities*. Annual reports bound in three volumes.

15. Separate File for:

   a) Santa Ines Papers; b) Deeds and Grants, c) Miscellaneous Maps.

16. *The Tidings*, bound set from 1903 onwards. Several incomplete years, bound and unbound.

Historical Clippings.

1. *Archbishop John J. Cantwell*, biographical. 1 vol.

2. *Archbishop Joseph T. McGucken*, biographical. 1 vol.

3. *Bishop Timothy Manning*, biographical. 1 vol.

4. *Bishop John J. Ward*, biographical. 1 vol.

5. *Right Reverend William Hughes*, biographical, 1 vol.

6. *Lay Mission Helpers*, historical. 1 vol.

7. *California Catholic Heritage*, historical. 1 vol.

Notes to the Text

1. This author was officially appointed archivist for the Archdiocese of Los Angeles on December 26, 1962.

2. Lord Acton.

3. July 20, 1963.

4. See Francis J. Weber, "The San Francisco Chancery Archives," *The Americas*, XX (January, 1964), 313-321.

5. For the location of all the mission registers, See, J.N. Bowman, "The Parochial Books of the California Missions," *Historical Society of Southern California Quarterly*, XLIII (September, 1961), 303-315.

6. *Codex Juris Canonici*, C. 375.

7. Joseph Sadoc Alemany was promoted to the newly created Archdiocese of San Francisco in 1853 and continued to occupy the metropolitan see for the next three decades.

8. Francis Mora retired in 1896 and returned to his native Spain where he lived until 1905.

9. George T. Montgomery was promoted to the coadjutorship of San Francisco in 1903 but did not live to succeed.

10. Thomas J. Conaty had been Rector of The Catholic University of America for some years prior to coming west and had been Titular Bishop of Samos since 1901.

11. During his thirty-year episcopate in Southern California, John J. Cantwell served successively as Bishop of Monterey-Los Angeles (1917-1922), Bishop of Los Angeles-San Diego (1922-1936) and Archbishop of Los Angeles (1936-1947).

12. Before coming to Los Angeles, J. Francis A. McIntyre had served as Auxiliary Bishop (1941-1946) and later Coadjutor Archbishop (1946-1948) of New York. He was named a cardinal priest in 1952 by Pope Pius XII.

13. Joseph T. McGucken served as Auxiliary of Los Angeles from 1941 to 1955. He was appointed coadjutor of Sacramento in 1955 and succeeded two years later. In 1962 Pope John XXIII named him Archbishop of San Francisco.

14 Timothy Manning has been Titular Bishop of Lesvi and Auxiliary of Los Angeles since 1946.

15. J. Wiseman Macdonald was long-time legal consultant to the southland jurisdiction.

16 These are copies of documents used in the preliminary cause for Fray Junipero Serra's beatification.

17. The original is in the Archives of the Archdiocese of San Francisco.

18. The originals of entries # p) and q) are in the Santa Barbara Mission Archives.

19. These interesting and valuable volumes were acquired by the author in 1962 as vital material for the eventual biography of the Right Reverend Thomas J. Conaty.

85

This address was delivered on October 11, 1970 for the dedication of the Santa Barbara Mission Archives. It later appeared in *Gazetta* for Fall of 1989.

The public inauguration of the new and modern facilities for the Santa Barbara Mission Archives has been, is now and ever will be widely applauded, especially in scholarly circles.

This archival collection, long recognized as one of the nation's most precious depositories for Hispanic-American materials, has been housed at Santa Barbara Mission, since 1833. Researchers first utilized the Franciscan treasures, as early as 1877, when agents of Hubert Howe Bancroft transcribed twelve folio volumes of about five hundred pages each. Since that time, serious and accredited scholars have compiled a whole library of books, brochures and pamphlets on discoveries in the Santa Barbara Mission Archives.

Among the carefully-catalogued documentary materials are annual and biennial reports of the missions, register books, inventories, correspondence of missionaries and civil officials and personal diaries dating from the 1767 Franciscan penetration into Baja California.

There were no fewer than 2,842 entries enumerated in the calendar of the archives, published in 1947, exclusive of reports, statistics, tables, lists and a considerable number of documents not belonging to the Californiana collection. Over the past two decades, the quantitative archival holdings have been tripled with an additional 8,000 pages of transcripts relating to the Serra Cause, 2,300 from the Alexander Taylor

Collection and about 1,000 from Rome and the Chancery Archives of the Archdiocese of Los Angeles. The nearly 2,000 original documents from the De la Guerra Papers are the most recent acquisition.

In addition to primary sources, the Santa Barbara Mission Archives possess a unique collection of printed materials dealing with every conceivable aspect of the multi-phased California missionary enterprise. The remarkably diversified assortment of newspapers, magazines, directories and other related historical ephmera is also extremely useful to researchers.

The growing interest in the archives evidenced in recent years by the increasing flow, to the Channel City, of professional and amateur historians, geographers and ethnologists rendered provision of more adequate and accessible quarters a matter of utmost urgency and civic responsibility.

The massive collection, housed for many decades in the small, second-story cell of Father Zephyrin Engelhardt, is now re-located on the ground floor of the recently-completed western wing of the central mission corridor, just outside the Franciscan cloister. Provisions have also been made for a highly select and relevant library to accommodate the immediate needs of researchers.

Erection of the new facilities, fully equipped with temperature control for better preservation of the documents, provides permanent quarters for the extensive materials pertaining to missionary activity on the West Coast. Not envisioned as a competitive agency to existing institutions, the Santa Barbara Mission Archives, with its unique treasures, will continue its accustomed role as a center for diffusing an understanding of the Church's pivotal role in Hispanic-American society. The purpose of the archives, "to preserve and serve the public," is now greatly enhanced and facilitated.

* * *

It is eminently appropriate that the Franciscans, who figured so prominently in colonizing this frontier outpost on the Spanish borderlands should also be the trailblazers for collecting, preserving and utilizing the records of that gigantic undertaking. Surely, no greater misfortune could possibly befall a people than to lack a historian to properly set down their annals; one who with faithful zeal will guard, treasure, and perpetuate those human events which if left to the memory of man and to the mercy of the passing years,would be sacrificed upon the altars of time.

A host of historically-orientated and socially-concerned friars must be accorded a portion of today's acclaim. Among those worthy of mention are such names as Owen Da Silva, Francis Guest, Finbar Kenneally, Eric O'Brien, Charles Piette, Albon Schwartze, Francis Borgia Steck, Joseph

Thompson and Antonine Tibesar. Three personages, however, deserve special recognition for their practice of the beatitude which states that "he who records the good deeds of others is himself a doer of good deeds."

The "Palou" of post-mission times was Father Theodore Arentz. Besides an innate love for the past and a natural ability for recording it, Arentz was a first-hand witness to much of what transpired at the important junctures of his order's history. In his various positions as pastor, missionary, provincial visitor, novice master, orphanage director and guardian, he methodically collected and saved all the newspapers, magazines, photographs and letters in any way related to Franciscan activities along the Pacific Slope.

Throughout his seventy-four years, Father Arentz was a lover of books, a promoter of studies and a hard-working chronicler. He had the foresight and took the time to preserve the accomplishments of the pioneers. He was a careful scribe. With tireless energy and a minute eye for detail, Father Arentz recorded, in a clear and legible hand, several thousand pages of history about the apostolic college, the commissariate and the province which otherwise would have eluded succeeding generations. It was Zephyrin Engelhardt, the second person of Santa Barbara's historical trinity, who effectively utilized the musty old archival materials locked away at the mission. After giving an organizational structure to the valuable holdings, to which he added several thousand pages of his own transcripts, Father Engelhardt breathed life into the Santa Barbara Mission Archives by allowing the documents to speak for themselves on the printed page.

With that inordinate passion for truth and accuracy characteristic of the German-born, Zephyrin Engelhardt composed a veritable library of historically-relevant volumes, each one painstakingly researched and thoroughly documented. What niceties he lacked in methodology, Engelhardt compensated for by his carefully exact style. Ever the crusader, the venerable friar was anything but a colorless compiler of records. His zeal in spreading the account of Franciscan accomplishments in the Far West was slowed by neither illness or advanced age. He had printers' ink in his veins.

Father Zephyrin Engelhardt was not, nor did he ever claim to be, a professional historian. He envisioned as his successor, a scholar more artistically-inclined and educationally-qualified than he. To that man would belong the duty of couching the story of the California missions in a style as readable as it was accurate. The mantle fell to Maynard Geiger, whose familiar figure has graced Santa Barbara since 1919.

Soon after returning to the mission with a doctorate in history, Father Geiger was entrusted with the office of archivist. Over the ensuing thirty-three years, a steady stream of books, brochures and learned articles has borne the Geiger imprint.

Subscribing to the adage that "there is no substitute for documents," Father Geiger continued the Engelhardt tradition which acknowledged that chroniclers, documents and history form one indispensable link in the flow of knowledge from one generation to another. His contributions as archivist and historian speak eloquently for themselves and, in defense of Father Maynard Geiger, there is no need to wave flags, explode fireworks or blaze forth with bands.

* * *

This modest, but wholly adequate archive-library, the life-dream of a friar as well-known among historians as is Junipero Serra to the general public, represents a measure of the Church's archival responsibility towards the descendants of a society it helped to inaugurate, nurture and bring to maturity.

The appreciation manifested today by city, state and nation, is a public affirmation of the very real sacrifices involved in erecting, and maintaining these facilities. Truly the friars and their generous benefactors have made a singular contribution which a most grateful people can only hope and pray will be worthily sustained for future travellers along *El Camino Real*.

86

The essay tells about "The Chancery Archives of the Archdiocese of Los Angeles." It is here reproduced from the *Records of the American Catholic Historical Society* LXXXII (September, 1971) 171-188.

Inasmuch as the fabric of modern civilization is anchored to the foundation of preceding generations, it follows that "both the security of its institutions and the means of further progress depend in a vital manner upon the safety and accuracy of its records."[1] The Catholic Church is no exception to that truism. Though firm in their reliance upon something beyond the human level, the People of God "can nevertheless ill afford to be neglectful towards the record" of their earthly accomplishments.[2]

The paucity of written treatises on or about ecclesial activities in the Golden State, prior to the 1960s, can be attributed, in large measure, "to the almost total absence of documentary evidence, especially for the Church in Southern California."[3] The relatively small quantity of papers left behind from the early decades prompts agreement with James Steele's lament: "one can only regret for the thousandth time, that the secrets of the dead, and what the dead leave behind them can never be told."[4]

The Chancery Archives of the Archdiocese of Los Angeles[5] can be lineally traced to 1842, and the arrival of Fray Francisco Garcia Diego, first Bishop of Both Californias. The few documents retained by that prelate were entrusted to his successor, Bishop Joseph Sadoc Alemany, at Santa Barbara, in December, 1850.[6] Alemany briefly resided at Monterey before his appointment to the archbishopric of San Francisco in 1853.

Even with the creation of a metropolitan province for California, the geographical extent of the earlier Diocese of Monterey, though considerably reduced, remained quite extensive. Most of the pre-1853 documentation remained in the archives of the metropolitan archiepiscopate.[7]

Thaddeus Amat, subsequently appointed Bishop of Monterey, lived at Santa Barbara during the early years of his episcopate. However in 1859 this Vincentian prelate had the diocesan seat transferred to Los Angeles and, from 1861 onwards, he resided in the south at the Asistencia de Nuestra Señora de los Angeles. A separate episcopal residence was erected in 1879 just north of Saint Vibiana's Cathedral, on Main Street. In 1888-1889, when Second Street was extended from Main, a three-story edifice was built at 118 East Second Street. Provisions were made in the basement area for the archival holdings amassed by Amat and his successors, Bishops Francis Mora and George T. Montgomery.[8]

Since 1898, and Bishop George T. Montgomery's establishment of a formalized curia, a growing concern has been given to the crucially important question of record keeping. What historical material survived the onslaught of subsequent decades can be credited to the solicitude of the Very Reverend Polydore Stockman and those who followed him in the office of chancellor in southern California:

1915-1918	Rev. Francis J. Conaty
1918-1924	Very Rev. John J. Cawley
1924-1938	Right Rev. Bernard J. Dolan
1938-1948	Most Reverend Joseph T. McGucken
1948-1956	Most Reverend Timothy Manning
1956-1962	Most Reverend Alden J. Bell
1962-1970	Right Reverend Benjamin G. Hawkes
1970-1986	Very Reverend John A. Rawden

Shortly after the turn of the century, Bishop Thomas J. Conaty purchased a residence at 717 South Burlington Avenue.[9] The archives continued to be housed at the Cathedral, however, even in the years following 1917 when separate quarters were acquired for the curia in the Higgins Building. The Cathedral rectory, severely damaged in the earthquake of March 10, 1933, was replaced soon thereafter with the present building. Portions of the Chancery Archives were incorporated at that time into the active files of the curial office which had since been relocated in the Petroleum Building at Olympic and Flower Streets. A sizeable share of the more antiquated files and documents was stored in a large walk-in safe provided on the basement level of the new Cathedral rectory. When the archdiocesan curia occupied its own building at 1531 West Ninth Street in August, in 1951, those remnants of the Chancery Archives still at the Cathedral were moved to the new facilities and integrated into the general files. Apparently no attempt was made to isolate the historically significant materials from the overall holdings.

There are only a few sporadic references to the archival holdings scattered among the surviving correspondence. For example, in 1908 Father Raymond Carodevall, an official from the Spanish Diocese of Vich, solicited Bishop Thomas J. Conaty's assistance in locating documentary evidence about Joseph Sadoc Alemany. On September 29, Conaty replied that "up to the present time, it has been impossible to get...the information you desire."[10] Whether any materials were subsequently sent to Carodevall is unknown, although the petitioner is known to have enriched his findings with California items acquired at the local level.

In the course of compiling his "Guide to the Biographical Sources of the American Hierarchy,"[11] the nationally recognized ecclesiastical historian Peter K. Guilday contacted Bishop John J. Cantwell in 1919 for confirmation about data used for the entries on Joseph Sadoc Alemany, O.P. and Thaddeus Amat, C.M.[12] Before answering the request, Bishop Cantwell mailed a query to the Reverend Zephyrin Engelhardt, O.F.M., who responded with a description of several sources, including the *Libro Gobierno*, which "used to be in the iron safe of the office."[13] Engelhardt's observations were sent on to Guilday, along with a one page typed addenda of the documentary items then constituting the Chancery Archives for the Diocese of Monterey-Los Angeles.

In 1923, after completing a preliminary survey on his projected doctoral thesis at the University of Louvain, Father Thomas K. Gorman told Bishop John J. Cantwell that he was contemplating "a study of the history of the diocese of Monterey-Los Angeles from the foundation just at the close of the Mission period down to the recent division." He felt that such a project "would prove interesting and serve to gather together some of the materials of our history that will be lost unless the work is done soon." Noting that his program would entail "some research in the archives of Propaganda and in Spain in connection with the lives of the Spanish bishops," Father Gorman presumed that "our own diocesan archives should contain considerable matter also."[14] Bishop Cantwell, however, doubted if Gorman "would be well advised in writing an essay" on the history of the diocese, inasmuch as "very little of real interest or great moment" had occurred since the collapse of the provincial era. Cantwell felt that the only significant accomplishment, effected "through the instrumentality of the Archbishop of San Francisco, was the issue of the Hague Tribunal in regard to the Pious Fund." The growth in Monterey-Los Angeles, said the prelate, "was very small and without interest."[15]

Cantwell's enthusiasm for an overall historical program was even further dampened a few years later with the publication of Frederick J. Zwierlein's *The Life and Letters of Bishop McQuaid*,[16] a work which confirmed a number of American bishops in their sentiments against prelatial biographies. It is unfortunate, in viewing Gorman's penchant for writing and personal interest in the region's past, that he was not encouraged to assemble the archives at that early date.

In late 1922, the Reverend Paul J. Foik wrote the Chancellor of the Diocese of Los Angeles-San Diego for "facts about the condition of archives" in California's southland.[17] In lieu of Foik's detailed questionnaire,[18] Monsignor John J. Cawley regretted his inability to provide any worthwhile information, noting only that "apart from some old mission records of the Spanish days, and the official records of the various Bishops, we have very little of importance in our archives." The chancellor admitted that "no archivist has ever endeavored to classify our documents," nor did he "see any hope of having one appointed in the near future." Interestingly enough, Cawley harbored an ambivalent attitude toward his own attempts "to preserve every document and have them put beyond danger of fire and theft,"[19] for, on at least one occasion, the chancellor and a companion were observed spending "a good many hours in the old archives in the Cathedral rectory taking out things they thought were not useful or edifying."[20]

Apparently at Cawley's behest the title of archivist was conferred upon Father Peter Hanrahan on November 29, 1927.[21] He was instructed to examine and put some sort of order to the holdings. The Irish-born priest recalls that the collection was then "a mass of unarranged material in a walk-in vault with combination lock at the old cathedral rectory." Though he made some preliminary plans, Father Hanrahan's pastoral commitments at Ascension Church demanded most of his time and he "gradually faded out of the work."[22]

Three partial, undated inventories have surfaced at various times, all of them indicating the general framework into which the materials in the Chancery Archives were classified at different junctures during these early decades of the century. The first is a four-page enumeration of items filed in eleven envelopes stored in the "Cathedral Vault." A second incomplete series is typed on stationery bearing the letterhead, "St. Vibiana's Cathedral." A final two-page inventory, discovered in the

Gleason library at San Francisco College for Women, refers to the register books of ten missions in the "Los Angeles Archives of the Catholic Church. Bishop's Residence." In each case, internal evidence favors a date considerably prior to the mid-1930s.

The initial reference to the Chancery Archives in the diocesan *Relatio*, a report submitted to Rome at five year intervals, appeared in 1924, when Bishop John J. Cantwell tersely admitted that "*documenta ab anno 1847 et pergamina et incunabula sunt.*"[23] Possibly on the strength of Father Hanrahan's verbal appointment as archivist, the bishop felt justified in stating in his 1934 *Relatio* that the "well organized" archives satisfied all the prescriptions demanded by the Code of Canon Law.[24]

Apparently a portion of the archival holdings pertaining to Central California were moved north at the time the Diocese of Monterey-Fresno was created in 1922.[25] Bishop John B. MacGinley, in a letter to the Apostolic Delegate, alludes to correspondence found "among the papers transferred from the Los Angeles archives to those of this diocese."[26] Available evidence indicates, however, that the majority of pertinent materials were only transferred to the Fresno chancery on April 12, 1935. A four-page typed inventory of items removed from Los Angeles on that date by Father James Culleton, enumerates the general subject-headings of files relating to the new jurisdiction.[27] As soon as he had indexed the holdings, Culleton provided a copy for the Chancery Archives at Los Angeles.[28]

An interesting allusion to the archival depository appeared in one of the formal addresses delivered at the inauguration of the new Metropolitan Province of Los Angeles in 1936, when J. Wiseman Macdonald told Archbishop Cantwell that it was "eminently proper and just that the opening archives of the new Archdiocese should carry, on their first pages, in bold words enduringly inscribed, permanent record of, at least, some portion of the remarkable work done" by the Church in Southern California.[29]

Early the following year, materials dealing with the parochial, personnel and property of the State's four southernmost counties were gathered into wooden boxes and shipped to the Most Reverend Charles F. Buddy, the newly installed Bishop of San Diego.[30] A second transferal of deeds pertaining to the Diocese of San Diego was sent the following month.[31] An amusing sequel to that archival dismemberment occurred when the Apostolic Administrator of San Diego was asked, in 1964, about "the possibility of cataloguing" his chancery archives. A proposal was made to employ a seminarian "who might qualify, in future years, as the officially appointed archivist."[32] In his negative response, the bishop reported "that for all practical purposes we have nothing for him to work on," noting that "the only records are those which were sent from Los Angeles at the time of the erection of the Diocese of San Diego and they have no historical value."[33] In any event, the inquiry must have unleashed a burst of archival investigation among those records having "no historical value," for on May 7, 1964, the *Southern Cross* triumphantly announced that the diocesan chancellor had discovered the eight page deed to Mission San Diego de Alcala, lost for twenty-eight years, when "it was misplaced" after being transferred to the new jurisdiction in 1936.

Responding to a survey from Thomas T. McAvoy, C.S.C., about the extent of archival holdings at Los Angeles, Bishop Joseph T. McGucken wrote that "here in the Chancery we have what we call archives but they are not open to the public and consist mainly in documents and ecclesiastical correspondence which may some day have interest as far as the history of this Archdiocese is concerned."[34]

The late Charles C. Conroy (1881-1953) was responsible for "what little there is recorded of ecclesiastical activities in Southern California"[35] prior to the 1960s. Conroy's publication of *The Centennial, 1840-1940*[36] demonstrated his incredible range of knowledge, tremendous patience for detail and amazingly vivid memory for the minutiae of the Church's growth. In the final years of his life, Conroy retained a desk at the Chancery Office, where he devoted his time to gathering materials for the comprehensive story of Catholicism in the Golden State. The chancellor confirmed, in 1944, that "Dr. Conroy is at present working on a history of the diocese and trying to locate sources of information on this point."[37] Two years later, the progress of his work was acknowledged in a nationally circulated journal which stated that,

> With the purpose of collating source material which may serve as the basis of a history of the Catholic Church in southern California, particularly in the American period from 1850 to date, Charles C. Conroy, professor of history in Loyola University, Los Angeles, has undertaken an extensive survey of archives and collections of correspondence, newspapers, and diaries in that field throughout the area in question.[38]

Conroy's work was further recognized in the *Relatio* for 1949, with the observation that "*historiographus laicus, in curia occupatus, curam documentorum antiquorum gerit.*"[39]

Despite the professional tone that characterized his historical style, Conroy exempted himself from many of that discipline's procedural norms. He followed, for example, the unorthodox practice of indiscriminately incorporating documents from the Chancery Archives into his own personal papers, thus effectively denuding the overall collection of its most valuable holdings. At the time of his death Bishop Joseph T. McGucken confessed to a correspondent that Conroy's materials were "in a hopeless tangle and I would not know where to begin to look among the papers on which he has been working."[40]

Shortly after his demise, Dr. Conroy's papers were gathered into cardboard boxes and placed in a storage area where this writer observed them on June 6, 1955. Sometime between then and 1961, most of the materials were burned, according to Mr. John Russell, the building superintendent.

A few remnants surfaced, in mid-1968, following a communication from John J. Conroy that he had discovered "amongst papers belonging to my deceased father, Dr. Charles C. Conroy, a number of files of documents and notes he was apparently working on at the time of his death."[41] Those materials, consisting of a dozen or so exceedingly valuable pieces of episcopal correspondence, were graciously returned and re-incorporated into the Chancery Archives.

In the fall of 1956, partly in reaction to the sad fate of Conroy's abortive historical activities and partly out of concern for the frightful state of his dishevelled papers, this writer presumptuously requested permission to continue the work inaugurated by the deceased historian.[42] The matter came before the archdiocesan consultors on December 5, 1956, where it was decided that "it would be better to wait until after ordination before such approval were given."[43] Surely "in retrospect this was a wise decision,"[44] for it provided several additional years in which to gain a familiarity with the sources available in the area's various California collections. A sympathizer noted that he "even knows of one seminarian in Los Angeles who dreams much of the day when he will, supposing ordination and a few other things, be allowed to have at the precious historical archives of the Archdiocese of Los Angeles."[45]

Shortly after this writer's publication in 1961 of a biographical monograph on California's initial bishop,[46] James Francis Cardinal McIntyre made provisions for his enrollment at The Catholic University of America for graduate studies in history, under the aegis of the respected Monsignor John Tracy Ellis.[47] Intimately involved in the Washington assignment was the understanding that serious attention would be given to a program for developing some sort of record management system for materials in the Chancery Archives which were still a "maze of disorganization and practically useless as reference tools."[48]

Before departing for the east, a cursory survey was made of the more historical items in the archival holdings. In order to thwart any further despoliation by well-meaning but indiscriminate "space-savers," it was decided to gather the older documents into six filing cabinets and to place them in protective storage at 416 South Wilton Place, in Los Angeles. That the very core of the collection was actually moved out and totally isolated for a considerable period of time, without causing any discernible concern or interest, is an indication of the disesteem into which those vital remnants of an earlier era had fallen.

Subsequent attempts to complete a dissertation on the life of a prominent California prelate, Bishop Thaddeus Amat, confirmed the suspicion that the sadly deficient Chancery Archives at Los Angeles had indeed been effectively depleted, through loss, alienation and carelessness, of their most resourceful documents. This unfortunate but unavoidable observation was conveyed to James Francis Cardinal McIntyre along with the suggestion that a personal visit to the major record depositories of Europe and the United States might shed some light on previously unknown materials useful to the story of ecclesial development along the Pacific Slope. The valuable holdings of the Roman Archives of Propaganda Fide,[49] for example, were known to have extensive correspondence from the early California bishops. While acknowledging that such a journey "would represent a considerable investment for the archdiocese," it was pointed out that the many documents still missing were absolutely indispensable for an accurate portrayal of the state's Catholic heritage.[50] The Cardinal warmly endorsed the proposal "with regard to a journey to Europe for the purpose indicated"[51] and repeated his earlier-expressed concern that the program of relating the Church's development in California be accomplished in total conformity with all the accepted professional norms.

Four months of feverish activity were spent canvassing several dozen civil and religious archival agencies in Ireland, England, France, Spain, Italy, Austria, Canada and the United States. Though the quantitative yield was not excessive, the search did unearth some "cornerstone" documents on a wide range of fugitive topics, events and persons. With the subsequent integration of those discoveries into the Chancery Archives, it had at last become feasible to chart an overall procedural outline for the history of Catholicism in Southern California.[52]

In November, 1962, the six files of historical materials were removed from storage and transported to west Hollywood, where they were reassembled in space generously provided by Monsignor John J. Devlin in the basement area of Saint Victor's Church. As soon as the newly acquired transcripts had been integrated with the existing holdings, "the first and undoubtedly most important step in the program"[53] was inaugurated by arranging the documents in chronological sequence. Each of the pre-1903 entries was catalogued and identified as to correspondents, date and place or origin, language and number of pages.

Short digests, entered on specially-printed call-slips, further narrowed the various items into the military, political, religious, commercial, maritime or Indian phases of activity in California during the Spanish, Mexican and American periods.

The long and tedious project of classifying the holdings into a Record Series plan recommended by the National Archives was complicated by the necessity of establishing and maintaining a basic uniformity between the current filing system and that used for retired documents. A description of the internal organization ultimately adopted with its major divisional units, was published by the *American Archivist*[54] and is now followed wholly, or in part, by such diverse ecclesiastical jurisdictions as New York, Detroit, Tucson, Corpus Christi and Miami. The archival master plan was officially mandated and given independent status with the public announcement, late in December, that "Father Francis J. Weber, biographer and historian, has been named archivist of the Archdiocese"[55] by James Francis Cardinal McIntyre.

Early in 1963, through the foresight of Auxiliary Bishop Timothy Manning and Monsignor Benjamin G. Hawkes, functional quarters for the archival collection were provided in the two-story annex built onto the northeastern end of the curial office. Upon completion of the new facilities in mid-April, the materials temporarily housed in West Hollywood were returned to 1531 West Ninth Street and, together with a considerable quantity of less significant data, arranged in their permanent location. In a simple but richly symbolic ceremony the Cardinal "blessed and formally inaugurated the Chancery Archives of the Archdiocese of Los Angeles"[56] as an autonomous collection, on July 8, 1963. Though precautions for providing adequate record management came late to the southland, most observers appeared to endorse the prognosis that the Chancery Archives of the Archdiocese of Los Angeles would "eventually constitute the largest collection of ecclesiastical documents in the Western United States."[57]

> In the years since our last report was submitted a trained priest-historian has been given custody of the archives and he has carefully organized the files in a strict chronological fashion.

It was also recorded that "Special quarters provided for the chancery archives in a recently added annex of the curial office were formally blessed on July 8, 1963."[58]

Primarily, the Chancery Archives exist to preserve and make available documents essential to the effective administration of ecclesial business for the Archdiocese of Los Angeles. As the final repository for the permanent records of the Church in California's southland, the collection is a treasure-trove for historians, economists and political scientists. Cardinal McIntyre agreed, from the very outset, that the Chancery Archives should be accessible to "qualified scholars whose work necessitates the use of Southern California's ecclesiastical archives."[59] A public announcement to that effect was made at the dedication of the new research facilities,[60] bearing only the proviso that concerned parties pledge, in writing, to observe the procedural guidelines drawn up in accordance with customary archival practices and canonical directives:[61]

1. Permission to use the Chancery Archives must be obtained from the Chancellor or his duly deputized Archivist. All persons admitted to the Archives will be accompanied either by the Chancellor or the Archivist. At no time will a person be allowed to remain alone in the Archives.

2. The Chancery Archives are not intended to serve the general public, and only those having a legitimate interest in their content will be afforded admission. Among those whose requests will be favorably considered are members of the ecclesiastical tribunal and duly recognized historians.

3. Permission to use the Chancery Archives is not to be construed as authorization to quote *verbatim* from materials contained therein.

4. Every researcher or visitor will fill out a registration card noting thereon the purpose of his work and the materials he wishes to consult.

5. No book, document or manuscript shall be removed from the Archives except for the purpose of repair or to be photocopied, and then only by the Archivist.

6. Should certified copies of any document be required, the Archivist will arrange to have the pertinent material photographed. It is understood that the cost of this process is to be borne by the interested party. Microfilmed or photo copied documents, when used, must acknowledge the Archives of the Archdiocese of Los Angeles (AALA) as their source.

7. No marking of any kind shall ever be placed on any book or document in the Chancery Archives.

8. No smoking is allowed while examining or working with documents.

9. Any violation of the above regulations will be construed as malicious.

At the same time, a form was drafted for those wishing access to the Chancery Archives on which the petitioner's particular competence, range of interest and specific objectives were outlined. Each applicant was then asked to sign an agreement of understanding covering six basic areas:

1. That the use of the Chancery Archives is a privilege accorded to me by, and can be revoked at the will of, the Most Reverend Archbishop of Los Angeles;

2. That only cases and materials concerning the subject of my search are to be examined;

3. That all copying of documents is to be done on the premises with pencil or typewriter. The use of ink is not permitted;

4. That smoking is not permitted while handling the documents;

5. That His Eminence, the Most Reverend Archbishop, has decreed that the penalty for unlawfully removing or maliciously damaging any document in the Chancery Archives is to be suspension, where that penalty has foundation.

6. That any removal of a document from the premises without the express consent of the Archbishop is to be described as unlawful and that failure to use reasonable care is to be considered as malicious.

The initial archival holdings were quadrupled within their first decade. In addition to tripling the drawer-space available for retired file storage, facilities were installed for fireproof storage cartons along the north and east wall surfaces. Specially constructed, recessed shelving was also provided for the issues of *The Tidings*, dating back to 1903,[62] and the extensive collection of national Catholic directories.[63] A bank of four functional thirty-drawer cases was added to accommodate such odd-sized and off-beat items as plot maps, souvenir folders, undated manuscripts and miscellaneous mementos. Oversize books, newspapers and pictures are neatly housed in a press cabinet. A large vault, the gift of Cass and Johansing Company, contains some of the more valuable books and manuscripts. The roll-top desk with a raft of assorted drawers, dating from the 1870s, was acquired from the Ritz Plumbing Service in Los Angeles, where it had been actively used for many years.[64]

As a partial and temporary response to the numerous written and oral inquiries about the precise nature of the archival holdings, a broad outline was drafted for distribution to interested scholars. A revised and updated version appeared in 1965 under the imprint of *The Americas* as "The Los Angeles Chancery Archives."[65] Unfortunately, the supply of the printed index was rapidly depleted. In succeeding years, "the more outstanding accessions are enumerated in a special section of the annual edition of the archdiocesan directory issued by *The Tidings*.[66] To serve the auxiliary function of providing guidelines for parochial retention and historical programs, "A Note on Parochial Histories" was published in 1964[67] and circulated to all the parishes in the Los Angeles jurisdiction.

In addition to the several hundred requests processed annually, a host of historians, archeologists, authors, ethnologists, playwrights, economists, sociologists, librarians, script writers, ecologists, genealogists and political scientists working on theses, dissertations, books and a myriad of other projects have been accommodated in the Chancery Archives during the first decade of its operation.

Formation of the extensive parochial monograph and periodical collection dates from April 18, 1963, when a questionnaire and appeal were mailed to every Catholic institution in the state for copies of "the more prominent books, pamphlets and brochures on or about" the Church's activities along the Pacific Slope.[68] The formidable quantity of historical items resulting therefrom proved to be most useful in furthering the overall course of scholarship in southern California.

The first major accession to the Chancery Archives was made early in 1963 when the extensive collection of transcripts from the Bureau of Catholic Indian Missions, amassed by the late Monsignor William McDermott Hughes,[69] was removed from storage in the Edward Laurence Doheny Memorial Library at Camarillo. The large assortment of materials pertaining to Bishop Thomas J. Conaty, also transferred to Los Angeles at that time, was subsequently gathered into thirty-six folders of sermons and addresses and one bound volume of press clippings covering the prelate's Worcester-Washington years. Since the appearance of the initial article on "California's Catholic Heritage"[70] in April, 1963, the Chancery Archives has been the depository for a wide range of items related to that widely circulated weekly newspaper column.

In November, 1963, an unpretentious cardboard box was unearthed in a little-used closet area of the curial office containing two certified typescripts of the long-lost *Libro de Gobierno del Vicariato de la Baja California*.[71] That portion containing the narrative of the pastoral visitation of Bishop Buenaventura Portillo y Tejada, O.F.M., from March 2 to April 6, 1881, was subsequently published as an appendix to this writer's *The Missions and Missionaries of Baja California*.[72] The extremely valuable collection of printed ephemera and personal papers of the Right Reverend John J. Devlin, utilized in the preparation of this writer's study on "John J. Cantwell and the Legion of Decency,"[73] was placed on deposit in the Chancery Archives late in 1964. In succeeding years a formidable amount of related items has been added to that significant holding. In May, 1965, arrangements were finalized to acquire the Thomas Workman Temple Collection of Historical Transcripts, part of an extensive survey made of early California, its missions, *padres* and people by the widely-known San Gabriel genealogist. The 2,000 typed pages, patiently prepared over a period of thirty-five years, are a treasure-trove for data on the *gente de razon* from sixteen of the twenty-one missions and several earlier foundations in peninsular California.[74]

At the conclusion of Vatican Council II, James Francis Cardinal McIntyre entrusted his enormous collection of conciliar materials to the Chancery Archives. Included were schemas, *quaestiones*, *decreta*, *relationes*, *animadversiones*, *constitutiones*, brochures, ballots, photographs, journals, commission reports and a considerable quantity of personal correspondence relating to the prelate's attendance at and participation in the four sessions.

A number of the documents used in preparing the life of the Reverend Anthony Ubach were presented to the Chancery Archives by Father Dennis Clark.[75] Covering the years 1864 to 1900,[76] the fifty-four separate items gave a whole new perspective on the extraordinary life of the Spanish-born Indian missionary, subsequently fictionalized as "Father Gaspara" in Helen Hunt Jackson's novel, *Ramona*.[77] Duplicates of the famed Alexander Taylor Collection of early California documents were acquired in the summer of 1966 through the kindness of Archbishop Joseph T. McGucken.[78] The master collection housed in the San Francisco Chancery Archives[79] contains over 2,560 letters,[80] bound in eight volumes and indexed. Practically all of the references to the "Archbishops Archives" found in early California source books pertain to items in the Taylor papers.

The already extensive assortment of correspondence and ephemera dealing with the history of taxation for private and parochial educational institutions in California was noticeably enhanced in May, 1966, by

George Engstrom's collection of related items which, when sorted and accessioned, added another fourteen volumes to the eleven previously on deposit in the archival agency. This noteworthy assortment of materials was acquired through the influence of the Right Reverend James H. Culleton, long-time Chancellor of the Diocese of Monterey-Fresno.[81]

A microfilm series of seventy-nine rolls of *The Monitor*, oldest Catholic newspaper on the West Coast, provided a healthy balance to the overall Californiana holdings. Founded in March, 1858, *The Monitor* has been the "official organ" for the Archdiocese of San Francisco since April 7, 1877.[82] The original files of the newspaper were destroyed by fire in 1906, "a factor which accounts for the wide gap in the rolls of film."[83] A transcript collection of twenty-four letters dealing with various aspects of the Catholic Church's history in California during the tumultuous years of 1848-1850, were donated to the Chancery Archives by the Reverend Columba Halsey, O.S.B., in June 1967.[84] The sixty-seven documentary pages figured prominently into Halsey's published article on "The Life of Samuel Eccleston, Fifth Archbishop of Baltimore, 1801-1851."[85]

Among the ephemeral additions to the Chancery Archives is a unique collection of death-memorial cards of the American hierarchy, clergy and prominent laity, which was accessioned in mid-1967.[86] An equally special-ized assortment of mission postcards,[87] acquired and featured in a series of articles appearing in the *California Herald*,[88] reflecting the tastes and sentiments of the areas when they originate, express the tone of California's provincial atmosphere.[89]

On November 29, 1967, the Chancery Archives fell heir to six reels of microfilm containing the Baptismal, Marriage and Burial records of the Plaza Church of Nuestra Señora de los Angeles, for the years 1826 to 1917. This valuable increment was made possible through the generosity of offi-cials at the Henry E. Huntington Library in San Marino. Another internally worthwhile acquisition was made in April, 1968, with the twenty-seven bound volumes (and index) of "Sermons and Addresses of the late Monsignor Thomas F. Fogarty," long-time pastor of Saint Brendan's Church in Los Angeles.[90] An assortment of thirty-four mission era docu-ments, reproduced from the scattered holdings of the Henry E. Huntington Library was presented to the Chancery Archives in June, 1968, by Dr. Doyce B. Nunis, Jr. Ranging in date from 1806 to 1851, the 290 pages con-sist mostly of private correspondence and missionary reports.[91]

Among the more recent documentary acquisitions is a rare, thirty-eight line broadside, dated September 19, 1836, carrying the authoriza-tion of the Mexican Congress for creation of a bishopric in the

Californias.[92] Included in the six articles are provisions and directives for selecting candidates, remunerating episcopal appointees and administering the Pious Fund.[93] In early 1971, Mrs. Anna Haws Calvert presented the Chancery Archives with her priceless, unbroken collection of Confraternity Notes, which she had amassed since 1944.[94]

Documents from the Chancery Archives have been edited and published in a number of scholarly journals, including *American Ecclesiastical Review*, *California Herald*, *Journal of Arizona History*, *Masterkey*, *Montana*, *The Magazine of Western History*, *Records of the American Catholic Historical Society*, *Coleccion Chimalistac*, and the *Utah Historical Quarterly*. Articles based on research in the Los Angeles collection have appeared in *Branding Iron*, *Pacific Historian*, *American Archivist*, *American Benedictine Review* and such prominent newspapers as the Los Angeles *Times*. Books, theses and dissertations researched wholly or in part from the Chancery Archives number into the dozens.

Archival activity in subsequent years has extended into a number of selected areas. Probably the most noteworthy of the extra-curial involvements associated with and sponsored by the Chancery Archives was the restoration of the *Bibliotheca Montereyensis-Angelorum Dioceseos* and its removal to more adequate quarters. The 1,760 volumes in that historic book collection were cleaned, repaired, catalogued and then placed on permanent display at Mission San Fernando. Formally inaugurated on November 21, 1969, by Coadjutor Archbishop Timothy Manning, the *Bibliotheca* is affiliated with, but operated separately from, the parent agency.[95]

Since January, 1963, a careful record of the administrative activities connected with the Chancery Archives has been filed in a series of *Register Books*. These volumes, indexed and bound annually, contain all the correspondence to and from the archivist, reports to the Chancellor, lists of purchases, visitors' forms, inquiries and documents relating to all the facets of archival business. By itself, that multi-volume series forms a valuable historical cornerstone for future historians in the Archdiocese of Los Angeles.

Although the historical collections pertaining to ecclesial activities in California now comprising the Chancery Archives are without peer, pertinent data is still being sought about the state's priests, religious, laymen and Church-sponsored foundations, as well as manuscripts, letters, pictures, scrapbooks, posters, maps, genealogies and histories of Catholic families, reports, descriptive literature, newspaper articles, parochial brochures, directories, gazetteers, theses and other related printed books and pamphlets. Present holdings, along with envisioned archival increments, will eventually assure the Archdiocese of Los Angeles of possessing "the most useful collection of ecclesiastical transcripts, photostats, microfilms and other precious documents on the Pacific Coast relative to the modern period."[96]

Notes to the Text

1. Owen C. Coy, *Guide to the County Archives of California* (Sacramento, 1919), p.1.
2. John C. Fitzpatrick, "The Preservation of Ecclesiastical Documents," *Catholic Historical Review*, I (January, 1916), 390.
3. Francis J. Weber, "Catholicity in California," *American Ecclesiastical Review*, CXLIX (October, 1963), 250.
4. *Old Californian Days* quoted in Edith Webb, *Indian Life at the Old Missions* (Los Angeles, 1952), p. 167.
5. Referred to by the early chroniclers as *"Archivo de Obispado."*
6. See Francis J. Weber (ed.), "Long Lost Ecclesiastical Diary of Archbishop Alemany," *California Historical Society Quarterly*, XLIII (December, 1964), 324.
7. See Francis J. Weber, "The San Francisco Chancery Archives," *The Americas*, XX (January, 1964), 313-321.
8. See Francis J. Weber, *A Bibliophilic Odyssey* (Los Angeles, 1969), pp. 13-14.
9. Francis J. Weber, *Thomas James Conaty, Priest-Educator-Bishop* (Los Angeles, 1969), p. 18.
10. Archives of the Archdiocese of Los Angeles (Hereafter referred to as AALA), Thomas J. Conaty to Raymond Carodevall, Los Angeles, September 29, 1908.
11. See *Catholic Historical Review*, V (April, 1919), 120-128.
12. AALA, Peter K. Guilday to John J. Cantwell, Washington, March 5, 1919.
13. AALA, Zephyrin Engelhardt, O.F.M. to Henry W. Gross, Los Angeles, March 16, 1919.
14. AALA, Thomas K. Gorman to John J. Cantwell, Louvain, February 20, 1923.
15. AALA, John J. Cantwell to Thomas K. Gorman, Los Angeles, March 12, 1923.
16. (Rochester, 1925-1927).
17. AALA, Paul J. Foik, C.S.C., to John J. Cawley, Notre Dame, November 29, 1922.
18. For a copy of the questionnaire, see "Proceedings of the Third Annual Meeting of the American Catholic Historical Association," *Catholic Historical Review* IX (April, 1923), 17.
19. AALA, John J. Cawley to Paul J. Foik, C.S.C., Los Angeles, December 7, 1922.
20. AALA, Thomas K. Gorman to Francis J. Weber, Dallas, April 20, 1961.
21. AALA, John J. Cantwell to Peter T. Hanrahan, Los Angeles, November 28, 1927.
22. AALA, Peter J. Hanrahan to Francis J. Weber, Alhambra, December 4, 1970.
23. p. 4.
24. p. 6.
25. AALA, James Culleton to Francis J. Weber, Fresno, September 6, 1963.
26. AALA, John B. MacGinley to Pietro Fumasoni-Biondi, Fresno, December 4, 1924.
27. AALA, "Files Taken from L.A. Chancery by Reverend J. Culleton."
28. AALA, "Diocese of Monterey-Fresno. Index to File B."
29. AALA, Manuscript Address, (Los Angeles, n.d.), quoted by Francis J. Weber, *John J. Cantwell, His Excellency of Los Angeles* (Hong Kong, 1971) p. 79
30. AALA, Joseph T. McGucken to Charles F. Buddy, Los Angeles, March 4, 1937.
31. AALA, Joseph T. McGucken to Michael O'Connor, Los Angeles, June 12, 1937.
32. AALA, Francis J. Weber to Francis J. Furey, Los Angeles, April 6, 1964.
33. "Notes and Comments," *Catholic Historical Review* XXXII (July, 1946).
34. AALA, Joseph T. McGucken to Thomas T. McAvoy, C.S.C., Los Angeles, August 14, 1944.

35. See Francis J. Weber, "Charles Conroy Knew Church Under Five Bishops," *The Tidings*, August 2, 1963.

36. (Los Angeles, 1940).

37. AALA Joseph T. McGucken to James W. Richardson, C.M., Los Angeles, May 22, 1944.

38. "Notes and Comments," *Catholic Historical Review* XXXII (July, 1946), 245-246.

39. p. 5.

40. AALA, Joseph T. McGucken to J. M. Byrne, Los Angeles, April 21, 1953.

41. AALA, John J. Conroy, to James Francis Cardinal McIntyre, Los Angeles, July 6, 1968.

42. AALA, "Minutes of the Council Meetings of the Archdiocesan Consultors, 1956-1957," pp. 968-69.

43. AALA, Harry Trower to James W. Richardson, C.M., Los Angeles, December 10, 1956.

44. Francis J. Weber. "California's Catholic Heritage," *American Ecclesiastical Review* CLIII (July, 1965), 14.

45. John B. McGloin, S.J., from a paper delivered during the annual meeting of the Catholic Historical Association at Saint Louis, in 1956.

46. *A Biographical Sketch of Right Reverend Francisco Garcia Diego y Moreno, O.F.M.* (Los Angeles, 1961).

47. Appropriately, a similar assignment emanated from the Archdiocese of San Francisco in the person of the Reverend James P. Gaffey.

48. Francis J. Weber, *A Select Guide to California Catholic History* (Los Angeles, 1966), p. xxiii.

49. See Francis J. Weber, "Roman Archives of Propaganda Fide," *Records of the American Catholic Historical Society* LXXVI (December, 1965), 245-248.

50. AALA, Francis J. Weber to Timothy Manning, Washington, April 7, 1962.

51. AALA, James Francis Cardinal McIntyre to Francis J. Weber, Los Angeles, April 19, 1962.

52. See Francis J. Weber, "California's Catholic Heritage," 9-18.

53. Francis J. Weber, "The Los Angeles Chancery Archives,' *The Americas* XXI (April, 1965), 410.

54. "Chancery Archives," XXVIII (April, 1965), 255-260.

55. *The Tidings*, December 28, 1962.

56. *Ibid.*, July 12, 1963.

57. Los Angeles *Times*, July 20, 1963.

58. *Relatio*, p. 12.

59. *American Archivist* XXVI (October, 1963), 549.

60. *Newsletter. The Historical Society of Southern California* II (Fall, 1963), 1.

61. *Codex Juris Canonicis* (Rome, 1919), Canon 375.

62. Ninety-four of these handsomely-bound volumes were acquired on an exchange basis through the kindness of Harold L. Hamill, City Librarian for Los Angeles, on August 7, 1964.

63. *Vg.*, 1833-1834; 1836-1837: 1840-1844; 1846-1847; 1849; 1851-1852; 1854-1859; 1864; 1866-1869; 1871-1896: 1903 onwards.

64. Los Angeles *Times*, September 17, 1966.

65. *The Americas*, XXI (April, 1965), 410-420.

66. Francis J. Weber. "Printed Guides to Archival Centers for American Catholic History," *American Archivist*, XXXII (October, 1969), 355,

67. Francis J. Weber, *American Ecclesiastical Review* XXXII, CL (February, 1964), 118-120.

68. Since 1963, the Chancery Archives has been listed in the *Directory of Religious Archival and Historical Depositories*. During 1967, the Chancery Archives was enrolled as holding agency by the Institute of Latin American Studies.

69. See Francis J. Weber, "Msgr. Hughes, Patron of Indians," *The Tidings*, April 1, 1966.

70. *The Tidings*, April 5, 1963,

71 See Francis J. Weber, "Baja's Lost History Found," *The Tidings*, March 14, 1969.

72. (Los Angeles, 1968).

73. *American Ecclesiastical Review*, CLI (October, 1964), 237-247.

74. *American Archivist*, XXVIII (October, 1965), 600.

75. "Anthony Dominic Ubach (1835-1907), Pioneer Priest of San Diego (1866-1907): A Study of His Influence upon the Rise of Catholicism in San Diego," (San Francisco, 1965).

76. San Francisco *Monitor*, July 21, 1966.

77. "News and Notes," *Catholic Historical Review*, LII (October, 1966), 424.

78. *American Archivist*, XXX (April, 1967), 401.

79. Los Angeles *Examiner*, September 17, 1966.

80. *Catholic Historical Review*, LII (January, 1967), 638.

81. AALA, James Culleton to Francis J. Weber, Fresno, May 10, 1966.

82. Los Angeles *Times*, June 18, 1966.

83. "San Francisco Monitor," *American Ecclesiastical Review* CLV (July, 1966), 55.

84. "The Life of Samuel Eccleston, Fifth Archbishop of Baltimore, 1801-1851," *Records of the American Catholic Historical Society*, LXXVI (June, 1965), 69-128 and LXXVI (September, 1965), 131-156.

85. *The Tidings*, June 9, 1967.

86. "Notes and Comments" *Catholic Historical Review* LIII (July, 1967), 279.

87. See Francis J. Weber, "The California Missions in Miniature," *Catholic Footprints in California* (Newhall, 1970), pp. 3-5.

88. XIV (June, 1967), 3, 15; XIV (July, 1967), 3; XIV (August, 1967), 4-5, 14 and XV (September, 1967), 13.

89. Francis J. Weber, "California Missions Are Postcard Favorites," *The Tidings*, April 5, 1968.

90. See Francis J. Weber, "Behold A Great Priest!" *The Tidings*, July 15, 1966.

91. Los Angeles *Times*, August 3, 1968.

92. *The Tidings*, August 7, 1970.

93. Los Angeles *Times*, August 8, 1970.

94. AALA, Anna M. Haws (Calvert) to Francis J. Weber, Redlands, February 1, 1971.

95. See Francis J. Weber, *Rebirth of a Library* (Los Angeles, 1970).

96. Francis J. Weber, "California's Catholic Heritage," *op. cit.*, 16-17.

87

This essay, entitled "Sources for Catholic History of California. A Biblio-Archival Survey," appeared in the *Southern California Quarterly* LVII (Fall, 1975), 321-335.

In large part the history of the Catholic Church is the story of mankind from the dawn of the Christian era. Her archives "are consequently a most valuable repository of human experience and of prime importance to an adequate understanding of the development of Christian civilization."[1] Locating and utilizing the records of prior generations, whether on the local scene or elsewhere, has always been among the most fascinating and rewarding of endeavors. Unfortunately, it is as true in the ecclesial sphere as anywhere that "throughout most of California's history permanently valuable records have been thrown out with the valueless."[2] What remains is not always accessible and even today a fairly large part of the manuscripts basic to California's history are scattered in private hands or forgotten in trunks, attics, and business files."[3]

This biblio-archival overview of the more important secular and religious depositories housing materials relevant to the Catholic phase of the state's history makes no claim at exhausting so broad a subject. Rather it demonstrates that "even in the most carefully compiled narrative merely the foam-bubbles that crest the wave-caps of events are visible."[4]

Beyond the heroic endeavors of such men as Hubert Howe Bancroft and Adolph Sutro, the first attempt to enkindle a public awareness of the need for collecting and preserving the priceless testimony of California's development can be dated from 1918, when John F. Davis regaled the

Native Sons and Daughters of the Golden West with *A Plea for the Collection, Preservation and Diffusion of Information Relating to the History of California*.[5] The apathy which delayed, for another two decades, legislation giving autonomous viability to a workable archival system was chronicled by Jacob N. Bowman in his report on the "Preservation of the State Archives," published in 1949.[6] A detailed study presented to the legislature, on January 9, 1965,[7] advocating a modernized program for restoring and preserving the historic documents on deposit with the secretary of state was little more successful in its long-term results.[8]

While a number of the more important collections[9] received attention by the Historical Records Survey Project in their volumes, *Inventory of the State Archives of California*, the only generally accessible finding-device for the overall parent depository, which one authority described as "entirely unworthy of the most populous state in the federal union,"[10] is an essay prepared over half a century ago by Edwin L. Head for the *Annual Report of the American Historical Association for the Year 1915*.[11] That historians of California's Catholic heritage have found little material of immediate value to their work in the state archives is only a minor comfort to those who recognize and appreciate the need for adequate record management in all areas of governmental administration.

Though the archival holdings at the county level are scarcely more esteemed, their contents have been more generously catalogued. In his *Guide to the County Archives of California*,[12] Owen C. Coy gave a brief historical and descriptive account of the contents in each of the fifty-nine counties[13] along with itemized lists in particular areas. The fifty-seven components of the *Inventory of the County Archives of California*, prepared at different times by the California Historical Records Survey Project, expanded the Coy compilation by outlining the organization and functions of the several agencies within their custody.

The *Guide to Depositories of Manuscript Collections in the United States. California*,[14] representative of an envisioned series on the holdings of seventy-four California depositories, contains notes about acquisition, scope and extent of the various archives. The program of the State Emergency Relief Administration for preserving 1,200 manuscript pages of the area's rapidly distintegrating documents is related by Marion Parks in an interesting essay on "Translating the Spanish Archives of Los Angeles."[15]

Such "fugitive" articles as J. M. Guinn's "The Old Pueblo Archives"[16] are useful to scholars and students. Therein is described the content of three quaint, ragged, time-worn volumes in the vault of the Los Angeles City Hall.[17] Two other related essays by W. W. Robinson, one a first-hand report on the fate of the Spanish and Mexican archives,[18] the other an outline of Indian *mores* between 1833 and 1850, as unfolded in the yellowing archival pages of the minutes of the *ayuntamiento*,[19] also shed considerable light at the local level.

Undoubtedly, "the richest source of information for the general history of California, and second in importance only with regard to mission history,"[20] was the monumental collection commonly referred to as the "California Archives." Included in that vast quantity of materials were royal proclamations, decrees, civil and religious records and reports, dispatches, letters, orders, laws, court proceedings, journals and diaries. The 289 volumes, each with an average of 700 pages, covering the period from 1768 to 1850, incorporated "everything pertaining to the government, the people, the climate, the soil, and the general character of the country."[21]

The "California Archives" were fused into a single collection at Monterey, in 1847, by Henry W. Halleck. In 1858, after having the documents re-arranged and bound, Edwin M. Stanton moved them to the San Francisco office of the United States surveyor-general where Hubert Howe Bancroft, Theodore H. Hittell, Zoeth Eldredge, Zephyrin Engelhardt and others utilized their contents. When, in 1876, Bancroft had the more important items transcribed for his personal files,[22] scribes filled no fewer than sixty-nine folio volumes. From the very outset, Bancroft must have realized that he "could hardly have written his History without access to these Archives."[23]

Subsequent scholars exhibited less concern, however, and it was only a proposal, in 1903, to place the "California Archives" on deposit at the Library of Congress that re-awakened local interest in the collection. The drama of the stormy, but successful campaign to retain them in the Golden State, spearheaded by Zoeth Eldredge, was only overshadowed by the devastating San Francisco conflagration of April 1906, which obliterated all but a "pitiable remnant"[24] of the priceless documents. Those few materials not totally destroyed were moved, in 1932, to Glendale, California, and, five years later, to their permanent home at the National Archives in Washington, D,C.[25]

The fact that "the ecclesiastical record centers in California have received proportionately more attention than those of any other State in the Union,"[26] owes its origin to Zephyrin Engelhardt, O.F.M., who located and described "The Sources of California Mission History" which served as the basis for his extensive study of *The Missions and Missionaries of California*,[27] as well as the subsequent sixteen volumes on the individual Franciscan foundations along the Pacific slope.[28] The Engelhardt tradition was sustained in this writer's treatment of "Archival Depositories" in *A Select Guide to California Catholic History,*[29] wherein eight curial holding agencies and eleven non-diocesan archival centers containing materials relating to the state's Catholic heritage were identified.

The inauguration, in 1969, of new and modern facilities for the Santa Barbara Mission Archives was widely applauded by historians who had long ranked that documental center among the most significant in the United States for manuscript material pertaining to the Hispanic era.[30] Mission Santa Barbara has housed the central archives of the Franciscans since 1833. Researchers first utilized the rich collection as early as 1877, when agents of Hubert Howe Bancroft transcribed twelve folio volumes of materials, each 500 pages thick. Since that time, scholars have published a whole library of books, brochures and pamphlets based on the annual and biennial reports of the missions, register books, inventories, correspondence of missionaries and civil officials and personal diaries stretching from the earlier days of Franciscan penetration into peninsular California.

In addition to primary sources the Santa Barbara Mission Archives has a unique assortment of printed materials on almost every aspect of the multiphased missionary enterprise. An extensive run of newspapers, magazines, directories and related ephemera has also proven extremely useful to researchers. The massive collection, formerly housed in the small cell and adjoining veranda once inhabited by Zephyrin Engelhardt, has been relocated on the ground floor of the recently completed western wing of the central mission-corridor, in an effort to accommodate the increasing flow of authors, historians, geographers and ethnologists. Provisions have also been made for a modest, but highly select and relevant library to serve the collateral needs of interested students.

The publication of Maynard J. Geiger's *Calendar of Documents in the Santa Barbara Mission Archives,*[31] enumerating 2,842 distinct items, exclusive of reports, statistics, tables, lists and a considerable number of documents not belonging to the California collection, was welcomed in scholary circles as "an outstanding contribution to the study of California mission history"[32] and a "distinct service to archivology."[33] Father Geiger has prepared a revised and much enlarged catalogue of that work, inasmuch as the quantity of holdings has tripled in the years since 1947. Over 8,000 pages of transcripts relating to the Serra Cause,[34] 2,300 from the Alexander Taylor Collection and about a thousand from Rome and the Chancery Archives of the Archdiocese of Los Angeles have been added as have several thousand original documents from the Reverend Joseph

Thompson's papers on, about and by José Antonio de la Guerra and his heirs.[35] This revised catalog, in manuscript copy only, can be consulted at the Santa Barbara Mission Archive-Library.

The prominence of the San Francisco Chancery Archives has long been acknowledged by western historians, many of whose footnotes bear the familiar code, *Archb. Arch.* The pivotal importance of that archival depository is a natural outgrowth of the state's ecclesiastical and jurisdictional development. Prior to 1936, San Francisco served as the metropolitan seat for all of California and very little escaped the attention of the residential ordinaries entrusted with governing the archdiocese in the years after 1853. The gradual reduction in size did not diminish appreciably its valuable historical documentation, much of which remains even now virtually unexplored.

A fairly well-organized curia has functioned in the Bay City since 1878, when Archbishop Joseph Sadoc Alemany instituted the office of chancellor in the person of Father Peter J. Grey. A progression of exceptionally qualified and able chancellors in succeeding decades established a tradition of efficiency in record preservation unequalled in any other part of the state.

Much of the system presently discernible in the archives, now located on the fourth floor of the Chancery Office, at 441 Church Street in San Francisco, can be credited to the late Monsignor Charles A. Ramm, who catalogued the collection's more outstanding materials shortly after the turn of the century.[36]

The most historically-treasured holding in the San Francisco Chancery Archives is the Alexander S. Taylor Collection, a group of papers ranging from 1770 to 1846, amassed during the years Taylor functioned as clerk of the United States District Court at Monterey. In 1854 Taylor offered his letters from the civil and religious authorities of both Alta and Baja California to the Library of Congress. "It has long been a painful memory to Washington officials that the generous bibliographer's offer was not accepted."[37] Some years afterwards, he presented 2,560 of the documents to Saint Mary's Library Association. There they were bound into eight volumes and chronologically indexed by John Ruurd, the court translator of Monterey County.[38] The collection subsequently passed to the Chancery Archives where it has remained ever since. In the 1940s the papers were microfilmed and prints placed on deposit at the Academy of American Franciscan History in Washington, D.C., and at the Santa Barbara Mission Archives.[39] Archbishop Joseph T. McGucken graciously permitted this writer to xerox the Taylor Papers, in 1966, for inclusion in the Chancery Archives of the Archdiocese of Los Angeles.[40]

Typical of the quality of other holdings in the San Francisco depository are three thick volumes of primary materials relating to the Pious Fund of the Californias which were given to the archdiocese by the descendants of the famous legal advisor, John Thomas Doyle. The bulk of the collection pertains to the diocesan period, that is, the years after 1840. Included therein are files of the various archbishops and bishops, parochial correspondence, clergy personnel records, letters to religious communities and the usual categories associated with ecclesiastical affairs.

The southern metropolitan jurisdiction was not as fortunate in the concern shown for its historical records. Prior to 1962 no serious attempt was made to organize or catalogue the documents in the Chancery Archives of the Archdiocese of Los Angeles and, as a result, much available primary evidence was lost or indiscriminately destroyed. On December 26, 1962,[41] the office of archivist was created and provisions made for separating the historical materials into a distinct collection to be housed in a new annex of the curia building. The Chancery Archives were formally dedicated by James Francis Cardinal McIntyre, on July 8, 1962, and made available to "qualified scholars whose work necessitates the use of Southern California ecclesiastical material."[42]

The vast amount of transcripts, photostats, microfilm and other precious historical items added to the meagre existing holdings in the earliest months of their autonomous existence prompted the observation that the Chancery Archives would "eventually constitute the largest collection of ecclesiastical documents in the Western United States."[43] Growth in content and quality during subsequent years has been phenomenal. Already, this writer's survey on "The Los Angeles Chancery Archives,"[44] published in 1965, is obsolete. The more important additions being added as time passes are catalogued in the annual publication of the archdiocesan Catholic directory.[45]

Several outstanding acquisitions are worthy of special mention. The Thomas Workman Temple Collection of historical transcripts, part of an extensive survey made of early California, its missions, *padres* and people, is one example. Over 2,000 typed pages include data on the *gente de razon* from sixteen of the state's twenty-one missions as well as several of the foundations in peninsular California.[46] Also now accessible in the southland for the first time, is a microfilm run of *The Monitor*, since 1892 the official Catholic newspaper for the Archdiocese of San Francisco. Included in the seventy-nine reels are issues dating back to December 14,

1861. As mentioned earlier, copies of the Alexander S. Taylor Collection have been integrated into the archives for researchers unable to investigate the originals in San Francisco.[47]

In addition to documentary holdings, the Chancery Archives house the largest museum of Catholic Californiana in existence. A wide range of historical mementos associated with the Golden State's religious and lay pioneers are attractively displayed in eight specially designed cases. A small but comprehensive collection of basic reference tools, including several hundred otherwise inaccessible periodical articles on the Church's activities along the Pacific slope. The Chancery Archives for the Archdiocese of Los Angeles, designated by early writers as *Archivo de Obispado*, has now come into its own.

Structurally, the innovative procedures used in the Los Angeles collection were early recognized. At the request of the National Archives, an organizational plan was drafted and, since its publication,[48] the format has been adopted totally or in part by a number of archdioceses and dioceses throughout the United States.

The internal worth of the more modest ecclesial archives scattered around the state varies considerably and is frequently determined by the ephemeral items that naturally gravitate towards agencies of that kind, some of which could be profitably utilized by historically alert students. One such collection is the Jesuit and Community Archives housed in the University of Santa Clara's Orradre Library. There, industrious Father Arthur D. Spearman, S.J. has gathered, over the past two decades, a remarkably extensive and well-catalogued assortment of documents and microfilm representative of practically every aspect of California's provincial era. Another worthwhile holding agency is that located in the Richard A. Gleeson Library, at the University of San Francisco. To the existing historical data associated with the earliest Jesuit activity in the Bay Area, Father John B. McGloin, S.J., has added the diversified documents and filmed transcripts from his own widespread discoveries in Europe and the United States.

Understandably, the paucity of personnel and lack of organization generally characteristic of the state's Catholic archival collections, be they diocesan, religious or institutional, militates against making their holdings accessible to researchers without definite restrictions. In most cases, however, satisfactory arrangements can be made for those interested and qualified parties willing to accommodate themselves to the schedules of local administrators.

There is copious evidence indicating a number of places outside California where materials relating to the state's Catholic history can be found. Forty such centers are enumerated in Edmund L. Binsfeld's study for the Church Records Committee of the Society of American Archivists.[49] Another twenty-three ecclesiastical "Manuscript Depositories" in the United States are listed by Msgr. John Tracy Ellis in *A Guide to American Catholic History*.[50] August R. Suelflow expanded to 162 the number of Catholic holding agencies in the latest edition of his *Directory of Religious Archival and Historical Depositories in America*.[51] Finally, there is this writer's treatise on "Printed Guides to Archival Centers for American Catholic History"[52] which focuses attention on those *fontes* of Catholic Americana for which at least some kind of printed finding device has been prepared.

In the *Handbook of Hispanic Source Materials and Research Organizations in the United States*,[53] "one of the indispensable instruments" of the trade,[54] Ronald Hilton zeroes in on the structural contents of many materials in various parts of the nation, much of it relating to California and the Hispanic theme.[55]

"Despite the substantial quantity of foreign material now available in transcript and authentic copy in American depositories, the researcher in many fields of American Catholic history must still have recourse to archives beyond our borders."[56] That conclusion is based on such works as Lino G. Canedo's informative essay on "Some Franciscan Sources in the Archives and Libraries of America"[57] which surveyed the extensive written testimony relating to the influence of the friars on the history of the nation. In his monumental *Guide to Materials for the History of the United States in the Principal Archives of Mexico*,[58] Herbert Eugene Bolton described 284 bundles of manuscripts dealing mostly with the Californias in sixty-five archives and regional depositories spread throughout the vast territory governed by Spanish and Mexican bishops between 1522 and 1850.

A general survey of the more useful private holding agencies, most of them religious, and few of them exploited by American scholars, is William L. Davis' article on "Some Neglected Archives of Europe."[59] John B. McGloin's treatise on the "European Archival Resources for the Study of California Catholic History,"[60] a descriptive memoir of an attempt to photograph materials pertaining to the American period of Catholic activity in the Golden State, provided a useful thumbnail sketch of the major centers in the area discussed.

For historians of California, no less than for those of the nation as a whole, the Roman Archives of Propaganda Fide are "the most valuable in the world"[61] for the richness of their contents. Organized in 1622, to oversee the expansion of the Catholic apostolate in under-developed areas, the Sacred Congregation of Propaganda Fide[62] supervises the activities of all missionaries working within its carefully delineated sphere of influence. Generally speaking, even today, a considerable number of residential bishops and practically all prelates in those territories beneath diocesan status are subject to the congregation and its cardinal-prefect, known in clerical circles as the "red pope."

Perhaps in no other country was the congregation more successful in fulfilling its purposes than in the United States, between the time of American independence and 1908. For that reason, the correspondence of this nation's prelates with officials of Propaganda Fide "make that congregation's archives more important for historians of the United States Church than all the other ecclesiastical record depositories taken together."[63] As an historical collection, the archives have been sporadically accessible to scholars only since 1863, when the present filing system was permanized.[64] In more recent times duly accredited researchers are routinely admitted upon presentation of a written request to the cardinal prefect outlining the purposes and scope of their scholarly interest.

In 1908 Carl Russell Fish devoted seventy-six pages of his *Guide to the Materials for American History in Roman and Other Italian Archives*[65] to analyzing the "practically inexhaustible"[66] resources of Propaganda Fide. Nicola Kowalski, O.M.I., updated and expanded the coverage of Professor Fish's work in 1961, with the issuance of his *Inventario dell'Archivo Storico della S. Congregazione de Propaganda Fide*. Since 1955, the Academy of American Franciscan History has been sponsoring the preparation of a systematic calendar of the Propaganda Fide documents with the patient and efficient collaboration of a leading European researcher, Anton Debevec. The initial volume of an envisioned series, covering the years between 1673 and 1844, was published at Washington under the editorship of Finbar Kenneally, O.F.M., in 1966.[67]

Few of the Church's archival centers in the Eternal City have any stated policy for admitting researchers. Fortunately, there are reasons to believe that little, if any matter relevant to the California scene exists in those depositories, with the exception, perhaps, of the Archives of the Sacred Consistorial Congregation which processes episcopal appointments and the Secret Vatican Archives[68] where this writer found a number of items pertaining to the activities of the *Patronato Real de las Indias*.

An often overlooked, but rich European collection of letters from California bishops and priests is housed at the Paris headquarters of the *Societe de la Propagation de la Foi.* That organization, founded at Lyons on May 3, 1822, "to promote the sowing of the seeds of faith in pagan lands,"[69] was especially active in the United States missionary apostolate in the years before 1912.[70] A goodly portion of the annual reports and other correspondence submitted by prelates seeking financial assistance is preserved in the society's archives.[71] Unfortunately, no guide is available and researchers frequently encounter difficulties in locating needed items. Abraham P. Nasatir's work, *French Activities in California. An Archival Calendar-Guide*[72] reveals some of the additional treasures hidden away in other Parisian archives and libraries relating to the California scene between 1700 and 1857.

The close relationship between Spain and its provinces explains the vital role that nation's manuscript depositories occupy in attempts to present an integrated and balanced account of Spain's far-flung colonies. William R. Shepherd's *Guide to the Materials for the History of the United States in Spanish Archives*[73] enumerated the general categories of several hundred thousand documentary sources pertaining exclusively to the continental part of the country on file in the Archives of Simanacas, the Archivo Historico and the Archives of the Indies. In 1910 James Alexander Robertson compiled a *List of Documents in Spanish Archives Relating to the History of the United States, which have been printed or of which Transcripts are Preserved in American Libraries.* Principal object of that 368 page study was "to show persons engaged in research, whether working in Spanish archives or at home, what portions of the Spanish archive material relating to the United States are accessible in the United States in the form of printed or manuscript copies."[74]

The *Archivo General de Indias*, with its unique collection of items relating to the Spanish dominions in America and the Philippines, received scholarly attention in Roscoe Hill's *Descriptive Catalogue of the Documents Relating to the History of the United States in the Papeles Procedentes de Cuba, Deposited in the Archivo General de Indias at Seville.*[75] That work was expanded a few years later by Charles E. Chapman's "A Description of Certain Legajos in the Archivo General de Indias,"[76] a survey of sixty-four "bundles of papers" in the vast Spanish depository. The following year the University of California Press published Chapman's encyclopedic *Catalogue of Materials in the Archivo General de Indies for the History of the Pacific Coast and the American Southwest*, a work whose 6,257 entries representing about 25,000 separate documents, two thirds of them relating to Hispanic times in California, may still be the "best and most scholarly guide to the original Spanish sources."[77]

Even the casual observer can readily conclude that the surface has only been scratched in the quest for documentary evidence about the Catholic contribution to California's history. Beyond the obvious archival centers here delineated and orders of less consequence, surely there are unknown and/or uncatalogued collections whose contents remain unexploited. If the Golden State's ecclesiastical historians view their work conscientiously, they must continue their painful, exhausting, frustrating and frequently unrewarding task of searching out, evaluating and integrating those "fugitive" sources which may noticeably effect the ultimate appraisal of Catholic activities along the Pacific Slope. For them to pursue any less assiduous course would reduce their role to that of "popularizers."

Notes to the Text

1. J. C. Fitzpatrick, "The Preservation of Ecclesiastical Documents," *Catholic Historical Review*, I (January 1916), 390.
2. W. N. Davis, Jr., "The California State Archives," *American Archivist*, XXII (April 1959), 191.
3. John Walton Caughey, *California* (Englewood Cliffs, N.J. 1964), p. 595.
4. Caroline Stevens Walter, "The Early California Missions," *Frank Leslie's Monthly* (December 1890), 743.
5. (San Francisco, 1908).
6. *California Historical Society Quarterly*, XXVIII (June 1949), 143-150.
7. A number of earlier reports were made over the years, such as the twenty-four page *Records Management for the State of California* (Sacramento, 1952), which briefly reviewed the records evaluation program in California for the Assembly Interim Committee on Governmental Reorganization.
8. See Walter C. Frame, *The Preservation, Organization and Display of California's Historic Documents* (Sacramento, 1965).
9. See, for example, David C. Duniway, "The California Food Administration and Its Records in The National Archives," *Pacific Historical Review*, VII (September 1938), 228-240.
10. Ernst Posner, *American State Archives* (Chicago, 1964), p. 60.
11. "The Public Archives of the State of California" (Washington, D.C., 1917), pp. 281-399.
12. (Sacramento, 1919).
13. Including the now-defunct Klamath County.
14. (Los Angeles, 1941).
15. *Historical Society of Southern California Quarterly*, XVII (March 1935), 28-30.
16. *Historical Society of Southern California Annual*, IV (1897), 37-42.
17. This description originally appeared in the Los Angeles *Times*, November 21, 1897.
18. "Abel Stearns on the California & Los Angeles Archives," *Historical Society of Southern California*, XIX (September-December 1937), 141-144.
19. "The Indians of Los Angeles As Revealed by the Los Angeles City Archives," *Historical Society of Southern California Quarterly*, XX (December 1938), 156-172.
20. Zephyrin Engelhardt, O.F.M., "The Sources of California Mission History," *The Missions and Missionaries of California* (4 vols.; Santa Barbara, 1912-1915), II, xxiv.
21. Zoeth Eldredge, *The Spanish Archives of California* (San Francisco, 1901), p. 3.

22. *Literary Industries* (New York, 1891), p. 252.

23. Charles F. Gompertz, "Attempt to Remove the Spanish Archives from San Francisco to Library of Congress at Washington, D.C.," (San Francisco, 1903), p. 561.

24. John Lombardi, "Lost Records of the Surveyor-General in California," *Pacific Historical Review*, VI (December 1937), 367.

25. See W. W. Robinson, "Land Grant Records That Survived A Great Fire," *Historical Society of Southern California Quarterly*, XXVI (March 1944), 38-41.

26. Francis J. Weber, "Printed Guides to Archival Centers for American Catholic History," *American Archivist*, XXXII (October 1969), 354.

27. (San Francisco, 1908-1915).

28. For the Franciscan's works, see Francis J. Weber, "Zephyrin Engelhardt, O.F.M., Dean of California Mission Historians," *Southern California Quarterly*, XLVII (September 1965), 235-244.

29. (Los Angeles, 1966), pp. 157-162.

30. See Maynard J. Geiger, O.F.M., "Mission Archive Building," *Provincial Annals*, XXIX (September 1967), 43-45.

31. (Washington, 1947).

32. Mathias Kieman, O.F.M., "Book Review," *Franciscan Studies*, VIII (June 1948), 205.

33. Roscoe R. Hill, "Book Review," *American Archivist*, XI (January 1948), 69.

34. For the interesting story behind the amassing of the Serra papers, gathered to further the beatification process, see Maynard J. Geiger, O.F.M., "In Quest of Serrana," *The Americas*, I (July 1944), 97-103. A list of the public and private archival holding agencies with materials useful to the study of early colonial period appears in Geiger's *The Life and Times of Fray Junipero Serra, O.F.M*, (2 vols.; Washington, D.C., 1959), II, 405-406.

35. See Maynard J. Geiger, O.F.M., "The De la Guerra Documents Come to the Mission Archives at Santa Barbara," *Provincial Annals*, XXIX (March 1969), 31-33.
A detailed description is also found in Fr. Geiger's "History of the Santa Barbara De la Guerra Family Documents," *Southern California Quarterly*, LIV (Fall 1972), 227-282.

36. For an outline of the holdings, see Francis J. Weber, "The San Francisco Chancery Archives," *The Americas*, XX (January 1964), 313-321.

37. Francis J. Weber, "California's First Bibliographer a Convert," *The Tidings*, April 10, 1964.

38. Zephyrin Engelhardt, O.F.M., "The Sources of California Mission History," *The Missions and Missionaries of California*, II, xxii.

39. Maynard J. Geiger, O.F.M., *Calendar of Documents in the Santa Barbara Mission Archives* (Washington, D.C., 1947), p. 253.

40. Los Angeles *Herald-Examiner*, September 17, 1966. A photostat set is also in the Huntington Library, San Marino.

41. *The Tidings*, December 28, 1962.

42. *American Archivist*, XXVI,(October 1963), 549.

43. Los Angeles *Times*, July 20, 1963.

44. See Francis J. Weber, "The Los Angeles Chancery Archives," *The Americas*, XXI (April 1965), 410-420.

45. *The Tidings*, May 28, 1965,

46. "San Francisco Monitor," *American Ecclesiastical Review*, CLV (July 1966), 55-56.

47. Los Angeles *Times*, September 17, 1966.

48. See Francis J. Weber, "Chancery Archives," *American Archivist*, XXVIII (April 1965), 255-260.

49. "Church Archives in the United States and Canada; A Bibliography," *American Archivist*, XXI (July 1958), 311-316.

50. (Milwaukee, 1959), pp. 7-12.

51. (Washington, D.C., 1963).

52. *American Archivist*, XXXII (October 1969), 349-356.

53. (Stanford, 1956).

54. Luis G. Canedo, O.F.M., "Book Review," *The Americas*, XIV (January 1958), 321.

55. Pages 4 thru 62 and 387 thru 391 deal with California materials. A Spanish edition of this valuable guide is available as *Los Estudios Hispanicos en los Estados Unidos*.
56. Thomas F. O'Connor, "Catholic Archives of the United States," *Catholic Historical Review*, XXXXI (January 1946), 427.
57. *The Americas*, XIII (October 1956), 141-174.
58. (Washington, D.C., 1913).
59. *Mid-America*, XXXVIII (January 1956), 15-37.
60. *Church History*, XXX (March 1961), 103-105.
61. Peter K. Guilday, *On the Creation of An Institute for American Church History* (Washington, D.C., 1924), p. 29.
62. Now known as the Congregation for the Evangelization of Peoples.
63. Francis J. Weber, "Book Review," *California Historical Society Quarterly*, XLVII (March 1968), 84.
64. For an historical sketch and outline of its holdings, see Francis J. Weber, "Roman Archives of Propaganda Fide," *Records of the American Catholic Society*, LXXVI (December 1965), 245-248.
65. (Washington, D.C., 1911), pp. 119-195.
66. John B. McGloin, S.J., "The Roman Propaganda Fide Archives: An Overview and Assessment," *Church History*, XXXIII (March 1964), 91.
67. *United States Documents in the Propaganda Fide Archives: A Calendar.* Five volumes have been published so far.
68. For a sketch of this agency's holdings, see Francis J. Weber, "The Secret Vatican Archives," *American Archivist*, XXVII (January 1964), 63-66. A more recent and thorough study is that of Maria Luis Ambrosini, *The Secret Archives of the Vatican* (Boston, 1969).
69. John F. Noll, "Relation of the Society for the Propagation of the Faith to the American Board of Catholic Missions," *American Ecclesiastical Review*, XCI (October 1934), 337.
70. Between 1822 and 1912, the society distributed $6,309.214.40 to financially underprivileged dioceses in the United States.
71. There were two councils of the society, one at Paris, the other at Lyons. Most of the Lyons documents were removed to Fribourg, Switzerland, around the turn of the century. Reports were submitted in duplicate, a factor which explains why the Fribourg collection so closely parallels that at Paris.
72. (Stanford, 1945).
73. (Washington, D.C., 1907).
74. William E. Dodd, "Book Review," *American Historical Review*, XVI (October 1910), 168.
75. (Washington, D.C., 1916).
76. *Hispanic American Historical Review*, I (May 1918), 209-230 and (August 1918), 352-371.
77. Henry Herman Evans, *Western Bibliographies* (San Francisco, 1951), p. 5.

88

This essay about the "Archdiocesan Archival Facility at Colma" appeared in *The Monitor* for August 24, 1978.

The prominence of the San Francisco Chancery Archives has long been recognized by Western American historians, many of whose footnotes bear the familiary code, *Archb. Arch.* The pivotal importance of the archival depository is a natural outgrowth of the ecclesiastical and jurisdictional development in the state. Prior to 1936, San Francisco was the metropolitan seat for all of California and very little escaped the attention of the four residential ordinaries entrusted with governing the archdiocese in the years after 1853. Its gradual reduction in size and influence did not diminish appreciably the archdiocese's valuable historical documentation, much of which remains even now virtually unexplored.

A fairly well-organized curia has functioned in the Bay City since 1878, when Archbishop Joseph Sadoc Alemany instituted the office of chancellor in the person of Father Peter J. Grey. A progression of exceptionally qualified and able chancellors in succeeding decades established a tradition of efficiency in record preservation unequalled in any other part of the state.

Much of the system presently discernible in the archives, housed until recently on the fourth floor of the Chancery Office, at 445 Church Street in San Francisco, can be credited to Monsignor Charles A. Ramm, who catalogued the collection's more outstanding materials shortly after the turn of the century.

The most historically treasured holdings in the San Francisco Chancery Archives are the Alexander S. Taylor Collection, a group of papers ranging from 1770 to 1846, amassed during the years Taylor functioned as Clerk of the United States District Court at Monterey. In 1854, Taylor offered his documents consisting of letters from the civil and religious authorities of both Baja and Alta California, to the Library of Congress. It has long been a painful memory to Washington officials that the generous bibliographer's offer was not accepted. Some years later, Mr. Taylor presented 2,560 of the documents to Saint Mary's Library Association. The letters were bound into eight volumes and chronologically indexed by John Ruurd. Subsequently, the collection passed to the Chancery Archives where it has remained ever since.

In the 1940's, the papers were microfilmed and prints placed on deposit at the Academy of American Franciscan History in Washington, D.C. and at the Santa Barbara Mission Archives. In 1946, Archbishop Joseph T. McGucken graciously allowed xerox copies of the Taylor Papers to be made for the Chancery Archives of the Archdiocese of Los Angeles.

Typical of the quality of other materials in the San Francisco Chancery Archives are three volumes of documents relating to the Pious Fund of the Californias which were presented to the archdiocese by the heirs of the famous legal adviser, John Thomas Doyle. In more recent times, the massive legal files of Andrew Burke and John F. Duff have been entrusted to the archives.

The bulk of holdings pertain to the diocesan period for the years since 1940. Included therein are files of the various archbishops and bishops, parochial correspondence, clergy personnel records, letters to religious communities and the usual run of categories associated with ecclesial affairs.

A brief descriptive guide outlining the major record collections in the San Francisco Chancery Archives appeared in *The Americas* XX (January, 1964), 313-321.

Shortly after his installation as the sixth Archbishop of San Francisco, the Most Reverend John R. Quinn asked this writer to draft a plan whereby the rich historical holdings could be brought into conformity with the statement issued on November 22, 1974, by the National Conference of Catholic Bishops on the accessibility of ecclesiastical archives.

It was suggested that the chancery Archives be moved to more commodious quarters in an unused wing of Holy Cross Mausoleum, at nearby Colma, California. An architect was employed to remodel the three designated rooms and during the last week of April, 1978, the Chancery Archives were installed in their new surroundings.

Father Kirby C. Hanson, Assistant Chancellor for the Archdiocese of San Francisco, worked on the project with the architect for several months. He also worked with the author in arranging the material for scholarly research. Father Hanson then selected and purchased the necessary storage equipment. After interviewing several applicants, Msgr. Daniel Walsh, Chancellor for the Archdiocese of San Francisco, selected the highly respected and superbly qualified James T. Abajian as archivist, a position he formally assumed on July 1st.

89

This ecumenical survey on "Catholicism among the Mormons 1875-79" appeared in the *Utah Historical Quarterly* XXXXIV (Spring, 1976), 141-148.

The history of the Catholic Church in modern-day Utah can be traced to June 4, 1866, when the first liturgical services were conducted at Independence Hall by the Reverend Edward Kelly, a priest attached to the Vicariate Apostolic of Marysville. Two years later, on March 3, 1868, Pope Pius IX erected the Vicariate Apostolic of Colorado and Utah and, on the following August 16, Father James P. Macheboeuf became ordinary of the newly-created ecclesial jurisdiction.

Shortly after his episcopal ordination, Bishop Macheboeuf visited Salt Lake City, where he was cordially received by Mormon officials. The prelate asked Father James V. Foley to assume charge of the city's small Catholic population, but the latter's tenure lasted only a few months.

When the vicariate was divided, in 1871, the area comprising Utah reverted to the Metropolitan Province of San Francisco. Archbishop Joseph Sadoc Alemany named Father Patrick Walsh to the Salt Lake pastorate, and it was he who built the original Church of Saint Mary Magdalene.

On August 14, 1873, the archbishop entrusted the eighty-five thousand square mile Salt Lake parish to Father Lawrence Scanlan (1843–1915), who was to become the anchor-chain of Catholicism in Utah.[1] To his dismay, the Irish-born pastor found that almost a century after Fray Francisco Atanasio Domínguez and Fray Silvestre Vélez de

Escalante had led the first white men through the mountains and valleys of Utah, there were only a scant eight hundred Catholics in the territory out of a population of eighty-seven thousand. And less than a hundred of them resided in the Salt Lake area.[2]

Scanlan was undaunted by the challenges facing him as pastor of the largest geographical region in the United States. Rather, he used that "distinction" as the opening wedge in his appeals to the *Society de la Propagation de la Foi* for financial assistance. Scanlan's letters to the *Societé* are historically pivotal inasmuch as they reveal both his own personality and the complex status of the nascent Catholic community in the predominantly Mormon territory.[3]

Two letters from Salt Lake City are especially interesting: the first, dated November 16, 1875, and the second, October 31, 1879. The latter appeal was sent in Scanlan's name by his longtime curate, Father Dennis Kiely (1848-1920). The documents are reproduced here from transcripts made by this writer and now on deposit in the Chancery Archives for the Archdiocese of Los Angeles.

Report of November 16, 1875

In my last report I most strongly represented to you, among other things, the great necessity of establishing in this Territory Catholic Schools, as a means—the only means-of saving to the Church the rising generation and of thus sparing to our successors in the ministry, the labor of converting to the Church those who, if in their early Christian education had not been neglected, should be her faithful members. In order to meet this necessity I implored your assistance and cooperation; and now I feel happy in being able to state that my appeal to you has not been made in vain. Through your generous contribution of more than one thousand dollars, and the assistance of God we have been able to bring here a handsome Colony of Sisters who have already firmly established themselves in Salt Lake City, the Capital of the Territory. The Sisters of Congregation of Holy Cross from St. Mary's, South Bend, State of Indiana arrived here on the sixth of last June. The outlook was then wild and gloomy, but, they were not discouraged. They—two daughters of the Holy Cross-and full of the Spirit of their high calling—came prepared to encounter and if possible to surmount every obstacle and hence, without loosing [sic] a moment in brooding over the hardships and crosses and suffering that stared them in the face, they at once set themselves to the unpleasant work of collecting funds wherewith to make a commencement. Through their great zeal and wonderful energy they succeeded in accomplishing their object. Accordingly a beginning was made: a very commodious lot of ground in the most desirable part of the city was secured, and about the first of August the corner stone of what is now known as the "Academy of St. Mary's of Utah" was publicly laid in the presence of a large assemblage of people. The Building is of brick, four stories high, forty feet wide and sixty long, and is the largest and most elegant educational establishment in the Territory. The School was formally opened by the Sisters on the Sixth of September, and since has progressed very rapidly, the number of pupils now being over one hundred, most of whom, of course, are Mormons or non-Catholics. The Sisters have also leased a building for the purpose of an hospital for the poor miners many of whom get sick from time to time and have hitherto died from want of proper care. It is the Sisters intention also to start very soon a school for small boys. This very flattering success of the Sisters here in so short a time constitutes the chief feature of the progress of Catholicity in Utah during the past year; and furnishes us the best proof that there is here a wide and fruitful field for Catholic operation. Of course, it is to be remembered that in establishing themselves so quickly and firmly here, the Sisters had to contract some heavy debts, which, however, they hope to be able to pay in the near future through their own heroic labors, the assistance of God and the generosity of the faithful-believing that those who have commenced the good work will see to its completion and that those "who have put their hands to the plough will not stop to look back."

During the last year also, I have purchased a handsome church lot in Ogden, the second city in the Territory. It cost $900 a third of which has yet to be paid. The Congregations in the several missions attended by us have increased a little since my last report. We have had about a dozen converts, fifty infant baptisms and ten mixed marriages. Many lukewarm and indifferent Catholics have been converted and are now practical members of the Church. On the whole the progress of Catholicity here during the year that is about to close has been very marked and encouraging indeed; and its present state is such, as to fill us with hope and inspire us with fresh zeal to continue with redoubled energies our feeble efforts in the future.

The Future

Judging from the past, this Territory presents a bright future to the Catholic Church, if only her wants are timely supplied. What are those wants? In the first place, there is need of at least another priest here. There are only two here at present who are wholly inadequate to meet the growing demands of the whole Territory. But, the difficulty is, that there is no means of support for a third priest-for even two cannot obtain a proper subsistence. We have to travel a great deal-sometimes hundreds of miles-on railways and stages, and this consumes the greater part of our little uncertain income; and hence, it is only by the greatest economy that we are able to support ourselves. No greater work of charity therefore could be done and none that would do greater service to the Church and the Saving of souls than to send another priest here, and contribute to maintain him. Another very pressing want is that of a pastoral residence. We have, at present, to live in a few small uncomfortable and unhealthy rooms attached to the rear of the Church, and are obliged to do all our own housekeeping. I do not mention this want through any personal motive, but on the grounds, that while this unpleasant state of things continues it is and will be very difficult to get priests to remain here. On this ground it is a want that should be supplied as soon as possible and in its behalf I most earnestly appeal to your charity. Of course, our means of collecting from the congregation this year is very limited, as the members have already contributed more than they could well afford to the Sisters.

I wish also to call your attention to the necessity of building a church in Ogden City. This is and always will be a city of importance, and consequently, its Catholic interests and wants should be attended to as soon as possible. The number of Catholics there is increasing and would increase more rapidly if there were a Catholic Church. There is also a number of Catholic children who if not attended to in time will be practically lost to the Church. In order therefore, to save the old and the young I intend with the help of God, to build a church, and also a school to be conducted by the Sisters. This is God's work and I most humbly appeal to you for aid. I promise you fruit an hundred fold. I will show you work done for every dollar you may be pleased to give me. I will endeavour to make the best possible use of it, to the advancement of our dear Church and the salvation of immortal souls. Encouraged then by your generosity in the past I renew my appeal for further help. I renew it in the name of the Catholic Church, in the name of hundreds of her children famishing through want of spiritual food; in the name of hundreds of the little ones of J Christ, who if not taught the principles of their Church will grow up infidels, and will at no distant day be her shame and disgrace and living monuments of her apathy and neglectfulness. Placing my best hopes in your generous feelings and love for the advancement of our great Common Cause I feel assured of meeting with a hearty response and have the honor to remain

Your Able & Ob Servant in J C

L SCANLAN
Pastor of St Mary Magdalen,
Salt Lake City, Utah

Report Of October 31, 1879

Since my last report the good work once begun through your aid in this Territory is still progressing, & each year, as it rolls into the past, is a witness of new Catholic institutions erected, & in use for the object for which they were designed within that space of time. The past year has witnessed the commencement, and completion of a Catholic Church, & Hospital. Within the past year the Church has extended her branches, deep & firm, not in one of the civilized places, which surround the beautiful city of Salt Lake, but far beyond the boarders [sic] of civilized life, in a thriving mining camp, which is 375 miles from Salt Lake, and 300 miles from any Rail Road.

Silver Reef

The place above referred to is called Silver Reef. Two years ago this place was a barren prairie. About that time some rich silver mines were discovered there, and the excitement created by these discoveries brought such an influx of people to the place, that in less than one year, it was a thriving little town of 2,000 inhabitants. In the mean time Very Rev Father Scanlan, Pastor of Salt Lake, visited the place & finding there a rich harvest for a new mission, immediately commenced to work.

His first work in the little town, was a church which he built with subscriptions raised in the place in addition to the aid received from the "Propagation of the Faith."

The church being completed, and seeing the great interest manifested by the people at large in the work which he had already commenced, Rev Father Scanlan, in order to further supply the demands of the people, who had petitioned him to establish a Sisters' School and hospital, found it necessary to accede to their demands, & try to supply their wants. Having from non-Catholics, & Catholics an assured promise of liberal support for future undertakings, he immediately set to work, & commenced a new building, which was designed for an hospital. The building, once commenced, was soon completed, & has been used for that purpose since last August.

The school, which was also one of the necessities of the place, could not be erected, as sufficient means could not easily be obtained. But in order to meet the earnest demand of the people, & further the cause of the Catholic Church, Father Scanlan so arranged his church that during the week the sisters could hold school therein, which they have done since last August with great success. Being the only school in the place, nearly all the children of the place attend thereat.

At present there are in Silver Reef one resident priest, & fur [sic] Sisters of the order of the Holy Cross. Two of the Sisters administer to the wants of the sick and three teach school in the church. Thus ended the past year in the Southern part of the Territory, where Father Scanlan spent the greater part of the year. He commenced, and completed two grand Catholic institutions, and saw the work for which they were designed carried on therein by fur [sic] self sacrifishing [sic] Sisters before he returned to Salt Lake.

Another great benefit to be derived from these institutions is, that it will extend the influence of the Catholic Church to places where it could not otherwise possibly reach: for whilst Silver Reef is but a mining camp it has a prosperous future of many years before it; and from that place the benign influence of the Catholic Church & its teachings will be felt in all directions.

Surrounding Silver Reef there is none but Mormon settlements. St. George, the great Mormon Center, and the only city in the Territory where there is a Mormon "Temple" (a place where all the secret ordinances of the Mormon Church are administered) is about 17 miles from Silver Reef. During Father Scanlan's stay in Silver Reef he had, by his works etc, attracted the attention of the St George Mormon church authorities, who, whilst opposed to his work, & the cause in behalf of which, he labored so zealously, could not help appreciating his zeal & sacrifice in the prosecution of his undertakings, and at the same time admiring him for his gentleness, & firm but unassuming character joined with his great ability. As a mark of their appreciation, they invited him to hold services in their "Tabernacle" (a place where their public services are held, & entirely distinct from the Temple) & explain to them the origin, nature, and claims of the Catholic Church. This invitation, which urged by his congregation to accept, he could not decline. In last May he celebrated High Mass (Mormon choir furnishing music) in the Tabernacle at St. George, before a congregation of not less than 3000 persons, all of whom with but few exceptions were of the Mormon faith. A correspondent, a good & worthy French Catholic, writing to your humble servant on the matter said "It was the grandest event I ever witnessed in the history of the Catholic Church. Before Mass Father Scanlan commenced by explaining the nature & meaning of the Sacred vestments, just the thing I wished to have done for the crowd that was present. After Mass he preached for two hours the ablest and most lucid discourse I ever heard. The truth of the Catholic Church he established beyond a doubt, and its history brief, but interesting from its establishment down to the present he gave in a graphic style. He has made an impression on the Mormons of St. George, that shall not be soon erased." The Mormon press, in alluding to the matter, spoke of it in the most favorable manner. This is an instance of how a mission in Silver Reef may & has been used as a great auxialary [sic] for spreading the light of the true faith amongst a benighted people.

Salt Lake

The Catholic institutions in the city of Salt Lake are all in a flourishing condition. During the year past four converts were received into the church. His Grace, Archbishop [Joseph Sadoc] Alemany, who made his Episcopal visitation here last September, confirmed 30 persons 8 males, and 28 females. Of this number 7 were adults. Of those confirmed 6 were converts to the faith, 5 of them adults.

St. Mary's Acadamey [sic] was never more prosperous, than it is this year. Pupils number 200, and of these 50 are boarders. During the past year more than $2500.00 has been expended in the completion of the institution. At present with its magnificent cornice, & beautiful porches & verandas recently put on it looms up above all other buildings in the city, & is, if not the most costly, the grandest & most stylish building in Salt Lake.

The Hospital of the Holy Cross is continuing its good & charitable work, under the management of its devoted occupants. Through it the Catholic Church has received more praise in this city, than it could otherwise possibly obtain. The Mormons never establish Hospitals, & when they see the good Sisters providing for the wants of the sick & needy, & for non-Catholics more than Catholics, the great truth is unconsciously forcing itself upon them, that The Catholic Church in her institutions is Divine, or otherwise those heroic acts of self-Sacrifice could not be so successfully carried on. The building, occupied by the Sisters as an hospital is only rented, & for the past two years, they have been visiting all the mining camps, in order to raise sufficient funds, with which to build a new Hospital.

Wants of Salt Lake

What Salt Lake seems most to need at present is an Orphan Asylum. Had such an institution been once established, it would live, thrive, & flourish, equally as well, if not better, than our other Catholic institutions, because it would have the sympathy of the entire community: & in addition to this through it a good deal of good could be accomplished. Several parties, whose husband or wife, as the case may be, has died, have applied to us, & asked that we place their children in some Catholic institution, but having no institution for such children, reluctantly, but necessarily we must refuse. Two such applications were made to his Grace Archbishop Alemany during his stay in Utah. I hope and pray, that before another year passes by, I may see such an institution, at least, commenced, & thereby have the consolation of knowing, that through it, many little children, who would be otherwise lost to the true faith, will be brought up in the bosom of the Catholic Church & that the voice of our good

Lord will be echoed in this desolate place. "Suffer little children to come to me for of such is the Kingdom of Heaven."

Ogden

The Sacred Heart Academy, which opened a year ago in Ogden, has had a prosperous school during the year past, & as bright a future awaits it, as that which has crowned St. Mary's Academy in Salt Lake during, the four years past. The pupils at present there number 150, & of these 15 are boarders.

On Sunday (Oct 5) his Grace made his Episcopal Visitation there. He dedicated the new church, which was erected since his last Episcopal visit, under the patronage of St. Joseph. He confirmed about 20 persons. Whilst there his Grace expressed himself as highly pleased with every thing. Ogden's next great need will be an hospital. For such an institution the inhabitants have already petitioned.

Other Missions Ready For Operations

There are many other missions around Salt Lake equally as important, as those already established, and which if attended to, would produce as much good fruit, as those which have been yielding a hundred fold.

Park City

Park City, a mining camp 40 miles from Salt Lake has a population of over 2000 persons. They are there not less than 20 Catholic families, twice as many as we have in Salt Lake with its population of 25000. & I have no doubt but the aggregate number of Catholics there is double what we have in Salt Lake. We visit there once a month but in such visitations very little can be accomplished. No lasting impression can be made on children, who, if not trained in, & habituated with Catholic practises, ceremonies & rites, will not when grown up be practical Catholics, or Catholics at all, unless the influence of parents is very great, which in most instances unfortunately is not.

The same remarks are equally applicable to another mining camp, called F'risco, which is 200 miles from Salt Lake. The latter place can be reached by Rail Road, the former can not.

Such is the present state of the Catholic Church & as the Society of the Propagation of the Faith has reason to congratulate itself for much of its progress, I hope in the future in its charity it will not fail to continue the good work so effectually begun. With feelings of the profoundest respect, I remain Your humble servant in Christ

D. Kiely, Assistant Pastor
St. Mary Magdalen's Church
Salt Lake, Utah

Notes to the Text

1. Indeed, as pastor, vicar apostolic of Utah, and finally bishop of Salt Lake, Scanlan served the people of God in Utah for over forty years, until his death on May 10, 1915. For further details on this remarkable prelate, see Robert J. Dwyer, "Pioneer Bishop: Lawrence Scanlan, 1843–1915," *Utah Historical Quarterly* 20 (1952): 135-58.

2. See Herbert Eugene Bolton, *Pageant in the Wilderness* (Salt Lake City: Utah State Historical Society, 1950), published as vol. 18 of *Utah Historical Quarterly;* William R. Harris, *The Catholic Church in Utah* (Salt Lake City: Inter-Mountain Catholic Press, 1909), p. 330.

3. Founded at Paris by Pauline Jaricot, the Society for the Propagation of the Faith was the most successful of several organizations established during the nineteenth century to sustain the material needs of Catholic activities in missionary regions. For a detailed account of the society's works, see Joseph Freri, *The Society for the Propagation of the Faith and the Catholic Missions,* (New York, 1913).

   Several of Scanlan's letters have already been published. See John B. McGloin, S.J., "Two Early Reports Concerning Roman Catholicism in Utah 1876-1881," *Utah Historical Quarterly* 29 (1961): 333-44, and Francis J. Weber, "The Church in Utah, A Contemporary Account," *Records of the American Catholic Historical Society* 81 (1970): 199-308, and "Father Lawrence Scanlan's Report of Catholicism in Utah, 1880," *Utah Historical Quarterly* 34 (1966): 283-289.

90

The following essay about "Ecumenism in California's Southland" is taken from *Front Line* V (Fall, 1966), 86-91. A slightly different version appeared in *Unitas* XIX (Spring, 1967).

A few years ago, shortly after the assassination of President Kennedy, a well-known Baptist writer observed: "Two Johns, one on the Tiber and one on the Potomac, have in different ways compelled some people to re-examine their attitude toward the Catholic Church and others to think seriously about it for the first time."[1]

This new awareness of Catholicism finds its correlate in a new awareness in Catholicism, of which one vitally important aspect grows out of the ecumenical movement, the desire of the world for Christian unity. Though concern for a united Christendom is as old as the controversies which originally tore asunder the family of Christ, Catholic thought on the subject reached the stage of codification only with Vatican II.

From here onward, according to the Archbishop of Montreal, "no Christian who is animated by the charity of Christ can look upon his separated brethren as strangers or enemies. He must avoid all that can hurt and widen the trench that separates us. He must rid himself of historical and psychological prejudices."[2]

The Decree on Ecumenism directs Catholics "to acquire a more adequate understanding of...their own history, spiritual and liturgical life, their religious psychology and cultural background."[3] With that exhortation in mind, this short treatise focuses attention on some of the positive contributions Catholics have made to Christian unity by briefly and simply examining the record of the American Church on the national and local scene, regarding religious liberty and ecumenism.

Some short reflections on the Catholic influence toward freedom of worship are necessary in this context in order to properly grasp the present-day ecumenical atmosphere - for where religious liberty and ecumenism are not closely aligned, there can be no meaningful movement to any other than an artificial or juridical unity such as that at Florence in the fifteenth century.

It was as far back as the early 1600s that a tiny band of Catholics first introduced the notion of religious freedom to the North American continent, a concept that has since become a vital cornerstone of this country's government. The originator of this plan, George Calvert, deserves, recognition "among the wisest and most benevolent lawgivers"[4] of all ages, for he was the first in the Christian world to seek religious security and peace by the practice of justice, and not by the exercise of power. By Calvert's actions, it came about that Catholics as well as Protestants were sheltered from intolerance and Maryland became "the first state in the world in which perfect religious freedom was enjoyed."[5]

To cite another example - the very first act of the initial legislative assembly of New York was the "Charter of Liberties and Privileges" engineered, inspired, and directed by the Catholic governor, Thomas Dongan. One hundred and six years before the adoption of this nation's Bill of Rights and 161 years before the last state (New Jersey) granted complete religious freedom, the Catholic-inspired New York charter declared "that no person or persons who profess faith in God, through Jesus Christ, shall at any time be disquieted or called in question, but all such may fairly and fully enjoy his or their judgments or consciences in matters of religion…"[6]

If similar acts in other areas were not commonplace, it is because the number of "papists" was extremely restricted throughout colonial times. Yet where they did appear, they came as champions of the freedom of religious worship and forerunners of today's ecumenists.

The Catholic pioneers of this country rejected from the very outset the European concept of *cujus regio, ejus religio*, and to their foresight can be credited the gradual evolvement of a climate which prompted a Catholic, Henry F. Brownson, in 1889, to tell a Congress of Laymen at Baltimore that "separation from the Church is no longer equivalent to outlawry, or privation of fire and water."[7]

Out of such comments as this grows this writer's suspicion that a detailed study of Catholic ecumenical involvement in the United States would demonstrate that the Catholic Church is a full sixty years ahead of parallel movements on the Continent.

Far from taking a defensive or apologetic stand about their Church's now-universal emergence in the struggle for religious freedom wherein true ecumenism must be nurtured, Catholics in the United States can and should point with pride to the spirit of brotherly love so nobly exhibited in the lives of their spiritual forebears. Bishop Thomas J. Conaty (1847-1915) caught the spirit of an earlier age when he stated that "the ideal American should be a broad-minded and just man, demanding liberty for himself, and desirous that it should be enjoyed by others."[8]

Once their nation was firmly established in the tenets of religious freedom, Catholics took the next logical step toward a united Christendom. The historical evidence of ecumenical overtures is especially impressive in California. One outstanding example is the broadminded, even heroic attitude of Francis Mora (1827-1905), Bishop of Monterey-Los Angeles. The Spanish-born prelate was a favorite target of the American Protective Association and was referred to by the APA as "that damn old foreigner at Second and Main."

While the bishop never hesitated to fight for essentials, he never engaged in useless polemics, preferring as he said, to pray "that God may bless them and give them the light to enter into His fold." When his broken health could no longer withstand the burden of persecution, Mora handed over the diocese to stronger hands but before entering his lonely retirement, the bishop had this advice for his people about their dealings with non-Catholics: "Give them always good example, for although of different religions, yet they are your brethren. Our creator is theirs. The sunshine and day fall alike on the field of Catholic and non-Catholic. God wishes the salvation of all. Be kind and considerate to your non-Catholic acquaintances, and let no animosity ever exist between you; have confidence in them. Such has been my endeavor always and I request you to do the same. I have never mentioned the name of Protestant in the pulpit - they are my separated brethren."[9]

By esteeming what was good in other Christian sects, Mora did not in any way minimize the uniqueness of the Catholic Church. He would have been the last to affirm what he knew to be false but, at the same time, the prelate recognized that much of Protestantism is good, mirroring as it does the stone from which it was hewn.

Mora's successor, George Thomas Montgomery (1847-1907) was long a respected figure in the cause for Christian unity. Even as a young priest in San Francisco, it was known that sentiments of respect for his aposto-

603

late were held by non-Catholics who respected the impartiality of his many activities.

Montgomery's popularity with those outside the Church carried over to the southland and though the memory of the APA still flavored the atmosphere, the bishop was given the unprecedented honor in 1901 of addressing the students at the Methodist-operated University of Southern California. His discourse, we are told by contemporary news accounts, was "loudly applauded by his intensely Protestant audience."[10] The local Catholic paper observed that through this address and other ecumenical gestures, a great change came over popular sentiment, so much so "that no public function is now considered complete without the presence and active cooperation of the Catholic bishop."[11]

As he was preparing to return to the Bay Area as Coadjutor Archbishop of San Francisco, it was noted that to Montgomery's broad-minded policy "is largely attributable the freedom of the diocese from religious factiousness, and polemical strife, and the existence of a happy and cordial *entente* between Protestant and Catholic."[12]

Bishop Montgomery was among the first to realize that involvement in ecumenism did not, in any manner, water down the doctrines of Christ. Though the prelate was conscious of a certain pluralism in the matter of salvation, he knew by faith that the fullness of God's teachings was present only in the Catholic Church. He would have agreed with C. F. Pauwels that "a strong faith in the divinity of the Church" is the first requisite for ecumenism since the Catholic Church must be seen "by faith as the real place of encounter between the divine and human."[13]

The Decree on Ecumenism, embraced and promulgated by Vatican II, is seen then as a natural flowering-forth, at the highest level, of that thinking which Bishop John J. Cantwell enunciated in his first pastoral letter: "...our mission, though primarily to Catholics is not to them alone. A Bishop of the Church of Christ belongs to all; hence it shall be our constant aim to lend our feeble assistance to every movement that makes for the salvation, the betterment and happiness of all the people irrespective of creed or other consideration."[14]

Fifty-six years ago, Father Paul James Francis Wattson, founder of the Franciscan Friars of the Atonement and considered to be the originator of the Chair of Unity Octave, wrote what might be taken as a guiding set of principles for those Catholics presently interested in furthering the tenets of ecumenism: "Charity towards our separated brethren, the faithful practice of our holy religion, unswerving orthodoxy, these are three things which must signally characterize the Catholics of America, if we

are to make our land altogether Catholic, but there is a fourth characteristic which American Catholics must emphasize more even than they
have in the past and that is personal loyalty, fealty and devotion to the
Successor of St. Peter, because he is the Sovereign Shepherd and the
Vicar of Jesus Christ. When the multitude of Protestants, who love our
Blessed Lord sincerely and who are trying so hard to serve and obey him,
come to realize that the voice of Peter is the voice of Christ, then they
will harken to His call and thus hearing the Divine Master speaking
through His Vicar, the problem of a reunited Christendom will be solved
and there will be ONE FOLD AND ONE SHEPHERD."[15]

Notes to the Text

1. Harvey Cox, "A Baptist Intellectual's View of Catholicism," *Harpers*, 225 (December, 1962), 44.
2. Emile Cardinal Leger, *Pastoral Letter* (Montreal, 1962).
3. Walter M. Abbott and Joseph Gallagher (eds.), *The Documents of Vatican II* (New York, 1966). p. 353.
4. George Bancroft, *History of the United States of America* (New York, 1882), I, 158.
5. J. L. Macdonald, *The Catholic Pages of American History* (Brooklyn, 1891), p. 9.
6. See John H. Kennedy, *Thomas Dongan, Governor of New York* (Washington, 1930), p. 31.
7. *Official Report of the Proceedings of the Catholic Congress Held At Baltimore, Md.* (Detroit, 1889), p. 32.
8. Archives of the Archdiocese of Los Angeles, Thomas J. Conaty, Address on the "Ideals of American Citizenship," not dated.
9. *Catholic Tidings*, October 24, 1896.
10. See Francis J. Weber, *George Thomas Montgomery* (Los Angeles, 1966), p. 17.
11. *The Tidings*, January 19, 1901.
12. *Ibid.*, February 7, 1903.
13. Quoted in Thomas O'Meara, "Towards a Pastoral Ecumenism," *Worship*, 39 (February, 1965), p. 103.
14. *Pastoral to the Clergy and Laity of the Diocese of Monterey-Los Angeles* (Los Angeles, 1918), p. 2.
15. *At-One-Ment*, V (1963 Annual), 6.

91

This essay, "Precedent for Ecumenism," appeared in the *Western States Jewish History* XIX (January, 1987), 158-160.

The cordiality presently existing between the Catholic and Jewish communities in Southern California has deep roots that frequently confront readers who page through the historical annals. The personages of Francis Mora (1827-1905) and Isaias W. Hellman (1842-1920) come immediately to mind. Those two Los Angeles pioneers practiced ecumenism decades before the word was even coined.

When the seventeen-year-old, Bavarian-born Hellman[1] arrived in Los Angeles, he found a city with a population of 4,000 people, of which three-fourths were Mexicans and Indians. He began clerking for the sum of twenty-dollars per month and slept under the counter of the store where he was employed. Shortly thereafter, he met Father Francis Mora[2] who came into the store one day to purchase some clothing. The two became close friends and Mora offered to help Hellman learn Spanish and perfect his English. It was a relationship that subsequently profited both the Church and the Synagogue. Hellman subsequently became a prominent merchant, banker and developer, while Mora went on to become the Bishop of Monterey-Los Angeles.

According to Hellman's son-in-law and executor, "the friendship formed then lasted throughout the lifetime of that eminent divine and Mr. Hellman from his youth continued to be the counselor and advisor on all financial matters pertaining to the welfare of the Church in Los Angeles."[3]

Hellman was involved in practically every innovative activity that touched the southland. He was among those who brought the railroad to Los Angeles, he helped to organize the Farmers and Merchants Bank and he was instrumental in founding the University of Southern California. During his years as president of Congregation B'nai B'rith (now the Wilshire Boulevard Temple), Hellman often sought out the advice of Father Mora. It was Mora who encouraged Hellman in his efforts to build a permanent structure for Jewish worship.[4]

Hellman was truly an outstanding man. In one account it is noted that "from the time the city of Los Angeles was a frontier village to the present day of its marvelous progress, he was in the foreground of the chief enterprises undertaken in the work of development.[5]

During the 1880s, the Diocese of Monterey-Los Angeles was in desperate financial straits. In 1887, Mr. Hellman came up with a proposal[6] for selling the valuable parcel of property on which the Old Plaza Church was located.[7] Hellman envisioned the site as ideal for commercial development. Mora and his Vicar General Father Joaquin Adam[8] favored the transaction, but because of opposition from the pastor and other influential parties, the sale was never consummated. Hellman, nonetheless, continued his interest in assisting the diocese and on numerous occasions he utilized his credit standing to guarantee Bishop Mora's notes.

On February 23, 1921, some months after Hellman's death, Bishop John J. Cantwell wrote a lengthy letter outlining the many areas in which Hellman's kindness and generosity had benefited the Diocese of Monterey-Los Angeles.[9]

At the head of Hellman's bequests in his last will and testament was a gift of $25,000 to the Catholic Orphan Asylum of Los Angeles. It was the last in a long series of benefactions stretching over the years between 1859 and 1920.

Notes to the Text

1. See Norton B. Stern, "Toward a Biography of Isaias W. Hellman, Pioneer Builder of California," *Western States Jewish Historical Quarterly*, October 1969, pp. 27-43.
2. For a biographical sketch, see Francis J. Weber, *Francis Mora. Last of the Catalans* (Los Angeles, 1967).
3. E.S. Heller, San Francisco, to John J. Cantwell, San Francisco, Archives of the Archdiocese of Los Angeles, February 25, 1921.
4. See Tom Owen, "The First Synagogue in Los Angeles," *Western States Jewish Historical Quarterly*, October 1968, pp. 9-13.
5. E.S. Heller, "A Biographical Sketch of Isaias W. Hellman," *In Memoriam – Isaias W. Hellman* (San Francisco, 1921), p. 4.

6. Peter Verdaguer to Francis Mora, Los Angeles, Archives of the Archdiocese of Los Angeles, October 4, 1887.

7. Marco R. Newmark, "The Story of Religion in Los Angeles," *Historical Society of Southern California Quarterly*, March 1946, p. 37.

8. For an overview of Adam's life, see Francis J. Weber, "Joaquin Adam y Tous," *Southern California Quarterly*, Summer, 1985, pp. 135-152.

9. The letter is mentioned in Heller's response to Cantwell, February 25, 1921, Archives of the Archdiocese of Los Angeles. Unfortunately there is no extant copy in Los Angeles.

92

This journal about "A Pilgrimage of Faith" was written to memorialize the ecumenical journey to Rome, Israel, Geneva and Taize by eighteen rabbis, ministers and Priests during the later months of 1974.

In a discourse delivered on May 23, 1974, Pope Paul VI said that the Church's twenty-sixth Holy Year provided "a most opportune period for spiritual renewal and for the promotion of Christian unity." It was a response to the Holy Father's exhortation that prompted the Los Angeles Council of Churches, the Board of Rabbis and the Roman Catholic Archdiocese of Los Angeles to endorse a unique inter-faith, pre-Holy Year pilgrimage to Rome, Jerusalem, Geneva and Taize, four centers of reconciliation, in the fall of 1974.

Included in the eighteen "representative" pilgrims chosen for the journey were three rabbis, four Catholic and two Episcopal priests, as well as ministers from the Presbyterian, Lutheran, Baptist, Methodist, Disciple of Christ and United Brethren persuasions. The group met twice prior to departure in order to map out the details of the journey. Since private and public prayer form the "soul" of the ecumenical movement, it was decided that a series of communal services would be interlaced into the already-packed schedule.

On October 21st, the polyglot collection of "divines" gathered at the Los Angeles International Airport to begin the saga of searching, out and studying, the common roots of their respective faiths. Shortly before embarking, Canon Harold G. Hultgren, Pastor of Holy Trinity Church in Alhambra, read a message from Episcopal Bishop Robert C. Rusack, conveying his "blessing and best wishes for the journey. Then Father Royale Vadakin, President of the Priests' Senate for the Archdiocese of Los Angeles, led the group in reciting the Holy Year Interfaith prayer composed by Cardinal Timothy Manning.

The first stop on the tour was Rome, where Msgr. Justin Rigali, a priest from California attached to the Vatican Secretariate of State, had provided choice seats for the papal audience of October 30th. In his address to the 8,000 people, read in four languages, the Pontiff called for a renewal of prayer in all its forms - personal, communal and liturgical. "Once the Christian family is revitalized and fortified with prayer," Pope Paul said there will be a "new spiritual, moral and social springtime" for the world. At the conclusion of the audience, the pilgrims were guests of honor at a luncheon hosted by the priests and seminarians at the nearby North American College.

Early the next morning, the group assembled in the tiny crypt chapel, at Saint Peter's tomb, where Cardinal Manning officiated at a concelebrated Liturgy of the Eucharist. It was an historic occasion for the Archbishop of Los Angeles was in the process of making his *ad limina* visit to Rome. In addition to several site-seeing forays around the Eternal City, the next two days were spent attending seminars at the Christian Center for Unity. Several interviews were also held with various curial officials, including an extensive session at the Sacred Congregation for Promoting Christian Unity.

The Christian pilgrims were especially anxious to see Israel so that, in the words of Pope Paul VI, they could "honor the mysteries of salvation" by visiting "the holy places where Christ was born, died, rose again and ascended into heaven."

The tensions of the Near East conflict were immediately obvious at Tel Aviv's Lod airport. Still visible on the walls of the terminal were the bullet marks of the 1972 raid, in which twenty-seven people were slaughtered by the so-called "Japanese Red Army." Israel was found to be "a nation going calmly about the business of daily living, while aware of the ever-present thrust of terrorism and renewed war."

In Jerusalem, the holy city and center of monotheism, the pilgrims hastened to the old sector and the Western Wall, which stands nearest to the defiled Temple sanctuary. There Rabbi Alfred Wolf of the Wilshire Boulevard Temple and Rabbi Paul Dubin of Temple Sinai read a pre-Shabbat prayer service partly from the traditional liturgy, partly from appropriate Scripture passages, including *T'hilim*, the Psalms.

The religion editor for the Los Angeles *Herald-Express* reported that "some people thought it strange to see ministers distinguished in clerical collars in that particular environment." He went on to say that "when they found that they were American priests and ministers traveling with rabbi friends to get a better understanding of the Holy Land and its people, they were greeted and blessed."

The following four days were devoted to visiting and praying at the Jewish and Christian shrines in and around the City of Peace. Through an arrangement with the Franciscans, the Catholic priests offered Holy Mass individually in the Church of the Holy Sepulchre where, by an agreement between the Latin, Greek and Armenian communities, the liturgy is still performed as it was in 1870. Canon Hultgren officiated at the Episcopal liturgy in the Chapel of Saint Abraham, in the Greek Orthodox Patriarchate, overlooking the Holy Sepulchre.

The Los Angeles clergymen took several walking-tours through the streets of the ancient city. Of special interest to the Christians was the *Via Dolorosa*, along which Jesus Christ passed enroute to Mount Calvary. Other sites in the area were the Dome of the Rock, the Pool of Bethsaida and the Chapel of the Flagellation.

The Catholic priests celebrated Holy Mass at all the major Christian shrines. At Bethany's Church of Saint Lazarus, Msgr. John A. Rawden, Chancellor for the Archdiocese of Los Angeles, was principal celebrant. Father John Cosgrove, Pastor of Saint Joseph's Church in Pomona, officiated at the crypt of Nazareth's magnificent new Basilica of the Annunciation and Msgr. Francis J. Weber, Archivist for the Archdiocese of Los Angeles, was the principal officer for the liturgy at the tiny chapel of the Nativity, at Bethlehem.

At the Memorial to the Six Million of the Nazi holocaust, one of the rabbis recited the Kaddish in English and Hebrew, the traditional prayer for close relatives who were lost.

Just before leaving, Jerusalem, the Reverend Bob Shepard, Pastor of Christ Church by the Sea, Newport Beach, and Rabbi Bernard King, of Harbor Reform Temple, in the same city, paid a final visit to the Western Wall, where they inserted into the crevices a series of petitions composed by their respective congregations.

The pilgrims were specially blessed in having with them the widely-known and highly-respected William Sanford LaSor, Professor of Scripture at Fuller Theological Seminary. Dr. La Sor's encyclopedic mind provided a veritable living-commentary on such vitally-important places as the caves of Qumran, where the Dead Sea Scrolls were unearthed and the Shrine of the Book, where they are displayed for public perusal.

Aside from the precious opportunity of visiting the sites where salvation history unfolded, the journey through the Holy Land provided valuable occasions for discussing theological and scriptural questions, as well as exchanging ideas about the more mundane problems confronting every community of believers.

Above the lake on which Christ walked, the ridge of the Golan Heights gives military mastery of the countryside, as it has done through all the wars and insurrections for the past three thousand years. At the border of the truce zone, Rabbi Paul Dubin read several passages from Holy Scripture and then led the Group in praying for a just and lasting peace between the warring factions separated only by a handful of United Nations troops. Informal prayer services were also conducted at the ruins of the synagogue in the mountain-fortress of Masada and in the historic synagogue of the Jewish mystics in Safad.

In Nes Ammim, the pilgrims observed an experimental program aimed at advancing Jewish-Christian relations. Staffed by Christian settlers from Holland and Germany, the small commune seeks to integrate the Christian life-style into the religious *mores* of Israel and Judaism.

Rabbi King, whose congregation in Newport Beach is named in honor of the victims of the Ma'alot raid, left the tour long enough for a visit to the school where twenty-one Israeli children were killed, in May, 1974, by the Popular Democratic Front for the Liberation of Palestine.

The pilgrims spent the night of October 29th at a Kibbutz in Upper Galilee, one of the 230 collective settlements operated under governmental aupsices. The Kibbutz at Ayelet Hashahar is considered among the most progressive and successful of the nationwide ventures and serves as a pilot project for fledgling foundations of more recent origin.

At Haifa, the clergymen visited the World Center of the Bahai Faith, located on the slopes of Mount Carmel. The golden-dome shrine and its impressively colorful gardens is the religious headquarters for believers in 141 nations. Another pleasant feature in Haifa was the reception accorded by the Arab-Jewish Cultural Community and Youth Center.

The pilgrims were exposed to a number of interesting personalities too during their sojourn. Interviews, for example, were scheduled with the Honorable Farah S. Al-Araj, the Mayor of Beit Jala, an Arab village on the West Bank, near Bethlehem; Archbishop William A. Carew, the Apostolic Delegate to Israel and officials at the Israel Institute of Technology and the University of Tel Aviv. Those and other personages provided a wide spectrum of background data on the area's political, religious and cultural complexities.

Fortunately, for the historical record, the Reverend Robert C. Walker of the National Conference of Christians and Jews assiduously taped all the interviews, addresses and conferences jammed into the hectic fifteen day journey.

After personally visiting the religious shrines of Israel, Catholics, Protestants and Jews alike could testify that it was a pleasant, temperate country of small wheat fields, thriving vineyards and grazing land for numerous flocks of sheep. It was easy to see how the Mediterranean Sea to the west, the Jordan river to the east and the brooding, heat-soaked desert beyond the river and to the south had shaped the economy, the living habits, the literature and the temper of the people.

Who could remain unmoved by so great a pilgrimage? Guided by faith along such paths, who could fail to return home a better man? For there unfolded the moving drama of our destiny, the primitive history of the human race, the philosophy of the saints, the legislation of a people chosen and governed by God.

Especially interested in visiting the Ecumenical Center, in the Grand Saconnex a suburb of Geneva, was Dr. Randall C. Phillips, Pastor of Wilshire Methodist Church and the past President of the Los Angeles Council of Churches. At the center, representatives of 252 Protestant, Anglican and Orthodox persuasions have been working together since 1948, in attempts to further the goals of Christian unity.

The Reverend A. Dale Rose, Pastor of Eagle Rock Presbyterian Church, utilized the opportunity provided at Geneva to learn what efforts the World Council of Churches was making concerning the war on racism and its dialogue with the Third World.

On November 2nd, the pilgrims journeyed through the French countryside to Taize, and the inter-denominational center founded by Brother Roger Schutz, in the early 1940s. There several Catholics and Protestants from a dozen different sects live as monks, bound together by the three vows of poverty, chastity and respect for authority. The ministers, rabbis and priests gathered in the priory church for the chanting of Vespers, followed by an address from the prior, Brother Roger. Afterwards, they hastily toured one or another of the multi-colored campsites for the Council of Youth, which were located in a field adjacent to the priory. Later that evening one of the monks explained the origins of the festival which had attracted upwards of 30,000 young people to Taize during the preceding summer months.

The next morning, several of the ministers conducted a communal prayer service. The Reverend Glen O. Balsley, Pastor of the Lutheran Church of Our Redeemer in Leimert Park, recited the Apostles Creed and Canon Oliver B. Garver, Jr., Assistant to the Episcopal Bishop of Los Angeles, read the scriptural selections for the twenty-second Sunday after Pentecost. The Reverend Jonathan Wilson, a Presbyterian minister, recited a prayer composed by one of his parishioners in La Canada. Dr. Horace C. Mays, Executive Secretary for the Los Angeles Council of Churches, explained several tenets of the Baptist faith and closed with a brief prayer for unity. The devotions were concluded with a handshake of peace, inaugurated by the Reverend Dale C. Whitney, Pastor of Geneva Presbyterian Church, in Long Beach.

The journey proved to be "a most intensive two weeks of relating to one another and of grappling with a multitude of impressions." Everywhere, the Los Angeles clergymen observed, in the words of Rabbi Wolf, "movements however rudimentary and fragile, toward greater openness among Christian churches and between Christians and Jews."

The 20,000 mile inter-faith, pre-Holy Year pilgrimage reached a safe and successful conclusion on November 4th. By the time the eighteen Los Angeles clergymen had arrived back in Southern California, they were unanimously in agreement with the observations of Episcopal Bishop Rusack that there is "no more fitting symbol of our hope than a journey to the historic homelands of our respective traditions."

93

"The Relics of Christ" is here republished from the *Review for Religious* XXI (March 1962), 79-88.

The spiritual value of a relic is directly proportional to the devotion it inspires in those who venerate it. Apart from this spiritual significance, the relic is merely a historical curiosity. It may or may not be of archaeological value to the museums of the world.

The official attitude of the Church regarding individual relics is one of extreme reserve. In most cases, the Church prudently withholds definitive judgment on even the most demonstrably ancient relics. In fact, while reluctant to proclaim the authenticity of a particular relic, the Church has not infrequently withdrawn from public veneration relics whose claims were found to be dubious or spurious.

In recent memory, this has happened in the case of "St. Philomena," center of a devoted cult for more than a century, though she had never been formally canonized and nothing actually was known of her life. Despite the many miracles attributed to the relics of this supposed second century martyr, unearthed from a catacomb in 1802, modern research shed doubt on the authenticity of the remains.

It should be noted that the decree of the Sacred Congregation of Rites in 1961 dropping the feast of St. Philomena from the liturgical calendar did not touch on the validity of the miracles attributed to her intercession. They may well have been genuine miracles performed by God because of the faith and devotion of those who prayed for them.

The oldest and most cherished of Christian relics naturally are those reputed to have been connected with the holy person of Jesus Christ

Himself. Those few that are still extant, for the most part, have sufficient historical documentation to merit scholarly attention.

It must be borne in mind that the honor and veneration given to these objects is directed primarily to Christ. Hence, in some cases where documentation establishes only doubtful authenticity, the Church is certainly justified in remaining silent, if it is understood that in so doing the Church is not giving positive approval and if greater honor and glory are thereby rendered to Almighty God.

Our approach to this obscure and sometimes controversial subject is that of the historian, who presents only the facts, leaving conclusions to the reader.

The True Cross

The Cross on which our Savior died has been traditionally the most precious of all Christian relics. Tiny splinters of the True Cross have been so widely distributed that, in the words of St. Cyril, "the whole inhabited earth is full of relics from the wood of the Cross."

St. Helena is credited with discovery of the True Cross in 327 A.D.[1] Early testimony of the fathers, among them Ambrose, Jerome, Sozomen, and Theodoret, recounts this marvelous event in copious detail. The Cross was found in an abandoned cistern near Mount Calvary. Identification as the True Cross, according to St. Ambrose, was easy enough since the *titulus* was still affixed. To commemorate this great occasion, St. Helena ordered a magnificent basilica to be erected over the Holy Sepulchre. She gave it the name of St. Constantius in honor of her son, the Roman emperor.

When Helena returned to Rome, the relics were placed in the Sessorian Basilica, Santa Croce in Gerusalemme. A substantial segment of the Cross was left in Jerusalem where it annually attracted thousands of devout pilgrims. It was captured in the seventh century by Khosru II, the Persian conqueror. When the holy relic was returned by Heraclius in 628, the feast of the Exaltation of the Holy Cross was instituted. The Jerusalem relic was divided many times. When certain of these fragments fell into the hands of the Mohammedans, the Crusades were inspired to restore them.

An extensive and intensive study of the True Cross was made and published in 1870 by Rohault de Fleury. After examination of all extant fragments claimed to be from the True Cross, he drew up a minute catalogue of them, with precise weights and measurements. His findings proved that if all known pieces of the True Cross were put together, they would constitute less than one-third of the original Cross. This effectively silenced skeptics who had scoffed that the total of supposed fragments was bigger than the Cross itself.

De Fleury's calculations[2] were based on a cross of pinewood weighing an estimated 75 kilograms. The volume of this cross would have been approximately 178 million cubic millimeters. Known volume of the existing relics does not exceed 40 million cubic millimeters. *0 Crux ave, spes unica!*

The Title of the Cross

There are many fanciful legends associated with the discovery of the True Cross by St. Helena. The manner of distinguishing the True Cross of Christ from those of the two thieves is usually related with colorful if not historically accurate circumstances. However, St. Ambrose testifies there was no problem in identifying the True Cross as the *titulus* or title-piece was still intact. Other writers corroborate this account, notably Sts. Cyril[3] and Jerome.

As has been the case with so many holy relics, the titulus was divided into several pieces. The Diary of Etheria locates a piece of the *titulus* in Jerusalem in 380 A.D. Helena undoubtedly brought a part of the title back to Rome with her. Regrettably, there is no further documentation available on the fate of the Jerusalem relic.

For some reason, very likely to protect it from invaders, the Roman relic seems to have been walled up in an arch of Santa Croce by Placidus Valentinian III in the fifth century. In the twelfth century it was accidentally unearthed by Gherardo Caccianemici, titular cardinal and later Pope Lucius II. The future pontiff placed his seal on the reliquary and replaced it in its hiding place.

In 1492 Cardinal Mendoza of Toledo rediscovered the relic which he immediately presented to the then Holy Father, Innocent VIII. A papal bull, *Admirabile Sacramentum*, was issued, after which the *titulus* was exposed for public veneration in Santa Croce.

The title-piece is of wood, about nine by five inches in size, and comprises two-and-one-half lines of faded inscription. Hebrew, Greek and Latin characters are discernible, all of which are printed in reverse, a practice common with the Romans of the time of Christ.

The Shroud of Turin

It is recorded in Chapter 27 of St. Matthew how Joseph of Arimathea wrapped the body of Jesus in a "clean linen cloth." No further mention of this funeral shroud appears in Christian literature until the time of St. Nino[4] (d. 338), who relates how Peter removed the shroud from the tomb shortly after the Resurrection. The fourteenth century Byzantine historian, Nicephorus Callista, tells how this Holy Shroud, soaked with the blood of Christ and bearing an image of His holy face, found its way to Constantinople: "Pulcheria, Empress of the East, having built a basilica at Blachernes in 436, piously deposited there the funeral linens of Our Savior, which had just been rediscovered and which the Empress Eudoxia had sent to her." Eyewitnesses to the presence of the Holy Shroud at Constantinople are recorded in the Annals of 631, 640, 749, 1157 and 1171 A.D.

During the Fourth Crusade, the Holy Shroud was surrendered in recompense to Otho de la Roche, Duke of Athens and Sparta. The Duke in 1204 sent the prized relic to his father in France. Soon after, it came into possession of the Bishop of Besancon. A fire caused minor damage to the shroud in 1349. Later that same year, it was stolen from its case in Besancon Cathedral and given to King Philip IV who in turn gave it to Geoffrey, Count of Charney and Lord of Lirey. There is documentary evidence that it was at Lirey in 1360.

During the Hundred Years War, the Holy Shroud was handed over by Geoffrey's granddaughter to the House of Savoy for safekeeping. In 1454, Pope Sixtus IV directed the Duke of Savoy, Louis I, to build a shrine for the shroud at his Chambery residence. During the troubled war years of the sixteenth century, the Holy Shroud was moved from town to town in France. It narrowly missed being destroyed a second time by fire in 1532, and in fact its corners were noticeably singed.

At the request of the aged Charles Borromeo, the shroud in 1578 was brought to Turin where it has remained for the past four hundred years. It is presently preserved in the black marble chapel specially built for it behind the city's beautiful fifteenth century cathedral.

Several pronouncements by the Holy See leave little doubt regarding the Church's official attitude toward the Turin Shroud. An Office and a Mass were formally approved by Pope Julius II in the bull *Romanus Pontifex* issued in 1506. Sixtus IV had previously stated that in this Holy Shroud "men may look upon the true blood and portrait of Jesus Christ Himself."

A remarkable discovery was made in 1898, when a photograph of the Turin Shroud revealed the faint, blurred image on the ancient linen to be an actual "negative" produced by vapors from a human body covered with spices. The negative of the modern photo–a negative of a negative, thus producing a positive–offered a far more pronounced picture of a human face than was previously recognizable.

Chemically, this "vapograph" was caused by the ammoniacal emanations from the surface of the body after an unusually violent death. It has been proved experimentally that these vapors are capable of producing a deep reddish brown stain which would vary in intensity with the distance from a cloth soaked with oil and aloes. Hence the image of Christ's face on the shroud is a natural negative.

This modern evidence, together with the identification of human bloodstains, prompted Dr. Paul Vignon to read a brilliant paper before the *Académie des Sciences*, in which he suggested that any explanation denying the authenticity of the Turin Shroud would be scientifically inaccurate.

It might also be mentioned that the impression on the shroud of the Crown of Thorns is in perfect conformity with the "helmet type" of crown displayed at Notre Dame Cathedral in Paris. Further, the nail wounds are not in the palms of the hands but in the wrists. It has been realized only in our own times that this was a physical necessity, for nails in the palms of the hands would not have been able to sustain the weight of a human body.

One of the major opponents and critics of the Turin Shroud was the anti-pope Clement VII, first of the Avignon Pretenders. His opposition apparently stemmed from a vague charge made by the Bishop of Troyes that the shroud was the work of a local craftsman skilled in the subtle art of simulating antique handiwork.

Other shrouds, thirty in all, each purporting to be the genuine article, have turned up through the centuries. Most notable are those still preserved at Besancon, Cadouin, and Champiegne. These shrouds likewise bear impressions alleged to be those of Christ's face and body.

However, the preponderance of historical evidence seems to leave no doubt that among all the claimants, only the Shroud of Turin has a valid pretension to authenticity.

The Pillar of the Scourging

The column of the Praetorium to which Christ was bound during His scourging was discovered in the Fortress of Antonia in 373 A.D., according to a chronicle penned by St. Ephrem. St. Paulinus of Nola,[5] writing after 409, refers to several relics of the Passion, among them "the pillar at which He was scourged." Philip of Brosserius saw the pillar in the Church of the Holy Sepulchre in 1285. Some time before the end of the fourteenth century it was broken and one part was sent to Constantinople.

An interesting Christian tradition, dating back to the fourth century, holds that Christ was actually scourged twice. St. John Chrysostom tells us this second flagellation took place at the house of Caiaphas after the mock trial.

This tradition finds prominent mention in early chronicles. The pillar used for the second scourging was reserved in the Church of Mount Sion, the Cenacle, where St. Jerome reported he saw it. During the Persian invasion, it too seems to have been broken into several pieces. The portion left at the Cenacle was lost in 1537. The other part was returned to a church subsequently erected on the site of the house of Caiaphas. Here it was venerated until the fourteenth century, when it completely disappeared.

In 1222 A.D., Giovanni Cardinal Colonna, papal envoy to the Orient, returned to Rome with a fragment of the Pillar of the Scourging, apparently given him by the Saracens. He enshrined it in his titular church of St. Praxedes, where it may be seen today. The Roman pillar is of marble, about two feet four inches high. It is probably one of the parts of the Praetorian column. Its counterpart in Jerusalem is of a different material and may have formed the lower part of the pillar.

The Holy Stairs

Among the many treasures brought back from the Holy Land by St. Helena was the marble staircase from the palace of Pontius Pilate in Jerusalem. It is still extant.[6] The stone steps number twenty-eight and are said to have been sanctified by the feet of Christ himself when He ascended this stairway at the Praetorium.

The stairway, reconstructed in Rome, originally formed part of the old Lateran Palace, leading into a chapel dedicated to St. Sylvester. When the Lateran Palace was torn down by Pope Sixtus V in 1589, the stairs were moved to their present location.

Today the *Scala Sancta* constitutes the entranceway to the Holy of Holies, an old private papal chapel.[7] In its present site, the *Scala Sancta* is flanked by additional stairwells on either side. Traditionally the Holy Stairs are ascended only on one's knees. The last pope to ascend the stairway in this fashion was Pius IX on the eve of his exile from Rome in 1870.

Pope St. Pius X decreed a plenary indulgence for those who devoutly ascend the *Scala Sancta* on their knees as testimony of their love for Christ. Replicas of the *Scala Sancta* have been erected at Lourdes and other centers of pilgrimage.

The Soldier's Lance

Mention is made of the soldier's lance in Chapter 19 of St. John in his account of the Savior's death, St. John relates that "one of the soldiers opened His side with a spear…" The first extra-Biblical mention of this relic seems to be by Anthony of Piacenza, who wrote that he saw the Crown of Thorns and "the lance with which He was struck in the side," in the Basilica of Mount Sion.[8]

A miniature of the renowned Syriac manuscript, illuminated by Rabulas in 586, assigns the name Longinus to the soldier whose lance pierced the crucified Christ. Cassiodorus and Gregory of Tours speak of a spear venerated at Jerusalem, which was thought to be identical with that mentioned in Scripture.

After the fall of Jerusalem in 615 A.D., several of the major relics of the Passion fell into the hands of the Persians. The *Chronicon Paschale* relates that a piece of the soldier's lance came into the possession of Nicetas, who enclosed it in an icon and presented it to Santa Sophia in Constantinople.

In 1241 the Holy Lance was given to King St. Louis for *Sainte Chapelle* in Paris. No trace of this part of the lance has been found since it was lost during the French Revolution, some time after its removal to the *Bibliothéque Nationale.*

The second and larger part of the shaft of the soldier's lance was reported seen by Arculpus in the Church of the Holy Sepulchre at Jerusalem about 670 A.D. Later it was taken to Constantinople, where Sir John Mandeville writes about it. It was sent to Pope Innocent VIII in 1492 in return for favors shown to the captured Zizin, brother of Sultan Bajazet.

At request of the French hierarchy, during the pontificate of Benedict XIV, an investigation was conducted to ascertain the relation, if any, between the two relics, one at Paris, the other at Rome. A papal brief, issued after the inquiry, concluded that both relics were originally parts of the same shaft.

Several other supposedly genuine Holy Lances are preserved in various treasuries of Europe, but none of the others offers a valid claim to authenticity. Even the story told by William of Malmesbury about the Holy Lance given to King Athelstan of England is historically inaccurate.

Since the tragic loss of the Paris relic, only the Roman lance remains. It is exposed each year for veneration during Holy Week by the Archpriest of St. Peter's Basilica.

Veronica's Veil

According to the historian Eusebius in his commentary on the Legend of Abgar and according to remarks contained in the apocryphal work *Mors Pilati*, several authentic portraits of Jesus Christ were made at vari-

621

ous times during His lifetime. The oldest and most authenticated of these images has been known to Romans for centuries as the *Vera Icon* or Veil of Veronica. So highly has this image been held in Roman esteem, that a Mass celebrating it was composed and inserted into at least one of the early Augsburg Missals.[9]

There is no reference in Scripture to a woman offering her veil to Christ during His Sacred Passion. But it is highly plausible that there was such a compassionate soul among those who followed Christ on His way to Mount Calvary. The incident itself is undoubtedly worthy of some credibility, since it has found its expression since very early times in the Christian devotion of the Stations of the Cross.

Apparently the holy woman in question, known in pious legend only as Veronica, found her way to Rome, where she presented her *Vera Icon*-True Picture-to Pope Clement I. The veil, ostensibly bearing the image of the suffering Jesus miraculously pressed into it, was venerated in several places until the pontificate of John VII who had it enclosed in an ornate reliquary. During the ensuing centuries, the Holy See has exhibited particular solicitude for this precious relic. It had been reserved to the Pope's own chapel, St. Peter's Basilica, where it is exposed briefly during Holy Week for veneration by the faithful.

The Holy Grail

A whole cycle of romantic legends has been woven about the theme of the Holy Grail,[10] but the legendary quests, inspiring though they may be, add nothing to the few slim historical facts available. Of the two notable "pretenders" to genuine Grailship, one alone merits serious consideration. And while the chalice displayed at Valencia is not generally accepted as genuine by historians, its proponents present a tolerable case in its behalf.

An account by Bishop Siuri of Cordoba relates that the chalice used by Christ at the Last Supper was brought to Rome by St. Peter soon after the death of Mary. It was used frequently at Papal Masses until the pontificate of Sixtus II. During the persecutions of Valerian, St. Lawrence sent the chalice to his native Huesca in the northern part of the Spanish peninsula where the Holy Grail remained until 713 when it was removed to San Juan de la Pena for protective custody during the Moslem invasion.

A deed of exchange, dated September 26, 1399, testifies that King Martin acquired the Holy Grail for his private chapel in the Palace of the Aljaferia. About 1424 the chalice was moved to Valencia by King Alfonso V. The chalice has remained at Valencia since the fifteenth century except for a brief period during the Spanish Civil War when part of the cathedral was burned by the Communists. It was restored to its chapel in the Metropolitan Cathedral at Valencia by the Franco government in 1937.

Artistically, the Holy Grail is Corinthian in styling,[11] made of agate or Oriental carnelian. The handles on either side are common appurtenances for drinking vessels of its period. The costly pearls, rubies, and emeralds were added much later.

The Crown of Thorns

St. Paulinus of Nola, writing early in the fifth century, is the first of the chroniclers to mention specifically "the thorns with which Our Lord was crowned." Other early writers allude apparently to this relic of the Passion, but their comments are vague and inconclusive.

Writing about 570, Cassiodorus speaks of "the thorny crown, which was set upon the head of our Redeemer in order that all the thorns of the world might be gathered together and broken." The pilgrimage of the monk Bernard establishes that the Crown of Thorns was still at Mount Sion in 870.

According to fairly recent studies, the whole crown was transferred to Byzantium about 1063, although many of the thorns must have been removed at an earlier date. The Latin Emperor of Constantinople, Baldwin II, offered the Crown of Thorns to St. Louis in 1238. After lengthy negotiations with the Venetians, the relic was taken to Paris and placed in the newly built *Sainte Chapelle* where it remained an object of national devotion until the French Revolution.

For security, the crown was placed in the *Bibliothéque Nationale* during the bloody days of the upheaval. In 1806, it was restored to Notre Dame Cathedral. It was enshrined in its present rock crystal reliquary in 1896.

All that is left to be seen today is the circlet of rushes, devoid of any thorns. What remained of the original sixty or seventy thorns were apparently removed by St. Louis and deposited in separate reliquaries. The king and his successors distributed the thorns until nothing remained at Paris but the circlet.

Reportedly there are more than 700 "holy thorns" scattered around the world. But only those traceable to St. Louis, to one of the emperors, or to St. Helena are genuine. Such authentic thorns are at Cluny, St. Praxedes in Rome, Santa Croce, and at Aachen, to mention but a few.

The Nails

There seems to be little agreement among Biblical scholars on the number of nails used to fasten our Blessed Lord to His Cross. Religious art of the early Middle Ages almost unanimously depicts the crucified

Savior with four nails. In the thirteenth century, however, it became increasingly common to represent the feet of Christ as placed one over the other and pierced with a single nail. Either of these methods is compatible with the information we have about the punishment of crucifixion as practiced by the Romans.

The earliest authors, among them St. Ambrose, speak only of two nails.[12] And it is a point of interest that the two oldest known representations of the Crucifixion, the carved door of Santa Sabina in Rome and the Ivory Panel in the British Museum, show no signs of nails in the feet The most commonly accepted opinion is that there were three nails that actually touched the body of Christ. This is borne out by the evidence of the Shroud of Turin. In addition, there were probably another three nails used for the *titulus*, the seat block, and the foot rest.

St. Ambrose and St. Jerome speak of the discovery of the nails in Jerusalem by Constantine's mother, St. Helena, in the third century. Sozomen notes in passing that St. Helena had no trouble identifying the nails.

One of the nails was fashioned into an imperial diadem for the emperor. This Iron Crown of Lombardy is now at Manza. Another nail was made into a bit for the imperial horse. This relic is believed to be the same as the one at Carpentas. A third nail was venerated for many years in Jerusalem before being moved to Rome's Santa Croce by Pope Gregory the Great.

Several European treasuries claim to possess one or more of the true nails, but their authenticity is clouded with the passage of time. Most of the confusion regarding the thirty or more known spurious nails can be traced to the well-intentioned Charles Borromeo who had reproductions made of the nails and gave them out as memorials of the Passion.

Conclusion

These, then, are the more commonly accepted relics associated with the holy person of Jesus Christ, our Savior.

Notes to the Text

1. Louis de Combres, *The Finding of the True Cross* (London: Trubner, 1907).
2. Charles Rohault de Fleury, *Mémoire sur les instruments de la Passion* (Paris: Lesort, 1870), pp. 97-179.
3. Philip Gonnet, *De Sancti Cyrilli Hiersolymitani Catechismus* (Paris: 1876).
4. Edward Wuenschel, C.Ss.R., *Self-Portrait of Christ* (Esopus, New York: Holy Shroud Guild, 1954).
5. See Letter 31 of Paulinus.

6. Herbert Thurston, *The Holy Year of Jubilee* (Westminster: Newman, 1949).
7. Philippe Lauer, *Le trésor de Sancta Sanctorum* (Paris: Leroux, 1906).
8. Francois Martin, *Reliques de la Passion* (Paris: Lethielleux, 1897).
9. *Sainte Veronique, apostre de l'Aquitaine* (Toulouse: 1877).
10. Nutt, *Studies of the Holy Grail* (London: 1888).
11. *The Holy Chalice of the Last Supper* (Valencia: 1958).
12. De Combres, *op. cit.*

94

This essay on "The Stations of the Cross" is here republished from *Cross and Crown* XV (March, 1963), 15-21.

The devotion of the Stations of the Cross is a typical combination of the gradual growth of practices of piety and the workings of the imitative tendencies of many popular Catholic devotions. It is a miniature pilgrimage to the Holy Land which can be made by those unable to participate personally in services at the ancient shrines.

Pious opinions to the contrary, the actual route of Christ's path to Calvary has not been marked from the earliest times. It is only in the Middle Ages that there is even a hint of the existence of a traditional Way of Sorrows. The earliest detailed account of a pilgrimage to the Holy Land is that of Lady Egeria written about 380 and discovered near the end of the last century.

Before the eleventh century there was no determined *via crucis* for those visiting Jerusalem, and Bishop Paul William von Keppler, an authority in the field, considers the first clear indication of a systematic route to be that contained in the French pilgrimage book *La Cilez Hierusalem* issued in 1187. But the stations, as we know them, continued to fluctuate in number and location, and as late as the seventeenth century such places as the house of Dives were included among the sites venerated on the road to Calvary.[1] In any event, by the early part of the sixteenth century at Jerusalem, the following of the Savior's path from Pilate's house to Calvary had become a special exercise of devotion.

The actual selection and arrangement of the stations "owes much more to the pious ingenuity of devotional writers in Europe than to the actual practice of Jerusalem itself."² It is the principal interest of this short survey to obtain an over-all view of the general historical aspects of the Stations of the Cross rather than a comparative analysis of the devotional growth in various parts of the world.

The palace of Pontius Pilate, his praetorium, and the garrison of the Roman soldiers, were situated on Mount Arca, northeast of and overlooking the Temple of Jerusalem. It is here that the *First Station* is commemorated. Pilgrims can still recognize, in the midst of the ruins, the council hall where our Savior was delivered over to be crowned, despised and outraged. Close by, at the northwestern extermity of the ancient buildings of the palace is the arch of *Ecce Homo* where Pilate traditionally presented Jesus to the people.³ The twenty-eight marble steps leading to the court proper are now at Rome and are known as the *Scala Sancta*.⁴

"And bearing the cross for himself, he went forth..." (John 19:17). It was the custom for those condemned to crucifixion to carry the cross on which they were to die. From the First Station to the Second the distance is 111 feet up an acclivity between the church of the Flagellation on the right and the wall of the *Scala Sancta* on the left. The precise spot of the *Second Station* is a few feet before the *Ecce Homo*, and custom places the Roman governor's tribune at this point. It was in this same general area that the door of the praetorium through which Christ carried his cross to Golgotha was located.

Passing under the arch of *Ecce Homo*, it is about 550 feet to the *Third Station*. The road slopes gradually and runs in an almost direct line to the intersecting point of the street coming from the Damascus or Ephraim Gate. At the end of the street there is a large pillar of red marble, about eight feet long, indicating the place where Jesus fell the first time under the oppressive weight of the cross. One scholar speaks of "an old wall of big square stones facing the north" and marking the area for future generations.⁵

Proceeding some distance further, the pilgrim arrives at the *Fourth Station* where an arcade designates the spot where the meeting of Jesus and his Blessed Mother took place. "The Evangelists, without speaking explicitly of this meeting, leave it understood in their recital by showing us the Blessed Virgin on Calvary at the moment of the death of Jesus; and the tradition which has been preserved of this fact, strengthened by the testimony of many great saints, dates back to the remotest antiquity."⁶ The Viscount Francois René de Chateaubriand mentions in his memoirs that "they showed me the ruins of a Church...[where] Mary, at first repulsed by the guards, met her divine son loaded with his cross..."

"And as they led, him away, they laid hold of a certain Simon of Cyrene, coming from the country, and upon him they laid the cross to bear it after Jesus" (Luke 23:26). Not far away is the Fifth Station at the end of a narrow sloping street which continues on, with various interruptions, to the foot of the hill ascending to Golgotha. Simon apparently had just entered by the Gate of Ephraim and was standing leisurely on a corner of the street. The soldiers singled him out as a non-Jew and compelled him to bear the cross of Jesus, alarmed as they were that their prisoner might expire before receiving the full measure of their cruelties. More probably a poor field laborer than the regal personage described by some, Simon took up the cross and thereby entwined himself forever in the gratitude of the Christian world. Simon was a native of Cyrene (modern Barca), a city of Libya in Africa. St. Mark (15:21) enlightens us further by saying that Simon's two sons were Alexander and Rufus. Both later were honored members of the Church of Antioch.

A tradition first found in the account of Lochner (1435) tells us that as the sad procession wound its way to Calvary a woman came from her house and, in the midst of the horrible concourse in which the depths of human wickedness and crime were set in play, fearlessly approached Jesus with a veil to wipe his bloody countenance. A low door at the left side of the street and a pillar of red granite indicate the *Sixth Station* and the house of this holy woman "or to speak more correctly, the place on which that house was built, for even the ruins of it have disappeared."[7] An account of this station, written in 1480, states that at first, in going from the Holy Sepulchre to Mount Olivet we passed before the house of Veronica, who, seeing our Savior being led to his curcifixion, lent him a fine cloth to cleanse his face."[8] Sometimes referred to as Berenice, but more widely known as Veronica (Vera-Icon), the young maiden was no doubt surprised to see her veil impressed with a very visible outline of the Savior's image. Cardinal Newman writes of this tender scene in touching words: "The relief which a Mother"s tenderness secured is not yet all she did. Her prayers sent Veronica as well as Simon—Simon to do a man's work, Veronica to do the part of a woman."[9]

The *Seventh Station* is marked by an incision in a stone wall along the gradually ascending pathway. A second fall of Christ is ascribed to this position. At the time this was the furthest extremity of Jerusalem. Calvary, now withing the limits of the the new city, was then beyond the precincts, as we are reminded by the words of the Apostle to the Gentiles, "Jesus...suffered outside the gate" (Heb. 13:12). There is an indication of an opening a few steps further along the same street, the old

Judiciary Gate. It was undoubtedly at this point that the official sentence was delivered by Pilate, which according to one reliable source reads as follows: "Conduct to the place of punishment Jesus of Nazareth, who provokes the people to rebellion, who despises Caesar, and who says falsely that he is the Messias, as is proven by the testimony of the ancients of this nation, and, with sham insignia of royalty, crucify him between the two thieves. Go prepare the crosses."[10]

"Now there was following him a great crowd of the people, and of women, who were bewailing and lamenting him" (Luke 23:27). It is about 150 feet to the area usually pointed out as the *Eighth Station*. A large column in front of a walled-up gateway marks the spot. In the time of St. Bonaventure (1221-1274) "there was still seen in this place the ruins of a church which was there constructed to preserve the remembrance of this fact."[11] This interesting passage illustrates that even before the crusades certain sacred spots were marked by oratories in order to immortalize the great drama of man's redemption. The meeting with the women of Jerusalem is mentioned in most accounts of the thirteenth and fourteenth centuries though it is usually considered as more closely associated with the coming of Simon of Cyrene.

The *Ninth Station* is included in the buildings erected after the death of Christ between the Judiciary Gate and Golgotha. Similar buildings mark the further trek of the *via crucis*, and it is necessary to return to the Seventh Station before proceeding to the Ninth. A short walk leads the pilgrim to the bottom of a yard area near the entrance of the Coptic Convent where a pillar lying at the base of a nondescript wall marks the place of our Savior's third fall.

All the remaining stations are located within the Basilica of the Holy Sepulchre. That part of the Way of the Cross comprising the first nine stations is about one mile in length; whereas the subsequent distance is quite short in actual walking distance. To arrive at the *Tenth Station* where "the soldiers...took his garments" (John 19:23), one must enter the Church and turn immediately to the right towards the eastern extremity. Two large pilasters sustaining a vault forming three arches rise in front of a chapel which has been erected in honor of this dolorous spoliation. Parts of the tunic of Christ have, by immemorial tradition, been associated with the cities of Tréves and Argenteuil. Studies made near the turn of the century indicate that both garments could be authentic. According to Rohault de Fleury the cincture of our Lord, a leather garment, is preserved at Aix-la-Chapelle, its extremities joined with the seal of Constantine.[12]

Two flights of stairs lead up to the *Eleventh Station* which is commemorated by a rock about eighteen feet high. The nearby walls are faced with marble, and it is here that Christ was fastened to his cross. The spot is marked by a large circle of marble incrustations of various colors.

The Twelfth Station, the actual place of Christ's death, is marked by a hole in the rock where the cross was planted. Rich ornaments decorate the wall behind a near-by altar surrounded by a multitude of lamps. Two dark round stones indicate the location of the crosses of the two thieves. Between the altar of the Crucifixion and that of the Erection of the Cross is a smaller altar commemorating the spot where the Blessed Virgin is thought to have stood.

The washing, embalming and interment of our Lord's body, subject of the *Thirteenth Station*, was probably performed nearby. A rock now venerated as the Stone of Unction is believed to be that on which these rites were carried out. "Some think," says Chateaubriand, "that it is part of the rock of Calvary, while others hold that it was brought there by Joseph and Nicodemus...it has been necessary to cover it with white marble and to surround it with a little iron balustrade for fear of being walked on..."[13]

"And Joseph brought a linen cloth, and took him down, and wrapped him in the linen cloth, and laid him in a tomb which had been hewn out of a rock. Then he rolled a great stone to the entrance of the tomb" (Mark 15:46). The tomb of Christ, the Fourteenth Station, was a favorite pilgrimage site for early Christians. Attempts made in 136 by the Emperor Hadrian to efface and desecrate this holy place were unsuccessful. However, the site was lost in later years and went undiscovered until the time of St. Helena, who happily came upon it during her search of the area. Despite its loss, "critical study does not err in locating Golgotha and the tomb of Jesus in the present Church of the Holy Sepulchre," according to the latest research.[14]

Each pilgrim who treks along the *via crucis* comes away with his own impressions, but none, perhaps, is more descriptive than that of Chateaubriand whose narrative is still regarded as classical: "We passed through all the stations to the summit of Calvary. Where can one find in antiquity anything so touching, so marvelous as the last scenes of the Gospel? These are no extravagant adventures of a Divinity estranged from humanity; it is a history, the beauty of which draws tears from the eyes, and whose consequences applied to the universe have changed the face of the earth."

Notes to the Text

1. The *via sacra* should be distinguished from the *via crucis*. The former was the route along which the curious were conducted in visiting the holy places; the latter is the traditional devotion with which we are familiar.

2. H. Thurston, S.J., *The Stations of the Cross* (New York: Benziger Brothers, 1906), p. 89.

3. Modern archaeologists believe that this arch was erected in the second century although it may have previously served as the entrance gate of the old fortress of the Antonia.

4. See "The Relics of Christ," *Review for Religious*,(March, 1962), p. 84 f.

5. Bernardin Surius, *Le Pieux Pélerin* (Brusselles: 1666), p. 441. Ludolf von Suchem (+ 1350) alludes to this as "the stone whereon Jesus rested a while when his strength failed him on account of his tortures."

6. Baron de Geramb, *Pélerinage á Jérusalem* (Paris: 1839), I, p. 323.

7. *Ibid.*, I, p. 324.

8. Charles C. Schafer, *Le Voyage de la Saincte Cyte de Hierusalem* (Paris: 1882), p. 75.

9. *Meditations and Devotions* (New York: Longmans, Green, 1893), p. 198.

10. J. J. Begel, *Last Journey and Memorials of the Redeemer* (New York: The Catholic Publication Society, 1880), p. 28.

11. *Vita Christi* (Antwerp: 1490), c. LXXVII.

12. Charles Rohault de Fleury is famous for his classical study *Mémoire sur les Instruments de la Passion* (Paris: 1870).

13. *Itinéraire de Paris á Jérusalem* (London: 1813), p. 222.

14. André Parrot, *Golgotha and the Church of the Holy Sepulchre* (London: SCM Press, 1957), p. 58.

95

"The Bulletin Apostolate" is here reproduced from *Worship* XXVIII (February, 1964), 174-177.

The use of the Sunday bulletin as an integral part of the apostolate comes highly recommended to the busy pastor, helping as it does to answer some of the problems brought on by hurried Mass schedules, crowded parking lots, abbreviated sermons and the other unavoidable results of our accelerated existence. Traditionally bulletins have several useful purposes. Most often they are used as the official organ for parochial announcements, thus diminishing or eliminating altogether the need for lengthy directives from the pulpit.

This is especially pertinent in view of modern research which tells us that most people do not retain, with reasonable accuracy, long and often unrelated facts such as those we frequently find in the weekly announcements.

But another of the bulletin's purposes, one which has only recently been exploited, is its use as an informal medium for conveying Catholic teachings on topics usually omitted in the normal sermon. Admittedly a more subtle form of approach, this indirect method has been used with favorable results by such groups as the Christophers in their thought-provoking "Notes."

A wide variety of formats is available from different publishers. The J. O'Brien Company of Peoria, Catechetical Guild of St. Paul, The Liturgical Press of Collegeville, Paluck Company of Chicago, Ligourian Sunday Bulletin of Missouri, to mention but a few, have attractive bulletin material at reasonable prices. Most of these commercial releases can be purchased in bulk several months in advance. Usually the front and rear pages are devoted to dogmatic, moral or liturgical instruction. The inner pages are blank and can be utilized for parish announcements. These popular and colorful bulletins are now used in the majority of American parishes.

Our own experience has shown the usefulness of a smaller format which will handily fit into missal, purse or pocket. In our West Hollywood parish, we developed a bulletin which has proven extremely practical and economical. It has been well received and has elicited a goodly portion of favorable comment with its dignified yet instructive appearance. We adopted a form measuring only 6 1/4 by 5 1/4 inches with a single crease down the center.

An artistic picture of the church together with a chart of the hours of services occupies the front page, while several selected advertisements fill out the rear. The two inside columns handily accommodate 500 words set to 8 point medium Spartan. In addition to the usual weekly announcements, we introduced a variety of *obiter dicta* into the bulletin without altering its compact size. A larger style of type would obviously be easier to read, but we found that popular sentiment overlooked this inconvenience in view of the worthwhile material which this arrangement allowed us to incorporate.

Certain qualitites will be discernible in a bulletin which has a widespread audience. The editorial style must be simple, dignified, readable, attractive, friendly, well balanced and succinct. Short paragraphs are the best eyecatchers:

> A RECENT STATEMENT of the Australian bishops states that "moral responsibility is to be imputed to the driver of an automobile who fails to act with reasonable care" on the highways.

Short, pungent commentaries are most effective and can even be used to include a particular announcement:

> FRIDAY of this week is the First Friday of the month, an excellent opportunity to begin or renew your pledge to the Sacred Heart. Jot down the 6:15 p.m. Mass in your appointment book — the life you save might be your own.

Dogmatic matters can be handled with no less dignity:

> WHAT DOES YOUR FAITH mean to you? Is it only a refuge in a storm? A burdensome duty on Sunday? An interruption to

your life like a knock on the door? An insurance policy against eternal fire?

YOUR FAITH is an engagement with a PERSON (Our Lord) which creates an obligation to OTHERS. Because we are becoming *numerically* less in the world, we must become *spiritually* more of an influence. We are not to isolate ourselves from the world, we are to help save it!

Depending on the week's schedule, your bulletin may contain from time to time as many as ten of these cryptic statements, each aimed at a particular segment of your congregation. The source material for these *obiter dicta* is limitless. Seasonal liturgy provides excellent subject matter on most occasions:

SATURDAY is the feast of the Epiphany, commemorating the visit paid to the infant Saviour by the Wise men from the Orient. Make it a point to pay your own visit to Christ today by attending Holy Mass. Normal weekday schedule will be followed.

Miscellaneous items can be gleaned from newsletters, pamphlets, public service releases, diocesan newspapers, (to say nothing of the ordinary theology manuals). Several weekly "filler services" are available at a nominal charge. Among the more useful sources for short Marian observations is the handbook of the Legion of Mary.

Our own bulletin is delivered to the rectory on Saturday evening. It is important to maintain a strict schedule, sometimes as far as ten days in advance, especially if the mails are used. This demands careful planning, but if managed efficiently unexpected developments can usually be anticipated. We needn't point out that it is unreasonable to expect the printer to meet his deadline unless he has the material on time, and that is particularly true when he is operating on a slim margin of profit. Misprints occur occasionally, but they are an occupational hazard which our people readily overlook.

You might ask about the effect of our system. An informal survey showed that well over 90% of our parishioners took the bulletins home. Well over half of these read the entire issue and many others read significant parts. This we regarded as a favorable indication of the programs usefulness. Four out of ten of those interrogated told us they kept the bulletins for their own reference. And while we didn't notice an outstanding or visible change in the mores of our fine people, we did have the satisfaction of making available one additional means by which they could advance.

It is wise to keep several collections of the bulletins for your files. They will serve the dual purpose of inspiring future issues and providing a handy journal of activities for the parish archives. Loose copies can be neatly bound at the end of each calendar year.

The financial aspect of this project obviously depends on the condition of the parish. In our parish of no more than 350 families, the advertisements not only paid all the printing costs, but in addition netted a modest profit during the first year. Advertisers were asked to sign up for not less than ninety days in order to avoid the cost of frequent plate changes in the ad layout. Multiplying the weekly bulletin order by twelve (approximately ninety days) will enable the printer to pre-run the front and rear page in large quantities, thereby reducing the over-all expenditure. In those parishes where the Legion of Mary or a similar organization is established, unused copies of the bulletin can be left on streetcars and buses, at neighborhood business houses and hotels, and in the homes of those contacted on parochial visitation.

It has been our experience that this combined system of announcement-instruction bulletin has not only increased parish efficiency but has given us a whole new apostolate.

96

This defense of "The High School Boarding Seminary" first appeared in *Emmanuel* LXXIII (June, 1967) and was reprinted widely by various vocational departments.

Almost half of the world's candidates for the priesthood are presently enrolled in this nation's seminaries.[1] Such statistics indicate that the future effectiveness of the Catholic Church in the United States, perhaps internationally, may well hinge on the training programs these institutions pursue during this vitally important postconciliar era.

Although no other country can boast a quantity of minor seminaries comparable to that of the Unites States, this proliferation of facilities has drawn fierce criticism in recent years. That many of the smaller prep schools offer little justification for autonomous existence is readily admitted by most competent authorities. Unfortunately, dissatisfaction with the admittedly large number of unqualified institutions has given rise to some misconceptions as to why an effectively operated minor seminary program is necessary, what it tries to do, and how it measures its results.

While there are several categories worthy of objective appraisal, this treatise is confined to the high school seminary as it operates in the overall clerical training program for the Archdiocese of Los Angeles. Though this institution, a boarding school, is serving the Church in Southern California well, structural variations surely would be needed for other areas of the country. The decrees of the Second Vatican Council leave considerable room for experimentation at the minor seminary, since these schools are much more dependent on local necessities than are their more advanced counterparts.[2]

Under its original title, Los Angeles College served the Diocese of Los Angeles-San Diego and later the Archdiocese of Los Angeles for the first twenty-eight years after its founding in 1926. Though boarding facilities were available, the institution was primarily a day-school until 1954, when it was moved to modern new facilities on property adjacent to the historic San Fernando Mission. Since 1961, under its new title of Queen of Angels, the seminary has functioned as the initial link of a tripartite system wherein the twelve year cycle is broken into equal periods of four years duration. This program has made it feasible to adopt a training period more commensurate with the natural psychological development of the candidates.

The whole high school seminary concept attempts to create a "controlled environment"[3] in which teenagers *tentatively* committed to the priesthood[4] are given the optimum opportunity for a spiritual, academic, social and pastoral formation fully in accord with the contemporary needs of the Church in California's southland as well as the opportunity to develop their own spiritual talents and individual personalities.

Development in the *spiritual* sphere is geared towards a life based on the Gospel ideal insofar as that can be realized in a normal teenage situation. Obviously the inchoate priest could find nowhere else the spiritual potential so fully explored and utilized as it is in the seminary atmosphere. Exclusive of personal guidance and private direction, about 8% of the day is spent at such tasks as morning and night prayers, Holy Mass, visits, rosary, Benediction, spiritual reading and private prayer. This allotment of time is surely not at all excessive in a school primarily designed to instill an intensive Christian formation in its enrollees.

In compliance with the council's directives, all religious exercises are based on the liturgy itself or orientated to it. Beyond the relatively few prayers recited in common, students are given opportunities and encouragement for those practices of piety commended by long usage in the Church.

Good habits, like bad ones, are acquired by repetition of similar acts and experience indicates that a reasonably fixed program, even in the spiritual life, is necessary for neophytes.[5] In the overall archdiocesan seminary system, however, emphasis on the disciplinary aspect of these obligations gradually gives way to one of personal responsibility as the candidate moves closer to the priesthood. The first impetus along these lines is given in the preparatory seminary.

Though the academic program does not vary substantially from that in other Catholic high schools, the tone of seminary curriculum leans toward that basic knowledge required in the fully accredited college and theologate. In order to insure an intellectually relevant course of studies, a continuous and realistic evaluation of procedures and techniques based on the rapidly evolving role of the priest in today's changing world has been devised by the faculty.

Students are encouraged and expected to use the 9000 volume library and to take full advantage of the sixty periodicals and journals which the seminary makes available. For the exceptionally gifted youngsters, special advanced classes are conducted on a voluntary basis and care is taken to maintain a proportion between curriculum requirements and intellectual capability. The daily schedule is so arranged as to spread out the time used exclusively for study purposes. A monitor is provided to supervise the younger boys while the older ones employ an honor system regulated by the internal sanctions of their student government. About a quarter of the seminarian's time is devoted to strictly academic pursuits. In addition to this, students can utilize free time for additional class assignments though this practice is not generally recommended.

Emphasis on the *social* or *communal* part of the youngster's formation grows out of the psychological principle that adolescence is a time when teenage boys are inclined to turn away from their home environment and the guidance of parents in search of emancipation from the so-called satellite status[6] of childhood. This movement toward societal independence, a vital part of the maturation process, can be encouraged ideally within a "peer group" whose interests, morals and goals are firmly based on a sound Christian foundation. The underlying concept of the high school seminary is rooted on the proven theory that the early teens represent the most impressionable period for cultivating a well-balanced interest in religious life.[7]

Studies indicate that physical separation from a healthy home environment poses a threat to teenagers only when it arises involuntarily out of parental rejection or some other unnatural cause. Since 1954, when the Los Angeles system changed from a day-school to boarding status, the first and second year students return to their homes on weekends and the third and fourth year boys monthly. Such a graduated program encourages a smoother transition from family orientation to adult psychic independence. Other means of family contact, such as letters, phone calls and visiting days are recommended. One recent survey demonstrated that the attitude toward parents was more mature in seminarians than in regular Catholic high school students despite the factor of separation from home.[8]

"There is no evidence of general deficit of maturity in a seminary high school student when compared to a non-seminary student."[9] Critics of the boarding system often overlook the fact that psychological maturity is rather well laid by the time prospective candidates appear at the seminary.[10] Adolescence does little more than apply the finishing touches by stabilizing the individual's outlooks, habits and other aspects of his character formation.[11]

Probably no era of history has seen a more generous youthful display of altruism in search of a better world than our own. For this reason the concept of *pastoral* service is an attractive challenge for the contemporary teenager. There is no reason why these youngsters with proper guidance should isolate themselves from the mainstream of dialogue with contemporary problems. Such activities as hospital visitation, Confraternity teaching, *etc.*, provide a useful and meaningful initiation to the apostolic work now considered an integral part of the priestly function. At San Fernando, for example, an elective (and fully credited) course has been inaugurated in the fundamentals of electronics whereby the students, after receiving the amateur radio licenses from the Federal Communications Commission, maintain scheduled liaison with the archdiocese's ninety Lay Mission Helpers in the outposts of Africa and Latin America.

Vocational research indicates that realism increases with age, so that, as the youth advances through the teen years, he views his role in life increasingly in the context of social responsibility. Especially is this true in an age which depends so much on youthful participation, and in a time when the council calls upon such activities and such apostolic youths to bridge the gap between the adult and juvenile worlds.

From the psychological point of view, the potential for permanent good at the teenage level far exceeds that of the more advanced institutions and that is why, all things considered, the minor seminary program provides such a richly fertile period for sacerdotal formation.

A high attrition rate is now and always has been envisioned in the high school seminary program. Yet, despite a refined screening process which accelerates the natural dropouts, it is significant that graduates of these institutions have a considerably higher rate of vocational perseverance than do their contemporaries in regular Catholic high schools, three-fourths of whom change their contemplated career *after* graduation.[12]

In an era when job specialization reaches as far down as the freshmen level in high school, it seems reasonable that a Catholic teenager be given the chance to test what he feels may be a vocation to the clerical state. Youngsters of today think more deeply about such things than did the present generation at a comparable age. They are seeking, as never before, a calling in life which affords them the best outlet for their interests, abilities, values and needs.

The kerygmatic approach to spirituality works on the assumption that youngsters grasp their involvement in the plan of salvation on a basis of progressive personal commitment. If the average teenager has grown into a conscious, meaningful sense of what this really entails, then a *tentative* commitment to Christ and His priesthood at that tender age by a select few seems quite reasonable.

Notes to the Text

1. For a statistical analysis, see *Catholic Seminaries in the United States — 1966* (Washington, 1966).
2. "Archbishop Garrone's Address to the West Coast Minor Seminary Rectors," (November 13, 1966), p. 1.
3. Melvin L. Farrell, S.S., "Let's Keep Our Minor Seminaries," *American Ecclesiastical Review* CLIV (May, 1966), 303.
4. An interesting insight to the "Certainty of Vocation" was written by Father Flavian F. Wilson in *Priest XXII* (May, 1966), 399-403.
5. Cf. Frederick R. Stenger, "The Decree on Priestly Training," *Priest* XXII (August, 1966), 645-653.
6. Carroll F. Tageson, O.F.M., "The Minor Seminary—Good or Bad," XXI *Way* (May, 1965), 7.
7. John F. Kinnane, "The Minor Seminarian: A Growing Boy," *Homiletic and Pastoral Review* LXV (February, 1965), 402.
8. Report by Vocational Office of the Diocese of Kansas City-Saint Joseph. See "Minor Seminary: We Must Be Doing Some Things Right," *The World Parish* (August, 1966), 1. Critics often fail to realize that the younger boarding students spend more time with their families each year (185 days) than they do at the seminary.
9. Francis J. O'Neill, C.Ss.R., "Are Seminarians Immature," *Liguorian* LV (January, 1967), 13. In another recent survey, Father Martin Pable reported that the charge about seminaries turning out "shy, socially inhibited and immature graduates" is totally unfounded. *National Catholic Reporter*, February 8, 1967.
10. One editorial writer has noted that it "is strange that this objection is not made of the many private schools and colleges in the United States" operating on programs closely paralleling that of seminaries. *Maryknoll* LXI (January, 1967), 35.
11. Andrew F. Greeley maintains that "there is no such thing as a normal social life for teen-agers, since teen age is by its very definition abnormal." *Emmanuel* LXXII (July-August, 1966), 322.
12. Joseph L. Kerins, "The New Breed of Americana," *Emmanuel* LXII (May, 1966), 207.

97

This essay on "The Meaning of the term 'Father' as Applied to Catholic Priests" appeared in *The American Benedictine Review* XVIII (September, 1967), 338-343. An abbreviated form subsequently was released by the *Catholic Digest* XXXII (June, 1968), 2-6.

One whole section of the Second Vatican Council's decree, "The Ministry and Life of Priests," is devoted to the sacerdotal role as pastor and father of the flock, towards whom the faithful are exhorted to show a practical *filial* love.[1] This concept of spiritual fatherhood has long been in evidence throughout the English-speaking world where priests have borne the richly symbolic title of "Father" for many decades. One contemporary writer feels that "no form of address is so widely used for a priest, and none so appropriate"[2] in expressing the priestly relationship towards the People of God.

During the years, the use of the term has been defended and explained by apologetical writers. Bertrand L. Conway in *The Question Box Answers* takes considerable pains to explain how the word "Father" is "fully sanctioned by Holy Scripture."[3] In his popular catechetical manual, James Cardinal Gibbons explains that "the priest is a father, because he breaks the bread of life to his spiritual children, whom he has begotten in Christ Jesus through the Gospel."[4] Sydney A. Raemers, in *The Convert's Manual*, states that the priest "is called 'Father' because, just as an earthly father gives physical life to his children, so the priest gives spiritual life to those entrusted to his care."[5] This theme is echoed in a more recently issued text which notes that the appellation is "used for priests, who are

641

regarded as spiritual fathers because they are the spiritual leaders of the faithful and the ordinary ministers of baptism, by which persons are born to supernatural life."[6]

That the matter recurs so consistently in apologetical tomes is indication enough of misgivings about the term among certain people. The most common objection comes from those who maintain that appropriation of the term "Father" to a priest violates the injunction echoed by Saint Matthew: "Call no man father upon earth; for one is your Father, and He is in heaven!"[7] Few scripture scholars, however, feel that Christ was here intent on reforming the then existing nomenclature of *rabbi*; rather they generally interpret his words as a rebuke of those taking vain complacency in the term. Father Louis F. Hartman, C.Ss.R., says that Our Lord was "condemning the spirit of adulation and complacency with which the great rabbis of His day were addressed."[8] He was simply insisting on a proper acknowledgement of the deity as the prototype of all fatherhood. Such an observation was certainly in order inasmuch as the "almost blasphemous pride" of the Scribes and Pharisees "evinced itself in their peculiarly arrogant use of perfectly legitimate titles which were meant to denote reverence and respect for their human authority as a reflection of the authority of God."[9]

An extensive reading of the inspired word indicates the particular suitability of the term "Father" as applied to those exercising the Sacrament of Holy Orders. One of the first times the word appears, in Judges 17:10, "father" and "priest" are used interchangeably. The identification of the two expressions hearkens back even further, however, perhaps even to patriarchal days when the father of each household performed the priestly duties for his own family unit.

This relationship, so common in the old covenant extends into the Christian era. Paul calls Timothy "my own *son in the faith*."[10] The Apostle of the Gentiles further endorses this unique identification when he speaks to the Ephesians about "that Father from whom all fatherhood in heaven *and on earth* takes its title."[11] One writer suggests that no other title "would suffice except that name which God appointed to all men who share with him the creation and the nurturing of life–above all, the life of grace which leads to eternal life in the home of the Father of us all–our God."[12]

Though Pauline by justification, the contemporary practice of referring to priests as "Father" is far more recent in origin, at least in English speaking countries. Ecclesiastical usage originally restricted the term to bishops who were known to their people as "Father in God," an appellation connoting not so much sacerdotal dignity as the position of teacher and master. This terminology found its way into the *Book of Common Prayer*[13] where the bishop is addressed as "Reverend Father in God," a practice also incorporated in the 1550 edition of the *Ordinal* in its outline of the "form and manner of making ordaining and consecrating Bishops, Priests and Deacons according to the Order of the Church of England." The term was not extended to ordinary priests of the reformed church, probably because of its already close association with members of Catholic religious orders.

The title of "spiritual father" was commonly used for priests acting in their capacity as dispensers of the Sacrament of Penance. This would account for the observation that "in old times there was the English phrase 'ghostly Father' which meant spiritual father. And it is just in this case, and in no other, that Catholics call their priest Father."[14] Close examination of the annals reveals that, as a title, the term "Father" was predicated only of Mendicant friars;[15] whereas monks and canons regular were known as *Dom*, a shortened form of the Latin *Domnus* or *Dominus*. From this latter term came such vernacular variations as *signore*, *dom* and *monsieur*.[16]

One historian relates that "even in Ireland in 1825 and for many years afterward, 'Father' and 'Mr.' were both used by Catholics" when referring to their priests.[17] This same authority notes in another context that the indiscriminate use of 'Father' became popular after Catholic Emancipation in 1829. Prior to that time Catholics had no legal standing and "it would seem that secrecy, once so necessary regarding the presence or even the existence of priests, made it obligatory to write or speak of them simply as "Mr.'" This evolved into "Rev. Mr." and, after the Emancipation, when greater freedom of expression was allowed, the title came into common use.[18] The earlier practice of reserving the term to religious gave way during persecution times when the artificial distinction between diocesan and regular clergy lost much of its practical significance.

Introduction of the term into England is usually attributed to Cardinal Manning. The Archbishop of Westminster wanted his priests "to call themselves 'Father' instead of the 'Mister' of penal days,"[19] and despite a lively newspaper controversy over the matter in the north, the prelate was successful in imposing upon the secular clergy the same appellation "which before this time in England applied only to members of religious orders."[20]

A Catholic newspaper in the United States observed in 1908, that the term "Father" was "time-honored because Catholics in all climes and in all ages have used this and nothing other."[21] As a matter of historical record, the title was very exceptional in this nation prior to the 1840s, a factor immediately obvious to scholars studying the letters and printed materials of those times.

In 1895, Martin I.J. Griffin noted, "It is really only since the stream of Catholic Irish immigration that 'Father' has become the universally used title."[22] Several years earlier, the same writer had remarked that "in this country the title has only become common or general within, say, fifty years or so, and only of occasional use, say, for about seventy-five years."[23]

Another early commentator on the question recorded that the practice became widespread only "after the church in the United States had begun to shake off the trammels of Protestant surroundings and influence and the laity had become more Catholic in spirit; say about 1840, the period of the decline of the Trustee System."[24] This authority went on to credit Bishop John N. Neumann of Philadelphia "with giving the earliest impetus in this direction, and when he was followed by such men as Archbishop [James F.] Wood, Bishop [John F.] Horstmann and other graduates of Roman institutions, the change became an accomplished fact."[25] The custom grew slowly and "up to the time, and in many cases for years after, the Third Council of Baltimore (1884), secular priests in this country were addressed as 'Mister' and 'Sir.'"[26]

Although the symbolic term "Father" can be justified scripturally, historically and etymologically, the continued use of the appellation is not without its critics. The editor of the Camden *Catholic Star Herald*, for example, prefers to be called "Mister Priest," feeling as he does that "dropping the title of 'Father' would create closer ties with the laity and help destroy the devil of paternalism."[27] This writer suggests, on the other hand, that the term "Father" has the very useful effect of reminding both the clergy and laity of the fatherhood of Christ as personified in those especially anointed to serve the People of God.

Noting that there is no closer, more potent nor more honorable a relationship than that which binds a child to its parent, the Archbishop of Baltimore was of the opinion that the title "Father" inspires deep filial love and confidence in the hearts of the faithful who recognize that in renouncing carnal fatherhood, the priest is able to concentrate all his affection on his spiritual offspring. Cardinal Gibbons further relates how "the boatman on the Lake of Geneva used to address St. Francis de Sales with great familiarity, by the title of *Father*. The Bishop of Belley, who happened to accompany him one day, instructed the boatman to call the saint *My Lord.* St. Francis rebuked the prelate, saying: 'Let them call me their father, and indeed they love me as such. O how much more good they do my heart, than those who call me *Monseigneur!*'"[28]

While the rather widespread practice of conferring strictly honorary ecclesiastical titles may well be a matter for continued discussion, such hardly seems the case with the tradition-laden use of "Father," for here, and perhaps only here, a title is bestowed "with the intention of inspiring a religious sense of duty rather than of conferring a prerogative."[29] Recognizing both the simplicity and grandeur of the title, modern-day society would be hard pressed to disagree with the sentiments voiced by James Roosevelt Bayley on his deathbed: "I am Archbishop; I have been bishop; but I like Father Bayley best of all."[30]

Notes to the Text

1. See Walter M. Abbott, S.J., *The Documents of Vatican II* (New York, 1966), p. 544.
2. Fulton J. Sheen, *The Priest Is Not His Own* (New York, 1963), p. 54.
3. (New York, 1918), p. 330.
4. *The Faith of Our Fathers* (Baltimore, 1917), p. 391.
5. (New York, 1961), p. 158.
6. Felician A. Foy, O.F.M., *1967 National Catholic Almanac* (Paterson, N.J., 1967), p.332.
7. Matthew 23:9.
8. *Encyclopedic Dictionary of the Bible* (New York, 1963), p. 759.
9. John V. Sheridan, *Questions and Answers on the Catholic Faith* (New York, 1963), p. 39.
10. 1 Timothy 1:2.
11. Ephesians, 3:14-15.
12. Thomas F. Rudloff, C.Ss.R., "Not Everybody Calls Me Father," *Liguorian* XXXXIX (August, 1961), 9.
13. (New York, 1929),p. 547.
14. "Some Things New and Old," *Catholic Mind* XL (August 8, 1942), 32.
15. This term, originally applied only to Franciscans and Dominicans, was later extended to include Carmelites, Augustinians, Servites, and others.
16. The *Oxford Dictionary of the Christian Church* (London, 1957), p. 495.
17. Martin I. J. Griffin, "Book Review" in the New York *Independent*, January 10, 1895.
18. "The Title of Priests," *American Catholic Historical Researches* XVIII (April, 1901), 83-84.
19. Shane Leslie, *Henry Edward Manning, His Life and Labours* (London, 1921), p. 457.
20. Edmund Sheridan Purcell, *Life of Cardinal Manning, Archbishop of Westminster* (London, 1896), II, 762n.
21. *Catholic Sun*, June 5, 1908.
22. "Annals of a Convent," *American Catholic Historical Researches* XX (July, 1903), 117.
23. "The Title of Priests," *Ibid.*, XVIII (April, 1901), 83.
24. Charles H. A. Esling, "Father Applied to Priests," *Ibid.*, XVIII (October, 1901), 174.
25. *Ibid.*
26. John V. Sheridan, *op. cit., p. 278.*
27. April 23, 1965.
28. The Ambassador of Christ (Baltimore, 1896), p. 10.
29. "On addressing a Deacon as 'Father,'" *Homiletic and Pastoral Review* XLI (March, 1941), 641.
30. *The Catholic Mirror*, October 13, 1877 as quoted in Sister M. Hildegarde Yeager, C.S.C., *The Life of James Roosevelt Bayley, First Bishop of Newark and Eighth Archbishop of Baltimore, 1814-1877* (Washington, 1947), p. 480.

98

The following essay on the "Relevancy of the Roman Collar" is taken from the *American Ecclesiastical Review* CLVIII (April, 1968), 228-234.

Though individual bishops and councils occasionally issued prescriptions for regulatory garb prior to the sixth century, papal concern was restricted to exhortations such as that of Celestine I, which advised clerics to distinguish themselves not by their dress but by their teaching, manner of life, and purity of mind.[1] Beyond scattered territorial directives, specific canonical legislation on priestly attire dates only from the Second Council of Nicea which declared all types of luxurious and gaudy apparel out of keeping with the religious state.

The various local and national regulations on sacerdotal garb were codified and promulgated in 1215, by the Fourth Lateran Council. Among other things, that ecumenical gathering gave formal approval to the already long-recognized *vestis talaris*, forerunner of today's cassock.

The Roman collar, introduced sometime in the sixteenth century, was a broad band of cloth attached to the soutane or cassock at the neck for the purpose of absorbing perspiration. According to one commentator, "originally it was nothing else than a shirt collar turned down over the cleric's everyday common dress in compliance with a fashion that began toward the end of the sixteenth century."[2] The cloth breast-plate, to which the changeable band or strip of linen (*collarino*) was affixed, was usually made of wool or silk depending on the prelatial rank of the wearer. Beyond variations in form, width, and texture, the Roman collar has undergone relatively few alterations over the past four centuries.

In 1624, Pope Urban VIII issued a mandate prescribing the Roman collar as part of the official clerical attire for the Eternal City. A century later, Pope Benedict XIII renewed his predecessor's decree and extended its use to all who had received the tonsure.

The diversity of sacerdotal apparel evident in the early years of the Catholic Church in the United States was a natural outgrowth of the practice many had of adopting the style of clothing prevalent in the areas of their origin. Already by the first years of the nineteenth century, however, "the clergy wore a neck gear called a 'chocker,' as can be seen from the pictures of the clergy of that period."[3]

In the *Pastoral Letter to the Clergy*, written by Bishop John England on behalf of the American hierarchy in 1829, priests were reminded that the very fashion of their dress was, in the eyes of the world, calculated to elevate or depress their character, and to extend or restrict their usefulness. Noting that in almost every recognized public association, such a subject was a matter of regulation, the Bishop of Charleston couched the obligations of the nation's priests in no uncertain terms:

> You are the officers of the militia of Christ. You bear His commission. Is it possible that there can be found one amongst you who would feel disposed to conceal the dignity with which he is invested? Such a renegade would be unworthy of his place. Can he presume to seek precedence in the church who is disguised in the world? Is he ashamed of that station to which he sought, with so much earnestness, to be raised?[4]

The biographer of John Hughes noted that in the 1840's, when the Bishop of New York walked in the street, "he dressed in plain black clothes, with no distinguishing mark except the purple Roman stock around his neck."[5] About twenty years later, in the United States and England, when the soutane or cassock was not worn outside the Church areas, the adapted form of the Roman collar began to assume the shape it now has and replaced the collar with wings, buttressed with cravat or choker.[6]

In an effort to unify ecclesiastical attire among diocesan priests, the hierarchy attending the Third Plenary Council of Baltimore made the wearing of the Roman collar prescriptive in 1884 by decreeing:

> We enjoin upon our priests as a matter of strict precept, both at home and abroad, and whether they are residing in their own diocese or outside of it, they shall wear the Roman collar.[7]

The Code of Canon Law, adopted in 1918, made no change in the use of the Roman collar in the United States, since, by allowing for an ecclesiastical dress "in line with the legitimate norms of the Ordinary of the Place," it served to perpetuate a practice already recognized on the national level.[8]

Available evidence indicates that the Roman collar, as a distinctive part of clerical garb in this country, has enjoyed rather wide approval. One expert, after considerable research, concluded, "There has never been any complaint from either Catholics or non-Catholics that it was an unbecoming garb for priests to wear."[9]

While allowing greater freedom for the particular mode of religious dress in individual countries, the Second Vatican Council reinforced the tradition-laden reasons for wearing some type of recognizable garb, *viz.*, poverty, dignity and protection, by attaching thereto the symbolic and practical value of serving as "signs of a consecrated life."[10] That the need for such outward manifestations still perdures is obvious from many sources. The Bishop of Rochester, for example, says that "unless the world sees a difference in the places we frequent, in our activities, and in the pleasures in which we indulge, in the language we use, in our dress, it will not respect our testimony."[11]

The total rejection of all forms of garb, advocated by and for priests in certain quarters, seems entirely at odds with such contemporary theologians as Yves Congar who characterizes the priest as a man "unlike others, by his dress and manner of life."[12] One cleric, quoted editorially in the Los Angeles *Times*, felt that there is "something paradoxical about a priest seeking to identify himself with the cause he serves while simultaneously renouncing the traditional garb which has come to be the most distinctive outward characteristic of it."[13]

While most recognized authorities defend retaining some means of identification for those in the active apostolate, there seems to be more questioning of the precise form of clerical clothing today than has been prevalent in earlier periods of renewal. In those cases where controversies have spilled over into the columns of the secular press, one is tempted to recall the pungent essay of Thomas Carlyle on "The Hero Priest": "Why should we misknow one another, fight not against the enemy but against ourselves, from mere difference of uniform? All uniforms shall be good, so they hold in them true valiant men."[14]

Much can be said in defense of the continued use of the Roman collar as the distinctive garb for diocesan priests in the United States. The increasing acceptance as a useful "sign" among non-Catholic clergymen is forceful evidence that throughout the nation the linen or celluloid neckboard fulfills most admirably its purpose as a conspicuous symbol of God's love and concern for His people.

But the Roman collar is not without its detractors. The five Jesuits at Fordham, for example, who recently exchanged their collars for business suits cited among other reasons, their opinion that "uniform clerical dress tends, for some, to paralyze communicational and interactional values."[15] The validity of that viewpoint deserves further consideration inasmuch as it fails to elicit wide support. A staff reporter for the Johannesburg *Star*, commenting recently on "the disappearing dog-collar" in his region, stated quite frankly that a clergyman who thinks the man-in-the-street admires him for appearing commonplace is "profoundly mistaken." To the complaint that the collar presents an obstacle in "getting to know people," or that "people will shy away from it," the African correspondent stated: "How much more will they shy away from somebody they have discovered to be hiding his identity ?"[16]

An amusing but effective footnote to the Fordham experience was the appearance on that campus the following week of a lay professor out-fitted in black suit and Roman collar. Dr. Irvin M. Arvin, assistant professor of theology, said his "experimental" garb was a "small protest" to the permission given the Jesuit faculty to put aside their clericals. The professor disagreed that "it contributes to scholarship or to a witness to adopt a disguise." He rejected the argument that priests can relate more to students when they dress in lay clothes. "In the academic area, I deny it very strongly," he said. "The students aren't that superficial."[17]

Another frequently heard objection to the continued use of the collar is echoed in the columns of the *National Catholic Reporter* by Father Walter Weiss. The Dodge City priest seemingly subscribes to the adage "that persons are helped only by persons they see as like themselves."[18] Not so, according to one outstanding layman who ridiculed the idea that "a priest by discarding his clerical collar and wearing a tie can somehow relate better to lay people." Such a theory, he believes, "belongs to that time in the past we had thought had long since ended, when lay people were considered to be little children, not quite smart!"[19]

An inner-city missionary, in a penetrating article on updating the clerical status, mentioned "the poor old Roman collar" as one of the vital links between Christ's priesthood and the downtrodden residents of ghetto areas. The writer observes that "in times and places of confusion and inter-societal conflict, the sacramental symbol of non-alliance with any other existing societal forms becomes especially valuable."[20]

The argument that priests prefer being heard "on the basis of what they say, rather than what they are expected to say"[21] is tantamount to admitting some invisible barrier between a rightly formed conscience and Catholic morality. Nor are the allusions made by one writer[22] to current clerical fashions in such countries as France, Germany, and Italy any more impressive. This is especially true to those who are inclined to wonder if the low ebb of Christian awareness in those nations is not more a result than a cause of their generally nondescript sacerdotal garb.

A final objection, from a theologian of Saint Mary's College in Kansas, centers on the Roman collar as counterproductive, insofar as it overwhelms, destroys or impedes any practical application as a sign.[23] It does happen occasionally that priests misuse their status and all that symbolizes it for personal gain, but isolated examples of men who confuse their external role with the need for internal perfection is not valid reason for altering the ground rules of the state itself, Admittedly, garb alone does not make the priest, yet as another writer recently noted: "Let's face it, the wearing of the collar has paid great dividends. One of the best has been that it makes Christ present to the people–to individuals and to groups." The same observer further pointed out that "in some locales the priest's only way to make Christ present is through his garb, particularly the Roman collar. I'm sure there could be another, maybe a better, way than the collar to distinguish the presence of a priest. But until that medium is found and accepted, the Roman collar is tops."[24]

One can sympathize with those who find that occasionally "there is something nice about being able to be lost in the crowd."[25] On the other hand, there is a little validity for habitual deportment along those lines, especially in view of the Vatican Council's concept of the priesthood as a chosen group *set apart within* the midst of God's people.

Whatever be his "accidental competence" in other fields, the ordained priest, in a dramatic and altogether decisive manner, "becomes the sign of the Church as no other Christian does,"[26] inasmuch as he manifests God's interest in and love for His people.

In this country where uniforms and badges are traditionally associated with special service, the priest, perhaps more than others, needs some readily recognizable sign of his sacerdotal role. Such recognition could hardly be more obviously demonstrated than by that neat, clean, handy, comfortable and distinguishing neckboard Americans have come to know and respect as the "Roman collar."

Notes to the Text

1. Migne, *P.L.*, 50, 431.
2. Walter J. Schmitz, S.S., "The Liturgy and Rubrics," *The Priest*, XIV (October, 1958), 846.
3. Henry J. McCloud, *Clerical Dress and Insignia of the Roman Catholic Church* (Milwaukee, 1948), p. 73.
4. Peter K. Guilday (Ed.), *The National Pastorals of the American Hierarchy* (1792-1919) (Westminster, 1954), pp. 52-53.
5. John R. G. Hassard, *Life of the Most Reverend John Hughes*, D.D. (New York, 1866), p. 327.
6. Francis Talbot, S.J., "The Collar Called Roman," *America*, XLVIII (March 25, 1933), 597.
7. *Acta et Decreta Concilii Plenarii Baltimorensis Tertii* (Baltimore, 1886), p. 41.
8. Canon 136. This was reaffirmed by a decree from the Sacred Congregation of the Council, July 28, 1931. See *Acta Apostolicae Sedis*, XXIII (1931), 336-337.
9. Bernard J. Ganter, *Clerical Attire* (Washington, 1955), p. 92.
10. Walter M. Abbott, S.J, (Ed.), *The Documents of Vatican II* (New York, 1966), p. 478.
11. Fulton J. Sheen, *The Priest Is Not His Own* (New York, 1963), p. 40.
12. *A Gospel Priesthood* (New York, 1967), p. 202.
13. Issue of November 18, 1967.
14. *On Heroes, Hero-Worship, and the Heroic in History* (New York, 1913), p. 129.
15. *National Catholic Reporter*, November 1, 1967,
16. Quoted in *The Crozier*, III (August, 1967), 4.
17. *Saint Louis Review*, November 17, 1967.
18. Issue of July 12, 1967.
19. Dale Francis in *The Twin Circle*, December 17, 1967.
20. Joseph F. Burns, S.M.M., "How Far Is Up?", *America*, CXVIII (January 6, 1968), 9.
21. Walter Weiss, "The Clerical Collar: Sign or Signal," *Catholic Digest*, XXXII (December, 1967), 105.
22. John McLaughlin, S.J., "Of Many Things," *America*, CXVII (October 7, 1967), editorial page.
23. Paul J. Weber, S.J., "On Wearing the Roman Collar," *America*, CXVII (April 15, 1967), 561.
24. John E. Leone, "Hurrah for the Roman Collar." *America*, CXVIII (January 6, 1968), 1.
25. *National Catholic Reporter*, November 1, 1967.
26. *The Church in Our Day* (Washington, 1968), p. 48.

99

"Is It The 'R.C. Church' or Not?" is the title of this essay which appeared in *The American Benedictine Review* XX (March, 1969), 93-98.

The penchant of many current writers for the term "American Catholic Church" is an obvious and possibly unconscious outgrowth of the recent trend towards administrative decentralization within the ecclesial structure. Nonetheless, the practice calls to mind the opposite extreme that developed in the years after the issuance of Leo XIII's *Testem Benevolentiae* in 1899. At that time, the Holy Father's widely circulated letter to James Cardinal Gibbons voiced the suspicion, then held by certain Vatican officials, that "there are some among you who conceive of and desire a church in America different from that which is in the rest of the world." The pontiff went on to emphasize carefully that the Church "is rightly called Roman, for where Peter is there is the Church."[1]

The uneasiness caused by the papal communique has continued to manifest itself, in varying degrees of intensity, even to present time. In fact, one of its most lasting effects, and one probably not at all envisioned, was the freezing of the term "Roman Catholic" into the vocabulary of American jurisprudence in such a way that practically all subsequent encounters with the civil realm have been executed in the name of the "Roman Catholic Church."

While the distinctive title of "Roman" was associated with Christians as early as the fourth century, the term "Roman Catholic" did not become popular until the post-Reformation era when, in a few countries, it came to signify those professing spiritual allegiance to the Pope. There is a complaint lodged in the annals, for example, in 1562, about certain customs revived at Oxford by William Hawle during a vacancy in the Wardenship, because their instigator was "known to be inclined to the Roman Catholic Religion."[2] The first recorded use of "Roman Catholic" in official English circles was found, according to one source, in a state paper of intelligence written by Queen Elizabeth's secret agent in the Papal States about 1564.[3] Thereafter, "the double name [Roman Catholic] seems to have been coined by the Reformers in England to support their claim to an equally valid Anglo-Catholicism."[4] In any event, the most vociferous objectors to the terminology have been those who regard the name "Roman Catholic" as "a British invention patented by an Act of Parliament."[5]

Whatever might have been its specific origin, there is no doubt that the term found favor, as Herbert Thurston charged, among those Protestant divines "who were unwilling to concede the name Catholic to their opponents without qualification."[6] The opposition, then, of English Catholics is an understandable by-product of their hyper-sensitivity to the implied fragmentation of the Catholic community seemingly allowed in the use of "Roman." That point of view is reflected in the writings of people like John Henry Newman who recorded that, as he drew nearer to conversion, he ceased to speak of the "Roman Catholics" and called them boldly "Catholics."[7]

In any event, the practice was stereotyped in such universally respected publications as *The Oxford Dictionary of the Christian Church* which categorically identifies the term "Roman Catholic" with that Catholicism which "has developed since the Reformation."[8] *The Oxford English Dictionary*, which most scholars regard as the ultimate authority on the history of usage, shows that "Roman Catholic" was viewed as a "conciliatory term, in place of *Roman, Romanist,* or *Romanish*" used in the 17th century.[9]

No apparent concern over the usage was evidenced at the Vatican until the Congress of Vienna in 1815, when Ercole Cardinal Consalvi, the papal legate, took public exception to a communique employing the *joint* term "Roman Catholic." He argued that the two words could be *separately* applied to the Church, which is Roman by reason of its necessary dependence on the See of Rome, and Catholic in view of its universal diffusion.[10].

Controversy about the appellation intensified in succeeding decades to the extent of provoking a lively and lengthy debate at the First Vatican Council during the early months of 1870. In the opening words of the proposed constitution *de Fide*, the Church was referred to as "*Sancta Romana Catholica*." Several emendations were offered, one prelate even wanting the term "*Romana*" deleted on the grounds that the expression might be construed as meaning the particular church in *Alma Urbe*.[11]

A more forceful objection came from William Ullathorne who felt that the designation might encourage those Protestants who "pretend that the Catholic Church is divided into three parts: the Romano-Catholic community, the Anglo-Catholic community, and the Graeco-Catholic community." Adoption of the term "Roman Catholic," conjectured the Bishop of Birmingham, would give the Puseyites further arguments to bolster their branch theory of ecclesial origin.[12]

In place of the proposed formula, Ullathorne suggested the use of either "Catholic and Roman" or "Roman, Catholic." The first of the English Benedictine's alternatives was rejected flatly. A subsequent vote on insertion of a comma between the two words was indecisive on the initial tally. The following day, Vincenz Gasser, the Prince-Bishop of Brixen, told the conciliar fathers that the term "Roman Catholic Church" means "the same as the Roman Church, that is, the mother and teacher of all churches, joined with the Catholic Church, that is, with that church which is in the whole world, and indeed so joined that the Roman Church is the Catholic Church and the Catholic Church Roman." To Gasser, insertion of the comma could not be tolerated because "that Church which is the mother and teacher of all churches cannot have or hold second place in the proper name of the Church." Following the intervention of the Bishop of Brixen, the council voted against the second of Ullathorne's alternate versions.[13]

No further action on the disputed phraseology was taken until the preliminary vote for the entire constitution on April 12. At that time, forty-four bishops, casting *placet juxta modum* ballots (favorable with certain reservations), offered to give their unqualified approval if the earlier question of "*Sancta Romana Catholica Ecclesia*" could be resolved. They suggested "*Sancta, Catholica, Apostolica et Romana Ecclesia*" as a tolerable alternative. At that juncture, Bishop Gasser offered yet another formula, acceptable to William Ullathorne, namely, "*Sancta Catholica Apostolica Romana Ecclesia*," a phrase allowing for a distinction between the name of the Church and its description. Such a compromise satisfied all concerned. From that time, the officially recognized name applied to the People of God has been the "Holy Catholic Apostolic Roman Church." In effect, then, in assigning to the term "Roman" a descriptive but not appellative connotation, the council clearly frowned on the use of "Roman Catholic" in conjunction with the name of the one true Church.

Although such outstanding theologians as T. Smyth-Vaudry triumphantly announced that the Vatican Council had "mercilessly shattered forever the mischievous dual name 'Roman Catholic,'"[14] the wishes of the conciliar fathers had little effect in those areas where the disputed terminology was already in vogue. That the issue continued to evoke occasional comment is obvious from any sources. At the annual conference of the Catholic Truth Society, for instance, in September of 1901, Herbert Cardinal Vaughan reminded the delegates at Newcastle that the term "Roman," when signifying a mere species of the more embracive "Catholic," was totally unacceptable. On the other hand, the Archbishop of Westminster warmly endorsed "Roman Catholic" when it referred to the Roman See of Peter as "the centre of Catholic unity."[15]

The practice in Maryland, and in the United States generally, seems to have been similar to that of England, and by the end of the eighteenth century many English-speaking Catholics were apparently content that the term "Roman Catholic" should be employed not only in their official relations with the government, but even to some extent in documents of a more domestic character.[16]

In succeeding decades, apologists have approached the subject from differing points of view, none of them attaching great importance to the terminology. Leslie Rumble, for example, felt that the term "Roman Catholic" involved a grammatical contradiction since "to use the word 'Roman' as a qualifying adjective of limitation or restriction is like speaking of the 'limited unlimited.'"[17] Bertrand L. Conway reflected the teaching of many theologians by equating the terms "Catholic" and "Roman," and using them interchangeably: "The adjective Roman merely accentuates the fact of the vital character of Christianity, having a local government on earth, whose head is the Bishop of Rome."[18] Another veteran apologist pointed out that "in the expression 'Roman Catholic' the word 'Roman' merely affirms that the Vicar of Jesus Christ, the Bishop of Rome, is the head of the whole Church and that all who are within the true fold are within his jurisdiction."[19]

The issue received no specific attention at the Second Vatican Council, which preferred to speak of the Church in such non-legal terms as "People of God." A footnote to the official text of the decree *de Ecclesia Mysterio* assumes, however, retention of the earlier council's terminology.[20]

Apart from the admittedly questionable intentions of the term's originators, "Roman Catholic" would certainly seem more appropriate than "American Catholic" as a designation of the one and only Church of Christ, at least as that body has been known through the centuries. While there might be occasional reservations on the part of certain theologians about identifying the primacy with Rome, most would recognize the historicity of the association which has perdured without interruption since Peter. That being the case, local custom, at least in the United States, would seem to justify retaining the term "Roman Catholic," provided that the reservations and distinctions outlined by the First Vatican Council are kept in mind.

One can hardly help thinking, in conclusion, that Saint Pacian of Barcelona (360-390) might have had the best answer of all when asked about his religious convictions: "Christian is my name and Catholic my surname."[21]

Notes to the Text

1. John Tracy Ellis, *Documents of American Catholic History* (Milwaukee, 1962), p. 542.
2. "New College Customs, 1562," reproduced in Philip Caraman, *The Other Face: Catholic Life Under Elizabeth I* (New York, 1960), p. 28.
3. New York *Freeman's Journal*, June 24, 1905.
4. Cronan Regan, O.P., "Signpost," *The Sign*, XLVII (May, 1968), 46.
5. New York *Freeman's Journal*, November 11, 1899.
6. "Roman Catholic," *The Catholic Encyclopedia* (New York, 1912), XIII, 121. M.E. Williams, "Roman Catholics," *New Catholic Encyclopedia* (New York, 1967), XII, 562-563 gives the same information.
7. Eleanor Ruggles, *Journey Into Faith* (New York, 1948), pp. 323-324.
8. (London, 1957), p. 1173.
9. (Oxford, 1944), II, 1750.
10. "The Name of the Church," *The Dolphin*, III (February, 1903), 135.
11. H.G. Hughes, "'Catholic' and 'Roman Catholic,'" *American Ecclesiastical Review*, XXVII (September, 1902), 243.
12. Cuthbert Butler, O.S.B., *The Vatican Council*, 1869-1870 (Westminster, 1962), p. 243.
13. Quoted in James Hennessy, S.J., *The First Council of the Vatican: The American Experience* (New York, 1963), pp. 155-156.
14. *Notes on the Divine Plan of the Church* (Montreal, 1906), p. 247.
15. John George Snead-Cox, *The Life of Cardinal Vaughan* (London, 1910), II, 238.
16. Herbert Thurston, "The History of the Name 'Roman Catholic,'" *The Month*, CXVIII (September, 1911), 301.
17. Leslie Rumble, M.S.C. and Mortimer Carty, *Radio Replies* (Saint Paul, 1940), II, 72.
18. *The Question-Box Answers* (New York, 1918), p. 129.
19. W. Herbst, S.D.S., *Twin Circle*, February 18, 1968.
20. *Schema Constitutionis De Ecclesia* (Rome, 1964), p. 17.
21. "*Christianus mihi nomen est, Catholicus vero cognomen.*" Quoted in F. Cayre, *Manual of Patrology and History of Theology* (Paris, 1935, I, 606.

100

This essay on "Altar Boys" and their place in the new liturgical life of the Church is taken from *The Priest* XXIX (May, 1973), 41.

The place of altar boys in the liturgical worship of God's People remains one of prominence and distinction. Indeed, Vatican Council II's *Constitution on the Liturgy* places "servers" on a par with "lectors, commentators and members of the choir" as exercising "a genuine liturgical function."

The high quality of performance demanded by the old ceremonial manuals emphasized the privilege of actively participating in liturgical functions. A. Croegaert, for example, stated that "a young man should be admitted to the service of the altar only if, after serious and methodical training in eucharistic devotion and ritual duties, he has proved at a practical examination that he is capable of performing them worthily."

Pope Pius XII instructed priests "to select carefully a number of good and well-intentioned boys from every class of the community, who will come forward of their own free will to serve regularly and reverently at the altar - an office which their parents, even those of the higher and more cultured class, ought to hold in great esteem."

It was not without reason that the same Pontiff referred to Mass servers as "the first seminary." A survey made some years ago, in Paris, revealed that 87% of the priests there were former altar boys.

The traditional importance of servers is attested by the 1917 *Code of Canon Law* which forbade priests to celebrate Mass without a server to assist and respond.

Though many of the functions once performed by servers have been as signed to the lector and/or commentator in the new liturgical directives, the altar boy retains a vital role which has been rather widely overlooked.

The recently-imposed minimum age of eighteen for permanent lectors and acolytes says nothing about servers, who most assuredly will continue to function, as they have for centuries, as an integral part of the Church's liturgical life.

The story is told about Thomas More, a server throughout his life. On Sundays he went to Mass with his whole family, and after seeing his wife and children into their pews, he went off to the sacristy, put on a cassock and surplice, and assisted the priest as his server.

One Sunday, when the Duke of Norfolk saw the Lord Chancellor of England, with hands folded and eyes downcast, leading the priest into the sanctuary, he murmured, in a tone loud enough for all to hear: "Good heavens, my Lord, you, an altar boy? You dishonor your office and the king by such deportment!"

"Not at all, your Grace," answered Thomas More, as he continued to the altar. "Your master and mine, the king, can take no offense because I serve a greater King, who is both his Master and mine - and yours too, I might add!"

What beautiful and meaningful sentiments for contemporary times.

101

This article on "The Crucifixion of Jesus Christ As Others Saw It" is taken from *Emmanuel* LXXXII (February, 1976), 98-104.

The story of humankind is incomprehensible without Jesus Christ or, as Martin Luther put it, "anything that one imagines of God apart from Christ is only useless thinking and vain idolatry."

In one way or another, all the problems of contemporary society can be traced to some form of alienation from the Savior. Their solution depends on a return to the full truth of the living God, the God of the Bible and of faith, the God of salvation history. There is nothing more urgent than doing all one can to know and make known the true God, whose last name is pronounced Jesus Christ.

Indescribably terrible as it was, the passion and death of Christ was the greatest and most blessed event in the whole of recorded history. It was the climax of the priestly work of Christ, the consecration and transformation of death. The journal of that first holy week is often more discernible through the prayer and study of others than through one's own reaction to the events as recorded by the Evangelists.

These reflections are on thirteen of the eye-witnesses to the Savior's ordeal, arranged in the chronological order of their appearance.

Judas Iscariot

Judas Iscariot, the son of Simon, always the last of the apostles enumerated, lives on in history as the ultimate example of faithlessness and treachery, the enigma of the New Testament. Few men ever had greater potential; surely none ever proved a more dismal failure.

The only Judean among the Galilean apostles, Judas was very likely born at Jericho. Certainly his life reflected the characteristics of that violently nationalistic segment of Israel. Judeans were a cold-blooded and hard-headed people, in contrast to their warm-hearted and generous-minded Galilean neighbors.

Throughout the early years of his association with Our Lord, Judas appears to have been a loyal, trusted and dedicated apostle. It was only when Jesus refused to adorn Himself with that earthly splendor of kingship that, as Luke says, "Satan entered into Judas."

The climax of his betrayal came on the Feast of the Passover. Unable even to wait for the conclusion of the Last Supper, Judas arose from his place of honor, to the left of Jesus, and hurried into the darkness of the night, as if to symbolize the gloom that must have enshrouded his troubled soul.

He became a partner to the most devastatingly-disastrous business deal of all time, that of selling Christ for a measly thirty pieces of silver, about $14, the going price for servants. The subsequent betrayal in the garden has enshrined the traitor's kiss as the symbol of all that is base and ignoble. The final, painful moments of Judas' life were flooded with unrest, remorse and ultimately, despair, a proof that "no man could be more akin to a devil than a perverted apostle."

In the natural order, Judas must have possessed a tremendous storehouse of human talents. He had many of the qualities that make for greatness: he was purposeful, bold, ingenious and methodical. Christ trusted him and exhibited special concern for him. Judas betrayed that trust and despised those favors. His tragedy is that of anyone who throws away or compromises his spiritual ideals.

The mysterious aspect of the whole frustrated narrative was not the selling of Jesus, but the despairing of his pardon. Judas showed his esteem for Christ, but it was an aborted esteem that stopped short of seeking forgiveness. Indeed that was the supreme outrage and the ultimate iniquity of Judas.

No one is sinless. Everybody, at one time or another, has betrayed Christ by preferring earthly to spiritual interests. How often has Christ been sold for even less than the thirty pieces of silver acquired by Judas? The difference is that he who believes in Christ confides in his mercy. The faithful man knows that God is always ready to forgive.

Mark Rutherford put it well by noting that had Christ met Judas with the halter in his hand, would he not have stopped him? Ah, I can see the divine touch on the shoulder, the passionate prostration of the penitent in the dust, the hands gently lifting him, the forgiveness for he knew not what he did, and the seal of the kiss from sacred lips. If only Judas had said: "I'm sorry."

Herod Antipas

A momentary reflection on the tragic figure of Herod and his relationship with Christ challenges human sensitivities. His kingly name deserves to be displayed in block letters on the world's marquees, for Herod Antipas surely ranks among the greatest failures of all time.

Scripture scholars surmise that during his youthful days, Herod was sent out to fosterage in the Manahen family, whose senior member was an elder in the synagogue at Antioch. Whatever minimal respect for holiness, scant knowledge of religious truth and limited interest for human betterment he had was acquired during those years spent away from home.

Herod ascended to the mostly-ceremonial throne of Israel while still in his teens. He proved to be a tolerable ruler only because of a masterful inactivity. His craftiness at avoiding decisions reached almost the stage of ingenuity. Had it not been for his part in the story of Christ's passion and death, Herod's name would be heaped with all the other historical non-entities scattered through the annals.

Weak man that he was, Herod leaned heavily on his ambitious wife, Herodias, the widow of his deceased brother. Already she had dispatched the principal threat to her position, by bringing about the death of the meddlesome preacher, John the Baptist. On that blood-drenched occasion, what vestige of good will there was in Herod died a shameful death.

Such was the caliber of the man to whom Christ was sent by Pontius Pilate on that historic Friday morning. Herod could have saved Christ. The tragedy is not that he failed to do so, but that he didn't even care enough to try. Oh, Herod was fascinated by Christ. The sacred writer says that he was "extremely glad" to see and talk with the one who had evoked such controversy and acclaim among the local populace.

Unfortunately, by that time in his dissipated life, Herod's spiritual senses were totally numb. It was only a vague curiosity that sparked his request for signs and wonders from Christ. Though confronted by a torrent of questions, Christ refused to answer. There really wasn't anything to say for, as Saint Paul later noted, "the sensual man does not perceive the things that are of the spirit of God, for it is foolishness to him and he cannot understand."

In his blindness, Herod interpreted the silence as a sign of stupidity. It was then that the king decided on having Christ mocked and returned to

Pilate dressed in the vestige of a fool. Herod's earthly demise was no less sad than his human sojourn. The conniving of his wife eventually cost him the throne and the one-time monarch ended his days as a restless, obscure wanderer.

How fascinated the Christian world has always been about the man who could have saved Christ, but did not; the man who could have led his people, but would not; the man who might have changed history, but didn't bother.

Herod personifies the men and women whose religion is little more than a tissue of superstitions, false beliefs and empty practices, the ones whose lifestyle ignores God and deifies mammon.

Pontius Pilate

For Pontius Pilate the passion and death of Christ marked the low point of an otherwise successful career as chief representative of the Roman emperor. He was in his seventh year as civil governor, military commander and chief judicial officer for the conquered Israeli people.

Pilate obviously hated and despised the Jews, but he was shrewd enough to fear them. And yet, experienced and astute official that he was, the procurator was no match for the unscrupulous and subtle religious leaders of the Sanhedrin. Pilate has marched through the annals of history as one who asked the right question for the wrong reason. And because he acted without the proper motivation, he didn't wait for an answer.

Uneasy before an innocence he couldn't penetrate, baffled by a justice he couldn't confront, and disgruntled by a pressure he couldn't resist, Pilate clumsily tried to side-step the issue by shrugging his shoulders. So he asked the question: "What is truth?" The answer stood there before him. The tragedy was that he didn't really want to see it.

When a man renounces the existence of truth, he finds a more demanding master that eventually enslaves him. Whether called popular opinion or majority rule, it brings no peace to one who has compromised with truth—and that Pilate blatantly did.

Though he little dreamed it, Pilate became, at that harried moment, the symbol of a world which, in every age, has felt hunger and emptiness of soul. Man craves for threefold peace: peace within himself, peace in society and peace in the world. Pilate's world felt the pangs of that hunger no less strongly than our own.

The first and most compelling of man's hungers is for that inner peace which only truth can satisfy. Christ, standing before Pilate, proclaimed the existence of an objective order of truth. It was as a witness to truth that he had been born into the world. The domain of truth has its own law, sanctions and imperatives. Men are free to adopt or reject it, but they cannot change it. And whether they accept it or not, they are unable to destroy.

The character of Pilate was paradoxical, insofar as he exhibited respect for truth, yet permitted it to be abused; demonstrated repulsion at wrong-doing, yet allowed it to occur and manifested sympathy for innocence, yet refused to sustain it.

Pilate's name is forever etched into the Apostles Creed for his part in the greatest perversion of justice ever recorded. "He suffered under Pontius Pilate, was crucified, died and was buried." No empty gesture of cleaning the hands could wash away the stain incurred by the blood of innocence itself. Pilate's sin was that of every one who strives to serve two masters: able to satisfy neither adequately, he was ultimately rebuffed by both.

While the Roman procurator sinned in ignorance and weakness, rather than in malice, his travesty of justice lives on to symbolize a world where man, rather than the God-man (Christ), is enthroned in the position of primacy.

Mary

Hidden away in that small cluster of people lining the *Via Dolorosa* was the Mother of Christ. In those sorrowful moments, Our Lady stood out as "the sign of hope and solace for the pilgrim people of God."

Although the early life of Mary is guardedly revealed by the inspired writers, that spotless maiden emerges from the dark Judean hills to become the mother of the Savior, a role which so closely united her with our Lord as to afford her the highest place in the Church after Christ himself.

Mary was not totally unprepared for her part in the redemptive process. Since that day in the Temple when Simeon had foretold the piercing of her soul with a sword, Mary had held herself in readiness for what would surely follow.

Her voice stifled with grief, her eyes filled with tears and her emotion fraught with anxiety, Mary remained steadfastly beside Christ. She suffered and all but died with her Son. For the salvation of men, Mary gave up her maternal rights over Christ to appease God's justice. For that, she may justly be credited with having an active share in the redemption of the human race.

In his sermon on the "Compassion of Mary," Bossuet said that God willed that Mary not only be immolated with Christ and nailed to the cross, but that she should be associated, as well, with the mystery accomplished by his death.

Liturgical traditions have long endowed Mary with the crown of martyrdom because of the agony that encompassed her heart. She suffered in proportion to her love for Christ. The cruelty of his executioners and the atrocity of their torments touched her own soul. Perhaps that's why, apart from Christ, Mary is the most appealing of all the figures described by the Scriptures. There is no other, beyond her Son, who has attracted so many hearts.

In his last will and testament, Christ committed Mary to his beloved apostle and, through John, to his followers. From that moment onwards, Mary became the mother of all Christians. The Church logically and necessarily venerates Mary in a way that allows contemporary believers to understand her pivotal role in the redemptive process. She makes the cross easier and more meritorious because of her pre-eminent charity.

Our Lady figures prominently in the history of salvation. In a certain way, she unites and mirrors within herself the central truths of the Catholic Faith. Her relationship to Christians is inseparably linked to the quiet but intimate role she portrayed at Calvary.

Throughout her whole life, but most especially during Christ's passion, Mary "lived an example of that maternal love by which all should be fittingly animated who cooperate in the apostolic mission of the Church on behalf of the rebirth of man." For this and other forceful reasons, Vatican Council II conferred on our Lady the most beautiful of her many crowns, the Motherhood of the Church.

Simon of Cyrene

Just for a moment, reflect upon Our Lord's passion and death through the person of that mysterious eye-witness, associated with the Fifth Station of the Cross. His service for the Lord was meant to be remembered because of its lesson for the people of God in other generations.

Simon was very likely a member of the Jewish community at Cyrene. Like all the Israelites, his supreme goal in life was to visit the Holy City for the passover Feast, an ambition he was about to fulfill. As he entered the Damascus Gate, he was confronted with the brutal spectacle of a frenzied mob, their passionate screams, blasphemous curses and boisterous shouts cutting the quiet of the midday air. A neatly-dressed centurion was approaching, with a contingent of Roman soldiers, followed by three prisoners locked in chains.

One of the condemned figures stood out from the others. On his bruised and quivering shoulders rested the vertical beam of a heavy cross. Encircling his brow was a crown of plaited thorns. Blood streamed down his face, giving it a mask-like appearance. Exhaustion and pain had reduced his gait to faltering, uncertain steps. Around his neck hung a wooden plaque, with a tri-lingual inscription: "This is Jesus of Nazareth, the King of the Jews."

Suddenly, human endurance reached its limit and the procession came to a halt. The Nazarene fell to the ground beneath the instrument of his crucifixion. The centurion, efficient officer that he was, hastily scanned the crowed for someone to assist the prisoner.

The choice couldn't go to one of the local leaders-that would be a gross indignity; it couldn't fall to a Roman soldier-that would violate military decorum; nor could such a burden be placed upon an ordinary Jewish bystander-that would further alienate an already shaky alliance.

Fearful that the repeated scourgings, loss of blood and crowning with thorns would prematurely snuff out the vital signs of his prisoner, the centurion's eye settled on a swarthy-looking, dark-skinned stranger from Cyrene. He sent for Simon and immediately "pressed" him into taking up the cross after Jesus.

How indebted the Christian world has always been to Simon for his service on that dreadful Friday afternoon. His presence is a perpetual reminder to the human family that the Cross of Christ is the badge of servitude, the condition of discipleship and the standard of suffering.

Whether, in reality, Simon was Jewish or pagan, wealthy or poor, black or white, young or old makes precious little difference when weighed against his unique role in the passion story. The facts speak for themselves: this insignificant stranger from a far-away Roman colony, was alone offered the opportunity of bearing the cross of humankind's redeemer.

Scripture scholars conclude, after careful study of the phraseology, that Simon did not initially undertake that task willingly. On the contrary he seems to have been done so with considerable reluctance. Yet personal inclination in matters of sacrifice can be of little consequence, inasmuch as the burdens enjoined by Providence are more efficacious than those of one's own choosing, provided, of course, they are accepted with the proper motivation.

That Simon's two sons later became leading figures in the Christian community at Rome, indicates that his unwilling impressment begot the very best of results, in a way unknown to the commentators.

The cross can be for contemporary man, as it was for Simon, the badge of servitude, the condition of discipleship and the standard of suffering. How, when and where our Lord beckons one from the crowd to take up that cross is unimportant. What really matters is a person's reaction. Even when the forces of nature incline one to turn and run away, as they did the Cyrenean, he can rise above those natural impulses to win, with Simon, a place of singular importance in the annals of God's kingdom.

Veronica

Since the Middle Ages, the story has been related of a holy woman from Jerusalem who fearlessly approached Jesus along the pathway to Calvary, with the head-towel or veil on which he wiped his bodily countenance. Upon receiving back the towel, the woman noticed the impressed portrayal of Our Lord's tortured face.

Identified in the apocryphal *Mors Pilati* as "Veronica," she is further associated with the woman spoken about in the gospel as having "an issue of blood." That same brave personage subsequently figured prominently in an Italian legend which told about Emperor Tiberius' cure from a serious malady after touching the sacred image. The veil was bequeathed to Pope Clement and his successors and is still preserved at Saint Peter's Basilica.

Very likely, the woman's name comes from the two Latin words *vera icon* (true image), the terminology used by the Romans in referring to the precious veil. Probably it was the towel customarily worn about the neck or over the shoulders.

A low door on the left side of the *Via Dolorosa* and a pillar of red granite indicate the place where Veronica is said to have approached Jesus. Today, a handsome church, erected by the Melchites, commemorates the event. The whole incident is worthy of credibility, insofar as it has found expression in literature and liturgy from the very earliest times.

In any event, the encounter of Veronica with Jesus takes its real importance from the lesson it teaches and the virtue it personifies. Then as now, it demanded a heroism worthy of imitation for an innocent bystander, and a woman at that, to step forward from a jeering and taunting crowd, with solace for a publicly-defamed stranger. Veronica's gracious act of wiping Our Lord's sacred face, buffeted as it was with insults, streaming with blood and covered with spittle, was prompted initially by sympathy, nourished with compassion and, ultimately, performed from love. Hers was a perfect example of a woman's spontaneity for religion and the virtues flowing therefrom.

The Veronica of contemporary times is known by her ready assistance to needy neighbors, patient response for rashly-conceived proposals and cheerful acceptance of foolish impositions. Cardinal Newman credited the Blessed Mother's prayers for sending Veronica and Simon to assist Christ, "Simon to do a man's work, Veronica to do the part of a woman."

Throughout the Christian era Veronica has epitomized the part of a woman by exhibiting a love not based on physical attraction. That pious woman serves to verify an old truism mentioned long ago in the Talmud, that "God did not create woman from man's head that he should command her, nor from his feet that she should be his slave, but rather from his side, that she should be near his heart."

102

"Why Church History" was first delivered to the Franciscan seminarians at San Luis Rey College on November 1, 1965. It appeared later that year in *The Evangelist* XXVIII (Summer, 1965), 6-8.

G K. Chesterton once said that our conquerors will not come with warships and brands but "books be all their eating and ink be on their hands." That being the case, perhaps a brief reflection on the intellectual life, as a vital part of the priestly apostolate, would be appropriate and timely.

There seems to be today, even at the minor seminary level, an intellectual reawakening within aspirants to the priesthood. Such has not always been the case. Until just a few years ago, one was considered completely out of step who brought up such matters as theology, philosophy, scripture, liturgy, or history outside the classroom. With some few exceptions, the average seminarian was decidedly anti-intellectual and, in many cases, he carried that attitude into the active apostolate after ordination,

Those few who tried to appreciate, for example, the learned encyclicals of Pius XII were bewildered to find this pontiff, surely the greatest teacher since Peter, so unheeded and unheralded. Paradoxically, that pope's outstanding writings on the Mystical Body, scripture, liturgy, and renewal of Christian worship came to full fruition only in the programs of his successor, a factor which recently prompted John Tracy Ellis to lament the "pathetic blackout" of the man during whose pontificate the foundations for today's *aggiornamento* were built.

If the seminarian of our time wants to see the priesthood restored to its rightful place as a dominant force in society, he must realize that people may continue to revere the unlearned priest, but they are attracted only by the learned one. They rightly expect holiness, but they will be led only by the educated *alter Christus* (other Christ). Without this learning, people will recognize the priest for what he really is - a fraud, even though he be a pious fraud!

Of course, there are many phases of the intellectual apostolate. During seminary days, the student has the privilege of sampling most of them. One aspect of the overall apostolate worthy of consideration is Church history; for, as one noted scholar recently remarked, he who "wants to be a good theologian...can never know Church history too well."

While it cannot be said, in agreement with Robert Fuller, that "history maketh a young man old, without either wrinkles or gray hairs." The temptation to bitterness and discouragement comes rather easily at these times. Certainly that temptation came to Isaac Hecker. To know the history of his life is to know how to react when faced with similar trials. Like this founder of the Paulist Fathers, others will eventually triumph if their cause is good and their spiritual life well-grounded.

Another purpose of Church history, one especially useful in our times, is its ability to broaden the horizons of those who pursue it. Church history demonstrates that every river has two banks, every opinion an opponent and a proponent. In these ecumenical days we have learned to tolerate the views of those outside the fold as of those not yet privileged by Almighty God with the wonderful gift of Faith. But there is more to ecumenism than that. By its very definition, ecumenism applies to members within the Church as well as to those outside. If liberty of conscience is granted to the nonbeliever, can we do less to our own brothers in Christ to whom we are united with very special bonds? The great Catholic reformers were always careful lest their liberal attitude in deciding what the Church should do in a given circumstance render them uncompromising in their own narrowness. A man who disagrees with another on matters such as racial relations or liturgical renewal must presume the opponent to be in good faith. Even though we know, or think we know, such an individual to be wrong, the true Christian would never impose his views on his neighbor, for he too has a conscience which, for him, is the *recta ratio* (right reason) of his actions. The student of Church history approaches such situations as this in the spirit of Montaigne, who noted that "opinions that are opposed to mine do not offend or estrange me; they only arouse and exercise my mind."

A knowledge of Church history will give a man a love and respect for the Church, almost unattainable elsewhere. He will gradually come to see that Catholicism down through the ages has been loved and hated, praised and reviled, but rarely has it been ignored. Perhaps the finest tribute ever written on the Church was penned by a man decidedly non-sympathetic to its doctrines. Lord Thomas Macauley stated that:

> There is not now, and there never was, on this earth a work of human policy so well-deserving of examination as the Roman Catholic Church. The history of that church joins the two great ages of human civilization... Nor do we see any sign which indicates that the term of her long dominion is approaching.

Finally, a knowledge of the Church's past will enable the priest and the seminarian to personally discuss, and apply present-day problems in an intelligent manner and in a way acceptable to educated men both within and without the Church. Men of our age, who know the pages of history , will be helped on the natural order to yearn for the obedience of Robert Bellarmine, the humility of Cardinal Newman, the zeal of Isaac Hecker, and the esteem of Thomas Macauley.

There is no reason why the average priest of today should not be welcomed in scholarly circles. His education, in length of years and scope of studies, measures up quite favorably with most of the Ph.D.s on secular campuses. If he is not accepted in those circles, he does himself and his cause a great disservice; for, like it or not these people are the leaders of society, and the impact of the priest as a molder of public opinion and morality must be made on this level before it can seep down to the grass roots.

Priests will be received by these people if they give evidence of having used their opportunities for study well; if, for example, they can look dispassionately at history, if they can discuss, maybe at times defend, the errors as well as privileging him with the experience of age...without the infirmities or inconveniences thereof," there is little doubt, as Pope John XXIII pointed out, that "only those who ignore history are condemned to repeat it."

There are all kinds of advantages attached to knowing the Church's past. A well-rounded knowledge of Church history, for example, gives the priest, among other things, a "balanced judgment." If, as Pius XI said, "it is no longer permissible for us to be mediocre," then also it is no longer acceptable for the priest, as a leader in society, to be swayed or influenced by emotion, pride, or prejudice in the making of his own conscience. The world of the 1990s no longer tolerates such narrowness.

History tells of many incidents to illustrate this point. One such case of a real, honest, balanced judgment was Robert Bellarmine, perhaps the most outstanding intellect in the Church during the 17th century. Bellarmine's support of Louis de Molina, however, was not universally appreciated, and he awoke one fine day to find himself exiled from Rome to the obscure Archbishopric of Capua. Although the appointment was a foolish one, an obvious political expedient to get a brilliant thorn out of the papal tiara, not a single word of reluctance is recorded on the part of Bellarmine. And, in an age when absenteeism was rampant, the archbishop literally dashed off to his new assignment. Three years of tireless activity at Capua made over that jurisdiction from one of the most backward to a model Christian community. Bellarmine would have stayed there the rest of his life had not a more virtuous pope recalled him to Rome and the cardinalate in 1605.

Here, then, was a man of balanced judgment, a prelate of great learning, a spiritual priest, one who, though he knew full well that the Holy Father was acting spitefully, had the virtue to accept the fact that Clement VIII, and not he himself, was the Vicar of Christ. Robert Bellarmine recognized that "the best and most effective servants of the Church have been those men who were able to submerge their personal interests in favor of the cause which they were supposed to serve."

One who lacked this "balanced judgment" was Johann Dollinger, a man who failed to see in history its necessary lessons of personal sanctity, without which even the priest is a whitened sepulchre. Dollinger, who lived through the first Vatican Council, had very strong feelings against the doctrine of papal infallibility. Perhaps his most powerful ally was John Henry Newman, who also thought a pronouncement on infallibility would be a disaster to the Church. But there was one, and maybe only one, difference between the outlook of these two men, one who died a heretic, the other a candidate for sainthood. It was a "balanced judgment," the ability Newman had to see himself out of context, a servant not a master, a realization that when the chips are down, the perfection of virtue does not consist in the quality of the work done, but in the perfection with which a man carries out the mandates of those whom he sees as God's representatives.

A student of Church history strives to be as "accurate"as is humanly possible. He is not given to broad, generalized, statements. Today the quality of accuracy is vitally important, for the careless juxtaposition of a single word could result, and has in the past, in the total misrepresentation of a man's views.

671

False or undocumented statements could easily undermine for non-Catholics the work of many years in the apostolate. Certainly then, it is not enough for priests to appear learned.

There is another useful purpose that Church history can serve. We recall what Chesterton said about surrender versus success: "In everything worth having, even in every pleasure, there is a point of tedium that must be survived, so that the pleasure may revive and endure. The joy of battle comes after the first fear of death; the glow of the sea bather after the icy shock of the water...All human vows, laws and contracts are so many ways of surviving with success this breaking point, this instant of potential surrender." In the history of the United States, there is one outstanding example of a man who did not surrender, one whose life has its lessons for those walking along similar pathways.

Isaac Hecker was this remarkable man, Expelled from the Redemptorist Order over a rather foolish misunderstanding, he later noted in a letter that "I have lived history in a few months...I have been cut and slashed at in every direction and before everybody up to His Holiness; and have lost any idea of ever having had any character at all. But the grace of God has guided me through it all, and thus far I am happy in having nothing to regret."

Almost everyone has been tempted, on occasions, to throw in the sponge, feeling betrayed by associates or misunderstood by superiors.

The temptation to bitterness and discouragement comes rather easily at these times. Certainly that temptation came to Isaac Hecker. To know the history of his life is to know how to react when faced with similar trials. Like this founder of the Paulist Fathers, others will eventually triumph if their cause is good and their spiritual life well-grounded.

Today, in this area of the apostolate, the era of street-corner preaching is as dated as Edsel automobiles and Dewey buttons. Christ and His Church must be carried to the acknowledged leaders of society first-there to be unfolded in beautiful and forceful logic. Those to whom the priest goes in this fashion want the truth, and not compromise. Taking the *corpus* off the cross, or making unhistorical claims about the blame for the crucifixion, does not win followers or even admirers. Those who seek to make the world safe for Christianity miss Christ's lesson about bringing the sword. Charity, the greatest of the virtues, must be united with truth before it takes on the absolute character of love.

The seminarian, tomorrow's priest, must be a revolutionary, for, indeed, Christ was the greatest revolutionary of them all; but, like Christ, he must always strive to elevate the people as he bends to serve them.

The ever-present temptation to view the Church as a solemn-high welfare organization, and little more, is not the logic a student of history would propose. Christ did not take the people out of the slums, he took the slums out of the people.

John Tracy Ellis, longtime professor of Church History at The Catholic University of America, was fond of saying that "after the priesthood of the altar, there is none greater than the priesthood of truth." That, in capsule form, is the message of this address.

103

This essay on "Pope Pius XII and the Vatican Council"was published in The *American Benedictine Review* XXI (September, 1970), 421-423.

The widespread failure to identify the late Pope Pius XII with the ide-als and accomplishments of the Catholic aggiornamento graphically illustrates how a lack of historical perspective can and does distort the public record. Renewal did not begin with John XXIII and, most assuredly, did not end with his demise. Rather, "its period of incubation took place in the pontificate of Pius XII. It developed because of, not in spite of, John's predecessor."[1]

Available evidence indicates that Pope Pius XII thought seriously on several occasions about calling an ecumenical council. World War II and the problems of the postwar years, as well as his own personal approach to the papacy, combined to delay the actual decision.[2]

The possibility of re-opening the First Vatican Council, or summoning a wholly new ecumenical gathering, was discussed by Pope Pius with Ernesto Cardinal Ruffini as early as 1939. At that time, the then Secretary of the Congregation for Seminaries and Universities, later to become (in 1945) archbishop of Palermo, encouraged the newly-elected pontiff, noting that the issues for such a convocation were "as abundant as they were at the council of Trent."[3] The cardinal subsequently recalled that the pope expressed favorable interest in the proposal and promised to examine it further.[4]

In 1948, the question was again actively considered by Pope Pius. "For two years commissions met to prepare the subjects to be discussed by the conciliar Fathers, including biblical studies, ecclesiastical celibacy, the use of the vernacular in liturgy, and the re-establishment of the permanent diaconate for use in mission territories."[5] For reasons not yet disclosed, but very probably related to his always-precarious health, the pope apparently took no steps to implement the proposals.

The pontiff's long-time confidant in the papal secretariate of state, Domenico Tardini, revealed that in 1956, with the partial recovery of his physical stamina, Pope Pius once again turned his thoughts to a council for which "certain studies had been undertaken by a small number of learned churchmen whose efforts would be utilized."[6] It was subsequently discovered from other sources that the envisioned council would have had five commissions, one each for dogmatic and speculative theology; practical and moral theology; missions; canonical discipline and liturgy and culture; and Christian action. A list of thirty-six names was drafted for a preparatory commission, including representatives of eighteen countries. A tentative list of sixty-five bishops from all parts of the world was drawn up to solicit ideas and suggestions for an agenda.[7] Among the concrete accomplishments of this planning was a 200 page schema written by Celso Cardinal Costanini on ecumenism which reached the pope's desk shortly before his death in 1958.[8]

Though no further action was taken, it is reported that among the documents John XXIII found at the time of his elevation to the papacy was his predecessor's detailed master plan for dealing with the world's manifold problems along with an elaborate prognosis. Written into the text were the words: *"concilio ecumenico."*[9]

How and to what extent these preliminary activities influenced Pius XII's successor to convene Vatican II is a question that must await the opening of Eugenio Pacelli's files to researchers. In any event, no less an authority than Augustin Cardinal Bea repeatedly stressed the more basic theme that "in many ways the Second Vatican Council would have not been possible without the long and faithful doctrinal preparation provided by Pope Pius XII."[10]

Apart from the part he may have had in actualizing the council, it is obvious from examining the many volumes of discourses, pronouncements and encyclicals of Pius XII "that in them there is already to be found everything which has now assumed visible form."[11] If one accepts the view that "the sixteen documents of Vatican II constitute the most remarkable message that God has sent, through his Church, to modern man,"[12] then a place of considerable prominence must be accorded the man whose teachings provided the outlines from which the conciliar decrees took their form.

The shadows of Pius XII are especially noticeable in Vatican II's three principal documents, namely, those on the Church, Divine Revelation and the Sacred Liturgy. The masterpiece of the council, its treatise *de Ecclesia*, was a theological refinement of the mysterious and vital relationship the People of God have to the Holy Spirit, the subject of the pontiff's monumental encyclical letter, *Mystici Corporis*. Godfrey L. Diekmann, O.S.B., recently observed that "we're apt to forget, as our memories are short, how quite revolutionary this document of Pius XII was" at the time of its issuance in 1943.[13]

Scripture scholars have long recognized their "immense debt of gratitude" to Pius XII for the atmosphere of joy and assurance with which he surrounded biblical studies with his precedent-shattering encyclical *Divino Afflante Spiritu*.[14] Indeed it was the work of this "architect and promoter of biblical renewal"[15] that provided exegetes with the theological basis for their controversial method of form criticism. Without the synthesis of a half century's research which the pontiff incorporated in his *magna carta* of Catholic Scriptural scholarship, the council would have had considerable difficulty in taking a clear and detailed stand on many problems, especially its remarkable pronouncement on Divine Revelation.

With the veritable litany of papal and curial pronouncements on various aspects of the sacred liturgy, it is sobering to hear a competent writer admit that even today "the most comprehensive official explanation of how the faithful participate in the Eucharistic sacrifice is still found in the encyclical, *Mediator Dei*, of Pope Pius XII."[16] It was interest in liturgical matters engendered by that encyclical which explains why the first completed work of Vatican II was its constitution on the Sacred Liturgy. Yet, time dims memories to such an extent that Pope Paul VI, in introducing and promulgating the new *Ordo Missae*, a generation after the issuance of the proto-liturgical directive, felt impelled to remind Catholics, in most forceful terms, that "the beginning of this renewal was the work of our predecessor, Pius XII."[17]

Quite obviously "Vatican II would not have been possible – or would not have taken the course that it did – without the preparations made for it under the earlier pontificate."[18] Hopefully, an historical-minded theologian will one day soon embark on an in-depth appraisal of the theological, scriptural, liturgical and pastoral indebtedness of the Second Vatican Council to Eugenio Pacelli whom the Patriarch of Constantinople's own newspaper predicted "would remain in history as the greatest of all Popes of Rome."[19] Then, perhaps only then, will the figure of Pope Pius XII emerge as the principal harbinger of a great new era for the People of God.

Notes to the Text

1. Robert A. Graham, "John Tracy Ellis on the 'Pathetic Blackout,'" *America*, 112 (March 6, 1965), 305.
2. Colman J. Barry, O.S.B., *American Nuncio: Cardinal Aloisius Muench* (Collegeville, 1969), p. 276.
3. Ernest Ruffini to John XXIII, *Acta et Documenta Concilio Oecumenico Vaticano II Apparando* (Rome, 1960), I, 124. See also Antoine Wenger, *Vatican II* (Westminster, 1966), I, 14, and Henri Daniel-Rops, *The Second Vatican Council* (New York, 1962), p. 58.
4. *Osservatore Romano*, November 1, 1959.
5. Francis J. Connell, C.SS.R., "In Review," *American Ecclesiastical Review*, 156 (February, 1967), 127.
6. *Osservatore Romano*, November 1, 1959. See also Domenico Tardini, *Memories of Pius XII* (Westminster, 1961), p. 82.
7. See Giovanni Caprile, S.J., "Pio XII e un Nuovo Progretto di Concilio Ecumenico," *Civilta Cattolica*, 117 (August 6-20, 1966), 209-227.
8. See *Irenikon*, 32 (1959), 309, and *Unitas*, 48-49 (1959-1960), 14.
9. Reported by Vincent A. Yzermans, *A New Pentecost* (Westminster, 1963), p. 298.
10. "Foreword" to *The Jerome Biblical Commentary* (Englewood Cliffs, N.J, 1968), p. viii.
11. Michael Schmaus, *Preaching as a Saving Encounter* (New York, 1966), p. 10.
12. Franco Pierini, S.S.P., *Catechism of Vatican II* (Staten Island, 1967), p. 9.
13. "The Liturgy and Personal Piety," *Sisters Today*, 40 (June-July, 1969), 552.
14. Ignatius Hunt, O.S.B., *Understanding the Bible* (New York, 1961), p. xiv.
15. Albert Cardinal Meyer, Intervention of November 19, 1962. Quoted by Vincent A. Yzermans, *American Participation in the Second Vatican Council* (New York, 1967), p. 108.
16. Charles E. Miller, C.M., "Explaining the New Offertory Rite," *Homiletic and Pastoral Review*, 69 (September, 1969), 925.
17. *Missale Romanum* (Rome, 1969), p. xvi.
18. Graham, p. 305.
19. *Apostolas Andreas*, March 6, 1957, quoted in the London *Tablet*, 210 (July 13, 1957), 46.

104

This essay on "Trinidad's New Sound" was written for *Our Sunday Visitor*, March 28, 1971.

The Tempo of Catholic Life in the independent nation of Trinidad and Tobago, most prominent of those Lesser Antilles known as the Windward Islands, approaches the ideal envisioned by the architects of the Second Vatican Council. An independent member of the British Commonwealth since 1962, Trinidad was etched onto the pages of history in July, 1498, when Christopher Columbus discovered, named and dedicated the Arawak kingdom to the Holy Trinity. For the past 81 years, Trinidad has been linked with Tobago, that colorful sister-island 21 miles to the north around which Daniel Defoe related the adventures of Robinson Crusoe.

The country's polyglot population, representing English, Scots, Welch, Portuguese, German, Spanish, American, Hindu, Muslim, African, Chinese and Lebanese ranks the residents of Trinidad and Tobago among the most racially integrated on the globe.

Always a dominant force in islandic life, the Catholic Church has exerted considerable political influence since April 30, 1850, when Pope Pius IX created an archiepiscopate at Port-of-Spain. The Catholic population has steadily increased over the past century until today it accounts for approximately 350,000 of the nation's 970,000 residents.

Though he attended and actively participated in the four sessions of Vatican Council II, Archbishop Finbar Ryan's attempts to implement the conciliar decrees were greatly hampered by the creeping disabilities of advanced age. On May 24, 1966, the 85-year-old Dominican prelate submitted his resignation to Rome, and shortly thereafter, returned to Ireland where he lives in retirement.

The ensuing 18-month vacancy indicates the care used in choosing a successor. Early in December, 1967, Father Anthony Pantin, a Holy Ghost Missionary, was summoned by the papal nuncio and abruptly informed that Pope Paul VI had named him Archbishop of Port of-Spain. Pantin recalls that the somber encounter was hardly lightened when his only request, "Can I continue to ride my bicycle?" was politely, but firmly refused. He was directed to mention the matter to no one, but the Prime Minister, until the press was duly notified. That was a tall order for a member of a family as closely-knit as the Pantins.

Ideally endowed by age, color and temperament, the 39 year-old priest, a native-born Trinidadian, would surely have been the popular choice had there been a plebiscite. His previous experience as missionary, religious superior and college administrator further enhanced his candidacy for steering a middle course between the racial, economic, social and religious complexities confronting the Church in the most southerly of the Caribbean Islands.

Fortunately, the organizational structure initiated and expanded by his predecessors provided Pantin with a solid foundation from which to launch his *aggiornamento*. Statistically, the Archdiocese of Port-of-Spain's secular and religious clergy staff 59 parishes and its religious women maintain 170 educational institutions enrolling well over 80,000 youngsters.

Except for a few years as a student and a short missionary stint on the Island of Guadaloupe, the new archbishop has spent his whole life on the 1,864 square mile Trinidad.

The pleasant, open and informal atmosphere generated by the young prelate is a vivid contrast to that of Archbishop Finbar Ryan, his Irish-born predecessor. A "princely man" by anyone's standards, Ryan personified the ecclesiastical demeanor Trinidadians had long associated with their spiritual leader. One priest captured the tone of those days with an amusing anecdote: He had approached "Count Finbar" about dedicating a new wing for his school. Stressing how much the Sisters wanted to have the archbishop in attendance, he delicately wondered if the ceremony could be conducted without the customary "splash." The prelate reared back in his chair and thundered his reply: "Father, if they don't want any 'splash,' they don't want the Archbishop of Port-of-Spain!"

The image of the Church in the Trinidadian capital has progressed considerably since the appointment of its new archbishop. At the same time, the last two years have brought extensive changes in the personal life of Anthony Pantin. While regretting the loss of those occasional moments of privacy he once cherished, he seems to have adjusted well to the hectic pace of his position. He lives very simply in a small section of the episcopal residence, next door to the Prime Minister, Dr. Eric Williams. An aunt looks after domestic needs, along with a caretaker who has worked at the "palace" for 34 years. The most foreboding thing about the home at 27 Maraval Road is a ferocious-looking German shepherd watchdog.

Perhaps more than any of his fellow-priests at Port-of-Spain, Archbishop Pantin recognizes the need for balancing local autonomy against ultimate dependence on the papacy. While unequivocally endorsing the canonical legislation regarding such matters as clerical celibacy, for example, Pantin shares the view of many Latin American bishops that some eventual accommodation is inevitable if the Church is to continue as a viable institution in the so-called "third world."

Pantin's handsome appearance, pleasant demeanor and articulate conversation belie the undiminishing fervor with which he is implementing the conciliar directives among the widely scattered Catholics in his 2,000 square mile archiepiscopate. Classified as a liturgical "moderate," he has encouraged, but not forced, such innovations as distribution of communion by laymen. At the same time, he views the reception of the Eucharist in the hands as something of a "novelty" for which there is no real, meaningful or practical need.

Pantin eventually hopes to consolidate the Dominican and Holy Ghost activities in Trinidad and Tobago with those of the diocesan clergy. The local seminary has been advanced to regional status as the first step towards providing the long-desired goal of a totally native clergy.

There are those among his official family who wonder if the archbishop's heart doesn't occasionally outdistance his head when he listens to the poor, finds work for the jobless and consoles the socially underprivileged. The extraordinary patience of his domestic staff is frequently stretched by the host of student leaders, Catholic intellectuals and seminarians who appear, mostly unannounced, at the episcopal residence for lunch or dinner.

Though he devotes little time to purely administrative functions, the archbishop has shrewdly surrounded himself with an elite corps of advisors. Just recently he demonstrated his concern for and appreciation of record management by calling on professional advice in organizing the valuable, but uncatalogued archival collection that has been collected over the past century.

There is a refreshing dash of informality in the archbishop's *modus vivendi*. He propels his own car, for example, through the congested streets of Port-of-Spain at a rate alarming even to a veteran of California's freeway system. When asked why there were no Monsignors in Trinidad and Tobago, the prelate quipped: "We already have two Canons and four Eucharistic prayers; surely that's enough for a little nation with a big mouth!"

Clearly Anthony Pantin is a rising star in the episcopal firmament of Central America. At forty-one, the "Lord Archbishop of Port-of-Spain," still among the world's most youthful prelates, embodies all the characteristics that the post-conciliar Church could expect of its readers.

105

"Who Is Leading?" is taken from *Friar* XXXV (April, 1971), 63-66. It had been given as an address to the Newman Club of Los Angeles on November 19, 1970.

The pitfalls associated with that elusive charism known as "leadership" were well expressed recently by a befuddled college professor who admitted he was never quite sure whether his students were following him or chasing him.

A considerable quantity of verbiage has flowed over the so-called authority crisis plaguing today's restless world. Inasmuch as "leading" and "following" are correlative terms, perhaps a modicum of attention could profitably be directed, not so much toward those who refuse to follow, as to that numerically smaller group which, in one way or another, fails to lead. Surely, it is altogether reasonable to wonder how the seemingly widespread reluctance to acknowledge and respect legitimate authority relates to the leadership-vacuum evident on so many levels of contemporary society.

While the basic mechanics of leadership don't vary considerably from one generation to another, their application must necessarily be adjusted to fit the times. In the 1970s, the "administrator" can be distinguished from the "executive" by his optimistic willingness to take calculated chances. The creativity predicted of true leaders, involving as it does an approach decisive enough to close none of the options, embodies the innate ability to penetrate and assess the heart of any situation through a middle course between the convergent and divergent reasoning processes.

While developing a climate conducive to growth, it must forge and sustain a meaningful dialogue between the decision-makers and those called upon to implement their directives.

The paramount quality associated with leadership and the obvious master-key to authoritative administration, is intelligence, which can harmonize the trinitarian concept of facts, ability to reason and intuition. Beyond a competence based on training and the gradual accumulation of experience and skill, the leader's mind needs enough resiliency to weigh, logically and objectively, all the alternatives before arriving at ultimate conclusions. To emotional balance, tested self-discipline and a strong sense of personal morality, must be added a fair, honest, frank, kindly, straight-forward and firm integrity.

Besides a personal fund of inventive ideas, the effectiveness of a leader can be hampered or furthered by his ability to inspire others with a measure of his own enthusiasm. Interdependence, or teamwork, figures prominently in the leadership montage, for without a sympathetic appreciation of the circumstances, ideals and limitations influencing his followers, there can be little of that harmonious *esprit de corps* so vital to any worthwhile undertaking. The self-actualized leader must also display a genuine concern for his subordinates, along with a trust in their capacity to attain the outlined objectives. Those rare individuals endowed by nature with the leadership charism, are generally warm, sensitive and cheerful persons, gifted with a sense of timing, alertness, imagination and foresight.

Inasmuch as human success is an unpardonable offense against one's fellows, that predominantly tiny segment of mankind displaying the leadership synapsis is seldom, if ever, appreciated. Charles de Gaulle was aware that the man who leads must go forward alone for, more frequently than not, even close associates attempt to shackle a "man born out of due time" by petty and jealous shenanigans. Super-competence has always been more objectionable to some than plain incompetence, for it militates against the first commandment of structured life: "Thou shalt not rock the boat!"

The names of Churchill, de Gaulle, Roosevelt, Pius XII, MacArthur and Adenauer are now consigned to the history texts. Today's uncertain, anxious and confused world suffers from a frightening percentage of faceless and forgettable personages in posts of strategic importance.

Despite the urgent appeals of Pope Paul the religious sphere reflects this contemporary vacuum. Rarely in the annals of history, has there been a more desperate clamor for strong, competent and balanced leadership than presently exists in the Catholic Church. And yet, while no one seriously questions the need for a responsible chain-of-command, seldom have the prospects on the local, national and international arenas been so barren.

Catholic uncertainty regarding the need, scope and obligations of leadership spans a wide spectrum. The first of the broad categories into which a portion of the Church's present-day "leaders" fall, the paternalistic, recalls the old divine right theory and its concentration of all decision-making prerogatives in a single man, along with the expectation (and demand) that everyone else fall dutifully into line, without being either consulted or questioned. This attitude, which can no longer be defended, much less advocated, gives indications of having reached its zenith. It is strongest at the parochial level, where a goodly percentage of pastors still rule "their" parish plants unencumbered, somewhat after the fashion of medieval fiefs. They alone make the important decisions, draw up the payroll, draft the schedules and appoint what titular officers are tolerated.

The distributive concept of leadership, developed extensively in recent times within religious communities, represents a first, faltering step in the commendable trend toward decentralization. As long as the absolutely vital distinction is maintained between a subject's inherent right toward self-expression and his natural proclivity to self-determination, progress toward human development and fulfillment, within a framework of responsible freedom, goes forward. The built-in weakness of this "committee" or splintered approach to authority, and one which has characterized practically the entire movement, is the tendency to oversimplify and short-circuit subsidiarity by scattering the reins of leadership so widely as to make them unrecognizable. The predictable results are frustrated subjects who are unable to affix their allegiance to any particular source, a factor which has given rise to many "identity-crises," a strictly post-Vatican phenomenon in religious life.

A by-product of weak, permissive and ineffective leaders is the "usurpator," one of those shadowy characters who cluster around authority-vacuums. An obvious example is that select, sacrosanct and omnipresent corps of theologians, known as *periti*, who haunt meetings of the nation's Catholic hierarchy. What they do, who they are and why they exist is one of the riddles of modern times. Their unchallenged manipulation of this country's episcopal conference must rank among the most accomplished usurpations ever recorded in ecclesiastical annals.

Today's most tragic ecclesial figures, those who cannot, will not or simply do not actively exercise the authority attached to their offices, are gradually allowing the lifeblood of American Catholicism to coagulate. Mostly, they have acquired their posts for talents other than leadership potential and, while the ability to lead naturally presumes the antecedent facility to follow, the fact remains that good followers only rarely evolve into effective leaders. This unfortunate category of headmen is about as useful to the flock as carved figurines on the prow of a ship are to navigators. Typical of this brand of leadership is the man who shrewdly calculates which direction the crowd is going and then, just before arrival at its destination, dashes around to the lead position.

Yes, the Church sorely needs leadership today; presently it has very little. Perhaps a contributing reason for the deficiency is a widespread unwillingness to admit that only a small segment of humankind possesses the natural and acquired requisites for exercising authority. Such rare gems must be ferreted out, properly trained and placed in posts of trust.

The leader is a lonely and courageous man, for as Friedrich Nietzsche stated: "Life always gets harder toward the summit–the cold increases, the responsibility increases." Harry Truman, a man of acknowledged leadership traits, put it a bit more bluntly when he observed that "if a man can't take the heat, tell him to get the you-know-what out of the kitchen!"

106

This essay on "The Trend Toward Titular Simplicity" appeared in *The American Benedictine Review* XXIII (March, 1972) 150-153.

Five years ago, this writer published an *apologia* for the continued use of the term "Father" by Catholic priests. That treatise endeavored to demonstrate how, in the light of Scripture, theology, liturgy and history, such an appellation retained a marked relevancy for current times.[1]

Perhaps a fair defense, etymologically, could also be made for the retention of descriptive terms as "Cardinal" and "Bishop," since in the visible structure of the People of God, both titles signify *real* rather than *honorary* designations. At the same time, however, such feudal and strictly secular titles as "Eminence" and "Excellency" seem peculiarly out of step in contemporary society.

Present-day ecclesiastical nomenclature is deeply imbedded in church history. Many features of ecclesiastical vocabulary, to say nothing of insignia, ceremonial procedure and ideology, were adapted from the imperial courts of the eleventh and twelfth centuries. Such practices in the secular realm hearken back as far as the Persian paganism of the fourth century before the Christian era.

Canonical recognition of such terminology is of more recent vintage. One authority notes that the title of address for cardinals dates from the early seventeenth century when the Sacred Congregation of Ceremonies under Urban VIII issued, on June 10, 1630, "a decree stating that the titles *eminentia, eminentissime and vestra eminentia*, along with *reverendissime* which was already in use, were from that day forward to be the proper and exclusive titles of the cardinalatial dignity."[2] Over succeeding centuries terms of address for lesser prelates took many different forms. The title "Your Lordship" was adopted in this country from England, where Anglican bishops were members of the House of Lords. "Your Grace" was the title given to dukes.[3] The term "Your Excellency," popular in the United States, is also an adopted title inasmuch as governmental protocol restricts its use to chief executives and certain diplomatic envoys. According to one commentator, that particular terminology avoids "the very definite lowering of the episcopal office that, in the minds of many, was involved in 'Your Lordship' or 'Your Grace.'"[4]

Canonical sanction was given to "Your Excellency" on December 31, 1930, when the Sacred Congregation of Ceremonies attached the form *Excellentiae Reverendissimae* to all patriarchs, nuncios, residential and titular bishops.[5] In one writer's opinion, the Holy See's chief motive for that decree was "so that no less honour may be imputed to her bishops than Mussolini allowed his prefects."[6]

Leo Cardinal Suenens was quoted recently as saying: "Everything which reminds people of the manners of an earlier age, the artificial etiquette of the Courts, certain bourgeois customs and conventions, marks of respect in so far as they are pompous and obsequious – all these now belong to the past."[7] Surely use of titles such as "Eminence" and "Excellency" is one area that has come under increasing criticism in these post-Vatican years by some who feel that those salutations misrepresent their bearers "as members of a privileged social class."[8]

Such universally respected churchmen as the lately retired Archbishop of Montreal believe that "the continuing use of ancient splendor is an obstacle to working for (the poor) in a spirit of the Gospel." Emile Cardinal Leger concedes that this splendor may have been necessary when some bishops held secular authority. In our time, on the contrary, "such display no longer fits into the normal pattern of public life and is out of tune with our spirit."[9]

Admittedly, special titles should be reserved to the hierarchy, sacramentally set apart as they are from the rest of the clergy,[10] but the continued use of an obsolete vocabulary in this regard tends to set up a barrier between them and the laity.[11] Perhaps John Cogley is right with his observation that "all the business of 'His Excellency' and 'His Eminence,' the elaborate vestments and uncomfortable courtesy-customs of another age" have no place in the Pilgrim Church of the 1970's.[12]

In recent years, a keen sensitivity to the inadequacy of Renaissance forms and protocol has resulted in scattered concessions. For some time, in Austria, the titles of "Eminence" for cardinals and "Excellency" for bishops have not been used. Each of the faithful is encouraged to decide for himself how he will address his bishop. Andreas Rohracher of Salzburg is on record as prefering "Father Archbishop."[13]

The trend toward simplicity is evident outside Catholic circles too. In the fall of 1968, the 460 Anglican bishops attending the decennial Lambeth Conference voted to "radically examine the honors paid to them in the course of divine worship, in titles and customary address, and in style of living." Suffragan Bishop Neil Russell of Zanzibar explained the action by asserting that "the picture of bishops as 'princes of the Church' causes public incredulity on their claim to being servants of God."[14]

While an instruction issued by the Papal Secretariat of State, on March 31, 1969, specifically tolerates *(adhiberi poterit)* retention of such titles as "Eminence" and "Excellency,"[15] the obvious tone of the directive indicates the inopportuneness presently associated with that terminology.

The fact is that while a considerable portion of people in the United States "love symbols of prestige and honor,"[16] most American churchmen "feel awkward with fancy titles" and are anxious to put them aside.[17]

Whether or not the priest of technopolis will continue to be called "Father" is an open question. It does seem, however, that ecclesiastics will not be called by less fitting titles much longer. "The sooner we dispose with all that red medieval trimming the clearer our role of service will be."[18] In any event, changes such as those introduced by the Austrian hierarchy are indicative of the trend to simplify those remnants of the past that have lost their meaning, especially those which distort the image of the bishop as a father and shepherd to his flock and a brother to his priests.[19]

Notes to the Text

1. See "The Meaning of the term 'Father' as applied to Catholic Priests," *American Benedictine Review*, 18 (September, 1967), 338-343.
2. Harry G. Hynes, *The Privileges of Cardinals* (Washington, 1945), p. 30.
3. Denver *Register,* February 8, 1931.
4. "Your Excellency," *The Fortnightly Review*, 38 (March, 1931), 61.
5. "Analecta," *American Ecclesiastical Review*, 84 (April, 1931), 388.
6. Yves Congar, O.P., *Power and Poverty in the Church* (Baltimore, 1965), p. 127.
7. Quoted in Richard M. McKeon, S.J., "The Church and Nobility," *Homiletic and Pastoral Review*, 65 (February, 1965), 398.

8. Bernard Haring as quoted in the Chicago *Tribune*, November 23, 1967.

9. Quoted in the *National Catholic Reporter*, May 11, 1966.

10. Joseph P. Kiefer in the Steubenville *Register*, July 29, 1965.

11. Congar, *op.*, *cit.*, p. 139.

12. Cleveland *Catholic Universe Bulletin*, January 5, 1968.

13. *Delmarva Dialog*, November 4, 1966.

14 *Central California Register*, September 5, 1968.

15. *Instructio circa Vestes, Titulos et Insignia Generas Cardinalium, Episcoporum et Praelatorum Ordine Minorum* (Rome, 1969), p. 11.

16. John V. Sheridan, *Our Sunday Visitor*, January 11, 1970.

17. Andrew Greeley, *The Monitor*, October 23, 1969.

18. Edward P. Echlin, S.J., "The Priest in the Secular Age," *Pastoral Life*, 16 (April, 1968), 222.

19. Raymond A. Tartre, S.S.S., *The Postconciliar Priest* (New York, 1966), p. 165.

107

"The Diocesan Workhorse" is the topic for this essay reprinted from *Twin Circle* for April 6, 1973.

In clerical circles, the term "work horse" refers to that flat-profile priest who touches all the bases of service to God's People. His versatility explains how, in his younger days, he came to drift through as many parishes as the Ohio River, pausing just about as long.

An ordinary student in seminary days, he learned much of what he knows from on-the-job training. Though he hasn't waded through all the footnotes of Vatican Council II, he suspects, and rightly so, that they only confirm what has long been his priestly lifestyle.

A tolerable preacher at best, his considerable effectiveness as a speaker derives more from his personal example than from his oratorical abilities.

He rarely attracts the Bishop's attention, except, perhaps, when occupying an adjoining seat at a Confirmation. He's the "used car" of the diocese. Though he likely has a lot of mileage left, the odds are that his frame is bent and his arches weakened by too many hours and too little rest.

A favorite of the Chancellor, his trunks are always packed. There's always a demand for him and he never fails to eagerly respond. He can cover for an ill pastor, substitute for an errant curate or fill in at a busy hospital with equal ease. He is, to modern times, what the strolling player was in Elizabethan days. Instead of a lyre, he packs along a chalice.

He's equally adept at giving vocation talks, conducting teenage retreats, moderating parochial societies and befriending grouchy pastors. Tireless priest that he is, he somehow manages to keep abreast of happenings in earlier assignments. Certain marriages just wouldn't be valid if witnessed by anyone else.

Though not young enough anymore to have all the answers, Father relates well to people of all ages. His outspoken defense of the Pope's teaching authority has not eroded his popularity in the confessional, even among teenagers.

Never too busy to pray, his breviary is hand-stained, his Rosary beads smoothly-worn and his meditation book in threads. His greatest and only anguish is that of not being a better priest. Though he squeezes in the daily holy hour, his spiritual "experiences" have precious little similarity to those he has read about in the lives of the saints.

He seldom takes a full day off, frequently gives away the bulk of his salary and hardly ever finds time for an uninterrupted vacation. Though he probably won't live long enough to enjoy it, he anticipates retirement, but only as a change of titles, not a putting aside of duties. He likes to recall that he was ordained "forever."

The worldly-wise consider him foolish and, by their standards, he surely is. Who else would volunteer to cover a neighbor's sick calls, offer an extra Mass for a vacationing confrere or defend a brother priest in trouble?

What he enjoys most is telling people about God. That's why he was ordained and that's the motivation of his daily life. He hankers for a parish of his own, only because there he could give freer rein to his pastoral enthusiasm.

One senses that such a priest knows more about "commitment" than the most exhaustive surveyor, the most talented theologian and the most gifted writer. After all, he IS the priesthood, this old "work horse" of the diocese.

108

This essay on the Holy Year, entitled "Jubilee rich in historical precedents" is taken from *Twin Circle* for May 10, 1974.

For the sixth and probably last time in this century, a Holy Year has been proclaimed for Roman Catholics by Pope Paul VI. The theme for the 1975 jubilee is "a reconciliation born of true conversion and repentance, a reconciliation of God with man and of man with his fellow man, a reconciliation bearing authentically human, ecclesial and ecumenical dimensions."

In former times, the local observance of the Holy Year took place throughout the Christian world during the 12 months following the celebration at Rome. That process has been reversed for the 26th and latest of the Church's jubilee years. The innovation was explained by the Holy Father as a means of honoring "the local churches, active members as they are of the one and universal Church of Christ."

The 1974-1975 observance is rich in historical precedents. The Christian "jubilee" derives from the ancient Jewish practice of a "sabbath" every seven years, during which there was to be neither sowing nor harvesting. When seven times seven years had passed, a trumpet or "*jobel*" was sounded to usher in the 50th or golden year.

That year was made sacred "by proclaiming liberty in the land for all its inhabitants" (Leviticus 25, 10). The Jewish practice was adopted by the Savior Himself, who announced, in the synagogue at Nazareth, "A year of favor from the Lord" (Luke 4, 19).

The first of the recorded Christian "Holy Years" was proclaimed by Pope Boniface VIII, on Feb. 22, 1300, in the now-famous bull,

Antiquorum fide relatio. Those who journeyed to the Eternal City within the appointed time were promised "great remissions and indulgences for their sins."

So successful was the proto-jubilee, according to Dante Alighieri's *Inferno*, that a strong barrier had to be constructed along the bridge of the Holy Angels, in order to keep the crowds flocking to Saint Peter's from mingling with and obstructing those coming in the opposite direction.

It had been the intention of Boniface to have a Christian jubilee at the beginning of each century. However, Saint Brigid of Sweden and other influential personages appealed to Pope Clement VI for a shortening of the 99 year interim since, as they argued, the average lifespan would not allow everyone to partake of the spiritual privileges attached to the jubilee.

Clement VI acquiesced and, in 1343, decreed that a Holy Year be proclaimed every 50 years, beginning in 1350. The number of pilgrims visiting the Roman shrines during that jubilee reportedly reached a million.

During the pontificate of Boniface IX, two jubilees were celebrated, the first in 1390, and another 10 years later. The earlier observance was largely frequented by peoples from Germany, Hungary, Poland, Bohemia and England, while most of those flocking to the Eternal City, in 1400, came from France.

Pope Martin V announced the fifth Holy Year for 1423, apparently in deference to a decree of 1390, calling for such a celebration every 33 years thereafter, to correspond with the human lifespan of Jesus Christ.

Fortunately, for mathematicians, the quinquagesima practice was restored by Pope Nicholas V, who designed 1450 as a year of thanksgiving for the end of the schism caused by the anti-popes. That jubilee is remembered for the catastrophe that occurred when a panic on the bridge leading to Castle Sant Angelo resulted in 200 pilgrims being trampled to death.

On April 19, 1470, Pope Paul III, "having regard for the shortness of human life," further reduced the interim between celebrations. From 1475, it became customary to observe a Holy Year four times each century.

The concourse of pilgrims coming to Rome, in 1500, is described in the annals as a "magnificent demonstration of the universality of the faith." Though the capacity of the city to house and feed so many visitors from all parts of Europe was severely taxed, Pope Alexander VI spared no efforts to provide for the security and comfort of the pilgrims.

The Holy Year of 1525, called by Pope Clement VII, was notable for the sharp criticisms of Martin Luther on the "Bull of Induction." The onetime Augustinian monks' ties with the Church had been decisively severed on Jan. 3, 1521.

Spiritual Results

It was part of an earnest attempt to bring about reform in the Church that motivated Pope Julius III to announce a Holy Year for 1550. There were discernible spiritual results, not the least of which was a temporary restoration of the Catholic faith in Queen Mary's England.

The innovative Pope Gregory XIII proclaimed the Holy Year for 1575. Pilgrims returning from Rome told about the revision of the Julian Calendar, which the pontiff introduced into most Catholic countries three years later.

The Jubilee of 1600 bore witness to the papacy renewed and updated by the Florentine Pope, Clement VIII. Over one million visitors crammed into the Eternal City for that year of grace.

So much in evidence was the "counter-reformation" during the *Anno Santo* of 1625, that Pope Urban VIII found it necessary, on several occasions, to caution extremists against inciting pilgrims with their inflammatory orations. It was shortly after the conclusion of that jubilee that Pope Urban solemnly dedicated the new Basilica of St. Peter.

Though physically weak and frail, the elderly Pope Innocent X insisted on proclaiming and presiding over the ceremonies for the Holy Year of 1650. Whenever possible, the pontiff personally greeted the pilgrims who jammed the confines of Rome.

The convocation of a jubilee year for 1675 was the most notable accomplishment of Emilio Altieri, who was already an octogenarian by the time of his election to the papacy as Clement X.

Pope Innocent XII died during the Holy Year of 1700, and was succeeded in the Chair of Peter by Clement XI. The newly-elected Vicar of Christ concluded the jubilee with the customary walling-up of the *Porta Santa* in the Vatican Basilica.

During the jubilee of 1725, Pope Benedict XIII discharged personally the duties of Grand Penitentiary and is said to have seriously considered (and happily rejected) the notion of reviving public penances for certain grave offenses.

Scholar Pope

The 18th of the Holy Years was announced and inaugurated by Benedict XIV, "the greatest scholar among the Popes," in 1750. During the months of the celebration, the pontiff called for a renewed interest in and observance of the Gospel message.

Pilgrims gathering for the jubilee of 1775 were greeted by Pope Pius VI who reminded them that personal holiness was to be the hallmark of those publicly demonstrating their commitment to the Nazarene through pilgrimage.

Owing to the Napoleonic Wars and the presence of a French army within the very shadows of the Vatican, the next jubilee was delayed until 1825, when Pope Leo XII designated the 120th of the Holy Years. The response of the Catholic world was enthusiastic, despite the misgivings of certain reactionary prelates and sovereigns.

The omission of the observances for 1850 and 1875 was again due mostly to political disturbances. Gioacchino Pecci, a young seminarian of 15 during the Holy Year of 1825, took an active part in the solemn celebrations at Rome. Then, 75 years later, in the evening of his own pontificate, Pecci, now Leo XIII, christened the present century by announcing a jubilee for 1900.

Pope Leo's proclamation was universally interpreted as the harbinger of better days for the Church. Though still a "prisoner of the Vatican," the venerable pontiff personally visited Saint Peter's and dispatched cardinalatial legates to the other three of Rome's major basilicas, to open the Holy Doors.

In 1913, Pope Pius X called for an "extraordinary" Holy Year of thanksgiving to commemorate the 16th centenary of the Edict of Milan, in which Constantine recognized the rights of Christians to worship in accordance with their consciences.

The 23rd *Anno Santo* was inaugurated by Pope Pius XI, in 1925. On that occasion, the Holy Father also announced his desire to resume the sessions of Vatican Council I with the "greatest international Christian congress...since the foundation of Christianity nearly 2,000 years ago." Eight years later, the same *Pontifex Maximus* called for another Holy Year, this one to "honor with unusual solemnity the 19th centenary of the Passion, and Death of our Divine Lord."

Pope Pius XII designated the Holy Year of 1950, on June 2, 1948, as a period devoted to "the sanctification of souls through prayer and penance." The 25th of the Christian jubilees brought unprecedented throngs of the faithful to the Eternal City.

On May 27, 1949, Msgr. Giovanni Battista Montini explained that the celebration for 1950 was to be looked upon as a "contribution to peace and fraternity." That same prelate lived on to convoke the next jubilee in his own name, as Pope Paul VI.

Christmas Eve

The Holy Father will tap three times at the sealed *Porta Santa* in the Vatican Basilica, on Christmas Eve, 1974, repeating the ancient formula: "Open unto me the gates of justice." At the third blow of the hammer, the door, walled-up for the last quarter century, will open, to signal the formal inauguration of the Church's 26th Holy Year.

Through that portal, and the similar doors in the other major basilicas, will pass hundreds of thousands of pilgrims in pursuit of the interior revival, which Pope Paul VI envisions will occur through reflection, prayer, penance, pilgrimages and the exercises common to the Holy Year festivities.

109

This essay "What's Right with America" appeared in the Ventura *Star Free Press* for July 11, 1975.

Catholics have every right to be proud of the American Republic as it enters the third century of its independent sovereignty. Indeed, those who would attack or belittle the American governmental process might do well to try the latest edition of the Statistical Abstract.

The median family income for Americans is now $12,000. Over 90 percent of the nation's inhabitants possess telephones. 80 percent have at least one car and more than 60 percent own their own homes. Oh yes, there's still poverty in the United States, but far less than ever before. In 1966, 15 percent of all Americans were officially classified as poor. That number has been reduced a third in just eight years.

The productivity of American industrial workers more than doubles that of their Russian counterparts and, in the area of agriculture, the figures are nine-to-one. Americans spend only 18 percent of their income for food, as opposed to the 30 percent required in England, 40 percent in Iron Curtain countries and 60 percent in the underdeveloped nations.

Taxes, of course, are high and irksome in the United States. Yet the total tax burden, and that includes income, sales and property, is only 28 percent per capita or the second lowest figure among the 13 leading industrial countries. And, in four of those nations, the tax rate soars beyond 40 percent!

Roughly 52 percent of all Americans 25 years and older have completed high school and 12 percent have finished college. Those figures are

697

indeed impressive when contrasted to 25 percent and 5 percent in 1940. More than a quarter of the nation's eligible young people are enrolled in college and two-thirds of that number come from families where neither parents has a college diploma.

American generosity continues apace, too. In 1974, a year of economic uncertainty and financial reverses, they contributed a record $24.5 billion to charity and that averages out to $120 for every man, woman and child.

The tremendous advancement of minority peoples in the United States is mirrored in the achievements scored by blacks. Within the last eight years, enrollment of blacks in college has increased by 80 percent.

In the past decade alone the number of blacks in professional and technical positions has grown by a whopping 128 percent, while the number of black managers, officials and proprietors has nearly doubled.

Black candidates elected to public trusts has soared by 152 percent in the last five years. There are now 26 black mayors and two black lieutenant governors. The Alabama State Legislature, formerly a bastion of Southern conservatism, now has 15 black members on its roster.

Forty percent of black families own their own home. The total income of black Americans has grown to $52 billion, a figure which outdistances the gross national product of all but nine countries in the world!

The expanded political clout of women is another gauge of America's continued growing-pains. Medical schools report female enrollees have doubled in just three years.

The recent elections resulted in a number of "firsts" for women at all levels of public service, including the first woman chief justice of a State Supreme Court, the first woman secretary of state and the first woman lieutenant governor.

The number of women in state legislatures rose by 19 percent in 1972, and by an additional 26 percent in 1974. Women last year were elected governor of Connecticut and mayor of San Jose.

There have also been landmark advances in the ecological sphere. Big business has voluntarily set aside massive funds for the commonwealth. The American steel industry, by way of example, now purifies more water every day than do the combined cities of New York, Los Angeles and Chicago.

The Environmental Protection Agency reports that smog concentrations are beginning to decrease. Sulphur dioxide levels have dropped in some areas by as much as 50 percent. The Fish and Wildlife Service recently announced increasing populations of many bird species in re-forested areas. Commercial fishermen last year removed 40 million pounds from the lately declared "dead" Lake Erie. New York newspapers proclaim that the Hudson River is cleaner now than in any time during the last 50 years.

Imperfections and inequities there must always be in any human society. Yet no system of government ever devised moves faster to eradicate its own inadequacies than that to which American Catholics proudly pledge their allegiance.

Happy birthday, Uncle Sam!

110

"A Farewell to Pope Paul" is the topic of this essay reprinted from *The Tidings*, August 11, 1978.

The long and difficult earthly sojourn of Pope Paul VI reached its full term on the Feast of the Transfiguration, in this year of Our Lord, 1978.

Looking back on this fifteen year pontificate, one is impressed by the similarity of his missionary journeys to those of the first Christian to bear his name, the great apostle to the gentiles, Paul of Tarsus.

Paul VI began his pontificate with a Pilgrimage to Jerusalem, where it all began for Christians. Then he visited the United Nations to dramatize the Church's concern for and involvement in programs for a better world. His subsequent journeys to Bombay, Fatima, Istanbul, Latin America, Africa and Australia were all undertaken for equally lofty motives.

Paul's visit to Geneva was of special significance for in that historical center of Protestantism he bore brave witness to his own office as Vicar of Christ, while expressing affection for those whom he honored with his presence.

The ecumenically-minded Pope felt it necessary to recall that Our Lord had placed Peter over the other apostles by instituting, in the person of Peter's successors, a permanent and visible foundation of unity, faith and communion. Thus motivated, the pontiff greeted the Protestant leaders at Geneva with the affirmation: "My name is Peter!"

History testifies that through the centuries Peter has presided over the People of God through his primatial successors. This he has done in virtue of Christ's memorable words: "Thou art Peter and upon this rock I will build My Church and the gates of hell shall not prevail against it. And I will give to thee the keys to the kingdom of heaven."

Peter was the cornerstone of that most wonderful institution the world knows as the Catholic Church. Succeeding vicars of Christ have given eloquent witness to the concern of Almighty God for His people and their spiritual needs.

For the primacy, Christ passed over John, His beloved disciple, James, His natural cousin and Paul, His most erudite follower. In selecting Peter as the Prince of the Apostles, His Vicar on earth, Our Lord clearly indicated that neither friendship, relationship nor learning were essential to the foundation of His church.

Primacy doesn't depend on a Pope's personal talents or virtues, but solely on the mandate of Christ, sustained by the Holy Spirit.

Peter's role as head of the Church is abundantly recorded in Holy Scripture. He functioned as Vicar of Christ, for example, when he called for the replacement of Judas, performed the first miracle, preached in the name of all the apostles, excommunicated the first heretic, presided at the Council of Jerusalem, visited the religious communities of Palestine and received the first pagan convert.

The passing of Paul VI gives the Christian family an opportunity for expressing its gratitude to Christ for the divine institution of the papacy.

None among the 263 successors of Peter has worn the tiara during more troublesome times than the good and gentle man whom we will remember in history as Paul VI.

He it was who took up the unfinished agenda of Vatican Council II and brought it to completion. And then, with painstaking dedication, he saw to it that every one of its directives was promulgated and implemented.

Forever the period between 1963 and 1978 will be known as the Pauline years. How good it was of God to send us a man of such holiness and zeal. A grateful people now implores for his happy repose.

The Pope is dead–long live the Pope! A vital chapter of ecclesial history is completed and another about to unfold. May the Lord provide for us as generously in the years ahead as he has in those just finished.

111

This essay on "The Life of John Paul" is here reprinted from *The Tidings*, October 6, 1978.

Today, we rejoice in the glories of the resurrection. Almighty God has called to Himself not alone His vicar here on earth, but one who typifies what Saint Catherine of Siena meant when she referred to the Holy Father as "the sweet Christ of this earth."

In the short but eventful days that Albino Luciani governed the People of God as Pope John Paul I, the bark of Peter felt a new but steady hand on the tiller.

And then, with the suddenness of a giant wave breaking on the stern of a ship, this 263rd chapter in the Life of the Church was abruptly terminated. Once again the flock is bereft of its shepherd.

That beautifully-contagious smile which the world so quickly came to know and love is forever frozen into the cold and impersonal annals of humankind.

God's plans for His people are not subject to committee hearings or public discussions. Often He finds it expedient to refocus world attention on the climactic part of Jesus' life–the pinnacle towards which everything led–Mount Calvary.

Death is the culmination of every life. Were it not so, there would be no point to living. With the death of Jesus, the world began anew.

So must it be with all Christians, especially that one known as the Vicar of Christ. It is a lesson underscored by Albino Luciani himself when, in his younger days, he recalled the advice of Socrates: "Ask not that you live long, but that you live well."

Seizing and utilizing the opportunities of life, however long or short, is the only adequate response that one committed to the resurrection promise can maintain in the face of death's mystery.

This Pope John Paul did in a most remarkable fashion. He needed only thirty-four days to imprint onto the universal consciousness the beauty, happiness and contentment of a truly Christian lifestyle.

With him the role of a follower of Christ took on a whole new image. His life was a public demonstration of the joys of faith, the consolations of hope and the radiance of charity.

Leonardo da Vinci surely had the likes of John Paul in mind when he noted that "just as well-filled days give joy to sleep, so too does a well-spent life give joy to death. For one who uses life well, death seems spontaneously, without the least pretense, to come not as the destruction, but as the fulfillment of life."

Historians will not remember John Paul for what he did, but for what he was–a kindly, open and radiant pastoral shepherd of souls who looked upon the Christian world as one gigantic parish.

After consigning the human remains of the Holy Father to the ground whence they came, we dispatch the cardinals back to their drawing boards in Michelangelo's Sistine Chapel with a commission to provide us with a new shepherd, in the mould of John Paul.

The orphanhood that fell upon the Catholic world last Friday morning is only a transitory cross. Just a century ago, when the great Pio Nono was called to his eternal reward, one of the great pioneers of the California Church said: "Fear not, Peter will live in his successors; Peter will speak forever from his chair."

112

This eye-witness account of the opening of Vatican Council II, entitled *"Tempora Mutantur et Nos Mutamur in Illis,"* was written for *The Evangelist* XXV (Fall, 1962), 14-15, 25.

A General Council of the Church is a noble theme for any historian, for it offers many attractions–important matters of universal interest long, widely and anxiously discussed; numerous mature and experienced men, often of the highest personal distinction, owing their positions to acknowledged merits; representatives of an intensely religious culture and of many races, nations and languages, detached from selfish pursuits, the nearest attainable substitute for a High Court or Senate of Mankind. Of such great Catholic assemblies of bishops there have been twenty in nearly two thousand years, always convened with extraordinary effort and affecting in some permanent way the general Catholic life.

This brief commentary is couched in references to the past, for in many ways an historian lives in the past and his opinions and thoughts are often colored, if not influenced altogether, by a healthy respect for tradition, coupled with a realization that time moves always ahead, never backward.

There was certainly much of the past evident in Rome on the 11th of October, 1962 – but much more of the present. Gone was the thunder of cannon on the Aventine which greeted the 744 prelates at the First Vatican Council. Also missing were the papal states, once thought an integral part of Church machinery. Rome itself had suffered a transformation beyond that of any other ancient center in Christendom. And yet, as the bells of the city's churches pealed forth, Rome seemed to possess that mysterious continuity which no disaster, not even the lapse of time, can interrupt or change or diminish.

From early morning, the six tribunes behind the tiers of episcopal thrones had been filled with theologians and canonists and a few fortunate observers. At precisely eight thirty the throngs outside the Vatican Basilica glimpsed the first of the solemn procession as it moved slowly down the Scala Regia, through the Portone di Bronzo, onto the vast square of Saint Peter's. In front walked the Sistine choir, followed by generals of religious orders, abbots, bishops, archbishops, metropolitans, patriarchs and cardinals, arrayed in shining silver copes and white linen mitres. Finally came the eighty-one-year-old pontiff, John XXIII, led down the Bernini staircase from the Sistine Chapel by his attendants and surrounded by the picturesque Swiss guards.

When the Pope, vested in radiant white silver garments arrived at the papal altar, he intoned the *Veni Creator Spiritus* and the ancient hymn of Urbanus Maurus was instantly taken up by the assembled prelates. On the altar, the four Gospels were opened, in keeping with the custom at all great synods from the earliest times.

In 1962 the governing body of the Church is far larger numerically than it was only ninety-two years ago and alignment of its members greatly differs from that of 1869. Roughly 37 percent of the Fathers at the Council represent Europe (whose total Catholic population is 210,000,000), about 33 percent represent the Americas (with a total Catholic population of 220,000,000), more than 11 percent came from Africa, and 8 percent from Asia and Oceania. Hence it can be seen that the center of influence is shifting from the European world, a factor which is due not only to the notable increase in representation at the Council but also to the composition of that representation. The last century has witnessed an unprecedented expansion of the Church in English-speaking countries as well as the newly emerging nations of Africa, all of which has brought with it, in the words of President Kennedy, "staggering problems which, from the human point of view, seem at times to be almost insoluble." And yet, as our first Catholic chief-of-state continues, "it is very heartening to know that the Council, in the words of Your Holiness, will strive to deepen the fellowship and love which are 'the natural needs of man' and 'are imposed on the Christian as rules for his relationship between man and man, and between people and people.'"

The First Vatican Council was held in the right transept of Saint Peter's where tiers of thrones had converted the 16th century basilica into a giant *aula concilians*. Elaborately surrounded with bright red carpets, gold brocades and pictures, the bishops formed eight rows along the two sides of the council hall. The papal throne was situated in the apse and the cardinals and patriarchs sat in a large semicircle on either side of the venerable Pius IX. A raised tribune was reserved for temporal princes and was occupied by such royal personages as the Grand Dukes of Tuscany and Parma.

Necessity demanded that the Second Vatican Council be held in a larger chamber. Hence seats were erected down the entire length of the basilica's nave, over 328 feet. The enclosure stops short of the canopied altar of the confessional which stands in the junction of nave and transepts, forming the basilica's giant Latin cross. An aisle eighteen feet wide separates the tiers of seats which face inward along each side of the aisle. All members with a deliberative vote have a seat, a desk and a prie-dieu.

The papal throne backs up to the confessional facing the entrance of the church and on the Pope's left are tables for the general secretariat. A pulpit to the right of the throne is used by those who address the assembly. Near the fully-vested statue of Saint Peter is a movable altar which is wheeled into place for Holy Mass.

Historically speaking, the opening of the Second Vatican Council is the culmination of plans begun forty years ago, for it was in an encyclical letter of December 23, 1922 that Pope Pius XI first set forth his hopes for re-convening the First Vatican Council which was never able to carry out its planned activities because of the unsettled political condition of Europe. Pius XI apparently wanted a Council from his earliest days as supreme pontiff but, as he said, he never received the "manifest sign" for actually summoning the world's hierarchy into session. Pius XI's Council would have completed action on the projected schemata of the earlier Council and would have devoted much of its attention to the subjects of unity and catholicity. The industrious pontiff even worked out a doctoral Program "which, in its teachings on the Church, the Pope, and the episcopate, continues that of the Vatican Council, and, in the Church's moral and social teaching, the subsequent papal pronouncements."

Soon after Achille Ratti's death in 1939, Msgr. Ernesto Ruffini, later the Cardinal Archbishop of Palermo, suggested that Pope Pius XII summon a Council to meet the radical changes in social conditions brought on by the advance of science and the need for re-emphasizing the religious and ethical principles of the 20th century. Apparently the plea had some effect on the pontiff, for Cardinal Tardini mentions in his memoirs that Pius XII had made preparations for an Ecumenical Council "at which, according with his instructions, a select group of ecclesiastics were working for several years."

Nonetheless, it remained for John XXIII to officially proclaim "the Ecumenical Council in obedience to an inspiration which we felt given in the humility of our heart as a sudden, unexpected motion…" the spontaneous flowering of an unexpected spring." Thus, for the second time in history, a General Council of the Church had been summoned by a John XXIII. The earlier Council had been called in 1414 by the pseudo-pope, an action subsequently validated when the two other papal claimants endorsed the proposal.

The Second Vatican Council will not be "a magic and immediate remedy" for all the problems facing the Church according to Giovanni Cardinal Montini, Archbishop of Milan. "We must guard against two illusions which could become disappointments for the future," he explains. To expect "the Council will decree radical and bewildering reforms in the present rules of the Church, to the extent of changing its century-old features and turning it into a completely new institution" would be no less wrong than hoping it "will remedy all defects, imperfections, and abuses which we find today in Catholic life."

As a matter of fact, the First Vatican Council only produced two constitutions, both of them doctrinal in content, after seven long months of labor. But with the greater preparation given to this Council, perhaps a larger volume of work can be expected. In any event, the Church is certainly in a transitional period. And as this author recently watched the precedent-shaking departure of the Pope on the Italian Government's presidential train for Loreto and Assisi, he could hardly deny that the Holy Father is leading the Church into a new era where tradition is the theory and progress is the practice.

Whatever be the Council's outcome, Pope John XXIII has long ago adopted the attitude of John Henry Newman, "nothing would be done at all, if a man waited till he could do it so well that no one could find fault with it."

113

This essay about Rabbi Eugenio Zolli's "Witness for Pius XII" is here taken from *The American Benedictine Review* XXVI (June, 1975), 227-230.

History rarely stays written. Scientific discoveries, new testimonies and fresh interpretations demand a constant updating of the human chronicle. Especially is that true for events less than a century old. Such vital evidence as personal memoirs, private correspondence, sealed archives and lost or misplaced records are often accessible only after the passage of several generations.

The relationship of Pope Pius XII to the persecuted Jewish Peoples of World War II is a case at hand. As the years roll on, the Holy Father's role becomes more clearly delineated. And time certainly seems to be favoring the Pontiff.

For one reason or another, the testimony of Eugenio Zolli (1881-1956), a crucial participant of the Jewish struggle for survival, has gone unnoticed. A native of Brody, in Austrian Gallicia, Israel Zoller rose to prominence early in life as an expert in Semitic languages and practices. At the time of his appointment as Chief Rabbi of Trieste, in 1914, he changed his familial name to Zolli.

This writer recalls that Dr. Zolli addressed the faculty and students at St. John's Seminary, in Camarillo, California, in the fall of 1953. The former Chief-Rabbi of Rome spoke extensively about the extraordinary efforts of Pope Pius XII for the Jewish inhabitants of Rome. Unfortunately, no transcript of that talk can be unearthed.

A little research confirmed that Zolli had journeyed to the United States as a Fulbright Award Scholar. He had conducted a Literary

Institute at Notre Dame University before coming to California's south-land as a consultant for a film script by the late John Farrow.

Aside from a brief and inconsequential interview in *The Tidings*, the official Catholic newspaper for the Archdiocese of Los Angeles, there is no further indication as to the tenor of Dr. Zolli's remarks at Camarillo.

Though this writer had some vague recollections of seeing and/or hearing about a published volume of Zolli's memoirs, it was only recently that a copy of this elusive book was located. Published by Sheed and Ward in 1954, *Before the Dawn* proved to be a charmingly-written series of autobiographical reflections. Certainly the contents of that volume must be entered as "evidence" in any fair and balanced portrayal of the Holy Father's concern for and aid to the persecuted Jewish populace.

Zolli's appointment as Chief-Rabbi of Rome came in 1940, not long after Eugenio Cardinal Pacelli's accession to the See of Peter as Pope Pius XII. Zolli recalled the Pontiff in moving terms and in one part of his book he reproduced the words of the "unique, serene and wise" Pius XII after the hostilities of World War II had begun: "The legitimate and just love towards one's own country must not close the eyes to the universali-ty of Christian charity which also considers others and their prosperity in the pacifying light of love!"

One can glean from Rabbi Zolli's reflections that when the German Army occupied the Eternal City, in September, 1943, he had vainly advised the Jewish community to disperse for reasons of safety. Zolli based that recommendation on his conviction that "the people of Rome…had intense pity for the Jews." He felt that "they would willingly have assisted in the evacuation of the Jewish population into remote vil-lages, where they would have been concealed and protected by Christian families" (p. 140). Apparently few if any of the Jews followed their spiri-tual leader's advice, and he himself felt constrained to remain with his beleaguered flock.

Rome's Chief Rabbi recalled how Pope Pius XII had "sent by hand a letter to the bishops instructing them to lift the enclosure from convents and monasteries, so that they could become refuges for the Jews." He went on to describe one convent where the Sisters slept in the basement, giving up their beds to the hunted Jews.

Zolli told of another haven, "the attic of one of the great churches in the center of Rome," which had been divided "into many sections, each bearing the name of the saint in whose honor the altar below" was dedi-cated. The refugees there were divided for the distribution of food into groups according to the names of the saints. The Rabbi further explained that practically all the schools, administrative offices, churches and con-vents of Rome had their "guests" (p. 188). To Zolli, there was no place of suffering where the spirit of the Holy Father had not penetrated. He reckoned that "volumes could be written on the multiform works of suc-cour of Pius XII" (p. 186).

Once, when his own financial resources had been completely exhaust-ed, the Rabbi approached the Vatican Secretary of State, Luigi Cardinal Maglione, for assistance. While acknowledging to His Eminence that "the Vatican had already spent millions in aiding fugitive Jews to reach safety," he pleaded that the New Testament "not abandon the Old." Zolli described how the cardinal hastily left the room and then, a few minutes later returned, after speaking directly with the Holy Father. The Chief-Rabbi of Rome was directed to come back shortly before one o'clock, when all the offices would be deserted. Two or three members of the lay staff would be waiting with a package of money!

Zolli concluded his portrayal of benefactions showered upon the Jewish people by every sector of Catholic Rome with the observation that "no hero in history has commanded such an army; none is more mil-itant, more fought against, none more heroic than that conducted by Pius XII in the name of Christian charity."

Those who might denigrate Zolli's testimony in light of his subsequent conversion to Catholicism will be interested in the former Rabbi's specif-ic observation on that point: "I do not hesitate to give a negative answer to the question whether I was converted in gratitude to Pius XII for his numberless acts of charity." He went on to say, however, that "I do feel the duty of rendering homage and of affirming that charity of the Gospel was the light that showed the way to my old and weary heart. It is the charity that so often shines in the history of the Church and which radi-ated fully in the actions of the reigning Pontiff".

In his final years, Dr. Zolli served as librarian and professor at the Pontifical Biblical Institute. The esteem in which he was held in ecclesial circles is indicated in a letter to James Francis Cardinal McIntyre. Therein Msgr. Giovanni Montini (presently Pope Paul VI) described the noted convert as "a devout Catholic of high repute."

Eugenio Zolli has provided what must be considered a weighty and convincing "intervention" for the record of Pope Pius XII and the Jews which he concludes in these words:

Many are the books by statisticians, generals, journalists, and many are the memoirs of individuals concerning this great war. The archives hold quantities of material for future historians. But who, outside of God in heaven, has gathered into his heart the sorrows and the groans of all the injured? Like a watchful sentinel before the sacred inheritance of human pain stands the angelic Pastor, Pius XII. He has seen the abyss of misfortune towards which humanity is advancing. He has measured and foretold the greatness of the tragedy. He has made himself the herald of the serene voice of justice and the defender of true peace. He took into his heart the pain of all the sufferers. He bent over the sorrow of all, and today he stands erect before the whole world saying, "The way you chose was not the just way. The true way is that which leads from the Gospel to Jesus. The good way is marked by a simple and clear word: from the Gospel, with Christ, towards the Kingdom of God" (p. 189).

114

"At the Feet of History" was an essay outlining the philosophy of history. It appeared in the *Homiletic and Pastoral Review* LXX (February, 1970).

Possibly nothing poses a greater threat to the survival of a free Western society than the increasing neglect of historical training in the curricular structure of contemporary universities and Colleges. Such a turn of events is all the more unfortunate since it is no less true today than it was when Cicero first pointed it out, that the very purpose of history is to explain the present, and to enable us to make intelligent judgment on the shaping of the future. Certainly "the higher man rides on the shoulders of the past, the more likelihood that his perspective of the present will be clear."[1]

Inasmuch as history must be defined in terms of men, their origin, life and destiny, those looking for a meaning and purpose in human activity must eventually conclude, as did Pierre Teilhard de Chardin, that "everything is the sum of the past and that nothing is comprehensible except through its history."[2] To the patient observer, the chronicle of man, far from being a chamber of horrors, becomes "a celestial city, a spacious country of the mind, wherein a thousand saints, statesmen, inventors, scientists, poets, artists, musicians, lovers, and philosophers still live and speak, teach and carve and sing."[3]

Studying human traditions carries a special significance for Christians since religion and history have always been closely united, almost as the soul and body; history representing the social framework of things and religion that special divine providence which has permeated human relationships from the very beginning. Those who wall themselves up within the contemporary milieu by severing the umbilical link of their religious heritage, open a breach which could (and very probably does) "account for that spiritual amnesia which, it is said, afflicts a generation suffering a cultural and spiritual identity crisis."[4] How many persons thus affected will ultimately repeat George Bancroft's observation: "It is when the hour of conflict is over that history comes to a right understanding of the strife and is ready to exclaim: Lo! God was here and we knew it not."[5]

If the Christian epic, a fascinating and integral part of history, could be written from an eternal perspective, thought Carlyle, it would be the one supreme chronicle, for it is, in design, the Bible itself continued. Whether it be the study of missionary endeavors, doctrine, magisterial teaching, forms of worship, discipline, public morality or day-to-day administration, the honest and sincere Christian, recognizing and taking account of the necessary human element, will love the Church's past, meditate on its history and explore the ramifications of its impact on the society in which it functions.[6]

The post-conciliar emphasis on "involvement" strengthens the characteristic dictum of ecclesial historians that all research that does not lead ultimately to a greater knowledge of the Divine Plan has lost its true purpose. In that vein, the Jesuit Cardinal, Jean Danielou, has noted:

> I love that Church which plunges into the thickets of human history and is not afraid of compromising itself by getting mixed up with men's affairs, with their political conflicts and their cultural disputes. I love that Church because it loves men and therefore goes out to look for them wherever they are. And I love best of all that Church which is mud-splashed from history because it has played its part in history, that Church of the poor which is denounced for its weakness by pharisees whose hands are clean but who can point to no single person they have saved.[7]

Foremost among the qualities one instinctively expects to adorn ecclesiastical historians are: accuracy in details, references, and quotations, along with objectivity in their presentation. Though "every man has a right to an opinion," Bernard Baruch pointed out that "no man has a right to be wrong in his facts." Accuracy, both in fact and transmission, must be a veritable personality trait of ecclesial historians. No amount of verbiage, no flights of brilliant oratory, no fascinating description, will compensate for the lack of accuracy and completeness in the presentation of the facts of history.

Lacking as they do the apologetical purpose of theologians, the Church's historians approach their work with the basic assumption that the growth of knowledge cannot in the long run be detrimental to religion. If they be intellectually honest men, they are "bound to be unbiased, objective, and sympathetic."[8] They are generally the first to acknowledge that "whenever people bury real history under the ornament of legend, fables take the place of truth–fables which elicit a smile from adult and reasonable people."[9] While carefully preserving an atmosphere of freedom, ecclesial historians exhaust all measures to insure against being consciously or unconsciously affected by accidental or environmental nuances. Once assured of an objective viewpoint, they are able to understand the difference between a picture and its frame.

By virtue of the intimate relationship between religion and history, the knowledge of the past has always been regarded as a peculiar appendage of the priest. That a theologian should be well-versed in history is shown by the fate of those, who, through ignorance of history, have fallen into error. Melchior Cano reasoned further that "theologians not expert in church history do not deserve the name theologians."

The awareness of and appreciation for the ecclesiastical heritage is, and has been, surprisingly widespread outside the fold according to the testimony of Friedrich von Schlegel, who regarded the Catholic Church as the greatest historical authority on earth. The German convert-philosopher explained his views by recalling that "from her seat on the seven hills she has watched the development of history of the past nineteen centuries; she has seen the rise and fall of nations and has lived as an eyewitness to record their deeds. Rome alone understands their history and writes their epitaph…"

Perhaps the Achilles heel of modern theology is its apparent fixation that history doesn't really count for much. If there was an element of weakness, for example, in Vatican Council II it stemmed from the fact that history was given short shrift by the Fathers. Pope Paul VI scored this when he noted that "it would be wrong to think that the Council represents a severance, a break–or as some believe, a liberation–from the traditional teachings of the Church… We must not sever the teachings of the Council from the doctrinal heritage of the Church." Quite logically, then, it follows that he who wants to be a good theologian, can never know Church history too well.

The relevancy of history in general and ecclesiastical history in particular, especially in a Western tradition preoccupied with the culture of science and overshadowed by the spectre of annihilation, is a question of concern. Obviously it can no longer be maintained, if indeed it ever was, that "history maketh a young man to be old, without either wrinkles or gray hairs; privileging him with the experience of age, without the infirmities or inconvenience thereof."[10]

The indisputable fact does remain, however, that learned men have always accorded a place of eminence to historical investigations. To them this study is one of the indispensable experiences of a balanced education. Among its multitudinous advantages they would regard history as contributing to the understanding of social progress; recognizing the individuality and personality of every man; uncovering the patterns and irregularities of past events, allowing for the inevitability of change and growth in human behavior; providing coveted antidotes of perspective; accounting for the frequently baffling contrasts between past, present and future; serving as a bridge between other disciplines; liberalizing the mind by deepening sympathies and fortifying the will and, finally, enriching the intellect through the cultivation of reading tastes.

The study of ecclesiastical history offers even further remunerations. Those immersed in the field agree that nothing is "more effective than the study of Church History in nourishing, sharpening and bringing to maturity the power and capacity of thinking with the Church."[11] One outstanding scholar rightly felt that

> Its influence on the theologian is great, as a man, a Christian, a student, a priest. As a man, he learns from it that the Church he serves has ever been the friend and uplifter of humanity, and has stood as a wall of brass against oppression and injustice: that slavery and barbarism have withered before its tread, and that Caesaro-papism and blighting Islam have been warded off by it alone from our Western society.
>
> As a Christian, he learns a broader, more discriminating charity from the sight of so much human weakness, so much discrepancy between graces and deeds, office and conduct, the "fair outside and foul within." He learns the almost irresistible power of circumstances, early training, climate, topography, prejudices, inherited trend of thought and character. As a student, his judgment may be trained to a quasi-mathematical precision by acute observation, his mental vision may be so sharpened by practice as to discover shadows and outline, and motion and life in what seems deep night to ordinary men "the dark backward and abysm of time."[12]

The annals clearly reveal, even among those not personally attracted to Christ or his teachings, that for nearly twenty centuries "the Catholic Church has been loved and hated, praised and reviled, but it has rarely been ignored."[13]

Far from subscribing to the antinomian view which portrays the chronicle of man as "just one damned thing after another," the "updated" ecclesial historian, professionally trained or not, sees the past, present and future ambivalently blended into orderly patterns of human behavior. To him, as perhaps to few others, the almost endless procession of years, decades and centuries forms a gigantic montage wherein the procession of God's people moves ever closer to that ultimate objective which alone gives purpose to human existence.

Notes to the Text

1. Paul J. Hallinan, "The American Bishops and the Vatican Councils," *Catholic Historical Review* LI (October, 1965), 380.
2. *The Future of Man* (New York, 1964), p. 12.
3. Will and Auriel Durant *The Lessons of History* (New York, 1968), p. 102.
4. *The Church in Our Day* (Washington, 1968), p. 11.
5. Quoted in "The Seminarians' Interest in Church History." *St. Meinrad Historical Essays* II (March, 1932) 200.
6. Henri de Lubac, S.J., *The Catholic and His Church* (New York, 1956), p. 17.
7. J. R. Kirwan (Trans. and Ed.), *Prayer as a Political Problem* (New York, 1967), p. 55.
8. Leonard Swidler, "The Catholic Historian and Freedom," *American Benedictine Review* XVII (June, 1966), 133.
9. H.W. Van der Vaart Smit, *Born in Bethlehem* (Baltimore, 1963), p. 80.
10. Thomas Fuller, "Epistle Dedications," *The Historie of Holy Warre* (Cambridge, 1639), pp. ii-iii.
11. Pius XII as quoted in "The Pontifical Gregorian University, October 17, 1953," *Irish Ecclesiastical Record* LXXXIV (August, 1955), 129.
12. Thomas J. Shahan as quoted in Peter K. Guilday, "The American Catholic Historical Tradition," *Catholic Mind* XVIII (June 22, 1920), 230.
13. John Tracy Ellis, *Church History and the Seminarian* (Saint Meinrad, 1961), p. 2.

115

This essay about the Archdiocese of Los Angeles was written for a brochure which was first distributed in 1991.

Though already launched toward its tricentennial, there is still something fresh and exciting about the one-time *Pueblo de Nuestra Señora de los Angeles*. The story of its progress, from Hispanic colonial foundation to international center for learning, art and commerce is as much a work of imagination as it is of history.

Historians and others maintain that more than any other major city, Los Angeles has achieved its unique place in human annals because a handful of pioneers – from the Kings of Spain to the barons of land, rail and industry – dreamt and decreed that it would be so, and because thousands of others, working people from Sonora and Indiana, Shanghai and Odessa, bought and built accordingly.

Los Angeles is not perched aside the confluence of major waterways or along a vital commercial route; it is not blessed with a great natural harbor or outstanding physical location; neither was it built atop some ancient center of human habitation or upon a pre-existing religious cult. About all the city ever had and continues to have is an unequalled place in human imagination. But, alas, that's what really counts when all the chips are down.

If New York is identified on bumper stickers as the "Big Apple," and Chicago as "gangsters gulch," then Los Angeles must surely be the city of the giant dream, the grand illusion and the hard reality.

Unimpressed by its own past and certainly not intimidated by that of its sister cities, *El Pueblo de Nuestra Señora de los Angeles* is a place where everyone is entitled to a second, even a third chance.

Angelenos have never measured the cost nor considered the contradictions of their accomplishments. Their quest for water, to cite an outstanding example, is a monumental feat of human ingenuity and skill.

Or, again, when pressing demands of new immigrants and the financial interest of aggressive developers converged in postwar Los Angles, the San Fernando and San Gabriel valleys blossomed forth with suburban housing tracts that defied demographers around the globe.

Probably no community in all of recorded history managed to house so many of its working-class and middle-income people so well, while continuing to provide them with amenities usually associated only with the wealthy. For the thousands who continue to pour into the area annually, Los Angeles is the community that invented itself. It remains the city of exceptions and exceptional "dreamers."

And why not? After all, was it not the "Dreamers of God" who began it all for *El Pueblo de Nuestra Señora de los Angeles?*

Even those outside her fold must accord the Catholic Church a special "historical pre-eminence" in discussions about the earliest days of Los Angeles.

The "Catholic presence" in the area now comprising the City of Los Angeles actually pre-dates the city by a dozen years. The very name derives from the diary of Fray Juan Crespi, who introduced the Feast of the *Portiuncula* into California's vocabulary.

And it was a group of Catholics, most of them predominantly Negro in racial strain, who effected the actual foundation of *El Pueblo de Nuestra Señora de los Angeles*, in the fall of 1781.

Fray Junípero Serra, the *Presidente* of the California Missions, first walked the dusty pathways of the *pueblo* the following year. Interestingly enough, he and his Franciscan companions initially objected to the establishment, feeling that premature Spanish towns would infringe upon the Indian and mission prerogatives. And they did!

In any event, despite the reservations of the friars, the *pueblo* has borne, from the very outset, the unmistakable seraphic imprint of those dedicated pioneers who came to share their religion and civilization with an aboriginal people.

Los Angeles continued for some years to be a "Catholic" enclave, with most of its inhabitants worshipping, at least sporadically, at the Old Plaza Church. Oh, that's not to say that the *pueblo* was, by any means, a virtuous city. Unfortunately, the Catholic Church has always been blessed (or cursed) with more than its share of renegades.

On January 17, 1837, just a year and a half after Los Angeles had been raised to the status of a city, the *ayuntamiento* or council passed, without a dissenting voice, a resolution declaring that "the Roman Catholic apostolic religion shall prevail throughout this jurisdiction."

While there is no evidence that this expressed but never enforced "establishment of religion" benefitted Catholics, it did provide adherents with a unique distinction in Western Americana's historical annals.

Plans were unveiled to open a Catholic school in the city in 1849 and two years later the institution opened its doors with twenty-six "scholars." Bishop Joseph Sadoc Alemany entrusted the administration of the school to the Picpus Fathers.

As late as 1853, Harris Newmark said that "nearly all the population was Catholic." Another credible authority noted that "up to 1854, the only organization in Los Angeles upholding any standard of morality whatever was the Roman Catholic Church. It erected houses of worship, hospitals and schools; it was the pioneer of all good works."

And while it all changed following the onrush of the gold seekers, Los Angeles continued through the decades to be a unique haven for religious-minded peoples of all creeds.

In a survey of local history published in 1967, Christopher Rand observed that "there are probably more religions in Los Angeles than in the whole previous history of mankind." And it all started with the Catholic Church, in 1781.

The geographical derivation of the 8762 square miles presently comprising the Archdiocese of Los Angeles can be traced to April 27, 1840, when Pope Gregory XVI created the parent jurisdiction from the already-established See of Sonora.

Boundaries for the gigantic Diocese of Both Californias were the Colorado River in the east, the 42nd degree of north latitude (Oregon line), the Pacific Ocean in the west and all of Baja California. The title was officially changed to Monterey in 1849.

The subsequent transfer of sovereignty in California made a further delineation of boundaries imperative. On April 17, 1853, Bishop Joseph Sadoc Alemany received word that the Sacred Congregation of Propaganda Fide had removed Peninsular California from its attachment to the Diocese of Monterey.

Several months later, on July 29th, Pope Pius IX created a Metropolitan District at San Francisco. The southern parallel of the parish at San Jose was fixed as the demarcation between the new Archdiocese of San Francisco and the larger but suffragan Diocese of Monterey.

The Monterey jurisdiction, which encompassed all of Southern California, remained territorially intact for the next seven decades. On July 8, 1849, Bishop Thaddeus Amat was authorized to move his episcopal seat to Los Angeles. At that time he was also permitted to add that city's name to the diocesan title.

During the subsequent years, there were a number of proposals for dividing the large and unwieldy Diocese of Monterey-Los Angeles. As early as 1866, Bishop Amat confided to a friend that he expected, "within a few years," to see another bishopric formed in the southland.

While no official action was taken by Amat, his successor, Bishop Francis Mora, petitioned the Holy See several times for a reduction of his jurisdiction. The proposal was shelved temporarily, in 1894, when Mora was given a coadjutor. Rumors of a division were revived after Bishop Thomas J. Conaty's death, in 1915, and were sustained by the long interregnum that ensued before the appointment of John J. Cantwell.

Early in 1922, Bishop Cantwell asked that the 90,000 square-mile Diocese of Monterey-Los Angeles be dismembered, with twelve counties formed into a separate jurisdiction. Pope Pius XI acquiesced and, in June, created the new Diocese of Monterey-Fresno. The larger area, known as the Diocese of Los Angeles-San Diego, embraced the remaining southland counties stretching to the Mexican border.

The final major alteration in the southland occurred on July 11, 1936, with the erection of a second Metropolitan District in California, at Los Angeles. Simultaneously, the four southernmost counties were fashioned into the Diocese of San Diego. Included in the newly formed Province of Los Angeles were the suffragan Sees of Monterey-Fresno, San Diego and Tucson.

In January of 1948, the Apostolic Delegate informed officials at Los Angeles that in order to avoid confusion with the older Archdiocese of Puebla, in Mexico, the southland's jurisdiction would henceforth be known officially as the Archdiocese of Los Angeles in California.

The archdiocese retained its geographical integrity from 1936 until June 18, 1976, when Pope Paul VI created a new diocese for Orange County. Remaining in the parent See were the counties of Los Angeles, Ventura and Santa Barbara.

Historical commentators are quick to observe that almost everything in Southern California has been imported—plants, flowers, shrubs, trees, water and even religion!

More than three decades ago, the late Carey McWilliams pointed to the unprecedented influx of peoples—a factor that today accounts for the multi-ethnic nature of the onetime *Pueblo de Nuestra Señora de los Angeles.*

The Indians were the first to inhabit the area. And though they are mostly gone now, they left an indelible mark behind in such names as Cahuenga, Malibu, Mugu and Pacoima.

Then came the Catholic *pobladores* from Sonora who laid out the original *plaza* on a bluff above the river named by Fray Juan Crespi to honor Our Lady of the Angels.

For a while after the war with Mexico and the discovery of gold, Los Angeles remained a small and insignificant town. But that was soon to change.

Statehood came, in 1850, and then, following the Civil war, the railroads reached out to touch Los Angeles, bringing newcomers from the south and midwest, many of them lured westward by the well-publicized sunshine.

The roots of the Bible were solidly transplanted by the great midwestern migration. Los Angeles remains predominantly Protestant, though the importance of the Catholic faith was first attested, in 1953, when the Archbishop of Los Angeles became the first cardinal in the western United States.

Though the city is famous for its revivalists and cultists, they have probably drawn attention out of all proportion to their numbers. Studies indicate that the great majority of churchgoers belong to the traditional faiths.

The Chinese and Japanese arrived; Poles and German Jews also came and many of the beach areas became popular resort meccas for English tourists.

Early in this century, the Mexican population began rising again, this time forming the bulk of the migratory work force. The Blacks, who presently constitute 12.5% of the population, began their treks in 1900.

And the waves of immigration roll on. In the last decade, Vietnamese and Koreans, with their distinctive contributions, have flooded into Los Angeles to join dozens of other Asiatic groups, like the Samoans, more of whom live in Los Angeles than reside on the Island of American Samoa itself.

The people thronging to the area have generally been an adventurous and inventive lot. In Hollywood, for example, creative minds have entertained and informed the whole world, reflecting both America's manifold problems and its unique promise.

A major port city, the aircraft and electronics industries expanded to meet the challenges of World War II and then spun around to handle contemporary transportation and communication needs.

This largest of the world's cities dedicated to Our Lady provides a haven for its perpetual transplants. It amazes, amuses and eventually absorbs. New arrivals are confronted with culture shock–the climate, the freeways, the lifestyles and the ethnic mix.

But one can rest assured that the new blood will keep Los Angeles alive, vigorous and growing as it begins inching toward its tricentennial.